# The Great Curse

# The Great Curse

## *Land Concentration in History and in Development*

ALBERT BERRY

OXFORD
UNIVERSITY PRESS

OXFORD
UNIVERSITY PRESS

Oxford University Press is a department of the University of Oxford. It furthers the University's objective of excellence in research, scholarship, and education by publishing worldwide. Oxford is a registered trade mark of Oxford University Press in the UK and certain other countries.

Published in the United States of America by Oxford University Press
198 Madison Avenue, New York, NY 10016, United States of America.



Library of Congress Cataloging-in-Publication Data
Names: Berry, Albert, author.
Title: The great curse : land concentration in history and in development / Albert Berry.
Description: New York, NY : Oxford University Press, [2024] |
Includes bibliographical references and index.
Identifiers: LCCN 2024037320 (print) | LCCN 2024037321 (ebook) |
ISBN 9780197782675 (hardback) | ISBN 9780197782705 |
ISBN 9780197782699 (epub) | ISBN 9780197782682
Subjects: LCSH: Land use. | Land tenure. | Agriculture—Economic aspects.
Classification: LCC HD156 .B47 2024 (print) | LCC HD156 (ebook) |
DDC 333.73—dc23/eng/20240903
LC record available at https://lccn.loc.gov/2024037320
LC ebook record available at https://lccn.loc.gov/2024037321

DOI: 10.1093/oso/9780197782675.001.0001

# Contents

## SECTION III: IMPLICATIONS OF PAST GLOBAL HISTORY FOR THE FUTURE IN SUB-SAHARAN AFRICA AND ELSEWHERE

# Glossary

**Economies of scale** exist when a higher level of production comes with a lower average cost in terms of resources utilized.

An **externality** is a cost or benefit that is imposed on someone who did not agree to incur that cost or benefit as part of an arrangement.

The **inverse relationship** refers to the typically negative correlation between farm size and land productivity.

The **marginal social cost of labor** is the cost in terms of foregone output and other benefits from the use of labor in its best alternative use to the actual one.

**Narrow efficiency** refers to a measure of economic efficiency that considers only one element of a productive unit's impact on total output but does not allow for its impact on other possible goals, such as the income of poorer people, a cleaner environment, and so on.

**Opportunity cost** is the loss of potential gain from other alternatives when one alternative is chosen. Thus, the opportunity cost of one firm's hiring a worker is the amount of output that worker would otherwise have generated in an alternative job.

**Social efficiency** is the ratio of benefits accruing to anyone in the society in relation to the opportunity cost of inputs used by a firm or group of firms in productive activities.

**Total factor productivity (TFP)** is the ratio of the value of output produced by a firm or group of firms to the total value of inputs going into that production, with the opportunity cost of those inputs measured either by their market price or in some other way that reflects their value in their best alternative uses.

# Introduction

Land is the key input for economies in the earliest stages of development, when seventy-five to ninety percent of the labor force is engaged in agriculture.[1] That access to land can be the source of much conflict—both physical and political—is thus not surprising. Often its distribution (whether by ownership or by control) is highly unequal, which typically implies severe inequality of income and welfare as well. Landlessness has been at the root of many of the world's most serious and persistent problems, including severe exploitation and the deprivation of political rights and basic human needs.

Over the course of economic development, the level of inequality typically shows a high degree of inertia, an inertia that seems generally to be stronger against decreases than against increases (Berry 2013). Thus, for example, contemporary Brazil owes its still extreme inequality to the distribution of land in the nineteenth century and earlier—a pattern that has remained intact even as the economy has shifted away from agriculture. Similarly, Taiwan owes its current impressive level of equality to the pattern imposed in part by a land reform in the early 1950s. With a gap of 0.3 between their respective Gini coefficients of income equality—0.6 in Brazil and 0.3 in Taiwan as of a decade or so ago—it is implausible to expect either economic policy or economic accident to cut that gap even by half in less than fifty to seventy-five years.[2] Levels of inequality become deeply embedded in economies, societies, and polities.

In a case like that of Brazil, a Gini coefficient of 0.6 implies that the top decile (i.e., the top ten percent) has an average income about forty to sixty times as much as the bottom decile, and the top one percent has about one hundred to 130 times as much. The bottom decile's average income is about one-tenth of the national average. Even if the national average is twice the

[1] Although a few economies have their historic roots elsewhere, usually in mining or in tourism, their share of the world's population is trivially small.

[2] The Gini coefficient, a standard measure of inequality, ranges from 0 (perfect equality) to 1 (total inequality, where one person has all the income). When measured at the country level, almost all cases fall between 0.3 and 0.6.

*The Great Curse*. Albert Berry, Oxford University Press. © Oxford University Press 2024.
DOI: 10.1093/oso/9780197782675.003.0001

poverty line, as much as forty percent of the population may be in poverty, whereas under an equitable distribution few or none would be. In short, such levels of inequality bring a huge welfare cost in terms of poverty and living conditions. Anything as clearly pernicious as a very high land concentration early in a country's development process invites analysis, explanation, and a search for remedies. It prompts three related questions: By what historical processes does it arise? What are its shorter- and longer-term implications for the country? What can be done about it?

Interpretations of land concentration vary widely; at one pole such concentration is seen as simply reflecting the distribution of political, military, and physical power—whoever has power gets the land (or keeps it). At another pole is the argument that economic efficiency eventually carries the day; therefore, high concentration signals the greater efficiency of larger units (e.g., through economies of scale) and thus contributes to high agricultural output. Many who hold this view do concede that land concentration contributes to income inequality, so steps like social welfare payments or other personal subsidies may be warranted to offset that effect. Over the last half-century or so the optimistic view that the concentration of a nation's land in large farms brings higher efficiency and output has been increasingly contradicted by the evidence that it more typically lowers efficiency and output. This, together with the near consensus that such concentration raises inequality, suggests that it is particularly prejudicial to lower income people. On all these matters there are "professional" views that rely on empirical evidence and/or credible theories, and "popular" views, which more often reflect intuition, a "status quo bias," and arguments coming from vested interests. Powerful narratives that defend the merits of the existing structure circulate within the political and social worlds. Other ideas get a less positive reception. Although the range of views on the implications of concentration has widened over the last several hundred years, reflecting changing settings and more empirical evidence, there has also been much continuity, going at least as far back as the debates around the British enclosures of the seventeenth to nineteenth centuries and coming right up to those debates currently ongoing in the context of Sub-Saharan Africa. There, a current counterpart to the large landholders who "enclosed" the land are the large foreign and domestic interests buying it up; their "land grab," occurring in an essentially capitalist world, can be seen as the most recent example of a long-standing pattern. The general character of the narratives created in this pattern's defense is largely the same as that of earlier times.

The long-dominant view that high levels of land concentration contribute to productive efficiency has deep roots in Britain, where the enclosures that amalgamated formerly common land into large estates were seen as increasing total agricultural output and promoting economic development and the Industrial Revolution. This belief was only convincingly questioned about thirty years ago as more detailed empirical evidence was brought to light. Parallel debates have played themselves out in the various corners of the developing world; there, too, the anti-concentration view has benefited from an increase in quantitative evidence, coming from agricultural censuses, surveys, and other sources. However, as was the case in Britain, general acceptance of the potential efficiency advantages of small agriculture never becomes very prevalent outside the group of analysts who probe the empirical information and beyond those with a good knowledge of the economics of agriculture. Of all the widespread misbeliefs around economic matters, this is among those with the greatest staying power and the highest social costs.[3]

In nearly all countries, whether they are now industrial or are still developing, history suggests that the course of change during the earlier phases of development has usually, and perhaps almost always, been dominated by the big landholders and their allies, sometimes modified by reactions from the small landholders when conditions permitted. It also suggests that a high level of concentration, rather than improving economic outcomes, is more likely to do the opposite. So, what can and should be done to rectify this social and economic flaw? In many parts of the world the answer today is "a limited amount" because economies have moved far enough into the post-agricultural/urban phase that a land reform undertaken now cannot by itself help in correcting the injustices and inefficiencies that a society or economy may be suffering. But many countries in Sub-Saharan Africa, and a few others around the world, are exceptions to this generalization. Accordingly, land distribution issues are especially pertinent in these locations.

[3] Most of the other highly damaging misbeliefs also involve areas in which alternative policy choices have very different impacts on the welfare of the rich and of the poor. One is the idea that tax cuts, even if focused mainly on the rich, help everyone by contributing to economic growth, job creation, and so forth. This concept is at the center of the so-called supply-side economics, a much-hyped idea from the Reagan era in the US. While presumably having some validity under certain conditions, it is usually incorrect. In other policy areas, like the role of counter-cyclical monetary policy, such differences in impact by income group are much less apparent, and so conflicting narratives are less prevalent.

This volume is divided into three sections. Section I provides historical and theoretical background. It briefly reviews the origins of land concentration (Chapter 1) and the typically inaccurate beliefs about its impacts, drawn from the early modern European experience (Chapter 2). The microeconomic basis of the efficiency and equity arguments in favor of small farms and of land reform (i.e., some equalizing form of land redistribution) is reviewed in Chapter 3. Section II reviews the major land reform experiences of the twentieth century, with special attention to the experiences of large countries and those which offer particularly relevant lessons (Chapter 4). Chapter 5 focuses on the experiences in communist countries while Chapter 6 focuses on the largely unsuccessful attempts in Latin America. Chapter 7 looks at a range of other cases, including the special successes of Japan, Korea, and Taiwan, and the tragic timing-failure in Iran. Section III looks to the future. Chapter 8 reviews the recent experience and current situation of Sub-Saharan African countries. Chapter 9 draws out the main implications of this study as a whole for current and future land policy.

The text uses a modest number of technical economic concepts, most of which are defined in the Glossary. None of the major conclusions are understandable only in terms of those concepts. The empirical findings which underpin the main starting point for the land reform arguments presented here are reviewed in Chapter 3. That starting point is the general superiority of the small family farm vis-à-vis traditional large-scale agriculture (the *latifundium* or *hacienda*), modern agribusiness type farming, and large state or collective farming when it comes to meeting a population's economic and social needs. That superiority can be best measured by the level of income earned by the typical person engaged in agriculture, the security of that income, and the quality of social setting that characterizes that system. It provides the valid logic for reforms that bring agrarian structure closer to such a system.

# SECTION I

# THE HISTORY AND MICROECONOMICS OF LAND CONCENTRATION

High land concentration is to be expected in the "law of the jungle" world described by James Scott (2017); it is accompanied by the various systems previously noted whereby underlings are exploited. If and when societies become more "civilized," the mechanisms of concentration typically evolve. Takeover by physical force becomes less acceptable as a way to maintain or increase concentration and it is in part replaced by less visible practices (e.g., legal theft or manipulation) or by more market-based mechanisms, such as easier access by large farms to credit and to accumulated profits from higher total incomes.

# 1

# Land Concentration

## Historical Origins, Socio-economic Effects, Political Logic, and Surrounding Narratives

### The Land and Labor Monopolization Model

For the millennia during which the world has essentially been agricultural and land has therefore been central to economic performance, its ownership and control has typically been highly concentrated. From the early days of settled agriculture in the Middle East, in China, and in the European countries, we know that land concentration was often high and that it underwent fluctuations, with gradual increases sometimes interrupted by sharper decreases in response to political pressures and conflicts.[1] Sometimes that pressure was enough to spark revolutions. Most of the time, however, a rich agricultural elite maintained firm control of "public policy."

Labor was the other key to production and wealth, so access to it was also important for those at the top. Under most settings, they could reap two benefits from (collectively) controlling more land. Not only did it provide greater income for them directly, but it also meant that less land was available on which workers could apply their own efforts, thus leaving more labor available to the rulers. A natural accompaniment to dominant classes living off the work of others is warring among such ruling classes, each trying to take what other ruling groups have. This dynamic does not qualitatively affect the need for each ruling class to have control over its "own" workers and be able to extract the benefits of their labor, although it does complicate the context in various ways.

Both distant and recent history suggest that high levels of land concentration are the result of a matching concentration of political and military power rather than of any economic influence like economies of scale. In his recent reinterpretation of the beginnings of agriculture, Scott (2017) goes a

[1] Linder and Williamson (2011).

*The Great Curse*. Albert Berry, Oxford University Press. © Oxford University Press 2024.
DOI: 10.1093/oso/9780197782675.003.0002

big step farther, in suggesting that the very logic and origins of the state itself have their roots in the potential for monopolization of both land and labor by a small dominant group of people; the state is in effect created as the instrument for that exploitation. This contrasts with modern positive narratives on government, which see its purpose as serving the population "governed"; within this latter narrative, governments composed of exploiters and thieves are seen as unfortunate deviations from the preferable and natural paradigm. The historical roots of the positive government narrative are, of course, also of interest. Many small groups have engaged in what may be seen as informal governance as a way to achieve needed collaboration among families and groups. Such collaboration may, under some circumstances, expand to the point at which the authority becomes more formally organized. Still, the history of large, highly organized government appears mainly, perhaps almost exclusively, to involve small, dominant groups learning how to control and exploit subservient populations.

A necessary condition for an elite to live very well off the labor of others is that those providing the labor be able to generate a surplus beyond their own minimum needs and that it be "collectable." As he probes the origins of hierarchical societies, Scott (2017) notes that the first settled societies in Mesopotamia, which took advantage of a rich wetland abundant in fish and land animals, preceded organized intensive agriculture by several thousand years and that, for the majority of the population, the transition to the latter system made life worse. He argues that there is a crucial, direct link between the cultivation of cereal crops and the birth of the first states; other crops were grown before but cereal crops seemed to foster organized states. Being more easily taxable than other food products, grain provided a convenient base on which a dominant group could live and prosper from the forced labor or slavery of underlings. In this reading of history, the implicit objective of dominant elites, and thus the condition likely to underlie the rise of states, was not finding the most productive form of agriculture but rather finding that form which allowed the elite to garner the most for themselves, without regard to the rest of the population as long as enough food was left to allow them to work effectively.[2] From this perspective, we are still struggling to turn the state from its original logic as an instrument of exploitation and associated repression into something more conducive to general human welfare.

[2] Other perspectives on the long sweep of socio-economic history are provided by Lucassen (2021).

We should perhaps not be surprised to find that the conversion remains incomplete, whether the government acts as partner to an exploitative private sector (as may occur under capitalism) or as the dominant decision-maker on nearly everything (as in centrally planned autocratic systems). And we should accept that, at best, any system will *de facto* be a combination of the exploitative state and the public-oriented state. Not surprisingly, some state institutions, like the military and the police, tend to be closer to the exploitative end of the spectrum than do others.

Many factors affect the trajectory of political systems and there have, of course, been exceptions to the "autarchy based on land concentration paradigm". Some natural settings do not lend themselves to the creation of states that could exercise near monopoly control over land and labor; their rarity gives special interest to the conditions under which they arise. Settings in which the collectable surplus is small pose upper limits on how large the elite class can be and how well it can live.[3] One such setting was the earliest settled agriculture of Mesopotamia, as described by Scott (2017). Another has been the nomad economy. Some small sub-regions have partially escaped centralized control by their isolation. One of Colombia's coffee zones presented such awkward mountainous terrain that it was not tempting to large owners because of the difficulty of access. Instead, it developed into an economy of relatively prosperous small landholders, even as good valley lands were quickly absorbed into a large farm system. Low-quality land has generally not lent itself to concentrated control because there is little or no surplus to be had above the subsistence needs of those who work it. When technological improvements or the introduction of more productive crops raise that potential, then this situation changes.

Some settings lend themselves to the development of more democratic structures, partly because the income gap between top and bottom is somehow limited. Where surpluses are substantial but not collectible, people may develop harmonious ways of living together. The proto-democracies of Greece have been the most studied (Hamilton 1993) in this regard. Over recent millennia, however, most such experiences have been short-lived. Small states not structured to control and repress their own populations are not well placed to permanently fend off invasion by states that are built for that purpose. Jan Lucassen (2021) refers to the violent displacement of

[3] "Living" here includes enough spending on defense to protect against other states and on domestic institutions to control the workers.

matriarchal and egalitarian communities in Europe and South Asia by warlike, patriarchal societies like the Yamnaya pastoral nomads of the Eurasian steppe from about five thousand years ago.

Labor's centrality to world economic history results from its being an input in the production of nearly everything that societies want to consume. Land is central because it produces the staple of life—food. In the earlier stages of that history, the technologies available for food production have often required so much labor that effective access to that factor of production is a necessary condition for any "non-laboring" class to exist. Circumstances determine the extent to which dominant groups try, in effect, to enslave others. When both land and labor are scarce, their relative scarcity determines both the income that would accrue to each were the economy to operate through free market mechanisms and the incentive to enslave when it does not.

To fulfil the goals of its beneficiaries, this "land and labor domination model" requires that the land be productive enough, either as a result of its own natural characteristics or with help from available technologies, to generate a surplus above what the workers must eat to survive plus whatever it costs to control them and their work effort. The model involves the actual or potential use of force to control the subservient population.[4] Control includes preventing workers from finding some other way to subsist. From the perspective of those at the top of the hierarchy, slavery or serfdom has been one natural option. Along with lack of freedom, such exploitation has usually also involved low income, hard work, and, frequently, personal abuse. Many regions, islands and backwaters can provide "refuges" for a few people to survive on their own, but an elite class need not worry about them as long as they cannot draw off too many of the workers it needs. States have established detailed rules to discourage the flight, escape, or theft of slaves. Thus the Code of Hammurabi from ancient Mesopotamia included harsh punishment for attempted flight by slaves, such as cutting off their hands or

[4] Many famous writers have dwelt on this aspect of society. An acute observer of the use of such force was Tolstoy. His 1903 short story, "After the Ball," involves a young man who loves a colonel's daughter. He also greatly admires her privately generous father until he sees the sort of punishment the army metes out to a Tatar deserter, with the girl's father leading the way. In the last years of his life, Tolstoy called for the dissolution of private property, the abolition of the state, and the end of military conscription. The government placed him under surveillance and his anti-war stance was given as one reason he was denied the Nobel Prize for literature by the Swedish Academy (Wilson 2020). He eventually came to view violence as a tool to maintain a social order that benefited only the wealthy and the ruling classes. His appeal for the abolition of institutions upheld and guided by the use of force is reminiscent of today's call for the abolition of the police. He called for the "rejection of coercion as the glue of the commonwealth" (Gustafson 1986).

the removal of their tongues (Scott 2017). Attempted flight from the slave-holding southern US states invited harsh penalties as well.

In contrast to this "slavery setting" in which people do not volunteer to work under harsh conditions but are forced to do so, an overabundance of labor can make it hard enough to find jobs providing even a subsistence income so that workers do not need to be coerced to work for the available employers. Such a "labor surplus" condition is the result of some combination of population growth, a relative scarcity of complementary inputs like land, and the presence of labor-saving technologies. When population growth dominates, development—usually defined as rising per capita output and income—does not occur. At the extreme, when the wage rate is pushed down to subsistence level, one is in the world of Malthusian economics. In that world, the population cannot grow further because as more workers put themselves onto the labor market they push wages to below the subsistence level and raise the death rate (e.g., through starvation and/or poverty-related diseases). In the simplest such world, a capitalist elite class controls all of the factors of production except labor (i.e., capital and land). When the marginal product of hired labor falls below the subsistence level people start to die of starvation/poverty.

The existence of surplus labor was a central concept in Marx's interpretation of capitalism and of Arthur Lewis's (1954) understanding of the development process. In that scenario another negative feature of life is economic insecurity—a central part of the Marxist model of capitalism. This challenge is dealt with in Lewis's labor-surplus economy mainly by families sharing within what he called the "traditional sector" of that economy. Most of the economies Lewis had in mind were still mainly agricultural in terms of where people worked. A traditional sector, made up of small farms and other informal activities in which most workers were self-employed, coexisted with a "modern sector," which was operated on a capitalist profit-maximizing basis. Surplus workers from the former sector went to work in the latter. Appendix 1.1 and Figure 1.1 summarize the essence of this model. The more land and other factors, and the better the technology at work in this sector, the higher the wage at which its laborers are willing to move to and work in the modern sector. Shrinking the amount of land available to it thus raises capitalists' profits.

The underlying logic of the monopolization model has thus been apparent in many situations less extreme than slavery. It was, for example, manifested in the so-called Wakefieldian principles, developed from

Edward Gibbon Wakefield's "theory of settler colonization," which argued that successful colonization hinged on the establishment of a minimum, or "sufficient," price on colonial land. Being "successful" meant both being profitable to prominent landholders like himself and beneficial to many lower income workers in England, which he considered to be overpopulated. His ideas impressed John Stuart Mill and other leading economists of the time. Wakefield spent the next few several decades promulgating them, first in the new colony of South Australia in 1836, and then in Canada and New Zealand in 1839.[5]

In the early decades of the European settlement of the province of Ontario in Canada, Wakefield's influence was present. Some members of the Upper Canada establishment wished to create—through immigration—a landless, wage-earning class whose presence would overcome the perceived problems of the high cost and scarcity of labor; that is, they favored a Wakefieldian theory of immigration which held that "immigrants should be denied easy, or any, access to land so that they would be forced to form a necessary pool of labourers" (Johnson 1990, 227–228).

Western economists came relatively late to the inherent logic of someone's buying an asset (like land) to keep it out of the hands of others, a delay which probably in part reflected the idea that competition was the natural condition for an economy. Such a blind spot has certainly not characterized businesspeople.

## The Growth Context: Who Benefits from Rising Per Capita Output and Income?

The last two centuries have seen the most rapid change ever experienced in the world's economy, in its population, and perhaps also in its politics. They make up the latter part of what is often referred to as the "Industrial Revolution," during which new technologies in agriculture, manufacturing, transportation, and other sectors opened the door to rising labor productivity

[5] Wakefield's theories were also at the center of a new imperial imaginary that had emerged in Britain by the 1850s, which established Australia and New Zealand as pastoral locations capable of restoring damaged British subjects. In spurring the vast expansion of migration to Australia and New Zealand, contributing to the genocide and dispossession of indigenous populations, and accelerating the destruction of local ecosystems, systematic colonization constitutes one of the most powerful and destructive examples of the ability of Victorian representations to permanently reshape the globe.

and higher average incomes. In the twentieth century, the phenomenon became increasingly global. Whereas previously per capita incomes had risen quite slowly at the global level, between 1850 to 2000 they jumped by 1.4 percent per year, or by over eight-fold in total (Roser 2013). The advances occurred first in what are often referred to as the "developed" or "industrial" countries. New technologies raised the productivity of the main economic inputs- land, labor, and capital. Increasing labor productivity and incomes were also due, in part, to the use of more capital per worker.

Some progress had occurred in a variety of places over earlier centuries, but the final global surge had its main roots in Europe. Historically, the first step toward such sustained growth was increased productivity in agriculture. Improved varieties of seeds were key in most places, together with better supplies of water and better cultivation practices. This allowed a rising share of the labor force to be shifted to the production of other goods and services for which people have an "elastic" demand as their incomes rise. Rising incomes increased life expectancy as people ate better and benefited from better health services, including the new medical technologies developed along the way, like sulfa and penicillin. At the global level, the increase in life expectancy over the twentieth century was from thirty-two years to over sixty-five years, due mostly to falling infant mortality. Rising incomes initially accelerated population growth as adults lived longer and more infants survived; for example, a family with ten births may have nine children reach adulthood rather than the five to seven that would have previously been more common. Later, the rising levels of education, urbanization, and female employment outside the home led to sharp declines in family size, which decelerated that growth. Until the beginning of the twentieth century, growth at the world level was very slow, usually under one percent per year. The economically more advanced, or industrial, countries, found mainly in Europe and the former British colonies (Canada, the US, Australia, and New Zealand), went through the high growth stage first.

The world has not fallen victim to a Malthusian outcome because population growth has been more than offset by some combination of an expanding natural resource base and technological change. Often the latter is key to raising output and income per person, although the form it takes matters greatly. When it is strongly labor-saving, as with machinery that directly replaces workers, this helps to keep wages low—perhaps at subsistence, and channels all, or nearly all, of the increased income to the owners of capital. When changes are labor-using and capital-saving, the result is the opposite—wages rise and returns to capital fall. What sort of technological improvements are made is thus pivotal to who gains the most from economic growth, a fact that highlights the question of who is in charge of coming up with new technologies. The answer is not simple, but part of it is cause for concern. When profit-maximizing enterprises are responsible for much of the search for new technologies and the choice among available ones, they must logically be expected to work in the interests of the shareholders (i.e., of capital) and, usually without realizing it, against the interests of the workers. From the perspective of those with land, labor-displacing technologies can bring major benefits by making labor so productive that little of it is needed to achieve high levels of output; a classic example arises in developing countries where an abundance of labor co-exists with access to the highly labor-displacing technologies developed in and for rich countries. This context renders slavery of little or no value to the elite because the market value of labor is so low. While they are not enslaved, the available options for many workers are underemployment and/or very low earnings, something that may be thought of as collective exploitation, à la Marx. This condition follows on the transition from some pre-capitalist labor arrangement, sometimes a very exploitative one and sometimes less so, to the capitalist counterpart—low wages and insecure employment and income.[6]

Rising average labor productivity in an economy provides greater incomes for someone—whether it is mainly for capitalists/landowners or for workers depends both on the source of the productivity increase and on how government and other institutional players affect the final distribution of gains. Rising productivity leads to another key change in the economy and society over time—the shift away from agriculture as the dominant sector and a move toward greater diversity, with bigger roles played by manufacturing and services. A related transition toward urban life occurs because these latter consumables are more efficiently produced in towns and cities. Rising incomes also bring increasing levels of education and changes in the political systems through which people govern themselves.

In this process of development the domination model tends eventually to give way, at least partially, to something more civilized. The paths vary.

[6] New technologies that raise land productivity make that resource more valuable and thus more attractive to hold. So, while labor-saving technological change benefits landholders at the expense of labor, when it also raises land productivity it provides a still greater incentive to for large landholders to tighten their control over that land.

Economic change interacts with the political and social settings and the changes within them. Some political arrangements foster economic growth better than others, and some foster equality. The initial motor for much societal change is economic, in particular increases in agricultural productivity which raise the surplus and shift more capital and labor to non-agricultural activities. A natural expectation is that equality of land distribution will promote or fit well with democracy and social progress, whereas a high concentration will be a deterrent.

Land rights and human rights are closely linked when an economy is predominantly agricultural; in that setting the only direct guarantee of a decent life for most people is access to land. The concepts of "equality" and "human rights for all people" are natural to a system of small owner-operated farms, whereas a system of large producing units brings inherent class distinctions and economic inequality. An equitable land distribution may thus be expected to contribute to the development of democracy. Ronald J. Herring (2009) argues that, in many rural societies, progressive politics can only emerge when agrarian reform has transformed the field of power. Such reform then becomes a necessary condition for many other types of advancement. One might also guess that, *ceteris paribus*, democracy early in economic development would raise the likelihood of an internally imposed land reform and of the other policies favoring small agriculture. But the dynamics of change are complicated. When there is pressure for reform and the system is not very democratic, the only political process available may involve force, whether applied by the military or by populist authoritarians. Understanding the causal processes that determine the evolution of land concentration has been a major challenge for students of history.

The degree of land concentration in the early stages of a country's economic development has lasting impacts on its subsequent evolution. A widely noted pattern in economic history is the extreme inertia over time in the level of income inequality; once high, it tends to stay high, and once low, it tends to stay low. Land concentration early in the process of development is thus likely to portend a long period of high income inequality, partly because it may not permit the development of a robust democracy and partly through purely economic mechanisms. The most interesting historical questions involve the nuanced interactions that occur when the political system is neither at the extreme of the pure domination model nor at that of a civilized democracy, and when things are changing over time, either internally through economic development or externally through the influence of other countries. Many alternative paths are elucidated by historical episodes, including some of the land reform attempts to be discussed.

While the concentration and deconcentration of land and the associated conflict have been features of history for millennia, their implications changed with the arrival of the Industrial Revolution, the onset of continuous growth in the world's per capita income, and the diminishing role of agriculture and land in the economy and in its total stock of wealth. The distribution of land became a less central direct determinant of income and welfare distribution. But the high degree of inertia over time in a society's inequality meant that, whereas a major redistribution of land in a still-agricultural country could put that country on track to have an enduring egalitarian character, a comparable reduction later in the development process would have much less impact. Similarly, preventing a rising concentration of land in a still-agricultural country where it was not yet extreme could avoid a long period of high income inequality. An advanced level of development diminishes the potential role of land reform as a tool to lower overall inequality; it also facilitates the use of other policies that may lower inequality. When they have great potential, the importance of land reform as a tool is likely to be small; when they do not, its importance remains.

## The Processes of Land Concentration

The implications of land concentration have changed with the developments of the last few centuries as societies have evolved away from feudalism toward capitalism and from feudal landlords to capitalist farmers and agro-industry. Accumulators of land have pursued their goal through various mechanisms. The enclosures of earlier centuries in Britain are one famous example.

As reviewed in Chapter 2, twentieth-century debates around the effects of the distribution of land had partial precursors in earlier centuries, including those around the enclosures. As now, there was awareness that the evicted tenants suffered and poverty rose, but it was widely accepted that, in terms of economic efficiency, this was a positive development and one that both preceded and helped to foster the Industrial Revolution. As the enclosures brought an end to an earlier configuration of life, the narrative on the inefficiency of production in the commons took root. Eventually, the captivating term "tragedy of the commons" appeared, together with an economic theory as to why common land available to all would be badly used (e.g., because it would be overused). Just as the idea that large farms achieve higher efficiency than small ones took a long time to be thrown into question by data demonstrating the inverse relationship (the systematically higher land productivity of smaller farms), so too did the idea that production under commons-type arrangements is, by definition, less efficient than private production take until the latter part of the twentieth century to be widely questioned within economics (Ostrom 1990, and others).

Karl Polanyi (1957) saw the enclosure movement as a pivotal step in what he referred to as the "great transformation" from an economy based on reciprocity and redistribution among people and groups to one built around a self-regulating market economy and the capitalist institutions that developed to support it. Competitive markets replaced those social interactions of earlier times:

> Enclosures have appropriately been called a revolution of the rich against the poor. The lords and nobles were upsetting the social order, breaking down ancient law and custom, sometimes by means of violence, often by pressure and intimidation. They were literally robbing the poor of their share in the common, tearing down the houses which, by the hitherto unbreakable force of custom, the poor had long regarded as theirs and their heirs'. The fabric of society was being disrupted. Desolate villages and the ruins of human dwellings testified to the fierceness with which the revolution raged, endangering the defences of the country, wasting its towns, decimating its population, turning its overburdened soil into dust, harassing its people and turning them from decent husbandmen into a mob of beggars and thieves. Though this happened only in patches, the black spots threatened to melt into a uniform catastrophe. (Polanyi 1957, 35)

As James Boyle (2003, 35) puts it:

> Some of these costs were brutally and relentlessly "material"—for example, the conversion of crofters and freeholders into debt-peons, seasonal wage-laborers, or simply, as (Sir Thomas) More argued in Utopia, and Polanyi argues 400 years later, into beggars and thieves. But other harms are harder to classify: the loss of a form of life; the relentless power of market logic to migrate to new areas, disrupting traditional social relationships and perhaps even views of the self or the relationship of human beings to the environment.

Sir Thomas More was an early critic of both Britain's agrarian system and its class structure. *Utopia* denounced private property, described the existing social order as a "conspiracy of the rich," and advocated a form of communism. He complained that many noblemen "lived like drones on the labor of others" with tenants evicted so that "an insatiable glutton may consolidate his fields" (Eagleton 2016, 412). This description is partially replayed in Robert Allen's (1992) reference to the parasitical character of the English agricultural elite who, instead of transferring their savings to underpin the Industrial Revolution, opted instead to live the good life.

Beyond his condemnation of people's personal behavior, More decried war as "fit only for beasts," and argued that armies should be disbanded, labor reduced to a minimum, and gold and silver used to make chamber pots rather than serving as objects of esteem and even worship. As Terry Eagleton (2016) notes, in its essence *Utopia* is very contemporary; the conspiracy of the rich against the poor was ever present and is still with us.

Colombia's history exemplifies many of the most damaging mechanisms of land concentration found in today's developing countries. The Spanish conquest saw wholesale displacement of indigenous groups by the conquerors. In this "law of the jungle" setting, physical power is the key to accumulation. In less extreme contemporary settings, such power is accompanied or replaced by other mechanisms, both legitimate (accumulation through purchase based on one's savings) and illegitimate (theft, legal chicanery, etc.). In societies in which ideas of justice and fairness are dominant both among people and in the institutions (e.g., the judicial system), accumulation occurs through legal mechanisms. Where that is less the case, much of it occurs unlawfully. And when the accumulation of land relies in part on the use of force, whether physical or political, it typically does so within a context where land is a particularly attractive asset for rich, powerful, and sometimes dishonest people. The last few decades in Colombia have seen a process in which those ending up with a disconcertingly high share of the land are of questionable moral standard—essentially self-selected as those most willing and capable of doing what needs to be done to acquire control over a property under the existing circumstances, or the ones willing to look the other way with respect to how the previous owner obtained it. This pattern has helped to keep the inequality of land distribution one of the highest in the world, and it has resulted in about a million deaths over the century (Berry, n.d.). In an economy in which markets function well, the most efficient producers tend to have access to inputs like land. But when both markets and the political system are seriously flawed, the process leads to a large percentage of income and wealth being concentrated in the hands of people with low moral standards, including drug traffickers, other perpetrators of displacement, and corrupt politicians and bureaucrats. According to one estimate, only ten to twenty-five percent of land currently in large farms in Colombia is likely to have been legitimately acquired.[7]

The frequency of land theft from small landholders in countries with weak judicial systems owes itself not just to land's being an important form of capital but also to the relative ease with which it can be stolen vis-à-vis other forms of assets. Successful theft (appropriation) of something to which someone else has as an equally strong claim involves the ability to seize the item without losing it again (e.g., through the courts or some other mechanism that helps the initial holder to reclaim it). Theft may occur through physical or legal means, the latter facilitated by a judicial system that responds to money, either in the form of bribery, pressure tactics, or the simple fact that richer people can buy success in the legal process by spending more. Most theft worsens inequality because the major acts are carried out by and for the wealthy, but some does go in the other direction. Inequality-increasing theft has lasting effects because the concentration of wealth it promotes tends to last.

Theft nearly always involves physical or financial assets. Ease of execution and who is most likely to be involved vary among subcategories. Key physical assets include land (rural-agricultural and urban), residences, factories, and commercial goods. Financial assets range from currency (the simplest form) to bank deposits, to other more complicated forms like bonds, stocks, and the right to pensions. Among physical assets, land stands out from, for example, factories engaged in manufacturing because in the latter case the asset is typically worth much less to most potential thieves than it is to the existing owner. Land is attractive because almost anyone can gain economically from it, whether as owner or as renter, not to mention the additional benefits (political and social) that it brings to some large owners in contexts like Colombia's. Another special feature, in contrast especially to manufacturing and financial capital, is that a not-insignificant share of land may be held by low income and, hence, vulnerable families; their share of manufacturing and financial assets is very low. A final advantage of farmland

[7] Berry (2017a, 278).

theft is that the rural setting often provides better cover against potential political or legal attention.

How unequal land distribution becomes in the earlier stages of economic development, how aggressively concentration is defended, and the way any attempts at land reform play out all depend greatly on who runs a country, and, in particular, on how allied they are with the landed elite or with the potential beneficiaries of a reform, as well as on their ethics and culture. To the extent that "bad people" get to the top and stay there, concentration is fostered, together with abuse of underlings; attacking these ills becomes more difficult. When concentration is increasing, it is unsurprising that some of those who try the hardest to accumulate land and do achieve this goal should be of below-average moral stature (willing to steal if it gets them where they want to go; lacking empathy for others). Once at the top, they establish and enforce laws that help maintain their position. More subtly, concentration tends to go with a class system in which those at the top are led to understand that this is their natural place—their due. Although such situations involve great inequality, a sense of shared interest and community may develop, for example in feudal systems in which both lord and serf take seriously their obligations and rights vis-à-vis the other group. How, from such a difficult starting point, can a healthy political system and culture be built? If it can be built, how long might it take?

## Aspiring Toward a Fairer Society: The Twentieth/Twenty-First Century Context

The process of economic development that encompassed the globe during the twentieth century had many implications on the land front. The world also became more democratic, less authoritarian, and less warlike, the latter especially after the end of World War II. The share of people living in countries with reasonably fair and open elections rose from about twelve percent in 1900 to fifty-six percent in 2000.[8] The unpromising aspect of this trend is that most of the still-agricultural countries remain less developed politically.

[8] In 1900, about 26.4 percent of the world's population lived under colonial rule (Roser 2016, 7). More refined measures of the quality of governance in terms of popular participation and of human freedoms also point to improvements.

Paradoxically, democracy may not be the best political setting for certain types of reform (see Chapter 4).

In the best of cases, economic and political evolution has been accompanied by civilizing trends and a greater presence of inclusive social democracy, where fairness and justice across all people become central objectives of at least parts of society. People who think like More are less rare than before; key ideas of the great religions can contribute to progress; a greater share of people have been educated on the flaws of the societies in which they live, which enables them to push for something better. Fear for the future of human society becomes more prevalent with the threat of climate change.

The evolution of humanity from a world in which a few methodically exploited the majority toward more progressive and socially oriented systems has altered the way pioneering governments and policymakers measure success. This evolution has gradually redefined the *good society*, including the way it is construed in economic terms. With the onset of more democratic systems and thinking, the *de facto* organization of the economy around the idea that the only thing that matters is the welfare of the elite tends to be implicitly shelved in favor of one that, by prioritizing total income or output as the appropriate goal, gives at least some weight to the welfare of everyone else. Under the former criterion, a high concentration of land is natural because it helps to maximize the welfare of those at the top. Under the latter, it is considered normal and acceptable as long as it does not have a negative effect on total agricultural output. The concept of economies of scale, part of the economic narrative brought to bear in defense of concentration, fits nicely into a conceptual framework where income distribution is not a major priority—the economic goal is maximizing total output (income) even if the great bulk of it goes to the top group. The more radical idea that the welfare of everyone in the society should be given reasonably equal importance is—outside the realm of philosophers and socialists—a historically rare and, for the most part, recent one.[9] This last step comes when a country tries to lessen inequality by giving more weight to a dollar earned or received by a poor person than to one received by a rich person. Doing so reflects not just the

[9] The Code of Hammurabi constituted a very detailed legal system and included such modern features as a presumption of innocence until guilt had been proven. For any given group penalties matched the crime, but they were greater when a given crime was committed by someone lower in the hierarchy against someone higher. A pattern that emerges in today's legal systems against their stated intent was consciously built into that one.

market value of production but also the social welfare it generates. The general appropriateness of this reweighting is widely accepted today, but how economic policy should be altered remains much debated. It has not yet been built into the standard measures of economic performance, like GDP per capita.

With respect to how agriculture performs, the shifting emphasis thus moves from "Are we the rich group exploiting the workers as fully as possible?" to an intermediate stage of "Is the sector contributing as much as possible to total output or income?" and finally to "Is the sector raising human welfare as much as possible through the food and income it generates?" Under the second and third criteria, efficient exploitation of one's underlings is no longer the explicit or implicit target; a narrative that puts the welfare of the elite at the top may still be present, but it now competes with others. And to the extent that the rest of the society does not judge agricultural performance positively just because the agrarian elite class lives well, that elite class may have to defend its and the sector's performance by those alternative criteria, such as total GDP generated, total supply of food provided to the population, or something similar.

Earlier in human history, then, some ecological conditions encouraged the creation of the land and labor monopolizing state. Periodically, battles ensued as those at the bottom challenged that structure. Which governing arrangement was best able to keep the economic elite from losing ground depended on the phase of economic development. It required both a form of economic management that facilitated extraction and one of political control that ensured stability. During the agrarian phase, democracy with high voting levels can be dangerous to the elite because the peasantry/workers are a large share of the population and usually prefer to operate their own land. However, the elite can often make pseudo-democracy work for them and thus avoid losing much land.

Within the last two hundred to three hundred years, global economic development has been accompanied by a political evolution toward wider popular participation in government and toward civilization, including a wider recognition of human rights and a narrowing tolerance for high levels of inequality. Inevitably, there have—in some places and at some times—been counter-pressures and counter trends.

Students of socio-economic organization see those last few hundred years as the period when European feudalism morphed into capitalism; that is, the feudal property morphed into the capitalist form and the serf became a paid employee. When feudalism was the *modus operandi*, the interactions between serf and lord, while they always involved a bargain or trade-off of some sort, covered a wider range (sometimes nearly all) of the aspects of the life of the serf. By the time agrarian capitalism prevailed, that relationship covered only the worker's labor. This shift coincided with and interacted with that from an agriculture-dominated economy to a more industrial one. Land reform took on a different character according to where society was in this broad transition (Bernstein 2002, 434). What it meant under a feudalistic system was "the displacement or transformation of parasitic landed property, of which redistributive land reform has been a major, if not necessarily exclusive, mechanism." Such a displacement was seen by people drawing on the European experience of modernization and post-feudalism (transitions to capitalism) in a variety of ways, specifically:

(i) the classic bourgeois view in which agrarian reform engineered (and ordered) by an enlightened state allows (encourages) development (modernization) of farming;
(ii) the Marxist view of social revolution in "backward" social formations, in which the abolition of predatory landed property by the agency of proletariat and peasantry (the worker–peasant alliance) prepares the way for forms of agricultural production that combine the economies of scale and technical advances of capitalist farming with social property and planning, *and* contribute to the project of industrialization and its accumulation imperative; and
(iii) populist views that attribute the central role in its emancipation to "the peasantry" (understood as a social class), proclaim the superiority-on technical and developmental, as well as sociological and moral-grounds of small-scale ("family") farming, and thus advocate policies to support such farming.

Throughout history, lessening land concentration through agrarian reform could naturally be seen as a form of social progress; it still can be seen that way today, although its potential to improve socio-economic equality naturally diminishes as the agricultural sector becomes less prominent. In a still-agrarian society, it is the natural and sometimes the only way to significantly lower economic and social inequality. As Herring (2000, 30) puts it, "agrarian reform remains a means of restructuring the field of power to which state functionaries respond, and therefore enables more possibilities for building an effective and responsive state, without which all other anti-poverty options—including growth—are reduced in efficiency."

As discussed in later chapters, students of agrarian reform have come up with many valuable insights on when it can happen successfully, how it comes about, and so forth. Social and political development tends to strengthen ideas like equality and respect for human rights. Sometimes progress involves ending one feature of the domination model before the others, such as where slavery and the range of abuses to which it subjects people are eliminated but hard work and low incomes remain. Some features may be framed as unjust in a given society, whereas others are not. An expansion of democracy—in the sense of a widening of the distribution of political power—may lead to some being tackled before others, and the agrarian elite may fight more to retain some than others.

Because a high concentration of land is seldom a historical accident but rather the result of a process in which those with power use it to accumulate and control that asset, it has predictable correlates. Whether in a feudal or a capitalist system, they include a high level of income and welfare inequality and a class system; that is, a sense of correctness/comfort/normality within that system for those at the top, which limits the level of generosity that might otherwise be felt for the rest of the population. When the system has shifted enough toward capitalism, a sense settles in that what one has is what one has earned, and that what one is now earning is the result of one's efforts (i.e., those with low incomes deserve what they get). The capitalist system tends also to accentuate the normal tendency toward interpersonal conflict or competition to show off one's high position, leading among other things toward much material waste in the production of status goods. Along with the inequality built into a system of high concentration comes, typically, a lower level of total output than would have been possible in a more egalitarian system because of a degree of economic inefficiency which, in agriculture, owes itself to the relative inefficiency of large farms and in some other sectors to the restriction of output in order to garner monopoly profits.

The implicit vision of the good society in a feudal or a capitalist system is naturally contested by others. Socialism and communism argue for a more egalitarian arrangement; the latter traditionally opts for centralized management of the economy rather than leaving a high share of production to private individuals and companies. Given the obvious flaws of both these systems in practice, their critics have generated many ideas on what a really good society would be like. This topic has been the natural theme of philosophers. As noted previously, an early modern version was that of More, articulated in his work *Utopia*.

The history of land concentration may thus be seen against a number of alternative versions of a good society, either those implicit in a given socioeconomic structure or those made explicit by thinkers and philosophers. The version corresponding to a feudal system with an agrarian elite at the top is the traditionally dominant one, defended by that elite. The capitalist model is defended by those who come to the top under its operating mechanisms; they tend to argue that it is the most efficient way to organize an economy for the good of the people as a whole. The communist model grows out of the critique that capitalism naturally impoverishes the working people and should therefore be replaced by a system organized to benefit them. Its political component has usually been vague, as reflected in the concept of the "dictatorship of the proletariat." Democratic socialism can be seen as an attempt to marry the better features of market capitalism and those of an approach more directly targeted at the welfare of the people. Other concepts of the good society can be much more directly aspirational, as with those which seek to encourage people to be "better," or those, like the "Via Campesina" vision discussed in Chapter 6, which aspire to promote such positive aspects of social life as community spirit, defense of the environment, and so on.

How much land distribution matters to the welfare of agricultural workers does vary markedly across settings. Available production technologies and the institutions that facilitate or impede land rental and share-cropping help to determine the level of group conflict because they determine to what degree the income of each contending group may be influenced by the *de facto* rules of the game with respect to land rights. At one extreme is an agriculture that relies heavily on labor and thus creates a high need for it, whether the land is owned by small farmers or large landholders. The rice economy of various Asian countries has fit into this mold during various historical periods. If markets are fairly competitive, then the distribution of income is not likely to be very unequal, as witnessed in cases like Indonesia or Taiwan.[10] At the other extreme are agricultural sectors like Colombia's,

[10] How unequal the income distribution will be in such cases depends on the share of agricultural income accruing to land; if it is high and land ownership is unequal, then inequality will still be considerable. But only if slavery or other less extreme contraventions of free markets for inputs and outputs are present can political elites greatly distort this market-based outcome.

where, for a good number of regions, there is a wide range of options in terms of what can be produced and how it can be done. Who owns the land then greatly affects how it is used. A large, absentee owner may engage in extensive cattle-raising, which creates virtually no jobs or income for labor, whereas a small landholder will produce food for own consumption and the local market. Although much more output would be produced if the land in large farms were rented out to small farmers, this usually does not happen because the institutions of the land market do not work well enough.[11] Under such conditions the distribution of land can have an enormous effect on the distribution of income (and on its total level).

## The Defensive Narratives and (One-sided) Economic and Well-being Debates

The frequency of extreme inequality of income and well-being due to concentrated land ownership creates powerful arguments to alleviate that condition, either by redistribution when it already exists or by prevention when it is at risk of becoming high. They boil down to the propositions that a shift from high to low concentration (or to collective ownership) will (i) improve the income and well-being of the beneficiaries of such reform; (ii) improve the overall distribution of income and welfare, both at the time and usually far into the future; (iii) raise total agricultural output and GDP; and (iv) create a better, more considerate society that is closer to those favored by philosophers of the past and present.

The counterarguments, distilled into various anti-reform narratives, are usually based on inaccurate interpretations of reality. The most frequent misbelief is that large farms are systematically the most productive, so the country will wind up with more output the greater their role. As discussed in some detail in Chapter 3, this idea is usually based on those farms achieving higher labor productivity—the wrong criterion for efficiency in an economy where labor is abundant and other factors, including land, are scarce. Applying the more appropriate criterion—land productivity—reverses the conclusion because it is typically lower on large farms.

[11] Limited levels of trust between potential participants discourage land rental, as does the limited potential to use the legal system if the other partner to a deal reneges.

Another popular argument is that there are better places to create new and remunerative jobs to raise the incomes of the many poor agricultural families, for example, in manufacturing or services like transportation. For this argument to have any validity requires careful calculation of how many jobs can be created in each sector, why the market has not already done so, and what policy interventions would help to do so. In most cases where a reformed, small farm sector could create many more jobs than it now does, and thereby reduce poverty, the main alternative is not well-paying manufacturing jobs but lower productivity ones in the non-agricultural informal sector. Such jobs are often less productive from an aggregate economic point of view than those in small farming because a larger share of them are found in monopolistically competitive activities where the income earned exceeds the contribution to national income.[12] In any case, economic logic points to the best solution for low-income workers being the maximization of total demand for their services, which implies taking advantage of all the options available, including those in the agricultural sector.

A third fallacious argument is that small agriculture need not be expanded through a reform because employment found there, along with that in agriculture as a whole, shrinks as an economy develops. Economies do eventually move into post-agricultural phases in which the incomes of the lower income groups are pulled up by their employment in other activities. But the real question is whether the failure to take advantage of the current output and employment creation potential from small-scale agriculture will either slow down overall development or keep the incomes of the lower groups below what they might have been. Usually, the answer is yes.

While some opponents of reform do recognize that their country suffers from high inequality of income and from poverty, they much less often accept the proposition that a shift toward smaller farm units could raise total output while also improving the distribution of the associated income and lowering poverty. They are seldom aware of the inverse relationship typically found between farm size and land productivity. On the contrary, they believe and argue that the small farm sector is inherently uncompetitive. What economists mean by this term usually refers to enterprises that will go out of business under fair market conditions (e.g., if they get the same price for

[12] The theoretical argument is presented in Avinash K. Dixit and Joseph E. Stiglitz, "Monopolistic Competition and Optimum Product Diversity," *American Economic Review* 67, no. 3 (1977): 297–308.

their products as do other producers and pay the same price for purchased inputs) because there are more remunerative economic options for them in some other activity (e.g., working on larger farms, working in urban activities, etc.). Wherever small farms are numerous, these conditions are almost by definition not being met—otherwise, the farmers would have moved with any assets they own to those superior options. Sometimes the concept in the minds of those who label these farms uncompetitive is that the average person working there earns less than others, such as those on large farms. This view incorporates two conceptual errors; first, it does not recognize that different people may earn different amounts because they have different skills; and second, other workers may produce more per person than do the small farmers (e.g., those working for large agro-industrial firms). This does not mean that they are operating more efficiently but simply that they work with more capital. Former President Cardoso's economic team in Brazil seemed to be suffering from this conceptual error (see Chapter 6).

Large-scale agriculture's defense against land reform is built partly on a failure to recognize the evidence of higher land productivity on small farms and also on a narrow definition of economic efficiency that does not allow for the relevance of income inequality, negative externalities like environmental damage, or the social advantages of certain ways of organizing production. Small farm communities are well known for the non-economic benefits they provide. The defense of large agriculture coincides in part with the critique of socialism and community activities and, often, with the "freedom of enterprise" arguments to the effect that firms should be able to do what they want with few or no controls, even if what they do hurts others.

It is hard to overstate the role of created narratives in shaping and biasing the understanding of land issues. They are built around a combination of misbeliefs (inaccurate facts), misunderstanding of economic concepts, and a tendency to believe what one wants (e.g., that one's large farm is more efficient than the neighboring peasant's small one) or what seems intuitively plausible (that same view). As highlighted in the discussion of specific reform attempts (see later chapters in this text), most decision-makers on agricultural issues are quite unaware of how peasants live, work, and think. That is a separate world that they cannot easily enter or understand, even if they are interested in doing so. The fact that little is written about that world, either in the social sciences or in literature, contributes to its opaqueness. In most countries, the peasantry itself has been mainly illiterate until recent times. A lack of deep curiosity on the part of everyone else contributes. Alexander Chayanov's major contribution on the Russian peasantry got little attention until decades after he wrote. Scott (1976) provided a very unusual breakthrough from outside the peasant society. A number of sociologists and anthropologists have taken serious looks at this world, but their views do not enter popular thinking. With few explanations or defenses of the peasant way of life—its virtues, hardships, and challenges—most outsiders have simply imposed on it their own inclinations, and in the process judged the typical peasant to be unintelligent, incompetent, and so on. This situation makes it unsurprising that, even among decision-makers with some empathy, wrong conclusions would be reached and bad policies chosen.

The lack of knowledge and curiosity about peasant life has an interesting parallel in the urban poor of lower-income countries, whose life also tends to go unrecorded and, in many ways, is misunderstood. Probably the biggest breakthrough, one which brought much new insight to its readers, was that of Carolina Maria de Jesus (1962). That this Brazilian slum-dweller's story would ever reach a wide public required not only that she keep a diary but also that her situation and writing attract the attention of a Brazilian journalist. How unlikely it was that this second condition be met is suggested by the details. She was discovered by Audálio Dantas in April 1958, when he was covering the opening of a neighboring city playground. After the ribbon-cuttings, a street gang stormed in and claimed the area, chasing the children away. Dantas saw de Jesus standing at the edge of the playground shouting, "Leave, or I'll put you in my book!" at which point the intruders departed. Dantas asked what she meant by "book." Although initially hesitant, she took him to her shack and showed him what she had written. He first ran a small sample in his newspaper, and eventually published the heavily edited version that became famous, and which some critics thought to be a fraud. Fortunately, the original manuscript was preserved. Its 1999 publication demonstrated that de Jesus was a livelier, more poetic writer than suggested by the Dantas edition. She had given interviews and made other newspaper appearances since the early 1940s, but these had not provided the breakthrough eventually achieved.[13] Because the urban poor have typically been more visible to the intellectual elite than the peasantry, they have appeared

[13] Wikipedia, "Carolina Maria de Jesus," https://en.wikipedia.org/wiki/Carolina_Maria_de_Jesus.

more frequently in novels, like Charles Dickens's *Oliver Twist.* Dickens would probably have focused less on this group had his father not spent time in a debtors' prison. Victor Hugo's *Les Misérables* also reflected on the harshness of life for the urban poor. But rural counterparts are very scarce.[14]

Because the "economics of land concentration" are relatively straightforward, with little serious argument in favor of large farms, how history plays out is mainly a matter of politics and the exercise of power rather than of the implementation of economic policies chosen carefully and in accord with the benefits they bring to society. This implies, among other things, that all progressive actors in the land drama need to deal with the political factors at work. And because the factors working against the prevention of rising land concentration may be less daunting than those standing in the way of redistribution to lower that concentration, the dominance of politics suggests the importance of the former approach, as well as the more obvious latter one. This may be especially true as countries get farther along in the development process and, as a result, become less agricultural. Later in that process, creating a push for reform often becomes harder because the share of total population made up of families aggrieved because of lack of land is relatively small; a push against further accumulation may be easier if the urban population becomes aware of the environmental damage it may cause.

## Appendix 1.1

### The Lewis "Labor Surplus Model"

In Figure 1.1 the marginal product of labor curves for the modern or capitalist sector (MPLm and MPLm') are drawn to the right from the left-side vertical axis; the corresponding curves for the traditional sector (MPLt and MPLt') are drawn to the left from the right-side vertical axis. When a sector grows, its MPL curve shifts in the indicated directions. At a point in time when the MPLm and MPLt curves describe the situation of the two sectors, the total amount of labor available (distance 00') is more than can be used productively in the two sectors together. The amount OE is hired in the modern sector

[14] Tolstoy was probably the most famous member of an agricultural elite who tried to get close to peasant life. He did so physically by undertaking much peasant work, like plowing, and socially by spending much time with the peasants, partly to make his writing about peasant life more realistic. His lifelong dream was to transcend or erase class lines and "cross over to the peasantry." Mohandas Ghandi was famous for revering the simple life, but he was not raised in the agricultural sector.

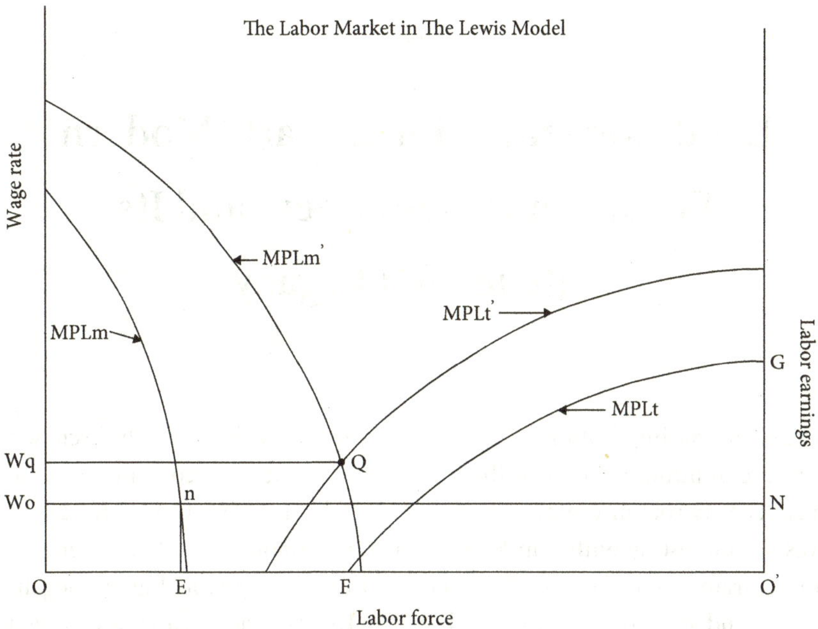


**Figure 1.1** The Labor Market in the Lewis Model.

and the rest remains in the traditional sector, with the amount EF having no potential productivity. The modern sector wage (OWo) is assumed to be just high enough to attract the needed labor from the traditional sector, often referred to as a "subsistence wage." With the growth of one or both sectors (here both are assumed to grow), the two MPL curves shift toward the center and intersect at point Q. The equilibrium wage rate, which equates the supply and demand for labor, is now above subsistence and surplus labor no longer exists.

# 2
# Land Concentration in Early Modern European Development and Its Intellectual Legacy

The economic implications of land concentration have been widely discussed for several hundred years in the European context. One contentious issue has been its role in the region's economic advance. The United Kingdom was an interesting outlier in Europe's history, famous for not experiencing an agrarian revolution, as did France or Russia, despite its highly inegalitarian land structure. Built around the English experience, a view emerged that larger farms were responsible for the agricultural productivity growth achieved during the early modern period, with the "enclosures"—whereby formerly common land was brought under the exclusive control of the manorial lord—being given much credit.[1] Enclosures increased the average size of the operating unit and decreased the share operated as commons. Many writers have linked enclosures to rising productivity through some type of economies of scale; others have argued that land under commons tends to be less productive; still others have pointed to the superior capacities and/or educational levels of the people in charge of the new, larger, and wholly privately owned units rather than of those running the smaller commons-based units. Traditional economic history often credits this earlier "agricultural revolution" with helping to pave the way for the later Industrial Revolution, which put the country on its path toward global economic leadership.

Although there have always been some dissenting opinions, the idea that large farms enjoyed a productivity advantage was accepted by most students of agrarian history until about thirty to forty years ago, when it was finally

[1] Enclosure refers to the consolidation of communal fields in Western Europe into delineated and individually owned and managed farms. Before enclosure, much farmland existed in dispersed strips under the control of individual cultivators only during the growing season until harvest; thereafter, it was available to the community for livestock grazing and other purposes. "Enclosing" the land involved establishing a hedge or fence to prevent common grazing and other uses.

*The Great Curse.* Albert Berry, Oxford University Press. © Oxford University Press 2024.
DOI: 10.1093/oso/9780197782675.003.0003

thrown into serious question, in particular by the work of Robert Allen (1992). Doubt was cast on the inherent inefficiency of land operated as commons at about the same time.[2] The durability of these two views underlines the power of narratives with deep roots in influential circles.

This combination of ideas not only endured for a long period as the standard English narrative, but it showed up everywhere else as well, including eighteenth- and nineteenth-century Europe, where peasant farming was widely seen as a stumbling block to development; twentieth-century Soviet Union and other communist countries; and, later, many developing countries. "For all those who contrast a traditional society with a modern one, for all those who argue that the traditional society must be overturned for development to occur, for all those who see inequality as the necessary price of growth, England is the classic case" (Allen 1992, 2). These views were shared by eminent historians like Arnold Toynbee (1884), for whom the large farms permitted scientific culture to replace the unscientific, and by textbook writers like Wilson (1984) a century later.[3] In the English case, virtually every detail of the intellectual construct that lasted for a couple of hundred years has eventually been shown to be either untrue or questionable.

In tracing English agriculture's shift from medieval to modern institutions, Allen (1992) explores their effects on productivity growth, income distribution, and overall economic development. He argues that contrary to the presumption of many historians, small-scale farmers in the open-field system were responsible for a considerable proportion of the productivity growth achieved between the Middle Ages and the nineteenth century. The process of enclosure and the replacement of these yeomen by large-scale tenant farming relying on wage labor had relatively little impact on the contribution of agriculture to economic development during the Industrial Revolution. Enclosures and large farms enriched landowners without benefiting consumers, workers, or farmers.

[2] A number of English historians had, over the years, expressed dissatisfaction with the conventional wisdom and, in particular, with the importance attached to enclosures. Among them was Havinden (1961); for more details see Allen (1992), who notes that while these studies did attract considerable interest from specialists, their scope was typically limited to the enclosures and it did not change the conventional wisdom on the bigger picture.

[3] Nobel prize winner Robert Fogel, a student of the economics of American slavery (Fogel and Engerman 1974) and a proponent of cliometrics (the study of economic history with a focus on quantification), attributed part of the progress of US agriculture to economies of scale and the increasing size of farms. In contrast, Earl Heady, one of the doyens of agricultural economics in the second half of the century in the US, at a talk at Yale University, Economic Growth Center (circa 1967), noted with a degree of puzzlement how difficult it was to quantitatively demonstrate any significant economies of scale in US agriculture.

Debates on the economic efficiency of large farms and the impact of the enclosures were well under way in Europe by the eighteenth century and were made more intense by the revolutionary settings in a number of other countries. In England, what Allen (1992) refers to as "Agrarian Fundamentalism" was the dominant strain of thought. It consisted of three claims: (i) that the ongoing technical revolution, which raised farm productivity, was the result of replacing the "traditional" or "feudal" peasant farms and open fields of the Middle Ages with large, private farms that included the formerly open but now enclosed fields; (ii) that this growth in agricultural productivity gave a strong boost to England's early industrialization, or was even a prerequisite; and (iii) that the growth in farm efficiency and the expansion of manufacturing could not have been achieved in an egalitarian society because there was an inevitable trade-off between growth and equity.

Early opposition to this Agrarian Fundamentalism was based on moral grounds. From the fifteenth century onward, critics of enclosure claimed that the large farms created thereby were an injustice, enriching the landowners at the expense of the poor. By the mid-nineteenth century, economic critiques were more common. William Thomas Thornton (1843/2019) used many examples to contend that small owner-operators were actually more efficient than tenant farmers. Alexis de Tocqueville shared that view, as did John Stuart Mill, but neither the cogency of the latter's arguments nor his considerable stature was enough to greatly weaken the fundamentalist consensus within English thought. Further, it is possible that his change of view toward the end of his life in favor of cooperative farms to achieve economies of scale did not help.[4] By the late nineteenth century, the debate had become intense in central and eastern Europe. Vladimir Lenin claimed that capitalist farms were more efficient and were driving peasants out of business in Russia. The persistence of the peasantry in Germany and France was attributed variously to their working harder than paid laborers, to their capacity to innovate, and

[4] Hollander (1985). Mill's opposition to the English and Irish agrarian systems stemmed primarily from the degree to which the division of society into rich and poor classes was unconnected to merit or effort but was rather essentially a result of conquest and violence. He favored social, political, and economic arrangements which presented everyone with an equal opportunity to achieve happiness (or income) and which rewarded them for diligence and initiative. Mill argued that the English government should actively promote small-scale agriculture in Ireland because property arrangements had created a very unequal distribution of income and had left many families on the margin of subsistence. And, while he accepted the presence of economies of scale in industry, Mill believed that, in agriculture, the division of labor yielded few benefits (Peart 1984). Mill foresaw nearly all of the arguments for small-scale agriculture which have been borne out by research since his time.

to other factors. In a comprehensive assessment, Doreen Warriner (1939, 99) demonstrated that Holland, Denmark, Switzerland, Bohemia, and western Poland achieved crop yields similar to those in the United Kingdom; she concluded that their labor productivity was comparable to that of large farms and that they offered "no hindrance to technical progress" (Warriner 1939, 7).

As noted in Chapter 1, when the enclosures brought an end to an earlier pattern of life, they were accompanied by a narrative on the inefficiency of production in the commons and the term' tragedy of the commons', together with an economic theory as to why common land available to all would be inefficiently used because overused. Only in the latter part of the twentieth century did this interpretation come under serious attack. In the process, many of the hypotheses underpinning the traditional argument have been weakened by an increasingly general rejection of the serious inefficiency of open fields. Carl J. Dahlman (1980) argues that the two major characteristics of this type of agriculture—scattered strips owned by individual peasants and extensive areas of common land—both fulfilled key economic functions.[5] Open fields are now widely viewed as an economically rational response to environmental and commercial considerations. Many of the techniques once derided by historians as inefficient, such as crop rotations, are now advocated by agronomists as part of sustainable farming technology in developing countries. The relative constancy in the technology employed by farmers in pre-industrial France led George Grantham (1993) to argue that no significant increase in labor productivity could have taken place until mechanization emerged in the early nineteenth century.

In deconstructing the intellectual edifice of Agrarian Fundamentalism, Allen (1992) drew a sharp distinction between two agricultural revolutions in England. The first, or "yeomen's," revolution was a product of the century of population decline and destabilization wrought by the Black Death of 1346–1353. An associated increase in labor mobility and in real wages and a sharp decline in rents led to enclosures and conversion to less labor-intensive pasture farming. "Between 1450 and 1525, about one-tenth of the villages in the midlands were destroyed via enclosures that eliminated small-scale agriculture and replaced it with capitalist relations" (Allen 1992, 14). But enclosures in the remaining open-field villages led,

[5] See also McCloskey (1991) and the review by Karakacili (2004).

ironically, to the consolidation of peasant agriculture. In view of the ongoing deterioration of the previous structure, the Crown began protecting the peasant farmers, especially through the extension of property rights by the courts, a legal transformation that ended the worst of existing feudal abuses and created the tenurial stability of the yeoman farmers who flourished under Queen Elizabeth and the Stuarts, and to whom Allen (1992) attributes much of the productivity growth in the early modern period. This "yeoman's" revolution (1600 to 1750) was marked by a doubling of corn yields; it raised England's national income and exerted downward pressure on food prices and upward pressure on wages. The benefits were thus distributed widely.

In contrast, the second, or "landlords'" revolution, which occurred mainly in the eighteenth century and consisted primarily of enclosure and farm amalgamation, did not increase output. It did, however, reduce farm employment, especially of women and boys. Despite their progressive farming, the yeomen were eliminated; the only beneficiaries were large landlords. The impact on income inequality was clearly negative. Allen (1992, 21) thus judges that "most English men and women would have been better off had the landlords' revolution never occurred."

On the matter of their contributions to industrial advance, Allen (1992) again contrasts the yeomen's and landlords' revolutions. Agricultural productivity growth can aid industrialization and economic growth, not only by supplying the needed food but also by providing savings to finance manufacturing investment. In England, most of the productivity gains of the landlords' revolution accrued to the large landholders as rent increases; instead of being savers, they were typically net borrowers, spending their fortunes on stately homes and elegant living. A concentration of agricultural wealth could, in principle, have been a boon in the financing of the Industrial Revolution, but he judges that, in fact, it was not, and that agriculture thus made little contribution to industrial capital formation.

Allen's (1992) revisionist interpretation of the post-medieval history of English agriculture is not a consensus view. Mark Overton (1996, 16), for example, maintains that "if the criteria for an 'agricultural revolution' are taken to be unprecedented changes in output and in the productivity of land and labour, then it is the period after the mid-eighteenth century that emerges as having such a revolution. It was during the eighteenth century that population was able to break through the ceiling of 5.5 million, that crop yields made a sustained improvement on medieval levels, and that land and labour productivity were rising together."

Given the lack of the aggregate output and input data over time normally used to settle such issues, analysts have resorted to a range of alternative approaches. One such method has been cross-section comparisons between production achieved in enclosures versus that in open fields. Allen (1999) defends this technique in his refutation of Overton's (1996) conclusions. Allen and Overton do agree that yields were independent of farm size, a view that contradicts the traditional wisdom. In reference to that "wisdom" he notes, "Many historians writing earlier in this century had a narrow view of the agricultural revolution—when it happened and what it consisted of. They emphasized the views of the eighteenth-century improvers who were enamoured of the institutions and innovations of their own day—hence the emphasis on the progressive role of the great estate, the importance of enclosure, and the productivity-raising effects of turnips, clover, and new sheep . . . . Recently, historians have placed the eighteenth century in a much longer historical context" (Allen 1999, 231). Such revisionism counteracts the general tendency in many areas of history to focus on certain allegedly key people and their discoveries and innovations at the expense of more general patterns of change. Reassessment has also been facilitated by the accumulation and analysis of quantitative information, which on many issues has occurred only in recent decades (see the discussion of late nineteenth-century Russian agricultural history in Chapter 5).

Gregory Clark (2009, 576) presents a third view, contrasting with both Allen (1992, 1999) and Overton (1996), to the effect that there was, in fact, no agricultural "revolution," in the sense of a period of much faster productivity growth, at least not since 1700. Clark (2009) concludes that productivity growth has been quite continuous over that time. He concurs with Overton and Allen on the need to downplay the institutions favored by some historians and the roles of pioneers of new techniques like Jethro Tull, Charles Townsend, and Arthur Young, whom he describes as "self-publicizing midgets" who were less important than "a broad swath of farmers across a broad sweep of time."

Another new twist comes from Eona Karakacili (2004), who finds that carefully recorded data from the Ramsey estates (in what is now Cambridgeshire) over the first half of the fourteenth century reveal that the labor productivity of crop workers was as high as anything recorded when more or less reliable aggregate data on output and labor productivity became available later in the pre-industrial period. These outcomes were achieved under conditions that, according to the traditional view, would result in quite low labor productivity: "much of the work was performed by serfs, in open fields, using medieval technology, during a time in which population pressures on land resources reached their peak" (2004, 43). In what they measure, Karakacili's (2004) numbers are much more reliable than those of most other sources; uncertainty does arise, however, with respect to how representative these estates were at the time.[6] If the Ramsey estates were close to being representative, Karakacili's evidence of labor productivity being as high in the first half of the fourteenth century as at the time of the Industrial Revolution, would refute the conclusion that the enclosures generated a productivity jump to previously unseen levels. As she notes, they might have contributed to a substantial increase if a decline occurred between the period to which her data refer and that of the enclosures, a matter that cannot easily be sorted out. But, even if rising productivity did occur over part of that period—either smoothly as Clark (2009) contends, or unevenly as posited by Allen (1992, 1999) and Overton (1996), the high productivity on the Ramsey estates would still tend to contradict the idea that such an increase was the result of the transition from the production practices on the Ramsey estates to those applied in the enclosures.

Even though information gaps will preclude a very detailed rendering of English agrarian history for at least some time into the future, the traditional narrative appears to be doomed by the breadth of plausible evidence that, one way or another, contradicts it. As noted below, the evolving knowledge about pre-revolutionary agriculture in Russia shares two key features with the English story: the traditional and widely accepted narrative had the numbers wrong with respect to productivity trends over the relevant period, and there was a presumption of inefficiency in open fields (communes), which, in retrospect, has proven to be wrong or implausible.

As discussed in some detail below, professional understanding has now laid to rest the sort of debates that continued for a couple of hundred years in England and elsewhere in Europe around whether the small farm could be at least reasonably efficient compared to the large one. For over a century, the "size and productivity" debate was necessarily based on limited

[6] The author opts to focus on numbers in the lower part of her range of estimates to counter this problem.

quantitative evidence. By the second half of the twentieth century, more information was available, and the balance of professional opinion was shifting further in favor of the smaller farm. Thus, Nobel prize-winning development economist Arthur Lewis (1955, 136) noted that, although the typical farm in Japan was only about two to three acres, output per acre was two to three times that of other parts of Asia. Output in Japan had increased by nearly fifty percent in the thirty years before the first World War, and it doubled again by the mid-1930s with no significant change in farm size. Lewis (1955) thus concludes that peasant farming was not an impediment to rising agricultural productivity. Since the 1950s, a wave of new quantitative evidence has emerged in many parts of the world and a consensus has emerged. Not only is smallness not an impediment to high land productivity; more often than not it is accompanied by an advantage on that front. Another Nobel Prize winner, Amartya Sen (1962), provided the first empirical evidence from India to show that land productivity in the Punjab was higher on small farms, a pattern that came to be known as the Inverse Relationship (IR). The Inter-American Committee for Agricultural Development did the same for several Latin American countries (e.g., Barraclough and Domike 1970), which, as Michael Lipton (2009, 66) puts it, "inspired two generations of productivity conscious reformers," including both liberal economists and some Marxists. These reformers argued that, because of the IR between farm size and land productivity, a transfer of land from large farms to smaller ones could be expected to raise total output. A World Bank policy paper (World Bank 1975) advocated for ceilings-based, productivity-conscious, and non-confiscatory land reform, citing evidence of the IR. By the 1970s, this relationship had arguably become one of the "stylized facts of development," accepted by nearly everyone who had looked at the issue and questioned only by a few, usually on weak grounds. Professional discussion has come to focus less on the existence of the IR and more on its implications; that is, on whether it connotes an economic efficiency advantage for smaller farms, how the relationship varies by context, what it means from an economic and social point of view, and how it changes as agricultural and overall development proceed. But among the various such stylized facts, this one has probably entered with the least force into the policy process. It has been confronted by the powerful vested interests stacked against land reform. Additionally, many people simply find it counterintuitive. As emphasized by Clark (1991), the traditional (pro large size) interpretation of the English story has permeated thinking around the world. Although a process of correction is underway among students of the issue, it is slow and always incomplete.

The detailed empirical evidence now available creates the potential for more effective policy-making in today's developing countries than would have been possible in the now industrial countries but, as discussed below, this empirical evidence runs up against many of the same barriers that confronted the astute observations of Mill and those others whose direct assessments led them to believe that the small farm could match or outdo the larger one. The relative weakness of "facts" as opposed to "preferred narratives" is apparent both in history and at present. The narrative in favor of large farms has two special advantages: it accords with most people's intuition, and it is the view held by most of the wealthy, the educated, and those with big interests in agriculture.

The political and analytical debates surrounding the size question do naturally differ across contrasting scenarios. In England, the preponderant view was that the larger units were more productive; most of the participants relied on their own observations and intuitions because detailed quantification was not yet the order of the day. With the issue widely assumed to be settled, it was only long after that history had played itself out that a new professional view emerged to the effect that the enclosures were unlikely to have been an important contributor to productivity growth whenever this did occur. The presumptions underlying the traditionally dominant theoretical construct turned out to be wrong or questionable, but those holding that view could be forgiven in part because there were few, if any, detailed numbers to draw on. Today's developing countries became the next arena of debate. Twentieth-century economists still refer back to Mill's views and others of the previous century, but the empirical evidence has come mainly from India, other Asian countries, and Latin America. Defenders of the status quo have relied more on diverting attention from the issue than on confronting the "facts" thrown up by the numbers, although there has been some of both. The discussion eventually came to be based on econometrics as tests were performed to check whether the observed IR was due to things like differing land quality, intensity of labor inputs, or other factors possibly at work. Like their earlier English counterparts, defenders of the existing structure have sometimes framed the issue as one of efficiency versus equality. In countries like Colombia and Brazil, the debate has had much in common with the debate surrounding climate change—an extreme dichotomy between those familiar with the evidence, among whom the discussion is often about non-central details, and those unfamiliar with the evidence and/or representing vested interests. Within the vested interest groups, some people have at least an inkling that their case is flawed.[7] The politics around land distribution have, for some decades, included fearmongering, as reformers are tarred with the socialist or communist brush. The term "land reform" has been denigrated in a way akin to socialism's long-time malignancy within US politics, or the recent disparaging of the "carbon tax" in Canada, the US, and other countries. Supporters of land redistribution thus must avoid the more poisonous terms used in the debate.

The last arena for these "small versus large" battles is Sub-Saharan Africa (SSA). There, the contest is much more recent, with most strong proponents of the smaller farm only emerging clearly on the scene over the last couple of decades. As the Latin and SSA debates heated up (to the extent that they did), the history of the East Asian success stories entered the picture and upended any simplistic views that small farms could never achieve high land productivity or dramatic productivity gains over time.[8]

As noted, the twentieth-century debates on land reform had a partial precursor in those around the enclosures of earlier centuries. There was some awareness that when an enclosure evicted former tenants it did harm them—the income distribution and poverty part of the phenomenon, but it was widely accepted that, from a purely economic or efficiency point of view, this was a positive development and one that preceded and helped to foster the Industrial Revolution.

A special feature of the British experience of rising land concentration was the unusual range of alternative opportunities available to people as the enclosures cut off their access to land and exercised a downward impact on their earnings. Absent either the Industrial Revolution or the possibility of emigration, shifting a population out of the existing agricultural operations would have been much more difficult. That the Industrial Revolution was not a strong "pull" factor is, however, suggested by the very harsh living

[7] A possible manifestation in Colombia was the lengthy (fifty-four year) gap between the one reasonable quality agricultural census of the twentieth century (in 1960) and the next one (in 2014), with the latter at one point being cancelled, allegedly for lack of funds but possibly as much in recognition that information like that generated by a census could be dangerous to the vested interests.

[8] Among the explanations as to why that sort of success could not happen in Latin America was that of a prominent Peruvian politician and writer to the effect that "Latins would not or could not work as hard as Asians" (personal comment).

conditions of urban workers, often noted to be worse health-wise than those of their rural counterparts. That it left a great and generally positive legacy can be accepted, while also speculating that it, and the possibility of emigration to opening countries, were among the reasons that the UK did not have an agrarian revolution during these times.

# 3

# Economic and Welfare Impacts of Farm Size and Tenure

## Measuring a Farm's Contribution

**NOTE: The many and serious problems in the measurement of "economic efficiency" are reviewed briefly in Appendix 3.1, with a special focus on those problems related to total factor productivity (TFP). Because it is not possible to know how serious these problems are in most of the cited studies, no overall attempt is made in this volume to identify the problems or to correct for them. It is left to the reader to keep in mind the possible resulting biases.**

* * *

Farm-size structure is one of many features that affect an agricultural sector's performance. Analysis of its impact begins with an appropriate definition of a good performance, identifies what directly affects that performance (amount of inputs like labor and land), and sorts out how aspects of the setting (e.g., security of access to land) come into play. Using level of output (value added) or the ratio of that output to inputs used (total factor productivity-TFP) as the measure of performance is overly simplistic. A more complete definition is needed to take account of how size structure affects other variables, especially the distribution of income and welfare. For an individual, a family, or a country, "performance" should reflect not only the participants' income, but also their economic security and their direct satisfaction from work activity and from the setting in which the work is carried out.[1] Relevant aspects of that setting include things like whether one manages one's own farm or works for someone else, how one is treated in that work, and so on. To judge the performance of agriculture at an aggregate level, the effects on the

[1] "Performance" more broadly defined should include not only a producing unit's contribution to human satisfaction at a point of time, but also its contribution to the growth of satisfaction over time.

*The Great Curse.* Albert Berry, Oxford University Press. © Oxford University Press 2024.
DOI: 10.1093/oso/9780197782675.003.0004

wellbeing of each person or family must somehow be summed up. When total value of income or output is the chosen measure, the implicit assumption is that one more dollar of income has the same value to each person or family; however, this is obviously untrue in any economy where income is unevenly distributed. So, some decision must be made on how much more weight to give a dollar of income received by a poor family than a dollar received by a rich family.[2]

The fact that maximization of output, or even of income, cannot plausibly be seen as the sole objective of any small farmer takes us into deeper issues of peasant life and behavior and to how it differs from other groups. Two common concepts associated with these discussions are "rationality" (i.e., basing decisions on the use of logic) and "economic efficiency." Much discussion has revolved around the matter of whether peasants are rational, despite the fact that no outsider could plausibly make a judgment without first knowing the subject's preference system(s). Although, in principle, that term typically refers to a decision-making process that allows an individual to reach the maximum level of benefit or satisfaction attainable under given circumstances, it is often treated as synonymous with "profit-maximization," which is thought of (loosely) as the basic criterion of a firm in a market-oriented economic system. Such a view implies that leisure has no value to people, that social interactions do not matter, that harming the environment does not matter, and so forth.[3] The more astute and in-depth analysts of peasant systems and behavior do, of course, take account of lifestyle preferences. A century ago, Alexander Chayanov[4] judged peasants to be rational actors and explained their behavior in terms of their dual role as family head and entrepreneur and their awareness of the possible drudgery of labor. He drew on a huge body of statistics on Russian peasant behavior and produced one of the most sophisticated analyses ever carried out. (As noted in Chapter 5, it was not at all persuasive for the Soviet decision-makers of the time.) Unlike the vast majority of commentators on peasant behavior, Chayanov recognized that it was not logical (or defensible) to judge peasant

[2] The path-breaking study by Chenery et al. (1974) suggested that economic accounting move in this direction.

[3] A few measures of economic efficiency do take fairly careful account of hours worked (and hence, implicitly, of the amount of leisure), but none, to my knowledge, have tried independently to assess the direct satisfaction a family realizes from the "peasant" lifestyle, whatever exactly that may be.

[4] His work is described by Greenwood (1973, 16) as "perhaps the most impressive political economy synthesis of peasant family farming ever done." A much later major contribution was that of Scott (1976), who delved into peasant behavior with a focus on Southeast Asia.

rationality without understanding what they value (their "utility function" in modern economic parlance). Any judgment of someone's rationality must reflect their psychology and their setting. Flagrant misuse of that concept fosters misuse of the term "efficiency"; it is not possible to judge how efficient a peasant has been in his economic activity until one knows what his goals are.

Meanwhile the gap between "economic rationality" and "social rationality"—where the former takes account only of the economic effects of one's activities, and the latter includes other effects as well—is wide when economic behavior has important impacts on the social interactions among people. A small farm system, where everyone has about the same amount of land, often provides a convivial setting, making those interactions unusually positive. This is in stark contrast to the situation of serfs in a classic feudal system, where hard work, low incomes, and a generally inferior physical quality of life are combined with abuse from the landowners (see Chapter 5 and Chapter 6), although the mutual consideration built into serfdom is sometimes better than the objectification that workers suffer in a capitalist system.

Just as peasants or small farmers have other motivations than income or profits, so, too, do large landowners. The mentality of the "rentier" class, which derives major social and political benefits from ownership, contrasts with that of "entrepreneurs" who seek access to land solely to make a profit from its use. Commercial agriculture (e.g., palm oil production) fits this latter mold. It is therefore less likely to suffer low land or labor productivity than may "rentier" agriculture. A third mentality is that of the speculator, who profits from purchases and sales and may not be very interested in achieving high productivity or profits. Thus, as one seeks to explain how a high level of land concentration affects productivity, it is important to distinguish possible motivations: exploitation of/control over labor; access to political and social status and power; living well, as per the landed elite; profits from entrepreneurial agriculture; and profits from speculation in land.[5] Such varied objectives among large landholders help to explain differences across settings

[5] One suggested source of bad rural and agricultural outcomes is the intensity of land speculation, particularly prevalent in countries like Colombia, where land is associated with local social and political prestige and has been relatively easy to acquire by displacing occupants through physical force or legal manipulation. While perhaps not as damaging in an urban setting, such speculation can still have negative impacts on economic growth. Kindleberger (1996) argues that as the focus of a country's economy shifts away from industry and toward finance and the frequently zero-sum character of many of its component activities, overall growth tends to slow.

in the relative performance of farms by size, as well as by changes in performance over time. Distinct motivations and behavioral patterns are not mutually exclusive. Thus, the property of a member of the landed elite may be quite productive if that family is able and willing to hire effective managers. If they do not, it is unsurprising that productivity will be low and will not rise much over time. An indirect way to "hire" managers is to rent the land, which may then be operated under various possible payment arrangements. Some provide strong motivation for the operator to achieve high productivity, although often they are less effective at spurring investment in improvements and/or in the taking of risks to achieve higher productivity. When a land reform is on the horizon, both its feasibility and its likely impacts can be affected greatly by whichever of these large-scale systems currently exists; in particular, a reform which passes ownership to former tenants without their having to relocate physically or greatly alter their operations is more straightforward and, as a result, more assured of success than one which involves new small landowners on land that they have not cultivated before.

The best benchmark of the performance of a given farming system is its *impact on societal welfare, measured by personal happiness, weighting that satisfaction plausibly across people and taking account of effects on future generations through environmental impacts.* Although such a broad-ranging criterion has not, to my knowledge, been used in quantitative assessments of the relative performance of different groups of farms, it would be expected under many circumstances to greatly favor the smaller units. Along with its economic inefficiency and its failure to provide good lives to workers, large scale agriculture has been a major source of damage both to natural resources, especially forests, and to the climate. Whatever other factors need to be considered in comparing performance between small and large farm systems, a key historical correlate of the latter must be borne in mind—the abuse of workers. It is argued in Chapter 6 that, in cases like Bolivia and Mexico, while the income gains to land reform beneficiaries were certainly substantial, even more important was the improvement in quality of life that came with the end of the sort of serfdom previously endured by these groups.

That both small and large operators may have a range of motivations and related welfare benefits beyond income earned does not render estimates of differences in productivity and income of no value, as long as they are recognized for what they are: descriptive statements that say nothing definitive about "efficiency" until interpreted against individual and social preference systems. The policy-oriented economist can still make administrative judgments as long as a reasonable guess can be made as to how small farms, for example, measure up against alternative uses of land in terms of those benefits and costs which cannot be readily measured, or of how much a group of farms contributes on other missing dimensions, like environmental impacts. Thus, if it is a reasonable guess that the family gets greater direct pleasure out of this form of life than would be enjoyed by those involved in the alternative uses to which the land could be put, *and* the evidence indicates that it produces more per unit of input, it becomes a safe bet that it is the most socially efficient way to use that land and the accompanying inputs.

Economists typically limit themselves to the income (or output) component of a firm's or a sector's performance. In this narrow analysis, the goal is to sort out how much various inputs contribute to output, as well as how various background conditions may affect output. When the main focus is on the direct inputs, the story may be summed up in the equation:

$$Q = f(\text{land, capital, pure labor, human capital; other})$$

where Q, the amount of agricultural output, depends on the amount of each listed input, as well as on other specified determinants.

Many other factors may affect output, including quality of land; availability of adequate water, including through irrigation; susceptibility of crops to pests; and distance from markets. Because how inputs work together to produce outputs may vary across institutional settings, understanding those settings matters. For example, it has been widely argued that secure access to the land one operates affects one's current and, even more, one's future productivity. To include this issue in a statistical analysis, one may add the variable "title" to distinguish between those farmers who have such security and those who do not. Many other background conditions may also affect the output of at least some farm operators.

When to the complexities in the definition of performance are added—those of identifying the above "production function" accurately in a given setting—it becomes evident that conclusions drawn about the determinants of performance are always subject to some degree of error. The final stage of any analysis involves guessing which gaps in our understanding are most likely to lead to incorrect conclusions and trying to fill those gaps.

Along with the need for a broad definition of how the performance of a farm or a sector affects those directly involved is the need to consider the possible impacts on others. This requires a distinction between "private efficiency" and "societal efficiency"; the former refers to how well the farm operator is able to satisfy family needs, while the latter also takes account of any impacts of that operation on other people. Positive and negative externalities are one source of differences between the two. When chemical wastes from one farm are channeled into a river only to then damage properties downstream, that farm is responsible for a negative externality, the value of which must be subtracted from the value of its output to convert its score on private efficiency to its score on social efficiency. And, whereas private efficiency includes impacts on family economic security, personal pleasure when operating/living on the farm, and so forth, some non-economic effects of owning/operating a farm have positive or negative impacts on others as well. Thus, when owning a large piece of land provides one with economic and social prestige that is, by definition, limited in quantity (the more one person has the less someone else must have), the benefits involved are part of a zero-sum or limited-sum game. Holding land for speculative purposes also often constitutes a zero-sum game because, if the actual owner did not receive the benefits of its appreciation, someone else would have.[6] Income earned from zero-sum games raises the private profitability of a farm but does not raise its social efficiency.

The remainder of this chapter discusses empirical evidence bearing on the broad question of which agrarian structures perform the best, with a focus on whether and when a system of mainly small family farms is superior to a system of larger farms. For most such broad questions there is no single simple answer; rather, it depends both on what the performance criteria are and on the specific setting. As just noted, one such criterion is the total amount of agricultural output generated or of income earned; another criterion gives greater weight to a dollar earned by a worker than a dollar earned by a rich farmer; yet another criterion takes account of the satisfaction generated directly by the activity performed for each participant and weighs these benefits across people in some meaningful way.

Because the simpler approaches are more commonly applied and easier to understand, the discussion typically begins with a look at the factors affecting

[6] The security against loss of wealth from inflation provided by owning land may be a zero-sum game if the benefits in question are the same regardless of the owner. However, if it leads to ownership by those who most benefit from the cited protection, it may contribute positively to overall societal welfare.

total agricultural output, and then moves to the more meaningful performance indicators. In a few cases, there is directly usable evidence on how systems perform against those broader criteria, but more often one must try to adjust the figures used in the narrow analysis to fit the more nuanced ones.

## The Impacts of Farm Size and Tenure

A key distinction in an agrarian system is that between who owns a piece of land and who operates it. Most empirical analyses of farm-size structure focus on the operated unit because it is recorded in most agricultural censuses and samples. But where ownership and operation are not systematically in the same hands it is important to take both into account. Agrarian reforms may or may not shift ownership to the "beneficiary" and they may or may not involve a change in who operates the land involved. A useful taxonomy for thinking about reforms thus distinguishes (i) who controls or owns the land; (ii) who operates the land; and (iii) any conditions imposed on the use of land, payments for that use, and so forth (see Table 3.1).

Any reform makes changes to the existing structure. The simplest takes land from a previous private owner "with clear title" to it and assigns it to a new private owner, also with a clear title, who may have been the operator before (e.g., a tenant or a sharecropper) or not. The new owner may or may not pay for the acquired land, and the former owner may be recompensed fully, partially, or not at all. Many reforms are less clear cut, usually because control of the land is less straightforward. For example, ownership may be vested in the state, but the land is "squatted on" (i.e., operated without title) in either small or large units. Ownership or control is often ambiguous because of a lack of legal records and an assumption of control by anyone who has been operating it for a period of time. Sometimes private ownership systems overlap with community systems, especially in Sub-Saharan Africa (SSA). In some societies, again most notably in SSA, community authorities (e.g., elders) are responsible for reallocating land among members according to perceived need and under a presumption of more or less equal access. Sometimes the operator of a piece of land does so under specified conditions. A renter or sharecropper may bargain with (or accept the orders of) the owner with respect to which products will be grown and how they will be grown. Landlords often allocate small amounts of land to the families

**Table 3.1** Agrarian Structures and Associated Working Conditions/Security

| Ownership/ Control | Operator | | | | | |
|---|---|---|---|---|---|---|
| | **Owner** | **Tenant** | **Share-cropper** | **Hired Labor** | **Squatter** | **Slave Labor/serfdom** |
| The state | — | Frequent in socialist countries | — | Some socialist countries | Frequent in many countries | — |
| Large private owner | In modern commercial agriculture | Frequent; conditions vary widely | Frequent; conditions vary widely | Frequent; conditions vary widely | Some cases of absentees owners or remote setting | Historically common in some countries; serfdom also common |
| Small private owner | A normal arrangement | Fairly frequent | Sometimes | Usually at a modest level | Uncommon | Unusual at any time |
| Community | May be jointly operated | Uncommon | Uncommon | Uncommon | Common | Rare |
| Ambiguous | — | Possible | Possible | Possible | Possible | Unlikely |

*Note*: It is usually unclear whether the land is owned by the state or a private individual of workers so that they can produce food for their own consumption, but they do not allow them to produce items for sale (e.g., coffee). In communist countries, the state typically maintains ownership even when land is allocated to families or groups of families, and it may control the way the land is used in various ways. This leaves the farm family with less than total control over operation.

The security of rights to a piece of land can thus be ambiguous for many reasons, from the fact that there may be overlapping and confused rights to it, to the possibility that the operator may be displaced by force regardless of any legal or custom-based title. The likely economic impact, as well as the other effects of a given land reform, depend on these and other details.

To identify with reasonable accuracy the impact of something like farm size on productivity and other relevant outcomes, one must understand the overall processes of causation leading to those outcomes; that is, what other factors besides size structure may affect results, as suggested either by plausible theories or by empirical evidence. These include how well input markets function (e.g., those for land, finance, labor, etc.), the supports offered and the constraints imposed by government and how they differ across farmers. Whether a given land reform brings an improvement or a worsening in some of these determinants of performance may thus be an important feature of the reform.

One commonly accepted contributor to agricultural performance is the security of access to land, and the institutions that provide it, like land titling.[7] Such security is especially important to relatively low-income families that are vulnerable to economic insecurity. At one extreme, having a title can be a total guarantee of continued access; at the other, however, it provides little defense against forced displacement. Titling is part of the "classic reform concept" whereby land is redistributed from large landholders to small farmers,[8] in a world where one's title to a piece of land is accepted by everyone and not breached by anyone. But often this is not the case, and power (physical, legal, social, etc.) can displace a current operator. Often public lands are titled under the implicit presumption that they will then be clearly under the control of the new titleholder and that the benefits

[7] Albertus (2021) looks at this issue in great detail.
[8] For a discussion, see Lipton (2009, ch. 3).

will mirror those of classic land reform. But, as experiences in many parts of the world make clear, who farms a piece of land is often determined by informal considerations. So, the impact of titling depends partly on how access was determined before; it can secure a plot for a small farmer, but it can also make it more likely that someone else will get that land (i.e., someone better connected to the levers of power). The early presumption of many observers from developed countries that a shift toward formal land titles would improve economic efficiency often exaggerated their effectiveness in settings where such titles were not the historical norm. Further, that presumption underestimated the merits of traditional and communal tenure systems. Eventually, empirical studies identified the latter error. Atwood (1990) used much evidence from Africa to question the then-standard view, noting both that the costs of titling could be high and that its effects could be the opposite of those expected.[9] As Cousins (2009, 1) notes, "From an analytical perspective, authority and power dynamics are key to understanding how tenure regimes work in practice."

A key institutional question is whether and how land tenure matters to performance. Arrangements vary widely, reflecting cultural tradition, economic logic, and other factors. Agrarian reforms, in attempting to alter outcomes in favor of the less well-off, emphasize different changes depending on the initial structure. The simplest involves transferring ownership from the landlord to the former tenant (and now small, independent farmer). Whenever relative scarcity makes land the most valuable factor of production, with an accordingly high rental, this transfers most of the farm-based income with it. In other cases, land goes to formerly landless families; this is a bigger change because the new small farmer may not have prior experience as a manager. Unsurprisingly, the empirical evidence suggests that the effects of tenure vary considerably across settings.

In summary, the design of an effective reform involves several distinct challenges. First, the use of more meaningful performance measures than GDP makes it harder to assess the current performance of different farm categories and to predict the impact of a given restructuring on each of them. Second, because we do not fully understand the causes underlying differences in performance across categories of farms, it is possible that, because some unidentified factor contributing to the good average

[9] Members of Wisconsin's Land Tenure Center, including John Bruce and Peter Dorner, were important contributors on these issues (Bruce 1986; Bruce and Dorner 1982).

performance of the planned recipient category, newly created farms that look like them will not perform as well as they do. These basic challenges, even to well-handled reforms, are then further complicated when administrative incompetence comes into play. If, for example, clearly more efficient large farmers have their land expropriated and redistributed to producers of clearly less than average efficiency for their smaller size category, output may fall—even if the overall pre-reform productivity of the smaller farmers was higher than that of the larger ones.[10] The performance of the reform sector may be negatively affected by the conditions laid out in the reform or in other ways that affect the productivity of the new farmers, a criticism made with respect to the reforms in Egypt and the Philippines. Given all of the ex-ante ambiguities and challenges, empirical tracing in the aftermaths of reforms is very important to check the validity of the information and understanding of those designing and implementing the reform.

Although reaping the potential benefits of a reform can be very challenging, the available evidence on performance differences by size sometimes suggests such huge gaps as to make it highly unlikely that even a half-way competent reform would not bring substantial net economic gains. Achievement of the main single such benefit—increases in the level and security of the earnings of lower income groups—is possible even if total agricultural output does not rise. If existing small agriculture yields up to five to ten times as much of that income per hectare as do large farms, failure to realize benefits from a redistribution that splits large farms into small units is extremely unlikely, even if total output falls somewhat (e.g., because of greater insecurity on the part of the large farmers as the reform is implemented). Reforms that transfer land from large landholders to former tenants or sharecroppers are even more assured of success as long as the large landholders' share of the income generated is high; when the original split is say fifty–fifty, this means that the former tenant's income will double on acquiring the land rights if production does not change; even if it falls by twenty percent, they will be better off by sixty percent. When the large

[10] One approach, employed for example by Adamopoulos and Restuccia (2020), involves drawing on the information (inputs and outputs, hence productivity by any definition) about each unit before the transfer of land and deducing what the impact of the reform was, assuming those features did not change. While useful, this approach can still mispredict for a variety of reasons. One reason is that, whenever a family's circumstances are changed, it is likely that there will be a learning period afterward during which the family moves toward its new equilibrium position under those different conditions. For those whose output adjustment as they move to their new equilibrium is large, the model understates their post-learning period productivity. This process is not to be confused with other sources of rising productivity over time, such as the appearance of better seeds.

landholders' share of the income generated is low, reform recipients would not gain nearly as much; if it were twenty percent, then that gain would be twenty-five percent. In such cases, the logic of reform is much less to begin with.

Empirical evidence on how productivity and other economic and social variables are related to farm size in the developing countries is presented in the following section. Evidence on how the level of land concentration affects overall agricultural growth, aggregate economic growth, income inequality, and societal welfare is reviewed in the section after that. Conclusions on the impacts of land distribution on aggregate variables like agricultural output and income, the wage rate, and the economic and social welfare of those engaged in the sector draw on the analysis of cases where that distribution changes over time (e.g., through reform) and on comparisons between high inequality and low inequality countries or regions. Hints are also provided by the systematic differences across farm sizes in the pattern of inputs and outputs. Thus, if a category of farms achieves very low productivity of both land and labor compared to another category, it is reasonable to assume that a reform that transferred land (and, presumably labor as well) from the first group to the second would improve the sector's overall performance. If, however, one category achieves higher land productivity and another has higher labor productivity, sorting out when such a transfer would be beneficial becomes more complex and requires taking account of the relative opportunity cost of each input. This more complicated picture is the norm.

## Economic and Social Implications of Land Concentration in the Developing Countries

Economists have traditionally judged the performance of an enterprise or a sector by how much it contributed to aggregate output (GDP). While not taking account of other possibly important effects noted above, this is a useful, albeit partial, indicator—a sort of first building block. The accepted measure of that contribution is total factor productivity (TFP)—the ratio of the value of output to the opportunity cost of the inputs. Frequently, not all of the data are available to calculate this measure correctly, so discussion often resorts to "single factor" productivity measures. Because the most frequently measured inputs are land and labor, land productivity and labor productivity are the two most frequently used measures.

## Stylized Facts: Land Productivity Falls and Labor Productivity Rises with Farm Size

In developing countries, smaller farms typically achieve higher land productivity and lower labor productivity than do larger ones. This combination implies a rapidly falling labor/land ratio with size—the most strikingly general relationship observed. The main immediate interpretation of this pattern is that the private cost of labor relative to that of land rises markedly with size, but other factors are usually at work as well. Neither land nor labor productivity is a reliable indicator of a farm's contribution to the GDP, but where labor is relatively abundant and land relatively scarce the former is more likely to be a good guide. Accordingly, the frequent presence of an "Inverse Relationship" (IR) between size and land productivity has provided a basis for the argument that small-scale agriculture is, in fact, more efficient than its large-scale counterpart. It has also provided a starting point for an ongoing and increasingly refined discussion around that issue. Discussion around the IR has contributed to a better understanding of how small-scale and larger-scale agriculture differ.

While details vary a good deal from case to case, the IR has been reported so frequently and often to such a marked degree (e.g., gaps of up to five-to-one and higher)[11] that it could not be simply the result of imprecise measurement. The main accuracy issue relates to whether and how land quality (defined broadly to include such other natural determinants of productivity as climate, water availability, prevalence of pests, etc.) varies significantly with size. If the measured IR existed only because small farms operated on better quality land (in the above broad sense of the term), then it would not suggest greater efficiency in the use of that resource.[12] Michael Lipton (2009, 83), however, concludes from his encyclopedic study of land reform and related issues that, although taking due account of land quality probably lessens the IR in some cases, overall it remains robust.[13] In much of Africa

[11] A recent analysis for Colombia reports an average land productivity advantage of about seven-to-one (after an adjustment for differences in land quality) between very small units of under one hectare and very large ones of two thousand to ten thousand hectares (Vergara and Zainea 2019).

[12] This measurement challenge is much more complicated than most others because determining quality, in the broad terms just referred to, is not easy. As with many other questions surrounding the IR, the land quality issue needs to be taken more seriously in some countries and settings than in others; in some cases, quality seems clearly to fall with size while in other cases it seems to rise.

[13] Most tests have involved cropped land, but small farms often get part of their productivity advantage from a higher share of land under crops than large farms have. In some cases, it is likely that there is endogeneity between small size and high land quality (Lipton 2009, 82). One of the most-cited studies questioning the IR is Bhalla and Roy (1988) for India, which finds mixed results.

and Latin America, the larger farms often appear to have the best quality land for endogenous reasons; for example, they use their political and economic power to gain access to well irrigated land. At the same time, they sometimes have the worst quality land, as a small amount of such land could not sustain a family economically.

The IR is best seen as the product of a set of direct causes and a set of indirect or underlying causes working through those direct ones. The former include the smaller farms (i) leaving less of their land unused, (ii) having higher crop per year ratios on a given piece of soil (e.g., more double-cropping), (iii) orienting their cropping patterns to higher-value items,[14] and (iv) sometimes achieving higher yields for a given crop.[15] Each of the first three relationships holds generally; exceptions are infrequent. The last one, around which much of the early debate revolved, is not systematically present; the difference often goes in the other direction, at least for part of the farm size range. When it does, its impact is typically outweighed by the other three factors. In such cases, a somewhat confusing pattern emerges in which overall land productivity falls sharply with farm size even as yields for specific crops are constant or rising with size, at least over certain size ranges. This pattern highlights the fact that, when the land productivity advantage of smaller farms is very large, it is not due mainly (if at all) to their achieving higher yields for given products, but rather to greatly differing product composition. Many tiny farms dedicate their land to vegetables, potatoes, and other high-value items including, notably, animals,[16] while many very large units engage in extensive cattle grazing. It turns out to be of little relevance whether moderate yield differences or economies of scale show up across different-sized farms either in the production of lettuce (or the other items favored by small farms) or in extensive cattle grazing; the IR emerges as a result of the huge differences in land productivity across products. Understanding the inverse relationship thus requires understanding the process of product selection, which clearly owes a great deal to the starkly differing availability of land and of labor as between very small and large farms; labor is a good deal more costly to large farms; the wage rate may be substantially above the opportunity cost of labor used on the small farms, and there may also be

[14] Or, more generally, an output pattern oriented to higher value products, including small animals and fowl and their products.

[15] See, for example, Lipton (2009, 72).

[16] In the Philippines, the presence of animals on smaller farms plays a big role in the higher land productivity of the smallest units.

a greater need to monitor hired labor to ensure good performance, which further adds to its cost. High land productivity on small farms also reflects the families' consumption of items whose production is very labor-intensive, such as vegetables and small animals.

The most commonly cited underlying causes of the IR include: (i) the lower opportunity cost of labor on small family farms, especially in settings with an important degree of labor surplus (as per the Arthur Lewis model), and the greater cost of or more restricted access to land; these factors explain the often much higher labor-to-land ratios on smaller farms; (ii) the bigger incentive that small, low-income farm families have, especially when alternative employment possibilities are limited or absent, spurring them to greater efforts to achieve high output; (iii) the lower average transport and other transactions costs when a high share of output is consumed on the farm and many inputs come from the farm; and (iv) the sometimes greater managerial capacity *cum* dedication of smaller farmers based on their experience and their incentive to succeed.

The relative roles of market imperfections, such as the differing costs of labor and capital,[17] and of differing transactions costs by size category, vary by setting. In Lipton's judgment, the main causal factor behind the IR is often transaction cost differences that, in developing countries, favor the small farms but, in substantially industrialized countries, favor the larger ones (Lipton 2009, 73). The small farm, especially one with a food deficit (many small farms do other things than their own farming and produce less food than the family consumes), experiences less (at the limit zero) cost in selling its products and less (at the limit zero) labor costs (when labor is in surplus supply). The IR can appear even when big and small farmers achieve

[17] A market is said to be working perfectly when all participants on the demand and supply side face the same price for the good or service, no participant is dominant enough in the market to be able to affect that price, and all participants have an accurate perception of the quality of the good or service. Analysts have debated whether a strong IR or a TFP which varies widely by size can be consistent with reasonably well-functioning markets. If markets work very well (including those involving land rental), there should be no significant aggregate output loss through resource misallocation across farm size groups (or any other groups); their TFP should be approximately the same, although land and labor productivity can vary somewhat. In fact, all markets do fall short of perfection to at least some extent; in many developing countries, the direct evidence of serious malfunction in most input and some output markets is strong (Binswanger et al. 1995). In any case, the more important issue surrounding land concentration is not whether the sort of total output loss suggested by the data is due to market imperfections, but rather what lies behind the even weaker performance in terms of generating benefits for those toward the bottom of the income hierarchy. Farm size comparisons in countries like Colombia and Brazil strongly suggest that the current agrarian structures did not emerge because of their efficiency, whether defined narrowly by total output generated or broadly by contribution to social welfare.

comparable levels of private efficiency, with reasonably similar TFPs. Because their transaction costs differ, their social efficiency also differs.[18]

## The Likely Impact of Land Redistribution on Agricultural Output

Whether the division of large farms into small ones can be expected to raise total output depends on what underlies the IR. Much evidence suggests that it mainly reflects a causal relationship from size structure to productivity, in which case it is quite plausible to expect an equalizing land reform to raise total output.[19] Still, calculations of the potential output gain must be based on reasonable assumptions about the productivity of newly created small units. There might be no gain, or even a fall, in total sectoral output if a piece of land is transferred from its large-scale operator to a new group of small farmers who are much less efficient than those who have operated for some time within that size range.[20] The new operators may well be less competent because they were formerly paid workers and thus lack experience in managing a farm—their performance would be expected to improve over time. In the case of reforms that increase the land available to formerly very small ones, such a lack of entrepreneurial experience is less likely to arise. New small farms created by a reform may also be less productive than existing

[18] Most analyses of the IR disregard the transaction cost advantages of smaller farms by, for example, measuring quantity of output of each item, with values summed up using either farm-gate or "market" prices. How transactions costs enter the picture can be seen by noting that the on-farm consumption of a kilo of corn requires the production of just that one kilo, whereas the consumption of that same kilo by a farm family, which buys it in a store, in effect requires it to produce more than one kilo of some comparable item, so that two transportation costs (to market and from market) can be borne. The failure to take account of transactions costs means that statistics comparing productivity by size are biased against smaller farms by an amount that varies according to how much home consumption they do and the height of transportation costs when the food is sold in the market. A farm that uses all of its output for home consumption and for which getting its product to market raises the price by fifty percent (i.e., the farm-gate price is two-thirds of the price on the market), when compared to an equally productive (in physical terms) farm that sells all of its output to the market is fifty percent more productive in terms of value in consumption per unit of land. The size of the adjustment needed data that take no account of the transactions cost advantage of small farms with high rates of home consumption varies greatly by setting, from almost nothing up to perhaps fifty percent.

[19] Early estimates of potential output gain by Berry and Cline (1979, 132–133) for Colombia, Brazil, and several other countries fell in the range of twenty to thirty percent. Colombia's greater farm size-related gaps in land and labor productivity today than in 1960 (the basis of those earlier estimates) suggest a bigger number now. In short, the negative effects of a high land concentration on total output, like those on inequality, may be substantial.

[20] The productivity figures used in many such calculations are in fact those of the existing farms in each given size category.

ones in the same size range if labor is not sufficiently abundant to induce the new ones to use as much of it as the existing ones do. Under the pre-reform conditions, with large farms occupying much land and employing few workers, the general surplus of labor in much of agriculture was substantially due to that low job creation on the large farms. A major redistribution should lead to a big increase in total demand for labor, and thus cut into the previous excess supply. If the new post-reform small farms apply less labor per hectare than their pre-reform counterparts, their land productivity would also tend to be lower. This predictable tightening up of the labor market—highly desirable in its own right because it will be a direct route out of poverty for many people—does mean that estimates of the output increase due to a major reallocation of land must allow for the general equilibrium impact of that reform on the labor market in the form of higher wages. Doing so is unlikely to reverse the conclusion that output will increase, but it scales down the estimated effect. Still, when the initial land productivity gap is large, there is little doubt that the land concentration is curtailing total output, as well as the demand for labor and the incomes of lower income groups.

A strong IR creates a persuasive case for redistributive land reform as a way both to reduce inequality and to raise total output; such reform would seem to be, in modern parlance, a "no-brainer" because there would be no trade-off between social justice and economic performance as commonly measured. As noted, its putative economic benefits lie partly in the direct effects (the higher incomes for the poor people who get access to more land) and partly in such indirect (general equilibrium) impacts as the increased total demand for labor and the associated rise in overall rural and urban wage rates.

Limitations on the output increases achievable through land reform mainly involve political factors. If the reform causes much conflict, agricultural output is likely to fall, at least for a period of time. Revolutionary experiences tend to trigger property damage with associated disruption of production; sometimes reforms are sabotaged by deliberate destruction of farm assets. And where the losers from a reform still wield considerable political power, they work to block the sort of policy support needed by the beneficiaries.

The best recipe for dynamic and equitable agricultural development begins with a conflict-free reform that leaves land reasonably evenly distributed and imposes a ceiling on the holdings of any one family such that the historical tendency toward concentration cannot go far.[21] Complementary

[21] When the agricultural labor force begins to fall as a result of industrialization and urbanization, the ceiling must eventually be raised.

to such a reform is a public support system built around the generation and diffusion of new technologies—largely crop varieties, but also breeds of animals, cultivation practices, and the like—that are size-neutral in their application. Investment in infrastructure (roads, communication systems, etc.) is also important and a credit system may be as well, especially in those cases where it helps to facilitate the adoption of new seeds and cultivation practices. It may be that the commonly observed biases of such support systems in favor of larger farmers can only be fully broken when there are few such farms left, such that everyone involved knows that they must work with and support small farmers.[22] The very presence of large farms can create an incentive or pressure to ignore the interests of the smaller ones.

The magnitude of the current land productivity advantage of smaller farms in countries like Brazil and Colombia is far bigger than anything suggested by the historical evidence from England or Europe, when it hinted at such an advantage at all. The debate there was centered on whether their performance was significantly inferior to that of the larger units; most analysis has suggested modest productivity differentials either way. Arguably, the key difference between these two settings lies in the abundance of land in the cited Latin countries and a few others, an abundance which has made it possible to dedicate much of it to extensive cattle rearing, the main single factor accounting for the extremely low land productivity of the large units.

The less marked IR that typically shows up in the countries of SSA (Chapter 8) than in many Latin countries (Chapter 6) raises the question of whether this region may avoid many of the damaging effects of concentration. As the most agriculture-focused part of the developing world, and as the least known and understood, how things unfold there is the main unanswered question of global agrarian history.

## Shifting the Measure of Farm-level Performance From Total Factor Productivity to Impact on Societal Welfare

As noted above, the two simplest and most common measures of performance in agriculture are land productivity and labor productivity.[23] The

[22] Too few studies have been undertaken on the factors that affect the behavior of research and extension systems vis-à-vis different sized farms to provide an answer to this question.

[23] The farm owner may use the rate of profit (i.e., level of profits divided by capital invested in the enterprise), but this is not a useful overall measure because it fails to account for the farmer's noncapital inputs and does not reflect any other benefits than those to the owner.

latter is useful when labor is scarce and other resources, including land, are relatively abundant. The former has its logic when land is scarce and labor is abundant, sometimes to the point where the additional output from applying more of it gets down to zero, as posited by Arthur Lewis (1954). Usually, no factor of production is in such excess supply that the additional output from applying one more unit of it reaches zero. In that case, the standard measure of a firm's contribution to agricultural (or total) output is TFP, which takes account of the amount of each input used and of its social opportunity cost (SOC),[24] measured either by its market price or in some other way designed to reflect its productivity in the best alternative use; it then compares the value of output to that of the inputs. While a potentially worthwhile indicator, it must be used with caution. Its precision depends on how the various input and output markets work and how one assesses the social opportunity cost of each input. Still, estimates by farm size can sometimes help to predict the impact on the GDP of a shift of resources between size groups.

How does economic efficiency, measured by TFP, vary by farm size, given the general pattern of rising labor productivity and falling land productivity? In the extreme case posited by Lewis, in which labor is in surplus to such a degree that its social opportunity cost approaches zero and there is thus no economic logic to saving on its use,[25] land productivity is likely to be a good proxy for TFP, whereas labor productivity is clearly not, and small farms have not only a land productivity advantage over large ones but a comparably large economic efficiency advantage as well.[26] In other situations, the two measures are likely to diverge and TFP can provide additional information; given its conceptual limitations, however, it is desirable to use both together and to attempt to identify the likely biases of TFP in specific settings.

As might be expected, TFP typically varies much less dramatically by farm size than does either land productivity or labor productivity; estimates point to much smaller differences across farm sizes (often falling within the range of zero to thirty percent) than those of single-factor productivity. It sometimes falls with farm size, sometimes rises, and sometimes follows a more complicated pattern, such as falling up to a certain size, and then rising.[27]

[24] See the Glossary for the definition.

[25] Achieving high labor productivity does not signal economic efficiency of an enterprise when the social cost of labor is or approaches zero. Rather, it suggests that the firm is contributing to excess supply in the labor market and hence to lower wages.

[26] The extreme contrasting case in which land has a zero social cost and labor has a high cost would imply the efficiency advantage was with the large farms, but this case is seldom discussed because it too obviously contradicts the facts in developing countries.

[27] As observed for regions of Brazil by Helfand and Taylor (2020) and in several African countries.

Because TFP is designed to answer the question "how does the presence of this productive unit affect the total output of the economy, it is conceptually appropriate only if the reference point at the aggregate level is GDP, a measure of national or regional economic performance that suffers many weaknesses, especially when the level of inequality is high such that nearly all (or even more than all) of the benefits of higher output go to the rich,[28] or when negative externalities are important. Accordingly, TFP, with its narrow focus on GDP, cannot tell us which type of farm contributes most to social welfare or which government policies do so. A more useful measure would also take account of a farm's impact on income inequality and poverty; an even better measure would reflect its impact on personal welfare or happiness. Because we are still in the early phases of developing refined measures of the effects of specific economic activities on happiness or welfare,[29] a more practical measure of the contribution of different types of farms would assign differing weights to the income received by people according to where they fall in the income hierarchy[30] (e.g., by categorizing income generated according to how much goes to low, middle , and high income people). In Colombia, as of 2014, the income accruing to a lower income group composed of paid workers plus that majority of small farmers who have relatively low incomes, was probably at least fifteen times greater per hectare on small units than on large ones, a result of total production per hectare (adjusted for land quality) being five times greater on the smallest units and of seventy-five percent to eighty percent of all income generated accruing to this group, while on the largest farms probably only fifteen percent to twenty-five percent accrued to it. In such cases, when the small farms generate so much more total income per hectare and its destination is so clearly the low-income group, there can be little serious debate as to which makes a bigger direct contribution to societal welfare.[31]

[28] Implicit in the acceptance of GDP as the correct measure of economic performance is the assumption that an extra dollar of income provides the same benefits to a poor person as to a rich one, which is manifestly untrue.

[29] See the literature on the determinants of happiness, including the annual World Happiness Reports (e.g., Helliwell et al. 2020).

[30] How much the weight should differ is a matter of judgment, so this approach can, for example, yield inconclusive results; on which of two types of farms is more socially efficient as judged by the income it creates, weighted according to who gets it. But it can certainly clarify how sensitive (or not) that judgment is to the decision on weighting.

[31] The noted combination of land and labor productivity differentials across farm size implies huge differences in the labor-to-land ratio; in Colombia, the figure reaches about forty-two-fold between units of less than one-half a UAF (a farm size large enough to provide an adequate level of income to a family, and defined with land quality in mind) and those of over ten UAFs.

Arguably, then, the most important stylized facts related to land concentration are the higher share of income generated going to relatively low-income families the smaller is the farm, and the greater the absolute amount of income generated; they imply that a redistributive land reform in a country like Colombia would greatly raise the absolute and relative income of those toward the bottom of the hierarchy.[32] The first of these factors has been the basis of the moral critique of the historically high concentration of land in England and elsewhere.

Standard aggregate measures of output and income not only fail to take account of distributional implications but also fail to incorporate most or all of the ecological effects caused by production or by consumption at a time when environmental damage, especially from climate change, is a major world issue. This failing is serious for those in many sectors of an economy, including agriculture, where smaller units are generally better protectors of the environment. There is much evidence of the great damage resulting from large-scale operations, such as when they intrude directly on forests or motivate others to do so by reducing their access to land. At best, family farms protect their environment out of concern with passing the enterprise along to the next generation in decent condition. And, as noted, the family and societal benefits derived from agriculture are not limited to the income earned from it; they include economic security, which explains why families do not maximize expected current income if this comes at a higher risk of that income falling below a minimum need. Preference for leisure, for the social benefits of community life, and other less economic objectives are also part of the picture. All this should be taken into account as one compares the overall benefits coming from different types of farming.[33]

[32] One concern is that although families who get land (or more land than they had before) through a reform will gain, the still landless families might lose. Dealing with this issue involves distinguishing between existing small farmers, landless aspiring farmers who may benefit from an agrarian reform, and agricultural workers who will not wind up with land. Because a land reform is likely to diminish the demand for paid workers (as large farms shrink and most new ones require little or no hired labor), it is a theoretical possibility that the paid workers will, as a group, lose (Berry 1971). Whether or not it happens depends on the country's agricultural structure and on the details of the reform/redistribution itself. For the case of Colombia, Thirsk (1976, 86) concludes that those initially landless workers who remain landless would probably not suffer and might be made better off by a reform.

[33] Wendell Berry has been a prominent advocate of the merits of more traditional rural life styles (e.g., Berry 2009).

## Small Farm Efficiency's Believability Challenge from the Negative Narratives

The limited believability of the superiority of smaller farms has several distinct roots. Some groups harbor an ingrained presumption against it, unsurprising in the case of the agricultural elites but also marked within the economic elite more generally, who tend to believe that owning much property, being a member of the educated class, and living a "civilized" life go together with economic/business competence; for them, it is implausible that the relatively uneducated peasant might be competent—a belief that makes them feel better about themselves. Given this underlying bias against such an idea, it could not be expected to garner many adherents in the absence of clear and comprehensible evidence; such evidence has been relatively scarce until fairly recently. Even when present, it does not persuade the vested interests (unsurprising) or those who, although less biased, tend to believe what they want to believe. The presence of considerable evidence that smaller units are or can be more productive does not even guarantee that the majority of professionals with some involvement in policymaking or implementation would be aware of and understand the economic and social implications of a more equal distribution of land. Thus, many agricultural extension workers, with only a partial feel for economics, believe it is more important to maximize labor productivity than land productivity and, therefore, that large units are more "productive." They and many others see US agriculture as the paragon of efficiency with its large farms and high labor productivity. As economies develop, labor productivity does indeed become an increasingly useful indicator of firm or sectoral efficiency because in rich economies it is likely to be reasonably well correlated with TFP. But it takes some study of economics, or a great deal of intuition, to understand that, at lower levels of development, labor productivity is not a valid indicator of efficiency whereas, among the single-factor indicators, land productivity and capital productivity (depending on which is the scarcer factor) are more likely to be. But even among those who recognize that TFP is a better indicator than labor productivity, many forget that neither of these measures takes into account the impact of farm-size structure on income distribution or, more broadly, on the social and economic welfare of those involved. Because much of this is unclear to anyone but an economist who has given it some thought or a very insightful outsider to the profession, it is not only the vested interests who use empirical evidence to argue that large farms are the preferable option, but also those who believe that labor productivity is tantamount to efficiency,[34] those who disregard the non-economic determinants of human welfare, and those who ignore negative impacts on the environment. Those who listen to economists to the point of adopting TFP as their indicator—duly adjusted for positive and negative externalities—are closer to the truth but, as noted above, this still gives no weight to poverty reduction and improving income distribution, an obvious goal in countries where inequality is high. In short, it is easy for many people to be honestly misled into accepting that larger farms are better for society than small ones. The more comprehensive are one's indicators of societal welfare, the more obvious is the case for the smaller farms, but few quantitative estimates based on such broad indicators are available.

The content and evolution of a group's beliefs and "narratives" (what it believes and what it says) naturally differ according to the group's own economic interests, as well as its knowledge; its concern about inequality, injustice, and abuse; and its sources of information. Most views are strongly influenced by what people want to believe and by the beliefs of those around them. Most predictable are the views of the large landholders who benefit from the land concentration and from government support. The narratives they create vary somewhat over time and place according to which opposing views they have to confront. Politicians naturally stick close to the stories of those to whom they are beholden for support. The various groups of "experts" presumed to rely more on knowledge and facts include agronomists; economists, particularly those who specialize in agriculture; and those agricultural economists who are especially conversant with the size issue and the implications of land concentration. Close observers of rural life, including some anthropologists and sociologists, bring another very useful perspective but they tend to be more distant from the policy discussion; economists and policymakers are too often unfamiliar with their findings. Interacting with experts and politicians and hence potential intermediaries between them are—the public servants who administer government programs.

The narratives of the large landholders typically emphasize two things: (i) the importance of property rights; land should thus not change hands except by mutual agreement; and (ii) the proposition that large-scale agriculture is more efficient economically and can thus contribute more to a

[34] For this reason, among others, the arguments of Ernst F. Schumacher's famous 1973 book *Small is Beautiful* were not by any means universally accepted by the public.

country's "development" than can its smaller-scale counterpart. Because strong class distinctions are a feature of most societies, psychological support for this latter view comes from the bias against/disdain toward peasants, not just by the well-educated elites but also by aspiring middle-class groups and by most public officials. Thus, while an awareness that the existing pro-large-scale model may be leaving many people in poverty does generate some support for policies to deal with it, the idea that the small-scale sector is or could in any meaningful sense be more efficient than the large-scale sector, is seen as quite implausible, if not ridiculous. Many people see peasants' poverty as the result of their own failings. The only obvious exception to these widespread misperceptions is the small group of people who either study agrarian structure in detail or are familiar with the presence of the IR and know some economics. As previously noted, even many agricultural economists, researchers, and extension workers fail to clearly understand why smaller-scale operations can be more efficient. Many are unfamiliar with the existence of the IR and many lack a clear grasp of how economic efficiency may be most meaningfully measured. On the other hand, a few people who simply know the sector very well from close contact, including the cited sociologists and anthropologists, are quite aware of the potential efficiency advantages of smaller units of production.

The deeply rooted confidence in the economic efficiency of large-scale agriculture shows up in the arguments raised when its worrisome effects are obvious. Thus, when its expansion replaces small farms and leaves former workers unemployed, one response is that it is, in any case, a better overall use of resources to create jobs elsewhere rather than trying to save the small farms. This perspective is not wrong by definition, but it is almost always the result of incomplete analysis; optimal policy on the employment front involves the creation of as many decent jobs as possible wherever this can be done most efficiently; the potential productivity of small farms usually points to that sector's being one of the best places to do so.[35]

On the other side of the debates, the direct voice of the peasantry is seldom, if ever, heard. It would be an understatement to say that the victims of the most oppressive agrarian systems have not been able to voice their own concerns or write their own history. Such a narrative would be the peasants'

[35] The general weakness and/or absence of well-thought-out employment policy in government reflects the lack of attention given in economics to employment creation as an objective, a weakness pinpointed decades ago by Dudley Seers (1969). That lack has facilitated the sort of loose thinking described here.

equivalent to Carolina Maria de Jesus's story of life in the slums of Rio (de Jesus 1962), a portrayal of the situation and life of the urban poor. The Tolstoys, Chekhovs, Dickens, and other great authors have told stories from a third-person perspective. The exploitation of lower classes by landlords in Brazil is a focus of several of the novels of Jorge Amado. Helpful as all of these are, they remain outsiders' accounts. Famed French historian Emmanuel Le Roy Ladurie pioneered a sort of informal movement to try to understand history "from the bottom up" by exploring the "mental universe" of peasants, workers, and others (Kandell 2023) instead of focusing on the leaders, generals, and the like.[36]

Meanwhile, a frequent gap in the case for land reform is that its focus on the welfare of a low-income group—the landless, for example—is too seldom accompanied by the case for its economic efficiency and its environmental advantages. Neither peasants nor many of their defenders on the ground are likely to understand that their farms are, in fact, more efficient users of resources than are the large ones nearby, or to understand why. The arguments for reform thus differ across supportive groups; most focus on small agriculture's potential to reduce poverty and inequality while a few focus on its economic efficiency. Although those concerned with the environment are usually aware that large agriculture wreaks most of the damage, many of them do not interact with the groups that emphasize the other two advantages of small-scale operations. Information on this threat is still partial and contested, but environmentally devastating practices, such as the exploitation of fragile Amazon basin lands and the excessive use of chemical fertilizers and insect poisons, are becoming better known.

Whose opinions matter the most and how do they change over time? The views of those who rely mainly on facts evolve as new sources and types of evidence appear. Agricultural surveys and censuses provide quantitative evidence on things like the relative productivity of different groups of farms. Studies of income inequality and poverty provide evidence on their causes. The most influential views, however, especially under authoritarian governments, are those of the elites and/or the military leaders. They may change marginally, although not necessarily in accordance with changes in professional understanding because that is not their base. In Brazil, pro-large farm arguments became stronger among some groups as the sector evolved

[36] Among his most noted works was *Montaillou* (Ladurie 1975).

from feudal to agro-capitalist and as it became more technology- and science-based and as its yields rose. In that case, the private media—typically supported by large, vested interests and, in any case, not inclined to probe much into complicated matters like the relative efficiency of farms by size—were a natural ally of agribusiness. Most people close to the government were convinced that agrarian reform would be detrimental; agribusiness was seen as so productive that its profits could be counted on to pay down Brazil's foreign debt and generate resources to invest in non-agricultural, pro-poor development policies.

## Effects of Land Concentration on Economic Growth and Inequality in the Developing Countries

How a high land concentration today affects a country's future involves its lasting impacts both on how agriculture develops and on how the economy as a whole evolves. These narrower and broader legacies are naturally interconnected; the latter is harder to predict.

### Land Concentration and Agricultural Development: Some Background Evidence

That land productivity is systematically higher on smaller rather than on larger farms at the early stages of economic development only partially invalidates the conventional wisdom on the merits of larger size as it does not guarantee that this advantage, when present, will persist into the future. It might have developed over a long period, with the pressure of low incomes forcing the farmers to reap the maximum potential from their limited land and available technologies. The small operators might be less adept at raising productivity quickly in response to new biological or mechanical technologies, especially if they are poorly educated and without easy access to information on those new options. The main ambiguity as to the economic implications of land concentration, especially in low-income countries, thus involves the dynamic side of things: under which agrarian structures can the fastest overall productivity increase be achieved? More important, under what structure can the largest income and welfare gains be reaped by today's poorer farmers and landless workers?

For most settings, the answer is less clear than are the immediate or short-term implications of size distribution previously discussed. On the productivity growth front, both small and large farm systems have sometimes done well and sometimes less well. Differences in farm characteristics and in levels of government support are the main factors involved. Just as differing motivations between small and large farmers may underlie productivity differences at a point of time, so may they also contribute to differing growth and productivity performances. Both the *modus operandi* and the productive performance of large-scale agriculture vary by setting and change over time; as with small farms, non-economic factors may affect how they are operated. Whereas the great majority of small farms are "worked" intensively because this is essential to the livelihood of the operators, motivations among larger farms are more varied. In the James C. Scott-type world, their logic is to control all productive assets—land, labor, and anything else that matters—with the benefits taking the form of political and social power, as well as economic wealth. The attitude toward the underlings is essentially exploitative. There may be competition within the elite group for control of the resources, and also competitive consumption aimed at demonstrating and maintaining social status. Owners of a large estate in seventeenth-century England had no need to vie with others for its control; this "landed elite" also worried less about the productive activities on its estates than about living the good life its advantages offered them. The mentality of such a "rentier" class contrasts sharply with that of the large entrepreneurs who seek access to land to make a profit from operating it or the speculators who aim to get a quick payoff.

The relative pace and pattern of agricultural growth achieved by different groups of farms depends on the relative capacities and inclinations of the farmers to take up new technologies;[37] on differences in the public sector support for each type; and on factors exogenous to current policy,

[37] A possible concern with reliance on peasant farming is the so-called perverse supply response, whereby a higher market price (or lower cost of inputs) will not generate an increase in marketed surplus but only an increase in family consumption and/or in leisure. Although such perversity may be consistent with standard economic theory, empirical studies have generally shown that both total production and marketed surplus respond in a strongly positive way to market signals like rising prices resulting from higher demand (Ozanne 1999). In any case it is not clear that such a pattern would slow desirable longer-term growth. It would suggest that this relatively low-income tier of the population does not feel a need for more income, in which case economic growth is less desirable than it would otherwise have been. On the other side of this coin, if a country relies on large-scale agriculture for growth, the fact that most of the income thereby generated goes to well-off people suggests that, in social welfare terms, such growth is less desirable than it would otherwise be.

such as climate change and international commodity prices. Among these determinants of growth public support has the greatest potential to vary by size, so politics is likely to be key. Some countries spend more on agriculture than others, some spend more efficiently than others, and some tilt the benefits more toward one group and some toward another. A government typically builds its policies around the interests of the groups that wield influence on it, including producers and consumers. A government under the control of a landed elite will select its spending options principally with the benefit of that elite in mind, whereas a country with an egalitarian distribution of land seeks a broader distribution of benefits.

One of the vicious circles that emerges within the agricultural sectors of very unequal countries reflects the fact that it is typically harder to provide good technical support for smaller farmers. This is not only because those farmers have less education, less access to credit, and the like, but also because the extension workers and others engaged in generating and dispersing new technologies are unfamiliar with that segment of agriculture and less capable of learning from those farmers and working together with them. One might then expect small farms to systematically slip behind the large ones over time. That a marked IR is usually maintained over time suggests that the effects of this bias are less than might be feared; however, they cannot be disregarded.

Along with the differing political sway wielded by groups associated with the agricultural sector, another major determinant of who benefits from public policy is the extent to which the optimal policy package varies between different groups—large and small farms, in particular. If it differs little (much), then whose interests dominate public policy matters accordingly little (much). Two important components of agricultural policy are investments in transportation and in technology. When large and small farms are scattered together in all parts of a country, the best transportation investments for the large farms may also be best for the small farms; when the opposite is the case, this will not be true. The same goes for technology and, in this regard, there is a major contrast between countries like Colombia, whose large farms produce a very different set of products from its small farms (although a few products, including coffee, are important to both), and those Asian countries where rice has tended to dominate, regardless of farm size. In the latter case, even when the larger farms have greater political clout, the benefits of policies designed around their interests will accrue in considerable degree to the smaller ones as well. In the former setting, in contrast, major positive spillovers from large-farm-oriented policies cannot be expected.

When the imbalance of political power in favor of the larger producers is greatest, even policies designed for the smaller farms are sometimes hijacked through corruption, as in the case over a decade ago in which the then-Minister of Agriculture in Colombia was accused of syphoning subsidy payments meant for small-scale agriculture toward larger farmers, whose political support he was currying for a future presidential run. When that imbalance is still greater, governments fail to protect vulnerable small farms from direct encroachment by larger ones. A quick reading of the economic history of countries like Colombia and Brazil, with their extreme land concentration in a context of formally democratic political systems, suggests that the agricultural elites have, from their own perspective, weighed in very successfully on agricultural policy: public sector support has favored them over smaller farms, decent agricultural output growth has been achieved so that the total income generated by the sector has risen, and its distribution has continued to favor them strongly.

Incompleteness notwithstanding, the available evidence on the relationship between farm-size structure and output growth does not weaken the case for small-scale agriculture. It includes data on relative productivity growth (including for land productivity, labor productivity, and TFP) by size category in a few specific countries, plus studies of the relative overall economic growth performance of countries with differing farm-size structures. The former information is too limited to support any general pattern, although it does demonstrate that when productivity (however defined) is rising at the sectoral level, it tends to rise in all size categories, and thus contradicts any idea that small farms do not achieve significant productivity increase. For Brazil, data for 1985, 1996, and 2006 from three regions—the North, the Center-West and the Southeast—while displaying the usual IR at each point of time, reveal significant increases in productivity over those two decades. For units of five to twenty hectares, the annual average increase ranged between about two percent per year and nearly four percent across these regions, with increases being fastest in the lower-productivity Northeast, whose smallest farms caught up to those of the other two regions over this period (Helfand and Taylor 2020, 8). In each of the three regions, TFP showed a U-shaped relationship with size, falling to a minimum in the one hundred- to five hundred-hectare size range in the North and the Center-West, but in a much lower size range (five to twenty hectares or twenty to one hundred hectares, depending on the year) in the Southeast. The percent increase in TFP tended to be highest in the largest size category. For the country as a whole, it also rose markedly from 1985 to 2006 (at 1.5 percent per year), with the biggest gains being achieved by the smallest farms (up to five hectares) at a rate of about 2.5 percent per year, and the largest farms (over five hundred hectares) at a rate of over two percent, while lower rates were achieved by the middle-size categories of twenty to five hundred hectares (Arias et al. 2017, 10, citing Helfand et al. 2015). Because these figures correspond to a context in which public sector support has generally favored the larger units, they reveal a considerable capacity of smaller units to do well even under circumstances tilted against them.

The Green Revolution experience of Asia also provides evidence on how different types of farms respond as important new options appear. In the Philippines province of Nueva Ecija, for example, it seems to have brought no lasting changes in the IR between farm size and rice yield. In some regions, larger farms initially reaped bigger output gains from the new varieties, probably due to easier adoption, but within about ten years the original IR had been essentially re-established (Berry and Cline 1979, 74). More generally, in those many countries where a marked IR still exists after a few decades of rising average productivity and yields in agriculture as a whole, one can deduce that any difference in those increases by farm size must have been of quite modest proportions; otherwise, the IR would have disappeared, or even been reversed.

Country-level data also make it clear that productivity increase is not the domain of any one agrarian structure. Brazil, for example, has achieved fast output growth with its highly concentrated distribution of land. The contrasting cases where land has not been highly concentrated offer evidence of the enduring advantages of small-farm agriculture. Among the greatest agricultural performances ever achieved are the post-land reform experiences of Japan, Korea, and Taiwan, each of which essentially put all the usable land into the hands of small family farmers and achieved historically high rates of agricultural growth (at four percent per year and more).

In some situations, there may be an innovation-related argument to have at least some medium or large farms, when these either develop new technologies themselves or provide a convenient testing-ground for them. Recent evidence from several African countries suggests faster productivity growth occurs on larger farms, probably at least in part a reflection of better public support (see Chapter 8). Gutiérrez Malaxechebarria (2014) explains how larger farms played a role in helping smaller ones take advantage of hillside irrigation in parts of Colombia.

## Broader Questions: The Effects of Land Concentration on Aggregate Economic Growth and Income Inequality

The impact of land concentration on agricultural growth is only one part of the bigger picture of its effects on overall economic and total income growth and on income inequality. On the latter count, there is little debate because land concentration clearly accentuates the inequality of both agricultural and overall income, and it builds inequality into a country's future. Its impact on GDP growth is less clear-cut and probably much more varied across cases. Possible differences in longer-term performance between small and large farm systems may result from what may be called internal firm dynamics, from changes that occur in agriculture's role as development proceeds, and from complementary activities of the state and private sector non-agricultural actors that affect the relative situations of smaller and larger farms.

On the first count, a key question is whether small or large units have an advantage over the other either in rates of savings/re-investment or in rates of productivity growth. It is reasonable to assume that larger units with higher incomes would find it easier to save and reinvest, either in their agricultural enterprises or elsewhere. This is consistent with the fact that high-income people generally have higher savings rates than do low-income people. This fact, however, does not imply that, with a given average income, the higher its concentration the higher will be total savings; for this to be the case, the marginal propensity to save has to rise with income, a much less assured outcome. The likelihood that land concentration will raise savings from agricultural income is further lowered when it leads to lower total agricultural output and income due to the IR, and thus provides less income from which the savings can be generated. Small businesses often do achieve surprising rates of investment as long as the needed finance is available (their own savings or loans from others).

A large farm system may more easily facilitate savings transfers to other sectors, especially industry, and thus contribute to the post-agricultural stage of growth. When large landholders are themselves interested in investing in other sectors, the savings-transfer process is less complicated and presumably more efficient; when the financial system effects the transfer, success depends on its efficiency. Agricultural elites willing and able to transfer savings to industry are thus a plus. Robert C. Allen (1992) argues that England's rentier class was not so inclined. In contrast, the coffee industry in Colombia is given credit for helping to finance the nascent industrial sector in Medellin, the major city of the province of Antioquia (Ospina Vasquez 1955). Some small farmers also engage in inter-sectoral savings transfer, usually to small, non-agricultural activities. The empirical record on who handles this challenge better is unclear. To the extent that the state is a major player in this intersectoral transfer, its capacity to tax agricultural income becomes pivotal. Where income or wealth taxes play a large role, the transfer might appear to be easier when income is concentrated. But large-scale agriculture is notorious for its ability to avoid such taxation. Maintenance of low prices is another strategy whereby states in effect tax farmers; it can be and has been used regardless of the size and income of farmers, but it can have significant distorting effects in the economy, and it can hold back agricultural growth.

Along with the "ease of transfer" question comes the broader political issue of whether powerful agricultural interests will welcome a pro-industrial policy in the first place.[38] It has often been argued that industrialization is slowed by the political weight of a landed elite naturally reluctant to cede its dominant role to other sectors, to pay taxes to fund their growth, and so forth[39] A preference to retain its dominance and the political capacity to do so has often been noted, as in India where it has been widely seen to have retarded overall economic progress, and in Brazil where President Getúlio Vargas struggled to make agricultural elites more accommodating on this front. The contrast between China and Japan is illustrative. Prior to the Communist revolution, Chinese governments were unable to tax the rural elite enough to promote overall growth, necessarily based mainly outside agriculture. In Japan, both after World War II and, more generally, from the late nineteenth century, that transfer occurred successfully. Anti-industrialization sentiments on the part of a dominant rentier class may be complemented by their negative attitude to agrarian reforms whose implementation could raise agricultural output and incomes. Rentier hostility to industrialization does not have a parallel among agro-industrial entrepreneurs because they interact closely with the industrial sector and bring a clear profit motive to

[38] Small farmers do not have the political clout to weigh in as directly as do *latifundistas*, nor a comparable economic motivation to block industrialization.

[39] Adamopoulos (2007) makes this argument in explaining the slower overall growth of Argentina (with a higher inequality of land) than of Canada.

what they do. Thus, it is possible that land concentration, while deterring overall growth under a rentier system, would promote it when the large units are commercial in nature.

The savings/investment and the productivity advances achieved by both smaller and larger farms are usually heavily influenced, if not dominated, by government policy, especially on the technology front. The relative performance of the two groups over time is thus likely to strongly reflect public policy in this area. New varieties, new cultivation practices, and the like are all classic "public goods"; economic theory suggests that their provision should be funded by the state so that they can be free and as widely disseminated as possible. The great success stories of healthy agricultural growth with maximal contribution to overall economic growth and welfare have involved strong public sector support on this front, especially the sort of development and diffusion of new varieties of crops that lay at the core of the Green Revolution.[40] When this function is either left to the private sector or carried out by the public sector but directed mainly at larger farmers, the outcome is likely to be much less positive.

As with their performance on the savings and investment fronts, agrarian systems can differ substantially in their growth and distributional legacies in the area of education (human capital). Large landholders, whether they live on their land or not, naturally tend to educate their own children well (usually in urban areas), but they invest little in the schooling of their workers' children, partly in the realistic expectation that doing so will increase that group's capacity to leave for other jobs (e.g., in towns and cities). Low local taxes, which they favor, help to hold down the level of schooling. In contrast, prosperous small farm communities tend to support education. Through this and other mechanisms, land concentration breeds greater inequality in the "human capital" of the next generation and, with it, income inequality. One possible effect of the undereducation of peasants' children is a lower rate of growth of output and income on small farms over time, especially when the education of the farmer or his/her children matters a lot to performance.[41] Although the most important assets of lower income groups in the early stages of growth are land and labor, access to education

[40] As with "merit goods" like education, whether the public sector actually produces the goods or services or simply contracts private agents to do so, the main point is that it guides their production and assures that they be freely available.

[41] Laszlo (2008) reports important income effects from education in rural families in Peru. Various authors have noted that children's education may pay off especially well when their parents have had little schooling.

and capital become more important in a modernizing agriculture and as the rural non-farm sector develops. By the 1980s, with technological progress well under way in some Asian countries, but less so in others, studies estimated an impact on productivity that varied from one to four percent per year of additional education (Hussain and Byerlee 1995). Across various studies reviewed, Dean T. Jamison and Laurence L. Lau (1982) found the average effect of the equivalent of four years of schooling to be 9.5 percent in modernizing environments but only 1.3 percent in traditional settings. Along with its direct contribution to the income of farm families, education is a key determinant of migration, which in turn is the major source of the remittances that support many rural households. Lack of education contributes importantly to creating poverty traps in many middle-income countries.

Transfer of savings for investment in other sectors is one of several linkages between agriculture and the rest of the economy. Other linkages include the demand for non-agricultural products and the efficient combination of agricultural and non-agricultural activities in the same household or locale. Overall, the growth-linkage effects between agriculture and other activities have proven most powerful when agricultural growth is driven by broad-based productivity increases in a rural economy dominated by small farms, as in much of Asia (Mellor 1976; Byerlee et al. 2005). The expenditure patterns of small- to medium-sized farm households are more likely to promote the growth of the local non-farm economy, including rural towns, because they spend higher shares of their income on locally produced items. These growth linkage effects strengthen agriculture's contribution to overall economic growth during the early stages of industrialization. The direct income gains from higher agricultural productivity are thus only one of the ways small farm families benefit from and contribute to growth.

Given the wide range of settings across countries and over time, land concentration has probably facilitated economic growth in some cases and slowed it in others; in-depth empirical analysis is required to determine which outcome is more common and what key factors are at work in each case. Several comprehensive studies have reported a negative association.[42] Their meta-analysis drawing on many existing studies leads Maria Cipollina

[42] Deininger and Olinto's (2000) finding of a negative impact of wealth concentration on economic growth comes from one of the more persuasive analyses in this area because of its use of fixed effects methods to control for intrinsic country heterogeneity.

et al. (2018) to conclude that land inequality is, on average, correlated with slower economic growth, a pattern they find to be more marked in developing countries.[43] They also find that analyses relying on panel data, which generally involve a relatively short period of time, typically report a less negative or even a positive correlation, suggesting that the more negative impacts of land inequality on growth operate primarily in the long term, possibly through stable institutional features. Such a negative link is especially plausible when an unequal land distribution impedes access to education for children, which in turn promotes larger family size and continued flooding of the relatively low-skill labor market.[44] The relatively recent time frame of the studies reviewed implies that the effects of land concentration being picked up correspond to a period during which the large farms in most countries have increasingly been of the capitalist rather than the rentier genre, and therefore possibly more likely to contribute to growth.

Distinguishing correlation from causation is difficult in this sort of analysis. As noted earlier, when growth occurs rapidly in large farm systems, it may be attributable to especially good access to public sector support; in other words, to political factors rather than to inherent economic advantages of larger farms. The meaning of any correlation between land inequality and growth is complicated by the pre-reform conflict and violence often resulting from that inequality and the conflict during the reform itself. Low land concentration may thus be good for growth as long as it does not bring too much of either of these forms of violence.[45]

[43] Cipollina et al. (2018) tested for "publication bias" (a bias toward reporting econometric findings pointing in a certain direction) and detected one favoring the negative result. Their own econometric analysis controlled for that bias.

[44] When this low education and large family size dynamic is at play as a result of land concentration, comparisons with cases of low land concentration and less population growth are most meaningful if they use the growth of per capita income as the test of relative success rather than the growth of the GDP. But the studies reviewed in the meta-analysis typically do not use such a per capita basis in their measure of growth.

[45] Neither our present understanding of the causal processes likely to affect the growth impacts of land concentration nor the comparisons across experiences of high and low land concentration countries points to a simple, general pattern. There have been famous cases in which land equality has preceded strong and egalitarian growth, with many plausible causal mechanisms suggested. But there may also be cases in which concentration has promoted growth, a plausible outcome where the large landholders belong to the agribusiness world and where strong public sector support for such small agriculture as exists is politically impossible. The review by Cipollina et al. (2018, 6) includes studies covering the period from 1960 to 2000, and therefore does not include much, if any, of the dynamics connecting land concentration to political activism and back to growth.

## Land Concentration and Societal Welfare

The central issue addressed here is how land concentration impacts societal welfare. Assuming that both good income levels for the poorer part of a population and income equality contribute to overall societal welfare, then high land concentration today could contribute to higher societal welfare in the future only if it generated much faster growth than would otherwise have occurred. This seems highly unlikely. Judging by the past record, land concentration today leads frequently to slower economic growth and, with great likelihood, to higher inequality in the future. Among countries that have achieved successful growth, current inequality contrasts starkly between those which started with a high land concentration and those with a low one. In the latter, fast output growth with an equalizing impact on income inequality produces very rapid growth of the income of those at the bottom of the hierarchy—a rate that fell in the range of six to eight percent per year in Taiwan over about two decades, essentially eradicating poverty over that short period.[46] This contrasts with an average wage growth in areas of high land concentration in Colombia of about one to 1.4 percent per year from 1950 to 2015, a rate considerably lower than that of agricultural output (Berry 2017b). In short, the post-land reform experiences of the East Asian countries, and more generally the record from cases like Denmark, Canada, Costa Rica, and Indonesia, where concentration has not been high over recent history, demonstrate the dynamic potential of relatively egalitarian agrarian structures and their much superior performance in terms of the resulting income distribution. Land distribution is generally more equitable in Asia, an important factor in the pro-poor impacts of the Green Revolution there. In socialist Vietnam (and also in China), the redistribution of land from collective farms and the security of land tenure have been strongly associated with poverty reduction and agricultural growth (World Bank 2003b).

These contrasting long-term outcomes reflect the fact that land concentration early in the development process typically has a major impact on economic and social inequality not only at that time but also far into the future. The roots of lasting inequality are established at this stage, including the economic, social, and political arrangements that maintain it over time. One

[46] Decades later Vietnam and China when they devolved most decision-making power to family operators, achieved comparable growth results. China's very fast agricultural growth peaked at over six percent during the 1980s and averaged 4.65 percent from 1980 to 2010, but instead of this contributing to overall income equality, the opposite occurred (see Chapter 5).

factor in that permanence is that several of the other forms of capital which become dominant in post-agrarian stages of development tend to be concentrated in few hands but, unlike land, cannot practically be redistributed to smaller firms for use by them. Productive assets of large manufacturing or commercial firms fall in this category.[47] In the case of human capital, which simply cannot be redistributed from one person to another, the level of concentration can only change gradually over the generations. The closest parallel in other sectors to the economic viability and efficiency of small farming is that of the small and medium enterprises found in commerce, manufacturing, and other activities; these often flourish best when they get their start in egalitarian agricultural settings. Because the distribution of human and other forms of non-agricultural capital can only change slowly over time, agriculture offers the only chance for a significant asset and income redistribution within a short period of time, and in the early stages of economic development when it most matters.

The unavoidable stability in the distribution of capital in the post-agrarian phases of development shows up in world economic trends. Both intra-country and overall world inequality have long been, and still remain, very high. Over the second half of the twentieth century, intra-country distribution tended more often than not to worsen, even though overall world distribution did improve somewhat due to the faster growth of lower income countries (Berry and Serieux 2007). Because of the difficulties confronting asset redistribution, most of the income equalizing attempts in the middle and later stages of development involve a progressive tax system and the provision of free or subsidized goods and services to lower income people; usually the latter is the more important. The level of post-tax-and-transfer income inequality is less than its pre-tax and transfer counterpart in nearly all countries, although this gap is much less in most developing countries than in the industrialized ones. Time trends in post-tax-and-transfer inequality have not been studied in enough countries to permit useful generalizations on what has been happening; the same is true for the arguably more important trends in the distribution of consumption. Although less extreme than for income, inequality of consumption remains very high in most countries and in the world.

[47] In a few countries, a partial step toward equalizing power and income in large-scale manufacturing firms is the inclusion of workers and/or union leaders in the decision-making apparatus. Curtailment of monopoly power also helps to reduce income inequality.

Histories like Brazil's and Colombia's underline the pivotal role of land concentration early in the development process as the foundation for enduringly high inequality. Although these two countries are no longer primarily agricultural, the level of inequality is probably about as high as when agriculture dominated their economies: in both cases, the Gini coefficient of income has been at or around 0.6.[48] Inequality based originally on the concentration of land has morphed into a broader-based phenomenon, and the unequal distribution of land is complemented by, and increasingly replaced by, inequality of human capital. This was notoriously the case in Brazil where, as of the 1980s, its inequality (as measured by differences in years of schooling) was among the highest in the world, and where the ratio of incomes of those with university to those with primary was about fifteen-to-one, compared to a figure of three-to-one in Sweden.

In light of the enormous inequality in land distribution in some countries and the political impediments to redistributive reform, are there alternative policy instruments to offset the damage that inequality wreaks? Various steps can, in principle, act as partial offsets, but most of them tend to be partly or wholly blocked by the same political barriers that prevent the reform itself. Sometimes, however, one or another can be employed, especially if they are seen by the power elites as needed to block bigger future reforms.

Some options involving agriculture aim to improve the potential of existing small farms; these include steps to improve the security of access to whatever amount of land farmers do have. Well-defined property rights can create long-term incentives for farmers to invest in productivity improvements and facilitate access to finance with low transactions costs (World Bank 2003b). Clear property rights and efficient land administration systems can, in some cases, lead to market-based land redistribution over the longer term (Mwabu and Thorbecke 2004). Reform of Indian land laws in the 1960s to provide security to tenants was an important factor in pro-poor growth. But in some cases, like that of El Salvador, ill-conceived land reform programs have aggravated the insecurity of land rights (World Bank 2004b). Secure property rights and efficient land administration

[48] For Colombia, see Alvaredo and Gasparini (2013, 46). This figure is higher than the standard estimates because it combines tax data with that from household income surveys. Its 2010 Gini coefficient of over 0.6 gave it the highest figure among all countries covered by such data as of that year (nearly all industrial countries but only a minority of developing ones), and certainly among the highest in the world. These data suggest that the top one percent of income earners received twenty percent of total national (disposable) income in both 1997 and in 2010. For the Brazilian data, see Chapter 6.

systems are important not only for pro-poor growth, but also to facilitate partial or total exit from the agricultural sector, which may eventually be important to increasing family income.

A frequently suggested option is a progressive land tax to discourage speculation and to reduce concentration gradually over time. When it can work fast enough to make a difference, and under what political constraints are complicated issues. Placing ceiling sizes on newly formed farms is another option. Investment in rural education and access to well-functioning financial markets stimulate farm productivity, rural non-farm growth, and migration.

Arguably the best offset to the lack of reform in cases where existing small agriculture employs a large share of the agricultural labor force is efficient public policy support on other fronts. But this is a very tall order—often impossible when power elites are still in place. More typically, investments in core public goods that would be pro-poor continue to be crowded out by badly chosen options, such as excessive subsidies (e.g., to fertilizer and irrigation) or heavy expenditures on what are essentially private goods (e.g., many livestock services) that mostly benefit large-scale farmers.

The bottom-line evidence on the success of effective antidotes to the absence of land reform lies in the infrequency with which high income inequality that is initially attributable to land concentration falls significantly over time. How much of this failure is due to the antidotes not being applied and how much to their limited effects when applied is a matter in need of further study. In any case, the record is not at all reassuring.

From the perspective of long-term economic and social welfare, the evidence leaves little plausible defense for high levels of land concentration and gives greater historical weight to the question of how such levels arise and how they maintain themselves even as countries become apparently more democratic and less accepting of inequality.

Fortunately, high levels of inequality do not block economic growth, so, over time, incomes of those at the bottom do rise. Poverty showed a marked downward trend over the twentieth century as the world economy and especially the lower-income countries grew rapidly. So did slavery, particularly that associated with agriculture, historically a major setting for this abuse but decreasingly so as mechanization replaced its function. Domestic service is now a much more important context for slavery. Quantitative evidence on sexual exploitation and other forms of related abuses is not readily available.

# Appendix 3.1

## Complexities in the Measurement and Understanding of Productive Efficiency

"Efficiency" is one of the most useful and most used concepts in economics, but it is also a very complicated one, both because there is no simple, obviously correct, or best definition of it and because, even when a definition is chosen, there are some measurement problems. As a result, almost any empirical discussion involving the concept is subject to error, and calls for the use of confidence interrvals.

Any attempt to measure efficiency (e.g., of difference firms or farms) must begin with the objective against which the measurement is occurring. In standard Western economics this is the maximization of national income or national product, without regard to positive or negative externality effects on others beyond the firm, to income distribution or to human welfare. (It is usually assumed implicitly that human welfare rises proportionately to income.). A useful distinction is between "narrow efficiency," defined by income generated, and "broad efficiency," which takes account of other factors like those just mentioned.

The other main complexities around the concept of efficiency involve potential measurement error or imprecision.[49]At the firm level, relevant concepts include both "single factor productivity" (e.g., labor productivity or land productivity) and "total factor productivity" (TFP), which compares value of output to value of inputs. Even in the former apparently simple measures, two common problems arise. The most obvious problem is simple mismeasurement, such as when a farm of five hectares is mismeasured and treated as having three hectares. Less obvious are the quality differences among the units of a given input. Land quality differences should be taken into account when comparing the inputs used by different farms; so should labor quality differences (i.e., the time spent by an accountant with a university degree is not obviously to be seen as having the same cost as an hour's work from an illiterate employee). The former challenge has been widely recognized and fairly often dealt with, whereas the latter one is seldom mentioned.

Whether measurement involves a single factor's productivity or that of all factors, measurement of quantity boils down to a measure of opportunity cost; what tells us how much more highly an accountant's time should be valued than that of an illiterate and inexperienced worker is what that person could earn in their best alternate use or employment. In measuring this value, economists typically resort to observed market prices (e.g., wages, rates of interest, etc.), but this approach is not fully satisfactory because markets are not perfect (i.e., for one worker the alternative use of his time would correspond to that observed wage, but another might simply become unemployed if the job they now fill were not available).

All of these problems are present in the use of TFP as a way to compare productive units. Standard practice is to apply the same cost to workers, whomever they work for, but this is theoretically invalid both because their quality may differ and because their alternative use may involve different markets. A common example of this problem arises when one tries to compare the efficiency of small family farms in a labor surplus economy (i.e., the opportunity cost of a worker's time may be as low as zero) with that of large farms. If

[49] For a review of various of the measurement problems, see Gollin (2018)

one accepts that the opportunity cost of labor is zero, then the relative efficiency is fully determined by land and capital productivity because the opportunity cost of these factors is indeed positive.

Correctly understanding which measures of efficiency are most useful brings additional complications and challenges. The main one in the discussion of farm size and efficiency involves the different meaning of labor productivity and land productivity. It is a key distinction because labor productivity virtually always increases with farm size, while land productivity usually falls. As previously noted, when the aggregate objective is the maximization of output, then TFP is the appropriate indicator; it reflects both land and labor (and capital) productivity. When the opportunity cost of labor approaches zero, land productivity and TFP show very similar patterns.

A major source of misunderstanding arises from the fact that the standard focus of people assessing how well a country is doing economically is labor productivity, as this is closely related to average income per capita. But achieving a maximum average labor productivity at a point in time (for the economy or a sector of it) does not imply the pursuit of a maximum labor productivity in each producing unit. When a set of large farms maximize their labor productivity by using very little of that input, this lowers its productivity in the rest of the economy, and for the economy as a whole.

# SECTION II

# THE MIXED RECORD OF TWENTIETH-CENTURY ATTEMPTS AT LAND REFORM

Land issues were either important or predominant in each of the Russian, French, Chinese, and Mexican revolutions, making these among the better-known attempts to reform agrarian structure over the course of the last two hundred years. The Russian and Chinese uprisings—historic moments in those two societies—wrought major effects, among them land redistribution and a rise in the incomes of most rural workers, but also the murder of many larger farmers and the much greater loss of life in the Great Chinese Famine of 1959 to 1961. Under the Marxist belief in the efficiency of large-scale collective farming, the Communist governments remade the agrarian structure in that mode. Its natural limitations contributed to the sector's underperformance for decades, and those limitations were amplified by the weak knowledge of agriculture and the impulsive and quixotic beliefs of Joseph Stalin and Mao Zedong.[1] The gradual redistribution of land after the Mexican Revolution provided important social benefits to many families, but the Revolution cost many lives and left a society far short of what its more idealistic backers had envisioned. These three experiences are discussed in some detail in this section of the book.

The earlier French Revolution was a pivotal step in the transformation of a formerly feudal society toward a modern one, as defined by standards of equality and liberty for all. By the time it occurred, a "seigneurial" system had largely replaced medieval feudalism; unlike the latter structure, its basis was

[1] All three of the century's great purveyors of death (Adolf Hitler, Joseph Stalin and Mao Zedong) suffered from a striking ignorance about the needs of agriculture in their respective countries. Hitler's coveting of agricultural land to the east followed from the regime's failure to understand the potential to raise the productivity of German agriculture through improved technology, a recipe that was so successfully deployed in many developing countries beginning just a couple of decades later.

almost entirely economic. Peasants who occupied land owned by a *seigneur* ("lord") had to pay feudal dues—in cash, produce, or service to the *seigneur*. In August 1789, the National Constituent Assembly abolished the remaining feudal-type privileges, along with the tithe, which had been a ten percent tax for the Church and was the main source of income for many clergymen. The peasants were still supposed to pay for the release of seigneurial dues, which affected more than one-fourth of the farmland in France and provided most of the income of the large landowners. The majority refused to pay and, in 1793, this obligation was also cancelled, thereby giving the peasants their land free. Although the revolution led to considerable land redistribution, its income-equalizing effects were not permanent. Instead, they were substantially offset by a reverse trend over the period from the 1830s to the 1860s (Morrisson and Snyder 2000). In retrospect, this precedent can be seen as another portent of how far final outcomes can be from the architects' original aims.

Chapter 4 examines key differences in the reforms undertaken or attempted during the twentieth century and how they may meaningfully be judged. Chapter 5 reviews the major reforms in communist countries—Russia, China, Vietnam, and Cuba. Chapter 6 does the same for Latin America's non-communist reforms, while Chapter 7 looks at the East Asian experiences (Japan, Korea, and Taiwan), along with India, Iran, and Egypt.

# 4

# Assessing the Success of Agrarian Reforms and Other Policies to Deal with Land Concentration

Land reform can be seen as one part of a process of modernization and civilization as countries enter a phase in which the abuse and extreme inequality that characterize many feudal systems become unacceptable. Thus, it is natural that many reforms—typically the bigger ones—are a part of broader societal advances that include extending education and health services to the lower classes and sometimes diminishing gender, class, and ethnic gaps. Where civilization does progress, the worst abuses are destined to end sooner or later. The question of interest here, then, is whether and when agrarian reforms are the best mechanism to hasten that advance. In the broadest terms, their contribution is measured by how much sooner societal abuse is curtailed and welfare improved because they have been undertaken.

In the agricultural stages of economic development the historic norm has been for the concentration of land ownership or control to be high, reflecting its role as the key economic mechanism that allows a small elite to benefit from the work of the masses.[1] That concentration varies over time, depending on changes in the capacity of those at the top to control and/or abuse, in the ability of the downtrodden to organize and fight back, and on exogenously determined changes of setting. One such change is population growth, which increases the pressure on the land, thus diminishing access for some families. If the elite resists getting less, then the poor will, and this may foment rebellion.

The phrase "land reform" has been used in strikingly different ways. Any discussion of experiences therefore requires some basic distinctions. Key among these are the context; the main actors, both those supporting and those opposing the reform; the agrarian and social structures that are

[1] Most exceptions have their own particular explanations.

*The Great Curse*. Albert Berry, Oxford University Press. © Oxford University Press 2024.
DOI: 10.1093/oso/9780197782675.003.0005

the final goal of the reform; the details of implementation; and the specific benefits sought. Redistributive agrarian (or land) reform has been the natural and most widely touted approach to dealing with excessive concentration of land. Its implementation is a direct remedy for that concentration. The corresponding "preventive" approach involves policies to avoid land concentration becoming too high.

## Broad Goals and Settings

Key features of a reform[2] are the source of the land transferred (currently operated land versus new or "frontier" land), the recipients (e.g., landless families, small farmers with too little land), the mode of transfer (e.g., involuntary expropriation, payment to former owners with or without a charge to recipients), and the coverage (e.g., in terms of share of land transferred). These features are related to the context and the broad objective sought in the reform; for example, as between a total shift from an existing hierarchy of private, large landholders to a collective type of agriculture, a major shift to a small farmer-based agriculture, a more marginal redistribution that does not greatly diminish the concentration of land holding, and so on. The proponents of agrarian reforms have varying goals, both for themselves and for their society, ranging from a modest nudging toward equality within a capitalist agricultural sector to a major change within such a system or a shift toward socialism and collectivism. The character of a reform is related to those goals, to the setting, and to the identity of the proponents and of the opponents with essentially defensive goals, which are sometimes to totally block the reform and sometimes to reduce its scope (e.g., as when the elite class accepts that landless families must be given some land to avoid a dangerous rebellion). With a reform-oriented government in power other proponents may be bolder; for example, it may be widely assumed that the reform will not only benefit the recipients of land but also the economy as a whole.

A major distinction among twentieth-century reforms is that between those carried out by capitalist regimes and those by communist ones. The latter are imposed by usually powerful authoritarian governments, whose vision of the good society is one of relative equality and a decent standard of

[2] For a detailed discussion of the goals of land reform, see Lipton (2009, ch. 1).

living for workers, and who favor large-scale production units because these are seen as fostering a communal way of life and/or because of a belief in economies of scale or in the lack of managerial capacity of workers operating on their own. Such reforms have been notable for the high coverage (the share of total land transferred and of the rural population benefited), for expropriation without payment, and for the (at least initial or fairly quick) shift toward communes or state farms as the unit of production.

Experiences falling in the capitalist category vary much more widely by setting, by the relative power and influence of the various groups involved (large landholders, the landless, etc.), and by the design. In some cases, the land distributed to beneficiaries comes mainly from unused, publicly owned land; in others, it is obtained by expropriating the land of current large landholders at low or zero prices. In still other cases, land is purchased by the state at market, or near market, prices and then transferred to the recipient, usually at a subsidized price. This last modality is commonly referred to as a Market-Assisted Land Reform (MALR). Distribution of land in a collective form has also taken place in a number of market economies, among them Peru and Venezuela, although this does not necessarily mean that everyone winds up a beneficiary.

Sometimes the recipients are former tenants or operators on public land, in which case the reform process is described as "land to the tiller"; in other cases, they were previously landless or operated smaller units elsewhere. If the land originally belonged to the state, the process is often referred to as "colonization." Both such colonization and other programs that involve little loss to former landowners are often labelled "pseudo-reforms." They are naturally favored by landlords because they do not much threaten their existing control; in fact, they may even increase it through the transfer of state land to close allies of the government, often illegally or by other corrupt means, as has happened in Bolivia, Mexico, Iran, and many other countries.

The contrast between the goal of an egalitarian family-farm system versus that of collectives or state-run farms reflects differing visions of a good society and differing ideas on what makes for an efficient economy. For some, the main goal is an egalitarian socialist society and for others it is a market-oriented capitalist system in which land is not highly concentrated. For still others, the goal is a simpler, more ecologically sound life, as exemplified by today's Via Campesina movement, which defends peasant agriculture and food sovereignty as a way of promoting social justice and dignity, while strongly opposing the corporate-driven agriculture that it sees as destroying social relations and nature.[3] Whatever visions energize them, reform experiences also reflect the domestic political setting and the presence (or not) of international actors.

Redistribution of land currently in use can radically change the concentration of land, as when it goes to poor, landless farmers. Transfer of publicly owned land to private hands, even when it benefits small farmers, typically does so without challenging the land wealth, social status, or power of large owners. It is a compromise between moving toward a radically more egalitarian structure and retaining the existing level of concentration. Cuba, China, Taiwan, and South Korea are examples of the former. Bolivia and Mexico are in-between cases, and Brazil and Colombia exemplify the latter.[4] The redistributive effects of reform are naturally greater when much land is expropriated and distributed to a large proportion of the rural population, especially the rural poor. The less paid out in compensation to landlords, and the less the beneficiaries have to pay for the land, especially if they include a large part of the rural poor, the greater is the redistributive impact. Agrarian reform also has a greater overall redistributive effect in countries with a relatively large rural economy and population. There is, naturally, an association between the types and aims of a reform and what sort of government carries it out.

The twentieth century saw major changes in the setting for reforms. Individual countries were advancing along the path from rural agriculture-based economies to more urban ones dominated by industry, commerce, and finance. Communism arrived as an important political/societal variant and, with it, came the Cold War between the capitalist countries and the

[3] This organization, founded in 1993 and now with representative groups in eighty-one countries, strives to forward the interests of peasants, small- and medium-sized farmers, those without land, rural women and youth, indigenous peoples, migrants, and agricultural workers. It is independent of political parties, economic groups, and other affiliations. Its founding was, in part, a response to the growth of agribusiness, the "globalization" of agricultural policies, and the feeling that small farmers needed to have and defend a common vision. At the 1996 World Food Summit, it launched its vision of "Food Sovereignty," seen as the right of people to healthy and culturally appropriate food produced through sustainable methods and their right to define their own food and agricultural systems. It prioritizes local food production and consumption, and a country's right to protect its local producers from cheap imports. It promotes agroecology and defends local seeds. The organization's ideal is small-scale sustainable production that benefits communities and their environment.

[4] Albertus (2017, 8) classifies "land colonization" and MALF as "pseudo-reform" because they are less aggressive and/or less complete than expropriation-based reform. They are designed to avoid tackling the unequal control of land; in fact, as he notes, they can promote it, as in cases where state colonization projects have created a new wave of *latifundism* when vast amounts of land are transferred, often illegally or by other corrupt means, to close allies to the government in power, as happened in Bolivia, Mexico, and many other countries. Such reforms are naturally favored by landlords.

communist ones, in particular the Soviet Union. Early in the century most of the attempted reforms were in heavily agricultural countries (e.g., Russia and Mexico). Later the market-based version appeared in countries in the middle stages of the transformation away from agriculture-based economies (Brazil, Colombia, Iran, etc.). By that time, the potential redistribution of income for the economy at large was less than it was in early twentieth century Russia or mid-century China.

The underlying distinction between traditional revolution-based reforms *cum* expropriation and the recent market-based model exemplifies the centrality of the political setting. In the former case, the land transfer is involuntary and can involve a high share of a nation's total stock of agricultural land. Such a surrender of land would not occur except under pressure. MALR involves, in effect, the voluntary sale of land by large landholders to families currently having none or too little, usually with a substantial subsidy provided by government (or international institutions). It can occur without the use of force or pressure; however, the extent of transfer is limited by the amount of subsidy funding available. Except in countries far enough along in the development process so that the value of agricultural land in relation to the country's tax potential and, ultimately, to its GDP is relatively low, the size of a reform is thus limited by fiscal constraints. The two types of reform are polar opposites, and most people are strong advocates of one or the other, but they may also be complementary; for example, in cases where the threat of uprisings or unrest encourages large farmers to accept compensation at below market values. The market model, which came on the scene late in the twentieth century, is usually attempted under considerable pressure for some type of reform, often manifested in illegal land occupations. To work smoothly, it relies on the bulk of the population abiding by the existing laws and respecting property rights, by even if much of today's property was earlier acquired by the use of force, legal manipulation, or other unjust practices. Which model is a better bet to yield societal benefits in a given country depends both on the agrarian structure and the politics. The creation of small farms through involuntary land distribution on a small scale tends to generate or be part of a self-reinforcing cycle of conflict: land is redistributed where there is a conflict, which puts pressure on the government to redistribute there; this in turn encourages groups to pursue conflict elsewhere (World Bank 2003, 127). Voluntary redistribution cannot achieve much unless large landholders are relatively disinterested in retaining their property and thus are willing to sell at moderate prices. Accordingly, the merits of MALR programs have been widely debated and criticized on the grounds that they reaffirm the property rights of elites, redistribute too little land to alter rural power structures, or reduce the role of social movements. The Word Bank has promoted such programs in Brazil, Guatemala, Colombia, El Salvador, Philippines, South Africa, Zimbabwe, and Namibia with mixed success in meeting their goals and with a modest scope. In each case, only a small fraction of land has been redistributed, benefiting only a correspondingly small fraction of the rural poor.[5]

Because land reform is, by definition, a political phenomenon, any theory designed to explain its presence and form must incorporate the strength, character, and organization of the forces for change and of those opposing it; the nature of the political system within which these forces do battle; and the dynamics of that battle, including which political groups are interested in, or prepared to collaborate with, the pro-reform forces and on which points, and which with the anti-reform forces. These broad background features largely determine what sort of reform is in prospect and what forms of support it will get. The benefits from any reform depend greatly on the availability of technical support. Also relevant is the availability of alternative and/or complementary policies, such as a progressive tax system that imposes a bigger burden the larger is the unit of land, or the greater the accumulation of value between time of purchase and time of sale (a feature designed to control speculation).

Michael Albertus (2015) concludes that the most redistributive land reforms occur under autocratic rather than democratic rule.[6] This pattern is explained at least in part by the significant share of major reforms that have occurred under communist regimes with the broad goal of income redistribution (Russia, China, Cuba, Vietnam, and Ethiopia). These reforms have, in the beginning, opted or pushed for collective production and, even when they later cede operational control back to the families, have maintained state ownership.[7] Most land reforms with major lasting impacts—a category substantially overlapping with the most redistributive ones—have also been carried out by authoritarian governments, often in the wake of a

[5] Many critics feel that such reforms do not provide net benefits at all. The discussion of the Brazil case in Chapter 6 suggests a more positive story.

[6] An insightful review and critique is presented by Kay (2019). Kapstein (2017), who focuses on international politics and specifically on US foreign policy, does not find strong evidence for Albertus's main thesis.

[7] This "property rights gap' is the theme of Albertus (2021).

revolution, and often applying much force. In China, the USSR, and Mexico the drive came from the inside; in Japan and Korea, it came partly from the outside. Most reforms attempted by modern-style democratic regimes (like Colombia, Chile, and Guatemala) have borne little lasting fruit.

Even among the non-communist countries, Albertus's (2015) hypothesis on the centrality of autocratic government to carry through significant reform is plausible enough; many factors would appear to contribute to such a pattern. In democracies, the rich have better access to voting than do the poor, they are able to spend more on elections, and they can greatly influence the opinions of many others and/or pressure them to vote a certain way. High levels of land concentration usually mean that the polity is dominated or heavily influenced by the agrarian elite. In such settings, one might expect a moderate, negotiated reform involving the distribution of currently public land but not much expropriation of private land. In those democracies with lower land concentration—a more natural fit—land reform is not on the table because it is not a matter of urgency. Autocratic governments, usually military, tend to be under less pressure to find a negotiated solution than are democracies, which gives them more independence. What they do then depends on their own character and preferences/ideology, how they came to power, and who exercises influence on them. Most are allied with the dominant economic interest groups, and thus are more inclined to repress reform than to support it (e.g., Brazil). Many are corrupt, making them natural allies of those existing vested interests. But a few, for a range of reasons, including the extent of public pressure and dissatisfaction, do advance serious land reform, as will be discussed in the contexts of Egypt and Peru. Relatively free from the pressure of the landed elite, they are better placed to effect major change. But the fact that a high share of significant reforms is carried out by autocratic governments does not mean that such governments are systematically more inclined to undertake reform. Arguably, they are more likely *both* to undertake major reforms and to be harshly repressive of pro-reform movements. Post-revolution autocracies have significant freedom to undertake large changes. If the revolution has an agrarian base, they are, in fact, expected to undertake major reforms in that area. Because democracies tend to reflect a range of views and to be more oriented to compromise, the reforms they do foster are likely to be moderate. Whether a country is democratic or not, land redistribution is most likely to occur when there are both coalition splits between political and landed elites and low institutional constraints on what the government can do.

The twentieth century saw major changes in both domestic and international political and economic settings, which in turn greatly affected the frequency, character, and outcomes of attempted reforms. The Russian Revolution not only altered the history of that country, but that of the world, by implementing an alternative model of how an economy and a society could be organized. The model—copied in the rest of the Soviet Union, China, Vietnam, and Cuba—included broad-ranging transformations of the agricultural system. A contrasting set of reforms, categorized by Michael Courville and Raj Patel (2006) as "postwar allied consolidations," were undertaken with the involvement of dominant political actors to secure democratic rule and thereby avoid communism, and to fulfill the needs of a growth model based on industrial expansion (e.g., South Korea, Japan, Taiwan, and Germany, a country to which many people of German lineage but living elsewhere returned after the war). The Cold War, an eventual result of Russian communism, created a new felt need on the part of the capitalist world to ease the social pressures and tensions arising from agrarian inequality in Third World countries by supporting defensive land reforms, most notably those undertaken by the US in various Latin American countries, the Philippines, South Vietnam, and elsewhere. By the 1980s, the shift in that capitalist world toward greater reliance on market forces was modifying the preferred form of reform toward the MALR.[8] Changes in domestic and international political settings and in ideologies (state-imposed versus market-driven reforms) were accompanied by the gradual change of economic setting as countries became less agriculturally oriented.

## Defining and Measuring the Success of Reform

In countries whose agrarian structure suffers from high land concentration, with accompanying slavery, serfdom, or labor subjugation through market forces, all of this underpinned by political and military power, the righting of such a multifaceted "wrong" would not be expected to come easily. And,

[8] As Kay (1998, 10) puts it, "The most significant symbol of the neoliberal winds sweeping through Latin America has been the change in 1992 of Article 27 of Mexico's Constitution of 1917, which had opened the road to Latin America's first agrarian reform and which enshrined a principal demand for 'land and liberty' by the peasant insurgents during the Mexican revolution. Before 1992 no government had dared to modify this key principle of Mexico's Constitution, but the forces of globalization and neoliberalism proved too strong to resist and the government took the risk of tackling this hitherto sacred cow."

indeed, it has not. The attempts have numbered in the hundreds, or perhaps even the thousands if one includes all of the uprisings, revolutions, and smaller scale reforms initiated throughout history. Those that got beyond the protest stage to some form of action are the center of attention here; they are selected with a view to the lessons they provide.[9]

Redistributive agrarian reform can be seen as the case par excellence in which farm size structure changes greatly and quickly. It requires unusual circumstances and typically raises major challenges. Even if there is a desire on the government's part to assist the new small farmers in raising their productivity—and there may not, either because the government is not solidly in favor of the new agrarian structure or it believes the farmers are naturally incompetent—it may still be difficult to develop the needed support apparatus.

Achieving an equitable distribution of land early in the development process has, understandably, been rare; original authoritarian-based concentration does not give way quickly to an egalitarian pattern. Although other redistributive mechanisms have more potential later, land reform and an associated transformation away from exploitative societal norms is the obvious, and probably the only, major corrective to early inequality in a society. To help put its role in perspective one can ask:

(i) How much can a reform affect societal welfare at various stages of the development process, and, in particular, when the starting point is a feudal agrarian society? Possible benefits include an improvement in social status/quality of life through the end of slavery/serfdom and the abuses associated with it; control over more land, thus raising beneficiaries' income and future economic prospects and lowering income inequality in the society; and a higher share of smaller farms, which can (although may not always) bring an increase in total agricultural output and in the rate of overall economic growth. A reform's impact depends on which of these potential benefits it yields, how large each of them is, the share of the potential beneficiaries actually reached, and the time profile of the benefits. Some reforms benefit only a small share of the aspirants, while others benefit a large share.

[9] Among the commentators on the history of land reforms are Lipton (2009), Herring (2000), Warriner (1969), Prosterman and Riedinger (1987), Powelson and Stock (1987), Ladejinsky (1977), de Janvry (1981), and many others.

Sometimes serfdom is ended for all, but only a few get full control/ownership of land. Sometimes the public sector provides little subsequent support for the beneficiaries, and sometimes it does better. Few aspects are clearly black or white. Each reform has to be judged in detail by its achievements and by the barriers it has to overcome. The benefits of a given reform depend on which type is attempted, the setting, the surrounding institutions, and, very importantly, the timing.

(ii) Of the negative phenomena associated with land concentration—income inequality, poverty, slavery/serfdom, abuse, and so forth—which can be most effectively corrected by deliberate "reform" and which less so?

(iii) To what degree have the reforms actually implemented been able to correct the injustices and inefficiencies they targeted? Over the last several hundred years, only a few cases have achieved near complete success; there have been many partial successes and some clear failures. Such a record is fairly typical of the various great challenges humanity has faced or faces, such as curtailing racism, criminality, and other forms of personal misbehavior.

(iv) Does the modest success rate mainly reflect unrealistic hopes, ineffective implementation, opposition stronger than what might reasonably have been expected, or other factors?

(v) In the absence of such reform, what alternative mechanisms and policies might raise broad societal welfare over time?

Assessing a reform's impact calls for the identification of one or more alternative routes that the country might have taken instead of the one actually followed. While one may say confidently that, after a given reform, a certain number of families previously without land then had it, and that it brought a higher income and/or other benefits, the key question is how such variables would have evolved in the absence of the reform. Sometimes plausible alternatives can be identified fairly clearly (e.g., the continuation of the status quo over a certain period). In some cases, economic or political logic points to other specific possibilities, but usually only limited confidence can be placed in the identification of any one of them. Sometimes broader trends, like urbanization and rising incomes around the world, narrow the range of alternatives. For example, it would seem unlikely that the extreme semi-slavery found in several of the Latin countries at the beginning of the twentieth century could have endured through it, given the ongoing economic and political trends. In that case, a proposed alternative to reform needs to specify when progress would have occurred on those fronts and what form it would have taken. An obvious option, as this trend was underway in many settings, is that semi-feudalism would have given way to wage labor as traditional haciendas were replaced by modern large-scale commercial agriculture. The alternative to reform would thus see workers operating under different conditions; assessment of its welfare advantage over serfdom can draw on a more general set of indicators. Empirical evidence on trends in income levels, wage rates, life expectancy, educational achievement, and other presumed correlates of welfare is helpful. Where a reform that redistributed a considerable amount of land leads to a short improvement in rural income distribution, but this is reversed as small agriculture stagnates and large agriculture booms, it would appear that the benefits did not last long. In contrast, a rapid and continuous rise in wages suggests a tightening of the labor market, possibly due to the increased access of small farmers to land.

A range of objective and quantitative information is available to help assess the immediate and latter impacts of whether and how a land reform is carried out. Few discussions detail the alternative routes not taken to better help identify the size of likely payoffs (or damages) from the reform.[10] For the cases considered in Chapter 5 to Chapter 8, while no organized attempt is made along these lines, relevant information is noted. The main, directly pertinent economic evidence refers to the incomes of landless workers (wages) and small farmers (earnings); data are sometimes available in a consistent form over time. More generally, data on the incomes of the bottom deciles of the labor force can give a relatively accurate picture of how those two groups are faring in terms of average income, poverty, relative income, and so on.[11] Thus, information on the absolute and relative income of the bottom sixty to eighty percent of the agricultural or rural (or total) labor force is likely to provide useful hints. Best of all would be to have data on the self-reported sense of satisfaction or welfare of the groups in question, but this is virtually never available around the time of twentieth century's actual or attempted reforms.

[10] With enough information on an economy's structure, it is possible to "model" how it would have evolved if the political actors had taken alternative policy steps. Such in-depth analysis is not normally feasible, although simple models can sometimes be useful.

[11] Unfortunately, as noted elsewhere, much of the available information on the income levels of small farmers is seriously underestimated (Forero et al. 2002). How the degree of downward bias varies with the circumstances is not yet well understood.

Data on relative incomes matters partly because it affects levels of satisfaction. There is some evidence of changes in the extent of abuse, much of which is related to those pre-reform patterns of serfdom that invite mistreatment.

The contribution of reform in a given country over a given period of time may be portrayed as in Figure 4.1, where the height of SW curves measures societal welfare over time under different circumstances; that welfare might, for example, be defined as the sum of the level of satisfaction of each person, with equal weights for each. A successful reform would be one in which curve SWr (societal welfare after reform) lies above curve SWw (societal welfare without reform) from the time of the reform onward, as portrayed by the combination of curves $SWr^1$ and $SWw^1$. In cases where income inequality was high because of the land concentration and agricultural output less than it might have been, the benefits would likely be large for a long time because growth would probably be faster, and distribution would be certainly less unequal. Where the inequality impact of land concentration would not have endured strongly into the post-agricultural stages of development, the benefits would be smaller at each point of time, as reflected in the vertical gap between curves $SWr^1$ and $SWw^2$. In cases where the reform was unsuccessful in either raising output or significantly reducing income inequality, and also

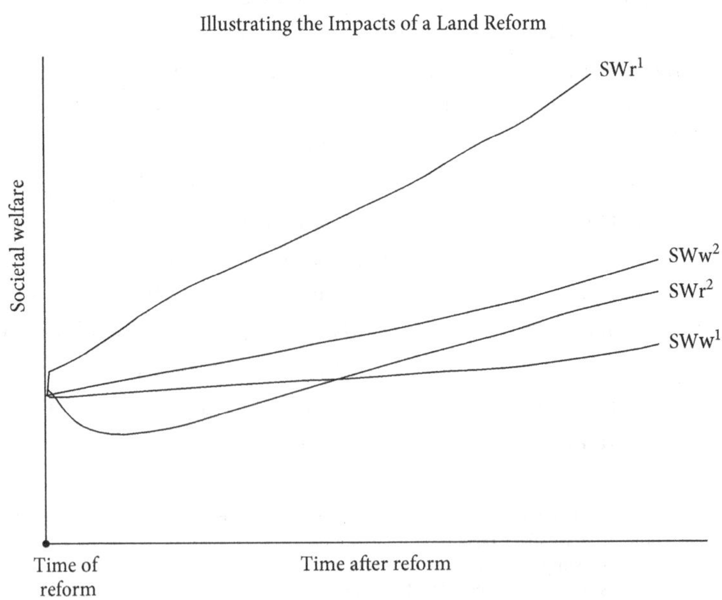


**Figure 4.1** Illustrating the Impacts of a Land Reform

where it also cost many lives, then the reform curve, say $SWr^2$, could be below the SWw curve. In short, many different dynamics could play out over time.

## The Outcomes and Their Associated Benefits

Enough significant attempts at land reform were made during the twentieth century to raise the question –"of what role they played in the world's evolution toward higher incomes and well-being during that period of dramatic change.[12] As of two hundred years ago, the share of the world's population living in countries or regions which either did not seriously need a land reform or had already experienced one was perhaps twenty to thirty percent; this included parts of North America, most of Europe outside Russia, much of Africa, and small populations elsewhere.[13] A great deal thus remained to be done.

Putting an end to slavery/serfdom has been the most widely achieved benefit, in part because it is, in principle, the most straightforward—certain customs can simply be ruled illegal—and, in part, because as societies become more civilized it is seen as the least defensible feature of a feudal agrarian structure. Two hundred years ago, a high share of the world's agricultural labor force (perhaps sixty percent) worked under such conditions, which translates to a high share (around forty-five to fifty percent) of the total labor force because economies were predominantly agricultural.[14] Today only a very small share of the agricultural labor force suffers this plight (probably well below five percent, depending on the precise definition) and a tiny share (perhaps one percent) of the total labor force, of which agriculture now forms only a little over a quarter. A drop from sixty to under five percent is indeed dramatic; in fact, agriculture is no longer a major site of the slavery/serfdom that does now exist. It is naturally hard to judge what part of this

[12] Albertus (2021) estimates that such reforms impacted over one billion people during the course of the twentieth century.

[13] The share of the world's agricultural population living in those countries was substantially lower, probably in the range of fifteen to twenty-five percent because they were atypically non-agricultural. China and India had nearly forty percent of the world's population, while Latin America and North America had a little under ten percent between them.

[14] In 1820, somewhere in the range of seventy-five to eighty-five percent of all workers were engaged in agriculture. With over two-thirds of the world's population found in Asia, this phenomenon's prevalence there largely defined its presence in the world as a whole. A rough estimate that eighty-five percent of the region's population was in agriculture, and that eighty percent of that population was in servitude, suggests the cited share of two-thirds for the world as a whole.

impressive decline, or of that occurring in specific periods, has been due to agrarian reform in its various definitions, but it has clearly been significant for some periods. Many of the reforms, which have brought mixed, modest, or delayed benefits on the economic front, have nonetheless put an end to the feudal order, as with those of Russia, China, Mexico, Bolivia, Ethiopia, and Iran, among others.

On the purely economic front, less success has been achieved. Although twentieth century attempts to reform or improve the distribution of land have been many, only a small minority have achieved a wide coverage of potential beneficiaries and effected the most desirable changes. One key element is that families gain immediate control of the land they work or of the product of that land. Over the twentieth century, Japan was the biggest success judged by number of families helped in this way, at somewhere between three and four million, or more than one-half of the country's six million-plus farm households as of 1950. At the world level, probably only one to two percent of the agricultural population benefited this way over the century. However, when to this modest share are added the families in China and Vietnam (and, in lesser degree, Russia), who eventually had access to land as a result of the earlier reforms, the share is much higher—probably fifteen to twenty percent, although some of the benefits were greatly delayed, especially those in China and Russia.[15]

Compared to the few major or complete successes, like the ever-cited East Asian cases, the number of failures, near failures, and partial successes has been large. Any simple assessment of the degree of success is complicated by the fact that some reforms have exacted very high costs on society, especially in the loss of life. Some have prompted reactions which have made things worse. Some socio-economic trends have cancelled out or prevented the potential benefits of reforms, such as where the growth of large-scale farming and agro-industry involves enclosure movements, the displacement of small producers, and the like. The main direct causes of limited economic benefits have been a low coverage of potential beneficiaries, the choice of a production system other than the small family farm, failure to provide the needed post-reform support to beneficiaries, and other structural flaws like the imposition of damaging regulations on the new farms.

Both the extent of reform impacts and the pattern over time vary greatly by region. Leaving aside the now developed, industrial countries—which

[15] Each reform's beneficiaries are taken as a share of world population when that reform occurs.

were already much less agricultural than the rest of the world in 1900—the biggest transformations have occurred in East Asia (most notably in China) and the USSR. In no other region has a sizeable share of land been wrested from the large landholders. In Latin America, that share ranges from complete in Cuba, down through to thirty to forty-five percent in Mexico, Bolivia, Chile, and Nicaragua, to tiny amounts in Colombia and others, and to none in Argentina and Uruguay.[16] The share for the region, adjusting for quality, is probably under five percent.[17] In South Asia and East Asia outside of the communist countries, it is again quite low, even though there have been a few important reforms, such as in the state of Kerala in India. In Sub-Saharan Africa, the outstanding case has been Ethiopia and the countries where land previously appropriated by Europeans was retaken when the countries achieved independence. In this region, the bigger issue is whether land concentration will be rising over the coming years.

The extent of land transfer through redistribution can be measured both by how much has been taken from the former agricultural elite and by how much has wound up in the hands of peasants, the difference being that which was expropriated but transferred to state collective farms, cooperatives, and so on, or which found its way into the hands of corrupt state officials and their acolytes. All the communist governments favored large producing units and collective farming. Some non-communist countries opted for collective operation, as in the case of the Peruvian reform undertaken by the military government of General Velasco. Another set of reforms were partial because the political battle was only partly won (Mexico, Bolivia, many others). Typically, as in China, the Soviet Union, and Vietnam, the large collective or state farm was a temporary (although long-lasting) phase, with most of the control and management of the land eventually being transferred to the farm family. Many governments have transferred public land to new, small landholders, sometimes to prevent or curtail redistribution through expropriation. The total amount transferred this way has not, to my knowledge, been calculated at a world level, nor as a share of all land received by this group.

Only a small minority of the many reform attempts have both undertaken the most desirable forms of change and implemented those changes on a big scale. Accordingly, those bringing the full list of potential benefits, including

[16] Some reforms, such as that of Chile, were at least partially reversed later.

[17] Transferred land has often been of lower-than-average quality, as in cases like Mexico.

fast growth of agricultural output, rapid income increases for the new peasantry, and lasting income equality—all this without any significant negative side-effects—have been very few. The greatest successes—Japan and its two former colonies, Korea and Taiwan—occurred at a special moment in world politics when Japan's new government, the US government, and its Supreme Commander General MacArthur were all persuaded that a broad-ranging reform was the best option.[18] Having both the country itself and the new world power on nearly the same page was a unique situation. During most of its decades of world dominance after World War II the US either opposed major reforms or advocated and supported modest ones which were neither built upon strong domestic pressures nor large enough to cause powerful pushback from the rural elites.

Weighing against the promise of reforms, and thus bolstering the power of opponents and potential losers, have been a number of circumstances. A key aspect of both existing power imbalances and the difficulty of attacking them through something like land reform are racial and ethnic divides. These often reflect the earlier creation of a socio-economic hierarchy, when one ethnic group defeated and enslaved another. They then help to maintain and strengthen the power imbalance by giving the group at the top an additional reason to understand their position above the "inferior" group as normal and appropriate. When all, or nearly all, of the serfs or landless families belong to the ethnic group perceived to be inferior, any movement to advance their situation takes on the character of a racial as well as a class struggle, making it harder to marshal outside support for the victimized group (e.g., from the nascent bourgeoisie) when it shares ethnicity with the agrarian elite. The group at the bottom sometimes coalesces and achieves unity precisely due to its racial homogeneity; often, however, it is fragmented into different indigenous groups. Such racial issues have played into and complicated many of history's agrarian reform attempts. In Guatemala, a lack of inclusion of indigenous peoples weakened the support for reform. In Mexico, Bolivia, and Peru the social hierarchy involved a powerful racial divide which no doubt worsened the abuse characteristic of feudalism, as well as limiting the early support from other social groups for the victims' cause.

Along with the typical domestic political power imbalance, another major deterrent to significant twentieth-century reforms in developing

[18] A more recent candidate for this "high success" category is the Vietnamese reform, with key advances in the 1980s and 1990s.

countries was Western (mainly US) fear of supporting (and/or willingness to undercut) anything that might look too socialistic in nature. Guatemala's modest attempt was thwarted by the American government. Chile's reform was reversed with support from that government. The US stance substantially diminished the chances for a useful reform in Brazil.

A perhaps less obvious barrier to success has been the weak understanding by those pursuing reform of the relative merits of differing possible arrangements after land has been wrested from the elite. The lasting belief in the merits of cooperative or communal production has influenced the outcomes where communist and left-leaning governments have been in power. The belief in economies of scale[19] constitutes either a powerful force against reform or a force to replace one form of land concentration—in the hands of a traditional elite—with another one, be it the large cooperative, the state farm, or the large agro-corporation. Suffering from both of these errors, the communist governments of Russia and China opted in their initial reforms for large state farms or collectives. As a result, those reforms failed to provide the potential benefits to the agricultural masses and, worse, led to devastating famines. The relative inefficiency of large communal and state farming has been clarified in part through those costly experiments. Such icons as John Stuart Mill had already identified and written about the merits of small, private units, but this did not reach or much affect the views of those involved in major decisions on agrarian structure. Even after the mid-twentieth century, when this fact was becoming more widely understood, apart from a few cases it had little impact on policy. It was counterintuitive to many people; it threatened the vested interests of the dominant owners; and, in a few instances, it clashed with the uninformed ideas of important leaders like Stalin and Mao. It did enter into the political discussions of land reform in countries like Colombia, Brazil, Chile, India, and the Philippines, but the main political and economic argument for such reforms was not that they would raise total output, but that they would lower poverty and inequality.

[19] Economies of scale exist when a higher level of production comes with a lower average cost in terms of resources used. They may be present for technical reasons, as where a chemical process occurs more efficiently when carried out on a large scale; because of the character of machinery (e.g., in agriculture); or through other mechanisms, such as the indivisibility of one of the factors of production. Thus, given that workers (or their families) are indivisible, it might be the case that a farm smaller than needed to keep one person (or one family) occupied would suffer lower productivity than a larger farm because it could not choose a labor input of less than one. But if labor is divisible because people can work simultaneously at more than one job, this consideration loses its potential relevance. In fact, it is standard practice for farm families to have jobs outside agriculture as well. In short, the concept is a complicated one and intuition is not a good guide.

Mexico and Bolivia became classic cases in which major reforms (redistribution of land) did occur, but their full potential benefits did not materialize because public policy was not oriented to supporting the beneficiaries.

Lack of the detailed understanding needed to design and implement effective reforms took many other forms as well. Most governments so engaged have seriously underestimated the complexities involved in transforming land tenure systems. As Kay (1998, 9) puts it, "the intricate dynamic processes set in motion by the agrarian reforms . . . frequently had unexpected and unintended consequences. Agrarian reforms often provoked dramatic counter reforms and neo-reforms following the social and political struggles they unleashed. Thus, the outcome of Latin America's agrarian reforms has been varied and has given rise to a more complex and fluid agrarian system." Some agrarian reforms that were intended initially for the benefit of the peasantry ended up favoring the development of capitalist farming, either because they were badly designed or because of power shifts over time.

A final contributing factor to "failure" appears when a country becomes substantially urban (hence, most workers are employed there) before its power structure becomes less antagonistic to reform. By that time, it is too late for such reform to have a major beneficial impact.

# 5
# Land Reform under Communist Regimes

## Russia/Soviet Union

Russia's nineteenth-century agrarian history set the stage for its 1905 and 1917 revolutions, the take-over by the Communist Party, and the subsequent course of events.[1] That history featured not only the usual conflicting interests by class and group, but also a striking level of ignorance about agriculture on the part of many decision-makers, and very costly misbeliefs on the part of some. Particularly noteworthy was the lack of knowledge about how agriculture was faring in the latter part of the nineteenth century, and of the capacities, preferences, and social settings of the peasants. This latter blind spot contributed to the standard view from the outside—including that of many well-meaning people—that peasant agriculture was not efficient, whether carried out on an individual or on a more communal basis. As in the case of the English enclosures discussed previously, it took a long time (about a century) for some of the misbeliefs of that time to be seriously questioned or overturned.

In Russia, serfdom was essentially a form of slavery.[2] Of its seventy-five million people just before the Great Emancipation of 1861, an official estimate was that 10.5 million people were privately owned, 9.5 million were owned by the state, and nine hundred thousand were under the Tsar's patronage (Kolchak 1987). Nearly one-third were thus in one or another of these forms of serfdom. As usual, the great inequality between lord and serf led to much abuse, and the practice of selling serfs was common. Some of the extreme cases of physical, emotional, and sexual abuse of serfs by the

[1] A helpful review of Russia's land reforms is Wegren (1998).

[2] As Blum (1967, 442) puts it: "In the early days of serfdom in Eastern Europe the seigniors had the right to exact as much as they wanted in goods and services from their serfs. But as time went by, the central power in all of the Eastern lands, save one, had ultimately intervened in the relation between the lord and the peasant, and had established norms beyond which the serf owners could not go. Russia was the one exception. The only restrictions the tsars placed on the seigniors were that the peasants 'must not suffer ruin' because of the demands of the lords, and that they be allowed enough time to get their own work done."

*The Great Curse.* Albert Berry, Oxford University Press. © Oxford University Press 2024.
DOI: 10.1093/oso/9780197782675.003.0006

landowners were publicized by *Kolokol*, the first Russian censorship-free weekly newspaper, which was published in Russian and French in London (1857–1865) and Geneva (1865–1867), with a circulation of up to twenty-five hundred copies. Although it was banned in Russia, *Kolokol* was well known and had a significant influence on the country's reformist and revolutionary movements of the 1860s.

Tsar Alexander II's Emancipation was a major step forward in Russia; it abolished serfdom and gave more than twenty-three million people new liberties. Former serfs were granted many of the rights of free citizens, including marrying without prior consent, owning property, and owning a business, although other restraints did remain. The group gained control of about half of the land they had previously cultivated. Until the beginning of the twentieth century, the vast majority held the land in communal ownership within the peasant communities (or "mirs"), which acted as village governments and cooperatives. Arable land was divided into sections based on soil quality and distance from the village. Households had the right to claim one or more strips from each section, depending on the number of adults in the family. The severe famine of 1891/1892 brought this post-emancipatory arrangement into question. It was abolished in 1906 as part of the market-oriented Stolypin reforms, which introduced the unconditional right to individual landownership and which encouraged peasants to buy their share of the community lands, leave the communities, and settle on their privately owned properties. By 1910, such private settlements accounted for a still very modest ten percent of all rural households in the European part of Russia; one reason was the resistance of some peasants to adopting this change (Kopsidis et al. 2015).

The Stolypin reforms reflected a wider reorientation of state policy toward the peasantry. Before the early 1890s, state policy had mainly sought to support the commune and provide security for the peasants against economic disruption, but the 1891 famine accentuated the fear that poverty was rising and that a greater integration into the market economy was needed to counteract this. Across the political spectrum, the dominant view was that peasants were backward and in need of new institutions and policies to steer them toward modern attitudes and practices. At times, the peasants themselves were knowingly involved in perpetuating these elite attitudes as when, in interactions with authorities, they pleaded poverty and ignorance. Those in power were typically unaware of what the peasants knew and how they perceived their own world.

Contemporary thinking thus attributed the alleged stagnation of agriculture at a low productivity level, together with crises like famine, to the general incompetence of the peasantry and to a badly structured agrarian system built around communes. That system, with its division of arable fields into numerous strips, was criticized by political and intellectual elites as a means of protecting an inept peasantry from capitalist dynamics, but also as something that impeded economic initiative and tied peasants to irrational and inefficient farming methods (Kopsidis et al. 2015, 426). The latter logic was built into the decrees issued by Prime Minister Stolypin between 1906 and 1911; they aimed to induce market-based agricultural growth by consolidating privatized parcels; it was presumed that individual ownership of land and the existence of a land market were necessary preconditions for healthy agricultural development.

Michael Kopsidis and colleagues challenge not only this latter view and the belief that the peasant farmer was of very limited capacity, but also the (related) conventional wisdom that agriculture had performed poorly during the latter part of the nineteenth century and thus contributed importantly to the economic problems the country was experiencing. They note that quantitative research on pre-revolutionary Russian agriculture was long dominated by the grand narrative of Imperial crisis and decline. Historians attributed the revolution to an autocratic political system, increasing exploitation of the peasantry, and economic stagnation. For Soviet authors, this picture of impoverishment and class struggle in the late-Imperial village justified the revolution's destruction of that system. In dramatic contrast, Kopsidis et al. (2015, 428–429) report that, "Rising levels of peasant consumption and steadily declining mortality, as well as significantly enhanced trade of agricultural products on national and international markets, combine to support arguments against the assumption of generally deteriorating living standards and deepening rural crisis in late-Imperial Russia." Recent calculations by Carol S. Leonard (2011, 241–243, appendix 1) point to a constant increase in output between 1861 and 1911, with a significant contribution from total factor productivity (TFP) growth during the 1870s, and then again for a period beginning in the 1890s.[3] Their analysis of the provinces of Vladimir and Iaroslavl leads Tracy Dennison and Steven Nafziger (2011) to conclude—on

[3] Needless to say, nineteenth-century data from Russia still suffers serious gaps and imperfections, so many conclusions and propositions must be seen in probability terms. See Nafziger (2017) for a discussion.

the basis of evidence on literacy rates, public health conditions, agricultural productivity, and other variables—that living standards were rising substantially faster than suggested by the dominant historical narrative.[4] One of the more persuasive pieces of evidence is the quite systematic increase in average height of military recruits from the early 1860s through 1893.

Belief in the universal superiority of private ownership to other property regimes, inherent in the Stolypin decrees and in many other agrarian restructurings around the world, has been brought into question, especially in recent decades, by the increasing body of empirical information. In this Russian case, Kopsidis et al. (2015, 441) conclude not only that peasant agriculture developed impressively during the late Tsarist period, but also that communal tenure was not an obstacle to adjustment or to growth. From 1892 to 1913, average crop yields on peasant allotments in the communes evolved similarly to those on private land, and slightly more than ninety percent of the observed yield growth on private land was realized in open fields. Clearly land titles were not the decisive factor for fostering welfare and growth. When peasant communes were hostile to the Stolypin reforms, this was typically because they saw it as a threat to their social and economic security. It remains unclear whether those reforms played any significant positive role in the rapid agricultural development of the years just prior to World War I; if so, it could not have been a definitive one.

Many explanations of the alleged backwardness of late-Tsarist Russia have built on the assumed economic inefficiencies of the peasant institutions created in the wake of the 1861 Emancipation. The reforms that ended serfdom endowed peasant communities with collective property rights and made them jointly responsible for tax and land payments. Historians like Alexander Gerschenkron (1965) argued that the communal property rights inhibited the development of a market for land and reduced the incentives for undertaking improvements to raise agricultural productivity, while the ties to the commune created by joint liability restricted labor mobility, which in turn "re-enserfed" the peasant population. In this view, the underdevelopment of the Russian economy, as of 1900, derived primarily from these institutional consequences of the allegedly "modernizing" reforms of

[4] The analysis draws on the many research publications over the post-emancipation period by the "zemstva"—new institutions of local self-government founded in the 1860s across much of European Russia.

the 1860s. For many students, these communal property rights have long symbolized the apparent backwardness of rural Russian society in the late nineteenth century. A century later, however, the reality looks very different on two counts. First, it now appears that the abolition of serfdom was, in fact, followed by substantial increases in agricultural productivity, industrial output, and peasants' nutrition (Markevich and Zhuravskaya 2018). In addition, recently compiled data and qualitative sources suggest that the new institutional framework provided much more *de facto* flexibility than scholars have typically assumed (Nafziger 2016). The oft-cited practice of repartitioning communal land was, in fact, relatively infrequent and, when undertaken, was generally done at low cost. Evidence from the Moscow province implies that this step was driven more by concerns over the distribution of associated tax burdens than the desire to reallocate productive assets.[5] Still to be clarified empirically is the extent to which communal land practices served beneficial insurance functions. As Nafziger (2016, 795–796) states:

> Even as repartitions possibly allowed some commune members to give up their land to pursue opportunities elsewhere, households typically retained ties to the village and often continued to pay shares of the collective tax and land obligations. Although this practice may have restricted labour mobility to more productive sectors and possibly limited productivity growth (perhaps until the liberalization of the Stolypin reforms), peasants may have willingly accepted these constraints to ensure future access to land and the old-age and unemployment support that the resource provided. Furthermore, communal land rights might have guaranteed the resources necessary to achieve a basic standard of living. Russian agriculture remained technologically backward into the twentieth century, but the rural economy appears to have avoided a Malthusian trap, even as population growth took off. Understanding whether or how communal practices may have prevented subsistence crises in the Russian context can inform discussions of communal forms of social insurance in other developing countries.

[5] Cross-sectional data on property rights and grain yield suggest a weaker causal link between communal land practices and agricultural productivity than typically asserted. The direct productivity impact of repartitions was probably small, and thus less consistent with the negative (Gerschenkron 1965) than with more positive interpretations of the institutional factors behind late nineteenth-century rural Russian development, like that of Gregory (1994).

Putting the impacts of the communal land redistributions in perspective, Nafziger thus argues that any direct economic consequences of this practice were of a second order when compared to the (generally negative) effects of geo-climatic conditions, poor infrastructure, underdeveloped credit markets, relatively low levels of human capital and technology, and the broader communal institutional context fostered by the Russian state.

Consistent with the views of specialists in late nineteenth-century Russia, like Nafziger and Paul R. Gregory (1994), many recent attempts in developing countries to formalize property rights by issuing individual land titles have yielded limited results (Bromley 2008a). Historians have increasingly questioned the presumption of a direct link between tenure regimes and development, with case studies in England and Germany suggesting that communal tenure did not impede the implementation of advanced technologies or agricultural methods. As noted below, the late 1970s Chinese de-collectivization and the introduction of the Household Responsibility System (HRS) within a communal land tenure framework established the base for impressive agricultural growth. Communal tenure does not appear to constrain farmers' ability to adjust effectively to market opportunities, although the lack of long-term tenure security may discourage some types of private investment. On the other hand, communal property is part of a more collective lifestyle, one which can bring major benefits in economic and social security and welfare, as well as some narrow efficiency benefits. James C. Scott (1976, 61) notes in the context of Vietnam that "the disappearance of village lands was a particularly vital blow to the community's protective fabric." Those lands were the source of community assistance to those in need.

The late-Imperial Russian case is of special relevance to the recent debate on whether and when commonly held property affects economic efficiency. Prominent in that debate has been the so-called tragedy of the commons, an idea developed originally by British economist William Forster Lloyd, and given twentieth-century popularity by American biologist and philosopher Garrett Hardin (1968). The "tragedy" refers to a situation in a shared-resource system where individual users, acting independently according to their own self-interests, behave contrary to the common good by depleting or spoiling the shared resource through their actions.[6] The publication of

[6] In liberal theories of ownership, land tenure issues have often been situated within the dichotomous "traditional versus modern" framework, where communal tenure is associated with

Hardin's paper met with much favorable reception; many economists and others found the idea intuitively plausible, and the article gave it a more rigorous conceptual base. It took a good number of years for the narrative to be somewhat rebalanced by the work of Elinor Ostrom (1990) and others. Like so many ideas, the fact that the cited "tragedy" could happen, and no doubt sometimes does, led to the drastic oversimplification that "the commons" is always an inefficient way to manage resources, even when, as in the Russian communes, individuals did not have the opportunity to do whatever they wanted on such land. The more serious thinking of recent decades has generated a growing consensus not only that "community" and "market" may be compatible with each other, but also that their successful combination can often provide better solutions than unrestrained private markets, especially in a context of weak or dysfunctional institutions. "In many developing societies, effective and flexible village communities may often be the only successful institutional framework to lower costs of market transactions, and to take risks of large investments in agriculture" (Bromley 2008b). The idea of the inefficiency of communal activities has a somewhat different history from that of peasant irrationality/incompetence, being more the product of a certain strand of economic thinking (individualist and/or neo-classical) than of a class-based intellectual superiority, but here, too, the narrative correction has been slow and, as always, partial, because many people are not aware of the revision.

The stereotype of the peasant as irrational and ignorant was a predictable feature of late-Imperial debates and it prevailed in Russian historiography for decades thereafter, as it has tended to do in most of the world; even today it remains little weakened among the agricultural elites of many developing countries, despite its coming under serious professional challenge everywhere.[7] Much evidence demonstrates that Russian peasants did not systematically reject technical progress and advice, that they did consciously use local institutions to achieve their private ends or for the regulation of local affairs, and that they participated in public negotiations to articulate their own interests. The complexity of their behavior is revealed in their reactions to unfolding events over a century in Russia/USSR. Still, it is not surprising that

irrationality and backwardness, and individual private tenure is linked with rationality and modern economic relations (Deininger and Feder 2009).

[7] Among the many later twentieth-century contributions to understanding peasant behavior were those of the anthropologist Manning Nash (1966) and the economist Theodore Schultz (1964).

many of the major participants in the late-nineteenth-century Russian drama were at least somewhat off-base in their interpretations of the peasantry and of what conditions made it more or less productive. As in the English case, it has taken a century or more for some of the earlier misconceptions to be either contradicted or thrown into question.

From the late nineteenth century, Russia was, in fact, the home of very serious quantitative analysis of the peasantry; sadly, this did little, if anything, for the quality of agricultural policy. During the 1870s, a basic apparatus was established for the collection and processing of data about the peasant economy—the *zemstvo* statistics (Harrison 1975, 393). The discoveries which began to be documented from this decade onward revolutionized many concepts and theories, and culminated in the "theory of peasant economy" constructed by the agronomist Alexander Chayanov and his school,[8] featuring the idea that peasant economic behavior in Russia was not consistent with the simple models of classical political economy driven by profit maximization, but rather reflected a "peasant rationality" based on the internally generated needs and resources of the peasant family and operating in an economy essentially without a labor market, as the family farm was operated by unpaid family labor.

As Mark Harrison (1975, 390) puts it, the neo-populist tradition to which Chayanov belonged:

> emphasised the viability of peasant agriculture and its ability to survive and prosper under any circumstances. There was no inevitable tendency for the peasantry to suffer the increasing economic inequalities and class antagonisms of bourgeois industrial society. The village was an overwhelmingly homogeneous community, able constantly to reproduce itself both economically and socially. Consequently, Chayanov saw the modernisation of traditional small farming as lying along neither a capitalist nor a socialist road, but as a peasant path of raising the technical level of agricultural production through agricultural extension work and cooperative organisation, at the same time conserving the peasant institutional framework of the family small-holding.

This view contrasted starkly with that of Vladmir Lenin, who postulated a situation in which capitalism developed within the peasant sector through

[8] See Chayanov (1966).

a process of socio-economic differentiation. He argued that this had been taking place in the Russian countryside in the late nineteenth and early twentieth centuries, with some peasants growing richer while others got poorer. He distinguished three initial strata: *kulaks* (the rich or well-to-do peasants), "middle peasants," and "poor peasants." This three-tiered structure polarized over time into a dualistic one as rich peasants became a rural *bourgeoisie* and poor peasants morphed into a rural proletariat, some of whom were landless, while others might continue farming a small plot of land but could not survive without wage income as well. Lenin argued that the "bourgeois" peasants were accumulating capital by exploiting paid non-family labor; that they owned the bulk of the draft animals, iron ploughs, and other means of production in the countryside; and that they were buying up or renting the land of impoverished peasants. As the principal challenger to those views, Chayanov tried to demonstrate that the agricultural statistics used by Lenin did not reflect an irreversible class polarization, while arguing that the peasantry could play a significant role in the future socialist society supposedly being built in the Soviet Union. He argued that peasants should be helped to prosper and modernize as individual family farmers through the establishment of cooperatives and should not be seen as the class enemies of the (still very small) Russian urban proletariat. He was a proponent of agricultural cooperatives, but he was skeptical on the efficiency of large-scale farms and maintained that the Soviet government would find it difficult to force peasant households to cooperate to produce a surplus. Chayanov's ideas were criticized by Joseph Stalin as a "defence of the kulaks." Preeminent in his field in the early to mid-1920s, he was accompanied by a circle of associated researchers and considered to be a founding member of Gosplan (the State Planning Committee), only to be excluded as it began to operate. Chayanov's view of the peasant may have been incomplete, but it was based on close and quantitative observation of behavioral patterns. His disagreement with Lenin had important political implications, and he was eventually executed by Stalin.

In the supremist of ironies, then, Russia was home to one of the great students of peasant behavior. That the Soviet regime cut short both his work and his life did not augur well for Soviet agrarian policy. A wave of relatively recent analyses of the Russian peasantry,[9] complemented by studies of Russian agricultural history and drawing on newly available information

[9] See Cox (2002).

for the pre-1900 period, sheds considerable light on the "quality" of contemporary policy. Judith Pallot (1999) notes that Russian bureaucrats, who had hoped to impose order upon what they perceived as a chaotic countryside, did not understand the multiple benefits of strip farming, periodic repartitioning of communal lands, private land exchanges, and common pasturage; nor did they understand peasants' risk aversion strategies.[10] A conventional wisdom has been that, with time, Stolypin's goal of encouraging peasant families to leave the commune and establish separate farms might have succeeded and contributed importantly to the growth of agricultural output. Pallot, however, argues that only in the north-west of the country did the experience conform reasonably to this expectation. Elsewhere the responses varied widely, including an actual strengthening of the commune in some places. Overall, they suggested that the peasantry tended to retain a collectivist outlook. Those supporting separation did so for a wide variety of reasons, often unrelated to any merits of private ownership and operation. Even where the Stolypin reform was adopted, peasants often maintained collective practices in their own farming.

The debates on how to organize agriculture played out in a very conflict-laden setting. Involvement in both World War I and Russia's own civil war greatly diminished the production and availability of food. Inadequate government understanding of the agricultural sector underlaid some of the war-related problems. An optimistic view of the country's war prospects relied on the assumed presence of a large excess labor supply in the countryside,[11] which fostered the belief that this excess could be mobilized into the army without any serious reduction of farm output. In fact, agricultural production fell by forty percent from 1913 to 1918, and hit bottom in 1921 at only forty-five percent of the 1913 level (Markevich 2005, table 1). Output fell fastest where more men were conscripted into the army. On top of the decline in aggregate output was the war's impact on the composition of grain crops and on the farmers' incentives to supply their produce to the market. War raised family economic uncertainty and, with it, the value of the sort of minimum income guarantee provided by access to communal land.

[10] She adds that, in their social engineering schemes, modern states still severely underestimate the practical agricultural knowledge of the people their reforms are designed to impact.

[11] A 1901 government commission estimated surplus labor at fifty-one percent of the rural labor force. Other independent studies reached similar conclusions (Markevich 2005). Such exaggerated estimates paid little attention to the economic activities of rural citizens other than the cultivation of cereals and revealed the woefully incomplete government understanding of agriculture.

Simultaneously, communal farms shifted efforts away from marketed crops toward subsistence ones (especially winter rye) for on-farm consumption. Finally, the wartime mobilization of industry reduced the supply of manufactured products available for peasants to purchase, further cutting the ability and incentive to produce.

Failing to predict or quickly detect the wartime shift in peasant behavior away from market-oriented operations toward home consumption led the Tsarist government to believe not only that sufficient grain existed in the country to feed the Russian army (true), but also that the task of getting enough of it to key groups (including the army) was merely a logistical problem (false). Although it developed a comprehensive state procurement system for grain, it could not purchase nearly enough of it. The deepening food crisis played directly into politics. The shortage of food in St. Petersburg in the winter of 1916/1917 led to the overthrow of the monarchy. Only in September 1917 did the Provisional Government (which ruled from February to October of that year) opt to double grain procurement prices; by then it was too late to prevent the Bolsheviks from overthrowing that government and seizing power. Their promise to solve the food supply crisis in urban areas was an important source of support for them.

When Lenin returned to Russia in April 1917, he promised the people "Peace, Land and Bread," the latter two items interpretable, respectively, as a promise to the peasants for the redistribution of confiscated land and a fair share of food for every worker. Shortly thereafter, however, the 1918 "Fundamental Law of Land Socialization" abolished private ownership of land and made it instead the "property of the whole people." In any case, the immediate steps of the Bolshevik government were not enough to overcome the economic crisis and the political struggle over grain distribution continued, helping to transform the Great War into Russia's Civil War. In June 1918, the now-ruling Bolshevik administration adopted the motif "war communism" or "military communism" with the goal of keeping towns (the proletarian powerbase) and the Red Army stocked with food and weapons. The system of distribution of food to urban areas was already failing when they took over, so they turned to violence, and eventually systematic coercion, to improve their access. Under Leon Trotsky's order, private trade in foodstuffs was abolished by confiscating stocks and shooting traders who resisted. By 1919, a system had been imposed under which the central government assigned compulsory quotas for each region; all grain not required for seed or to meet peasant consumption was to be transferred to the state at fixed prices far below market value.[12] In response, the peasants reduced the area sown, worsening the food balance further, and the relationship with the regime degenerated into sporadic violence. Because they continuously overestimated rural food stocks, the Bolsheviks were unable to collect the assigned quotas; they then blamed the peasants for withholding it. At first, they specifically accused a minority of richer peasants, the so-called kulaks, of speculating in food by withholding it intentionally to push up its price. Because rural food stocks were smaller and more scattered than the government believed, such measures tended also to victimize many ordinary peasants without improving supplies. The government implicitly recognized this when it moved to a system of collective responsibility by villages and whole regions for compulsory grain deliveries. Black markets developed in which urban residents bartered their products and property with peasants for additional food (Harrison and Markevich 2012).

The objectives of the Soviet strategy of forced procurement of agricultural commodities, socialization of land, and nationalization of other industries have inevitably been a matter of much controversy. Some have argued that its sole purpose was to win the war, others argue that it was designed as a transitional step toward socialism. Still others propose that it was an attempt to move directly to a communist system of centralized control, which the leaders expected to generate an immediate and large increase in economic output. Although the approach was largely successful in its primary purpose of aiding the Red Army to halt the advance of the White Army and in reclaiming most of the territory of the former Russian Empire,[13] the urban population did experience severe hardship, as total agricultural and food production kept falling until 1921. Workers began migrating from the cities to the countryside, where they had a better chance to feed themselves. Between 1918 and 1920, Petrograd lost seventy percent of its population, and Moscow lost over fifty percent. A series of workers' strikes and peasant rebellions broke out all over the country. A turning point came with the rebellion at the Kronstadt naval base in early March 1921. It startled Lenin because Bolsheviks considered Kronstadt sailors to be the "reddest of the reds"

[12] Application was partial because large areas of Russia remained outside Bolshevik control, and poor communications meant that even those regions loyal to the Bolshevik government often had to act on their own, lacking orders or coordination from Moscow.

[13] America and other Western countries supported the White Army, but their effort was both unsuccessful and of questionable legality, as a result of which it appears very little in the US historical narrative, but much more in that of the Soviets (Carr 2020).

(Harrison and Markevich 2012). Christian (1997, 237), summarizes the state of Russia in 1921 as:

> A government claiming to represent the people now found itself on the verge of being overthrown by that same working class. The crisis had undermined the loyalty of the villages, the towns and even sections of the army. It was fully as serious as the crises faced by the tsarist government in 1905 and February 1917.

The ruble collapsed and a barter system increasingly replaced money as a medium of exchange; ninety percent of wages were paid in goods. Food requisitioning, combined with the effects of seven years of war and a severe drought, contributed to a famine that caused between three and ten million deaths (with an average estimate of perhaps five million). Communist officials could not blame the 1921/1922 famine on the usual enemies. Food purchased abroad all went to cities, not to peasants. US President Herbert Hoover's offer of $62 million worth of American food was accepted, helping to feed up to eleven million people.

The bleak state of affairs, topped off by the Kronstadt Rebellion, convinced the Party and Lenin of the need to retreat from its socialist policies to maintain power.[14] In March 1921, the New Economic Policy (NEP) was introduced, including the return of most agriculture, retail trade, and small-scale light industry to private ownership and management. The peasantry was allowed to own and cultivate land. The NEP reintroduced a measure of stability to the economy, although it was dogged by the government's chronic inability to procure enough grain supplies to feed the urban work force. How food should be divided between the peasants and the urban population posed a continuing challenge; the reallocation of land in 1921 did not end the shortages in the cities. Even though grain production had nearly returned to pre-war levels by the early 1920s, the large estates which had formerly sold to urban markets were no longer there, and the peasants who now operated that land increased their own consumption, a natural outcome of any "land to the tiller" reform. As a result, by one estimate, city dwellers were getting half the grain that had been available to them before the war (Kenez

[14] By 1921, Lenin was in poor health. He died in 1924, after leaving his testament on the personal qualities of his comrades, particularly Trotsky and Stalin. He recommended Trotsky for the position of General Secretary of the Communist Party, while advocating Stalin's removal, arguing he was ill-suited for the position. His views did not hold sway.

1999).[15] Stalin claimed that the needed grain had been produced but was being hoarded by kulaks. Undoubtedly some farmers were holding onto their grain because of low prices and their own consumption needs. Instead of raising those prices, the Politburo adopted an emergency measure to requisition 2.5 million tons of grain. The seizures further discouraged the peasants. When less grain was produced in 1928 than before, the government again resorted to requisitions, and much of the grain was now being taken from middle peasants because the kulaks did not have enough. Some of the poorer peasants moved to the cities. By 1929, there were violent episodes of resistance, together with massive hoarding (burial was the common method) and illegal grain transfers. The resulting shortages prompted Stalin to eliminate the private ownership of farmland and to collectivize agriculture under state control. This abrupt policy change, accompanied by the massacre of several million of the country's most prosperous private farmers, marked the end of the NEP. It was followed by the re-imposition of state control over all industry and commerce by 1931.

The nationwide program of collectivization began in November 1929 and continued during the 1930s with the creation of both collective and state-controlled enterprises. By the early 1930s, over ninety percent of agricultural land had been collectivized; rural households entered collective farms with their land, livestock, and other assets. Some critics have described the arrangement as neo-serfdom; among other things, it relied on a sort of *hukou* system which tied peasants to the land. The leadership expected an immediate increase in output of food, thereby resolving the urban food crisis that had been worsening since 1927, along with the shortage of raw materials for processing industries and of agricultural exports. Instead, in 1932/1933, the country suffered what was probably its most severe famine, with an estimated death toll of seven to ten million people. The hardest hit region—the Ukraine—suffered 3.5 to four million deaths.[16] The later famine of 1946/

[15] Conquest (1986, 87) states that, before the revolution, the peasants, who controlled only 2.1 million square kilometers of land, divided into sixteen million holdings, produced fifty percent of the food grown in Russia, and consumed sixty percent of the food produced. After the revolution, they controlled 3,140,000 million square kilometers, divided into twenty-five million holdings, produced eighty-five percent of the food but consumed eighty percent of what they grew (implying that they consumed sixty-eight percent of the total). The share of food left for the non-farm population thus fell from forty to thirty-two percent.

[16] The full range of estimates is even wider, reflecting both differing care in the use of data and political stance. Stalin admitted to Winston Churchill in Yalta (1945) that his collectivization policies had cost the lives of ten million people over four years. It is widely assumed that he would have not exaggerated the figure, as the general Soviet policy was to conceal and downplay such issues.

1947 caused about 1.5 million deaths. As in China, the famines were substantially attributable to chaos and to governmental mismanagement. They wrought particular devastation on the peasantry. Grain-producing regions suffered the most because they lost a larger share of the food they produced. Another great irony lay in the fact that the peasants knew how to deal with famines by storing appropriate amounts of grain. The state, less competent and less concerned with the welfare of the peasants, and more dedicated to achieving rapid industrialization, gave less thought to future supplies.

By the 1932/1933 famine, the trajectory of events in the Soviet Union was a matter of much interest in the West. Even writing about the famine, and more generally about life in Russia, was becoming highly controversial. Journalist Walter Duranty of the *New York Times* downplayed the famine and its death toll; according to Sally Taylor (1990), that coverage led directly to President Roosevelt's officially recognizing the Soviet Union in 1933. When Malcolm Muggeridge and Gareth Jones criticized Duranty's story, they were later banned from returning to the Soviet Union.[17]

Apart from the death toll of the 1932/1933 famine, much debate has surrounded the causes and nature of possible Soviet government complicity in it. Like the late-nineteenth-century development of Russian agriculture, exploration of this issue was long constrained by a lack of inside information. Popular media and most historians from outside the country came to describe the famine as "man-made," or even a "genocide" perpetrated intentionally by Stalin against Ukrainians and sometimes other national groups to destroy them as nations.[18] Revisionist writings of the last quarter-century, drawing on new archival documents—including formerly secret records of the Politburo and correspondence between Stalin and some of his top lieutenants relating to the decisions taken in this crisis—and with a generally more analytical approach, argue that the famine was not limited to Ukraine or to rural areas, nor was it the intention of Stalin and others in the Soviet leadership to create such a disaster. R. W. Davies and Stephen G. Wheatcroft (2004) see it as the culmination of a crisis that began with the economic disruption created by the massive investments under the first five-year plan

[17] Jones's articles were alleged to be the inspiration for Orwell's *Animal Farm* (Wikipedia "Soviet Famine of 1932–33").

[18] The best known such exposition is Conquest (1986) but, as Tauger (2004b) notes, it can also be found in many textbooks of Soviet history, on the history of famines, and on genocide. Another strongly negative take on the government's actions in Ukraine is Applebaum (2017), which Tauger (2018) criticizes for leaving out much important information, drawing unjustified conclusions, and making false claims.

(1928 to 1932) and the simultaneous and related food supply difficulties from 1927 to 1929. Soviet leaders had expected that the plan, together with the collectivization of agriculture, would increase food production;[19] but two years of natural disasters and disruption lowered harvests drastically and forced the government to ration food in inadequate quantities to most groups. The authors attribute the reduced harvests to four factors: (i) the increased area under crops, which disrupted the 1920s crop rotations and brought soil exhaustion; (ii) the decline in draft capacity due to lack of forage and to collectivization, which facilitated the spread of epizootics and killed many horses; (iii) disaffection of the peasants which, combined with the decline in draft capacity, lowered cultivation quality; and (iv) the exceptionally bad weather. The Soviet government's initially confused responses—the overestimation of harvests and the attempts to impose high procurement quotas—were moderated as their costs became apparent. Quotas were reduced and some of the procured grain was returned to villages for food and seed. Although trying to feed the cities as well as possible, they also made significant efforts to support agricultural recovery. The single key factor behind the famine crisis was the decision to industrialize at breakneck speed. Even though some of their actions contributed to the famine crisis, for the leaders it was unexpected and quite unwelcome.

On another widely debated aspect of this period—how hard life was for the peasantry and whether the Soviet system constituted in effect a neo-serfdom—Tauger (2004b) argues that, at least when compared to early modern pre-revolutionary Russia, when serfdom was part of a whole complex of controls designed to limit not only the geographical mobility of the population but also its economic and social mobility, the Soviet system of the 1930s constituted an easing in the latter regard. Although working conditions for peasants in 1933 were certainly made very severe by the famine, evidence of their resistance is anecdotal and does not suggest that it was occurring on a massive scale (Tauger 2004a). Meanwhile, many workers and peasants were educated for, and promoted to, responsible posts, although of course many others became victims of the witch hunts extending from the 1930s to the 1950s. No Russian peasant had ever advanced far in the hierarchy before 1917, but under the Soviet regime four men of peasant origin became rulers—Stalin, Nikita Khrushchev, Leonid Brezhnev, and Mikhail

[19] This excessive optimism was shared by Mao's government in the early years of its rule in China. It reflected, in part, the understandable belief for those sharing the Communist ideology that central planning could outperform the capitalist market system.

Gorbachev. Of former peasants who stayed on the farms, a good number acquired technical knowledge and skills that they later used to help increase farm production significantly over the 1950s to 1970s, despite the perverse influence of Trofim Lysenko and other favorites of Stalin. Between 1897 and 1939, the literacy rate of Russia's rural population (aged nine and up) jumped dramatically from twenty-six to eighty-four percent, and then on to ninety-eight percent in 1959 (Mironov 1991, 245). The increase was especially notable for women, jumping from thirteen to seventy-seven to ninety-eight percent; for men, the rise was from thirty-nine to ninety-two to ninety-nine percent.[20] The levels for peasants would have been somewhat lower than these rural averages but would have followed similar trends.

Stalin's personal blunders on agriculture undoubtedly wrought serious harm; collectivization came along with a number of bad technical choices. He allowed his favorite "scientist," the semi-educated charlatan Lysenko, to attack and hinder the serious scientists who were trying to develop new higher productivity hybrid crops; they went out of favor, with one of the most famous, Ivan Pavlov, dying in prison in 1943, a few years after challenging Lysenko. The matter of whether collective farming did eventually bring some advantages through economies of scale remains open, but if it did so, they were no doubt more than offset by the inefficiencies built into the system.

From the late-nineteenth-century tsarist government to the 1930s Soviet regime, whoever was in power saw an agricultural sector that underperformed relative to what it (the government) wanted and expected. In the late nineteenth century, the rising demand for food associated with urbanization and industrialization, together with increasing consumption by the peasants, helped create the illusion that output was growing very slowly, if at all. In fact, as Andrei Markevich and Ekaterina Zhuravskaya (2018) conclude, the end of serfdom was responsible for a substantial increase in agricultural productivity and in peasants' nutrition, as well as in industrial output. When production did, understandably, suffer some declines during the turmoil of wars and revolutions, governments did not predict them at all well. Under Stalin, who misunderstood both agriculture and the peasantry, but still made the key decisions, it was unsurprising. Ironically, the Russian peasantry was inclined to communal activity and was at least reasonably

[20] His estimates for 1847, derived from various sources, were fifteen percent for men, eight percent for women, and eleven percent for the two combined.

capable of technical advancement; however, a degree of resistance was a foregone conclusion, given what it understandably saw as mistreatment by a state whose demands pushed it toward hunger and starvation. Another great irony was that the country not only had one of the century's most famous experts on the peasantry (Chayanov), who, with colleagues, collected more detailed information than existed in almost any other developing country of the time, but the country also had him in government for some years before he drew Stalin's ire and was executed. Nikolai Bukharin, one of Lenin's key associates, was another very talented member of the Bolshevik team, whose differences with Stalin usually saw him justified. Much of the tragedy associated with the aftermath of the Russian revolution could probably have been avoided if the right people had had more authority and the wrong ones, especially Stalin, had had less. Perhaps the greatest irony was that a socialist government, which might have been expected to defend and promote the welfare of the peasantry—the lowest income group in Russian society—was caught between its political and ideological reliance on and dedication to the (urban) proletariat and its reliance on the peasants for food. Failure to understand the dynamics of agricultural production, including overoptimism about the impact of collectivization on output, together with the objectively dire conditions brought by conflict and weather, assured that this would not be an easy relationship. Some of the abuse suffered by peasants reflected pressure on the bureaucrats to fulfill their food quotas, compounded by their own weak understanding of peasant behavior generally and especially around the urgency of storing food. Had the late tsarist government understood the peasantry better, the Bolsheviks might never have come to power. Had the Bolsheviks, and especially Lenin and Stalin, understood the peasantry and agriculture better, something less bloody and much more effective than the Soviet collectivization might have spared many people.[21] These were, admittedly, new and complicated settings for decision-makers. It was not a time for self-confident ideologues but rather for careful, informed decision-makers willing to draw on the knowledge of others, as well as their own.

One clear lesson from the Soviet experience is that leaders who stifle debate are prone to major errors. Stalin dominated the decision-making

[21] In the Great Leap Forward of 1958–1962, Mao Zedong undertook a sort of replay of the Soviet experience, with collectivization, attacks on the Chinese equivalent of the Russian kulaks, and an acceptance of some of Lysenko's ideas. Each of these leaders shared two personal characteristics that manifested themselves in their misdiagnoses of agriculture: incompetence in that area, and great self-confidence. Many other politicians, at other times and in other places, have shared this combination.

process, and it could be a death sentence to disagree with him. His authoritarian tendency, his self-confidence (he was indeed well-read on many things), and his paranoia probably all contributed to his mistreatment of intellectual opponents like Chayanov and Bukharin. Like Chayanov, Bukharin was a dedicated citizen and a serious intellect; on intra-group intrigue, however, he was not a match for Stalin and some of the other operatives high up in the party. When, prompted by the grain shortage in 1928, Stalin reversed himself and proposed a program of rapid industrialization and forced collectivization because he believed that the NEP was not working fast enough, Bukharin was worried that the plan would lead to "military-feudal exploitation" of the peasantry. He preferred a more moderate approach to industrialization which would simultaneously allow the peasants the opportunity to become prosperous and generate greater grain production for sale abroad. He pressed his views throughout 1928 in meetings of the Politburo and at the Communist Party Congress. He was executed in 1938.

Many apparently chance events were part of the scenario around the Bolshevik revolution, the reorganization of agriculture, and their unfolding through the Stalin period. The same might be said of earlier conflicts that did not lead to an overturn of the government. Interactions among power bases have much to do with whether land reform occurs and what its final economic, political, and social impacts are. In elucidating peasant relations with the state, with the landowners, and among themselves, David Moon (1999) contrasts those pressures for reform that played a role in ending serfdom and in overthrowing the imperial regime in the twentieth century with earlier revolts that backfired by provoking the landowning class to react in ways that consolidated its power. He emphasizes the inherent conflicts among peasants, such as those between communal elders who could enrich themselves at the expense of neighbors by taking advantage of their close links with local officials. Such details help to desimplify the concept of a homogeneous peasantry often found in the historiography.

Under Gorbachev, Russia finally undertook a partial reversal of its collectivization, when the 1990 Law on Peasant Farms denationalized the land. Many Western scholars and Russian advocates of the reform anticipated that family farms would re-emerge in large numbers. In fact, many fewer candidates took up that option than they expected, a lack of enthusiasm attributed variously to inadequate rural infrastructure, which could limit the processing and marketing services available to individual producers; the fear that families striking out on their own might lose eligibility for those social services traditionally provided by the local corporate farm instead of the municipality; and the very long period that had passed (half a century or more) since families actually had the experience of independent farm management. Operating practices inside large agricultural enterprises remained largely unchanged despite the formal reorganization. The present structure includes the still-dominant corporate farms, together with the new "peasant" farms and the traditional household plots, long noted for their high land productivity compared to that of large collective farms. From 1990 to 2006, there was a modest shift from the formerly dominant corporate farms to the individual private sector: as of 2006, household plots and peasant farms together controlled about twenty percent of agricultural land and forty-eight percent of cattle, up from two percent and seventeen percent, respectively, in 1990 (Rosstat 2008, 445 and on). Their share of gross agricultural output showed a bigger increase—from twenty-six percent in 1990 to fifty-nine percent in 2005. Generating fifty-nine percent of agricultural output on twenty percent of the land meant that the individual farms (including the household plots) were achieving land productivity 5.7 times greater than that of the corporate farms.[22] Because the distribution of the income generated by the large collective farms differs greatly from that of large private farms in capitalist countries, where much and sometimes nearly all of it goes to capital, the former are likely to be the better of the two options from the workers' point of view.

Gorbachev's great and lasting achievement was to collaborate with Ronald Reagan and Margaret Thatcher to end the cold war (as then understood). But both his *perestroika* ("economic restructuring") and his *glasnost* (increased openness and transparency in government institutions and activities) either failed to produce the hoped-for benefits and/or were partly rolled back. Whatever its possible longer term merits in terms of economic efficiency and growth, the transition toward a more market-oriented and internationally open economy brought some very negative short- and middle-term outcomes, and essentially reversed the progress the USSR had made toward equality. Privatization of public sector capital encouraged theft of formerly state-owned resources, and in the process created many of the billionaires for which Russia has since become famous. The other side of this coin was the demise of the social protection system that had been part of the centrally planned socialist economy; it coincided with a macroeconomic downturn

[22] Part of this gap may be due to land quality differences. Another part is certainly due to the very high productivity of the household plots.

at the time of the transition to produce a striking increase in inequality and a dramatic jump in poverty. The Gini coefficient of inequality probably rose from about 0.3 to about 0.5 between the pre-*perestroika* and post-*perestroika* periods. When it occurred, this was the biggest increase in inequality ever recorded anywhere in such a short time span. Economic and political power was then used to block further reforms of corporate governance. Some oligarchs joined the government, thereby deepening the system's crony capitalist character. Russia and some of the other former socialist republics came to be kleptocracies and plutocracies, adopting and exaggerating some of the worst features of capitalism. A major factor at work was their inability to quickly develop those institutions and practices that long-established capitalist countries use to curtail the natural excesses and weaknesses of that system, including controls on the theft of public resources and a range of social protection policies that function within a generally capitalist framework (e.g., unemployment insurance).

## The Chinese Experience

### The Pre-reform Setting

Land reform, a recurring theme in China's history, was on the horizon in the early decades of the twentieth century. Leaders, most notably Sun Yat-Sen, the first head of the Kuomintang (Nationalist Party of China) and the provisional first president of the Republic of China after the ousting of the Qing dynasty, were advocates of "land to the tiller"; but their ideas were only very partially implemented by the National Government under Chiang Kai-shek (1928–1949), which tended to ally itself more with landlords and businessmen. In the 1940s, the Sino-American Joint Commission on Rural Reconstruction carried out promising land reform and community action programs in several provinces, with the involvement of famous expert Wolf Ladejinsky; these, however, were overtaken by the Communist Revolution.

When it came to power in 1949, the Chinese Communist party (CCP) inherited an agrarian system with low average productivity per worker because of the scarcity of land, but with a number of compensating pluses. Farm technology was complex; for example, it included water sharing systems, and there was a tradition of recording what was done—features fostered by the fact that such a high man-to-land ratio made attaining a good level of land productivity essential for survival. In the judgment of Dwight Perkins (1986), China's premodern development had created values and traits favorable to growth, including a disciplined labor force and managerial personnel who could work effectively together. But the tax level was inadequate to allow major public investment initiatives. The economic surplus in the hands of landlords and the urban well-to-do was hard to tap because they were the mainstays of the traditional government. Ts'ui Liu and John C. H. Fei (1977, 379) attribute the dramatically more successful economic development of Meiji-era Japan (1868 to 1912) than of China over that same period and the first decades of the twentieth century to the fact that Japan transferred much of its agricultural surplus to the industrial sector through a reformed and flexible land tax system that provided over eighty percent of government revenue. China's governments of the time showed no enthusiasm for such a system.

From a developmental perspective, agriculture prior to the Communist government's land reform could be characterized by a high level of waste. Victor Lippit (1974) estimates that roughly twenty percent of the national product was used for luxury consumption by the landlords, a scenario akin to Robert C. Allen's (1992) description of Britain and its landed elite. This class lacked either the willingness and/or the incentives and skills to invest its surplus in agricultural or industrial activities. Although the land reform redirected some of it to the poor, the government simultaneously manipulated the price of farm products relative to those of consumer and industrial goods so that much or most of it found its way back to the state and was used to fund investment. These resources, together with greater political stability than characterized the pre-revolutionary period, explain much of the country's post-Revolution surge in economic growth.

## The Maoist Land Reform

Although the number of beneficiaries of the reform realized by the Communist government was huge, in keeping with China's large population, the share of land changing hands was moderate—about forty-three percent, according to John Wong (1973).[23] The recipients, mainly landless workers, got an average of just one-sixth of a hectare. Only the surplus held by the

[23] A detailed analysis by Schran (1969, 22) agrees with this number.

landlords (four percent of the population), plus that belonging to temples and other institutions, was redistributed, while land owned by the larger group of rich peasants was not.[24] The reform was limited in scope for both political and economic reasons. Mao was fearful that a broad attack on the sizeable group of prosperous peasants would generate too much opposition. He was also aware that, with a fragile rural economy, a substantial disruption of the activities of this group could seriously reduce the supply of agricultural products to the cities. Wong (1973) argues that while the Communist leadership wanted to stamp out feudalism, they were planning to allow rural capitalism, as represented by this "rich" peasant economy, to grow spontaneously for a while. This intermediate stance owed itself to previous reform experiences during the Revolution, which gave the CCP leadership both a relatively good understanding of the issues involved, and well-developed organizational skills and administrative expertise. As Ben Stavis (1978, 68) puts it, "Rare is the government which carries out land reform with this much practical experience. Rare are 20-year pilot programs."

China's land reform benefited from a strong political commitment to the transformation of the society. It was implemented effectively through a combination of central leadership and mass participation, expressed through a wide range of local organizations. Peasant associations were set up at the township level, while land reform committees and peoples' tribunals were established at county and higher levels. Peoples' militia and special land reform police supplemented the regular army to discourage landlords from violently opposing the reform.[25] Timing was orderly, something not to be taken for granted since when landlords begin to organize resistance a reformist government may be pushed to move too quickly from the perspective of efficient implementation; ultra-radical forces, fearful of compromise,

[24] Schran (1969, 18) estimates that "very large farmers" making up eight percent of the households owned 17.6 percent of the land, while landlords (four percent of households) owned 28.7 percent of it. These two groups thus owned about forty-six percent of the land. Stavis (1978) notes that some Chinese statements have claimed that landlords and rich peasants, constituting about ten percent of the rural families, owned seventy percent of the land. In the initial redistribution, one estimate puts the land transferred at 46.7 million hectares, with this going to three hundred million families of formerly landless families; the latter figure is implausible because the country's population in 1950 was just 552 million. Possibly the number referred to people rather than families. Wong (1973, 129–130) puts the number of recipients at about 430 million, a figure that referred to the total number of people, and was the equivalent of about one hundred million families.

[25] The Chinese success, based on a combination of central and local leadership, is consistent with the findings of Montgomery (1972); in an analysis of twenty-five land reforms (not including that of mainland China), he found that peasants' productivity and welfare gains were best served through the devolution of authority to carry out land reform to local political organizations.

may also push for haste. Because of both the prior experience of the CCP and its overwhelming victory in 1949, such pressures were moderated. Implementation was carried out on a regional basis, and it was extended over six years. Roughly one-quarter of China had already experienced reform in the context of revolution from 1946 to 1948; the rest did so over 1949 to 1952, except for regions inhabited by minority groups, where it tended to be delayed. Several stages were involved, beginning with rent reduction. To initiate the redistribution per se, cadres selected a pilot village in each county to gain experience pertinent to the specific needs of that locality (Stavis 1978, 73). Rather than classifying people simply on the basis of the size of holdings or income, the CCP stressed the source of the income—whether earned directly through one's own labor or through that of others, in the form of rent, interest, or profits—because, in practice, the distinction was often difficult to make. Final judgments were made at public meetings with mass participation. Cadres then handled the details of computing surplus lands, determining how much land each family would get, and assigning specific plots to families. Inspection teams formed at various administrative levels were sent to check up on the implementation.

China's land redistribution probably had at most a modest positive impact on aggregate agricultural output; little could be expected because the land was already farmed intensively[26] and the reform could not quickly modify the basic technology. Reduced levels of conflict probably contributed to the healthy 4.1 percent annual increase in output from 1952 to 1958, while TFP was probably rising at 0.75 percent per year or less (Lin 1990, 1233, 1245). Yields did not rise significantly until the 1960s, when modern inputs became more generally available. The reform did, however, succeed impressively in raising the consumption of many people through its redistributive impact; it also improved the economic security and stability of the great majority, so that on average welfare rose markedly. Security was boosted by the government's vigorous efforts to ensure that people got the basic necessities, by effective rationing and big increases in grain storage, and by a concerted effort to improve public health. These important advances of the 1950s were largely one-shot in character[27] but did constitute one of the notable cases

[26] As one Western visitor phrased it in the 1930s, "not a blade of grass was out of place" (comment of Professor Jacob Viner in his History of Economic Thought course at Princeton University, 1960).

[27] After a thirty percent increase in real wages from 1952 to 1957, there was no further advance through 1971 (Perkins 1975, 137), an unsurprising outcome given the presence of much surplus labor in the country.

in history where income redistribution was the key to a substantial increase in the welfare of the majority. Inequality in pre-revolutionary China was no higher than what many developing countries have suffered but, given the very low average income, it was enough to keep many people in poverty and be a major cause of the political turmoil that had hampered growth (Perkins 1975, 128).

Stavis (1978, 69) argues that, although from a strictly economic point of view the land reform was of modest proportions, its social and political dimensions made it profoundly radical and revolutionary, "a crucial first step in the destruction of the political power of the rural elite." It transformed both rural and national politics, and it was, in his view, an important step in a psychological transformation of peasants from a mode of passivity toward a greater realization of their potential influence within the society. It was also a milestone in the struggle for gender equality in China. Women and girls received the same share of land as men and boys, reinforcing their claim to property rights. Women, often the victims of sexual exploitation and abuse in earlier times, were frequently the leaders in public meetings to criticize landlords and strip them of their status.

The status and treatment of serfs had varied little over the millennia; they were always open to both bad fortune and to abuse of many forms. By one judgment, "extreme serfdom generally made slavery unnecessary . . . because the serfs, theoretically free but in practice subject to the most cruel serfdom, worked as slaves" (Preece 2010, 858).

Political inequality, typically closely linked to unequal land ownership and often an important obstacle to agricultural development, was significantly reduced. A typical precondition for rural local organizations (including local government, farmers' cooperatives, and so on) to effectively serve the interest of small farmers is a reasonably equitable distribution of land (Uphoff and Esman 1974, 72).[28] A lack of political and social connections often prevents tenants and small landholders from obtaining credit or buying fertilizer. Busy extension agents tend to concentrate their efforts on larger farmers. Farmers close to the margin of survival may be afraid to risk new cultivation techniques or to grow more crops in an unstable or exploitative market. While in some cases the large landowners may be innovative leaders in modern agricultural techniques, in other cases they may subtly oppose agricultural improvement; they may have no desire to see irrigation projects

[28] Their results are based on an analysis of eighteen Asian case studies.

developed if they do not expect to control them. Such projects might increase the viability of small holdings and the demand for labor, and thus the bargaining power of laborers. Poorer classes can usually expect little justice in disputes involving land ownership, settlement of debts, or water rights.

In summary, the Chinese land reform from 1949 to 1952 was carefully and effectively carried out. It brought substantial economic benefits to the recipients of land and significantly reduced income inequality; its most notable impact, however, was to end China's style of feudalism, reduce social and political inequality, and thereby improve the overall welfare of the rural population. By 1980, life expectancy had experienced a dramatic increase from around forty to forty-five years in 1950 to about sixty-five years. Data ambiguities cloud the timing of this increase. While many sources show little improvement prior to the early 1960s, Kimberly Singer Babiarz and colleagues (2015, 39) conclude that the largest advances occurred during the 1950s.[29] The famine associated with the Great Leap Forward must have had a significant downward effect for several years. In any case, it is clear that by the 1970s a major increase had taken place.

Considerable debate has surrounded the number of deaths attributable to the land reform; most estimates fall in the range of eight hundred thousand to three million. Starting from the lower figure (based on Mao's estimate of those executed by the state), and noting that not all of them were landlords, Stavis (1978, 75) comes up with a figure of a half million for the latter group, amounting to 2.5 percent of the landlord class and 0.1 percent of the rural population as a whole. He notes that there were also many unofficial and illegal killings of landlords by angry peasants. But he suspects that some of the higher figures circulated have been essentially propagandistic.

## Industrialization and the Great Leap Forward

As in the Soviet Union, China's land reform coincided with the beginning of its major effort to industrialize and generate a growth surge. The huge increase in capital formation was impressive in light of the country's very low level of per capita income, which many contemporary experts viewed as an almost insuperable obstacle to achieving really high savings and investment

[29] These authors use a range of sources to undertake an interprovincial analysis of the period from 1950 to 1980.

rates. Until 1952, Soviet-type forced draft methods were part of the story, including the introduction of high sales and profits taxes on consumer goods. Taxes, only two percent of the GDP in the nineteenth century, rose to thirty percent after 1949.[30] The government expanded education rapidly and directed the university population away from the humanities and social sciences into engineering and the natural sciences; thousands were sent to study in the USSR.

Aiming to keep everyone reasonably fully employed, a natural challenge in such a heavily populated country with a long history of urban unemployment and rural underemployment, the government undertook a mass mobilization of rural labor to expand the infrastructure, fuel industrial growth (e.g., through the backyard furnaces) and find new ways to raise agricultural output. As a result, the first burst of growth in agriculture did not rely significantly on new technologies. By the mid-1970s, the regime's initial employment goals had been achieved, with urban unemployment lower than in most of the less developed countries (LDCs) and rural seasonal idleness was much reduced (Rawski 1979).

Shortly after the Communist takeover in 1949, and the ensuing redistribution of land, came the 1955/1956 decision to almost fully socialize the economy, except for the smallest trades and industrial producers. In the case of agriculture, various arguments were put forward including, as always, the idea that the sector was characterized by economies of scale, but also Mao's view that collectivization would produce group enthusiasm leading to greater productivity, raise socialist consciousness, and help to link peasants to the Communist Party (Albertus 2021, 299, citing Pryor 1992, 52–55). Others felt that collectivization might be needed to protect individual small farmers from abuse or even dispossession by richer ones. Debates emerged within the party as to how and how rapidly to collectivize agriculture. Experiments with cooperatives were being carried out even as the 1950–1953 reform proceeded; over the years, three levels emerged: "mutual aid teams," "elementary cooperatives," and "advanced cooperatives."[31] By 1957, the number of advanced cooperatives had greatly increased (Lin

[30] The land reform may also have contributed significantly to national savings. Lippit (1974) estimates that after the reform about forty percent of the agrarian property share of net domestic product, for which his median 1933 estimate was seventeen to nineteen percent, went to increased consumption by the poor, with the remainder siphoned off for government current and investment expenditures. This amounted to about seven percent of 1952 net domestic expenditure financing about forty-five percent of net investment.

[31] Details of this process are presented by Albertus (2021, 299).

1990, 1231). Overall, this process was successful: it confronted little active resistance from the peasantry, was accompanied by good output increases (the cited average of 4.1 percent per year from 1952 to 1958), and it left some labor available for construction projects. This encouraged the leadership to adopt a bolder approach. Although significant, the economy-wide progress achieved over the first Five Year Plan had not, by 1957 or 1958, added up to the "great economic transformation" sought by Mao—a quick conversion from an agrarian economy to a socialist society through rapid industrialization and collectivization.[32]

Not all of the leaders agreed with Mao's next steps, as evidenced by major debates within the party,[33] but Mao prevailed and the country embarked on the biggest single mistake of the Chinese Communist regime—the Great Leap Forward (1958–1962), which included the forced collectivization of farmers into large communes of five thousand or so households (Lin 1990, 1232), the abolition of private ownership of land, and the ensuing Great Famine of 1959–1961. The famine was the combined result of a decline in agricultural and food output and inefficient distribution of what was available through an increase in the amount of grain requisitioned from the communes to feed the urban population, other forms of maldistribution, and even some exports to finance capital goods imports. Following as it did on the initial success of collectivization from 1952 to 1958, the sudden collapse of production from 1958 to 1960—by about twenty-five percent for all agriculture and thirty percent for grains—has naturally been the topic of much debate. It seems to have been due in part to unfavorable weather, but mainly to management inefficiencies, including a worker incentive problem arising from the unwieldy size of the communes. Output reduction and mismanagement fed on each other, as well as on a flow of misinformation based partly on the leadership's translating its optimism into publicized "facts," and partly on reports from lower levels that were unduly positive out of fear of disclosing bad outcomes or contradicting the leadership.

Three successive years of bad weather was the original official explanation from the Communist Party for the calamitous fall in output, but most

[32] Mao's belief that more could be achieved than the seven to eight percent aggregate growth performance over this first five-year plan came in part from his own observation of what he saw as the economic benefits of mass mobilization. However, he and some close advisors also expected big efficiency benefits from shifting the economy toward a more collective character.

[33] Thus Zhou Enlai, among others, argued for a reversal of collectivization in 1957 when the Party's response to some grain crop failures was to increase the proportion collected by the state to guard against future shortages.

students have concluded that weather made, at most, a modest contribution, perhaps a third. With management becoming the responsibility of the large communes in 1958, inadequate preparation and implementation by central and local officials took its toll; local cadres were ill equipped to handle the complicated administrative task of so large an entity. Some policy errors were due to overconfidence in the sector's performance up to that point and in how it would perform when fully collectivized. Many farmers were assigned to engage in the production of steel in backyard furnaces as the Great Leap Forward began in 1958 and fifty million prime agricultural workers left farms to work elsewhere. As a result, farming activities were neglected in some areas. The sown acreage of grain was reduced by nine percent in 1959 as planners shifted land to such non-food crops as cotton, sugar cane, and beets; meanwhile, grain exports were raised. Communal mess halls were initiated and workers now had to eat there; they were, in effect, encouraged to overeat because they were unable to save food at home.

Prior to the crisis, the grain procurement quota had been kept under thirty percent of the total output, but with the authorities expecting production to grow, they raised its absolute level from 58.8 million tons in 1958 (29.4 percent of the total) to 67.4 million tons in 1959, which turned out to be 39.7 percent of a fifteen percent lower total. Although the quota was then reduced to 51.1 million tons in 1960, this was still a high 35.6 percent of the falling output. Only in 1961 did the share requisitioned get back down to 27.4 percent (Lin 1990, 1238). The excessive quotas reflected the over-optimism of top state officials and contributed to the "illusion of superabundance." Party members started to report excessive production due to pressure for success from those at the top, even as actual production was beginning to fall. By 1960, the Party claimed that the state granaries had twenty-five billion tons when in fact they had 6.3 billion (Hua 2011). Food availability in rural areas dropped dramatically. Well distributed, there was still a (barely) adequate supply; but overprocurement and poor distribution within the country produced the famine.[34]

Once the exaggeration of crop yields was in play—encouraged, among other things by the "Mass Line" (one of the three banners which told people to, "go all out, aim high, and build socialism with greater, better, and more

[34] Meng et al. (2010) show that, in contrast to most other famines, there were in this case more deaths in places that produced more food per capita. They argue that the inflexibility in the centrally planned food procurement system explains at least half of the deaths from the famine.

economical results")—later reports did not dare to contradict them. Politics entered the picture in a variety of other ways as well. Conspiracy theories circulated to the effect that peasants were only pretending to be hungry. Saving grain for the family to eat was seen as unacceptable. Peasants were unable to speak out given the dangerous setting in which they found themselves. Local party leaders conspired to cover up shortfalls and put the blame on others. It has been said that, for a time, Mao himself was kept unaware of the starvation villagers were suffering. In a visit to Henan province in 1958, local officials showed him fields which had allegedly achieved huge yield increases through "sputnik launches," but it was all faked (Becker 1997). In a pattern similar to the massive 1932/1933 famine in Ukraine, doctors were prohibited from listing "starvation" as a cause of death on death certificates. The over optimism of the leaders, which induced them to focus increasingly on other objectives than grain production, was thus not immediately corrected by the facts of falling production and masses of people dying in the rural areas.

Another source of incompetent management were Mao's own ideas. Following in Stalin's footsteps, he was persuaded by Soviet pseudoscientist Lysenko to pursue "close planting" on the grounds that stalks of the same species did not compete with each other,[35] and by Lysenko's colleague, Terentiy Maltsev, that deep plowing was a good practice because the most fertile soil was well under the surface. The first idea was not in and of itself wrong, but it was when taken to extremes without the proper understanding of how to do it; the second was basically wrong. In the "Four Pests Campaign," citizens were called upon to destroy or scare away sparrows and other wild birds that ate crop seeds. On balance, this effort appears to have been counterproductive as it led to an explosion of the vermin population, especially crop-eating insects, now without predators.

Along with weather and the incompetent overall planning and management, a third hypothesis places the blame on the system of large communes, together with the prohibition against workers leaving them, both dating from 1958, and the incentive problems to which this combination gives rise. Until 1955, the majority of households were either in the mutual aid teams (with an average of 8.4 households per team in that year) or were not yet in cooperatives at all. In 1956, this structure changed sharply; 84 percent of those households in cooperatives (now the great majority of the total) were in the "advanced cooperatives," with an average of almost two hundred

[35] Lynch (2008, 57).

households in each (Lin 1990, 1232). The next major change in late 1958 put nearly everyone in a commune, with an average of five thousand families. Because aggregate output did not fall until 1959, it is plausible that the early stages of the collectivization process did not have a significant negative impact on output, and that it was the switch to these giant communes that did. As noted, the earlier upward trend in output is believed to have made those at the top overconfident that the collectivization experiment was living up to their expectations.

Some combination of incentive problems and other forms of mismanagement in the newly established large communes is widely accepted as explaining a good deal of the output decline. Dwight Perkins and Shahid Yusuf (1984, 79) see the low work incentives as a significant problem: there was little connection between an individual's effort and the value of their work points, which determined their earnings. Effective supervision from above was not feasible, nor was it provided by fellow villagers because they, too, saw little connection between the efforts of other village members and their own work points. The estimate by John McMillan et al. (1989) that the reversal from the production team system to the HRS between 1978 and 1984 increased total factor productivity by thirty-two percent is consistent with the "other side of the coin" proposition that the switch to large-scale communal farming contributed strongly to the collapse from 1959 to 1961.[36] By the time of the later corrective reform, the production team system in use typically consisted of twenty to thirty neighboring households, something similar to the situation in the mid-1950s during the shift to larger sizes (Lin 1990, 1231).

Although accepting that bad policies and weak management—including the switch to the huge communes—did definitely contribute to the severity of this disaster, Lin (1990) argues that if they had been the main cause then the policy reversal in 1962 would have brought a quick recovery of agricultural productivity to the level prior to that switch. Most problems were recognized within a few years, so by the end of 1961, the majority of the previous harmful policies had been reversed: the mobilization of labor for irrigation projects was abandoned, production decisions were decentralized to

[36] Different studies have come up with a range of estimates of the share of output growth acceleration after the adoption of the household responsibility system that was due to price increases and the share due to rising efficiency through decollectivization. Lin (1992) puts the latter share at one half, whereas McMillan et al. (1989) put it higher, although some of the gap is due to differences in what is included in measured output.

production teams with an average size of twenty to thirty households, communal kitchens were abolished, and the state compulsory grain procurement quota was lowered to its pre-crisis level. But only in 1964 did output again approximate the pre-crisis high achieved in 1958. Lin (1990) attributes the delayed recovery to the special motivational problem that arises when collectives lack supervision *and* do not allow individuals to leave them. In the absence of supervision, performance depends on a "self-enforcing contract," in which each person disciplines himself; such discipline is more likely if the effects of its absence are clear. In the context under discussion, Lin argues that a self-enforcing agreement can only be sustained if the members of the collective have the right to leave it when others do not honor their agreement. At the initial stage of collectivization movements like China's, the right to withdraw tends to be respected and most members do "self-enforce"; that is, they fulfill their responsibilities, partly in recognition of the fact that if many do not then the dedicated ones will leave, and a downward spiral will occur. But zealous political leaders, encouraged by the initial success of the movement, tend to see the individual members who withdraw as enemies whose right to withdraw must be curtailed in defense of collectives in general; the safety valve is then removed, as happened in the fall of 1958. Lin (1990) argues that when the lack of self-enforcement comes on gradually then agricultural performance also declines gradually, but if it happens swiftly then an agricultural crisis—like the one in the Soviet Union between 1929 and 1932 and that in China between 1959 and 1961—follows immediately.

The relative roles of the factors contributing to the disastrous collapse in output and how they interacted with each other remain something of a mystery, partly because so much was changing so fast. Without relatively solid evidence on how and when weather issues may have been important, it is hard to definitively link the decline with other elements, such as the incentive problem in general, the compulsory character of membership in the collective, and the changing levels of requisition. To the extent that increasing requisitions were a source of output decline, the timing of the awareness of them would matter and could interact with the prohibition of withdrawal from the commune to magnify its effect. In any case, it is clear that some of the hypothesized causes did play a role, and that the combination was lethal.

In the most supreme of ironies, China's carefully implemented land reform brought significant economic gains and major political and social advances for the direct beneficiaries, but very soon thereafter a combination of ineffective and careless planning, together with Mao's egomania, generated the greatest loss of life ever experienced from a single famine; most estimates have fallen in the range of twenty-five to forty-five million deaths.[37] Although the subsequent Cultural Revolution took many additional lives (perhaps two to three million), its total was small beside this one. Accepting a figure of thirty million deaths for the famine associated with the Great Leap Forward, China's total death toll from it, from the violence associated with the reform itself, and from the Cultural Revolution was about 6.4 percent of its 1960 rural population, or 5.3 percent of the total population at that time. The toll may have reached as high as seven to eight percent of the rural population, depending on one's estimate of deaths due to the famine.[38]

## De-collectivization

After the bad harvests from 1959 to 1961, control over production and income-sharing decisions was returned to small groups of no more than a few dozen families; this, perhaps together with an increase in managerial experience, raised the efficiency of the commune system. Then, beginning in the late 1970s, China began an experiment that transferred most of the rights and responsibilities for the management of land to the families who operated it; the typical units were quite small, reflecting the country's high labor-to-land ratio. This reform, together with others instituted under Prime Minster Deng, was highly successful; agricultural output grew dramatically, averaging above four percent per year over the quarter-century period 1979

[37] Johnson (2018, 4) came up with this range after surveying the various serious estimates. Banister (1987) used Chinese demographic statistics to produce a figure of thirty million. Ashton et al. (1984) concluded that, along with thirty million excess deaths, there were thirty-three million lost or postponed births from 1958 to 1961.

[38] The enormity of both the human benefits and the human costs of the reform path taken in China invite comparison. Clearly the best outcome, bringing the benefits of this one (or more) but without the human costs, would have been far superior to what happened. But if the only route to substantial progress had been this one, was it worth it? In terms of its impact on years of life lived, the answer is positive; if each of the than 980 million people alive in 1980 was living ten extra years, the positive contribution would come to nearly two billion years. If each of those unnecessarily killed (say thirty-six million) lived twenty-five years less as a result, the total lost years would be nine hundred million years. Such comparisons based only on years lived do not, of course, allow for the special human loss from execution or starvation. And they involve speculation as to which elements of what happened later were attributable to the reform.

to 2004.[39] The benefits went primarily to the lower income part of the population, making this arguably the single biggest factor in bringing eight hundred million people out of poverty. Part of the income boom was due to the unfulfilled potential for output under the previous collective management system, part to a lowering of tax rates on agricultural incomes, and part to the rising non-agricultural incomes of these families. An initial and dramatic burst of output growth from 1985 to 1989 (at an average of eleven percent per year) was due to a combination of rising efficiency as incentive and organizational problems were reduced by the switch to household responsibility, together with a rapid rate of technological advance which shifted the productivity frontier outward. The key elements of this latter advance included research on new seed varieties, chemical fertilizers, and control of plagues, and were accompanied by important investments in hydraulics, flood control, and small-scale irrigation through pumps and tubes. Extension services were improved; in 2006, a pilot program was launched to stimulate more interaction with farmers at the local level. Rural electrification facilitated the use of some productivity-enhancing technologies. The efficiency of the input and output markets was substantially improved. Removal of state requisitioning of food at low prices allowed prices to rise and thereby provided one more incentive to increase output. The jump in agricultural productivity and income generated a burst in related local activities.

China's current agricultural structure is relatively effective in taking advantage of economies of scale where these do exist, without having many large production units. Further, a system in which the farmers are not owners of the land has not impeded very fast growth. The initial guarantee of access to one's plot for fifteen years that came with the Household Responsibility Reform was later raised to thirty years. Some recent threats to family land rights have, however, raised concerns. Despite the general pattern of small-scale operations, there has been considerable support for what Jan Van der Ploeg and Jingzhong Ye (2016b) refer to as "capitalist agriculture," with examples showing up since the 1980s and 1990s. The basic attraction of this for the land buyer is the potential profits from speculation, especially where the property is located near an expanding urban area. Not surprisingly, this option can be attractive to party *apparatchiks*, which helps to explain why the state may not resist the trend very forcefully.

[39] Deng also relaxed some controls on rural–urban migration. When attacked by Party members as "ideologically retrograde," his supporters responded with the call to abandon dogmas and "seek truth from facts" (Albertus 2021, 303, citing Unger 1985, 591).

## Summing Up

In any case, China's post-1980 experience is one of the great success stories of small-scale agriculture and its potential for rapid poverty reduction. It followed on the earlier experiences of Japan, Korea, and Taiwan, and slightly preceded a comparably dramatic one in Vietnam after a similar shift from collective to family-oriented farming. The synergy between a prospering small-scale agriculture and the rural industry in China is also reminiscent of the experiences of other Asian countries, like Taiwan and Indonesia. The share of the rural labor force engaged in off-farm work rose from ten percent in 1978 to twenty-one percent in 1988, as the rural TVE enterprises absorbed sixty-seven million workers.

As in the case of Russia and other newly communist countries, it was to be expected that China's new leaders would want to transform a traditionally exploitative system. Distributing land to those without it was a natural first step, followed by an exploratory search for something more collective in nature and whose benefits would be more or less equally shared. During this stage (1952–1958), agricultural policy under the CCP was a strange combination of the apparently cautious and competent testing of a succession of steps toward cooperative farming and the sudden and ill-advised switch to large scale communes in 1958. A major factor in the discarding of caution was the overconfidence (on Mao's part in particular) that, because the introduction of cooperatives had been accompanied by rising output, a switch to much bigger units would bring even bigger benefits. Misinformation from farther down in the administrative hierarchy fed into it. An appropriate recognition that some activities, like many investments in irrigation, could be better carried out on a large scale was not matched by an awareness of the possible lack of disciple that can come with group production and egalitarian sharing of benefits. The rather subtle difference between a cooperative with self-supervision from which people can exit and one which they cannot leave would understandably escape most people.

Perhaps least forgivable was the general failure to take account of "peasant knowledge." Among the many faucets of peasant behavior about which outsiders are typically unaware is the management of the risks (climatic, plant disease, etc.) that their activity entails. Both Russia and China suffered the lethal combination of a collectivization that put too much control in the hands of people with insufficient knowledge of how best to deal with such risks and how to manage agriculture more generally, together with a matching unwillingness to accept peasant behavior as substantially knowledge-based and sensible. The overconfidence of those who innocently expected collectivization to bring big production gains, based on the presumptions that they could manage farm activities better than could the peasants, and that communal farming would bring economies of scale, came with the failure to understand the peasants' natural need to have a store of food (if necessary hidden from requisitioners) to handle future eventualities. This combination, together with the desire to move ahead with rapid industrialization, pushed governments to extract a very high surplus from agriculture at the rather obvious risk of creating a crisis or even a famine; this set of conditions was akin to a carton of explosives waiting to detonate. Under such circumstances, either bad weather or any other quick deterioration of conditions is likely to take a heavy toll.

As in many other countries where agrarian reform has been part of a larger social transition, China's revolution brought important changes in the areas of education and health, both of which appear to have yielded significant benefits. These contributed directly to the country's rapidly rising life expectancy and to falling inequality. Probably they also had a significant positive impact on economic growth, although this is harder to judge.

The mortality decline and the associated increase in life expectancy from forty to forty-five years in 1950 to about sixty-five years in 1980 is among the most rapid and sustained ever documented. Many explanations have been proposed, including the arrival on the scene of the famous "barefoot doctors" during the late 1960s; widespread public health campaigns (childhood immunizations in particular); improvements in water, sanitation, and nutrition; and gains in educational attainment. Babiarz et al. (2015), comparing evidence across the country's provinces, conclude that the expansion of education during the 1950s, together with the large-scale public health campaigns, jointly explain roughly fifty to seventy-five percent of the reduction in China's infant and under-five mortality rates between 1960 and 1980. That the expansion of post-primary school enrolment during the 1950s corresponded with a large decline in mortality after 1960 is consistent with a large literature reporting better infant and child survival among more educated mothers. One explanation involves cognitive capacity; better-educated people process information more efficiently and thus benefit more from the diffusion of knowledge about health. Other contributing factors were the general improvement in food consumption and living standards (outside the years of the great famine). A substantial share of the improvement was thus linked to non-medical factors.

Given that China, in 1980, was a predominantly rural country, for major improvements in health and education to show up at the national level it was important that public policy in those areas not be too heavily tilted in favor of urban residents. After the Communist takeover, and especially during the subsequent Cultural Revolution Period (1965–1975), much medical skill was transferred to the countryside and health services improved, contributing to the major gains in that area.[40] Similarly in the realm of education, a rural push took place during these early post-Revolution decades.

## The Post-revolution Trajectory of Inequality at the Economy-wide Level: Impressive Decline and Dramatic Increase

The path of inequality since the Revolution provides one of the great ironies of Communist China—its dramatic failure to leave a long-term legacy of income equality despite the original intent to attack the unfairness and inequality for which capitalism is widely criticized and the striking early success on that front. From a moderate level of inequality during the early decades of the century, but one whose poverty costs were high because of the country's low average income, the Revolutionary government achieved a major improvement in a short span of time. By the 1970s, inequality was quite low by the standards of developing countries, with a Gini coefficient probably in the range of 0.25–0.3. Over about two decades, the country achieved labor-absorbing growth, with the effect of greatly raising the incomes of those toward the lower part of the income hierarchy. Income differentials by level of education were kept low, partly by design. But the fast growth period since the introduction of market reforms came with a large and rapid increase in inequality. Poverty fell further; in fact, it fell very rapidly during the early 1980s as the country moved toward family-based agriculture, although that descent has since slowed. Major issues still under discussion are the factors behind this reversal in the inequality trend, the extent to which it was

[40] The famous system of "barefoot doctors" drew on local workers selected by their comrades to be given several months of medical training (Birn et al. 2009, 603). Because they became a significant component of medical service only in the late 1960s, years after the largest mortality reductions had already been recorded, they may not have been a major contributing factor (Babiarz et al. 2014).

inevitable if the country was to pursue pro-market reforms, and the degree to which it was due to the legacy of certain policy decisions during the central planning era.

China's land reform was one of the several major economic transformations realized by the Communist government which together substantially reduced income inequality. Reforms to education and health contributed to a more broadly defined equality. The historic pattern of much higher incomes and living standards—including much better access to education—in urban than in rural areas was tackled, with at least temporary success in some respects. Some of the shrinkage of the urban–rural educational attainment gap occurred during the Cultural Revolution (1966–1976),[41] which is well known as a period of intense and complicated conflict.[42] A favoritism toward those with the "appropriate" class backgrounds continued from the Revolution until well into the 1980s, being strongest during the Cultural Revolution from 1966 to 1976, when Mao pushed a radical decree whose aim was to make political recommendation and class background the primary determinant of progress through the education system (Unger 1984). The Cultural Revolution was probably the most drastic major attempt in history to reduce the intergenerational transmission of educational achievement; it raised rural levels of education and narrowed the urban–rural gap (Hannum 1999, 202). As a result, the ubiquitous link between social origins and educational attainment appears to have been substantially weaker in China at that time than in other comparable countries for which such data are available (Evans et al. 2016). At the same time, considerable chaos and confusion plagued the system, resulting, among other things, in serious quality problems.

The phase during which income inequality was low turned out to be short. Albeit via somewhat different mechanisms from those of the USSR/Russia, China's transition to a more market-based economy has also been

[41] China began the twentieth century with an extremely low level of education. Men born around 1900 averaged two years, and women less (Deng and Treiman 1997, 422). By the birth cohort of 1945 (i.e., those finishing primary school by the late 1950s), the figure for men had reached 6.5 years. The next seven to eight years showed no net gain, after which the upward trend returned until a downturn from 1960—the cohort in school during the Cultural Revolution. The large gap between urban and rural men—about four years around 1930 (seven versus three) had started to shrink in the 1940s—by 1950 it was down to about 2.5 years (eight versus 5.5); it continued to fall in the 1950s and, by 1962, it had reached two years (about ten to a little over eight).

[42] Yang (2021) describes it as a triangular battle between Mao, the bureaucrats and the conservative Red Guards they supported, and the rebel Red Guards whom Mao relied on to undercut the bureaucrats blocking his plans for social and economic transformation.

accompanied by a huge increase in inequality. The period since the dramatic growth take-off has probably featured the sharpest increase in inequality ever seen anywhere, as the Gini coefficient rose to somewhere in the range of 0.5–0.6.[43] The country's leadership has become increasingly worried;[44] it stresses the goal of a "harmonious" society, with rising inequality seen as a threat to this goal and a precursor to social instability. In 2013, the government released its Income Distribution Plan, also known as the 35 Point Plan.

Much research has sought to understand why income inequality has skyrocketed after reaching such a low level in the 1970s. Among the generally cited factors are a large and rising urban–rural income gap; a gap between the coastal provinces favored by trade liberalization and foreign investment and the rest of the country; a rising dispersion in educational attainment and a rising income differential by level of education; a rising share of income accruing to capital, perhaps related to the increasing role of monopolies; and a probably rising share derived from corruption/grey income. These factors interact among themselves. Each invites an analysis of what lies behind it in terms of economic structure and government policy, and of what links, if any, it has to the agrarian reform. The answer remains somewhat unclear (for more details see Appendix 5.1), but it is safe to say that the urban–rural income gap has played a role and that it has been accentuated by the policy of limiting rural–urban migration; a rising level of crony-related corruption has also contributed. This suggests that the inequality surge was not at all inevitable; had limits on migration not been imposed, corruption kept more in bounds, and the premium on education kept to a middling level, inequality would probably have risen much less. In any case, such increase as occurred cannot easily be blamed, directly or indirectly, on the land reform because its impact, especially after farm operations were returned to families, was strongly positive—it contributed directly and strongly to the income increases of those toward the bottom of the income hierarchy.

[43] As in many, if not most, countries, both the level of inequality and its increase over time are likely to be somewhat understated due to underreporting of income at the top, although the failure to properly incorporate the income of rural-to-urban migrant families has probably worked the other way in this case. Zhou and Song (2016, 2) report an increase in the Gini from about 0.28 from 1982 to 1984 to something approaching 0.5 by 2009. One estimate from a Chinese university put the Gini coefficient at 0.61 in 2012 (Wu 2014, 2).

[44] Early in this process Perkins (1986, 63) noted that the reforms themselves would be at risk if they were seen to be fostering inequality.

## The Land Reform's Legacy

A summing up of the contribution of China's land reform under the CCP is especially difficult because it initially brought great benefits, then caused enormous harm, and, finally, after the shift from the large commune to the small production team system, contributed greatly to the very rapid post-1980 growth of output and incomes that drastically reduced poverty. Many conditions were, from the beginning, nearly ideal for the contribution to be large. The number of potential beneficiaries was enormous, and the government had much knowledge on how to proceed organizationally; hence, the large short-term benefits to the direct beneficiaries and the significant contribution to the rapid industrialization and growth of the country. It was the first step in a process which brought overall income inequality in China to a quite low level by the 1970s. But an enormous number of lives were lost, a small minority as a direct result of the reform and a huge number as a result of the famine associated with the Great Leap Forward. Then, after becoming a world leader on the equality front, the country lost this distinction and morphed into a high inequality case during the post-agricultural phase of development. However it might compare to a capitalist regime in this stage of development, China's autocracy was certainly not the answer to keeping inequality low.

Although both China and Russia did eventually get rid of the problem of private land concentration, they did so at huge social and human cost. Had they been willing to undertake something more akin to the land reforms of Japan, Korea, and Taiwan, the outcomes would have been enormously better in both economic and human terms. In the additional just-cited irony, the income equality achieved through the restructuring of agriculture and of the economy as a whole was lost during decades of centralized authoritarian rule, with both countries now suffering greater inequality than before their respective revolutions.[45] In contrast, inequality has remained relatively low in Taiwan, Japan, and Korea.

One lesson from the enormous inequality reversal suffered by China in the midst of the great growth burst is the ease with which the equality benefits of land reforms and related progressive policies can be so totally reversed. During the country's agrarian phase of development, the Communist

[45] For the case of Russia, see Nafziger and Linder (2013). For that of China, see Benjamin et al. (2008) and Piketty et al. (2019).

government opted for central planning and large production units in agriculture, the sector to which these alternatives are least suited. Then, in the midst of a sensible switch toward smaller units in agriculture and a decentralized and generally more market-oriented approach, it also pulled back from its strong public sector presence in education and health, where private markets have many flaws. And it failed to let the market operate in the regional allocation of people, probably at serious cost to the lower-income families in the country.

One broad interpretation of this post-revolutionary history is that the early egalitarian orientation of the government, which Mao did try to maintain through the Cultural Revolution, later gave way to other deeper-seated tendencies and beliefs within the government to favor people like themselves, to elitist beliefs, to the demeaning of the rural population, and so on. Although this rebalancing of forces did not eradicate policies designed to benefit the lower income groups, the new preference for markets, the *hukou*-based restrictions on mobility, and the natural inequality arising from the large firm structure and other factors came to carry the day. Education came to play a much bigger role in inequality; probably the rising shares both of grey income and capital income did as well.

As with any other specific case history, the overall impact of China's land reform depends both on the identifiable effects—in this case, enormous benefits and enormous costs—and also on which alternative possible pathways one compares it to.[46] Had the economy advanced well under a market-based system without major land reform, one major group (the beneficiaries of the actual reform) would have remained worse off for perhaps a few decades (the length depending on how that different polity would have evolved in a modernizing world); another major group, most of the forty million or so who died in avoidable famine or in conflict, would have been clear winners. Among alternative but plausible scenarios, the one against which this actual history compares least favorably is what might have unfolded had the reform suggestions of Wolf Ladejinsky and others prior to the Communist triumph been implemented. The gains for the large group that did benefit from the CPP's initial reforms would presumably have been somewhat larger (Ladejinsky knew more about how to establish a productive

[46] The reform was part of a structural shift in the economy toward large units and centralized control, so distinguishing the impacts of the steps taken within agriculture from what happened overall creates analytical complications.

small-farm system than did the CPP); the death toll from the reform itself, the famine of 1959–1962, and the Cultural Revolution would have been avoided; and agriculture would have performed very well, not just after 1980, but over the whole post-1950 period. Rural poverty would have been erased much earlier. Whether the economy as a whole would have grown faster over the medium- to long-term is harder to judge, as are the relative trends in economy-wide poverty. Much would have depended on the political trajectory of the country, but had it had been akin to that of Taiwan, the initially equalizing impact of land reform on income distribution might not have been lost later on. At a personal level, the contrast between Ladejinsky and colleagues on the one hand and Mao on the other, is dramatic. The former was the epitome of an expert professional whose decisions were based on much knowledge and experience; Mao was highly intelligent, but overly self-confident, unable to select the best advisors and thus subject to scams.

That China's major equalizing land reform, together with other equality-inducing policies, did not leave a medium-term legacy of income equality makes it an especially interesting experience from which to learn. A natural point of comparison is Taiwan, whose very successful reform was followed by fast and equitable growth. Rural–urban migration was rapid during the burst of growth. At the same time, the prominent early role of small enterprises outside agriculture, often in rural areas, provided a complementary base for that equitable growth. In China, centralization and size worked in the other direction, as did the *hukou* system, which could be seen as a failure to end an aspect of serfdom—the lack of freedom to move according to one's preference. Although the switch to an independent small farm system via the household responsibility reform worked against rising inequality and coincided with the last observed decline in that inequality, it was not nearly enough to carry the day in the midst of the other major changes described.

## Vietnam

In Vietnam, many of the direct effects of the twentieth-century reforms of agriculture were broadly similar to those in China, but the experience differed dramatically on two fronts. First, the human toll associated directly with the reform was not enormous. Instead, the country was a victim of the American attempt to contain communism, which did cost about 3.3 million to 3.4 million Vietnamese lives, the great majority from the North; nearly eight percent of the total Vietnamese population died during this conflict and nearly fifteen percent of the North Vietnamese population. Underlying the advance of communism were the perceived injustices associated with unequal land distribution. The successful expulsion of the French in the 1950s drew much support from the fact that the communist Viet Minh movement had adopted a policy of land confiscation from rich landlords and its distribution to poor and landless peasants.[47]

A second contrast with China (and with Russia) is that, although markets have, over recent decades, been given a greater role in resource allocation, inequality in Vietnam has not thus far risen to the high levels of those other two countries, an outcome that challenges the common hypothesis that a sharp upswing is inevitable when such a structural shift takes place. Between 1993 and 2012 inequality seems only to have risen marginally, while the bottom forty percent of the population enjoyed a phenomenal surge in average income at nine percent per year (World Bank 2014). The sequence of reforms undertaken bears many similarities to that of China, even though it was complicated by the different paths taken in the North and in the South. Vietnam's post-1980 experience has arguably been the most successful agrarian reform of the last half-century. One notable feature was that, after pursuing collectivization at a time when evidence of the risk of its lowering productivity was emerging (especially from China), the country was able to reverse course quickly and implement a very productive small-farm system.

The pre-Revolutionary setting for Vietnam's agrarian reforms was French colonialism, experienced during the roughly six decades from the 1880s to the 1940s. It involved much displacement of small farmers from their land onto rubber and rice plantations, with low wages and harsh working conditions. The colonial state thus endangered what Scott (1976) considered to be the peasantry's twin norms: reciprocity and the right to subsistence. In pushing peasants to the edge of food crises, it fostered revolts. The early twentieth century saw accelerated changes in land tenancy and distribution. Village common property and unclaimed forest land, previously accessible to poorer villagers and very important for some of them, now had to be sold to pay the heavy collective taxes imposed by the French regime (Mcelwee 2007, 59). Large landholdings were being consolidated into the plantations of wealthy French and Vietnamese owners. New, burdensome taxes not based

[47] Pryor (1992) provides a comparative analysis of agrarian reform in communist countries, including Vietnam.

on production levels or amount of land were particularly resented, especially the head tax, described by Scott (1976, 93) as "the ultimate in regressive fiscal measures. It falls indifferently on rich heads and poor heads in good times and in bad, with the result that its actual burden on the tax-paying family fluctuated widely from season to season."

Significant social protest eventually erupted in the Central Anna province in 1930, after droughts and floods in 1929 and 1930 led to failed harvests. Increasing communist agitation, local unrest, and the threat of starvation created a volatile combination. Although the French attributed the unrest to the incipient Indochinese Communist Party, the great majority of people incarcerated for being "red peasants" or "communists" claimed that they had protested against high taxes, not for an end to French colonialism or the establishment of a communist government. Others cited the corruption of forest guards (Mcelwee 2007, 93). Such evidence is consistent with Scott's view that peasant rebellion often grows out of threats to subsistence and that interfering with a local moral economy can have serious consequences.[48] There is no doubt that peasants' reaction to their plight, and to the French policies that aggravated it, were key factors in promoting revolts and in the ultimate victory of the Vietnamese. In the immediate post-colonial years, it is probable that overall inequality in the North was moderate, as suggested by the 1953 figures on land distribution and that after a redistribution in 1956 it was relatively low. In the south, inequality remained significantly higher, but by how much is not known.

During the anti-colonial war (from 1946 to 1954), communist policies were designed to benefit the rural poor in the Viet Minh zones of influence. These policies consisted mainly of measures like rent and tax reductions, debt annulments, and the periodic redistribution of village-held communal lands, although the basic inequality of landownership was not significantly altered. As of 1953, the Vietnamese Communist Party (VCP) calculated that individuals classified as landlords and rich peasants accounted for three percent of the rural population and owned almost twenty-two percent of the land, an average of nine times more than the rest of the rural population

[48] As between these two factors, Luong (1985) argues that the threat to subsistence levels is often a less important cause of protests and demands than are strong social ties (primarily due to village endogamy) and local associations (such as Buddhist and age-cohort associations). As Mcelwee (2007, 93) notes, the implicit normative rules over the "right" to wealth are in constant renegotiation, with that "right" being particularly weak in cases of what appear to be ill-gotten or corrupt gains. Much of the rural unrest in Vietnam seemed to be spawned not by peasants alone, but by cadres and others acting as whistleblowers who highlighted the immoral misappropriation of state or peasants' funds.

(Raymond 2008, 46).[49] The great scarcity of land meant that many of the farmers who employed landless field laborers did not themselves own much. A redistribution that allocated even a very small amount to all families required expropriation from a large number of peasants with quite modest but still above average holdings; many of this group of "middle peasants" had, in fact, received land as part of earlier redistributions. This delicate context of the 1953 Land Reform Law led to many farmers being punished or killed arbitrarily, and ultimately forced VCP leaders to concede in 1956 that "errors," "excesses," and "injustices" had been committed.[50] Despite the considerable social upheaval and widespread violence during the land reform, agricultural production rose; annual per capita production of paddy rice made a quick recovery, jumping by over sixty percent between 1954 and 1958 (Raymond 2008, 46).

The VCP followed up its 1953 redistribution with a drive to consolidate the North Vietnamese farmers into mutual aid teams (MATs); their number peaked at over 150,000 in mid-1956, but by a year later had fallen to less than half that, as households went back to the tradition of exchanging labor only during the harvest. The next step was the creation of production cooperatives; members were organized into teams overseen directly by brigade leadership committees and indirectly by cooperative management committees. Managers awarded work points for each member's labor, with brigade leaders responsible for calculating and recording those points, which were originally supposed to reflect the difficulty and quality of work performed as well as the quantity. The impossibility of applying the former criteria to hundreds of members led quickly to the points being based solely on time spent on collective labor, which naturally reduced the incentive to work hard. When it established the production cooperatives, the VCP did permit households to produce certain crops on "five percent" plots corresponding to the five percent of the land available to the family, which was seen as part of a supplementary "family economy." They quickly became an important source of food and income; from the early 1960s through the early 1970s, households earned much of their income from their cultivation of these plots which, although not officially provided with any state-supplied

[49] While striking, this degree of concentration was nothing like that prevailing in many other countries, including the majority of those in Latin America.

[50] An early estimate, based on an extrapolation from the report for the Red River Delta, states that one of every 160 village residents had been executed—implying a national total of nearly one hundred thousand deaths. This was later scaled down to half that by various scholars and, more recently, to something in the range of fifteen thousand by authors like Moise (2001).

resources, often achieved yields two to three times those of the cooperative land (Raymond 2008, 49).

Despite such local information, as well as evidence from China's recent experience, Le Duan, the general-secretary of the VCP, declared in a major 1974 party conference that small-scale, family-organized farming could not meet Vietnam's economic needs. He ordered that cooperatives be consolidated and enlarged to redistribute manpower and reorganize production "better and more rationally" (Raymond 2008, 50–51). Predictably, this step did not halt the ongoing downward trend in North Vietnam's per capita rice production. It no doubt contributed to an overall economic malaise which continued even after the military victory over South Vietnam in 1975.

South Vietnam's reform history prior to 1973 was also notable for what went right and what went wrong. Land was less scarce and its concentration was higher than in the north. Shortly after its support for the successful reforms in Japan, Korea, and Taiwan, the US advised Ngo Dinh Diem's new government to undertake a land redistribution, among other policy changes. In 1955/1956, land rental was capped at twenty-five percent of production and ownership at one hundred hectares of rice land. Under this program the government acquired 422,000 hectares over the period from 1958 to 1961 and distributed 244,000 (Dacy 1986, 112). For a land scarce country, the ceiling was extremely high, and the land redistributed comprised less than ten percent of the total (Prosterman 1967, 35). Farmers were required to pay for land acquired, and the program was riddled with corruption and inefficiency (Tucker 1998, 219). To make things worse, in political terms, this feeble attempt suffered from direct and unfavorable comparison with what the Viet Minh had already been doing in the regions of the South that they controlled. Many peasants believed that the US army and the South Vietnamese government were on the side of the landlords, an understandable view given that their military operations to clear communist insurgents from an area would often result in landlords reclaiming territory previously abandoned or confiscated and redistributed by the Viet Minh or Viet Cong. Although this reform program technically remained in effect until 1970, it was largely unused after 1960 as the Viet Cong insurgents either took over or disputed the South Vietnamese government's control of most of the rural areas. In 1967, late in the game, land expert Roy Prosterman proposed a "land-to-the-tiller" program which had the potential to compete with the Viet Cong for the allegiance of the peasants. Under it, all agricultural land would be owned by those who worked it, and landlords were to be compensated fully for land given up, with payment guaranteed by the US.[51] In March 1970, the South Vietnamese government began to implement something like this proposal, with individual landholdings limited to fifteen hectares. By the end of 1973, about 1.2 million hectares, or nearly forty percent of the cultivated area, had been titled to 953,000 poor or landless farmers.[52] By the war's end in 1975, the US estimated that land tenancy had practically disappeared and that the living standard of farmers had increased by thirty to fifty percent (Dacy 1986, 113). Under any other circumstances, this would have been a very successful effort. But it failed to have a decisive impact on the war because it was "too little, too late" (Elliott 2003, 372). In that respect, it bore an eerie similarity to the above-cited 1950s Sino-American program, launched in 1949, by which time the Chinese Revolution had advanced too far to be turned back.

The South Vietnamese government's ongoing reform was replaced at war's end by a VCP attempt at collectivization, especially in the highly productive Mekong Delta. It followed the model applied two decades earlier in the North with similarly disappointing results on the productivity front, and in the face of much opposition from the farmers, many of whom had just been beneficiaries of the "land to the tiller" program. They resisted collectivization in a variety of ways: some refused to perform collective labor, some wrecked machines and slaughtered livestock before they could be expropriated by the VCP, and many sold grain on the free market at prices far above those paid by the state for what it requisitioned. In the Mekong Delta, state food procurement decreased by more than half between 1976 and 1979. The state's inability to collectivize agriculture in the south left it unable to appropriate large quantities of grain (Raymond 2008, 51), and inefficiency in production exacted a high cost in terms of poverty and economic insecurity. Farms, at an average size of just 0.63 hectares, were among the smallest in the world. About seventy-five percent of the labor force was employed in agriculture, and over eighty percent of the poor were located in rural areas (Huong et al. 2016, 477).

As the party proceeded with its attempted collectivization in the south, national rice production fell by over seventeen percent in the three-year period from 1976 through 1978, and food in the North became increasingly scarce.

[51] Prosterman (1967, 22–44) estimated that the land-to-the-tiller program could be implemented for just $900 million—less than the monthly cost to the US of the Vietnam War.

[52] In total, the United States financed $339 million of the total $441 million the reform cost (Brocheux 2000, 89).

The first policy reversal, Directive 100 of 1981, permitted households to take over the planting, tending, and harvesting of crops (i.e., the labor-intensive phases of cultivation) on land contracted from cooperatives for one to three years in exchange for delivering to the cooperative a specified quantity of grain at each annual harvest; farmers still had to purchase seeds, irrigation, fertilizers, and plowing and pest control services from the cooperatives. Crops in excess of the quota could be sold to the cooperative at a higher bonus price or on the free market. Although this directive did improve the situation of farm families and led to a large short-term increase in output and in state procurement, farmers still tended to find it advantageous, where possible, to operate outside the official system.

Per capita food production continued to stagnate in the North throughout the 1980s. At the beginning of 1988, several provinces, including Hanoi, confronted food shortages, and severe hunger threatened over 3.5 million people. By the late 1980s, this threat had pushed the party to start encouraging private, family-based production—part of a package of economic reforms that became known as the Doi Moi or "renovation." It had taken the evidence of disappointingly low output levels and slow growth, together with widespread hunger, to fuel such a policy reversal; the decision-makers tended to be blind to the micro-level evidence of flaws in the collective system. Chad Raymond (2008, 56) reports one farmer saying that the cooperatives had "too many expenses. So if the harvest was bad then we didn't have enough food to live on." A farmer who served on the village People's Committee said that "the upper levels of the state didn't know anything about agriculture." Greater respect for and interest in what the farmers knew could have helped to shape much better policy sooner and to curb conflict and resentment. In any case, Vietnam did, with only a modest delay, achieve a major U-turn from the collective land use system installed at the end of the war. The Doi Moi program of 1986 officially launched the switch from a socialist-controlled economy to a regulated market economy and it launched the most radical land reform of modern times. It transferred decision-making powers over farm inputs and outputs to households and freed up input and output markets. The bulk (eighty to eighty-five percent) of the country's agricultural land area was scheduled for effective privatization over a relatively short period. Initially, the collectives and local cadres still set production quotas and allocated land across households for fixed periods; households were not initially free to transfer, exchange, or sell their allocated land, but they did become the residual claimants on all output in excess of the contracted quotas. This reform was similar to China's HRS, which was introduced in the late 1970s. Two years later, the government introduced the 1988 Land Law, which mandated the breakup of the agricultural collectives, the allocation of land to households by administrative means, and the liberalization of output markets. The 1993 Land Law introduced official land titles and permitted any kind of land transaction (Ravallion and van de Walle 2008, 180). Although land remained the property of the state, usage rights could be legally transferred, exchanged, mortgaged, and inherited. In transferring most of the control over the land to the farmer, the 1990s reforms sought to raise productivity by allowing transactions to improve allocation among users and the consolidation of very small plots, and by promoting better access to credit. Sales to the government at below market price were ended in 1990, with a view to raising incentives. Contract duration, initially fifteen years, was extended to twenty years in 1993. When they did get started, the market-oriented reforms were implemented faster than were their Chinese counterparts. Each reform was, in part, the legalization of already frequent customs, although collective practices were not ended. The state did maintain tight control over which items were produced, with implementation by the communal authorities. A much-debated 1998 resolution removed restrictions on the size of landholdings and on the hiring of agricultural labor. Economic efficiency was clearly the primary objective of these reforms, which were admitted to have their risks.[53] While freeing up land markets is widely expected to promote economic efficiency, policy-makers in communist countries have worried that it would encourage capitalism by re-creating a rural proletariat of poor workers. This concern has, for example, inhibited the liberalization of agricultural land markets in China.

Judged not only by the growth of agricultural output, but also by overall economic growth, poverty reduction, and the level of inequality, the Vietnamese reforms of the 1980s and onward have been a major success. Breaking up the collectives and returning to family-based farming quickly put an end to the food crisis. After decades of decline or, at best, stagnation, a persistent upward trend in the per capita availability of food grains got underway. After the policy switch, agricultural growth averaged an impressive 3.6 percent from 1987 to 2019 (World Bank, n.d.). The sector's share of

[53] The still poorly developed markets for other inputs were likely to limit the efficiency gains from simply freeing up land transactions alone. Pervasive market failures fueled by imperfect information and high transaction costs could have stalled the process of efficiency-enhancing land reallocations during the transition. And there were concerns about their fostering rising inequality.

GDP dropped from forty to forty-five percent to fourteen percent as overall growth surged at an average of 6.75 percent per year and the economy rapidly diversified.

The record on income inequality appears equally impressive. Between the final communist victory in 1975 and the beginning of the pro-market reform process in the 1980s, it may be presumed that inequality remained relatively low.[54] Judging by the reasonably comparable estimates available since 1992/1993, this period has not seen much change either.[55] Dwayne Benjamin and colleagues (2017, 32) judge that inequality, whether of per capita income or of per capita consumption, changed surprisingly little from 2002 to 2014 given the major structural changes underway in the economy and the high rate of growth.[56] Rural income inequality rose moderately—the Gini increasing from 0.341 to 0.365, while its urban counterpart experienced a more marked decline from 0.365 to 0.313. These offsetting trends, combined with a reduction in the gap between rural and urban incomes—a major contrast with the Chinese story—account for the stability and slight decline overall.[57] The combination of dramatically high growth and relatively stable inequality meant that poverty fell dramatically, from 66.4 percent in 1993 to 19.8 percent in 2006 in rural areas, and from 58.1 percent to 15.9 percent overall.

That inequality should have remained at low to modest levels since the 1970s is a matter of importance, given the central role played in Vietnam's nineteenth- and twentieth-century political history by the sensitivity of low-income people to unacceptable shocks perpetrated by the economic elites or

[54] Considerable attention has, however, been directed to gender inequality, which is not reflected in the standard figures.

[55] Although McCaig, Benjamin, and Brandt (2009) suggest that the Gini coefficient of per capita income inequality fell sharply between 1993 (at 0.450) and 2002 (0.378), their consumption inequality figures show the opposite trend, from 0.326 to 0.365. The enormous gap between these two Gini coefficients in 1993, and the sizeable one in 1998, appear to be implausible, giving weight to the idea that the story told by the consumption figures is the more accurate one. World Bank figures agree with the interpretation that there was little change in the Gini coefficient for income between 1992 and 2002.

[56] The Gini coefficient for the former was 0.375 in 2002 and 0.360 in 2014, although it had reached 0.396 in 2010, while that for per capita consumption was 0.342 in 2002 and 0.336 in 2014, after hitting a peak of 0.38 in 2010.

[57] Most of the rising rural income inequality derives from different group outcomes, such as that between the Kinh majority and ethnic minorities. Although incomes rose for minority households, they grew more slowly than for the Kinh. Moreover, inequality rose more within the ethnic minorities than within the Kinh. Understanding rural inequality dynamics therefore requires further research on the determinants of the livelihoods of minority households. On the other hand, migration across locations has played a role in decreasing the importance of location for income (Benjamin et al. 2017, 44).

the rules they applied. Even if it was not particularly high by world standards, in such a low-income agricultural economy those toward the bottom of the hierarchy are especially vulnerable, permanently engaged in security-oriented behavior, and highly sensitive to changes that put them at risk.

Both economic and political explanations have been advanced to explain why inequality has apparently remained at low to moderate levels in the wake of the market reforms of the 1980s. On the former front, the continuing relative equality of land-based earnings has no doubt been a significant factor, especially in the earlier years of this period. Crops remained a substantial share of total national income—forty percent in 1993 and 25.9 percent in 2006.[58] A relatively equal distribution of education, especially in the North, also played a role, as did the fact that many families were able to supplement their farm earnings with income from other activities. Additional likely factors include a rapidly increasing ratio of labor-intensive exports to GDP.[59]

Considerable debate has arisen around how well the various market-oriented reform steps were designed and what role they played in the equitable growth that followed. In their detailed statistical analyses of the 1988 and 1993 reforms, Martin Ravallion and Dominique van de Walle (2008) probe several questions, including (i) how close did the land allocation in 1988 bring Vietnam to an equitable allotment, similar to the sort sought by the 1954 redistributive reform immediately after the War of Independence from France; (ii) whether this allocation came at a large cost in terms of aggregate efficiency; and (iii) how things evolved subsequently when the land market was freed up in 1993 and, in particular, whether the market-based reallocation of land raised inequality as well as efficiency? Their analysis is, to my knowledge, the most detailed to date around these important questions.

Both the initial allocation of land and other assets in 1988, and the timing and details of the subsequent freeing of markets, reflected a concern with equity as well as efficiency. The need to avoid extreme inequality was coupled with the worry that an overly egalitarian allocation would leave too much land in the hands of relatively unproductive farmers. Given the decentralized character of the reform's implementation, there was also concern about possible capture by local elites, an apprehension subsequently heightened by the considerable number of local protests against their actions. Ravallion and van de Walle (2008, 176) conclude that such capture was not great, noting

[58] McCaig et al. (2009, table 11).

[59] For a perspective on likely future trends from around 2000, see Fritzen (2002).

that judged by "its impact on average consumption and consumption inequality, the observed allocation of land was roughly equivalent to giving every household in the commune the same irrigated-land equivalent per person" and had a significantly more equitable outcome than one would have expected from a competitive privatization at market-clearing prices. Such an outcome suggests a successful effort to protect the poorest and reduce overall inequality at the expense of some loss of aggregate output and consumption. That the land allocation did not unduly favor households with government or semi-government jobs[60] may be explained in part by a sort of pro-reform coalition between the farmers and the reformers in the central government to prevent local capture during the decentralized allocation. The farmers, direct losers from the collective system and the source of much resistance against it, desired a reform that they saw as fair. The central government helped to shift the balance of local power around the time of the reform by actively promoting farmers' organizations and using the press to channel complaints and expose corruption. The memory of previous redistributive land reforms undertaken before collectivization (such as the South's land-to-the-tiller program introduced in 1970) may also have helped to define a relatively equitable standard.

The 1993 law that fostered free transactions in land-use rights was designed partly to guard against a possible rise in inefficiency after the initial equitable allocation, but was accompanied by the concern that, even given such an egalitarian starting point, market mechanisms might generate excessive inequality in the distribution of land and of rural living standards. In any event, the same features that helped ensure an initially equitable allocation may have moderated any disequalizing effects created by the new market forces. Other policy reforms that provided new opportunities for diversification and growth, such as the increasingly outward orientation, no doubt also affected the legacy of the agrarian reforms.

Ravallion and van de Walle (2008) do conclude that land transfers after the 1993 law were successful in attenuating the initial inefficiencies resulting from the 1988 administrative assignment by moving land from less efficient to more efficient producers and thereby raising total production. The adjustment was

[60] This conclusion seems to be at odds with the frequent reports of abuse by local officials. A limited number of large deviations from the efficient allocation do show up and could reflect such misbehavior, such as in some of the "hot spots" which experienced protests against alleged abuse of power by local elites in the late 1980s and 1990s. But the evidence suggests that such abuses were not frequent.

not rapid, with an average of one-third of the initial gap between the actual allocation and a maximally efficient one being eliminated over five years; it was quicker for those households that started with the least cropland relative to the "efficient amount" for them.[61] The market-driven correction also proceeded more effectively for households with long-term roots in the community, male heads, better education, and more land in other (non-annual crop) categories. As the authors note, these findings tend to contradict the common view that land markets are very thin in developing rural economies, locking small landholders out of the credit market and preventing their acquisition of more land.[62] The Vietnamese setting was indeed unusual; Ravallion and van de Walle (2008) suspect that, even as late as the 1990s, the history of landlord suppression back in the 1950s would have made most farmers wary of appearing to hold large, unproductive holdings. Local governments may also have helped to make the land market work better for the poor; cadres (particularly in the North) continued to reallocate land in some communes and were undoubtedly reluctant to let a landless proletariat emerge in their villages, even though this did happen in a minority of cases. Faster adjustment for the land poor may have reflected their greater desire to get more land or the fact that markets work better in situations where nearly everyone has the same amount of land, comparable access to credit, and so forth. Market imperfections would naturally be expected to be greater when the potential number of families with whom one may trade is smaller because of a wide difference in the amount of land families have.

The authors were unable to reach a conclusion as to whether the more efficient land distribution brought by the free land market raised inequality, as expected by some. The very rapid rate of poverty reduction suggests that even if post-1993 re-allocation of land did play a negative role on that front, its impacts were greatly outweighed by other poverty-reducing processes at work. The years after the reforms did see an increase in the share of landless agricultural households, from 8.4 percent of the rural population in 1993 to 13.6 percent in 2004 (Akram-Lodhi 2010, 571). This fact's implications have generated considerable debate and concern. How landlessness fits into the picture is complicated. Ravallion and Van de Walle (2008, 179) report

[61] The information on a family's labor supply and the efficiency of its farming activities allowed the authors to estimate how much land that family should have for the distribution of land among all families to maximize total value of output.

[62] Government efforts to make credit more available had some considerable success, as the share of agricultural families receiving formal credit rose from was 21.7 percent in 1993 to 35.6 percent in 2004 (Ravallion and van de Walle 2008, 161).

that its frequency rose among the poor and that this group was responsible for most of the increase. But in absolute terms such post-reform landlessness was higher for the rural non-poor. Typically, it was not the currently poor who responded to the new opportunities for selling (or buying) land and acquiring land titles; instead, it was the relatively well off. Access to formal credit appears to have improved overall, although more markedly for better-off households; it seems to have partially displaced informal credit. Meanwhile, the poor experienced the highest rate of urbanization, a standard pathway out of poverty in a fast-growing economy. The authors find little evidence that rising landlessness undermined the gains to the poor from the relatively equitable assignment of land-use rights achieved at the time of decollectivization.

"Even in the South's Mekong Delta—where there are signs of class differentiation—poverty has been falling among the landless, albeit at a lower rate than for those with land. However, we find no sign that this pattern is emerging elsewhere in Vietnam; indeed, as a rule, the landless are enjoying similar (or even higher) rates of poverty reduction as those with land. On the whole, rising rural landlessness appears to be a positive factor in the process of poverty reduction, as farm households take up new opportunities, notably in the labor market" (Ravaillon and van de Walle, 2008, 179-180).[63]

Vietnam's case has been one of the most interesting and important experiences of an agrarian reform building a dynamic small-farm system; it provides a recent and dramatic example of success on all fronts, like Japan, Korea, and Taiwan only a half-century earlier. The shift from collectivization brought large gains in agricultural production while also preserving, or

[63] Akram-Lodhi (2010), in contrast, interprets rising landlessness as a negative outcome, and emphasizes the need to look not just at land but at other agricultural assets as well. He also draws attention to possible problems with the data. Reputable Vietnamese academics conducting fieldwork when the Living Standards Measurement Study (LSMS) was being implemented have reported that the local authorities in charge distributed the surveys to senior members within the community, who completed them, rather than interviewing the households: "The surveys were then returned to the local authorities and the results reviewed in order to ensure consistency with data that are routinely relayed to provincial statistical offices. In the process, some quite significant irregularities may have been generated; for example, it has been suggested that the extent of rural diversification and rural non-farm employment was significantly overstated. Of course, it must be stressed that these reports may be anecdotal, which would not undermine the validity of the LSMS. However, it should be noted that the LSMS suggests that most land is rented out at no charge; but in the fieldwork that I have conducted in more than twelve provinces over a ten-year period this has not been witnessed" (Akram-Lodhi 2010, 571). While they appear not to be serious enough to place great doubt on the output and inequality trends indicated by the official data, these concerns highlight a need for further probing.

even advancing, equality within that sector. It also set the stage for a dramatic burst of aggregate economic growth, during which, like those three countries—but unlike China and Russia—it has generally retained a low level of overall inequality. This combination led to a dramatic drop in the rate of poverty, which was still very high in 1993 when nearly two-thirds of the population fell below the poverty line, and concentrated in the countryside where 70.9 percent were classified as poor compared to 39.8 percent in the cities. By 2006, only 6.5 percent of the national population was so classified—8.4 percent of the rural population and 1.2 percent of the urban (McCaig et al. 2009, sec. 10).[64]

The post-1990 reform steps appear to have been very well chosen. The initial allocation in 1988 provided a high degree of equality, which, in turn, offered a good base from which the introduction of a free market in land could provide positive results. Accepting this positive take on Vietnam's experience leaves the important question of why its inequality trend has diverged so much from that of China, another single-party regime with a broadly similar agrarian reform experience. Both economic and political/institutional factors appear to have been at work. On the former front, Vietnam has benefited from a greater ability of rural households to access off-farm opportunities, especially in small and medium enterprises, and from the ability of those staying in agriculture to shift to higher value crops. Lower barriers to entry of new firms and fewer restrictions on individual mobility—in contrast to China's *hukou* system—have also probably been important. Better access to labor markets and wage earnings have helped to keep inequality down in Vietnam, whereas in China the inequality of those earnings has increased significantly, especially as a result of widening differences in educational attainment and widening income gaps by level of education, especially at the university level (Benjamin et al. 2017, 43).

Edmund Malesky and colleagues (2011) highlight differences in elite political institutions between the two countries, arguing that those in Vietnam force greater accountability upon the leadership, resulting in higher equalizing transfers across provinces. Vietnam features broader and more diverse governing coalitions; critical economic decisions are taken in its 160-member Central Committee, while China has relied primarily on its twenty-four-member Politburo. In addition, Vietnam has greater electoral

[64] These figures differ slightly from those cited above (Benjamin et al. 2017) due to modifications made subsequently by the authors.

competition for leadership positions both within and outside the party. It does so through more open nominating procedures, direct elections of the general secretary, and higher candidate-to-seat ratios. These differences arose in the late 1980s and resulted in a diffusion of political authority in Vietnam and a concentration in China. A critical distinction between the two regimes is the percentage of their budgets devoted to public spending, especially to the large-scale expenditures in poorer jurisdictions known as equalizing transfers, which go toward education, infrastructure, social welfare, and poverty alleviation programs. Such transfers represent six percent of the GDP in Vietnam but only two percent in China. In 2006, these transfers were two hundred percent larger than locally produced revenue in the median Vietnamese province and over seven hundred percent in the poorest, suggesting a significant redistributive effect.

## Cuba

In the lead-in to its 1959 revolution Cuba was, like Chile, one of the higher-income, more urbanized countries of Latin America. Under thirty percent of employment was found in agriculture, which was heavily focused on sugar. The large US presence was concentrated in that industry, as well as in electricity and oil. Employment on the sugar plantations was mainly wage labor, with a large share of seasonal sugarcane cutters coming from urban areas. There were only about forty thousand peasant farmers (Ghai, Kay, and Peek 1988).The goal of a series of laws implemented between 1959 and 1963 was to break up large holdings and to transfer the land to the peasants who worked it, to cooperatives, and to the state. The 1959 agrarian reform law focused on small, independent farmers. A 1963 bill established a maximum of sixty-seven hectares that could be held by one person; by this time about seventy percent of arable land had been expropriated. Castro's government gave ownership to an estimated 160,000 tenants, sharecroppers, and squatters. The plantation sector was taken over by the state. With time, the original state farms were amalgamated into even larger units, eventually becoming giant agro-industrial complexes. That model fostered the use of advanced technology with a high level of purchased inputs, which helped to raise the output of sugarcane and other crops typically produced on a large scale.

Almost two decades after the revolution, the government initiated a campaign to encourage peasants to form agricultural and livestock cooperatives

(CPAs); within a decade, over two-thirds had done so, despite having earlier resisted being incorporated into state farms. CPAs outperformed state farms, provided an example to them, and eventually led to the latter's transformation (Kay 1988b, 20). Not long thereafter, however, the break-up and economic crisis of the Soviet Union, Cuba's major source of aid and trade, altered the setting drastically by decreasing availability of some inputs and raising the price of food. In 1993, the government implemented another reform, which decentralized production and shifted it toward smaller-scale operations, transferring many state farms to their workers who then became the new collective owners of these Basic Units of Cooperative Production (UBPCs), modeled after the CPAs. In the face of this change, the CPAs and small-scale farmers, previously thought of as less modern and efficient, now showed themselves to be more resilient and adaptive by shifting back toward some more traditional techniques and by innovating new low-input ones. The need to increase the food supply also led the government to make land available to interested urban dwellers and to transfer up to thirteen hectares of idle rural land to individual small farmers.

As in the other communist countries previously discussed, a broad majority of the rural population appeared to benefit from the post-revolutionary restructuring of agriculture, part of a major and permanent overhaul of society; in Cuba, unlike the Soviet Union and China, that impact on equality carried into the long term as well. Unlike them, expropriated land came mainly from large agro-industrial corporations—a good number of them American—and very few people lost their lives. Cuba's agrarian reform strengthened the Castro regime; it was, unsurprisingly, popular. But the country's post-reform growth was far weaker than that of the other communist countries, especially China and Vietnam. World Bank data on per capita GDP show a decent average increase of two percent per year from 1970 to 2020; population growth averaged about 0.5 percent and GDP growth averaged about 2.5 percent.[65] Growth was presumably slowed somewhat by US sanctions but sped up by USSR support. It is hard to judge the longer-term impact on the modest number of immediate beneficiaries of the reform. The modest growth of per capita income was accompanied by the development of very impressive health and education systems (Birn et al.

[65] Although many countries grew faster over this period, few had slower rates of population growth. Thus Brazil, whose GDP grew at an average of 3.3 percent per year, had a population growth rate of 1.7 percent, with the result that its per capita GDP grew more slowly than Cuba's, at just 1.7 percent.

2009; Gasperini 1999). The notable health system has been reflected in the country's relatively high life expectancy of 78.3 years, only 1.5 years below that of the US.

## Appendix 5.1

### What Explains China's Sharp Rise in Income Inequality after the 1970s?

As noted above, factors contributing to the dramatic increase in income inequality from its very low level in the 1970s are large and rising income gaps between urban and rural residents and between the coastal provinces favored by trade liberalization and foreign investment, and the rest of the country; a rising dispersion of educational attainment together with and a rising income differential by level of education; and a rising share of income accruing to capital or derived from corruption/grey income. Each of these interacting factors invites an analysis of what lies behind it, either in terms of the structure of the economy and/or of government policy, to better understand the lessons this post-land reform reversal on the inequality front may have for other reforming countries. What links, if any, does each have to the agrarian reform?

On the policy front, the major shift since the revolution has been the increase in the role of markets, a transition dating to the early post-Mao years with the arrival of President Deng as the key decision-maker, and encouraged by the tightening of the labor market and the difficulty enterprises had in recruiting. It includes a major entry into global markets. Because this transition tracks the reversal from low to high inequality, it is usually presumed to have contributed to the latter. Its importance is best judged after reviewing the factors directly at work to gauge how and to what extent it was responsible for each of them.

One important scenario has indeed been the labor market. When China's inequality was at its low point in the mid-1970s, the earnings differentials across levels of education were very small compared to that of capitalistic countries; they have risen sharply since then. Another major contributing factor to the currently very high inequality has been the large—by some estimates enormous—urban–rural income gap, a gap that, after an initial reduction under Communist rule, rebounded sharply. A prime contributing factor has been the inability of people to move as they please within the country—a feature of the former systems of serfdom. Since the educational gap between urban and rural areas has widened from the 1980s onward, these two factors have reinforced each other. Thus, although the land reform was part of an initially equalizing set of structural changes, the rural population has slipped farther behind the urban one since the pro-market reforms of the 1980s. The societal tradition of an urban superiority complex has presumably contributed to this outcome.

The underlying goal of limiting rural-to-urban migration to the level deemed necessary to implement the industrialization strategy[66] has been enforced through the

[66] Control of migration reduced the amount the state needed to invest in urban infrastructure. Rural industrialization through subcontracting was seen as a partial offset.

household registration (*hukou*) system—which in principle sets the number of urban households, rations food, and allocates urban housing. Without urban registry a household has restricted access to public services, such as education and health care, and its members typically wind up with lower-paying jobs. Despite the restrictions, the share of urban to total population has risen rapidly, from about twenty percent in the late 1970s to fifty-four percent by 2015; the stock of rural–urban migrants has increased rapidly from less than five million in 1978 to more than 250 million by about 2015, accounting for fifteen percent of the total population and over a quarter of the urban population. Some levers of control were dropped or loosened during the pro-market reform period as urban enterprises demanded more workers for the relatively unskilled jobs that urban residents did not want. Still, the *hukuo* and other institutional and social barriers have both kept migration far below its natural level given the country's rapid development[67] and also prevented those who migrate without urban *hukou* from doing as well as they otherwise would have.

It is generally accepted that the reduced flow of migrants due to the restraints has contributed to the large rural–urban earnings gap, which is further accentuated by subsidies to urban dwellers and by the inability of farm families to either use sale of their land to facilitate a move to an urban area or use its continued ownership as insurance against the economic risks entailed in such movement. The migration barriers also accentuate the gap between the earnings of "migrants" living in urban areas and urban "natives." As well as helping to maintain and probably enlarge the inequality gap between urban and rural residents, the compromise solution of allowing more and more migrants without *hukou* has been very disruptive of family life. At the time of its implementation, the potential of this control system to contribute greatly to inequality probably escaped nearly all of those decisionmakers whose goal was to cut poverty and inequality. By the time its impact was becoming clear, policy was, in any case, less equity-oriented than before.

The issue here is how large a role the very high rural–urban income gap has played in the rise of income inequality. According to official statistics, the average urban-to-rural income ratio[68] has been one of the highest in the world, at over 3.0 during the first decade of this century. Between 1978 and 1983, it fell from 2.5 to 1.8, the lowest level of the past four decades and a reflection of the Chinese government's replacement of collective farming with the household responsibility system in 1978 and its raising of agricultural prices. These two policies were mainly responsible for the very rapid growth of rural incomes. Since then, the ratio rose nearly continuously to a peak of 3.3 from 2006 to 2009, and then fell slightly in the following years (Zhou and Song 2016, 6). During this whole period, absolute incomes have been rising rapidly in both rural and urban areas. Given the speed of urban income growth during China's three-decade economic boom, it would have been extremely difficult for the rural incomes to keep up. Between 2002 and 2007, for example, rural incomes grew at an average annual rate of more than seven percent, but urban ones were rising at eleven percent (Sicular 2013). Still, the *hukou* system, the failure to provide land ownership rights to farmers, and other policies no doubt did contribute to the expanding income gap.

[67] The special arrangements governing Chinese land may also act as a constraint on migration. Farm households only have land-use rights, but they cannot sell their land.

[68] Defined in China as the ratio of per capita disposable income of urban households to per capita net income of rural ones.

Understanding the role of this gap in accentuating overall inequality is restricted by ambiguities in the evidence, both as to exactly how large it is (due to standard measurement problems), and to how it has moved over time, at least since migration without *hukou* became a major phenomenon from the 1990s onward. Most such migrants are still counted as rural households because they are registered that way, even though they live in urban areas. This leads to misestimates of the urban–rural gap because the income of these rural migrants is not included in either the official rural or the official urban household income surveys (except to the extent that their remittances are reported by the receiving rural household). Jinjun Xue and Wenshu Gao (2012) suggest that the gap may be overstated by as much as forty percent, in which case the 3.3 figure for 2006 to 2009 would fall to about 2.3, a little below the official figure of 2.5 for both 1978 and 1998. The rural–urban gap would then contribute substantially less to (actual) national inequality than present estimates suggest, and its rise would contribute less to the increase in that inequality level.[69] Still, economic logic suggests that the constraints on movement must contribute significantly both to overall inequality and to the urban–rural gap.[70] Even if the gap is somewhat overestimated, it is likely high by international standards. The structure of the migration control system is consistent with a significant upward impact on the urban–rural gap; while overstated due to the cited data problem, that gap is understated because of subsidies that favor urban dwellers in the form of better pensions, better health system, and so on. In any case, it is, at best, one part of the story of increasing inequality in China, as both rural and urban inequality have shown an upward trend since 1978 (Xue 2012).

## Regional Factors

China exhibits enormous spatial disparities in economic activities, natural resource endowments, local government policies, and other factors affecting income levels and economic growth; many studies conclude that these factors have contributed to the rising inequality.[71] Some suggest that a rise in regional inequality can be attributed to trade liberalization (initiated in the 1980s) and to fiscal decentralization (Kanbur and Zhang 2005). Freer trade enabled the coastal provinces to exploit their geographic advantages as well as benefit from preferential treatment (e.g., through the creation of export processing zones). This regional element interacts with the rural–urban gap because the coastal provinces are more urban than the inland ones. Like the urban–rural gap itself, its effect may be exaggerated due to the cited measurement issue related to the *hukou*, as GDP per

[69] Their estimates refer to the provinces of Zhejiang and Shaanxi. Note that the overall increase in the national Gini coefficient will have been somewhat exaggerated due to this measurement problem. Other factors, like the non-inclusion of "grey income," will probably work much more strongly in the other direction.

[70] Inclusion of the non-*hukou* migrants fully into the figures would have an unknown (pending more data) effect on national per capita income. With the families of migrants included in the rural population (as they are now supposed to be), inclusion of their full urban-based income would raise their reported incomes.

[71] According to Hao and Zheng (2009), income inequality between inland and coastal regions grew rapidly throughout the 1980s. They find that inland–coastal inequality accounted for more than sixty percent of income inequality across Chinese provinces in 2000, making it the largest contributor to inter-provincial inequality.

capita is understated in migrant-sender provinces and overstated in migrant-receiving ones. After carefully addressing this issue, Chao Li and John Gibson (2013) conclude that, when this factor is taken into account, Chinese economic reform does not appear to have been associated with rising regional income inequality after all.[72] The issue remains to be settled.

## Education

Among the main direct causes of rising income inequality has been a rapid transformation in education's role in it between the 1970s, when the income advantage it provided was very modest, and the last couple of decades, by which time it had become large and similar to that of a typical capitalist country. The amount of "human capital" has also grown rapidly over the reform period; the illiteracy rate fell from 33.6 percent in 1982 to 4.9 percent in 2013, and the number of regular undergraduate and college graduates per year exploded from 0.17 million to 6.25 million. The dramatic increase in the inequality of labor earnings reflects the combination of a rising dispersion of educational levels and a sharp increase in the income differentials associated with level of education. Returns from an additional year have risen from being very low in the 1970s to something much higher now; they were still increasing over the first decade of this century. Compared to people with junior high school or less, graduates from senior high school, technical school, and college earned four percent, seven percent, and fourteen percent more, respectively, in 1998; by 2009, these gaps had jumped to eighteen percent, thirty-two percent, and sixty-one percent, respectively (Meng et al. 2013).[73] There is also a great disparity in the quantity and quality of education that urban and rural children receive and a gap between the attainment of the children of migrant workers and of urban residents (Golley and Kong 2013). A 1980s wave of reforms in educational finance and curriculum increased the barriers to social mobility for rural children (Hannum 1999, 202). The reimplementation of a dual-tiered system crystallized class boundaries along urban–rural lines for school-aged cohorts of the 1980s and on. Especially now, with a high share of children attending university and having a degree, the *hukou* system plays importantly into a pattern of great inequality between rural and urban children by determining who is able to attend and who has access to a high-quality institution.

Another increasingly powerful phenomenon is the inter-generational transmission of education within the household. It tends to reproduce educational inequality, and, with it, income inequality, over the generations. By one estimate, whereas about seventy-five percent of urban children go to university, the corresponding share for rural children is just fifteen percent.[74] Cronyism is another part of the institutional structure determining who gets to go where.

[72] Li and Gibson (2013) conclude that regional inequality in terms of the GDP declined almost continuously during 1978 and 1990. About one-third of this decline was reversed over the next three years in the early 1990s. Regional inequality fluctuated thereafter and by 2010, the measure was back at the low levels previously seen in 1990.

[73] If the average difference in the number of years attained by a college graduate compared to someone with a junior high and below education was eight, this would correspond to an average income gain of about six percent for each additional year of education.

[74] *The Economist*, May 29, 2021.

Changing gaps across the population in the levels of education or the human capital gained from it have clearly been important in the country's rising inequality. One contributing mechanism may be the increasing share of national income going to capital and its implications.

## Corruption and Grey Income

Widespread corruption affects both actual and measured inequality, which differ because "grey income" [75] (e.g., the "collection" by some officials of huge amounts of money at the weddings of their children and relatives) is likely to be both unequally distributed and underreported.[76] Using an indirect method to gauge the grey income of Chinese households by income level,[77] Xiaolu Wang and WingTthye Woo (2011) estimate that, as of 2008, the share of income unreported rose from about eleven percent for the lowest income group to nearly seventy percent for the highest group, and was about forty percent overall—a high figure compared to estimates for other countries (whose numbers, of course, also involve much guesswork). With the top ten percent of urban households taking in sixty-three percent of all unreported income by these estimates, their estimated income was sixty-five times that of the poorest ten percent, in contrast to the ratio of twenty-three reported in the official data. If Wang and Woo (2011) are fairly accurate in their analysis, this grey component of income contributes strongly to the urban–rural gap and it implies that this gap is less overstated than the above-cited data problems resulting from the *hukou* system suggest, or perhaps even understated. Even if unreported income were half as high as their estimate, it would still suggest a substantially higher level of inequality because it is distributed so unequally.

Part of the rising role of grey income has no doubt reflected an increasing share coming from corruption, financial and real estate speculation, and favoritism in access to rents from public property.[78] It is probable that these forms of capital-related income have become more concentrated over time, but even if they have not, their rising share of total income has been disequalizing because capital incomes accrue to people higher in the income distribution.

[75] The latter term, coined in China, refers to income that the government does not officially know about and on which the recipient has not paid taxes.

[76] As of 2009, the World Bank's Worldwide Governance Indicators ranked China 148th on "control of corruption" and 220th on "voice and accountability" out of 235 countries (Knight 2013).

[77] Using urban household income and expenditure data collected in their own surveys, they estimate how the share of expenditure on food varies with reported income level to estimate the grey income of the households.

[78] The speculative profits arising in a situation of feverishly fast growth coupled with crony capitalism bring high levels of corruption, apparent in all levels of government. The state continues to hold residual property rights to at least half of the net worth of the economy. Corruption has been made easy by the ill-defined property rights, decentralized administrative authority, and the absence of democratic checks and balances (e.g., an independent judiciary, a free press, or political competition). Unlike the USSR, large corruption associated with the disposition of formerly stated-owned companies has not been a big factor in China.

## Functional Distribution of Income: The Rising Capital Share and Its Causes

The capital share in national income in China has increased sharply over the period of fast growth while the share of low-skilled labor has fallen; Zhou and Song (2016, 13) estimate that the former rose from about forty-five percent in 1995 to nearly sixty percent in 2009.[79] It is a contributing factor directly or indirectly, through the sources previously discussed, to the rise of inequality. A broad interpretation is that the rapid increase in the capital share reflects China's "capital-oriented" model, which, compared to most countries at similar levels of development, has given greater emphasis to capital and technology-intensive activities and less to labor intensive ones.[80] The tendency has various roots, among them a greater need for economic independence (e.g., an ability to produce high technology defense-related equipment) than other developing countries, and a proclivity toward larger firms. In the post-agricultural phase of development, China has more or less retained the orientation to large size, which it eventually gave up in the agricultural sector. Like Taiwan, it initially had considerable activity in labor-intensive export industries, but then moved more quickly toward capital-intensive ones. In non-agriculture, large monopolies brought relative capital-intensity in the choice of technology, together with monopoly profits, higher salaries than received in other firms,[81] and the capacity for more financial corruption that characterizes larger firms.

Very fast growth may itself promote a high capital share as many new entrepreneurial opportunities are opened up, creating high capital incomes, at least for a period, while wages tend to lag behind. It could thus be argued that the rapid increase in inequality, due partly to the very fast growth and to the rapid increase in educational inequality, was also a result of the pivoting toward a more private-based management of the economy in which some large state enterprises morphed into large private ones with resulting high levels of capital intensity and low use of labor relative to capital, and to the state's undertaking one major intervention to block market forces—the control of migration in one of the few areas where such forces would have brought a less unequal outcome than did state control.

[79] This is consistent with the findings of Piketty (2014) for many other countries showing the functional distribution of income moving in favor of capital owners at the expense of low-skilled and, to some extent, medium-skilled labor. According to Piketty, the fundamental cause of the rising income inequality globally is that the return to capital has been persistently higher than the growth rate of the economy, leading to an increasing share of capital and a decreasing share of wages in national income.

[80] Thus Piketty et al. (2019) note the sharp increase in net private wealth from 1978 to 2015, while net public wealth stayed about constant; the former's share of total net wealth rose from about thirty percent to about seventy percent. They argue that China's rapid growth has relied on a model that particularly rewards various forms of capital, including finance and real estate. Because income based on private wealth is much less evenly distributed than that from public wealth, this factor may have played a significant role in raising inequality of income.

[81] Thus Sicular and colleagues (2011) find that monopolistic industries (e.g., electricity) pay more than those that are competitive (e.g., textiles). By their calculation, this division accounts for 8.2 percent of the total income gap among workers; only differences in education emerge as a more important source of inequality.

# 6

# Land Reform under Capitalist Regimes in Twentieth-Century Latin America: Varying Degrees of Failure

Apart from Russia, China, and Vietnam, other twentieth-century agrarian revolutions or reforms occurring by the 1960s were those of Mexico and Bolivia in Latin America and of Iran and Egypt in the Middle East. A serious attempt at reform was initiated in Guatemala, and later ones occurred in Chile, Peru, Nicaragua, and El Salvador. Various Indian states have also pursued reforms. Within Sub-Saharan Africa (SSA), those of Ethiopia and Zimbabwe have been notable. Each experience provides lessons on the conditions conducive to significant benefits.

Much of the interest in and study of Latin America's twentieth-century reforms reflect the severe inequalities and injustices that characterized their agrarian systems, and the associated hope that correcting them could greatly enhance the population's welfare. Although all shared a history of extremely concentrated landholding, their experiences varied in many other ways, including the nation's stage of social and economic development when reform was attempted.

Two features common to many of the region's countries were a large amount of land—unlike China, Vietnam, or most Asian countries—and a strong racial divide between the descendants of the Spanish or Portuguese conquerors and the indigenous peoples and those of African descent. The former condition provided the setting for the very extensive use of much of the land on large farms and the latter helped to shape the various forms of servitude and abuse which arose. Although, as elsewhere, land quality varies greatly within most of the countries, which makes measurement of its concentration complicated and imprecise, most estimates identify this as the highest land concentration region, with Gini coefficients typically falling in the range of 0.85–0.9 (see Table 6.1).

*The Great Curse.* Albert Berry, Oxford University Press. © Oxford University Press 2024.
DOI: 10.1093/oso/9780197782675.003.0007

**Table 6.1** Gini Coefficient Estimates of Land Concentration by Country

| Country | Gini coefficient and years | Average size (Hectares) |
|---|---|---|
| Colombia | 0.85–0.88 (1950s–2010s) | 23.3(1990) |
| Brazil | 0.83–0.86 (1950s–2010s) | 70.7(1980s) |
| Mexico | 0.75(1960–1970s) | 41.4(1980s) |
| Costa Rica | 0.78–0.84(1960s–1970s) | 38.3 (1970) |
| Kenya | 0.77–0.82 (1960s–1980s) | 2.5(1980s) |
| Tanzania | (0.79) (1960s) | 2.8(1990) |
| Senegal | (0.40–0.50) (1960s–1990s) | 3.6(1980s) |
| India | 0.59–0.68 (1950–2010s) | 2.0(1977) |
| Taiwan(post-reform) | (0.40–0.47) (1960s) | |
| Korea(pre-reform) | 0.72 | |
| Korea(post-reform) | (0.30–0.38) | 0.9(1980s) |
| China(pre-revolution) | 0.70(1930s) | |
| China(post-revolution) | 0.19–0.21 (1970s–1980s) | <1(1980s) |

The enormous size gap between the largest and the smallest farms (whether these latter are owned, held in tenancy, or provided by the landowner for the production of food) has usually meant that they are farmed very differently. Large holdings have tended to underuse the land by farming it in an extensive manner and often leaving a significant proportion uncultivated. Small farms (*minifundios*) have been very intensively farmed. By the 1950s and early 1960s, when systematic measurement of productivity began, output per agricultural worker was typically five to ten times higher on *latifundios* than on *minifundios*, while production per hectare of agricultural land was roughly three to five times higher on the *minifundios* than on *latifundios* (Barraclough 1973). Drawing on such evidence, some proponents of agrarian reform argued that land productivity could be increased more easily by redistributing land than by making costly investments in modern technology, which might also displace labor. Reform was also expected to leave a better legacy on the income distribution front than a reliance on modern technology; worries about the impacts of such technology were accentuated by the fact that land tenure and labor structure had begun to change in worrisome ways prior to the implementation of most of the agrarian reforms (Kay 1998, 14).

The most far-reaching reforms were typically the outcome of social revolutions, as in the cases of Mexico (1917), Bolivia (1952), Cuba (1959), and Nicaragua (1979). A few significant reforms were undertaken by elected governments, including those of Chile during the Frei (from 1964 to 1970) and Allende (from 1970 to 1973) administrations, or by military regimes such as that of General Velasco Alvarado in Peru (from 1969 to 1975). Less wide-ranging efforts were typically the work of civilian governments. By the time most reforms took place, the countries had been experiencing gradual modernization of the *hacienda* system in the direction of capitalist agriculture. Accordingly, the social relations of production had also begun to change, with labor-service tenancies giving way to wage labor. Some landlords sold part of their estates to finance improvements on the remainder of their property, thereby advancing a process of "transformation from above" (Kay 1988a). This trend often gained further momentum as a result of agrarian reform. Ironically, many such reforms contributed more to the modernization of the *hacienda* system and its transformation into capitalist farming than to its elimination from below through the redistribution of land to peasants; in so doing, they accelerated an already established path from the traditional landlord system to agrarian capitalism more than they fostered the development of peasant farming (de Janvry 1981; Kay 1988a).

Like those involved in agricultural policy around the developing world, most of the designers of the Latin American reforms seriously underestimated the productive potential of the small peasant farm. They also underestimated the existing presence of peasant farming, such as sharecropping and labor-service tenancies, within large, landed estates.[1] The former weakness led them to downplay the potential of generalized peasant farming; the latter led them to underestimate the difficulties of organizing collective farming and the pressure that beneficiaries would exercise within collective enterprises for the expansion of their own family activities. The new managers of the collective reformed enterprises, generally appointed by the state, had far less authority over the beneficiaries than the landlords had before them and were thus unable to prevent the gradual erosion of the collective enterprise from within; the collectivist feature of the reformed sector was typically overstated and often more apparent than real. Thus, in Peru, about half the agricultural land of the reformed sector (collective and state farms) was in fact cultivated on an individual basis. In Chile and El Salvador, the figure was about one-fifth, and only in Cuba was it insignificant (Kay 1998, 9). This reflects the

[1] National census data generally failed to record, or to record accurately, the number of peasant tenant enterprises within the *hacienda* system, something Kay (1998, 9) refers to as the "internal peasant economy."

varying degrees of capitalist development and proletarization of the agricultural labor force in each of these countries before their respective reforms. Differences between types of pre-reform estates, such as plantations and *haciendas*, were also reflected in the character of post-reform enterprises. Thus, prior to expropriation, the large coastal sugar plantations in Peru were capitalized and employed largely wage labor, whereas the domestic-market-oriented *haciendas* of the highlands relied much more on tenant labor. A government initially oriented toward centralized and collective management systems found these much easier to set up on the expropriated sugar plantations than on the highland *haciendas*, where a process of "decollectivization" followed fairly soon (Kay 1998, 18–19). The socialist countries which opted initially for collective or state farming later assigned more authority to the individual farmer or to smaller groups by decree. In Latin America, the process of correcting the original error was more gradual and often informal in nature.

As has been common elsewhere, a number of Latin American governments implemented timid redistributive reforms and then failed to support the peasant sector to an adequate degree. Rhetoric dominated in cases where governments were either too weak to implement substantial reforms and/or had the underlying intention of promoting larger-scale capitalist farming.

## Mexico

### Revolution, Reform and Their Impacts

During the colonial era, Mexico's economic elite expropriated indigenous lands to convert them into *latifundia*. Over the nineteenth century, land concentration became extreme; the final phase of this process occurred under General Porfirio Díaz (1876–1880 and 1884–1911). As of the 1860s, most land was either in relatively self-sufficient *haciendas* or in small subsistence plots farmed by indigenous or mestizo people. Díaz saw this structure as a barrier to his goal of modernizing the country; the indigenous and mestizos were understood to be innately lazy, unproductive, and incapable of adapting to modern ways of producing or of responding to economic incentives. As in many other cases, this elite belief rested on the presumed inferiority of other races, and provided grounds for pushing ahead with what was essentially an enclosure movement that displaced many people and created a rural proletariat available for use on the large farms. Later, at the beginning of the tweniteth century, a burst of economic growth based on agricultural exports contributed to another wave of displacement and pushed the pre-reform land concentration to an astronomical level; the estimated Gini coefficient was 0.96.[2] Díaz planned to build Mexico's agricultural future around a modernized version of the existing *haciendas*. The extreme inequality and poverty associated with this concentration, together with the resentments of displaced farmers, served as the spark for the particularly bloody Mexican Revolution, which ended Díaz's long-standing dictatorship. A legacy of the Mexican Revolution was the agrarian reform from 1920 to 1950. As of 1910, about half of the rural population were debt peons working as resident laborers on *haciendas* and smaller *ranchos* under a variety of arrangements. Less than eleven thousand *hacienda* owners controlled fifty-seven percent of the national territory and held most of the fertile and irrigated land, while residents of free agricultural villages had land on the periphery, often on mountainsides and unirrigated flat areas (Albertus 2021, 9, citing Sanderson 1984, 18–19).

Díaz resigned and went into exile in 1911; pressures for revolution were intense during his last years in power and over the following decade, as both the economy and political order eroded. Falling living standards no doubt contributed to the revolutionary setting. In Tutino's (1986) interpretation, however, this factor must be accompanied by a sense of rage in the face of lost economic independence, together with the feeling that this loss is the fault of a visible elite or of the state and is not being compensated by a new source of income or mobility. Another catalyst may be a perception of state weakness or a division among the elites which could prevent a rapid and effective response to insurrection. These latter conditions were met during the transition from the Díaz dictatorship. The rural poor interpreted their worsening economic condition as the fault of the elites; new laws which denied peasants rights to their traditional common lands brought a rapid loss of autonomy, and many families were forced into an insecure position in which they combined farming on marginal lands with seasonal employment on the *latifundios*. Simultaneously with this set of conditions creating the potential for an explosion,[3] there emerged the so-called Regeneration movement, pushing for a grand renovation of Mexican society, including

[2] Eckstein et al. (1978, 2).

[3] Tutito compares the early twentieth-century revolution with the 1820 uprising under Hidalgo, which did not meet the cited conditions.

agrarian reform and education for all. It helped to promulgate the New Constitution of 1917. In 1929, what became the PRI (*Partido Revolucionario Institucional*-Institutional Revolutionary Party) was founded; from 1928 on, the presidential term was set at six years, without the possibility of more than one term—Díaz had ruled for twenty-seven consecutive years. Reflecting the dominant, albeit temporary, power attached to the presidency in this new system, each incumbent—rather than the party or its chief—selected his own successor. As it evolved over time, the party had little clear and sustained ideology beyond maintaining power; elections were held but the party was quite willing to rig them. Peruvian novelist and politician Vargas Llosa dubbed it the "perfect dictatorship." It balanced the interests of the different groups in society. Only in recent decades did it gradually morph into a three-party system in which vote rigging ceased to be the rule.

After a period of much violence between groups (mainly from 1910 to 1920), costing well over a million lives,[4] together with the onset of the Great Depression, Lázaro Cárdenas became president in 1934. He was a good conflict manager and his domestic stature rose when, after a dispute between the US-owned oil industry and the unions representing its workers, he nationalized it in 1938 without opposition from US President Roosevelt.[5] He dedicated much attention to agrarian reform. The party maintained political control for decades and, although suffering incompetence and much corruption at times, it did achieve a degree of continuity in agrarian policy and a few other areas. Reform was an ongoing political process, with new redistribution often the result of new protests (Assies 2006, 42, 45). Over several decades much land was transferred from large landholders (*terratenientes*) to *ejidatarios*, members of the traditional communal grouping of Mexican indigenous peoples. By 1970, after fifty years of such piece-meal redistribution, about half of the land under cultivation had been transferred (Eckstein

[4] Estimates of excess deaths during this period ranged from 1.0 to 3.5 million people, in a country with just fifteen million people at the time (McCaa 2001). The wide range reflects the notorious failings of Mexico's 1920 population census and the differing biases among those undertaking the estimates. McCaa (2001) concludes that the toll was around 1.5 million from 1910 to 1921, while there were an estimated 350,000 net emigrants and an estimated decline in births of almost six hundred thousand.

[5] In retaliation, the oil companies initiated a public relations campaign against Mexico, urging people to stop buying Mexican goods. Although many foreign governments did close their markets to Mexican oil, US President Roosevelt had just issued the Good Neighbor Policy, aiming to improve US–Latin American relations. Mexico did suffer—the peso was devalued and prices jumped by twenty percent. Soon thereafter, the Mexican treasury minister met secretly with an American intermediary to set up a barter deal also involving Germany. By 1940, the war in Europe guaranteed international demand for oil (Schuler 1999).

et al. 1978, 36). As of 1992, about half of the rural population, or 3.5 million families, lived in *ejidos* (Binder 2015).

Redistribution almost always faced heavy resistance from the large landholders, the Church, and other elements of the society. It slowed markedly after the Cárdenas administration, which achieved nearly half of all the redistribution undertaken through the 1950s. In most of the subsequent governments, the forces for reform were much weaker, while many regional and local politicians, together with many powerful private interests, opposed it strongly (Hamilton 1982, ch. 9). The normal pushback from the large landholders and other conservative forces was accompanied by that of some of the revolutionary generals who, after the conflict, had granted themselves *haciendas* as well as communal lands. Many military chiefs also started to use their troops to accumulate land by illegal eviction of peasants (Flores Perez 2015, 2).

Through it all, the land structure remained quite bimodal, and many of the *ejidos* were too small or located on land too poor to easily generate a good living. Apart from the redistribution itself, public policy favored the large farm sector in greater or lesser degree. Public investment was eventually provided to support the new "commercial agriculture," support that in the early PRI years would have been politically risky (Reynolds 1971, 153).

Cárdenas promoted the collective *ejido*—previously a rare institution—at least partly to justify the expropriation of large commercial estates (Knight 1994, 82). In fact, however, operation nearly always remained in the hands of the farmers themselves, a double benefit because it presumably brought greater efficiency than if the operation had been collective, and it avoided the corruption characteristic of such *ejidos*. Over time, the performance of the *ejido* sector depended on access to complementary resources and an adequate peasant organization and institutional setting.[6] The Cárdenas period saw relative success on both fronts; the failure of many *ejidos* was traceable to the lack of one or usually both of them. While the *ejido* provides a potentially useful framework for peasant organization, it is not a guarantee against political manipulation or other institutional deficiencies. Only in 1970 was a special agency established for *ejido* promotion and organization. Government support was typically deficient.[7] The sector was clearly disfavored relative

[6] See Eckstein et al. (1978) for a detailed analysis.

[7] Gates (1981) discusses in detail the problems that plagued the National Plan of Irrigation Works for Rural Development (*Plan Nacional de Obras de Riego para el Desarrollo Rural*) in the region of Campeche. Although she feels that it was a sincere attempt to support peasant agriculture, all of the

to the private one in terms of access to credit and other inputs (Heath 1992, 701), reflecting, in part, the prevalent idea that it was, by default, a sort of subsistence activity. As in many other cases, the political allies of the reform movement have had little confidence in the capacity of the *ejidatarios* and have behaved paternalistically toward them. Both *ejidatarios* and private borrowers have confronted the dirigisme approach of the National Credit Bank (*Banco Nacional de Credito Rural—Banrural*), founded in 1975, which decided what crops and inputs were appropriate for the farmer. As John Richard Heath (1992, 699) states:

> Moreover, until 1990 inputs such as seed, fertilizer and pesticides were provided in kind by *Banrural* on the assumption that loans would be misappropriated if farmers were given cash with which to purchase inputs. Partly in order to achieve scale economies in procurement, the bank operated with a standardized input package that was insensitive to regional variations in input requirements and prices. Farmers were thus given little opportunity to boost yields by carefully tailoring the input package to the precise needs of their land. They had little confidence in the quality of the inputs provided, preferring to buy from commercial manufacturers. To make matters worse, *Banrural* often failed to deliver inputs on time: farmers frequently complained that fertilizer and pesticides arrived too late in the crop cycle to be fully effective.

As elsewhere, there is plenty of evidence from Mexico that many small farmers can not only organize current production activities effectively but can also play an active role in technological advance. Thus, in a community in the state of Chiapas, small farmers modified an improved maize variety—until then perceived as affordable only to the wealthy—into one appropriate for all, including the poor (Bellon and Risopoulos 2001).[8]

Judging the *ejido* sector's performance is challenging because of incomplete and confusing empirical evidence and because of differences in setting and support, both over time and between it and other subsectors of agriculture. There is little doubt that the *ejidos* did experience many limitations

standard deficiencies were apparent, including technical, administrative, and (critical to success) the lack of communications with the supposed beneficiaries.

[8] During a nine-year period, this variety became "creolized" through farmers' management, which fostered hybridization between improved and local varieties.

which would be expected to reduce their productivity; virtually all authors agree that much of the challenge for them was the lack of technological and other support from the state, a lack also suffered but usually in lesser degree by small private farms, explaining part of any productivity gap in favor of the latter. Barriers notwithstanding, the sector seems to have achieved substantial advances in production, productivity, and incomes. From 1950 to 1970, for example, the productivity growth achieved appears to have been good, albeit probably less than that of small private farms (Yates 1978, 602).[9] After these decades came a less successful stretch.[10] Over the 1970s and 1980s, output growth was fastest for the private middle- and large-scale farmers, as government policy continued to favor commercial agriculture through major investments in irrigation and the provision of subsidized credits.

Still, as of the 1970s and 1980s, the relative productivity of the private parcels within the *ejido* sector to similarly sized private farms (i.e., those under ten hectares) outside the sector seems to have been surprisingly good, given the latter's more secure tenure and ability to mortgage or lease out land, thereby facilitating better access to credit. Heath (1992, 705) concludes that "the available data fail to demonstrate that *ejido* parcels are less productive than private holdings."[11] One reason for the roughly equal productivity was that the land reform legislation on collective organization had not been carried into practice. If all *ejido*s had been organized collectively in line with the legislation, it is probable that there would be as large a gap between the productivity of collective and private farms as seen in countries like China and the Soviet Union. Happily, the truly collective farm never had a significant presence in Mexico. Case-study evidence on the relatively few collective *ejidos* highlights the prevalence of corrupt management and resource misallocation (Heath 1992, 705). Still, the comparable productivity

[9] Yates's figures imply an average annual growth of 6.5 percent in the output per hectare on private farms—about the same for small (under five hectares) as for large ones, while *ejido* productivity increased at a lower, but still substantial, 2.3 percent per year. The former figure is so large as to appear implausible.

[10] Agricultural production as a whole increased by 325 percent from 1934 to 1965, or 4.8 percent per year, the highest rate in Latin America during this period (Kay 1998, 10). Since then, Mexico's overall agricultural growth has been weak (Thiesenhusen 1995).

[11] In reaching this conclusion, the author carefully reviews the available data and the analyses undertaken over the previous couple of decades. Comparison between overall *ejido* and private farm performance are complicated by the fact that the big majority of *ejido* land (seventy-three percent according to a 1988 survey, see Heath 1992, 704) was in common use (e.g., grazing, forests) with low productivity, partly due to free access and the resulting overgrazing. Although Yates (1981, 134) concluded that by 1970 crop output per hectare was about forty percent higher in small private farms than in the *ejido* sector, Heath suggests that much of this difference results from the inclusion in the data of the *ejido* common land.

of privately operated *ejido* parcels with that of private farms is surprising; it suggests that the disadvantages faced by the *ejidos* either were not as great as they may have appeared or had less impact than might have been expected. Possibly access to credit was less important to productivity than is often assumed. The fact that the productivity gains from the liberalizing reform of the 1990s appear to have been small to modest is further evidence of relatively good productivity before it, and the limited transition to complete private rights when this option appeared reveals that the communal aspects of the previous system did have important payoffs to those involved.

The very low incomes of the peasants in the 1920s could no doubt have been raised more rapidly had their land base been increased considerably more than it was, had public sector support been better than it was, and had there been no damaging property rights gaps. A continuing puzzle, whose resolution would require more detailed evidence on the evolution of Mexican agriculture, is the relative roles of these three factors in limiting the income growth of poorer groups. Least clear is the potential of better property rights, whose benefits come from: (i) control over decisions on inputs and outputs; (ii) better access to credit or other inputs; (iii) ability to sell or rent land; and (iv) clear control over land into the future, leading to greater investment. A good outcome by international standards would have involved a fivefold increase in total (agricultural and non-agricultural) income per person for *ejido* families over the period from 1925 to 1980 (i.e., three percent per year); for agriculture as a whole, the actual increase in output was about 2.76-fold, or 1.86 percent per capita per year, and the income increase for the reform beneficiaries was probably not too different from this. That an improvement in property rights could produce a large share of the difference between three percent and under two percent is unlikely.[12]

Evidence that *ejido* agriculture was no less productive at given points of time than the rest of the Mexican system does not establish whether the reform raised or lowered overall agricultural productivity or growth. Low productivity of the sector as a whole could be a pernicious effect of the agrarian reform if, as many have argued, the reform and the tensions around it exercised a brake on both the private and the *ejido* sectors by discouraging private and public investment in agriculture. Thus Heath (1992, 706) judged that:

[12] Conclusions from the impact of the liberalizing reform of the 1990s in Mexico itself, and from the experience of China and other countries, suggest that this would be unlikely.

> In one respect the agrarian reform has indeed failed: the threat of expropriation has not been sufficient to induce large landowners to adopt a more intensive (rather than land-extensive) approach to agriculture; nor has it removed the speculative, recreational or prestige motives for holding land. There is an ineluctable trend toward land concentration that the land reform authorities have been unable or unwilling to prevent. Among smaller properties some measure of concentration is probably desirable on efficiency grounds; but at the other end of the scale, the consolidation of large estates has not been conducive to the full employment of land. In 1981 . . . 27% of the land in private farms was left out of production: on farms of five hectares or less the proportion was a mere 6%, indicating that underemployment is overwhelmingly a large-farm problem.

This negative assessment of the degree to which the *modus operandi* and the socio-economic contribution of the large-scale sector had improved over time contrasts somewhat with the more optimistic take of Clark W. Reynolds (1970) two decades earlier.

Michael Albertus et al. (2016) report that the extent of reform was associated with slower overall economic growth across states over the period of 1940 to 1992. Remaining to be sorted out is the degree to which that slower growth was a direct result of the inefficiency of reformed agriculture, or was due to growth potential being less where reform occurred, to state support for agriculture (and perhaps for development more generally) being weakest where it occurred, or to other factors.[13] It is common in developing countries undertaking reforms for political and institutional factors to weaken technical and other support through a combination of political and institutional mechanisms. Albertus et al. (2016) note that the Mexican reform sector was a major political supporter of the PRI, which preferred to keep tight control over it; one way was to limit private property rights. Avoiding having the sector grow too fast could also have been beneficial to the PRI.

## The 1980s Reform

From the beginning of the 1980s, Mexico suffered an economic crisis, substantially the result of its dependence on natural resource exports, especially

[13] Albertus et al. (2016) attempt to take account of some of these possible complicating factors.

oil. By the early 1990s, with both the *ejido* sector and agriculture as a whole stagnant, recovering a degree of dynamism had become an important goal. Some people blamed the agrarian reform for the stagnation. Many assumed that the lack of individual rights to land left the *ejidatarios* at a disadvantage (e.g., when they needed credit), and that their capacity to invest was correspondingly weakened. There was also considerable ambiguity as to the rights and security enjoyed by this group, which depended a great deal on local authorities. The growing belief that the *ejido* structure needed more space for market forces was built into a new reform, implemented in 1991 under President Salinas, who was one of the early non-PRI presidents and an economist known for his neo-liberal thinking. A balance was sought between raising efficiency and incomes and protecting the sector's members from unscrupulous land speculators who were expected, given the chance, to scoop up any desirable land available for sale. Freeing land use from at least some of the existing restrictions was expected to release untapped potential.

This new reform (known as PROCEDE)[14] established the boundaries of each *ejido* and of each individual plot within it. The certificates received by the *ejidatarios* allowed them to employ outside workers, rent their land, or leave it uncultivated—previously dangerous moves that could invite the reassignment of the land to someone else. Sale of the land was now permitted, but only to other members of the *ejido*. Members of a given *ejido* could, however, vote to make their land rights totally private ("complete domain"), in which case the land could be sold to anyone. As of 2005, such conversion had occurred on just one percent of the land (Assies 2006, 53); by 2010, it had taken place in ten percent of the *ejidos*, although the move seemed to be more related to urbanization and the rising value of land than to other motivations, such as greater efficiency of land use. The generally low take-up was consistent with the fact that *ejidatarios* have always placed considerable value on their communal way of life and on family economic security (Assis 2006).

The partial freeing of markets did open up new potential and benefit many members. By 2010, a range of economic effects were showing up, although their aggregate impact appears to have been modest, at best. Alain de Janvry et al. (2015), whose study covers the period from 1993 to 2006, confirm that PROCEDE increased the incentive to invest, as predicted by the technocrats

[14] *Programa de Certificación de Derechos Ejidales y Titulación de Solares* (Program for the Certification of Ejidal Rights and Land Titling).

who designed it, and facilitated the consolidation of plots into a single property (not previously permitted). It also accelerated the out-migration (especially of youth) to find employment elsewhere; this was more marked for families with less land or with land of lower productivity, making resource allocation more efficient and beneficial overall. It has presumably had an upward effect on average farm size, thereby raising family incomes, something reflected empirically in an increase in family consumption. Although the evidence from this study and from Pedro Olinto et al. (2000) does suggest significant welfare benefits for many families and uncovers little evidence of damaging effects, it does not point to the big impact on production expected by the reform's proponents, a contrast that exemplifies the frequent weakness of policy thinking around agrarian structure and its implications.[15] PROCEDE was based mainly on assumptions linking free markets to economic efficiency; those effects appear to have been considerably less than expected, although other beneficial effects have probably been more important.

Mexico's agrarian reform clearly contributed to the long-term stability of the political system, although not necessarily to its democratic development. For many decades, the PRI successfully co-opted the peasantry as part of a balancing act between them and the other groups in the society. In recent decades, its hegemony has been challenged by a variety of political forces and its grip over the peasantry has loosened. A high level of dissatisfaction was evidenced by the Zapatista rebellion in the southern state of Chiapas. On January 1, 1994, the Zapatista Army of National Liberation (EZLN), an indigenous organization, declared war on the Mexican government, demanding "work, land, housing, food, health, education, independence, liberty, democracy, justice and peace." That dissatisfaction reflected, among other things, the limitations of Mexico's decades long reform; it was partial, in that it never reached enough of the appropriate beneficiaries, and it did not support the *ejidal* sector in nearly the degree needed to generate dynamic, continuing productivity and income growth. Probably there was a modest medium-term trend toward equality in the distribution of land, but not a definitive one. And this is one of the numerous examples of a reasonably large reform failing to bring a significant and lasting reduction in overall income inequality, if indeed there was one at all.

[15] The small impact on productivity was, however, predicted by Heath (1992, 706) in his analysis of the performance of the *ejido* sector.

## Legacies of the Reforms

It remains unclear exactly how overall inequality has changed during the decades since the Revolution, but it was clearly quite high then,[16] and is high now. David Felix (1977, 112) posits a Gini coefficient of 0.61 at the end of the *Porfiriato* period in 1910, and the best estimates for around 2020 are not much different. The most interesting issue from the perspective of this study is whether and how inequality was affected by the drawn-out, post-Revolution redistribution, and the recent redistribution of PROCEDE. It probably fell during the former period (Felix 1977), although by how much remains a matter of speculation (see Appendix 6.1). By the 1950s and 1960s, it was probably rising again, leading to a sky-high Gini coefficient of 0.59 by 1968, according to Alice Krozer and Juan Carlos Moreno-Brid (2014, 2). Trends since that time are unclear, with some sources pointing to a net decline and others not. If the 1968 figure of 0.59 is not overestimated, overall inequality was very high around that time. That it rose sharply in the preceding decade or so would suggest that it fell as the reform was occurring but began to rise as redistribution came close to a halt and industrial growth took off. In that scenario, the equality benefits of the reform were short-lived.[17] As for the impact of the liberalizing reform of the 1990s, it is unclear, and it would not seem to have been large.[18]

Like many other reforming countries, Mexico under the PRI sought to raise the educational levels of the former underclass. The context, however, was complicated. Being liberated from their *haciendas* and *pueblos* allowed *mestizos* and the indigenous population to migrate to larger communities

[16] In fact, Alexander von Humboldt, were he to revisit today's Mexico might suggest that his take of over two hundred years ago (von Humboldt 1811) was not far off base for the present. He reported that "Mexico is the country of inequality. Nowhere does there exist such a fearful difference in the distribution of fortune, civilization, cultivation of the soil, and population . . . . The capital and several other cities have scientific establishments, which will bear a comparison with those of Europe. The architecture of the public and private edifices, the elegance of the furniture, the equipages, the luxury and dress of the women, the tone of society, all announce a refinement to which the nakedness, ignorance, and vulgarity of the lower people form the most striking contrast."

[17] If so, the parallel with China and some other reform experiences is of interest, through the impact of rural–urban migration as industrial (or post-agricultural) growth accelerated. China's deliberate limiting of that migration clearly pushed inequality up. In Mexico, a combination of the *ejido* system's discouraging its members from leaving and a possibly lower tendency of indigenous than non-indigenous people to do so could both have been at work.

[18] It is generally assumed that adjustment of the SEDLAC figures to allow for unreported income leads to an increasing gap between the former and the true figures, in which case it is quite likely that overall inequality has risen since the early 1990s. This is not surprising because any positive effect of this reform would not likely be very great, while other factors pushing inequality up were more powerful.

where rural schools grew rapidly.[19] The Ministry of Education tackled the so-called Indian problem—their lack of integration into the society—by teaching them in Spanish and imparting the same secular worldview to them as to other students, one that emphasized community development, modernization, and incorporation. Public schools became a vehicle in the pursuit of political change, including the creation of national worker and peasant organizations and the consolidation of an authoritarian single-party regime. Although some teachers saw themselves as part of a "mystical crusade for the nation, modernity, and social justice," many ministry personnel retained the traditional attitude of contempt for the *campesinos* and the rural culture. In the 1930s, during the Cárdenas presidency, there was a push for "socialist education" at all levels. The schools became a source of anti-religious ideology, which fueled resistance from Catholics. Cárdenas eventually backed away from this goal. Despite good intentions, the complicated politics of Mexico's post-revolutionary setting was not a venue within which maximal benefits for indigenous peoples could easily be generated. The use of Spanish as the language of instruction helped keep their desertion rates high. It was not long before investment in education took on a distinctly urban bias; by 1970, only nine percent of rural primary students completed the four grades available in most schools (Felix 1977, 113–114). An initial move to address rural medical challenges was also short-lived; by the 1940s, a strong urban bias was present there as well (Albertus et al. 2016, 195).

The great positive lesson of the Mexican experience, nonetheless, is the enormous potential of such a reform for raising the socio-economic welfare of a population through a transition from serfdom, poverty, and abuse to a much better economic, political, social, and psychological status. Among the many worrisome lessons are the high levels of violence and death that can accompany such a societal upheaval, and the tendency of a government relying on political support from the reform beneficiaries not to allow sufficiently for their needs or to understand and have confidence in their economic potential and, as a result, to be less beholden to them politically than to the still-existing class of large farmers. Albertus et al. (2016) posit that the PRI may have preferred that the *ejidatarios* not become well-off quickly in case it would have weakened their ties to the party.

[19] The improvement in educational opportunities coincided with a significant reduction in the infant mortality rate, from 222 per 1,000 births in 1920, to 125 per 1,000 births by 1940, although the relative roles of education and other factors are unknown.

Mexico provides one of the clearest examples of a reformist party (PRI) that does not understand the economic potential of the beneficiaries of its reform, or that is happy enough to see some of that potential unfulfilled. Later PRI governments, like that of Salinas, clearly lacked such insight. But weaknesses notwithstanding, the case demonstrates that a government committed to reform can still make a big positive difference. The gains for the beneficiaries were great—perhaps a fifty to one hundred percent increase in income above what it would have been under the old system. But they were very modest gains compared to those achieved in Korea and Taiwan, partly because, in the latter cases, the burgeoning agricultural sector helped to foster rapid growth in related non-agricultural rural activities. A final lesson is that socio-economic institutions, like the Mexican *ejido*, have a valuable protective role against potentially damaging encroachment by members of the outside, and historically exploitative, society. A less predictable effect was a shift in the attitudes of some large landowners, who gradually came to value real estate more as a factor of production than as a store of wealth or of prestige (Reynolds 1970, 152). Many people came to use more intensively the smaller extensions of land they had after some was expropriated; with the former underclass of indigenous peoples now liberated from their control, land did not so automatically bring status and power. This shift away from a feudal-type system toward agro-capitalism was typically both gradual and partial.

Although the details differed greatly, there are interesting parallels between Mexico's reform experience and those of Russia and China; among the most obvious is that, many decades after the reform, there was a partial reversal to give more space to market forces and more decision-making power to the producers themselves. The initial reasoning behind collectivization also differed, with Russian and Chinese reforms being propelled by a belief in the general merits of collective economic behavior, whereas in Mexico, the *ejido* was seen more as a natural configuration for the country's indigenous peoples but not for the rest. Of the three, only China ultimately, if implicitly, accepted the potential efficiency advantages of small farms relative to larger ones. Another striking parallel was the failure of all three to lay the institutional basis for a durably egalitarian society, although the details and social costs of their current forms of inequality vary considerably.

On the political side, Mexico illustrated how a unique political party/dictatorship with agrarian reform as one platform and the beneficiary group as a major support could, after the Revolution, walk the line between conflicting class interests. It was also the only Latin country of which it might be said that a government engaged in a serious land reform found the US as much of an ally as an opponent, something that reflected the early timing of the reform and the presence of Franklin Roosevelt in the White House. But, as the PRI quickly morphed into a party whose main focus was maintaining power rather than the pursuit of any specific ideological or social aims, its preserving a disproportionate interest in the rural poor became increasingly unlikely; both its power base and its leaders were increasing urban.

The Mexican experience can be seen more as a success, with a large increase in welfare and a substantial one in income for the luckier beneficiaries, or more as a failure, with improvements far short of what they might have been even for this group, continuing albeit diminishing poverty for those who did not receive land, a slower rate of agricultural growth than would have been possible, the failure to put the country on a path toward low income inequality, and many deaths. What the likely alternative path might have been politically is central to guessing which is the more persuasive judgment. It does not appear that political bad luck, such as the loss of a key progressive politician at the wrong time, kept the country from better choices than those it made.

## Bolivia

The long lead-in to Bolivia's 1952 revolution and its 1953 land reform was one of brutal mistreatment and abuse of the indigenous peoples, especially after the defeat of the Spanish by Bolivar, and despite his own attempts to improve their economic and social position.[20] He abolished slavery, forced labor, and the indigenous tribute payment; his broad objective was to turn the rural population into yeoman farmers, with individual ownership over the plots they operated within their community's territory. But his decrees of 1824 and 1825 were quickly countered by the elites, who, from 1826 onward, were able to block any further parceling of land. The process of breaking up the communities and taking their land was greatly accelerated in the second half of the century. Many conflicts dotted the country's history up to the mid-twentieth century.

[20] See Bonifaz (1955, 1–5).

The most widespread and dangerous indigenous revolt occurred in the context of an 1899 civil war between Liberals and Conservatives; indigenous peoples sided with the Liberals and helped them to win, in the process invading land and slaughtering *hacendados* in several regions. When no reforms were forthcoming, they resumed invasions and killings, but their rebellion was quickly and brutally stamped out. Such insurrections left white people with a legacy of fear of the indigenous peoples (deShazo 1972).

The period leading up to the epochal 1952 revolution was marked by growing social unrest and economic decline. Defeat by tiny Paraguay in the Chaco War of 1932–1935 had a major impact on the thinking of both intellectuals and army officers, partly by underscoring the extent of corruption and inefficiency within the Bolivian army; it contributed to a reformist coup within that institution. Coups and countercoups continued up to the revolution of 1952.

Scarcity and low quality of land in the *altiplano* meant that, at midcentury, over eighty percent of the country's labor force was still involved in low productivity agriculture. Ownership of cultivable land was extremely unequal; by one estimate ninety-two percent was held in estates of one thousand hectares or more (Wagner 1989a). Although the labor force was still heavily concentrated in agriculture, there was also a large mining industr a famously rich elite whose wealth came from that sector, and the count strongest union with its base there.

## Revolution and Reform

As early as 1946, domestic turmoil was aggravated when trade union leaders issued a call to the working class for a permanent revolution and violent armed struggle. In response to labor's steady radicalization, the government resorted to increasingly repressive measures, including the dismissal of seven thousand miners. By 1952, the country's economy was in rapid decline while social unrest continued to grow. In the early 1950s, the National Revolutionary Movement (*Movimiento Nacionalista Revolucionario*, MNR) emerged as the dominant force for change. It espoused a working-class ideology, support for indigenous rights, and an extensive agrarian reform. Like the Mexican Revolution, this one was multi-faceted. Along with the land reform, the Revolutionary government nationalized mines, gave miners' syndicates a say in business operations, and abolished the existing literacy and property requirements to vote (Ferragut 1963).

Although various revolts led to a considerable loss of life, the death toll over the whole revolutionary process was nothing like that in Mexico. Probably it helped that most of the great *hacendados* and tin magnates left the country. But the Revolution was also a hesitant one, moderated by intense pressure from both the left and the right within Bolivia, as well as by outside pressure from the US. By nationalizing the mines, reforming the agrarian system, and initiating universal suffrage, the MNR did eliminate a powerful traditional elite and transform part of Bolivian society, but it failed to control the new forces unleashed or to institutionalize itself as the PRI had done in Mexico. In 1964, the army overthrew the MNR government and shifted the country back toward the right again. But the major benefit of the Revolution—the emancipation of the indigenous peoples from their historic bondage—could not be reversed.

The land reform begun in 1953 was partial, as it was essentially limited to the heavily populated highlands; it transferred only part of the land; and it transferred land titles not to the beneficiaries but to unions affiliated with the National Confederation of Peasant Workers (CNTCB), which was politically controlled by the MNR (Albertus 2021, 117). As a result, it did not lay the basis for a strong and effective support system for the beneficiaries.[21] The Agrarian Reform Law abolished forced peasant labor and established a program of expropriation and distribution of rural property from the traditional landlords to the indigenous peasants. Compensation was in twenty-five-year government bonds. Only estates with low productivity were to be completely redistributed, while more productive medium-sized farms kept part of their land and were encouraged to invest in raising agricultural production. At first, the government was unable to prevent the unauthorized occupation of some lands by peasants. Eventually it earned their co-operation, partly through the creation of the Ministry of Peasant Affairs and the organization of peasants into syndicates (Wagner 1989b). But redistribution was gradual, and by 1970, only forty-five percent of peasant families had received title. More reform projects followed in the 1970s, 1980s, and beyond. Distribution

[21] Ironically, it was in Paz Estenssoro's later presidency (from 1985 to 1989) that, as part of a neo-liberal adjustment plan financed by the World Bank, steps toward improving property rights were undertaken (Albertus 2021, 158). His neo-liberal policies were met with much protest.

among recipients was not fully egalitarian, partly because of differing land quality across the highlands.

## The Disastrous Follow-up

As in Mexico, a newish large-scale agriculture flourished in non-indigenous sections of the country, especially in the Santa Cruz region, which today is a major producer of sugar, cotton, and soybeans. In the more corrupt of the rapidly rotating governments, large parcels were handed to speculators and swindlers who, for legal purposes, posed as agricultural entrepreneurs. Broad disparities in land ownership thus persisted. In the east, autocratic officials frequently spurned indigenous claims to land, encumbering their efforts with unfathomable red tape. Under the dictatorship of General Hugo Banzer (1971–1978), thousands of hectares were handed out to friends and cronies, part of which remained uncultivated, sometimes held as collateral to obtain loans for other purposes. The even more repressive, but fortunately short-lived, dictatorship of Luis García Meza, who came to power in what has been referred to as the "cocaine coup," was arguably the bottom of the barrel in terms of Bolivia's post-revolutionary governments. Of ultra-conservative, anti-communist persuasion, García Meza endeavored to install a Pinochet-style dictatorship designed to last for twenty years. He outlawed all political parties, exiled opposition leaders, repressed trade unions, and muzzled the press. He was backed by former SS officer and Nazi German war criminal Klaus Barbie and by Italian neofascist Stefano Delle Chiaie. Other foreign collaborators included professional torturers allegedly imported from the notorious Argentine dictatorship of General Jorge Videla. The Minister of the Interior, Colonel Luis Arce Gómez, cautioned that all Bolivians who opposed the new order should "walk around with their written will under their arms." The most prominent victim was congressman, presidential candidate, and noted orator Marcelo Quiroga, who was "disappeared" soon after the coup; he had been the chief advocate of bringing former dictator Banzer to trial for human rights violations and economic mismanagement. Like García Meza, Arce Gómez was deeply involved in drug trafficking. He subsequently spent many years in jail, both in the US for drug offenses and in Bolivia for human rights abuses. Some of the deaths for which he was directly responsible were linked to the notorious "Operation Condor," a US-backed campaign of political repression and state terror involving intelligence operations and the assassination of opponents, implemented in 1975 by the right-wing dictatorships of Chile, Argentina, and Uruguay but extending its operations to many other countries.[22] These post-revolutionary regimes showed how far Bolivia still was from stable and decent governance.

Their limitations notwithstanding, and despite such horrendous regimes as that of García Meza, the reforms left impressive improvements for the mainly *Aymara* and *Quechua* communities of the western highlands. Anthropologist Arthur McEwan (1975) judged that the reform would have been a great step forward, even if it had yielded no economic benefits at all. In any event, it brought great cultural and political change, communities began finally to manage their own affairs, and many social indicators showed marked advances. For the first time in the nation's history, an attempt was made to incorporate the *Aymara* and *Quechua* peasants (at least sixty-five percent of the population) into national life. The Bolivian state increased its role in rural areas; an extensive public health campaign specifically included indigenous groups and their economic status improved markedly. On the northern *altiplano*, their new access to land raised peasant incomes and food consumption.[23] Market access to goods and services had always been very limited. Sales to the cities initially declined, but as a new commercialization system developed this impact was reversed and greater peasant participation was evident in the local markets, as was the use of cash, replacing an earlier pattern of barter. New fairs appeared. Some peasants took a while to adjust to the new reality and to be convinced that the changes would not be reversed.[24]

Whether output rose or fell on the redistributed land or in the aggregate (i.e., including that from the land that was not redistributed) is less clear. Some authors have contended that total output was maintained or increased; others argue that almost a decade passed before it recovered its pre-reform level (Thiesenhusen 1995).[25] Several factors were working to lower aggregate output; others raised it, including the transfer of previously under-cultivated lands to reform beneficiaries. Some land went temporarily out of production, when owners opted not to use what they still had or when small

[22] Wikipedia, "Luis García Meza."

[23] In 1950, the average *colonato* (a term referring to an agricultural laborer who, although legally free, was in practice bound to the will of the patron/owner of a large estate) consumed fifteen hundred calories per day (Ferragut 1961, 30).

[24] For an overview of the revolution and its impacts, see Grindle and Domingo (2003).

[25] Eckstein et al. (1978) concluded that land productivity on redistributed land had risen due to the reform but that a greater rise in consumption had, for a while, reduced the sales to urban markets. Burke (1971, 316) agreed that production had risen, and found no indication that the former *haciendas* benefited from significant scale economies.

indigenous-operated plots suffered declining yields because it became harder to get manure or other inputs.[26] A few local unions forbad the *campesinos* to cultivate the land of formerly abusive landlords to discourage their return or continued operation of the land they still controlled. Some local markets were slow to adapt, and some new farmers needed time to learn the ropes. As usual, many observers assumed from the start that the new peasant farmers would not be efficient producers, so when the supply of food to La Paz shrunk in the years immediately after the reform, this was accepted to be the cause. From a longer term perspective, it may not matter much which of the cited factors prevailed over the post-reform decade because (i) there was little or no evidence suggesting that the beneficiaries themselves were suffering income or consumption declines, except for those whose access to inputs fell substantially; and (ii) in the longer term the combined likelihood that land cultivated would increase and/or that land productivity on the cultivated area would increase appears to have been high.[27]

The remarkably unstable government suffered by the country for several decades after the reform contributed to its typically being quite short of both human and financial resources. The large mining industry remained a major focus of attention; as of 1977 it generated about eight percent of the GDP, sixty-seven percent of exports, and an unusually high (for mining) six percent of employment. With the lack of continuity from one government to the next, and the disinterest of most of them, it is no surprise that the reform beneficiaries were not provided with strong technical support, that overall agricultural policy was weak, and that the income of beneficiaries did not rise dramatically—probably less than their counterparts in Mexico.

[26] Output certainly fell on some large farms, as noted by Clark (1968); his study of fifty-one formerly large properties in the northern highlands revealed that seventeen of them lay idle for varying periods after the Revolution. All but five were absentee-owned, and farming was generally a secondary activity for the owner.

[27] Experiences naturally differed across regions and *ex-haciendas*. Joseph F. Dorsey (1975, 11), drawing on the analysis of Marcelo Peinado (1969), reports that over the fifteen-year interval between 1950/1951 and 1965/1966 the total production on the former *hacienda* Toralapa rose by over one hundred percent, or by 5.1 percent per year (in metric tons), to more than triple its prior level, with this increase due to an even bigger increase in land under cultivation. This combination of effects meant that output (in tons) per hectare cultivated fell. Prior to the reform, potato output per hectare was estimated to be twice as high on the *hacienda* land, something Dorsey (1975, 12) suggests was due to its favored conditions in terms of land quality, irrigation, fertilizer, and the like. (He considered such a yield advantage abnormal because the 1950 agricultural census showed average production per hectare to be inversely related to farm size). After the reform, with total potato area up by over fifty percent, average yield was about the same, presumably due to the incorporation of poorer land as area rose. Most striking was the dramatic increase in the land under cultivation on this former *hacienda*. Before the reform some *haciendas* had been cutting back on the number of *colonos* in response to their own needs for more land or from fear of the rising agitation among the *campesinos* (Dorsey 1975, 83).

Agricultural growth after the reform came, in large part, from the colonization of the eastern lowlands, a process typically encouraged by the state and designed to boost commercial farming and export agriculture in the Santa Cruz zone. According to Musgrave (1981, 242), as of the mid-1970s, agriculture still employed two-thirds of the labor force but generated only twenty percent of the GDP, implying a labor productivity just one-eighth that of the rest of the economy—a huge gap.[28] The reform did not end the strongly bimodal feature of agriculture; rather it changed its character.

Meanwhile, new *campesino* protest movements maintained the pressure for additional land distribution and for other improvements. A signal event in 1990 was a march on La Paz by eastern lowland indigenous groups from the areas of Santa Cruz and Beni, who had previously been neglected in the allocation of reform benefits. The increasing deforestation of their region by logging, cattle ranching, soybean farming, and land speculation threatened their livelihood. Their demand for recognition of rights to ancestral territories earned wide public support. A new wave of land protests followed, along with the first call for a new constitutional assembly. Resolution of land conflicts was a permanent challenge to governments. Conservative President Gonzálo Sánchez de Lozado included a modest amount of land titling and other initiatives in his first term plans (from 1993 to 1997), but his goals went largely unfulfilled, despite millions of dollars contributed by the European Union. Much dissatisfaction remained when Evo Morales (from 2006 to 2018) came to power as the first indigenous president, promising to allocate more land to the indigenous communities and *campesinos*, a promise that predictably led to bloody clashes.

Bolivia's post-revolution history is often divided into the pre-Morales period of about half a century and the Morales period. Despite the many limitations and failures, the short- and medium-term benefits accruing during the former half-century appear to have been great. Although the economic gains were probably less than those in Mexico, the non-economic ones were enormous in what was, according to Philip M. Raup (1967), one of the most archaic and backward social systems in the world. The reform put an end to the most serious human rights abuses that were a natural product of a traditional system that imposed few limits on the behavior of those land owners who might be labeled "natural abusers/exploiters." One of this group was

[28] This gap was probably exaggerated by defective national accounts, which usually understate the output of small family agriculture. But even if such an understatement was about thirty percent (fifty percent), the gap with non-agricultural labor productivity would still be a very high 5.5 (4.1).

probably surprised when, after the reform had passed some of his land to new small farmers, the latter group opted not to cultivate his remaining land as before, out of contempt for his personal behavior (Clark 1968, 163).

Bolivia's story is, in many ways, typical of agrarian reform experiences. Although the 1950s reform brought great benefits, because political power remained very divided much was also left undone. A few subsequent reforms added important benefits. But corruption and cronyism contributed to new waves of land concentration. To the extent that the descendants of the 1950s *campesinos* have reaped major benefits, the land redistribution itself appears seldom to have been the direct cause. More significant was another major achievement of the Revolutionary government—making primary education available to nearly all children in rural Bolivia. Along with land, this is the most valuable gift to former serfs, something typically and deliberately absent in slave and feudal societies because it is not in the interest of the dominant class to permit it. Although it does not usually raise family income or welfare immediately, it can begin to yield productivity and other benefits fairly soon[29] and it can have a major effect on future income and welfare. Before 1953 rural schools were almost exclusively limited to communities of small landholders and freeholding indigenous families, but typically unavailable to the children of tenants on the *haciendas*. Until the early 1960s, school construction, and even payment of teachers, was the exclusive responsibility of the community. In 1956, new legislation laid the foundation for a public education system that remained in force until the late 1980s, including a six-year primary cycle. The gross enrolment rate in primary schools showed a sharp upward shift from the early 1950s; it had risen only from eight percent in 1900 to twenty-eight percent in 1950/1955, but by 1960 it had reached forty-three percent, and by 1970, seventy-six percent.[30] The adult literacy rate jumped from 31.1 percent in 1950 to 63.2 percent in 1976.[31] In each case, the rural rate would have been somewhat below these figures[32] but its percentage increase probably greater. Progress has been fairly continuous over the subsequent decades.

It is probable that, over the 1950s and 1960s, income inequality in Bolivia fell somewhat. It is virtually certain that poverty fell significantly, and it is

[29] As shown by Laszlo (2008) in the case of Peru.

[30] Estimates by Peres-Cajias (2017). The gross enrolment rate is the ratio of all children in a given schooling stage (e.g., primary) to the number of years involved in that education.

[31] These data may not be fully consistent over time because sources were not necessarily reliable over the first part of the century.

[32] In 1945, eighty-four percent of all indigenous adults were illiterate (DeShazo 1972).

obvious that the quality of life rose for many people. No adequately organized data are available to track the post-revolution economic trajectory of the current and former serfs. Given their low share of national income both before and after the reform, it is not surprising that 1970s figures still showed a huge gap between those at the top and those at the bottom.[33] For 1975, the Musgrave Mission (Musgrave 1981, 110) estimated a national Gini coefficient of 0.52, comparable to other high inequality cases in Latin America, and with estimated income shares of 2.6 percent for the bottom decile and twelve percent for the bottom forty percent. For several decades thereafter, inequality remained quite high and sometimes rose. A dramatic increase pushed the Gini coefficient for the period from 1995 to 2007 up to around 0.6, far above its level from 1988 to 1995 (probably under 0.5); as discussed below, this was followed by a sharp decline to a low of 0.44 in 2017 (WIID, n.d.).[34] The estimated share of the bottom forty percent, probably a good indicator of how *campesinos* were faring relative to others, appears to have reached a low of about eight percent around 2000, before climbing up to 12.5 to 14.0 percent from 2014 to 2018.

Overall, then, the evidence suggests that inequality at the national level stayed high from the 1970s, then rose to an even higher level for a period around the turn of the century, before finally coming down.[35] Clearly, although it did much for the beneficiaries at the time, Bolivia's agrarian reform did not set the country on a path of either declining or low inequality in the middle term; this is unsurprising given the number of right-wing, military, corrupt, and incompetent governments over that interval, the lack of attention to the needs of *campesino* agriculture, the prominence of the mining

33 The share of national income that changed hands due to Bolivia's 1950s reform and the later ones has no doubt been very modest, similar to the story reported by Webb and Figueroa in (1975) the case of Peru.

34 See UNU-WIDER World Income Inequality (n.d.). While these figures may not be fully comparable over the period, the general pattern is likely to be that shown. Other countries of Latin America have also experienced declines in household-survey based inequality estimates since around 2000, but Bolivia's is much more marked than most of them. Broadly consistent with the WIID data, Aristizabel-Ramirez et al. (2015, 3) report a decline beginning in the period from 2005 to 2008 (with the Gini coefficient falling from somewhere in the range of 0.55–.60) to under 0.50 by 2009. As of 2017, the World Bank's estimate of a Gini coefficient of 44.4 for Bolivia put it thirty-sixth highest among the 159 countries with available data. Bolivia has not yet been included in the World Top Incomes Database, so it remains to be seen how top incomes have been affected by the general decline in inequality showing up in the household surveys.

35 These indicators are hard to estimate with any precision in countries like Bolivia, which have a large family agricultural sector, a large informal sector, and much income going unreported. But, unless estimation errors have changed sharply over short periods, the data from the 1970s leave no doubt that inequality worsened.

sector, and the economic disorder which followed on the sharp economic fluctuations leading up to and during the 1980s crisis, when informality jumped and real wages declined by forty to fifty percent (Horton 1994, 135).

## The Morales Period

Evo Morales's ascent to the presidency (in 2006) as leader of the Movement for Socialism Party (*Movimiento al Socialismo*, MAS), which he had led since founding it in 1998, signaled the beginning of a new phase. At that time, five percent of property holders still owned seventy percent of the country's arable land (Dangl 2007, 95), but most large properties were now found in the eastern region. Initially, Morales proceeded cautiously on the agrarian front, not wanting to unnecessarily unsettle the *status quo* or curtail efficient commercial operations. A modest land reform measure only narrowly passed in the legislature in 2006, with the dominant eastern elite vigorously opposing it. Many landowners circumvented the new regulations by claiming that family members were also farming and were thus entitled to their own individual parcels; some claimed that their land was being used as an ecological preserve.

In an early success (in 2007), the government granted the *Chiquitano* indigenous group permanent land titles in Monte Verde, its ancestral territory of almost 2.5 million acres located in the department (province) of Santa Cruz. Oxfam, the UK relief agency, welcomed this historic move and congratulated the indigenous group for its persistent efforts over more than a decade that had led to this peaceful transition. Illustrative of the nature of the conflict was the demand that the president of the Pro Santa Cruz Civic Committee, Branko Marinkovic, return twenty-seven thousand hectares, which he was charged with illegally appropriating through the use of false documents. Easterners were worried that reform would flood the lowland communities with impoverished indigenous immigrants from the western highlands, thereby tipping the region's social and political balance. Opponents of reform charged that Morales would impose the beliefs and practices of the Andean indigenous communities in some form of "communist model." The wealthy of Santa Cruz and other eastern regions have systematically threatened to use force to defend their property, and they have announced the formation of armed defense committees to guard it against the landless peasant movement (*Sin Tierra*) founded in 2000.

Although doing little on the agrarian front, Morales's government did achieve much for Bolivia's indigenous peoples, beginning from a still very low base. It had the good luck of enormous financial resources due to the high prices of oil and other commodity exports and to its nationalization of the oil and gas industries. During most of the period since 2000, the country has achieved robust GDP growth (eighty percent from 2000 to 2014, or 4.3 percent per year), partly reflecting the commodity boom. As important as the fast growth has been, the sharp decline in inequality and in poverty has perhaps been more important; the latter fell dramatically from 60.6 percent of the population in 2005 to 38.6 percent in 2016, while extreme poverty (those living on less than $1.25 per day) fell from thirty-eight to 16.8 percent.

Explaining the recent fall in inequality remains a work in progress. It began somewhere in the period from 2000 to 2005, gained momentum from 2007 to 2011, and continued through at least 2017. Estimates of poverty show parallel trends. Progressive social and economic policies were implemented, some of which affected people's incomes directly. More important have been major changes in the distribution of labor income. Workers with less education benefited more than those with higher levels, and their gains were especially notable in the informal sector.[36] From 2001 to 2013, the real minimum wage increased by one hundred percent and average real earnings by over thirty-five percent.[37] Unemployment fell from 8.5 percent in 2005 to under four percent in 2013, the lowest in Latin America. Non-labor income, including that of most informal sector workers (of whom few are paid) and most farm workers, rose more strongly in the rural areas (Vargas and Garriga 2015, 17), suggesting that many in the small farm sector were gaining substantially. Meanwhile, workers with thirteen or more years of education (i.e., post-secondary) lost in absolute terms (ibid, 22); in the economy as a whole the earnings premium from having more education was thus sharply reduced.

Over the longer term, and especially during the period of extreme income inequality, that premium was great not only in the formal sector, but

[36] This may be seen in part as a recovery from the sharp declines in informal sector incomes during the crash of the 1980s.

[37] In their analysis of the decreases in inequality and poverty observed from 2005 to 2014, Vargas and Garriga (2015) note that, as of 2014, Bolivia still had the lowest minimum wage in South America (US$240 per month). An important caveat in guessing its impact involves coverage; it directly affects only workers in the formal sector, which represent about one-quarter of the workforce. Its effect could be substantially greater to the degree that there is a "lighthouse effect" on the informal sector, in which case a hike in the minimum wage may provide a higher reference salary for part of that sector.

in the informal one and overall.[38] As of 2001, the gap in labor income between those with 16 or more years of education and those with none was 7.3-fold in the formal sector, 5.5-fold in the informal sector, and about 6.9-fold overall (Vargas and Garriga 2015, 22), implying an average benefit of about twelve percent in income for each additional year of schooling. By 2013, these earnings–education gaps had shrunken greatly; in the formal sector, the top-to-bottom ratio was just 2.7; in the informal sector, 3.9; and overall, about 4.5-fold, for an earnings differential of about nine percent per year.[39] As a result of this sharp swing, while average labor income increased by thirty-six percent from 2000 to 2013 (Vargas and Garriga 2015, 11, 22), it fell for those who had completed secondary or more, especially from 2006 to 2013. This may have reflected a rapid change in the educational composition of the labor force, as the relative supply of highly educated people increased rapidly.[40] The combination of trends suggests a considerable improvement in the share of national income going to people of indigenous descent.[41] The sharp decline in the economic return to education from 2001 to 2013, a very infrequent phenomenon, remains to be analyzed more deeply, both to understand its causes and to sort out possible implications for other countries.

Given the enormous decline in agriculture's share of employment since 1950, from a little over sixty percent to about thirty percent in 2020, a key question is how well the former *campesinos* have fared and are faring in the non-agricultural labor market. Broadly speaking, the recent evidence on this point is reassuring since most of them are likely to be in the informal sector where incomes have been rising quickly. Arguably, that sector is more competitive than the formal one and hence an easier place for an indigenous person to enter and operate successfully.

Labor-market gains for the lower income groups have been complemented by a set of social policies, including: (i) the *Juancito Pinto* program, designed

[38] Muriel and Jemio (2010) present a detailed analysis of the labor market and its trends, with focus on the period from the early 1990s until 2006, during which inequality tended to rise.

[39] The earnings ratio of 2.66 for the formal sector seems implausibly low when compared to other countries, raising the possibility of data problems. Nonetheless, it is highly likely that a sharp narrowing did occur.

[40] After a mass literacy campaign that used Cuba's 'YES I CAN' program to educate 850,000 people, illiteracy—at thirteen percent when Morales became president—was declared conquered in 2008. The country ranked second only to Cuba within Latin America in the share of the GDP spent on education.

[41] It also raises the question of whether, over time and with differing government policies, the decline in the relative income of more educated to less educated people will be reversed, as occurred dramatically in China after the 1970s; during the decades since then, China's inequality has risen from very low to quite high, a huge jump over a short period.

to increase school attendance and reduce child labor, which, as of 2017, had reached two million children, providing $28 annually upon the completion of the school year; (ii) the *Juana Azurduy* program, designed to combat maternal and infant mortality and malnutrition in children under two years of age, which saw chronic undernourishment in children fall sharply from twenty-seven percent when the program began in 2009 to sixteen percent in 2017, and a halving of infant mortality between 2008 to 2017; and (iii) the *Renta de la Dignidad* (Dignity Income), a payment to the nine hundred thousand Bolivians over sixty years of age, who would otherwise receive no pension. Incapacitated and disabled people receive $36 monthly.[42]

Due to the combination of rising incomes, social support programs like those discussed, and an improved health care system, life expectancy increased from sixty-four to seventy-one years over the Morales years. Almost seven hundred members of the Cuban medical brigade came to work in the country and about five thousand Bolivians obtained medical degrees in Cuba. Many new hospitals and health centers have been built. Another dramatic development saw the extension of electricity to sixty-six percent of rural homes by 2015, up from twenty-five percent in 2001. Both of these advances are likely to have substantially benefited the lower income and indigenous groups.

Bolivia's economic growth remains substantially mineral-dependent, a condition which typically raises the level of inequality because mining creates so few jobs relative to output. In this case, however, its presence provided both the organized labor union support for the 1952 agrarian reform and ultimately, under Morales, financed a much bigger flow of benefits to lower income groups than is normally the case in mineral-based economies controlled by an elite. One major channel was the public programs just discussed.

In light of the recent economic improvements realized by lower-income families and the associated decline in inequality during the Morales administration from 2006 to 2019, many observers find it ironic that this indigenous labor leader, with roots in agriculture, should not have pursued major benefits for the landless through agrarian reform—something that was promised and expected; instead the benefits came through the other mechanisms cited. There has been very little redistribution through the

42 More than 4.8 million Bolivians, nearly half of the total, have benefited from these last three programs (Gomez Sarmiento 2019).

expropriation of private landholdings, and the relatively little state property redistributed has usually been land with low agricultural potential. Clearly the landed elites of the eastern region have posed a challenge to any extensive reform that impinged on them. Another explanation involves changes in the balance of agrarian forces and in the class composition of the MAS bloc over time. Initially, between 2006 and 2009, the indigenous–peasant social movement alliance (called the Unity Pact) pushed for a genuine transformation of the Bolivian rural class structure, and the agro-industrial elite battled the central government openly through "an autonomist and regionalist destabilization campaign, headquartered in Santa Cruz"—the most dynamic center of economic wealth and power in the country, and one that affected the rest of the lowland departments (Webber 2116, 331). By 2010, however, the idea of autonomy in the lowlands had been given up. Subsequently, what Webber refers to as "a novel agro-capital–state alliance" emerged. Productive land was increasingly being concentrated in the hands of national and transnational agro-industrial enterprises devoted to soy production and its derivatives and destined for export. Rich peasants in the coca, soy, and quinoa export sectors have been among those benefiting from incorporation into the wider, transnational commercial crop value chains, and from political absorption into the coalition between the state and industrial agricultural capital.[43] Webber's reading of this outcome corresponds to what Lenin expected to follow from the post-feudal evolution in Russia, with capitalism developing *within* the peasant sector through a process of socio-economic differentiation. Alexander Chayanov (1966) disputed this view. Historically, which route is followed depends on which subgroups the state support system helps the most. Interpreting the trajectory of Morales's government in this way helps to explain the apparent policy shifts on the land front and the loss of backing from his usual supporters for what they came to view as his excessive dedication to continued growth through oil drilling in regions populated by indigenous groups, and his encouraging (or failing to curtail) land clearing for cattle ranching. A spike in slash-and-burn clearing was linked to fires in the *Chiquitania* regions. These trends may portend longer-term damage to the

[43] Webber sees these modifications of class alliances over time as corresponding to Antonio Gramsci's theoretical concept of "transformism"—a programmatic convergence of historically oppositional forces on the Right and Left and a taming of political contestation from the popular social movements through their partial absorption into the bureaucratic apparatuses of the state. In this perspective, passive revolutions do not culminate in total restoration of the *status quo ante*, but neither do they allow for radical change.

peasantry and to the environment due to the government's failure to rein in extractive industries (including, sometimes, large-scale agriculture).

Another, partially overlapping, interpretation is that progressive elements within the government and the society came to conclude that, among the political and economically feasible policy options to improve the welfare of those toward the bottom of the socio-economic hierarchy, redistributive land reform was no longer a promising one. Certainly, it is easier to spend an abundance of oil revenues on the sorts of programs noted above than to fight a land reform battle.

Further detailed analysis will be required to sort out what has underlain the trajectory of the income and welfare of the lower deciles since the Revolution, especially that of the indigenous peasants and their descendants. There is reason to believe that a prominent role in the recent apparently sharp improvement in their incomes and the sharp fall in inequality is associated with better returns to middle-level education and the decreased payoff to higher levels.[44] Vargas (2012) concludes that the advance in education was the most important factor in the falling level of inequality, more so for example, than the *Renta Dignidad* and *Juancito Pinto* programs. Arguably, therefore, the greatest legacy of the 1953 reforms was to put the country on a path toward more education for the lower income groups, a process which may have borne its main fruits only recently, delayed by the economic chaos through which the country passed in the 1980s, and possibly strengthened by a decrease in the race-based income differentials that previously existed. If this is the case, it will be even more important to understand exactly what the impact of the 1953 reforms was in that regard. Without them, would the educational levels of these deciles have remained well short of what they are now? Also crucial is to understand why the income differential across the educational scale has shrunk. The faster increase in the supply of those with higher levels of education has presumably been one factor. Have government policies under Morales (e.g., a change in government hiring practices, or exogenous changes in economic structure) also had a significant impact?

[44] In what may seem ironic, a boost to the education of the rural poor beginning decades ago may later pay off for that group through a falling rate of return to education in general. Where education is narrowly limited to an elite group, market forces assign a high value to it because of its scarcity, while those with little or no education are part of a large labor supply whose market price is thus very low. When more and more of this latter group advance on the educational hierarchy, while this reduces the payoff to those who do achieve a high level, it diminishes the supply of those with lower levels and thus raises their market-based wage.

Regardless of the next turns in Bolivian history, important gains have been achieved. The reforms brought by the 1950s Revolution were clearly a step toward more peasant participation in political and social life and hence indirectly to things like the election of an indigenous president. From a highly repressive society in the 1940s, it has evolved into a much more democratic one. The post-revolution land redistribution had a major positive effect at the time, but overall income inequality rose markedly in the middle term. One possible message to be gleaned from this latter fact is that, in a Bolivia-style democracy evolving out of a system featuring a powerful non-indigenous agrarian elite and a large indigenous underclass, only with a strong indigenous presence in politics is inequality likely to be brought down in the medium term. In this case, major improvement only occurred when an indigenous person took the reins in a very favorable fiscal context. It was not the result of contemporary agrarian change; instead, the main direct contributing factor was the rising labor incomes of those with below university education. Active social and economic policies were also important; in 2014, the three main tools mentioned above—the *Juancito Pinto*, *Juana Azurduy*, and *Renta de la Dignidad* programs—accounted for 1.5 percent of the GDP and a much higher share of the income of lower income groups. The very rapid increase in social spending was facilitated by the combination of the oil and commodities boom and the nationalization of the oil and gas industries, which put a much higher share of the income from those sectors directly into government coffers and greatly enlarged the country's spending capacity. This situation may be reversed if the oil and gas industries shrink quickly in the coming years. Currently, much economic and political uncertainty shrouds the country. It will become another test case of the extent to which important social policy advances can withstand political backlash and the strains of fiscal stringency.

Speculation as to the net gains of the 1950s reform involves guessing how the international setting might have differed had the reform not occurred when it did. Its timing corresponded to the early years of the US's "nation-building" projects in the Third World, when economic aid, so successfully applied in post-war Western Europe with the Marshall Plan and in Japan, Korea, and Taiwan, was seen as the main tool. Bolivia was the first of these experiments in Latin America. The US deployed both economic and military aid to contain the Revolution and to support "institutional development"; Bolivian officials sometimes channeled the aid to their own purposes (Siekmeier 2011). The complexity of US–Bolivia interactions over this period is reflected in, among other things, the joint campaign to capture Ernesto "Che" Guevara in 1967 and by Bolivia's decision not much later (1971) to expel the Peace Corps. Had the original revolution and reform not occurred, it is quite possible that some alternative would have taken place with USAID support, more akin to that provided by Presidents Kennedy and Johnson to Colombia. It probably would have been much less beneficial, at least in the short- to medium-term, and its impacts might, on balance, have been negative. Much later, US embassy cables revealed Washington's attempts to create divisions in the social and indigenous movements that made up Morales's support base.

## Peru

Like the other Latin America countries with large indigenous populations, Peru has suffered extreme inequality in the distribution of land and of income,[45] leading also to economic inefficiency (Hunt 1972). Famous novels have highlighted the atrocious injustice within rural society, among them Ciro Alegría's 1941 classic *El Mundo es Ancho y Ajeno* (*The World is Wide and Distant*). Peru became one of the few cases in which a military government undertook a reform designed to strip power from the traditional landed elite.

### Rising Conflict into the 1960s

From the time of independence in the early nineteenth century, the economic system has been characterized by a relatively high dependence on exports—mainly minerals and agricultural products—especially sugar and cotton, sectors which generated considerable wealth and financed the purchase of imports. Peasant-based exports played little role, and highland agriculture was the economic home to a large, low-income indigenous population (Berry 1989b). This socio-economic structure bore a considerable resemblance to that of Bolivia.

[45] As of 1950, the Gini coefficient for land was estimated at 0.88, close to current estimates for Colombia and significantly higher than those observed in most developing countries. Eckstein et al. (1978, 2) cite a range of 0.60–0.69 for a group of other countries for which data were available. Albertus (2021, 208) reports that, as of the 1961 agricultural census, the largest one percent of landowners had eighty percent of private land; the eighty-three percent of farmers with under five hectares had only six percent of the land.

The inequality led to a long history of conflict between the highland peasants and the *latifundistas.*[46] From about 1850, the latter moved to incorporate formerly community lands, sometimes through purchase, sometimes by deception (e.g., taking advantage of their control of the local courts), and sometimes by force (Sheahan 1999, 62). Many invasions by indigenous groups were aimed at restitution, so conflict was virtually permanent. Expulsion of sharecroppers against strong resistance was frequent from the 1940s. From the mid-1950s, the lower-income rural population entered more and more into politics and the number and impact of conflicts rose further.

During a period of liberal economic policy, between 1950 and 1966, overall income inequality rose. While average real income per capita rose by four percent per year in the modern sector and by two percent in the urban traditional sector, that of the rural traditional sector advanced by only about one percent while the peasants of the Sierra, accounting approximately for the bottom thirty percent of the income hierarchy, experienced practically no gain (Webb 1977, table 3.7). This growth pattern, with the average income in the rural traditional sector dropping an additional sixty percent behind that of the "modern" sector, was a natural harbinger of political tension. From 1960 to 1963, invasions in the central and southern highlands were accompanied by strikes in the sugar plantations of the coast.[47]

A short-lived military regime following the 1962 coup attempted to calm the peasant insurgency; a land reform was decreed, but without plans for large-scale implementation. The elected government of Fernando Belaúnde (from 1963 to 1968), which represented the country's reformist bourgeoisie, redistributed some land in the areas of greatest conflict. Although the government passed a reform bill in 1964, the opposition in congress was able to keep funding very limited, so only twelve thousand families benefited (Sheahan 1999, 149). This bourgeoisie lacked the power to impose its will on the oligarchy and it was also wary of mobilizing the peasantry in support of an expansive reform.

[46] A valuable analysis of peasant resistance and its interface with politics is Smith (1991).

[47] In his analysis of why peasant movements arise, why some are more radical than others, what factors determine a movement's success, and why some movements are able to sustain growth while others cannot, Tullis (1970) constructs a theoretical framework using three independent variables—information processing, group solidarity, and relative centrality, and he applies it to the Peruvian experience.

## The Velasco Reform: Big Benefits and Much Foregone

The next relatively progressive military government, that of Juan Velasco (from 1968 to 1975), did undertake a significant reform in response to political pressure from radical peasant movements and a crisis in agriculture. The regime was serious in its objectives of improving both the economic and the social conditions of the targeted groups.[48] It characterized itself as "humanist-socialist," with a commitment to fundamental structural change in pursuit of economic development and social justice in a way that was neither communist nor capitalist (Stephens 1983, 59); it aimed to eliminate class struggles and end the marginalization of the masses.[49] Behind such impressive stated ambitions there were, unsurprisingly, serious differences of opinion on practical goals and policy steps, both on the agrarian front and on others. The land reform set a strict upper limit on landholdings of 150 hectares or less (depending on the setting), and transferred about fifty percent of the total farm area to about one-third of rural families, which were mostly organized in various types of cooperatives in the hope of preserving productivity while improving rural income distribution. Although farm size structure did not change greatly, the feudal vestiges of the *hacienda* system were eliminated. The reform was supposed to support ongoing industrial development as Peru moved into the import-substituting stage, by contributing to the growth of a market-oriented rural middle class, the transfer of agrarian capital to the industrial sector, and the conversion of some former *hacienda* owners into industrial bourgeoisie by cutting their links with land.

A key component of the reform was the conversion of the large coastal farms into production cooperatives, with the intent of achieving higher productivity and better conditions for workers now under collective management. Cooperative arrangements were also adopted in the highlands, although they gave more scope for private operation of plots. Although little land was formally allocated in private plots, the outward appearance of collectivism concealed the fact that much was, in fact, cultivated that way (Kay 1982, 153). The final configuration was, however, seriously unequal in its impact across groups. In the large coastal units, the former permanent employees were favored. Coming off worst were the *comuneros* (highland indigenous communities); this largest and poorest group before the reform

[48] A useful discussion is provided by Korovkin (1990). Rozman (1970) reviews the political involvement of the Peruvian military.

[49] Albertus (2021, 209) reviews political aspects of this military government.

was basically excluded from its benefits (Figueroa 1976, 172). Some of these indigenous communities invaded the reform-based collective or state farms, contributing to the emergence of the Shining Path (*Sendero Luminoso*) movement, with its devastating consequences for the social and political fabric of Peru.

The government's opting for cooperative rather than individual farming units reflected the standard view that economies of scale were significant, along with the idea that this was the best way to avoid food shortages, as suggested by the positive experience of Yugoslavia with agricultural collectives and cooperatives. Cooperatives were also seen as a way "to build social solidarity and elevate peasants' attitudes of themselves and their role in society" (Albertus 2021, 211, citing Cant 2012 and others). Another objective was to retain social control to avoid problems that might arise from negative peasant reactions. The considerable negative reaction from peasants to the failure to allocate rights individually (Lastarria-Cornhiel 1989, 142) did, in a way, confirm this need for social control.

Along with the land reform, a significant effort was made on the educational front, important among other reasons because literacy was necessary to vote; it also provided an important social demarcation between the rich and the poor. For the rural areas and for many of the urban poor, opportunities for education were "abysmally low" until well after World War II (Sheahan 1999, 21); as of 1970, forty-seven percent of the labour force still had three years or less (ECLA 1984, 113). Public spending on education did rise rapidly during the 1950s and 1960s as the economy expanded, and again during the Velasco years, when the mass media were used to invite the participation of the populace in this venture. But progress was not maintained during a subsequent period of economic chaos. Part of a post-1975 spending plunge took the form of falling teachers' salaries, which, by the early 1990s, had dropped to a fraction of their 1975 level (Saavedra et al. 1997, 14); this contributed to the well-known quality problems in education. Teacher absenteeism was notable, especially in more remote regions.

Through a combination of design and administrative flaws, the economic benefits from the Velasco administration's land reform effort fell far short of hopes. The cooperative system suffered many of its usual incentive problems, including the insufficient link between income and work effort. To implement its plans, the government set up a large bureaucracy which, although lacking experience in agriculture and in marketing, did not pass much authority on to the cooperative members themselves.[50] It also failed to provide resources or adequate technical training to beneficiaries, and its continued adherence to a cheap-food policy aimed at urban dwellers limited the reform sector's profitability (Kay 1982).

In the wake of the high expectations came a reality of underperformance, corruption, and peasant dissatisfaction fueled by conflicts with the government-appointed managers. From the beginning, there had been much resistance to the new model in the highlands. By the end of the 1970s, many cooperatives were either bankrupt or heading that way (Lastarria-Cornhiel 1989). In the 1980s, subdivision into private plots was legalized as long as it was supported by a majority vote of the members. Most did opt for this alternative although, plausibly enough, some maintained cooperative arrangements to handle the purchase of machinery and for buying and selling other inputs or outputs.

Institutional conflicts abounded. The Velasco government set up a peasant organization, the National Agricultural Federation (*Confederación Nacional Agraria*, CNA), which became something of a rival to the autonomous peasant organization, the Campesino Federation of Peru (*Confederación Campesina del Perú*, CCP), founded in 1947. The CNA itself became increasingly independent of the government, demanding a more radical expropriation process and a greater say in running the reformed enterprises; the government responded by dissolving it in 1978.[51] Meanwhile, reform units experienced land invasions by highland communities (*comuneros*), as well as suffering the violence perpetrated by the Shining Path (*Sendero Luminoso*) guerrilla movement in the 1980s. The invasions subsided when the government transferred some of the land to the communities. Although the Shining Path was partly spawned by the agrarian reform context, it failed to take root in the countryside, especially in those regions with the greatest agrarian reform activity (Kay 1982).

The reform's aggregate economic effects appear to have been small. Microeconomic studies suggest little impact, either positive or negative, on productivity (Malmed-Sanjak and Carter 1991). Agriculture continued to

[50] McClintock (1981, 345-348) contrasts the very limited willingness of the relevant governments in Peru and in Chile to assign decision-making power to the *campesino* federations with the case of Yugoslavia where self-management was the norm. Federation members had little confidence in their own leaders because of their limited decision-making power.

[51] The CCP supported the expropriation of the *haciendas* but criticized the formation of super-cooperatives and defended the right of the *campesino* communities to recover lands adjudicated to them. In 1987 they did manage to recover 2 million hectares in Puno department.

grow slowly for the next couple of decades. Some have blamed the reform for this, but Sheahan (1999, 67) emphasizes that the stagnation preceded the reform. The first post-military government (Belaúnde's administration from 1980 to 1985) gave less emphasis to the sector. The short-term impact of the reform on income distribution was also small, with only one to two percent of national income changing hands;[52] it benefited one-third of all agricultural families, or a little under one-sixth of all families in the country (Webb and Figueroa 1975). The workers in the coastal operations wound up faring relatively well, but in the highlands the majority did not (Sheahan 1999, 64). The former landlords had decapitalized the farms when they realized they would be giving them up, another factor contributing to the slow growth of the sector.

All such limitations notwithstanding, the agrarian structure was left much less unequal by the reforms and there were widespread improvements in overall welfare. Based on interviews with many people who had lived through reforms undertaken during the last three decades of the twentieth century, Peruvian anthropologist Enrique Mayer (2009) concluded that, in breaking the unjust and oppressive *hacienda* system, they made as big a contribution as did the freeing of slaves in other places. One reflection of those gains was the reduced support for the Shining Path in reform zones and a dampening of subsequent conflict, effects which appeared to be due to the reform's facilitating counterinsurgency and intelligence gathering, building local organizational capacity later used to deter violence, undercutting the Marxist left, and increasing the opportunity costs to peasants who supported armed groups.[53]

The benefits from reform could clearly have been much greater had it been better designed, broader-ranging, and better implemented. According to Jolyne S. Melmed-Sanjak and Michael R. Carter (1991), the most damaging flaw was the inefficiencies implicit in the collective organization, even though these weaknesses did contribute over time to a shift toward independent farming units and were thus self-correcting. Instead of benefiting one-third or less of agricultural families it might have reached twice that many, delivered much greater benefits on average, and as a result redistributed

[52] The low figure is, in part, a result of the relatively small share of agricultural income in total national income at the time and in part of the fact that it was not the lowest income groups who most benefited.

[53] In reaching this conclusion Albertus (2020) uses a combination of data on all land expropriations under military rule from 1969 to 1980 and data from the Peruvian Truth and Reconciliation Commission on rural killings during Peru's internal conflict from 1980 to 2000.

a significant three to four percent of national income and cut income inequality considerably more and sooner than it did.[54] A picture of the potential benefits from a better structured reform accompanied by complementary investments can be inferred from the recent dramatic income gains in some remote areas of Peru following on a burst of growth in agriculture, a big increase in non-agricultural activities, and a considerable inflow of public and private remittances from those now working elsewhere. Webb (2013) attributes much of the boom to transportation improvement, which over ten years cut the time required to get produce to a city from 8.8 hours to half that. Annual family income growth, an estimated 1.4 percent from 1900 to 1994 leapt to 7.2 percent from 1994 to 2011,[55] a rate similar to that achieved in the golden age post-reform periods of Korea and Taiwan. The enormous improvement in the quality of life was reflected in the share of households with electricity which, after a gradual increase from 2.9 percent in 1972 to 29.2 percent in 1998, then leapt to 72.5 percent in 2012 (Webb 2013, 207).

These recent achievements suggest that, under conditions similar to those of the East Asian success stories, including a small family farm structure, Peru's land reform could have been a dramatic success in at least some of the remote areas. And, had it come a few years earlier, been better designed, and been more inclusive of various indigenous groups, it might have left such an unpromising setting that the *Sendero Luminoso* would not have arisen in the first place; certainly, it would not have been able to wreak the damage it did. *Sendero* had its roots in the1970s among university-based idealists, and it expanded greatly in the chaotic and, for many people, distressful 1980s. A 2003 report of the Truth and Reconciliation Committee blamed it directly for thirty-five thousand to forty thousand deaths from 1880 to 2000.[56] Peasants suffered especially from its brutality. Its goals were to replace Peru's political institutions with a communist peasant revolutionary regime, while resisting any influence from other Latin American guerilla groups (like the

[54] Eventually the failure to provide individual property rights was largely corrected, beginning in the 1980s and reaching a peak in the 1990s Fujimori years with programs supported by the IMF and the World Bank (Albertus 2021, 224). By this time, however, the potential gains of two decades had been foregone.

[55] Webb (2013, 160).

[56] Because its violence interacted with that of other actors, attribution is difficult. The Committee's official estimate is that there were between 61,007 and 77,552 deaths during this "time of fear." It attributed fifty-four percent of them to *Sendero Luminoso*, 1.5 percent to the Túpac Amaru Revolutionary Movement (a Marxist revolutionary group also operating at this time), and the remaining 44.5 percent to the police, the military, other political parties, security forces, and the government (especially under Fujimori). The majority of the violence was targeted at indigenous populations.

Tupac Amaru Revolutionary Movement) and from foreign ideologies (apart from that of Mao). Its basic strategy was to bring down the "imperfect democratic institutions" by force, in the process destroy the economy, and in the meantime thwart any government attempts to assist the population. With its early bases in revolutionary university youth and in Maoist ideas of the 1960s (when founder Amibael Guzmán visited China), the ideology was not at all rooted in Peru's rural reality. Guzmán played the role of the *Sendero*'s military and spiritual leader; its organization was more that of a hierarchical cult than a cell-based, horizontally structured institution (Council on Hemispheric Affairs 2008). Its role in Peru offers a partial parallel to that of *Fuerzas Armadas Revolucionarias de Colombia* (FARC) in Colombia; in each case, a serious agrarian reform could, in all likelihood, have avoided the great tragedy wrought, directly or indirectly, by the presence of a guerrilla group.

While Mexico and Bolivia and perhaps Peru can be classified as partial successes because they did yield major benefits, Guatemala and Colombia, both of which at some point or points have appeared close to serious reform, cannot.

## Guatemala's Daunting Setting for Reform

Guatemala underwent a nearly continuous social tragedy over the twentieth century, interrupted by one moment of real opportunity when the progressive government of Jacobo Árbenz (from 1951 to 1954) attempted a limited reform to an extremely unequal and backward agrarian system. It would have expropriated about one-fifth of the country's arable land and benefited close to one-quarter of the peasantry (Brockett 1988), in the process transferring unused land held by the United Fruit Company to new small farmers. Unfortunately, these were the McCarthy years in the US, with the associated hysteria around communism; the Eisenhower administration, heavily influenced by the Dulles brothers, was very susceptible.[57] The American intervention was followed by (led to, according to most observers) half

[57] Both of the Dulles brothers had worked with or for United Fruit in the 1930s. It is noteworthy that the previous Truman administration had also authorized a plan to topple Árbenz in 1952, with the support of notorious Salvadorian dictator Anastacio Somoza, but backed off when too many details became public (Schlesinger and Kinzer 1983).

a century of violence and around three hundred thousand deaths (United Nations 1999).

As of 1955, close to seventy percent of the labor force was still engaged in agriculture and income inequality was severe. A successful reform could thus have had a major impact. Since then, the country has for the most part remained an economic underachiever and a political and social disaster, featuring much corruption and violence, one of the highest levels of inequality and one of the weakest social expenditure performances in the world. It illustrates the sort of catastrophe that can follow on failed land reform, and the immense potential risk of living in the shadow of the US at a time when its government is averse to anything that may be tainted with the socialist/communist brush, and when its leadership is particularly weak on issues like land reform.

Guatemala's historic oppression of its majority indigenous population has had many similarities with Peru. After conquering the Mayas in Guatemala and the Incas in Peru, the Spanish invaders left a feudal system whose trappings remained long after the introduction of capitalist property relations in the nineteenth century; the rural *latifundios* combined the worst features of feudalism and capitalism (Proyect 1998). The introduction of coffee cultivation in the later nineteenth century was instrumental in laying the contemporary foundations for the semi-feudal oppression of the Maya,[58] who were displaced from their communal lands to make way for coffee and then forced into various binding work arrangements. White overlords in each department inhabited by Mayas processed requests for forced labor. This system gave way to a form of debt-bondage in 1894, which in turn was replaced in 1934 by a set of "Vagrancy Laws." Many tricks were employed to suck the victims into forced labor. During periods of labor shortage, the police would throw large numbers of people into jail for petty offenses and impose heavy fines that they could only work off by picking coffee on the plantation. Another tactic involved alcohol: "When partway drunk, an Indian will sell his soul for more liquor: upon this the *finca* [plantation] system is based.... So effectual are the familiar devices of colonial exploitation, alcoholism, easy credit, debt indenture, and liability for debts to the third generation, that once caught in the system, escape is difficult" (Bunzel 1940).

[58] The contrast with coffee's positive contribution in Costa Rica highlights the difference that setting makes.

## The Tragic Reversal of the Árbenz Reform

In the 1940s, an emerging class of urban professionals and merchants sought to modernize Guatemala and break what it considered an excessive dependency on coffee exports. Their Nationalist Party (*Partido de Integración Nacional*) was similar to such others as the APRA in Peru and the Peronists in Argentina; their goal was not socialism, but modernization and industrialization within a national framework (Proyect 1998). The working-class movement, which had some links to the Communist Party, supported it. Indigenous groups were secondary players; although Árbenz's *ladino* reformers wished to end their oppression, they were not seen as equal partners. This left a gap in Árbenz's social base, limited the potential of his movement, and may have contributed to its eventual defeat.

Guatemala's near reform left important lessons both because of the dire aftereffects of failure and because of the impressive internal forces that were mustered to do away with the traditional oppression of the underclass. As of mid-century, the distribution of land was extremely unequal: two percent of the population was said to control seventy-two percent of the arable land. Most of the landless were poor, indigenous peoples who had been treated as subordinate for hundreds of years, had become increasingly dependent on wages from plantation work and, according to some observers, had also become increasingly impoverished. The election of Juan Jose Arévalo in 1944 ushered in a period of democratization and liberal reforms—the so-called Ten Years of Spring; the constitution of 1945 stated that the government should protect communal land and pursue policies leading to a more equitable distribution of wealth. Only in 1944 were the Vagrancy Laws, the final mechanism of forced labor, brought to an end. On becoming president in 1951, Árbenz's goal was to transform the economy into an independent form of capitalism. He was aided politically by the Communist Party of Guatemala (*Partido Guatemalteco del Trabajo*, PGT), which, like many other such movements, believed that some amount of capitalist development was a necessary prelude to a communist revolution/government. He disagreed with some of their schemes, including the organization of producer cooperatives. His proposed agrarian reform law gained widespread support among popular organizations and in some of the national press, while being opposed by the large landowners association (*Asociación General de Agricultores*), some elements within the military, the Catholic Church, and much of the business class (Gleijeses 1989, 455–458).

The plan entailed redistribution of land from at most seventeen hundred estates to about one hundred thousand families or five hundred thousand people—one-sixth of the country's population (Gleijeses 1991). According to Decree 900 of 1952, just over six hundred thousand hectares of farmland—including a little under half of the 222,000 hectares owned by United Fruit—were to be redistributed through a process that authorized the transfer of all uncultivated land on estates larger than about 270 hectares, and on estates of ninety to 270 hectares where less than two-thirds was cultivated (Trefzger 2002). Properties of less than ninety hectares were exempt. Landowners were to be compensated in government bonds. This was by no means a harsh reform.

Union representatives began to travel through the countryside to inform people of the new law. To prevent their doing so, landowners closed private roads going through their property; the government then announced that all roads would become public. By 1954, more than three thousand local agrarian committees (*comités agricolas locales*, CALs) had been formed to administer the allocation of land at the local level; their existence and role represented a substantial increase in political influence for rural people. The law also increased the power of the President and of the new National Council (DAN).

Opposition came not only from landowners but also from groups who felt excluded or discriminated against. Some peasants seized land without going through legal channels, believing that the law provided them with a mandate to do so. There were rumors of peasants illegally occupying territory or burning pastures or crops so that the land would be declared uncultivated and hence subject to expropriation. Other incidents involved peasants acting in self-defense or in retaliation against landowners who sought to disobey the law or to intimidate them. A new crisis arose in 1953, when the Supreme Court ruled that the lack of judicial oversight for the reform made it unconstitutional and blocked further implementation. Congress, with Árbenz's urging, voted to impeach four judges, a step which provoked anti-government demonstrations.

The US government saw the reform as a communist threat.[59] Although the State Department recognized its limited dimensions, it feared that

[59] For the expropriation of its holdings United Fruit was to be compensated in bonds worth $627,572, the value of its land as reported for tax purposes. However, the company now alleged that it was worth much more, and it lobbied the U.S. for intervention. The State Department, on behalf of the United Fruit Company, claimed a figure of $15,854,849 (LaFeber, 1993, 76).

implementation would reinforce communist influence in the country. Various forms of pressure were exerted, some from private companies like the Wm. Wrigley Jr. Company, which announced that it would no longer purchase Guatemalan chicle. The US worked to develop relationships with members of the Guatemalan military, while instituting an arms blockade that made some in that military fear a security crisis or even a US invasion. The CIA intensified propaganda campaigns to isolate Guatemala among Central American countries, and to convince its population that the Árbenz regime was on the brink of collapse. In June 1954, Árbenz was overthrown by a multi-faceted operation involving a small army led by exiled general Carlos Castillo Armas, a US Naval blockade, bombardment by CIA planes, and a sophisticated CIA strategy of psychological warfare intended to demoralize Árbenz and provoke military defections (Bowen 1983). Although Castillo's attack was repelled, Árbenz resigned and Castillo became president, quickly reversing the bulk of the land redistribution that had occurred and destroying government documents pertaining to Decree 900. Two new land laws were passed, which transferred small amounts to a very modest number of families. Castillo also ended government support for labor unions and denounced their members as communists.

Debate continues as to the relative importance of the factors that blocked this reform, how promising things were before the coup, and what the reform's long-term impacts might have been had it proceeded. On the first point, observers have placed differing weights on the broad anti-communist stance of the US, its protection of national economic interests (the United Fruit Company), the domestic opposition of large landholders, and other factors. Many have judged that the reform was on a good path to succeed when it was subverted (Trefzger 2002).

There has also been considerable disagreement as to how much land had been expropriated and redistributed and how many families had benefited by the time of Árbenz's fall. José Aybar de Soto (1978) estimates that approximately twenty-four percent of Guatemala's total population did benefit directly from the reform (i.e., over seven hundred thousand people). Piero Gleijeses (1991) puts the figure of direct beneficiaries at about five hundred thousand. Jim Handy (1994) is more conservative, concluding that only nineteen percent of those eligible to benefit did receive land. All three agree that the reform was a quick success that significantly improved the lives of many Guatemalan peasants. Handy argues that the Mayan Indian population, in particular, were winners.

The optimistic view of these authors and a number of others sees the reform as not only benefiting many families and favoring the indigenous population, but also raising agricultural output, rural wages, and, in general, the quality of life. In contrast, Douglas W. Trefzger (2002) argues that the program was less encompassing than sometimes claimed due to discrimination in favor of the *ladino* minority in the distribution of land,[60] and that agricultural wages fell markedly from 1950 to 1955.[61] Whose views are closer to the truth on these matters may never be sorted out with precision. That some decline in output would have accompanied a process of substantial change, considerable uncertainty, and some conflict would not be surprising. Nor would a modest degree of bias against the indigenous peoples in the process. But the evidence that this reform was relatively well designed, together with the record from other such experiences in Latin America and elsewhere, provides much confidence that the final outcome, absent the coup, would have involved major social benefits, most notably the end of *de facto* servitude for a large group of people, the avoiding of hundreds of thousands of deaths in the years that followed, increased incomes for the vast majority of the people, and a significant increase in output, if only from peasants putting to use land that was previously left uncultivated (including that of United Fruit). In the best of cases, whatever the initial size of the beneficiary group, subsequent bouts of redistribution would have occurred as well. Reasons for pessimism were the power of the agrarian hierarchy and/or the US to successfully stand in the way by fomenting conflict in the former case and penalizing the country in the latter. The gap between the hopes of supporters and the actual outcomes probably explains part of the disagreement on how the reform was actually progressing in the lead-in to the coup.

Unpersuasive critics included Ross Pearson (1963, 227) who explained, and to a degree defended, the subsequent reform plans of the Castillo Armas government, arguing that although the Árbenz plan had considerable merit,

[60] His statistical analysis finds that "*ladino* departments," with 35.8 percent of total population benefited from 52.6 percent of total land expropriations while the Indian departments, with 64.2 percent of that population, benefited from only 47.4 percent of the expropriations.

[61] His figures indicate a decline of twelve percent over that period, made up of a sharp drop of twenty-two percent from 1950 to 1952, and then a partial recovery over the next three years. That wages would fall in the midst of a controversial reform seems hardly surprising; had the reform proceeded, they might well have continued to increase.

its administration was focused on speedy distribution and political expediency, as a result of which many beneficiaries were not getting enough land to provide a decent livelihood. Rapid distribution has, however, characterized most of the successful reforms, such as those of Japan, Korea, Taiwan, and China; sometimes there is a trade-off between getting the job done quickly and getting it done at all. The author posits that with average quality soil about twenty hectares were needed to provide the decent livelihood sought and that there simply was not enough to go around, an argument made to defend many "defensive reforms." When providing a high share of families with a reasonably sized farm requires that a high share of all land be transferred, it is tempting for the opponents to push for a number of beneficiaries small enough so that even if each is provided with a decent amount of land, the share transferred is minor. This both limits the scope of the reform and permits the claim that it is being "done right," even though the great majority of families are getting nothing. It predictably brings less overall social and economic benefits than does an egalitarian distribution.

The external (US) and domestic concern that the agrarian reform and other steps being pursued by this government were putting the country on the road to communism appear, in retrospect, to have been seriously exaggerated; as noted above, this was a period of particular US susceptibility to such thinking. While the reforms of 1944 to 1954 received strong support from the left, including the Communist Party, the eventual outcome of the process would quite probably have been no more revolutionary than the Costa Rican "revolution" of the same period. "That Árbenz was considered a radical—and in the Guatemalan context he certainly was—tells more about the nature of reactionary despotism in Central America than about him. Mild as the Árbenz reforms were, especially the land reform, they provoked the fury of the landed oligarchy" (Dore and Weeks 2007, 3). The long period of civil war that followed the coup pitted indigenous and poor Guatemalans against landowners on the economic front and a leftist guerilla insurgency against the military on the political one. Much good land was awarded to military officers and rich landowners tied to the military, thus maintaining or exacerbating the level of concentration. The period saw a deepening of the agro-export economic model, partly through further displacement of indigenous peoples from their land. One consequence was rural to urban "push" migration, as the big plantations became increasingly mechanized.

## Conflict and Genocide

In the 1960s, a guerrilla movement developed out of a coalition of groups, including the Communist Party. Like Árbenz's reform movement, it failed to sink deep roots within the "Indian" population, concentrating its efforts instead in predominately *mestizo* zones. The Guatemalan Communist Party saw the indigenous population as "culturally backward" and not having revolutionary potential (Proyect 1998, 2). After this movement had been defeated, one of its factions, the Frente Guerrillero Edgar Ibarra (FGEI), argued that any armed movement was bound to fail unless the indigenous population was involved in its leadership, an idea incorporated into the thinking of the "Guerrilla Army of the Poor" in the 1970s, which centered its activities on the highland Indian communities. The ferocity of the 1980s guerrilla war reflected the combination of a people fighting for their cultural and economic survival and a merciless army driving peasants off their land to make room for agro-export activity. In the words of Proyect (1998, 3):

> The countryside was the scene of a massive Indian, peasant and semi-proletarian resistance to a genocidal counterinsurgency war. Hundreds of thousands of highland Indians were exterminated and driven into flight away from the violence . . . . The guerrilla movement in Guatemala . . . was defeated by a "scorched earth" policy. Over 440 villages were entirely destroyed. Well over 100,000 civilians were killed or "disappeared." There were over 1 million people displaced persons, including 200,000 refugees who fled to Mexico. Accompanying these population displacements was the deliberate destruction of huge areas of the highlands, including by forest fires, in order to make sure that the region could never function as a theater for revolutionary operations. The consequent environmental despoliation was monumental, even to the extent of modifying climate and rainfall patterns.

## Market-led Agrarian Reform in a Context of Ongoing Tragedy

After decades of violence, a peace accord was reached in 1996. One of the most controversial but also essential components was increased access to land by those with too little of it. The state was charged with this task, setting the stage for the market-based, World Bank-supported land reform whose implementation began in 2000. In a setting like Guatemala's, it would be overly optimistic to expect major benefits, even if implementation had proceeded very successfully, because such benefits would require much more land than large owners could plausibly be expected to sell. Even if it worked perfectly, which it typically does not, a Market Led Agrarian Reform (MLAR) is not a good bet to achieve much in such an inegalitarian society, and in Guatemala's unpropitious setting it did not. The chronic land shortage was exacerbated by a "coffee crisis" beginning around 2000. Farmers who traditionally migrated from their small plots to seek harvesting jobs on plantations now found no available work. Dismissed workers could also be expelled from their homes and the land they had cultivated for decades (Viscidi 2004). Desperate groups of poor farmers occupied idle lands or refused to vacate plots which they had traditionally cultivated. Non-agricultural opportunities remained quite limited in most rural areas.

What was needed in this setting was a wide-ranging reform, such as that espoused by several *campesino*, indigenous, religious, and human rights organizations across Guatemala, who, to that end, formed the Agrarian Platform (*Plataforma Agraria*). This institution has advocated for the expropriation and redistribution of land taken illegally during the armed conflict and the taxing of idle land to force owners to create jobs or turn the property over to landless agricultural workers. Redistribution would be complemented by government provision of technical assistance, credit, and market information to small farmers. Instead, what appeared was the market-based version. Susana Gauster and S. Ryan Isakson (2007) conclude that the latter strategy did not improve poor Guatemalans' access to land but rather, paradoxically, burdened many of the intended beneficiaries with debt and even made them worse off. Over its eight years of operation, it facilitated the distribution of just four percent of agricultural land, most of it overpriced and of little productive potential due to poor quality. Given its dependence on the repayment of loans, market-assisted land reform is unlikely to benefit the neediest peasants. It targets those with the greatest entrepreneurial potential, but too often does not provide the necessary training or guarantee appropriate quality of land. It can create so many transaction costs for land-hungry peasants that many drop out of the process.

The failure of Guatemala's market-assisted reform can also be attributed in part to its vision of land as nothing more than a commodity. While there may be plenty of willing buyers, most wealthy landholders are unwilling to sell their property even at what seem to be reasonable prices (Gauster and Isakson 2007). Land is a source of political power and social prestige, as well as providing security against the instability of Guatemala's export-oriented economy. Meanwhile, the importance of ownership to the rural poor also involves not just a path to improving their economic but also their political and social well-being. For the predominantly Mayan majority, it is a means of cultivating maize and beans for food security and simultaneously fulfilling their cultural heritage. The many non-market-related benefits from land can make it simplistic to lay the groundwork for a major redistribution toward small landholders around economic considerations alone. Possibly Guatemalan policymakers had come to this realization, when they replaced what would have been the second of three planned World Bank loans with a land rental program that dealt with some of the immediate needs for land, but ultimately tended to benefit the agrarian elite through the state-subsidized land transactions it fostered.

The current Guatemalan constitution, promulgated in 1985, while stressing the sanctity of private property, does theoretically open the door to a more comprehensive reform through its Article 40, which permits the expropriation of land to meet social needs, so long as owners are justly compensated in due time. But everything then depends on how "justly" is defined. True justice will only be served when Guatemala's indigenous population recovers the stolen land that is their heritage. Gauster and Isakson (2007, 1535) also note that the 1996 Peace Accords call for a "firm and lasting peace," something that "will not be achieved until the inequitable distribution of land, which underpinned the civil war and continues to be the source of political conflict, is resolved." "Just compensation," as that condition is likely to be applied in Guatemala, is inconsistent with a lasting peace. As Carlos Camacho Nassar (2010, 2) puts it: "the inequalities of agrarian structure are at the root of the economic, social, political and cultural contradictions which generated the war during the last four decades of the last century . . . . To defend an archaic and racist bourgeoisie, the country suffered what were perhaps the most atrocious military dictatorships in the history of the continent."

To date, the country has not made amends for those horrors. It still has one of the most skewed land distribution patterns in the world and the second most inequitable in Latin America—roughly two percent of the population owns seventy percent of all productive farmland. Although long-term growth has been moderate (an average of 3.8 percent from 1960 to 2019

(World Bank, n.d.), the rapid population growth of nearly 2.4 percent per year has left only a modest increase in per capita income of under 1.4 percent per year, a rate at which it takes fifty years to double that income, something which took only about ten years for Taiwan's rural population when the country was at the height of its post land-reform growth burst. Guatemala's fast population growth is, in part, a result of low levels of education. The enduring impacts of its sad history show up today in very high rates of poverty and extreme poverty. As of 2016, Guatemala and Nicaragua were the only countries of Latin America where the latter rate exceeded fifteen percent, while Guatemala and Honduras were the only ones where poverty exceeded fifty percent (CEPAL 2018, 81).

Guatemala's experience invites comparison with that of Bolivia. Prior to the reform movements of the 1950s, both were characterized by brutally oppressive agrarian systems. Bolivia's reform ended the worst of the oppression and went a considerable way to raising the living standards of the indigenous peasantry. Still, poverty and overall income inequality remained very high into the twenty-first century, the large farm sector remained strong, and the quality of governance was on average weak. Under the administration of Evo Morales and with the benefit of large mineral revenues, however, income inequality has fallen sharply and poverty with it. The death toll from land-related conflicts since the 1950s was modest by comparison with cases like Guatemala and Colombia, despite a number of oppressive governments and considerable conflict around land at times. In Guatemala, most of the approximately three hundred thousand deaths were at the hands of a vicious military which undertook massacres and, in essence, genocide. Both there and in Bolivia, a growing commercial agricultural export sector was behind much of the continuing battle for land; in Guatemala, this led to the clearing of indigenous zones, whereas in Bolivia, the Santa Cruz zone where commercial agriculture has flourished was not traditionally the home of many indigenous peasants. The factors underlying the enormously different outcomes remain a matter of interest: how much was due to different US involvement over time or to a greater worry about communist presence within Guatemala; how much to a possibly stronger progressive movement in Bolivia; how much to a stronger large farm pressure group in Guatemala, including United Fruit; and how much to a differently oriented military?

Whatever the causes of the failure, it is hard to imagine a much worse trajectory of events than what actually happened in Guatemala. Even if the 1950s reform attempt had fallen short on many dimensions, such as the initial inequality of treatment among ethnic groups and the inadequacy of technological support for rising productivity of the new small farms, the net benefits would have been huge and the contrast with the actual course of events almost unfathomable.

With the recent election of progressive candidate Bernardo Arévalo in 2023—the son of former President Juan José Arévalo, as President-elect, some degree of optimism for the country's future has returned.

## Colombia

Colombia's recurrent attempts at agrarian reform provide one of the world's most complicated and tragic stories on this front. The recently ended civil war between the government and the guerrilla group FARC lasted fifty-two years. About one million deaths have been the result of land conflict since 1900 and many millions have been displaced.

### The Challenging Setting

Land conflict and the associated violence had their origins in the historic inequality of access to land—more specifically in the lasting grievances of peasants who had been dispossessed of land they considered to be theirs.[62] More than half a century before the birth of FARC, land conflicts were part of the civil wars which recurred every thirty years or so, and which were finally brought to a temporary end by the National Front, a sharing of governmental authority between the competing Conservative and Liberal parties (1958–1974). The most famous wave of violence (known as "La Violencia"), occurring mainly in the 1940s and 1950s and claiming two hundred to three hundred thousand lives, was originally portrayed by most historians as a battle of "hereditary hatreds" between members of those rival parties. No one doubts that this factor was quite important, but a second round of analysis (Sanchez 1977; Legrand 1986) clarified how central the interaction was

[62] In the prominent role of felt grievances—as opposed simply to not having land when others have a lot of it—Colombia's known history bears important parallels with those of Vietnam (as emphasized by Scott) and Mexico (as stressed by Tutino 1986) but no doubt also, albeit perhaps in lesser degree, to those of many other countries including Peru, Brazil, and Guatemala. Widely publicized narratives have not included those of the victims of dispossession, while outsiders to these events, even those searching to do so, cannot easily get at the truth.

between land issues and the political confrontations. A key background element was the growth of the coffee export industry, which raised the value of land in some regions. Many participants in the conflicts had either land acquisition or its recovery after dispossession as their main objective, and much land changed hands under the fog of the ongoing political violence. The National Front greatly calmed the political battle but by no means ended the rural conflict, which has experienced resurgences from the 1980s on. By then, the main direct actors were the guerrillas, the narcotics industry, the paramilitaries who initially defended large farmers from threatened kidnappings, various public officials whose interests overlapped with some of the above, and a very corrupt judicial system as it applied to rural land. Behind all this was a political system still heavily influenced by agrarian elites. The upshot has been another two hundred to three hundred thousand lives lost and up to five to seven million people displaced, mostly from rural areas and many of them small farmers.[63] Meanwhile, Albertus (2021, 58) estimates that between 1930 and 2000, the government distributed two to three million hectares of land in reform projects, a maximum of four percent of the land registered in 2000. For every ten hectares distributed, three to five people died in mainly land-related violence and twenty-five to thirty people were displaced.

Unlike Guatemala, a politically fragile and very underdeveloped country in which an elected government had only one real opportunity to advance on the land front, Colombia has a history of nearly continuous, albeit flawed, democracy since the first years of the twentieth century, a fact that lends it special interest among nations attempting to resolve the problem of excessive land concentration. There has been much in-depth analysis of its agrarian problems, resulting in an impressive understanding of them. Reasonably serious attempts at limited reforms were undertaken or begun in the 1930s, the 1960s, and the 1990s, respectively. Despite considerable effort dedicated to the task of improving the quality of rural life, the outcome—at least with respect to land distribution and to the physical and economic security of the rural population—has been a resounding failure. The most recent measures

[63] Colombia has, for several decades, been among the world's top four or five countries in terms of the absolute number of displaced people and has at times had the highest homicide rate. It is also among the most dangerous countries for journalists and civil rights activists. In 2019, it led the world with 106 murders of activists, about one-third of the world total. (The Philippines was the second deadliest country with forty-three killings, followed by Honduras, Brazil, and Mexico). Targeted violence against community leaders opposing environmentally destructive mega-projects has spiraled since the 2016 peace accords.

of land concentration suggest that it is as high or higher than ever before (with a Gini coefficient of above 0.9 according to one recent estimate),[64] while income inequality is among the half-dozen candidates for the world's highest (with a Gini of around and perhaps above 0.6)[65] and, as noted below, the hopes built around the 2016 peace agreement with the FARC continuing until recently to be crushed. Major protests of early 2021 were among the latest manifestations of unrest as the country suffered the impact of COVID-19.

Violence and injustice have long been integral parts of Colombia's social construct; land concentration has been and remains both cause and effect of both.[66] Most small farmers threatened by violence cannot escape it by residing in urban areas, as absentee landlords can and have. As in Brazil, the particularly weak rule of law within the agrarian system and outside the cities more generally, plays into the hands of violent and abusive mining and forestry industries and invites their aggressiveness. It is not surprising that the inequalities and injustices that go with land concentration should make elections more violent, a notable feature of Colombia's history especially in the 1930s and 1940s, and periodically since then. Even today, that concentration contributes to both electoral violence and fraud against voters in rural areas. Where violent actors have close ties with state officials and political elites, their presence is manifested primarily in fraud; otherwise, it takes the form of physical aggression. Land concentration deters democracy and political reform in these, among many other, ways (Nieto-Matiz 2019, 276).

Although underplayed in some early histories, land has been a main cause of the Colombian conflict since at least the late nineteenth century and has long been recognized as such by those close to the issue. Maria del Pilar López-Uribe and Fabio Sanchez Sanchez (2018) judge that the main facilitating factor has been the historically weak enforcement of property rights, allowing peasants to be dispossessed of their lands by large landholders, in many cases with the informal approval of the State. Some of the resulting grievances have taken a legal form, in which the peasant filed a

[64] Ibáñez et al. (2012).

[65] An estimate based on an adjustment of household survey data to take into account the high incomes those surveys typically fail to record (see Alvaredo and Gasparini 2013).

[66] Thus the National Center for Historic Memory (CNMH 2013), which studies Colombian armed conflict, asserts that "the appropriation, use, and possession of land have been the driving force of the origin and persistence of armed conflict." Berry (2017a) reviews the major interactions among land, violence, and injustice. Land concentration has been associated with fraud, violence, and clientelism in many contexts, including nineteenth-century Germany and today's Sub-Saharan Africa (Klaus and Mitchell 2015).

petition for land protection or restitution; others have led to invasions and violence.

While recognized worldwide as a violent country, something relatively easy to observe and measure, Colombia is less well known for its injustice and extreme inequality—of income, of wealth in general, and of agricultural land in particular. Violence and injustice have here been tightly linked in rural areas, in a context of weak property rights. Much of that violence and injustice has been associated with misappropriation of agricultural land—dispossession through theft, extortion, and legal manipulation, among other mechanisms. The currently extreme concentration of land is largely a product of these illegitimate means. The percentage of today's large properties acquired through fully legitimate means (i.e., without involving blood, dispossession, or any type of fraud) probably falls in the range of ten to twenty-five percent, depending on the definition of legitimacy applied (Berry 2017a, 278); a broad definition would include only accumulation that has not involved any current or recent violence, coercion, bribing of bureaucrats, legal manipulation, or similar means.[67] By an even broader definition that includes the fairness of state allocation of public lands and the regulations that determine who winds up with what, little or none of the land currently in large farms could be judged to have been free of some injustice, if only in the "unfairness" of original allocation. In summary, fairness in twentieth-century Colombia around matters of rural land has been in short supply, not only in absolute terms but also in comparison with most other countries.[68] The state has been unable to prevent a huge number of injustices, and it has often facilitated them. This failure to protect vulnerable small farms from direct encroachment by larger ones has underlain the displacement of several million people from small units, through either physical violence or legal manipulation; therefore, the large-farm sector has taken much of the land it wanted. Fortunately for the small farmers, it has not

[67] Many transactions involve a buyer who is formally innocent of fraud or other illegitimate behavior but a seller (or intermediary) who has engaged in it. Under a narrow definition of legitimate accumulation, no illegitimate transfers of this or of more obvious kinds could have occurred over several decades. Even before the conflict and violence of the last decades, this percentage was probably low. An agronomist who knows the country well once told me that he had yet to find a large property created without somehow taking advantage of settlers, of ambiguous laws, or of other inappropriate means.

[68] As discussed, the high degree of rural violence is a key factor distinguishing Colombia from nearly all other countries. That violence goes hand-in-hand with injustice when, for example, it is the means of displacing people from the land they previously held. It also reduces the capacity of the judicial system in general.

wanted it all, in particular the land on steep slopes, the land whose quality leaves it of little value for large scale operations, and so on. This history fits well with Scott's hypothesis of a state designed to help an elite extract an agricultural surplus. And it explains why, since its foundation, FARC has put the land issue at the center of its political agenda; its leaders have often cited the expansion of the *latifundio* through violent dispossession of peasants as their *raison d'etre.* They have demanded the takeover of large properties that they claim have been consolidated through legal fraud as well as physical dispossession (Faguet et al. 2000).

When did inequality become so high in Colombia and why did it remain so? Prior to about the middle of the last century quantitative details are scarce but many known features suggest that it was always high (Melo 2012). In the still very agricultural society of the early twentieth century, a significant share both of total income and of that of the richest group was generated in agriculture; because land was very unequally distributed, land-based income was as well. Meanwhile, local elites discouraged education for the populace, with the result that, in the late nineteenth century, Colombia was one of the least educated countries among those with similar income levels.[69] The resulting inequality of "human capital" complemented the high concentration of land as sources of a very unequal distribution of agricultural income. This in turn largely determined overall income inequality and, given its notorious stability over time in most countries, thereby set the historical pattern for what was to come.

## The 1930 Attempt and "La Violencia"

The first setting for reform came in the 1930s. The impacts of the Great Depression and of the displacement of small farmers during the coffee export boom, which had begun a couple of decades earlier, led to serious rural unrest. Its focal point was Central Colombia, where squatters (*colonos*) were creating a small-farm-oriented structure whose importance was rising relative to the larger-scale estates characteristic of the previous period. In this context, land "entrepreneurs" targeted the parcels farmed by these squatters for appropriation, assuming they had been chosen for fertility, access to

[69] The comparison is among countries for which data are available. See Ramirez and Salazar (2007).

market, and the like. Unexploited terrain and absentee ownership were common. Property rights institutions could not easily distinguish between public and private lands, or decide who had rights to the latter (Flores 2014, 17). Regulation of land conflicts largely devolved to local governments, with mayors playing an integral role (Legrand 1986, 74). Both mayors and judges tended to be sympathetic to large landholder (*hacendado*) claims.

The unrest worried political leaders both because of its destabilizing impact and its possible dampening effect on agricultural production, especially of food crops at a time when their supply appeared insecure. Several prominent observers blamed the perceived stagnation of the food supply on the concentration of land in the *latifundios* (Lopez 1927; Uribe 1936). Important figures in the Liberal Party saw the dissatisfied squatters and small landholders as a political resource on which they might draw. The threat to the rural elite was signaled by a wave of invasions of large farms beginning in the late 1920s, many in response to earlier dispossession. It helped to lay the groundwork for the reform attempt formalized in Law 200 of 1936 during the administration of President Alfonso López Pumarejo (from 1934 to 1938). Public sector support for small farmers had been manifested in the country's first colonization program and by an emblematic 1926 Supreme Court decision, the so-called *Prueba Diabolica*, which, in assuming that every plot was public unless and until proven otherwise, applied a narrow definition of legal possession; this made it harder for large landholders to reclaim lands invaded by squatters and more generally cast doubts on the legitimacy of their titles. Although Law 200 was the final step in a process which had the stated (and for many participants real) objective of facilitating peasant access to land, in fact its reversal of the *Prueba Diabolica* requirement helped to validate the existing land concentration and to reduce the costs of further accumulation for anyone who could claim to be occupying a plot. Its legal aspects were advantageous to landlords; transaction costs around that legalization process "greatly favoured wealthier (and larger) farm operators, especially in a context in which landed elites could mount much political and economic power in defense of property" (Torres 2020, 2). Thus, despite its progressive declared intentions, it has been widely seen as having facilitated the appropriation of land by the agrarian elite, while allowing and facilitating the ongoing eviction of peasants (Machado 2009; LeGrand 1986). Further, it provided an incentive for large landholders to expel current squatters to avoid future claim-related conflicts. To top things off, it was accompanied by a vagrancy law that facilitated the removal of expelled squatters.

These latter features reflected the fact that by the time Law 200 was passed the balance of power was shifting back toward the landlords. The experience exemplifies how what is, or what appears to be, a serious attempt to reduce inequality in the access to land can instead wind up doing the opposite because of landlords' capacity to adapt to ongoing institutional changes in a way that leaves them the main beneficiaries (Torres 2020). That capacity involves the overlap between the economic (landed) and the political elites and the noteworthy ability of landowner associations to organize collective action in defense of "their" property. While the strong resistance of the landed elite was interfering with López's original plans, the push for reform lost much of its initial impetus as his government came to focus more on the Liberal Party's potential among the urban populace rather than the peasants. Not only did this reform attempt fail to bring a better distribution of land but, through its perverse effects on large landholder behavior, it fed strongly into the escalating rural violence centered in the 1940s and 1950s ("*La Violencia*") and to the creation of the largest guerrilla group—the FARC.

As the coffee boom proceeded, each side in the battle for land intensified its tactics. The Communist Party of Colombia helped to create collectives and squatter organizations in permanent colonies. Simultaneously, there was a major increase in the adjudication of state lands (Legrand 1986), and much displacement of families within the coffee zones, especially those that were still being settled. In the process, formerly peaceful *campesinos* were motivated by repeated violent expulsions to take up arms. FARC, established in 1964, grew directly out of the agrarian mobilizations of the 1920s and 1930s; for FARC, land issues were always central.[70] Adolfo Molano (1992, 210) cites its ability to slow the rate of expropriation of peasant land by large landowners and to provide certain public goods as reasons for its ability to survive its difficult early years. The Colombian army's attempts to crush the guerrillas had only mixed success; for example, although it retook the area around Marquetalia (the most famous of the so-called independent republics established by the guerrillas) it failed to kill or capture many guerrillas or to seriously dent their fighting power (Flores 2014, 23).[71]

The many factors contributing to "La Violencia" have been widely debated. No one doubts that both land conflicts and the "hereditary hatreds"

[70] For example, a solution to the land issues was the main demand enunciated by FARC in the peace negotiations of 2016.

[71] Palacios (2006, 193) notes that the FARC's collective level of organization, discipline and cultivation of local support networks far exceeded anything the Colombia military had previously seen.

between Liberals and Conservatives played important roles.[72] In a careful statistical analysis, López-Uribe and Sanchez (2018) conclude that, on the land front, the main direct cause was the historically weak enforcement of property rights, which invited large landholders to displace peasants who felt entitled to the land they had been cultivating. Dispossession then bred a strong sense of personal grievance. The main operative mechanism was not the resulting inequality of land distribution, nor the economic condition of the dispossessed families, which was often seriously aggravated,[73] but this sense of grievance.[74] Its intensity and the related conflict was amplified by the so-called hereditary hatreds between Liberals and Conservatives.[75] The eventual scale of the conflict during "*La Violencia*" was fostered by the level of earlier and ongoing displacements and, as noted, led to the creation of the FARC.

## The Tragic Failure of the 1960s Attempt

Colombia's 1960s reform attempt was one of several occurring in the context of the Cold War, US fear of communism, the recent Castro take-over in Cuba, and rural protests and uprisings in other countries. Like the 1930s attempt, it did not significantly alter land distribution and, through that failure, indirectly facilitated decades more of violence. It played out in the country's imperfect democracy, after two decades of intensifying violence rooted in the conflict around control of land and the partisan rivalry for political power at the national and regional levels, where the payoff to that power depended substantially on facilitating the control of land. Among the elites, "*La Violencia*" created fear of a political breakdown that could generate widespread rebellion. A flash point was the murder of leftist leader Jorge Gaitán in 1948, leading to an uprising and to enormous destruction in Bogota (the *Bogotazo*); this, together with the presidency of hard right Conservative Laureano Gómez soon thereafter (1950 to 1953), fueled further political conflict and induced leaders of the two parties to invite General

[72] An early review of possible factors contributing to the wave of violence is provided by Pollock (1975).

[73] Loss of income was typically accompanied by loss of food security, and sometimes also by loss of an adequate food supply in the community (Reyes 2016).

[74] This conclusion mirrors that of Scott (1976) in the case of Vietnamese peasants during the French colonial regime (see Chapter 5).

[75] An early review of possible factors involved is Pollock (1975).

Rojas Pinilla to calm things down. After his four-year stint as President, those parties cooperated during the sixteen-year bipartisan compromise known as the National Front, which included shared control of state institutions and alternating presidencies.

The 1950s and 1960s brought a focus in the richer industrial countries (the so-called First World) on the need for "Third World Development," and an early stage of post-war thinking about the steps needed to achieve it.[76] A popular and often dominant strand of thinking saw this development as involving the use of modern technologies and practices to transform traditional communities and put an end to the feudal structures within which they lived.[77] Such thinking underlies the justifications for and the formulation of land reform policy. A "developmentalist state" was expected to "modernize" those subjects whose "traditional" character was seen to go hand-in-hand with their serf-like status and constitute the main cause of their poverty.[78] Colombia was one of the first developing countries included in a World Bank-led plan to promote development; it was the first to receive a World Bank mission after that institution's creation, a mission headed by soon-to-be government advisor Lauchlin Currie.

The land reform policy, implemented a decade after the World Bank mission (although not based on its set of proposals), was designed to preserve the existing pattern of extreme land concentration in the more densely populated areas of the country, while creating new agricultural space for the large group of land-seekers produced by the great displacements of the 1930s, 1940s, and 1950s. The focus on colonization of new (public) lands avoided any significant loss of land or power by the traditional agrarian elite.[79] In one common ruling group perspective, what was needed was to take a dangerous

[76] The 1950s saw the first phase of what became known as "development economics" with the works of such pioneers as Arthur Lewis (1954), Ragnar Nurkse (1953), and Paul Rosenstein-Rodan (1961). But its key elements had not yet much found their way into government thinking.

[77] Thus part of the general development agenda of a number of Latin American countries in the 1960s was the abolition of "pre-capitalist" forms of land tenure and agricultural labor relations through land reform (de Janvry 1981).

[78] Such thinking corresponded to the "modernization" view on what development of Third World countries involved, as exemplified by Rostow (1960). For a discussion of its interface with the Alliance of Progress, see Ish-Shalom (2006). Kapstein (2017) reviews US foreign policy in the Cold War context, when the promotion of land reform became a significant instrument. Poverty and inequality were seen as the main causes of rebellions and uprisings. They had to be tackled to avoid the increasing spread of communism and to prevent revolution. Through land distribution and the "land to the tiller" policy, the aim was to create a conservative peasantry and a bulwark against communism, as well as to promote overall political stability.

[79] Villaveces and Sánchez (2015) review the quantitative history of public land adjudications over the twentieth century.

group that threatened the land rights of that elite, and whose resentments contributed to the strengthening of the communist-supported guerrillas, and to create a life for them good enough to defuse the threat they embodied.

The key features of this Colombian experience, beginning in the 1960s, involved a government not inclined or in a position to implement a major redistribution of already operated land, but also without an easy and cheap alternative way to provide the tens of thousands of displaced farmers with satisfactory life conditions.[80] The Cold War was a dominant feature of the international setting; for the US, the central goal was keeping communism at bay. A third element at play was the widespread belief that the part of the rural population viewed as a political threat was incapable on its own of becoming a major positive contributor to agricultural and overall development; to prevent its morphing into an even-greater threat, conditions had to be created in which its backwardness would not expedite that outcome.

American support came via the Alliance for Progress and drew on confidence generated by the successful US-backed reforms in Taiwan, Japan, and South Korea during the early post-World War II years (Dorner 1992). Its aim was to finance and mobilize local political will to carry out various social reforms, including those around land, to alleviate rural poverty and counteract the spread of communism among the region's rural poor.[81] Most of the money spent on the reform came from US assistance (Duff 1968), justified by the view that land tenure conditions were the main obstacle to political stability; that is, that in the absence of improved opportunities, the accumulating discontent could generate a full-scale rebellion, and the belief that the social problems of Colombia could affect general hemispheric order.[82] Security was thus the main direct rationale for the policy. Colombian president Alberto Lleras (from 1958 to 1962) shared this take on the problems to be solved, as did the ruling elites. Various projects meant to alleviate the "distress and unrest" of rural populations were carried out under the reform. Partly because the policy was mainly organized in response to

[80] The rural violence was spurring very rapid rural to urban migration, making Bogota the fastest growing city in the world (at about eight percent per year) within its size range over the intercensal period from 1951 to 1964. This stretched the capacity of the cities to absorb the people forced to move, and it fed a strong preference on the part of urban dwellers against more arrivals.

[81] Such calls for reform from Washington had precedents in the World Bank's role in the reconstruction of Europe and in Harry Truman's developmentalist discourse since the early 1950s.

[82] In the words of Jorgenson (1963, 25): "It seems one of the major lessons to be learned from past foreign assistance is that unless the wants of the dispossessed in the rural distress areas are met . . . we shall continue to have centers of dangerous discontent—more Laos, more Viet Nams, and more Cubas."

a broad perceived threat to the national order, to hemispheric security, and to Western culture, it tended to lack the specificity of design needed to guarantee improvements in the welfare of this specific target group or its successful inclusion in the broader society (Galvis 2009). That the support for newly created colonies was inadequate to produce systematically good incomes for enough families, plus the fact that most of those who did get land were physically separated and thus harder to control, laid the groundwork for guerrillas, drug industries, and others to move in and exert their own power.

In retrospect there was very little prospect of a reform that would produce a big payoff, defined as large and rapid welfare improvements for most of those in the bottom quarter or third of the country's income distribution, together with the lasting benefits that typically accompany a substantial decrease in inequality. The defining features of the country's own society and agrarian structure, and the timing of the uprisings and revolts that contributed to the reform, weighed too heavily against this outcome. On a scale from zero to ten, where the latter would imply major economic, social, and political benefits in both the short- and long-term, what actually happened would merit a score of close to zero. The direct benefits—including those from the integrated rural development program (DRI) and various other successful initiatives were significant, but the social costs of not doing more—expressed in terms of violence and insecurity—were and remained enormous, and the country was left with a deep and abiding inequality which now rests not only on the traditional sources (mainly land concentration) but also on the profits from illegal industries or activities (drugs, unregulated mining, etc.) and on corruption and use of force.

The range of possible outcomes from the 1960s reform depended on six main political forces then directly at play: the right-wing and more rural-based Conservative party; the more centrist and partially industrial bourgeoisie-based Liberal party; the rural protestors, some simply wanting a piece of land but an increasing share having institutional support from the guerrilla groups backed by/connected to the Communist party; those guerrilla groups, of which the FARC was the largest; the large landholders opposed to change; and the US government. A major reform, like those of East Asia, was not on the table, both because of Colombia's political configuration, wherein the two rival parties shared (though with differing intensity) an interest in blocking it, and because the pressures for serious reform were not strong enough by themselves to carry the day and did not have the backing of the country's military—which in any case had no recent history of uninvited political involvement, or of the US government.

A comparison with Brazil's experience highlights the greater role of protesters in that case than in Colombia, and the probably greater role of social and religious groups as well. Each of the three groups identified by N. Patrick Peritore and Anna Karina Glave Peritore (1990) as supporters of reform in Brazil—the Church radicals, the secular radicals, and the agrarian populists—appears to have been weaker/less present in Colombia. Some church-based groups did provide support but much of the hierarchy was firmly on the side of the landed elite. The 1960s "awakening" of the Latin Church, symbolized by the 1968 Council of Latin American Bishops in Medellin, saw Catholic leaders from across the region examine how Vatican II should be implemented there.[83] Previously, Colombian Catholic leaders had encouraged the poor to retain their dignity by continuing in their existing tasks, implying that "poverty was less a product of the social structure . . . than a result of the faulty habits of the poor" (Levine 1981, 85, cited by Estrem 2016, 51). The Pope's new view, however, was that the poor should no longer be seen as individually deficient, but rather as victims of structural deficiencies. "In the end, although the Council forged a new path for the broader Latin American Church . . . Colombian leaders were among the least responsive to its results, remaining staunchly on the periphery of this new social-revolutionary mentality in spite of hosting the conference on their own turf" (Estrem 2016, 52). Although a shift in views among many at or near the top of the world hierarchy was underway, it was relatively slow in Colombia and came too late to influence the views of those who mattered on contemporary issues of justice like agrarian reform. Outliers like Father Camilo Torres, co-founder of the sociology department at the National University (*Universidad Nacional*) in Bogota, joined the guerrillas; he was killed in 1966.

Because policy in Colombia was arguably determined by a narrower group in and near government than was the case of Brazil, it is probable that their views mattered more. Neither the concept of the "competent *campesino*" nor the idea that small farms could be more productive than large ones

[83] In a significant break with the Church's tradition, the conference's agenda did not begin with doctrine followed by recommendations for application but rather with observations about society followed by "theological reflections" on those conditions. Instead of downplaying the importance of class structure, it drew on a movement across the region encouraging those in lower classes to push for improved social conditions (Estrem 2016).

was at all common. And whereas in the lead-in to the 1930s effort around Law 200 there was some recognition that unproductive *haciendas* might be responsible for inadequate food production, by the 1960s a new commercial component of agriculture was expanding and showing promise (Atkinson 1970).[84] At its creation in 1961, the Colombian Institute for Agrarian Reform (*Instituto Colombiano de la Reforma Agraria*—INCORA) included on its Agrarian Reform Committee members of the landed elite, the armed forces, congressmen, and a maximum of two peasant representatives among a total of fifteen members (Albertus 2013, 204). This board selected zones for reform projects and was strongly influenced by resistance from the landed elite (Duff 1968).

In light of this political constellation, the best that could be hoped for was a very modest transfer of land from large unproductive units to small ones, accompanied by a well-designed and supported colonization program and by an improved support system for the small-scale sector in general. Debate continues on how much benefit such a reform could have brought; given that much colonization on fairly productive land was still possible, it was probably substantial. Had it brought *campesino* standards of living up substantially and also successfully protected the new communities from predators who wanted their land or would abuse them in other ways, the benefits would indeed have been quite large. But building such successful communities in newly settled regions would have involved a considerable investment (especially if the displacement of indigenous groups was to be avoided), which the ruling elite was unlikely to make unless it felt under immediate threat of revolution. The second, and major, benefit from success on this front would have been avoiding the deaths of two hundred thousand or more people and the displacement of millions, phenomena that have again come to be synonymous with Colombia over the last forty years. In retrospect it is clear that the only path to assured success was a quick and substantial transfer of land that also laid the political foundation for continued support to the now expanded small-scale agricultural sector, combined with a future allocation of still unsettled lands that did not permit a reconcentration. Such a trajectory was not politically possible. In the reality that unfolded, the reform attempted was far too limited to effect the needed change in agrarian structure. The ongoing allocation of public lands also appears not to have made much difference; thus,

[84] As of the late 1940s, Lauchlin Currie, head of the 1949 World Bank Mission to Colombia, observed that much of the best land near Bogota was in large, relatively unproductive cattle farms (International Bank for Reconstruction and Development 1950).

Colombia still has one of the highest land concentrations in the world, with any downward effect from the reform process being offset by factors working in the other direction. Data on the size distribution of adjudications over the period from 1901 to 2012 show that a little over one-third of the land fell in the range of one hundred to five hundred hectares, a little under one-third in larger units, and about one-third in smaller ones,[85] a distribution less unequal than that existing at most points of time, but far from an egalitarian one.[86] That a sequence of well-executed land allocations could have brought much gain is suggested by the detailed analysis of Faguet et al. (2020). They conclude that, more often than not, and specifically in municipalities with few or no *latifundia*, the effect of public land distribution was to increase the average size of rural properties (as expected), to advance overall development, and to decrease land inequality, a combination that raised the social status of the poor, fostered their greater participation in local and national politics, and eventually led to more investment and expenditure on public services and to higher local taxes. In contrast, in municipalities with high initial land concentration there was a "pernicious *latifundia* effect" whereby large landholders used their power to capture land intended for the poor and probably also to strengthen their grip on local politics. These municipalities featured lower public investment and service provision, increased poverty, and less development.[87] Whatever has been the net effect of the adjudications on Colombia's rural population, much more might have been achieved had the favorable outcomes in those municipalities without prominent landed elites been present everywhere. Still, the adjudications could not by themselves substitute for a major redistributive reform; they could not distribute enough land fast enough to satisfy the needs, nor could they assure that the recipients would include enough of those *campesinos* who had previously been dispossessed of what they considered to be theirs to greatly reduce the associated resentments and thereby remove the fuel for future invasions and conflicts.

In any event, the land reform was implemented (or impeded) by a series of governments, beginning with that of Alberto Lleras Camargo (from 1958 to 1962). The major effort was undertaken by the generally impressive

[85] Based on Villaveces and Sánchez (2015, 28).

[86] At least not unless land quality was much lower on the large units adjudicated than on the smaller ones.

[87] Faguet et al. (2020, 1). Although the *latifundistas* appear to be affecting outcomes negatively in the cited municipalities, the authors find little evidence that their power is channeled via elections. Other means may include informal or illegal ones.

administration of Carlos Lleras Restrepo (from 1966 to 1970). Lleras Restrepo had support from some sectors of the bourgeoisie and attempted to add that of the peasantry (Zamosc 1986, 47–51), among other things by promoting peasant organizations, building a link between them and the state, and undertaking a more vigorous land reform. Although INCORA did not wind up transferring a great deal of land, other institutional innovations had interesting potential, including the ANUC (*Asociación Nacional de Usuarios Campesinos*/National Association of Peasant Users), a group designed to act as spokesperson for the small farm sector, but which could also organize and/or support occupations of privately held land by the peasants themselves. The slow pace of land allocations in the early years contributed to the creation of ANUC in 1967, which also reflected the somewhat smaller influence of the landed elite than in the two previous governments. Beginning in the early 1970s, ANUC councils invited a set of land invasions where reform demands had not been met.

Spending on this reform was not inconsequential; Tamayo (1970) reports that land redistribution cost the state 0.5 percent of GDP in 1970 (seven percent of the national budget)[88] but that less than twenty thousand families benefited. Many critics, including supporters of the third reform attempt of the 1990s, have judged that the efficiency of spending in this one was low. In any case, the opening for even a modest continuing reform ended with the subsequent administration of Misael Pastrana (from 1970 to 1974); it not only spelled the doom of any major land redistribution, but it put the brakes on the agrarian reform process in general, as emblemized by the 1972 Chicoral Agreement (*Acuerdo de Chicoral*) which undercut the progressive forces put in play by the previous administration. Pastrana's government promoted rifts between subgroups of ANUC and began repressing that institution when it came to be deemed a threat to the elite (Zamosc 1986).

This limited 1960s reform faced the traditional challenges that make substantial benefits hard to achieve. The standard views, mostly erroneous, that downplay the potential of small-scale agriculture were very present. The pursuit of fast urban development as the best solution to rural poverty associated with a lack of peasant access to land is another ubiquitous argument, even in countries with relatively high endowments of that factor; in these latter cases, it is usually nothing more than a vested interest talking point unsupported by economic analysis. In the Colombian case, a more serious

[88] However, as noted above, most of the spending was supplied by US aid.

claim based on the development theory of Currie (1966) linked fast overall economic growth to increased spending on labor-intensive urban construction and related non-agricultural sectors, and thus suggested that a properly designed strategy could quickly reduce the number of low-income workers in agriculture (small farmers and paid workers) by absorbing them into more remunerative urban jobs.[89] The theory rested in part on the proposition that many urban dwellers needed better housing.[90] The strategy was put temporarily into play by the Pastrana government, and although it was then largely left aside by subsequent administrations, it served to weaken the apparent centrality of land reform to successful economic and social development. In retrospect, the timing of the Pastrana administration gave some credence to the view that Colombia was unlucky in that between two of the governments with the greatest interest in resolving rural problems through support for small farming—those of Lleras Restrepo (1966–1970) and Lopez Michelson (1970–1974)—came one with a contrary perspective.

As for the level of confidence in what small agriculture could do and the capacity to support it, Colombia's situation was more typical. A decent support system for small farmers in general, including those given access to land in the reform, had not yet been developed as of the 1960s (Felstehausen 1969). Systems basically designed to foster the success of large-scale agriculture are naturally less effective—if so at all, in assisting small farming. A major barrier in countries where children of small farmers do not attain post-secondary education in significant numbers is that too few of the technicians, especially the extension workers, have had a childhood that helps them to understand the small farm setting.[91] The weak support system went hand-in-hand with a deep-seated and lasting misunderstanding—even among most of the proponents and implementers of some type of land reform, with respect to the typical capabilities of the peasant and landless groups. Although the strength of this view varied over time and across groups, it was always there to some degree. Peasant capabilities also naturally varied across individuals, families, and groups, but given modest levels of support, there was much

[89] The theory is presented, among other places, in a 1972 Planning Commission document (*Departamento Nacional de Planeación* 1972). For background on Currie and his impact, see Sandilands (1990); for a critical view, see Brittain (2005).

[90] The issue debated by serious economists was whether such a strategy could draw in enough rural workers fast enough to make a significant dent in the rural labor surplus; that is, could the sector grow fast enough and long enough to deal with that rural surplus of labor.

[91] A Canadian expert in Colombia in the 1960s noted somewhat facetiously that if a group of extension workers was parachuted anywhere into the rich Cauca Valley they would starve for lack of practical knowledge about agriculture.

more potential than assumed by outsiders.[92] In general, agricultural policy aiming to facilitate modern capitalist progress saw this group as unpromising because of its inability to perform in that world of markets and of advancing technologies. Within such a belief system, land reform was seen primarily as a way to solve a number of interconnected social, political, and economic problems. INCORA, for example, framed its own task not just in the narrow terms of providing land to those needing it, but as part of the overall quest for development: "The problem that the Colombian land reform seeks to solve . . . is not a critical land tenure situation, but rather the standard of living of the peasant" (INCORA, n.d., 1, cited by Galvis 2009, 518). The defining problems of rural areas were seen as relating in the first instance to "public order, peace, security [and] criminality"; in the second instance to underperforming components of agriculture; and in the third instance to illiteracy, helpless children, and so on. As Galvis (2009) emphasizes, matters like inequality and marginalization were not generally seen as direct sources of concern, but rather ones that deserved mention when they were causally linked to one of these priorities, especially security.

This perspective on agriculture and development represented the less informed end of an extremely wide spectrum of views; for those who held it, the basic problem was not the existing concentration of land but rather the incapacity of the marginalized population. At the other end of the spectrum were people much closer to reality, including economists like Arthur Lewis, Theodore Schultz, Bruce Johnston, John Mellor, and many others, along with sociologists and anthropologists who worked in the field, like the Colombian Orlando Fals Borda (1955); none of them saw peasants as a barrier against economic and social advance—more often they were seen as the key movers thereof. Reflecting the former view, a functionary of the Colombian Ministry of Agriculture opined that "The inhabitants . . . have a socio-cultural level very similar to the state of barbarism . . . live in an undoubted state of infra-civilization . . . . [The settlers] still have infra-structural costumes and habits. They are people that in reality are in the protoplasm of contemporary civilization, but not reaching yet its nucleus . . . . The level of production . . . can be considered as . . . of clear natural and gatherer profile. . . . Absence of machinery, primitive practices of labour, and near absence of constant capital" (Alameda 1962, 29, 30, cited by Galvis 2009, 521). This perception of

[92] One factor in the collective capacity of small farmers is the degree to which they learn from each other, watch each other try new things, and so forth. Outsiders are typically not much familiar with this phenomenon.

threatening subjects lacking certain desirable attributes facilitated a strategy that helped to reproduce marginalization on the frontier. In the words of soon-to-be President Alfonso López Michelsen, quoting Felipe Herrera, first president of the Inter-American Development Bank (IDB): "The Latin American agrarian problem is not so much to distribute land as it is to distribute people" (Lopez 1961, 83, cited by Galvis 2009, 521). The state thus engaged in sending to the frontier those pushed out of conflict-ridden, high-density rural areas (a process known as "directed colonization") and sought to assist "on-their-own" settlers in public lands ("spontaneous colonization").[93] For many or most of them, "spontaneous" was a misleading word because their movement was very much related to the violent eviction of tenants and brutal dispossessions during "*La Violencia*." These refugees from the violence were not provided with the tools needed to succeed (Machado 1984), and were frequently pushed farther into the hinterland by extensive cattle ranchers who took advantage of their weak position. The political reality was that their economic success was never a priority either for the US or for the ruling elites of Colombia.

The focus on the shortcomings of the allegedly "backward" subjects allowed for an imaginative but inaccurate narrative in which their relocation provided a solution both to their problems and to the threat they represented to the nation. For this to work well, however, the spaces for settlement had to be empty and virtually ready for use, which often required the forced displacement of indigenous peoples.[94] President Alberto Lleras's reference to these places—"It is true that we still have vast territorial extensions barely open and that are a remarkable patrimonial reserve for the new generations of Colombians" (Lleras, n.d., 5)—was an example of the prevalent rhetoric (Galvis 2009, 524). Some Colombian and international officials did suspect that such an initiative would repeat the process of marginalization that had created the need for it in the first place, with tragic consequences for the

[93] Galvis (2009, 521) cites as a prime example the colonization projects in Caquetá, in which "titled land, built basic infrastructure and provided some sort of assistance to settlers, but always failed to consolidate this over the longer term, allowing the same structures of rural marginalization to be reproduced in a more difficult frontier environment."

[94] Unlike Guatemala, Bolivia, and Mexico for example, Colombia does not have a large, purely indigenous population—one recent estimate puts it at about four to five percent of the total population, while nearly half are classified as *mestizo*. Indigenous groups may at times have been mistreated as badly as those in some of the other countries, but they have not typically provided a strong base for national political action. They do provide clear examples of the differential treatment of peasants across ethnic lines. The *hacienda* is most concentrated in regions where such populations are prevalent (Faguet et al. 2020, 6).

whole country (Rodríguez 1960, 9). Many of the places in which such colonization took place turned out, by the late 1980s and 1990s, to be war-torn, reliant on illegal activities, or both.

The reform did include a modest transfer of already cultivated land to new farmers,[95] but the land-owning class's success in securing a high compensation for expropriated lands restricted the state's ability to expropriate much. By the late 1960s, another factor was working against that approach—a shift in the conditions placed by the US on how resources should be spent in such programs; the Johnson Administration emphasized colonization rather than parcelization (Duff 1968, 168). With its greater potential in theory than in application, this approach exemplified Torres's claim that plausible-sounding plans backed by people concerned with the peasants' welfare can easily backfire due to the power of the elites. Ventures such as the 1961 reform that created INCORA and Law 60 of 1994, which decreed that future allocations of public lands to private citizens should have an upper limit defined as a family agricultural unit (*unidad agricola familiar*, UAF), were clothed in the thinking of public welfare and improved equality. In both cases, the aftermaths differed greatly from the espoused plan and large landholders wound up with much of the land allocated.

That the sort of redistributive land reform needed to resolve Colombia's rural-based problems was not even on the table owed itself to the political constellation and to two prevalent and related beliefs. On average, governments were much more beholden to the entrenched landed elite than to those in need of land and of physical and economic security. As noted, an entrenched belief in the inferiority of the rural masses and their incapacity to be effective farmers was standard fare, not just among the rural elite but among relatively educated people, some of whom genuinely wanted to assist the rural underclass toward a better life while also reducing the political threat it posed. Related to this belief was the presumption that small-scale agriculture could not be as efficient as its larger-scale counterpart. The (always muted) professional debate on the relative productivity of smaller and larger farms in Colombia was at the time hardly present; the idea of smaller-scale agriculture having any economic advantage was as implausible to most people who thought about the issue as it had been in England a couple of centuries earlier. Only years later with the analysis of the 1960 agricultural census did strong quantitative evidence arise in favor of the "inverse

[95] A valuable study of the details of the 1961 reform is included in Bagley (1979).

relationship" (IR) (the pattern of higher land productivity on smaller farms), but it never became a widespread belief, just as it has not in other countries where the data are equally unequivocal. Such evidence was hard to square with the deeply felt belief in the inferiority of the uneducated peasant. Around the world, some students of agricultural economics were becoming aware of this relationship, such as in India's Punjab region where Nobel Prize winner Amartya Sen (1961) publicized it.

The belief in the relatively uncivilized state of the rural masses was a useful component of the broad picture being painted, in which that group was in need of help to become both more productive and more civilized. As in Russia and elsewhere, the idea of a peasantry that knew things that others did not or that could be more productive than educated farmers, would not—to put it mildly—have been an easy sell. By the early 1970s, there was some awareness of it in Colombia—among other places, in INCORA, and much more within US agencies like AID (with its expert support from the University of Wisconsin Land Tenure Center)—but the broad outlines of the reform effort had already been created and the implementation process was under way. And even a fairly widespread recognition of the existence of the IR among the professionals would not have been enough to seriously offset the resistance of the agrarian elite to a significant redistributive reform.

Finally, yielding to the idea that large amounts of land now in elite hands should be given to protesting rural masses would have appeared and would, to some extent, have been, a bowing to the communist rebels whose sweep was expanding. The idea of helping the group at the bottom by providing them with land which did not have to be taken from existing large farms and would thus not damage the agricultural sector seemed very sensible to many. Few would have doubted the sincerity of Alfonso Lopez Michelsen in his above-cited comment.

As the Colombian story unfolded in the second half of the century, it was thus not yet possible to make a persuasive argument for small-scale agriculture on the grounds of economic efficiency. The poverty-reducing potential of land redistribution was more obvious. The situation of supporters of small agriculture was thus akin to that in England and other European countries a century or more earlier: even if their observation and their intuition were good, they lacked persuasive general evidence of the efficiency of small farms, so their only strong argument was based on concern for the poor. But the levels of inequality and poverty in Colombia, while obvious to some, were also in the early stages of quantification, and discussion remained limited.

The poor's urgent need for more land was often countered by the idea that "lots of land was available," an implausible argument in contexts like Britain. Only a few decades later did the serious debates on relative efficiency by farm size deepen both internationally and in Colombia. Even as they did, few engaged in them; both political power and popular intuition remained very much on the other side. Major decisions on reform were made in the 1960s, after which it was too late for positive correction. Time passed and the potential social and economic contributions of a well-designed reform diminished as the country became more developed and urbanized. By then, more than at the time of the enclosures in the UK, the idea that size accompanies efficiency had many confirming examples in other industries and, as always, was given clout for non-economists by the fact that more money could always be made in a big company, the most direct advantage of size.

## Efforts during the New Setting of Violence: Guerrillas, Narcos, and Paramilitaries

Like Guatemala, Colombia thus needed a moderately successful reform by the 1960s to pave the way for a decent socio-economic performance over the rest of the century and beyond. When that success was not forthcoming, a new and tragic scenario emerged, one in which several hundred thousand more people have died, millions have been displaced, and Colombia's status as one of the world's most violent countries has been restored. Not only did the major reform that would have answered the need for land felt by many victims of earlier violence, displacement, and mistreatment not eventuate, but the festering resentments based on those experiences helped pave the way for the new wave of violence, beginning in the mid-1970s and typically associated with birth of the illicit drug industry, strong guerrilla groups, and paramilitary forces.[96]

Another continuing element of the context for Colombia's violence was land informality; leaving rights unclear invites the law of the jungle to prevail. For the rural poor, obtaining formal rights to the land has been blocked by prohibitive legal requirements, including such things as having a survey done and paying legal fees (Sanchez et al. 2010). Opaque and unclear land

[96] For an analysis of the role of dispossession as a source of grievances in Latin America, see Saffon (2015).

rights have, unsurprisingly, been accompanied by an extreme level of corruption among the notaries responsible for adjudicating land issues and prone to cooptation by local powerbrokers. Their power was so deeply entrenched that President Lleras Restrepo backed away from attempting to reform the system even though he was well aware of its character and its negative impacts on the policies he was pursuing. Many other state institutions involved in the land issues have also been highly corrupt.[97] A strong positive state presence has been missing.[98] A sometimes corrupted military; the strong local influence of *gamonales*, which contributes to widespread corruption within the police force; and the willingness of too many participants to use violence have all contributed to the state's failure to protect the rural population when it was under physical, economic, or legal threat from more powerful agents. Policymakers have sometimes been reluctant to take what would otherwise be socially desirable measures for (legitimate) fear of violence, a fear underlined by the very high rates at which union leaders, journalists, and activists have been murdered.

By the late 1970s, the guerrillas could draw on a share of the drug bonanza as well as the accumulated resentments of those victimized earlier. A strong link connected FARC rebel activity during the beginning stage of this new wave of violence (from 1974 to 1985) to the much earlier peasant dispossessions by large landowners during the export coffee expansion (from 1916 to 1946); it was activated by the access to weapons and military experience provided to small peasant groups by exposure to the previous wave ("*La Violencia*") and by the ideological cohesion afforded by the communist party.[99] The peasant grievances held by the victims of land dispossessions during the export boom thus underlay both the consolidation of FARC and its later activities (Lopez-Uribe and Sanchez 2018).

Meanwhile, the drug industry was able to draw not only on a large supply of people willing to engage in production, transport, and intermediation, but also on an already developed comparative advantage in illegal activities, something that fit easily into a setting characterized by the lack of rule of law.[100] Drugs and land concentration have been part of many vicious cycles.

[97] For a recent review of corruption in Colombia, see Cepeda (2015).

[98] Authors like Flores (2014) dispute the idea of a weak state, noting that the political class has achieved some of the goals important to it. In many respects, it is not so much the degree of government impact but rather its composition and who has access to it that matters.

[99] Molano (2015) presents a detailed story of the evolution of the FARC.

[100] Some of the entrepreneurial skills which came to the drugs sector had been honed by the production of emeralds, a notoriously gangland-type activity. The general disrespect for law also creates a natural setting in which such activities can thrive (Thoumi 2021).

The flourishing of this industry certainly owes much to rural inequality and injustice. Its presence, then, makes it harder for the state to deal with land issues and with other injustices and sources of conflict, not only because it complicates any setting, but also because it takes official precedence among problems to be dealt with even by well-meaning governments (and by foreign ones like the US), thus crowding out the needed responses to other problems. Most governments oversimplify the challenges it poses—partly because their publics do so, and thus miss the nuances involved.[101] It fosters a setting of rural violence, creates a new and powerful group (the drug lords) interested in acquiring rural properties, and makes it dangerous for anyone to resist them.[102] In providing an attractive setting for the development of the drug sector, Colombia's socially and economically dysfunctional agricultural system wrought enormous damage.

Various forms of cooperation (and at times competition) have linked the drug industry, the guerrillas, and the paramilitaries who arose initially as a defense group to protect large farmers from kidnapping at the hands of the guerrillas, and then morphed into an independent power group characterized by unusual brutality. Also involved, of course, have been corrupt politicians. The recent conflict-ridden decades have provided the worst chapter in a history marked by striking continuity in that regard. The modes of settler eviction broadened; the actors became more numerous with the arrival of drug lords, paramilitaries, guerrillas, agro-industry, and mining; and the last wave of violence generated more displacement than any previous one. Further, beginning in the 1980s, land became literally an "instrument of war"[103] and of political power in a war context, not to mention a convenient mechanism for the laundering of drug money. Drug lords and paramilitaries increasingly secured control of local political bases at the expense of the traditional agriculture-based elites (Reveiz 2007). Large-scale commercial agriculture and industrial-scale mining have interacted with various of these purveyors of violence, in effect subcontracting forced displacement to them.[104] Many

[101] On the complexities of drug policy and the frequent incompetence that characterizes it, see Thoumi (2015). An extreme case was the Trump administration's pressure on the Colombian government to "stop the flow of drugs," an accentuation of the long-standing American view that the producers rather than the consumers are responsible for handling the problem, and assuming implicitly that this is as simple as turning off a tap.

[102] The power and sweep of the drug sector is at the center of what Reveiz (2007) refers to as Colombia's "second government."

[103] See Reyes (2008).

[104] All of this is part of what Webster (2012) refers to as a ruthless competition for land leading to the violent displacement of millions of rural people and involving the Colombian army, the guerrillas, and "shadowy paramilitary forces that are often associated with local business interests."

of the displaced are from indigenous and Afro-Colombian communities engaged in gold mining. Sometimes organized crime collaborates with industrial mining by attacking the communities of traditional miners and driving them away, often into poverty and illegality. Jesuit Father Javier Giraldo argued that the security of foreign resource companies was "only effective with the protection of enormous contingents of paramilitaries secretly co-opted by the armed forces and by the government security agencies" and who "when faced with local resistance to resource projects do not hesitate to murder the leaders of this resistance" (Webster 2012).

In the twentieth century's second major wave of violence, occurring during the drug period, the role of resentments related to dispossession or to lack of access to land and leading to what one may call "defensive violence" is often seen as less obvious than the factors creating openings for profitable or "aggressive" violence. The "feasibility model" (Collier et al. 2009) interprets this wave as essentially due to the drug trafficking, the difficult topography, and a weak state. Although this interpretation provides useful insights into the violence since the 1980s, it cannot account for the creation of the FARC,[105] whose presence remained a factor of importance during this post-1980 wave.[106] Historic and/or contemporary land issues have been involved in this recent wave in several other ways as well. The huge ongoing land dispossession has inevitably given rise to new resentments and reactions on the part of the dispossessed. Meanwhile, resentments from early century dispossessions were still in evidence as this recent wave got started.[107] Finally, even if their role has been secondary in the maintenance of the violence after those first years, land issues may still be an important indirect source

One of the most famous cases occurred in the municipality of Marmato, where Father José Reinel Restrepo was murdered after speaking out against a plan by a Canadian mining company to have the town moved to make way for an open-pit gold mine (Webster 2012).

[105] See Flores (2014, 10).

[106] López-Uribe and Sanchez (2018) propose two mechanisms through which earlier land dispossession may contribute to the creation of guerrilla groups like the FARC: military feasibility is fostered by civil war periods when peasant groups have access to weapons, and the ideological politics of rebellion is developed with the guidance and support of revolutionary groups that may generate political awareness among the peasantry and foster the formation of rebel groups.

[107] Peasants' claims have remained mostly unchanged during the twentieth century. But the opportunity to pursue them without the use of violence only became possible when both a window of political opportunity and the economic resources appeared. Faguet et al. (2020) conclude that the differences in the intensity of armed conflict at the municipal level during its early stage (1974–1985) were due to differing frequency of the much earlier (1914–1946) peasant dispossessions by large landowners that led to the rise and persistence of grievances, with this link mediated by the exposure to the previous civil war, "*La Violencia*," which gave peasant groups access to weapons and military experience and by an ideological cohesion coming from the communist party (Molano 2015).

because the conditions under which each of the guerrillas, the drug industry, and the paramilitaries arose is arguably attributable to the historic inequality of land. It remains a legitimate question whether a high level of land conflict could ever occur if that asset were more or less evenly distributed, absent enduring ethnic conflicts. The main issue is not whether a certain degree of inequality of access to it and/or resentments from dispossession is a necessary condition for serious conflicts over land—it is—but rather within what range of inequality or perceived unfairness this becomes a serious factor, what additional factors enhance or detract from its role, and so forth.[108] The historical centrality of dispossession in conflicts like Colombia's stands out. Land conflict has been fed by peasant reaction to displacements and/or peasant invasions based on a feeling of having a legitimate right to land currently under someone else's control.[109] In that context, to judge that inequality and perceived injustice had played no role in the more recent conflicts would be to say that if, as of the 1930s or the 1950s, everyone had operated the same seventeen hectares of land, there would still have been a conflict. If so, this would make Colombians unique in the world in their proclivity to violence. In fact, it appears more likely that distributional issues and the resentments they foster among dispossessed families have been central to nearly all of the conflicts. The issue to be sorted out is whether and when a reaction to dispossessions and perceived unfairness coming from the bottom is more important than moves at the top that serve to retain or increase that high level of inequality. Within such distinctions, and as one studies the detailed chronology of any given conflict, it is often necessary to distinguish between the sources of apparently minor changes or provocations that contribute to conflict and the broader bases of antipathy and willingness to do battle that

[108] A statistical analysis among conflict-ridden countries all of which suffer a significant level of land inequality—the case of some of the studies supporting the feasibility model—might not find it to be a significant determinant of violence since the difference between a Gini coefficient of 0.65 and one of 0.8 might not matter greatly to the generation of conflict; in such an analysis, the factors that are central to the feasibility model would emerge as the relevant ones. But such analyses do not contradict the hypothesis that the difference between a low level of land inequality and a relatively high one (say a Gini of 0.65) is central. Cross-country statistical analyses like some of those that support the feasibility model must, in any case, be interpreted more as presenting interesting hypotheses to be tested in individual countries than as providing strong evidence on the causal process in those countries. Their results rely on very strong assumptions (e.g., that the countries involved are identical except with respect to the variables that are formally part of the analysis) and thus often turn out not to be robust over different time periods, different groups of countries, and so on. Taken in conjunction with historical and other types of in-country analysis, such exercises can be useful.

[109] Perceived injustice—associated with, but not identical to, inequality—has always played a role in the violence associated with land in Colombia. It results when a powerful group confronts another group which either feels it has some power or is desperate and feels it has been treated unjustly (Legrand 1986).

may help to sustain it once initiated. Categorizing conflicts by sources runs a risk of oversimplification unless it takes account of the historical details of each conflict.[110] As Cramer (2003) notes, the socio-political relations in which inequality is embedded are key. Formal and informal institutions define the set of rules and procedures by which economic rights are specified, allocated, and enforced, and they determine the nature of competition and, in particular, whether it degenerates into open conflict.

That having avoided high land concentration in the first place would also have avoided the violence Colombia has undergone does not, of course, mean that lowering the concentration somewhat through land reform would greatly reduce violence. Albertus and Oliver Kaplan (2013) question whether targeted land reform like Colombia's could have substantially reduced levels of civil conflict by mitigating the contributing factors. They judge that the capacity of politically powerful landholders to block most large-scale reform projects resulted in an enduring, low-intensity, and geographically dispersed reform that, in turn, encouraged continuing, albeit low level, insurgent activity. Larger-scale reforms, only implemented in areas that threatened serious violence and had the potential to harm elite interests, did reduce guerrilla activity. But the elites successfully lobbied for INCORA to focus on projects where they would be least disturbing to the existing land structure. The authors thus conclude that while land reform can be an effective counterinsurgency policy up to a point, doing so at a sufficient scale to end the conflict is very difficult because it threatens the status quo. As that threat grows, the elite bring to bear powerful political and physical resources to counteract it.

As homicide and forced displacement once again became major features of Colombian life, with the former rising rapidly during the 1980s to a peak around 1990, and the latter escalating about a decade later to peak in 2002,[111] income inequality was also advancing toward possible peaks in the late 1990s and 2010 (the last year for which fuller information estimates, including tax-based information, are available).[112] A jump in national-level inequality over the 1990s and the likelihood of its remaining extreme (possibly the highest

[110] Authors like Flores (2014) and Hough (2011) provide valuable information at this level of detail for Colombia and FARC, as do histories of the guerrilla group, like that of Leech (2011).

[111] The timing of the displacement of families through legal manipulation is harder to identify than that associated with violence.

[112] Because the more complete data that include estimates for the top earners are only available for selected years over this interval, it is not clear whether there were other peaks between the two cited and, if so, whether the level of inequality was higher than for those two.

in the world) through at least 2010, suggests that the conflict has again been a factor at work. Land concentration also seems to have been increasing from the 1980s, with no sign of reversal at least into the last decade (IGAC-CEDE 2012). Once again, violent conflict around land came with great suffering and injustice as well as with high and rising levels of inequality.

The early 1990s, with its very high rural violence fuelled by the deadly mix of guerrilla groups, the drug industry, and the paramilitaries, provided the context for the World Bank-supported "market-assisted" land reform (MALR), an approach reflecting the contemporary popularity of market mechanisms. The "negotiated land transfer" to aspiring small landholders involves a subsidy equal to the difference between the price at which the owner is willing to sell and what was deemed a reasonable contribution by the "buyer." Whatever its potential under more favourable circumstances, operational and design weaknesses quickly left it far short of its goals in this case, and Colombia's early 2000s fiscal constraints then helped to put it on the back burner. Its strengths were a capacity to contain administrative costs, which had been high in INCORA (Deininger 1999, 655) while potentially reaching a significant number of families through a strategy of first targeting municipalities that posed less complicated challenges and then, aided by a learning process, moving to more complicated cases. With a reasonable budget—one still quite small in the context of the costs of Colombia's rural violence, it would have been possible to improve the land access of say four hundred thousand families (compared to the 250,000 recipients of INCORA projects from 1960 to 1988 (about nine thousand per year on average).

Peasant organizations had little involvement in this MALR (Law 160 of 1994). The previous year they had presented an agrarian reform bill, which was not voted on in Congress (Hollinger 1999, 161–168). After widespread mobilization, the government did incorporate them into the negotiations around Law 160. Due to their pressure, the planned subsidy was raised from fifty to seventy percent of the price of land. Even though they rejected the MALR approach in principle and defended a state-implemented redistributive reform, various peasant organizations, including ANUC, did act as intermediaries in the land transactions, sometimes competing among themselves in the process (Mendes Pereira and Fajardo 2015, 7).

Although both its aspirations and its achievements were modest relative to the challenge in Colombia, this MALR effort (Law 160 of 1994) has provided useful lessons on program execution, especially in such difficult contexts. Its initial target was to finance the purchase of one million hectares by seventy-five thousand families over four years, but it quickly fell behind schedule and, by the end of 1997, less than twenty thousand had been financed. The World Bank identified three errors/problems in that initial effort: the subsidy (around seventy percent of the total land cost, with a maximum of US $21,000) was too high, arguably stimulating a sort of conspiracy between sellers and purchasers that led to the overvaluation of the property; the income ceiling for entrants to the program was also too high, leaving too few opportunities for the poorest families; and INCORA's decision-making and implementation procedures were overly centralized, resulting in a lack of community access to information, local participation, and involvement of the private sector in the provision of services and credit (Mendes Pereira and Fajardo 2015). The link with INCORA was seen as a source of "resistance" within the broader state apparatus to the provision of needed funds because its bureaucracy was widely considered to be inefficient and resistant to innovation. Another weakness lay in the failure to work out the details of projects before land was purchased, something that reflected the lack of autonomy and protagonism of the purchasers.

Initially poor results led to adjustments. In 1997, a pilot program was begun in five municipalities with the aims of: (i) formulating a "municipal agrarian reform plan" to identify situations where the possible supply of land to the program was three times the potential demand, a condition it was hoped would prevent the overvaluation of land prices; (ii) seeking partnerships at a local level with NGOs which could provide technical assistance and with private financial institutions willing to provide credit to the farmers; (iii) creating better procedures to select beneficiaries, including greater publicity about the project and a local register of applicants with details about their prior agricultural experience and socio-economic situation; (iv) designing projects *before* land acquisition, to be able to inform potential beneficiaries about their economic potential; and (v) monitoring and assessment of project impact (Deininger 1999). These modifications reflected the Bank's assessment that the beneficiaries lacked the needed experience and capacity; accordingly, it mounted a training program for preselected candidates. Even with all of this, a large majority of beneficiaries were found to be in a condition of chronic default (World Bank 2003b, 147).

The degree to which the various difficulties emerging in the context of this reform were due to the chaos and instability in many regions of rural Colombia is a matter requiring in-depth study. It competed with other priorities, like dealing with the drug industry, and Colombia-style democracy did not provide a good political base from which to effectively confront such a complicated reality and policy challenge. Whatever its actual and potential merits and weaknesses, the MALR fell into the "too little-too late" category with respect to the resolution of rural Colombia's enormous problems.

The Peace Process, which in 2016 ended the fifty-two-year conflict between FARC and the government, brought one more effort to confront the land issue. Its major goal was to pave the way for the re-entry of the guerrillas into the society and the economy, and to help deter other continuing conflicts around land. Its "land fund" of three million hectares was designed to provide one base by which ex-combatants could re-enter the economy. But a report presented in August 2020 by opposition senators and representatives pointed to almost no progress having been made toward the goals set, and to a worsening of the rural setting. As of January 2021, "statistics on violence remain staggering and, what represented a great and historic opportunity for Colombia, has witnessed an incomprehensible stagnation on some of its key points" (Open Democracy 2021). There was a significant increase in the murders of social leaders and in forced displacements. On the issues of victim reparation and land endowment, the report found that, at the present rate, it would take the government forty-three years to compensate all of the conflict's victims, while only 0.08 percent of the targeted three million hectares of the Land Fund had been allocated.

Now, in 2023, a new opening has arisen in the context of the left-leaning government of former guerrilla Gustavo Petro. Consistent with the general inclinations of this administration, its goal on the agrarian front is to bring significant rather than marginal change. It remains too early to guess at the likely outcomes, either immediate or longer-term.

## Retrospect

Twentieth-century Colombia, with its history of violence, injustice, and periodic support for reform, together with a relative abundance of analysis of both the agrarian system and income inequality, provides a natural setting within which to ask a central question: what might have happened, especially in the post-1950 period, had the early twentieth-century distribution of land been very different, with a Gini coefficient of say 0.4 (low to medium inequality) instead of 0.8–0.9 (extremely high)? The likely answer is that almost all of the things that went wrong would have been avoided.

Countries with a low land concentration almost never suffer from serious internal rural conflict unless it is ethnic based. Colombia's early waves of violence could be seen in that way, as the "hereditary hatreds" pushed people to do battle with an intensity often associated with ethnic animosity. The fact that, over the decades, those party-based hatreds have faded dramatically suggests that they were never acting alone. A land Gini coefficient of 0.4 would have implied much easier access to the resource, a much wider base of family farming, and much less poverty. Under such conditions, the logic that spawned the creation of FARC would simply not have been there, nor would the lingering resentment of peasants that helped to fuel that organization and the conflicts of the last decades. If to this positive scenario were added a reasonable degree of public support for the small-farm sector—even the moderate level achieved in the 1970s—farm and rural incomes would at each point of time have been much higher than in fact they were, and the country's potential for developing a comparative advantage in the drug industries (marijuana and cocaine principally) would have been greatly reduced, if not absent. Prosperous small-farm agriculture is not the natural base for such industries. Without the guerrillas or the drug industries, rural security would have been reasonably good and there would have been no reason for the creation of the ultimately brutal paramilitaries. The income trajectory of the working population in agriculture, instead of struggling up at an average of a little over one percent per year over sixty years (and thus doubling), would have probably grown by at least 2.5-3.0 percent per year, hence by a total of 4.4-fold to sixfold (Berry 2017b, 281). Many lives and much suffering would have been avoided, and Colombia would have looked forward with confidence to the future. Instead, there is a sad story of what might have been, given the wealth of natural and human resources that this country possesses, and its stark contrast with what actually unfolded. The actual benefits have been modest; in contrast, some of the societal costs of not achieving more are all too measurable. The most extreme are the deaths and displacements; about a million and five to seven million, respectively. Some of the less extreme forms of loss have been quantified in monetary terms; Anna Maria Ibáñez and Carlos Eduardo Vélez (2007) report a large lifetime loss of income suffered by survivors of the violence, to which must be added the enormous psychological cost of the traumas experienced.

The second big question raised by this agrarian history is, given the bad starting point early in the century, what conditions or policies could have brought significantly better results than those achieved? Forces against change have been notoriously strong, but the country's twentieth-century development altered political and economic structure in many ways. Were some periods more promising than others? Were some approaches/projects more promising than others at certain points of time, opening windows of opportunity, and did some people or groups have much better chances to bring about beneficial change than did others? How long did the window of opportunity have to last for a breakthrough to occur?

Among the competing narratives around Colombia's experience since the 1940s wave of violence, the most positive, in terms both of how one judges this society and gauges the potential of others like it, is that the cost of a lack of positive policy continuity has been high and that bad luck has played a significant role. In several of the windows of opportunity it seemed clear that at least two successive reasonably progressive governments were needed to make a significant difference. Most reform experiences have involved policy changes during the process and the aftermath of redistribution, due to a combination of changing conditions, learning about what is not going according to plans/hopes, and shifts from a government with one perspective (e.g., representing one interest group) to one with a different perspective. Although these modifications are always present to some degree, they take different forms, for example between democracies and autarchies. Important policy shifts can occur when it becomes obvious that the existing path is not as good as an alternative, as happened when Communist regimes shifted from collective production to a small unit approach. Such shifts have typically brought large benefits. Most others come when control of government moves from one group to another—a frequent phenomenon in democracies as an incoming party replaces the one previously in power—and occur sometimes as control shifts between military and civilian or between autocrats. The fallout for land reform attempts varies from case to case.

Colombia's twentieth-century history involves various forms of government alternation, mainly between parties after an election and therefore at least somewhat unpredictable. However, in the case of the sixteen-year National Front Agreement (1958–1974) during which the presidencies and other high political positions were alternated between the two parties involved (the Liberals and the Conservatives), it was predictable. The pattern of succession has arguably mattered most during two intervals: that National Front period and the immediately ensuing years, and the two decades of the twenty-first century. The first of these saw the reform steps taken mainly by the Lleras Restrepo administration (1966–1970) reversed by that of Misael

Pastrana (1970–1974) with its *Acuerdo de Chicoral* in defense of large properties. While the benefits of fifteen to twenty years of policy continuity would certainly have been much greater than those actually achieved, the bigger question is whether they would have been enough to deter the arrival of the drug industry and to diminish the still festering resentments from the many dispossessions in the first half of the century. Without a significant level of redistribution, necessarily over the fierce opposition of the landed class, and without much support from the available technical economic arguments in its favor, this would not have been a likely outcome.

Half a century after the Lleras reform, another unfortunate political sequence starkly illustrated the need for continuity. The Juan Manuel Santos government (from 2010 to 2018) achieved peace with the FARC guerrillas and organized a Rural Mission (*Mision Rural*) headed by noted economist José Antonio Ocampo to advise on agricultural and agrarian policies to foster successful termination of that conflict, including a modest transfer of land. But Iván Duque's government (from 2018 to 2022), widely seen as following the path of former president Álvaro Uribe (from 2002 to 2010), sabotaged the peace plan and its rural components to the highest degree possible. In the process, the areas previously controlled by the guerrillas became contested, homicides rose, social activists died in large numbers, environmental depredations multiplied, and the eventual achievement of a degree of peace and justice became a less realistic dream. Had one more positive administration succeeded that of Santos, there would have been six years within which to pursue the guidelines set by the Mission, and reversing some of its advances would have been much harder.

Some other initiatives undertaken over several decades beginning in the 1960s did bring considerable benefits, and even provided models copied in other countries. The country's impressive Integrated Rural Development Program (IRDP) showed what could be done through effective support for the existing small-farm sector. The benefits of many such efforts were eroded over time, rather than reversed. Overall, their benefits in Colombia were more than offset by the negative effects of the drug industry, the still heavy clout of the large-farm sector, the corruption of important institutions of government, and the land question's gradually slipping from its earlier prominent position among major public policy issues.

The background political setting has evolved a great deal since the earlier reform efforts. Between the first two (1930s and 1960s), when the polity was built around the two traditional parties and in most respects very top-down and centralized, and the last three—the 1990s MALR effort, the post-Peace Treaty plans to distribute land to former FARC members, and the Petro government's current project—the political system had become more "democratic" and the population had shifted from mainly rural to mainly urban. This evolution has impacted the trajectory of events, and it may have increased the diversity across administrations. Opposing interests on land and on dealing with rural violence and the FARC have played out in a democratic context where the details of electoral processes can have a good deal to say about who gets elected. By the last few decades, the traditional two-party system had given way to something more complex; this, and the changing views and perspectives of the voting public, created a complicated story in which a former M-19 guerrilla leader, Petro, could be elected mayor of Bogota and, later, president of the country.

The most influential opponent of land reform over recent decades has been Uribe, president from 2002 to 2010 and still a prominent participant in politics, recently through his protégé, Duque. Uribe has arguably been Colombia's first modern populist, able to exploit the potential of television to reach the population and achieve very high approval ratings. His skills, together with the natural bias of most media against the guerrillas over the long period of the civil war, intensified the ill will toward them, but much less toward the paramilitaries and other bad actors. Much of the current urban population knows little about the last century of Colombia's rural history; its perceptions are inevitably determined by the information easily available and mainly focused on the day-to-day challenges of their own lives. Ongoing urbanization left a majority of the electorate with little understanding of the rural reality and heavily influenced by a political narrative that placed excessive blame on the guerrillas for what had gone wrong. Under such circumstances and the current democratic processes, Colombia's electorate cannot be relied upon to vote for the sort of healing processes the country needs. This was reflected in the over fifty percent opposition in the referendum vote to approve the peace deal worked out between the Santos government and FARC in 2016. In terms of political leaders, the country has been in need of a Nelson Mandela but has instead had an Álvaro Uribe.

Some have interpreted the recent political battle between the forces for reform and those defending the interests of large-scale agriculture, the oil palm industry, the cattle ranchers, and others as the latest manifestation of the long-standing intra-elite battle. They see Santos as representing the entrepreneurial and centralist urban elite engaged with the process of modernization and Uribe as speaking for "an amalgam of regional elites, usually land rentiers, controlling the structures of the state at the regional level and highly reliant on large-scale landed property as a means for ensuring political and economic power" (Coronado 2019, 15). The gap in preferred agrarian policy between these two groups—originally the Liberal and Conservative parties respectively—was apparent during both the 1930s and the 1960s reform attempts. For the first group, a redistributive land reform represents a minor direct inconvenience and may even bring some benefits indirectly, whereas for a good number of rural elites it can have a significant negative impact on their political and economic power. These latter continuously resisted the Santos government's 2011 Land Restitution and Victims Law through both legal and informal strategies. Members of the rightist *Centro Democrático* Party (of Uribe and Duque) have tried to amend it, in particular its *bona fide* principle which directs the judiciary and administrative authorities to presume "good faith" on the part of the victims. Those currently controlling the land the "victims" claim must prove that they have followed due diligence in acquiring the rights to that land, which poses a major problem both for those who have engaged in land dispossession themselves and those who obtained ownership rights to dispossessed land at low prices. Their response has included both the use of force and the threat of it.[113] Meanwhile, the Duque government stalled the enforcement of the agrarian chapter of the 2016 Peace Agreement with its goal of formalizing seven million hectares and distributing three million to landless and nearly landless peasants. It aimed to modify the agrarian law so as not only to impede the enforcement of the peace agreement but to roll-back a key institution in the Colombian agrarian legal framework: the prohibition against granting to people not classified as agrarian-reform beneficiaries ownership rights to "*baldíos*" in amounts exceeding 450 hectares. After becoming President in 2018, Duque placed loyalists in prominent positions; in an extreme example, he appointed a former secretary-general of the oil palm federation as director of the Land Restitution Unit.[114] In some cases,

[113] In 2016, amid threats against peasants demanding land restitution by so-called Anti-restitution Armies, the former General Attorney, Alejandro Ordóñez, and the president of the Cattle-Ranchers' Federation, José Félix Lafaurie, conducted a public hearing in one of the most problematic regions for the enforcement of the policy. They referred to the restitution as "the first steps towards delivering the territorial control of the country to illegal armed actors" (Reyes 2016).

[114] In the Urabá region, one of the most affected by land dispossession, land restitution judges ruled that twenty-five oil palm companies could not prove due diligence and good faith regarding purchases of land currently under oil palm plantations (Coronado 2019, 16).

incumbents have resigned in light of the change of setting implicit in Duque's government. Gonzalo Sánchez de Lozado, a famous student of land issues and associated violence, resigned the leadership of the *Centro de Memoria Histórica* (Center for Historical Memory) in 2018.[115]

Sergio Coronado (2019, 119) also sees the Duque government as representing the re-emergence of right-wing authoritarianism in Colombia, and links it to the rise of far-right populism elsewhere in the Americas.[116] In much of this group's discourse around the Land Restitution and Victims Law of 2011 and the Peace Accord of 2016, a focus on justice is implied to have a cost in terms of efficiency; it has been alleged that "state actors are obliged to allocate property rights over rural lands to subjects that could not be considered by mainstream parameters as the most efficient holders" (Coronado 2019, 16). Most people accept those "mainstream parameters" and the idea that large-scale operations are more efficient economically.

How much good might have been achieved through Colombia's land reform attempts with better "luck" on such fronts as the sequences of governments will always be a matter of speculation. Colombia's land reform history is one of the few involving a more or less continuous democracy. Chile is the closest parallel from Latin America. It had an earlier and more pronounced socialist presence within its system, while in Colombia the political competition over the twentieth century was essentially between the right and the center. That setting arguably left little space for a major reform and meant that even a minor one would require a good deal of luck to be successful. It was in this context that the insightful political economist Albert Hirschman (1963) explained his theory of "possibilism," an approach grounded in sensitivity to context and hence to the limitations of what was possible, but also to the idea that more might sometimes be achievable than met the untrained eye. Key to the Colombian context of the early 1960s was the threat to such a country of having to choose between communist takeover (as per the Cuban revolution) and a degree of reform that would otherwise not appear to be politically feasible. He critiqued the presumption that on the matter of land distribution there was no middle ground between

[115] Among his recent studies is Richardson et al. (2012).

[116] Populism was strikingly apparent in Petro's recent opponent for the presidency. Rodolfo Hernández is a real estate magnate and former mayor of Bucaramanga who promised great things, especially getting rid of corruption, but was short on sensible ideas as to how to do so. He had appeared out of nowhere politically and welcomed comparisons to Trump and Bolsonaro.

revolution and the maintenance of the status quo, suggesting that a centrist approach could help to stave off revolution and garner support from the United States and other industrial countries. It would involve a more than marginal land reform. The degree to which Hirschman's hypothesis was correct cannot be known because it involves too many counterfactuals, and also depends on how much redistribution would have been seen as a "success." One key question is the extent to which what genuine possibilities were, in fact, undone by events that were avoidable.

## Brazil

Like Colombia, Brazil is a prime example both of historically extreme land concentration without significant redistribution over time and of economic and social inequality enduring long after the agriculture-based phase of development. In spite of *campesino* movements and protests, some governments disposed to help, support from the Catholic Church at times, and a competent group of technocrats who have, when possible, worked to support family farming, the current state of agriculture, the economy and the society are very distant from what they might have been had agrarian history unfolded more positively. Efforts to change the agrarian structure have been substantial in absolute terms but small in relation to the challenge. Despite the presence of the landless workers' movement (MST) and, at one point, three consecutive governments which appeared to have some concern for small agriculture and the rural poor, land distribution has not improved; instead, the Gini coefficient measuring its concentration appears to have increased between 1967 and 2006.

### Early History

As a major country having experienced, at best, marginal land redistribution, Brazil is a laboratory for the study of how the economic sources of inequality evolve between that land-based starting point and the later stages of development, and for the potential of other pro-equality strategies to make up for the absence of an early redistributive reform in agriculture. One such substitute, for which Brazil was among the experimenting countries, has been market-based land reform. Others include *Bolsa Familia* (Family

Grant), which offers cash payments to low-income families on condition that their children stay in school, and pensions for the elderly in rural areas.

Brazil was notable for its rapid economic growth and diversification over the course of the twentieth century, with an especially impressive burst during a post-World War II period of import substitution.[117] Today, it is a middle-income developing country with a slowing population growth rate—dropping from nearly three percent per year around 1960 to 0.6 percent at present—and continuing rapid urbanization. Agricultural employment peaked around 1970 and the sector's share of the total labor force fell rapidly from almost sixty percent in 1950 to forty-four percent in 1970, a little under twenty percent in 1990, and a little under ten percent today (World Bank, n.d.). Strong economic growth did reduce poverty substantially; in recent decades, social programs have also helped on that front. Since 1980, however, growth has on average been slow and the economy has suffered considerable volatility; the "lost decade" of the 1980s was followed by a brief growth spurt, but recently the pace has again faltered, with an average of just 0.5 percent per year from 2012 to 2022. Inequality has remained very high, making it unsurprising that levels of dissatisfaction have, on occasion, surged as well.

The agricultural sector has always been and remains extremely unequal. In 1995, the roughly half of farms with less than ten hectares had 2.2 percent of all the land, while the 1.0 percent with over one thousand hectares had 45.1 percent of it, and were thus on average about one thousand times larger than the bottom half.[118] Recent numbers put the inequality of land distribution at or near the highest in the world, with a Gini coefficient of around 0.85–0.87 (Bauluz et al. 2020, 10);[119] one estimate suggests an increase between 1967 and 2006 from 0.836 to 0.872 (Robles 2018, 6). With land concentration so high, both production and income generated are also highly concentrated in the larger units. As of the 2006 agricultural census, the 84.4 percent of all agricultural enterprises classified as family farms accounted for only 24.3 percent of all cultivated land, generated 38.0 percent of output, and employed 74.4 percent of all agricultural workers (12.3 million people). Although their

[117] Average overall and per capita growth was especially good from 1930 to 1980, at 5.7 percent and 3.0 percent respectively.

[118] Farms of one hundred to one thousand hectares (9.7 percent of the total) had 34.9 percent of the land. Thus the top two categories, with 10.7 percent of the units, had a little over eighty percent of the land (Robles 2018, 18).

[119] Although this probably overstates inequality as measured by land value, the latter is clearly very high as well. For most of the few other countries with estimates of inequality by land value, Bauluz et al. (2020, 11) find that it is usually greater than that by area, but for Ecuador and Guatemala, the two Latin American cases, the reverse is true.

share of total output is modest, the family farms produce a high share of such food items as beans (seventy percent), cassava (eighty-seven percent), coffee (thirty-eight percent), corn (forty-six percent) and rice (thirty-four percent), reflecting the very different composition of output by farm size; they also make a significant contribution to the overall production of animal-derived food: fifty-eight percent of milk, fifty percent of poultry, fifty-nine percent of pork, and thirty percent of cattle. Overall, land productivity was 1.8 times higher on the family farms than the large ones, and labor intensity (workers per acre) was about nine times higher. Much land on large farms is dedicated to extensive cattle grazing and much goes unused;[120] in contrast, land on small farms is intensively used. As far back as data are available, the IR between farm size and land productivity has been quite marked; as of 1973, the ratio of value added to reported value of land was about three times higher on farms of up to ten hectares than on those of one hundred to one thousand hectares (Berry 1985).[121] Small-scale agriculture has at times experienced healthy increases in both land and labor productivity, as occurred during the 1970s (Berry 1989, 188).[122] Brazil has been a very extreme case of land concentration coupled with consistently much lower land productivity on the larger farms than on the smaller ones.

In the midst of slower overall economic growth since 1980, the pattern of agricultural expansion has often been highly labor-displacing. In the 1970s, when the GDP grew at 8.7 percent per year, agriculture expanded at a striking 4.4 percent per year. But, as a result of technological modernization, the sector's employment experienced its first reduction, from 13.3 million in 1970 to 13.0 million in 1980. The 1990s and 2000s saw another extraordinary increase in agricultural production, particularly for global markets, again with reliance on advanced technology and increasing yields, and rapidly falling labor-intensity. The growth of agribusiness is usually attributed to public investment in research (through *Embrapa*, the Brazilian Corporation for Agricultural Research) and to the expansion of cultivated area (Rocha et al. 2012). The country was or became the world's largest exporter of sugar,

[120] As of 1976, the unused arable land in the *latifundios*, at seventy-five million hectares, was half as great as their total cultivated area and twice that in the hands of the 2.7 million *minifundistas* (Peritore and Peritore 1990, 378).

[121] In a more detailed study by zone in Northeast Brazil, Berry and Cline (1979, 46) find that this relationship varies considerably across zones, but the ratio for the smallest size group (up to ten hectares) always considerably exceeds that for the largest one.

[122] Arias et al. (2017, 10), drawing on estimates by Helfand et al. (2015), note that from 1985 to 2006 TFP increases were fastest in the smaller farms and the larger ones.

ethanol (from sugarcane), beef, coffee, and orange juice, and the second largest (after the US) in soybeans and poultry meat. Over these two decades, agricultural employment fell further in absolute terms. The sector's growth pattern has thus continued to foster high income inequality through its low demand for labor. Had employment been, for example, twenty-five percent more than it was through the post-1950 period, the urban informal sector would have grown less, and rural non-agricultural employment would probably have expanded faster.

Along with the extreme concentration of land and of income, the most striking features of Brazil's agrarian history have been the unequal access to education, to health care, and to other sources of personal welfare, together with the extreme levels of abuse, injustice, and violence that go with such a system.[123] In the education and health areas, the picture has been similar but perhaps even more extreme and certainly more enduring than in Mexico, Bolivia, and Peru. The absence of a major reform has enabled personal abuse and income inequality to endure. In those other three countries, the underclass of poor agricultural workers was largely indigenous, whereas, from the nineteenth century onward, a much higher share in Brazil were of African slave origin; it was the largest single destination of the transatlantic slave trade. Slavery ended formally only in 1888 but, as elsewhere, the pattern of dominance and oppression has persisted; the country remains the setting for much open mistreatment of the poor, many of them of African or mixed blood.

Brazilian society, like any other, downplays the darker elements of its own history, including slavery (Miles 2019).[124] Its racial problems and discrimination have often been viewed as less severe than those of the US; the considerable racial mixing contributes to its sometimes being pictured as a "post-racial society." Many outcomes, however, belie this interpretation; for example, income differentials by race appear to be comparable in the two countries, as is the gap in life expectancy vis-à-vis "whites." Although such a formalized group as the Ku Klux Klan is not in charge, death

[123] Income inequality and violent crime are associated across countries. Fajnzylber et al. (2002), in an analysis covering the period of 1970 to 1994, report a positive correlation both within countries and (especially) between them, and note that the correlation reflects causation from inequality to crime rates. A similar conclusion is reached by Bourguignon (2019).

[124] In his many stories, Brazil's most popular twentieth-century novelist, Jorge Amado, describes much of the country's reality, including social relations between classes in rural areas. He was arrested in 1935 for leftist activities, his books were burned, and he then spent several years abroad, sometimes in exile. His descriptions of sexual behavior scandalized the upper classes.

squads—generally made up of off-duty or retired policemen and encouraged by impotent courts—have operated in Brazil since the 1960s, when they killed not just known or suspected criminals but also opponents of the military regime. Inequality has been accompanied by a persistently weak social structure. Officials monitoring child abuse have claimed that hundreds of deprived, destitute minors were being murdered every year; a report by Amnesty International (1992) observed that police were illegally arresting, torturing, and raping street children. These societal flaws were laid bare in an extreme fashion during the 1980s economic crisis, when death squads hired by businesspeople to "rid the slums of crime" killed many street children. Rodrigo Sousa Filho, coordinator of the National Street Children's Movement in the state of Rio de Janeiro, said that "Kids are being gunned down without question, as if they were wild dogs." Grinding poverty, family disintegration, and police corruption contributed to the increasing brutality during that crisis. The drug industry has helped to maintain it. In 2017, Fortaleza, a northeastern city of 2.7 million, became the youth murder capital of the country as 414 adolescents aged ten to nineteen were killed.[125] To a very difficult situation was then added a government particularly weak on matters of justice; President Bolsonaro backed mass incarceration, immunity for police who kill in the line of duty, and a lower age of criminal responsibility. Its history of slavery has reinforced both the social abuses associated with Brazil's agrarian system and those that accompany its urban slums.

Whether through traditional feudalism or some alternative mechanism, keeping everyone else from settling on open land has been a permanent goal of Brazil's agrarian elite because it keeps labor costs low. Slavery, once the most profitable means of doing so, was harder to apply to non-black, non-indigenous peoples. Enclosure has at times been a common strategy to keep land from the masses. Peasants have never found access easy, but rather something that had to be fought for and defended (Fernandes 2013, 271).

The struggle against slavery, expropriation, and exploitation was manifested in territorial disputes that continue to the present. One famous battle featured religious missions organized by Jesuit priests and the "Thirty Guaraní Peoples" who lived on common land, each village having a few thousand members. They continued their struggle against slave hunters and the armies of Spain and Portugal until suffering final defeat in a bloody 1756 massacre in which Sepé Tiaraju, the Guaraní icon of indigenous resistance,

[125] *The Guardian*, December 14, 2018.

lost his life. By then, with the native population of Brazil decimated, indigenous slavery was being substituted by the African variant.

By the late nineteenth century, Brazilian large landholders were drawing mainly on the supply of "free labor," composed of small landholders or squatters and black former slaves who had been freed or had bought their freedom. Many of this group were employed on large farms as bondage workers; the period of bondage was a challenging thirty-eight years. The "Land Law" of 1850 had enshrined the principle of private property and ruled that access to land was only possible through purchase in money. In this context, aspirants had two main options: to work on large farms to save and buy land, or to occupy already claimed lands, many of which had themselves been illegally obtained by landowners through the falsification of title documents. In 1888, abolition ended 350 years of slavery and certified various forms of dependent labor relationships with European immigrant *colonos*. Until the post-war period, this shift from slave to free labor was probably the most important transformation in Brazilian agricultural history, but the persistence of labor dependency and controls on access to land made even this normally momentous change less significant than it might have been.

Meanwhile, the inter-class battle for land included diverse forms of resistance against private enclosure. Peasants and former slaves established the village of Canudos in 1893 on an abandoned farm in Bahia. The village's economic organization was cooperative, with a common fund reserved for use by the more vulnerable segments of the population, particularly the elderly and disabled; in this it resembled a religious commune. These features helped attract new arrivals until the population eventually reached about thirty thousand. Canudos's very presence challenged the established order of submission to the *latifundistas*, so the perpetrators were declared enemies of the state. It was continuously attacked by military expeditions and by the Brazilian Armed Forces; the local government of the state of Bahia felt pressure from landowners to take action against the settlement because of labor shortages, while the national government was unhappy with the implicit show of autonomy. The final siege occurred in 1897; the Brazilian army slaughtered the survivors and destroyed the entire village. A similar outcome befell a peasant movement which grew out of a large government concession to the Brazil Railway Company that forcibly dispossessed thousands of families; by 1914, the movement comprised more than fifteen thousand people. The families were attacked by gunmen of the Railway Company and the Brazilian Armed Forces. Accusing the government of killing peasants and workers, and handing land over to foreign companies, peasants began to attack large farm holdings and cities and to take control of parts of the railway. The final battle/massacre took place in 1916 (Fernandes 2013, 276).

## The Goulart Opening

A few decades later the setting had changed enough to permit a signal event in Brazil's agrarian history—the formation of the Peasant Leagues (*Ligas Campesinas*) around 1945, with the help of the Brazilian Communist Party (*Partido Comunista do Brasil*, PCB). They became a force in defending those with little or no land. In 1947, the government of President Eurico Gaspar Dutra declared the PCB illegal and embarked on a campaign of violent repression. The Peasant Leagues re-emerged in the state of Pernambuco in 1954 as an autonomous organization. At the end of the 1964–1984 military dictatorship, the current landless workers movement (*Movimento dos Trabalhadores Rurais Sem Terra*, MST) was created.

From mid-century onward, there was continuous discussion of and pressure for agrarian reform, but the early 1960s administration of João Goulart provided the only possible opening for major action. It was nearly simultaneous with Colombia's best chance and just a few years after Guatemala's. In Brazil, with a large landholders' oligarchy even more notoriously strong than Colombia's, the effort was quickly terminated by the military coup of 1964. After that failure, a game-changing reform became impossible as large capitalists gradually replaced the traditional *hacendados*, and the country's economy shifted rapidly toward non-agricultural activities. Much protest and activism during this period, together with support from a few political groups, has achieved modest gains but major reform has not been on the table.

The son of a rancher and one himself, Goulart was a protégé of Getúlio Vargas, the complicated political figure who, as president (1930–1945) during troubled and dramatic times, attempted to bring various groups together to shift the country away from what he saw as its excessively plantation-based economy to a more industrial one. He was up against the "old Republic," dominated by the landed interests, which showed little interest in promoting industrialization, in the welfare of the masses, or in an emerging middle class. Widely perceived as Brazil's most influential twentieth-century politician, Vargas was a populist—the first president of the country to draw widespread support from the masses—while also being a staunch anti-Communist; he saw off a Communist revolt by a left-leaning segment of the military in 1935.

Goulart's own plans included not only a land reform to expropriate and redistribute non-productive properties larger than six hundred hectares, which he linked to the doctrine of Pope Leo X111's encyclical "*Rerum Novarun*," but also an educational reform to combat adult illiteracy, drawing on the pioneering teaching and method of Paulo Freire and on a large planned increase in spending on education; a tax reform to limit the outward transfer of profits by multinational companies with headquarters abroad; and an electoral reform to extend voting rights to illiterate people and low-ranking military officers. This was indeed a wide-ranging manifesto.

His plans were naturally met by a strong negative reaction from many better-off Brazilians and were seen as extreme by much of the military and by the US government, whose ambassador (Lincoln Gordon) believed that Goulart was collaborating with the Brazilian Communist Party. America's precise role remains somewhat unclear; years later, in 1976, Gordon stated that the US had been prepared to intervene militarily to prevent a leftist takeover. It was particularly upset by Goulart's independent stance on international affairs—he had resumed relations with socialist countries and opposed sanctions against Cuba—and by his limiting the amount of profits multinational companies could transfer out of the country. There is no doubt that America financed Goulart's electoral opponents, funded public works projects of his leading gubernatorial enemies, and by, late 1963, was broadcasting its view that he was opening the way for the radical left to gain power. By the 1950s and early 1960s, there had been a rightward shift in the American political scenario, as the progressivism of the New Deal gave way to militarism, anti-Communism, and a strong "Southern" influence within the political establishment (Pereira 2018). The administration's confidence that it could entice revolutionary Latin American regimes toward the center through diplomacy, as it felt it had in the wake of the 1952 Bolivian revolution, gave way to an increasingly aggressive approach, reflecting especially the perceived failure in dealing with the 1959 Cuban uprising. Emphasis shifted from positive economic incentives to destabilization and replacement of recalcitrant governments; support for the Brazilian coup signaled the beginning of a wave of similar US actions in the region. Recently declassified US documents lead Pereira (2018) to conclude that US policymakers were not deeply informed on Brazil, its leaders, or its politics, nor did they have a well-planned scheme to deal with Goulart. Until 1963, they were not yet confident in the ability and willingness of the Brazilian military to carry out a successful coup; only then did they throw their weight definitively behind the plotters. Pereira suggests that US officials might have been willing to let President Goulart see out his term if, for example, he had complied with their demands to remove leftists from his government and adjust his economic policies in favor of US economic interests; any such interpretation will remain provisional until more US government documents—and perhaps Brazilian ones as well—are declassified. Skidmore (1988) judges that the main impetus for the coup came from the Brazilian military officer corps and much of the Brazilian public, including the middle class as well as the traditional right. In any event, retrospect does suggest that a coup was quite likely; the Brazilian military leaned strongly that way and the US was unlikely to oppose such a step.[126]

## Post-Goulart

In contrast to Peru, where a military government undertook the country's major agrarian reform, Brazil's 1964–1984 regime was particularly hostile to the peasantry; it put an end to the *campesino* leagues, was closely allied with the agricultural power groups, and supported large agriculture and mechanization. An estimated 1.5 million peasants were expelled from their land from 1960 to 1980 (Peritore and Peritore 1990, 378).

Interacting with this regime's approach was a signal event in the history of developing country agriculture—the post-World War II Green Revolution. Agricultural scientist Norman Borlaug received a Nobel Peace Prize in 1970 for his role in a break-through expected to prevent many people (estimates reached a billion or more) from starving to death. But whether and where it did greatly reduce food shortage and poverty depended on the context.

[126] The second controversy around Goulart has been the cause of his death in 1976, allegedly of a heart attack, at a time when he was dividing his exile between Uruguay and Argentina. Later reports, in particular one from a former member of the intelligence service under Uruguay's dictatorship, alleged that he was poisoned by the Brazilian government. In July 2008, a special commission of the legislative assembly of Rio Grande do Sul, Goulart's home state, concluded that there was strong evidence that he was deliberately assassinated with the knowledge of the Ernesto Geisel military government. In 2013, however, forensic experts in Brazil undertook a postmortem, failed to find traces of poison in his remains, and accordingly judged that he had probably died of a heart attack, although given the time that had passed since his death, they were not able to rule out poisoning.

A large beneficial effect required not only that land productivity increase substantially but also that enough of the associated increase in income go to poorer families. As Sen (1981) would clarify a few years later in the context of famines, when families do not get enough food it is not usually because their country or the world cannot produce enough of it but rather that their own incomes are inadequate to allow them to buy it. Lack of financial capacity to purchase food lessens the market-based incentive to produce it. In settings like that of Brazil under the military dictatorship, the Green Revolution and associated policies promoting capital intensive practices (more fertilizers, irrigation, etc.) can cause more harm than good.[127] Its net impact on agricultural workers and small farmers, and on labor as a whole,[128] may have been a significant factor in the marked increase in income inequality during the dictatorship. In contrast, where small producers dominate the agricultural sector, as in the East Asian tigers, and later in China and Vietnam, the Green Revolution did greatly diminish poverty levels. The best guarantee of widespread food security is a small-farm system in which families satisfy their own food needs. In a large-farm system, little of the income gets to those toward the bottom of the hierarchy and often little food is produced.

The military regime that overthrew Goulart in 1964 established its own land reform as a matter of so-called national security (Lambias 2008, 7). To address growing social tensions, President (General) Castelo Branco promulgated a Land Statute calling for the expropriation—based on "social interest"—of *latifundios* over six hundred times bigger than the typical size in areas of heavy conflict. In 1971, as another part of a clearly nonconfrontational policy, the Brazilian Institute of Agrarian Reform (*Instituto Brasileiro de Reforma Agrária*) was replaced by the National Institute of Colonization and Agrarian Reform (*Instituto Nacional de Colonização e Reforma Agrária*, INCRA), which emphasized colonization as the answer to peasant unrest. But those few receiving plots lacked the needed government support (credit, infrastructure, etc.) to integrate them successfully into the market.

When José Sarney, the first civilian president after the dictatorship, took over in 1985 on the death of Tancredo Neves and aspired to fulfil Neves's

[127] This argument is made by Welch (2006, 38). Labor-replacing machines in such a context are referred to as "inappropriate technology," a concept widely discussed in the economic literature.

[128] These effects are analyzed in depth by Bustos et al. (2016), who find that the introduction of genetically engineered soybean seeds in Brazil was strongly labor-saving, and thus led to a decrease in the share of employment in agriculture, consistent with its lowering wages there and in manufacturing, and in its raising manufacturing's share of total employment.

progressive promises, there were widespread expectations of positive change. The policies of the military regime were under considerable attack and a range of groups were pressuring for land reform.[129] Organized civil society was becoming increasingly involved in discussion of policies for sustainable rural development and food security. Trade unions, the newly created Workers' Party (*Partido dos Trabalhadores,* PT), the Landless Movement (MST), and other broad social movements all contributed to this democratization process and to the activism on the land front. Sarney's administration created the Ministry of Agrarian Reform and Rural Development (MIRAD), with the promise of providing land to 1.4 million landless families by 1989, and to 7.1 million by 2000, using mainly public property though with some expropriation of "idle private land." Accompanying public support was to take the form of agricultural research oriented to peasant agriculture, extension, inputs, and a special credit program (PROCERA), which was seen as fundamental to raising agricultural output and to providing long-term stability.

Supporters drew optimism from the range of groups that had mobilized against the military. Another positive signal was the new 1988 Constitution, which incorporated many laudatory goals and included the directive that land should serve a social function; unfortunately, this was accompanied by the idea that property rights were to be protected by guaranteed compensation for landlords. thereby making social justice by itself insufficient grounds for expropriation (Welch 2006, 42).[130] While many did see the new constitution as a potential support for agrarian reform, a group of younger landlords—many of them livestock producers and worried by the apparent passivity of their traditional representative organizations—founded the Rural Democratic Union (*União Democrática Ruralista,* UDR). UDR militants adopted the posture that farmers were under siege from invading slum-dwellers who had no vocation for agriculture but were being stimulated into action by MST agitators. The UDR organized private militias to repel the occupations attempted by the landless. It also helped to resuscitate and fortify the so-called Rural Caucus (*Bancada Ruralista*) in the legislative assembly. Given that many politicians were themselves large landowners, this group had much influence on the upper levels of decision-making,

[129] At this time, the share of Brazil's labor force found in agriculture was around twenty percent; by 2000, it had fallen to 16.5 percent (World Bank, n.d.).

[130] This constitution also became famous for offering benefits that would cost the country much in future, especially the generous civil servant pensions.

an influence reflected in the resignations of consecutive Agrarian Reform ministers under political pressure, and in the new constitution's approval only after a downscaling of the land reform plans. MIRAD was abolished in 1989 and responsibility for handling land tenure issues was completely transferred to INCRA, which focused on colonization and was influenced by the military-controlled National Security Council. The anti-reform pressure was successful. By 1992, less than one percent of the farmland had been redistributed, less than ten percent of the initial proposal. Of the 1.4 million families scheduled to be settled in the short-term plan, only about ninety thousand were (Robles 2018, 9), followed by another sixty-five thousand during the subsequent Fernando Collor de Mello-Franco administration (1990–1994) when land reform was squeezed out of the political agenda by the corruption and the impeachment of Collor de Mello. Relative to the needs, the settlement over this decade was tiny.

Although the idea of "social purpose" was written into the 1988 constitution (e.g., landlords were to comply with environmental conservation laws and labor legislation), land was also to be used economically and rationally (i.e., productively); in fact, only the productivity aspect was given weight in the allocation process (Lambais 2008, 9). The inability and the lack of political will of the legislators to determine the strict sense of "social purpose" or to weigh in seriously on how "productive land use" should be defined helped the anti-reform groups, as did the fact that agribusiness was one of the few healthy components of the economy in the midst of the 1980s recession, systematically producing thirty-five to forty percent of the country's exports. Sarney, like others, was loathe to create instability for that sector. In short, the political backing needed for real reform was not enough to overcome the powerful opposition, and Congress greatly limited the funds available for land settlement.[131]

The supporters of agrarian reform at this time had less political clout than might at first glance have appeared. Peritore and Peritore (1990) distinguish three broad groups—the Church radicals, the secular radicals, and the agrarian populists—each of which supported some type of agrarian reform; unfortunately, their doing so for different reasons often put them at odds over implementation.[132] On the ground, three main pressure groups

[131] Robles and Veltmeyer (2015) review the agrarian reform process under Sarney and Collor de Mello-Franco.

[132] The church radicals were skeptics with regard to parties and political processes in Brazil, seeing the agrarian issue as a moral question and wishing to promote mass movements leading to redistribution within a Christian framework that excluded violence and class struggle; emphasis on

pushed for reform—the workers' party (PT), the National Confederation of Workers in Agriculture (*Confederação Nacional dos Trabalhadores na Agricultura*, CONTAG), and various subgroups of the Catholic Church. Both the background supporters and the online pressure groups were divided over aims and implementation; in contrast, the right was able to create a strong coalition. The government was too fragmented and weak to mediate the conflict toward a positive outcome. The contrast between proponents and opponents exemplified a common problem of social reform movements. Support is built on a variety of moral and social grounds; when they do not fully coincide, this impedes coordinated action. In contrast, groups pursuing their own self-interest and unencumbered by moral issues can more easily work together.

Along with clearly differing stances across them, some of those support groups have experienced internal disputes and changes in overall posture over time. CONTAG is a corporatist organization of rural labor unions founded in 1963 with roots in the communist party; that party, in turn, has the longest institutional history of action on behalf of Brazilian peasants, beginning with its popular front strategy in 1928 (Welch and Sauer 2015, 1111). Its early history of collaboration has made it suspect in many branches of government and on the political right and has also contributed to confusion as to whether it supports agrarian reform, as opposed simply to the welfare of workers—the traditional role of a union and of communist ideology. Welch and Sauer argue that in fact it has remained committed to reform that privileges individual property rights, family labor and production,[133] although its precise definition of reform and especially its actions

the centrality of passing property from one class to another was unwelcome. Secular radicals saw the issue as one of practical politics rather than morals. They were willing to use existing legal and political means to bring change, and were happy with Sarney's goal of a system of rural property and land use that would promote social justice, progress, and welfare for the rural workers and the gradual extinction of both the *minifundia* and the *latifundia* (Peritore and Peritore 1990, 385). They preferred reimbursement for expropriated property at the declared tax value. They were critical of the military government's promotion of large-scale agriculture on the northern frontier but did not strongly reject the conservative goal of capitalist modernization. They were political pragmatists whose central goal was collective or cooperative property. Finally, agrarian populists promoted direct action to occupy and cultivate *latifundia* in collective and cooperative systems. The family farm was seen as desirable but not viable in the Brazilian economy. They felt it necessary to occupy lands, given the degree of immiseration of rural workers.

[133] This conclusion challenges that presented by Martins (2002), who claimed that CONTAG was historically committed to "class struggle against capitalists and landlords" whereas the CPT and MST saw "no need for radical systemic transformation and adhere[d] . . . to a communitarian vision in which capitalists and workers enjoy[ed] a tension-free parity of esteem' (Welch and Sauer 2015, 327).

have at times changed with the socioeconomic and political setting. Seeing little need to abandon capitalism *per se*, it has endeavored to harmonize peasant interests with a system of market-oriented family farming. It only came to officially recognize the legitimacy of land occupations in the mid-1990s. The delay in doing so reflected, among other things, the considerable differentiation across its grassroots constituencies between agricultural employees, small farmers, and the landless, together with the organizational structure of CONTAG itself, in which national decisions have rarely been seen as instructions to the entire movement. In the 1990s, CONTAG's continued commitment, combined with the actions of the MST, largely account for such priority as agrarian reform has had in Brazil's new period of democracy. Some of its views have been controversial within the left. Whereas the MSL opposed market-based land reform as something undermining the goal of redistribution, CONTAG decided to support it when the government adopted some improvements in the program, including an end to the settling of families on unproductive land (Lambais 2008, 25).

Meanwhile, the large landholders naturally constitute a formidable opponent in a country like Brazil. In the face of what appear to be serious threats, they and their allies have responded quickly and effectively, a fact underlying the pattern detected by Albertus et al. (2018, 557) between land inequality, rural unrest, and landowner organization. "Isolated threats to landed elites in the form of land invasions are difficult to repel, generating a positive relationship between landholding inequality and one-off land invasions. By contrast, sustained, broader local threats triggered by nearby land reforms catalyze landowner organization to repel land invasions, leading to the reverse relationship." As a result, there is no unidirectional association between land inequality and unrest/invasions.[134]

By the arrival of the new constitution in 1988, the Washington Consensus in favor of globalization and freer markets had become increasingly influential. The World Bank was funding many studies on how to liberalize agricultural policy and enhance the sector's global competitiveness. Participation in international agreements protecting intellectual property rights were opening the door to genetically modified (GMO) seeds, such as Monsanto's Terminator, which resisted pests and needed less water than did normal hybrids and which stimulated further expansion of the agricultural frontier

[134] Their conclusion is based on a statistical analysis of municipal data on land concentration, municipal-level data from Brazil's land reform program, and the universe of 9,400 land invasions staged by several million individuals over the period 1988 to 2013.

and facilitated mechanization. Public–private partnerships were expanded in research and development, infrastructure investment, and other areas. From 1990 to 1994, many agricultural jobs disappeared. Most commentators blamed the victims and attributed their problems to a dearth of needed skills, although the former head of *Associação Brasileira do Agronegócio* (ABAG), an agribusiness association founded in 1993, admitted later that this period was a brutal "agrarian desettlement" (Welch 2006, 43).

A lack of major progress on inequality under two generally impressive presidents—Fernando Cardoso and Luiz Lula da Silva—reflects the challenging barriers in the way. Coming to power a decade after Sarney's failed attempt, Cardoso (1995–2002), a notable intellectual who might have been expected to provide support for a serious land reform, was instead cautious; he believed the cost would be high and, in light of the urgent need to tame inflation and end an ongoing recession, he gave precedence to the fiscal challenge and successful negotiation of the foreign debt (Robles 2018, 17). He appears never to have been convinced that a reform could make a big contribution to national welfare, but instead saw the agrarian question more as a historical anachronism, along the lines of such "death of the peasantry" exponents as David Lehman (1978). Spokespeople for his government commented at the end of the 1990s that a reform was unwise because the small units were not competitive and could not much increase the incomes of the rural poor; priority should thus be given to creating more remunerative higher-skill jobs, which with time would shift the land reform issue into the background, a view held also by former American ambassador Gordon (Smith 2009, 259).[135]

Although Cardoso's election, under the banner of constructing a "new Brazil," did bring the issue of access to land back onto the agenda, this was mostly because of the increasing demands of the MST and the need to contain the sort of social tension that culminated in a massacre of MST militants by the state police in 1998 and 1999. The number of families settled increased with the creation, in 1999, of the Agricultural Development Ministry (*Ministério do Desenvolvimento Agrário*, MDA). Land allocation was almost completely a matter of response to conflict.[136] By 2002, the government had

[135] For a more detailed look at the economics of this argument, see Chapter 3. It is almost always put forward by those defending large-scale agriculture, as noted above in the context of Colombia.

[136] According to Heredia et al. (2005), ninety-six percent of the settlements that took place during Cardoso's presidency resulted from conflict, eighty-nine percent of it initiated by the peasants, sixty-four percent in the context of occupations, and twenty-nine percent of resistance.

settled 592,141 families; in this tension-laden process, 271 peasants were murdered. Cardoso did see land reform as an instrument for poverty reduction, and also undertook useful steps like raising taxes on unutilized land. MDA's mandate included the promotion of rural sustainable development, support for family agriculture, agrarian reform, and new rural settlements. Two of its most important ventures were the National Programme for Strengthening Family Agriculture (*Programa Nacional de Fortalecimento da Agricultura*, PRONAF) and the Food Acquisitions Programme (*Programa de Aquisição de Alimentos*, PAA).

PRONAF is the oldest social assistance program in Brazil, dating back to 1954, and one of the largest (Rocha 2009). In 2009, the Lula de Silva government scaled up the potential for PAA's reach by legislating that at least thirty percent of the funding for the national school meals program had to be spent on purchasing food from family farms. Around that time the national school meals program was serving over forty million children per day throughout Brazil and was administered in every municipality. This legislation had the potential to significantly boost local food production on family farms and appeared after a few years of operation to be having some success.

His ambivalence notwithstanding, Cardoso's eight years in office did see land settlement regain a new, albeit limited, momentum. By the end of his mandate up to five percent of land had been redistributed—although much of it appeared to be of marginal quality, and six hundred thousand families settled, with what appear to have been broadly satisfactory results in terms of income gains.[137]

While not opposed to small-scale agriculture, Cardoso saw the MST as a threat to democracy, viewed land occupation as a violation of property rights, and sought to penalize the landless workers involved (Robles 2018, 21). This stance naturally created a tense relationship with the MST and some other reformist groups; it also undercut such potential benefits as might have accompanied the direct participation of land reform beneficiaries in its design and administration. Being seen by some as insincere in his stated concern for the welfare of the landless was the cost of his "weighing the balance"; after leaving office he commented that had he not been president he would probably have been marching with the protesters, but in the former role he had to consider the impact of "land invasion scenes" on the nation's

[137] Heredia et al. (2005) judge that across states, one to five percent of the land was redistributed, with the exception of Pará, where the figure reached a striking twenty-five percent.

economic stability. While this very thoughtful president did empathize with the condition of the landless workers, he probably never understood the potential economic advantages of smaller scale agriculture and the extent of welfare gains that an equalizing reform could bring. Even if he had, however, policies might not have been very different. As noted, the economic setting posed very serious challenges. Other members of his government were much more negative on land-related issues; one minister of agriculture categorized the MST as a terrorist organization. The conventional wisdom was that size went with efficiency, and the negative distributional effects of an agrarian system like Brazil's were not at all well understood. Those effects are mainly indirect, through the general downward pressure on lower skill wages, rather than direct; as a result, few people intuit them correctly.

The Washington Consensus with its neoliberal train of thought provided a more independent element of logic to support the view that large-scale agriculture was the best option available to the country. This way of thinking formally accepted GDP maximization as the sole goal of economic policy and gave little or no attention to income distribution or poverty; it also exaggerated both the effectiveness of free markets in solving all problems by generating fast growth, and the degree to which exports would raise that growth, all while worrying little about negative externalities such as environmental damage.[138] At the time of Cardoso's presidency, the ideology was widespread and he seemed generally to accept its premises, including deregulation of the agricultural sector, closing some government support agencies, eliminating subsidies and repressing unions, which were seen as an "imperfection" in the labor market. The new technologies at this time involved mainly agro-chemicals and seeds, along with labor-displacing mechanical harvesters. Production for export soared and the rural labor movement was weakened (Welch 2006, 37).

Under Cardoso, Brazil provided the setting for an important test of market-assisted land reform (MALR); while that setting did involve conflict, it was less severe than in such other World Bank projects as those in Guatemala and Colombia. A key objective of his government was to break the link between land occupations (mostly organized by the MST) and land expropriation. The reform was essentially limited to the creation of new rural

[138] As with all such prevalent modes of thinking, the Washington Consensus umbrella has incorporated both subtle and not-so-subtle thinkers. Its popular and simpler manifestations appeal to the latter end of the spectrum.

settlements (in 1996 and from 1998 to 2002) in the hope of alleviating social tensions and calming pressures provoked by social movements. Its implementation occurred in a broader context of the criminalization of land occupations and moral disqualification of the peasant movements, especially the MST. The federal government and the mainstream media collaborated in this process (Pereira 2007, 41). After its 1997 launching and a 1998 assessment that revealed serious weaknesses, the program was re-started with the important support of the CONTAG and expanded to the Northeast, the South, and the state of Espírito Santo (Lambais 2008, 20). CONTAG support was conditional on modifications, including a decrease in interest rates, extension of the loan repayment period and, most importantly, the exclusion of unproductive lands from the program. The resumption of World Bank grants was very important because the evaluations suggested that such up-front funding was needed to establish the new communities and secure the land.

While no one would argue seriously that a MALR begun around the turn of this century could transform Brazil with its extreme land concentration into a Latin American Taiwan, this does not mean that such a reform cannot provide very meaningful benefits. The National Land Credit Program (PNCF), aimed at providing access to land along with needed infrastructure, assisted over ninety thousand beneficiary families between 2002 and 2012. A recent study (Helfand et al. 2019) concludes that it achieved its primary objective of fostering remunerative activities, albeit with some delay. It took an average of four years to trigger a significant increase in agricultural production; one estimate puts that increase at about US$400 per person after five to six years, a gain of around seventy-four percent relative to the baseline production of non-beneficiaries. Relative to the control group, total earned income (including that from non-agriculture) rose less—by an estimated US$325 per person or about thirty-seven percent.[139] Taking repayment of the PNCF loan into account, however, beneficiaries could face a trade-off between current consumption and asset accumulation, as the impact on disposable income (net of payments on loans) was negative in the early years, and might only become positive after five or six years of ownership; although their net wealth was rising, most or all of the beneficiaries' initial increases in income went to debt payments. Eventually many would be able both to make

[139] The income gain is roughly equivalent to what a poor household would have received in 2010 through the conditional cash transfer program *Bolsa Família*, in exchange for ensuring that two children remained in school.

these debt payments and raise consumption, but some were likely to fall into arrears on their payments, in which case they lost access to a source of family farm credit. Helfand et al. (2019) judge that the grace period for repayments should be extended beyond the current two years, the repayment period lengthened to reduce the annual payments, say from the current fourteen to seventeen years to twenty to thirty years, and access to technical assistance and other loans improved. In addition, they suggest that medium-term impact evaluations be undertaken instead of focusing only on the first few years. Their general conclusion is thus optimistic, but cautious. The program does much better than claimed by its harsher critics, but a good deal less well than would be desirable and feasible with a better organized support package. Dylan Fitz (2017) reaches broadly similar conclusions from an analysis of the reform's impact in Northeast Brazil. The provision of an average of 7.5 hectares to participants had a positive impact on income, although its effect on rural poverty was less clear since, while beneficiary households did transition successfully into agriculture, control group households also saw an increase in their (labor) income; that both groups wound up with higher incomes probably owed something to the rapid economic growth experienced by Northeast Brazil during the 2000s, to an increase in minimum wages, and to *Bolsa Família* transfers.[140] While rebutting claims that the Land Credit program simply traps landless farmers under mountains of debt, Fitz (like Helfand et al. 2019) finds evidence that beneficiaries may be left too much on their own. MALR programs are typically designed with the expectation that owning land will by itself give beneficiaries access to credit, insurance, technical assistance, and other needs. On these counts the evidence is mixed. Just twenty-seven percent of them received PRONAF credit (in theory available to all land reform beneficiaries) and only five percent got private loans. Fitz opines that, without doing more to overcome credit market failures, the long-term effectiveness of the program may prove limited; greater credit access might allow larger investments like those in irrigation.

Although the analyses undertaken to date provide broadly positive evidence that MALR in Brazil can "work,"[141] it remains unclear whether such

[140] Even if the overall economic status of the two groups wound up being approximately the same, the reform program could be contributing to both by creating one more way for them to be productive and earn higher incomes. A contribution to the aggregate income of the larger group does not always imply that the direct beneficiaries of a program do better than non-beneficiaries.

[141] See also Lambais (2008).

programs could be expanded to a point where they would have a significant impact on rural and overall poverty; the level achieved was not nearly large enough to do that. And, without a major reduction in the overall degree of land concentration, it would be impossible to provide enough good quality land and unlikely that there would be adequate technical and other support for reform beneficiaries.

Because of its labor movement roots and the personal support candidate Lula da Silva traditionally showed toward the landless movement, there were widespread expectations that his Workers' Party government (2003–2011) would make agrarian reform a major project. Instead, it kept a relatively low profile on this front, especially in the first years. As a result, the MST switched back from an initial collaboration mode to its traditional pressure tactics.[142] The party, with only partial control of the state bureaucracy, was forced to make compromises. The appointment of ABAG president Roberto Rodrigues as Minister of Agriculture was an early indication that the policy tilt in favor of large farms would not be greatly altered. Agribusiness and the landed elite continued to receive the lion's share of government resources channeled to the sector through generously subsidized credit, debt equalization, purchase and price guarantee schemes, infrastructural investments, and so on. Meanwhile, the Ministry of Agrarian Development continued to operate on very limited funds. For this administration, like its predecessors, agro-exports were seen as the path to development; agrarian reform policies could, it was hoped, help to make peasant agriculture more market-oriented and successful, but were clearly not central to overall economic success. Lula da Silva's financial advisors argued that Brazilian growth would be helped by maintaining the orthodox neoliberal policies, and that it would be foolish to confront the international community with appeals for debt-relief if it were not doing so. The administration did differ from Cardoso's in its perspectives on and actions toward peasants, particularly those linked to the MST, with which it cultivated broadly positive relations. It also increased

[142] This shift back toward active land occupation to target the agro-export complex, including sugar cane plantations and productive eucalyptus forests, was undertaken both to gain territory and to change the terms of debate. MST accepted that many agro-export plantations were highly productive but argued that they failed to fill their social function by employing few people, used what was in effect slave labor, and damaged the environment with agro-chemicals. In contrast to profit-oriented agribusiness, family farming was touted as producing better nutrition and much more employment—small farmers were responsible for generating seventy percent of the total in agriculture.

by fourteen-fold the budget of PRONAF, the Cardoso government creation designed to assist small farmers.

As occurred in Colombia, a reasonably positively oriented government was then followed by a starkly negative one—that of Jair Bolsonaro, from 2019 to 2022, who wrought havoc on the country in many ways. Recent slow growth, a lack of trust in corrupt politicians and other factors paved the way for his campaign as the strong man who would correct all of these ills. Instead, he encouraged the cutting of the Amazon forests, thereby creating an environmental danger for the world as well as Brazil, and he failed to seriously tackle the poverty challenge. Soon after taking power, he cancelled the National Council for Food and Nutrition Security (*Conselho de Segurança Alimentar e Nutricional*, CONSEA) which, since its creation in the 1990s, had helped to curb poverty and hunger and led to Brazil's removal in 2014 from the list of undernourished countries in the World Food Programme's Hunger Map. Prior progress on this front was slowed or reversed as the recession of 2014 to 2016 cost many people their jobs. Then came the COVID-19 challenges, whose mismanagement by Bolsonaro's administration—including the espousal of non-cures, disparaging of masks, and so forth—caused avoidable deaths numbering in the hundreds of thousands. As of late July 2021, Brazil had over half a million deaths (official figures) and the world's highest death rate among large countries, at 2,590 per million. COVID-19 highlighted the weaknesses of Brazil's social safety net and its policy response, including steps such as raising the *Bolsa Familia* allowance in April 2020 to help deal with sharply higher food prices. Bolsonaro's "right to govern" attitude resembled that of Trump. Fortunately, on narrowly losing the 2022 election, he did not foment a coup to retain office. Another term would presumably have greatly aggravated the damage already done. His coming into office can be seen partly as a reflection of the long-lasting grievances and dissatisfaction that flow from the poverty and extreme inequality that a land reform may have been the only way to partially resolve. It was also indicative of the deep polarization present in Brazilian society, as in so many others.

## Summary of Reform Experiences

Except for the Goulart opening in the early 1960s, the defining questions of Brazil's agrarian history have always been whether minor improvements would be possible and whether they would make enough difference to be worthwhile. That opening itself was a result of prior political and social progress plus the accident of his succeeding to the presidency when the also left-leaning Jânio Quadras resigned in 1961.[143] A (perhaps the) key factor in the negative outcome was the hardline stance of the country's military; its history of collaboration with the ruling elites, together with its willingness to be involved in politics (Stepan, 1973b) came into play at that time and in the military dictatorship that followed.

The limited impact of the various other land reform measures was a natural result of their being designed mainly to "appease immediate claims, defuse local conflicts, and, above all, avoid major confrontation with large landholders" (Carter 2015, 24). The various organizations of this latter group remained very powerful and continued to exert the dominant influence on government policy. While the MST and other peasant and rural labor movements had access to the Ministry of Agrarian Development, responsible for agrarian reform and family farming, the landed elite and agribusiness interacted with the far more powerful and better-resourced Ministry of Agriculture. The "modernization" of Brazilian agriculture made the country an agro-export powerhouse. The persistence of the extreme land concentration through it all reflects the state's continued and strong support for agribusiness. Post-1985 democratic governments have provided generous economic incentives for it to open new frontiers, even as it has evolved toward a socially and environmentally destructive pattern of monoculture.

Although the MST has demonstrated much vibrancy, it has not had enough political clout to weigh heavily in the outcomes and has suffered from the fragmentation and decline of pro-agrarian reform forces. Still, Cristóbal Kay (2019) judges that the struggles of the rural labor movements were responsible for whatever advances did occur, and that when mobilizations and pressures waned so did those advances. He gives particular credit to the MST, which by organizing and mobilizing the rural poor contributed to the democratization of rural society and the country as a whole. Despite tensions and disagreements between them and the Workers' Party (PT) governments, the latter helped to make this achievement possible, by refusing to repress and criminalize these organizations and movements as had been the case in the past. The MST repertoire involved a range of activities including land

[143] As well as being to the left of the Brazilian political establishment, Quadras was also considered to be unpredictable.

occupations and demonstrations, protest camps, road blockades, occupation of buildings, long-distance marches, and hunger strikes. Without these actions, often taken in collaboration with other rural and urban popular organizations, he judges that far less land would have been redistributed and fewer civil, social, and political rights would have been extended to the rural poor and other disadvantaged groups. The MST retained a significant degree of autonomy despite its many dealings with various government institutions and the Workers' Party.[144] Women played an increasingly important role in its mobilizations and other activities; they also established their own rural organizations. At times, the MST engaged in acts of invasion but at other times it followed the legal path. It has included a group of technocrats and experts who have themselves developed technologies for use in small-scale agriculture (Pimbert 2005, 33). As expected, it has systematically been the object of harsh criticism from the right. As a result, it has been a permanent defense mechanism for the landless poor. While its various collaborations with the government did help to achieve modest progress, they may have diminished the chances of major success.

On the other side, the agribusiness boom has helped to forge a new triple alliance of "old" and "new" large landholders, chemical–agricultural transnationals, and the national government. Agribusiness has become an integral part of what Wilder Robles (2018, 24–26) refers to as a broader neoextractivism often pursued by Brazil's national government which, as in previous centuries, is displacing indigenous peoples, creating enclave economies, lowering labor standards, damaging the ecosystem, raising inequality, and opening Brazil's economy to the volatility of global commodity prices.

As reviewed below, income inequality both within agriculture and overall has remained extremely high, with no apparent long-term trend. The questions of general interest raised by the Brazilian story are (i) what alternative policy approaches might have been followed? and (ii) how different might the outcomes have been from those actually achieved? An important sub-question is how much luck it would have taken under either Goulart or Sarney to cut the level of land concentration enough to yield large societal benefits. What combination of aggressive pressuring (e.g., via occupations)

[144] Comparable rural organizations in many other Latin American countries lost legitimacy with their members when they became entangled in patron–client relationships and, at the extreme, became tools of government policy or pawns of political parties.

and collaboration would have produced the best outcomes? These questions confronted participant institutions at many points in time and now need to be addressed by historians. After the 1960s, there was, in retrospect, little chance of a major reform; the historical question is which modest steps could have brought the largest benefits.

## Possible "Models" for Brazilian Agriculture and the Narratives Built Around Them

Broadly speaking, two starkly contrasting models for the organization of Brazilian agriculture stand out, with many in-between variants. The dominant one is the "bigger is better" agro-industry view that was actually pursued. What many would see as its mirror image is that of the *Via Campesina*, the international peasants' movement that came on the scene in 1993 as an organized institutional critic of all that was wrong with the standard Brazil-type model, and which now has member organizations in eighty-one countries. *Via Campesina* criticizes Brazilian agribusiness as environmentally unsustainable—particularly because of its role in the Amazon region and its high use of harmful chemical inputs—and as socially damaging because of its failure to help reduce poverty and improve food and nutritional security. In contrast, agrarian reform is seen as promising ecologically sustainable development, dignified labor, community cohesion, wholesome food, peaceful social relations, equality, decentralized power, and democracy.

In Latin America, *Via Campesina* has drawn much of its energy from opposition to globalization, to the associated weakening of protectionist legislation, and to cutbacks of some existing rural programs, all this in the midst of the damaging effects of the lost decade of the 1980s (Welch 2006, 50). This context gave rise to a new generation of more autonomous peasant organizations, who perceived their similar problems as largely coming from beyond the borders of weakened nation-states. *Via Campesina* had its base in these autonomous organizations, first in Latin America, and then globally. It has increasingly defined itself in opposition to transnational corporations, has given particular emphasis to food sovereignty, and has tried to provide small farmers with a platform from which their voices may be heard. As in most Latin countries, including Brazil, the twentieth century's early peasant support movements relied in part on local Communist parties—an obvious ally in terms of shared interests/goals and often an institution with some power.

That affiliation influenced their views on how to aid peasants and landless workers. Thus, although some landless movements support small-scale agriculture as a solution to their problems, this has not always been the case. Views on large agroindustry have also varied with place and time.

A narrower model, overlapping substantially but not totally with that of *Via Campesina*, does focus mainly on the potential economic efficiency and social benefits of family farming and the fact that, even when judged by the efficiency criteria of capitalist market thinking, it can often outperform both old-style haciendas and modern agro-industry. Along with this, it brings various social benefits, like mutually supportive communities, and private ones like economic security for families, but does not have natural links to socialism or any political leaning. In fact, communities of small farmers often lean toward conservative parties and stances, one of the factors underlying the support for such a system by General MacArthur and the US government in their backing of the reform in Japan, Korea, and Taiwan. In Brazil, views on the family agricultural sector have become somewhat more accurate and hence more positive since the 1990s, due in part to extensive research by INCRA in collaboration with the United Nations Food and Agriculture Organization (FAO) (Rocha et al. 2012).

Narratives built around any model naturally play on its alleged strengths. Brazil's economy has historically been reliant on "big agriculture," from sugarcane, cocoa, and coffee plantations to large soy and fruit production and extensive cattle operations. Small, family production has always been widely seen by policy makers and many others as a marginal, and even dispensable, part of the sector. As a result, the most predictable views to appear in standard narratives are those of the large landholders who benefit from land concentration and government support. Pro-large farm arguments became stronger among some groups in Brazil as the sector evolved from feudal to agro-capitalist, as it became more technology and science-based, as yields rose, and so on. The early years of the twenty-first century saw its public aura reach "hagiographic proportions," with major news magazines celebrating its capacity to "save" Brazil (Welch 2006). The private media, typically supported by large, vested interests and, in any case, not inclined or able to probe much into complicated matters like the relative efficiency of farms by size, were a natural ally of agribusiness.[145] Unsurprisingly, most

[145] As Welch (2006, 56) puts it: "The major corporate media is closely tied to agribusiness interests and regularly promotes agricultural capitalism while denigrating agrarian reform in a constant barrage of calumny."

people close to government were convinced that agrarian reform would be detrimental. Agribusiness was seen as so productive that its profits could pay down Brazil's foreign debt and generate resources to invest in non-agricultural, pro-poor development policies. And, in fact, the share of the population in poverty did fall during the most recent growth boom. In 2004, the Lula da Silva administration counted on agro-export earnings to normalize Brazil's relationship with the international banking community and free the country from years of IMF supervision.

On the other side of this fence, awareness of the quantitative dimensions of small agriculture has increased somewhat; agricultural surveys and censuses provide quantitative evidence on things like the dimensions of and the relative productivity of different groups of farms. Until the 1990s, however, there was little recognition of the family farm sector's contribution. As in Colombia, most people, aware of the widespread poverty among small farm families, saw them and their demands for agrarian reform and land settlements as a "social problem" that needed to be dealt with (Rocha et al. 2012). Recognition among the few experts that smallness can have efficiency advantages is also relatively recent; the first broad supportive empirical evidence for Brazil came from the survey of 1962/1963 (Cline 1970). That view gradually spread to a larger, but still tiny, group of people close to agrarian issues. Other weaknesses of large-scale agriculture, especially its contribution to deforestation, chemical pollution, and the like, have garnered much more public attention, with Brazil figuring prominently in the wave of international attention to environmental misdeeds. Although information on this front remains partial and somewhat contested, environmentally devastating practices like the exploitation of cheap-but-fragile Amazon basin lands and the use of more chemical fertilizers and poisons are coming to popular attention in Brazil, as well as elsewhere. Soybean expansion into the Amazon appears already to have brought more destruction to the region than the much-criticized cattle ranching did in the 1980s. Despite this, a popular narrative in Brazil sees any major new road or railway line into undeveloped land as facilitating the "arrival of civilization." President Lula da Silva inaugurated a trans-Amazonian road project to the Pacific Ocean that passed through the Brazilian and Peruvian forests.

Some of the rural movements are cognizant of and proponents of the small farm's economic efficiency when that term goes beyond the "generation of profits"; others are not, understandably given the weight of allegedly informed opinion against this view. In fact, some of those who are aware of the facts on this issue may not want to push them too strongly to avoid looking uninformed. When all is taken together, the balance of opinion seldom changes much, and remains weighted very heavily in favor of the *status quo*. For a strong redistributive reform to be implemented by an elected government requires an unusual setting on the part of the decision-makers, as was the case in post-war Japan and a few other countries in lesser degree.

The Brazilian land story and the views expressed around it exemplify many normal responses and beliefs—most of them inaccurate but in greatly varying degrees, from the acceptance not only by large farm supporters but also by some *Via Campesina* spokespeople that agribusiness is more productive (generally true only if labor productivity—the wrong indicator—is used) to the view that it would be the best way to bring people out of poverty—highly improbable in a context like Brazil's, but not a total contradiction of terms.

Given the charisma and persuasiveness of some of Brazil's presidents and their main advisors over the last few decades, this group's understanding of land issues is certainly a matter of importance. Even though major change in land distribution was not politically possible, it is very likely that societal welfare would have been significantly improved by substantially more resettlement of landless people than did occur, and by greater support for those that were settled and for the already existing small farm base. Whereas a president's understanding of why small agriculture may be more efficient than large might not have paid off in policy, as both the political power of the large landholders and general doubts about small agriculture would have helped to make a major redistributive reform impossible, a belief that small farming has a role to play and can be made much more productive by a strong support policy could have paid off. Understanding that extremely ineffective support policy can in principle make it impossible for small farms to be successful may thus be very important.

## The Trajectory of Income and Welfare Distribution Compared to What They Might Have Been

With both the sector's share of the labor force and its contribution to the country's wealthy class falling over time, agricultural policy and, more generally, the policies affecting the rural population might be expected give somewhat less weight to the welfare of the large landholders and thus become somewhat more "progressive." As well, if progressive policies are generally easier to adopt outside agriculture, one might expect its declining role to facilitate the partial correction of the extreme income inequality whose historical roots are in that sector. Over the decades, several national governments and a range of Brazilian states have indeed adopted a variety of forward-looking policies. Most of the evidence, however, suggests that the current level of inequality is about as high as in most periods of the past; certainly, it remains extreme (See Appendix 6.1).

Even though income data itself provides little grounds for optimism that Brazil's bleak inequality picture has finally begun to improve, the relatively fast growth over extended periods and a variety of social policies have helped those at the bottom and lowered poverty. Trends in post-tax and transfer inequality, which take into account the changing benefits from public services as well as changing tax burdens, are needed to get a better picture. As of 2009, taxes amounted to a relatively high thirty-five percent of the GDP, with over two-thirds of that revenue spent on social programs. These proportions are similar to those of OECD countries and well above the Latin American averages. However, in contrast to most OECD countries, where tax and benefit systems reduce income disparities quite significantly, this has not been the case in Brazil. Overall, social spending bears little relation to need, especially in the case of pensions, which account for eighty-five percent of total benefit-related expenditures but are concentrated on a relatively small group of non-poor people (Higgins and Pereira 2014).[146] The targeting efficiency of other much smaller programs is very good, but their budget share is quite small and their impact on poverty is correspondingly limited. On the tax side, the predominance of indirect taxes limits potential distributional benefits, as does the fact that the most affluent groups have been the main beneficiaries of tax concessions and of the difficulties in enforcing tax compliance and the resulting avoidance.

Given the very low incomes of the poor, even the modest absolute spending undertaken via the current well-targeted benefits programs does have a real impact on their situation. Among the well-regarded social programs is the *Bolsa Familia*, a highly targeted, conditional, cash-transfer program that

[146] This conclusion is consistent with that of Chu et al. (2000) to the effect that the redistributive effects of tax-benefit systems in developing (and transition) countries are much more limited than those observed in developed countries. What is special about Brazil in comparison to most other developing countries are the high tax-to-GDP ratio and the high level of social transfers going to the middle and upper-middle income groups.

reached twelve million families in 2010 (about a quarter of the country's population) and, by raising participants' incomes, contributed directly to increasing food and nutritional security and to reducing the severity of poverty; as much as eighty-seven percent of the transfer is spent on food (Rocha et al. 2012, 520). Impressive results have also been achieved by the rural pension program established in 1988; all women over the age of fifty-five and all men over sixty-nine receive a monthly benefit equivalent to the minimum wage, irrespective of their past social security contributions. Taken together, Brazil's federal income transfer programs have been credited with reducing the incidence of malnutrition by almost thirty percent (Monteiro et al. 2006). By targeting the lowest income groups, they help to reduce the worst features of income inequality. In 2006, during Lula da Silva's first administration, the National Law on Food and Nutrition Security (*Ley Orgánica de Seguridad Alimentaria y Nutricional*, LOSAN) required the state, with the participation of organized civil society, to formulate and implement policies to ensure the "human right to adequate food." This experience helped to institutionalize the practice of including civil society in Brazil's process of policymaking, implementation, and monitoring in the area of food security; in 2010, an amendment added the Right to Food to the country's constitution (Rocha et al. 2010, 524–525). Between 1995 and 2008, during the presidencies of Cardoso and Lula da Silva, over twelve million Brazilians are estimated to have moved out of poverty (Ituassu 2010), with the incidence of extreme poverty falling from 17.4 percent in 2001 to less than nine percent in 2008 (Barros 2009). This was accompanied by rapid social progress in a number of other areas: infant mortality rates were halved from fifty-five per one thousand in 1996 to twenty-four per one thousand in 2007; the share of children under the age of five without adequate access to water declined from thirty-nine percent in 1992 to twenty-two percent in 2008; and the percentage of children aged seven to fourteen years who were not attending school fell from twelve percent in 1992 to two percent in 2008 (Barros 2009).

In summary, Brazil combines (i) an extreme high level of pre-tax and transfer inequality, due mainly to the extreme concentration of income from capital and to the limited supply of jobs that reimburse people decently for the skills they have, this in turn due to the lack of remunerative jobs in agriculture and elsewhere and to the low levels of education of much of the population; (ii) a well-designed and hence efficient set of social protection programs; but (iii) a level of spending in those programs far too limited to make up the gap between market-determined income levels and what people need for a good life. The substantial economic growth, although it has not generally reduced inequality, has not shrunk the income share of those at the bottom, as far as is known.[147] There has thus been notable progress in reducing poverty, as well as hunger and other manifestations of food and nutritional insecurity. Clearly, though, the inequality legacy of its agricultural history is still very present despite much evolution in economic structure and serious efforts to curb it, some of which have had a significant impact but never nearly big enough to change the overall picture of one of the most unequal societies in the world.

On the matter of what can best make up for the lack of an expeditious agrarian reform, Brazil's experience suggests that:

(i) with respect to income inequality, whether pre- or post-tax and transfer, nothing is likely to make up for the lack of it; that is, inequality will probably remain very high for at least fifty to one hundred years after an economy ceases to be predominantly agricultural;
(ii) high payoff, pro-poor steps like the rural pension, the *Bolsa Familia*, and other programs can bring major benefits in the reduction of poverty and malnutrition, although unless such steps are carried out on a very large scale—one that is politically implausible in a country with such a high concentration of income—those hardships are likely to remain much worse than they would have had a major agrarian reform been achieved;
(iii) more direct substitutes for redistributive land reform, like market-based reform, can also bring real benefits but, like the cited social policies, ones that are very small in comparison to those of a redistributive reform and that cover a much smaller share of the poor population than do policies like *Bolsa Familia*.

[147] There remains some inevitable uncertainty about the income and welfare levels of the bottom couple of deciles, which include most landless workers and small farmers, along with informal sector workers outside agriculture. Their share of recorded national income is miniscule—recent estimates put that of the bottom quintile (twenty percent) at about three percent, so mismeasurement of their incomes does not greatly affect overall indicators like the Gini coefficient. But small changes in absolute terms can be very important to this group; thus a twenty-five percent increase in its average income would amount only to 0.75 percent of estimated national income. Such changes are hard to identify because incomes can easily be mis-reported in the cited categories, even if social security benefits are not. This remains one of the chief gaps in the story of Brazilian inequality and welfare over time.

The available evidence on Brazilian agriculture suggests that the combination of a more equal distribution of land and a good public sector support system for small farmers would have led to greater agricultural output and employment at each point of time, to higher earnings for those farmers, and to higher agricultural wages. The impact on total GDP is harder to guess but would also almost certainly have been positive as well. Income earned by the relatively poor segment of the population, arguably the most important single indicator, would have been much higher than it has been, probably by two to three times.[148] The positive impact on the demand for and use of labor would have raised not only agricultural wages but those in other sectors as well, contributing to a strongly positive income distribution effect overall. Education would have advanced faster and been more equally distributed. The physical and social environments would have benefited.

As noted above, smaller farms have been shown to have higher output and labor use per hectare than larger farms since organized data became available.[149] The typically large land productivity gap by farm size reflects an enormous differential in labor intensity. For example, in 1950 farms of five to ten hectares applied twelve times more labor per hectare than did those of one hundred to one thousand hectares, which in turn applied a high multiple in relation to those over one thousand hectares. By 1980, the former ratio had risen to 16.2 as the labor intensity slipped by a quarter for the one-hundred-to-one-thousand-hectare category (Berry 1989, 189). As of 2006, the agricultural census points to a labor-to-land ratio nine times higher on the family farms than on the agribusiness ones (based on Rocha et al. 2012).[150]

The combination of differences in land productivity and in labor intensity across size categories throws light on the shares of income generated in a given size category going to better-off and not-so-well-off people. On owner-operated family farms, the latter group receives nearly all of it, whereas on large, mechanized farms they get very little of it. If seventy-five percent of the income generated on family farms in 2006 went to relatively low-income families while the corresponding figure for agribusiness units was thirty percent, then the income received per hectare by those families would be nearly five times greater on the family farms; were the shares eighty

[148] This figure draws, in part, on a comparable calculation for Colombia (Berry 2017a).

[149] Agricultural censuses have been a main source. Helfand and Taylor (2020) confirm that the IR was present in Brazilian agriculture as of 2006, more markedly in the North than elsewhere.

[150] These figures are not fully comparable across the years because they refer to different size groups, but the gaps have clearly remained very large.

percent and twenty-five percent respectively, the ratio would be six.[151] The "socio-economic efficiency" of land use, measured this way, almost certainly falls sharply throughout the full size range.[152] As noted in Chapter 3, even such big differentials understate the advantages of the family farm system for lower-income families because it provides not just income, but also economic and food security.

Much less certainty surrounds the matter of how various possible reforms would have affected total agricultural output. In assessing a productive unit's contribution to the GDP or the impact of a shift of resources between sectors or groups of firms, a conceptually useful indicator is "total factor productivity" TFP, as discussed in Chapter 3.[153] Studies elsewhere show that this indicator sometimes falls with farm size and sometimes rises. According to regional estimates for 2006 by Steven M. Helfand and Matthew P. H. Taylor (2020), it decreased with size over most of the range (up to one hundred to five hundred hectares in the North and Center-west), but to a lower size level in the Southeast, where it rose strongly with size above the twenty-to-one-hundred-hectare category. From 1985 to 2006, TFP rose markedly overall (at 1.5 percent per year), with the biggest gains achieved by the smallest farms (up to five hectares), at about 2.5 percent per year and the largest (over five hundred hectares) at over two percent, while lower rates were achieved by the middle-size categories of twenty to fifty-five hectares (Arias et al. 2018, 10, citing Helfand et al. 2015).

[151] Land productivity was 1.8 times higher on the family farms than on the agribusiness units; this, together with the assumed shares of income going to the lower income group, provides the cited figures.

[152] Although Helfand and Taylor (2020) do not attempt to estimate this particular indicator, their data on land productivity per hectare also suggest that it falls sharply over the whole size range. Even in the Southeast, it seems likely that income per hectare for the lower income group would fall by at least fifty percent between farms of five to twenty hectares and the largest ones, and that in all cases except the Southeast it would be much higher on the smallest farms than on the large ones. Further analysis would be needed, especially for the Southeast, to take account of the use of other scarce resources, especially physical and human capital, to clarify whether there is any part of Brazil in which (at least as of 2006) large farms yielded more benefits per unit of scarce resources used for low-income families than did small ones.

[153] TFP levels provide clues on how a redistribution of land would affect total output. In the 1960s or 1970s, increases of five to twenty-five percent could probably have been attained, judging by Cline's estimate of twenty-five percent for a total land redistribution that created a system of small family farms (Cline 1970). Berry and Cline (1979, 132–133) also estimate a gain in the range of twenty-five percent. Such figures may exaggerate the productivity gain that would result when a piece of land is transferred from its large-scale operator to a new group of small farmers; for example, because that new group would probably not be as efficient as those who had operated for some time within that size range, it leaves little doubt that land concentration typically curtails total output significantly, along with its even greater negative impacts on labor demand and the incomes of lower income groups.

Much speculation and guesswork inevitably surround any attempt to assess the costs to Brazil of not having had a serious agrarian reform. While there is no doubt that the agrarian structure contributed to the very high level of inequality a century ago, for example, and no doubt that it contributed to that level remaining high over the century, less assurance can be attached to estimates of the potential agricultural output benefits from various levels of reform at given points of time; these also could have been large depending on the productivity advantage of smaller farms (substantial) and on whether the state would have been willing to provide the needed advances in technology, infrastructure, and so on to a sector not including many, if any, large landholders (unclear). In short, it would be hard to mount a serious economic case against a major land redistribution in a country where the IR between size and land productivity is as strong as it has been in Brazil. The potential benefits from reform might, of course, not emerge for political reasons, and if conflict around the reform were severe enough, there might be no gain in aggregate agricultural output and perhaps, in the extreme, no welfare gain for poorer people. The argument that the poverty and dissatisfaction due directly to high land concentration will pass as development proceeds is generally true—unless failure to reform greatly impedes overall economic development, which is not the case in Brazil. If reform neither speeds up nor slows down overall development and the creation of jobs in other sectors, then the issue is simply one of how much welfare is lost by the low-income landless group before those alternatives become available to them. If the pattern of agricultural development (i.e., its low labor-intensity) is passed along to other sectors, this adds one more permanent negative effect on income inequality and the welfare of the lower income population.[154]

To summarize, while both incomes and living standards have indeed risen for those at the bottom of the distribution in Brazil, including those working in agriculture, the long-term improvements appear only to have been roughly comparable to those of people higher in the distribution, as overall inequality appears not to have changed significantly. Had the reforms that were actually carried out (e.g., colonization, better credit, etc.) been more extensive and better executed, even without an expropriation-based reform, average incomes of the working part of the agricultural population and

[154] But the opposite could happen if the failure of agriculture to create many jobs pushes down the wage rate and leads other sectors to be more labor intensive. If land reform is not politically possible, more equitable development may require that a state focus on middle (appropriate) technologies outside agriculture.

other groups that form part of the overlapping labor markets could probably have been fifty percent higher. With a significant agrarian reform, it seems likely that incomes at the bottom would be two to three times what they have been and are. Such income increases would guarantee an enormously better standard of living with significantly less inequality, less informality in employment, and a more generally accessible health system; as a result, Brazil would not be so close to the bottom among nations in terms of its response to the COVID-19 pandemic.

## Chile

Chile's reform experience unfolded in a country widely seen as the most successful democracy of the region, where centrist and leftist political groups vied with those on the right. It suffered a political crisis when the socialist government of Salvador Allende was removed in 1973 by a right-wing military coup soon after implementing a package of reforms, including prominently a restructuring of the agrarian system. The experience drew much international attention due to the heavy US involvement and intervention, the viciousness of the Chilean military under Augusto Pinochet, and the extreme policy reversal from the reformist steps of Allende to the "Chicago school" neoliberalism of the military government. This dramatic sequence left much uncertainty as to what the economic, political, and social legacies would be when the country returned to democratic rule, as it did in 1990.

### A Dangerous International Setting for a Major Reform

The US had a wide range of economic interests in Chile, including mining and the telephone sector.[155] The Cold War had been around a good deal longer than at the time of its 1950s interventions in Guatemala and Iran. By the lead-in to this coup, Chile was much less agricultural than the Latin American average; only about 26.5 percent of employment was found there

[155] International Telephone and Telegraph (ITT), the largest single American investor in Chile, was the major owner of the Chilean Telephone Company and funded the right-wing newspaper *El Mercurio*. Its CEO made a famous remark at the time to the effect that it was a bad omen if ITT could not do what it wanted to in Chile without interference from the government, a comment that those on the left found revealing and helpful to their political cause.

in 1970. Although important exports came from the sector (wine, especially), mining was dominant. By the late 1930s, the country had become a net importer of agricultural goods.

Chile was long one of the more inegalitarian countries in Latin America and hence the world. As best can be determined, the pattern of change from pre-reform to the present involved an initial rise, which probably helped to lay the groundwork for the reforms, a fall due to them, then a dramatic increase after the coup to a historic peak around the end of the 1980s due to the neoliberal policies and other factors, followed by a possible decrease. Despite the probably substantial net increase in inequality from before the reform to the present, the healthy rate of economic growth left the poverty rate dramatically below its early 1960s level.[156]

From colonial times until the moderate 1965 reform introduced by the centrist government of Eduardo Frei, land concentration was high.[157] Demands for reform had been present since the early twentieth century but were not high profile until the 1950s. Pressure accentuated when the large *haciendas* undertook a great deal of labor-saving mechanization between 1935 and 1965; whereas in 1935 about sixty to seventy-five percent of the rural population of central Chile lived on large properties, by 1964 this figure was down to thirty-five percent (Kay 1981, 70). Employment of workers on *haciendas* fell by about twenty percent in absolute terms between 1955 and 1965, and landlords increasingly found it more profitable to employ wage labor than *inquilinos*[158] such that the share of wage laborers within the agricultural labor force rose dramatically from seventeen percent in 1955 to forty-one percent in 1965 (Kay 1981, 71) and the *inquilino* share fell from its maximum of forty-five percent in 1935 to twenty-five percent in 1955 and then down to twelve percent by 1965. The structure of agricultural employment was thus in very rapid flux.

[156] The World Bank's series shows a fall in the incidence of poverty (with the line at $1.90 per person per day (PPP) from 11.4 percent in 1987 to less than one percent since 2010. With a line of $3.20 (PPP), the drop is from 28.4 percent to 0.7 percent in 2020. Scott's (1997) study of small farm households points to a small net decline in that group's inability to meet basic needs from about three-quarters to about two-thirds between 1967/1968 and 1985/1986. Scott guesses that the fall may have been due to a combination of increased payments from targeted welfare programs, but that any gains through rising agricultural productivity were modest.

[157] Judging by figures unadjusted for quality, it was one of the highest in the world. World Bank (1978) put the Gini coefficient at 0.94 as of 1936. But quality differences were enormous, so the actual degree of concentration was substantially less (see Valdes and Foster 2014, 14–15). The large farm category included the very low productivity units in Patagonia, for example.

[158] An *inquilino* is a worker on a Chilean landed estate who is given the use of a small plot of land, implements, seed, and a small wage in return for his labor.

By the early 1960s, mounting pressure from agricultural workers provided the backdrop to the Frei and Allende reforms. Slow growth of agricultural output was also a broad concern: it had stagnated from about 1950 onward, averaging only about 1.5 percent per year from 1945 to 1965 and not responding to government efforts to boost it. Support for some sort of reform came also from the Catholic Church and the US Alliance for Progress. Future president Frei declared that both *minifundia* and *latifundia* were detrimental to the health of Chilean agriculture. The modest 1960s reforms of Jorge Alessandri and Frei were followed by Allende's more sweeping reform from 1971 to 1973. The latter shared with Guatemala, in 1955, a major US intervention to overturn the reform on the grounds that it signaled the country's descent into socialism/communism.

Right-of-center President Alessandri's 1962 effort, supported by John F. Kennedy's newly founded Alliance for Progress, consisted of a modest distribution of some state-owned land and some large estates to *campesinos* as small landholdings (Valdes and Foster 2014, 1). The much farther-reaching reform of the centrist Christian Democratic government of Frei expropriated fourteen hundred land holdings with 3.5 million hectares, or about eighteen percent of the country's agricultural land; one hundred thousand *campesinos* became members of four hundred collectives, in whose formation some communists and socialists were engaged. Meanwhile, the Catholic Church began, in the 1960s, to distribute its lands to *campesinos*. Frei's reform was designed to stimulate agricultural production, raise peasants' standard of living, and gain their political support (Kay et al. 1981, 76). Agricultural production did initially accelerate to a peak of 4.6 percent per year between 1965 and 1968 (Kay 1982, 143). One complementary policy was to pressure landlords to modernize; in fact, the bulk of the output increase came from them. Those whose land was expropriated, however, withdrew most of their machinery and livestock from operation. About seven percent of rural laborers benefited from markedly increased incomes. The organization of workers into trade unions forced many employers to respect the minimum wage and social security provisions. The downward trend in employment on former *hacienda* land was reversed, as employment rose by twenty-one percent on expropriated farms in the wake of a shift toward more labor-intensive crops. Along with its various benefits, this reform diminished the government's capacity to contain peasant militancy, demands for higher wages, and expropriation (Kay 1981, 70). The combination of heightened expectations and the realization that, by itself, this reform alone could not benefit a great number turned many into supporters of Allende's Popular Unity party and government.

On coming into power in 1970, the Allende government's plan was to expropriate all Chilean *latifundia*, including almost all farms of over eighty "basic irrigated hectares," a quality-adjusted measure of land quantity (Belisario 2007). By 1973, forty percent of land so measured was in the reform sector; the share in farms with twenty hectares or more had fallen from 77.6 to 36.6 percent (Kay 1981, 80). That forty percent of land produced just over one-third of output, using something over one-fifth of workers; its below average land productivity and its relatively low labor intensity were related to a variety of organizational inefficiencies. As expected, the reform lowered income inequality within agriculture and, together with other policies, especially the nationalization of mining, contributed to a fall in inequality at the national level.

But by the end of 1973 Chile was suffering an economic crisis with multiple causes, together with hyperinflation due, in part, to a large expansion of the public sector. The fiscal crisis limited expenditures in all sectors, including assistance to collectives and small farms. In contrast to the positive growth rates of agriculture during the initial more moderate expropriation under Frei, the sector shrunk from 1970 to 1973 due to a fall in production in the commercial, non-expropriated sector together with an underutilization of land in the *asentamiento* (settlement group or collective) sector. That output should fall during the conflictual setting of expropriation and changing patterns of operation is not surprising, but design flaws also played a role, in particular the serious incentive problems common to collectively managed agriculture.[159] Whereas the agrarian reform period from 1962 to 1973 saw only modest changes in land use (e.g., changing output composition) attributable to expropriations and *asentamientos*, more marked changes emerged after the structural reforms following 1973 and the close of the agrarian reform experiment.

## The Pinochet Coup

The military coup that overthrew Allende is one of the best-known events of the Americas during the post-1950 period. Still, who did what and how

[159] These are described in some detail by Valdes and Foster (2014).

much was known by whom are not yet fully clarified. Certainly, this military government was willing and anxious to terrorize what it considered to be the dangerous parts of its population. The battle around reform was unlike those of Bolivia, Peru, and Colombia, where the aspirants to land (or more of it) were seen as the hostile interest group—the typical situation in cases of land reform—and the fear of a socialist or communist takeover, while always a concern for some people, was less central. In Chile, the capitalist elite was very apprehensive. The large landholders naturally worried about losing their land, and saw the landless and troublemakers as enemies, but the military and its right-wing allies were especially worried about the socialist leaders and their followers.

As a relatively ethnically homogenous country (like Argentina and Uruguay), Chile was less susceptible to class- or ethnic-related abuse within its pre-reform system than many other countries; such abuse is typically inflicted by one ethnic group on another. For Pinochet's government, the thousands of victims held famously in the stadium in 1973 were not peasant leaders, but educated radicals about whom the fear was their socialist or communist leanings; one was an American filmmaker and journalist, allegedly murdered with knowledge of the CIA because he "knew too much." There was also fear about the continued loyalty of military personnel to the new regime. These concerns were a factor in the regime's notorious brutality, evidenced early in its "Caravan of Death," an Army squad that flew by helicopter to order or personally carry out the brutal executions of at least seventy-five individual communists held in Army custody in certain garrisons; eyes were gouged out with knives, and jaws and legs were broken. The killings were often designed so that the prisoners would die slowly. This episode was startling in many ways, among them the fact that many of the victims had voluntarily turned themselves in to the military authorities and posed no immediate threat. The squad's apparent aims were to instill "terror" in potential opponents, as well as to ensure loyalty to the military leaders. According to a 1991 government commission (Rettig) report, Pinochet's government killed at least 3,197 people and tortured about twenty-nine thousand, with two-thirds of this happening in 1973. The later Valech Report (2004) indicated that 1,312 were exiled, with some of them then pursued all over the world by Operation Condor, a cooperative plan between the intelligence agencies of various South American countries, assisted by a CIA communication base in Panama. Pinochet argued that all this was necessary to save the country from communism. Some political scientists have attributed the relative bloodiness of this coup to the stability and resilience of the existing democratic system, which therefore required extreme action to overturn.

The US provided material support to the military government after the coup, although criticizing it in public. A document released by the CIA in 2000[160] revealed that it had actively supported the military junta after the overthrow of Allende and had accepted many Pinochet officers as paid contacts of the CIA or the US military, even though some were known to be involved in human rights abuses. The CIA also maintained contacts with the Chilean secret police agency (DINA), which participated in Operation Condor.

The regime's approach was successful in keeping it in power for a lengthy period of seventeen years and in keeping the overall death rate low—compared for example to that of the contemporary Argentine dictatorship—through a combination of fear and a strong power advantage over potential opponent groups. The order that resulted made it either popular (with some) or at least not in widespread disfavor, especially when economic success started to appear in the 1980s.

On the agricultural front, the Pinochet coup brought a counter-reform. Of the lands expropriated during the reform, about thirty percent were returned to the former owners, five percent were auctioned off, and the "reformed lands" owned by cooperatives were divided into individual properties. But many *campesinos* now sold their lands due to the lack of capital or credit. The post-reform reconcentration left the pattern of ownership in 1997 more unequal than it had been in 1955 (Rytkonen 2004). By the agricultural census of 2007 the 1,430 farms with two thousand hectares and up (half a percent of the total) had seventy percent of the land (Berdegue and Fuentealba 2011).

Alberto Valdés and William Foster (2014) see both the Frei and Allende reforms as a restructuring of agriculture involving "not just land redistribution but also an economic rationalization of what was thought to be a conservative, traditional, and inefficient system of *inquilinaje*, or labour tied to estates, by transforming extensive landholdings into large cooperatives and collectives."[161] The reforms were based on the view that agriculture was

[160] Entitled "CIA Activities in Chile." For a discussion, see Castellanos (2006).

[161] As these authors note, one political-economic motive for the initial push for land tenure reform in Chile was to reduce the political power of large landowners (the *latifundistas*), whose electoral influence: was linked to their control over land. An important 1958 reform that made voting secret reduced the influence of landowners on how their workers voted. The 1966 agrarian reform law was likely approved because of the prior change.

performing poorly due to a precapitalist, semifeudal land tenure system that was inefficient and unresponsive to normal economic incentives; it was replaced by a relatively dysfunctional system of collectively operated units. Design and coordination problems created incentive problems and misallocation of resources—especially labor—within the enterprises. In addition, the policy planners' narrow focus on staple goods turned out to be out of line with the country's shifting comparative advantage toward higher-value products; identifying these new opportunities required entrepreneurship and high per-hectare capital investments. These factors played a major role in the eventually rapid growth of the sector and, in the view of Valdes and Foster (2014), tended to give an advantage to medium and large farm operations in fruit and horticultural crops. The composition of production changed considerably, and land productivity increased significantly. From 1955 to 1976, yields per hectare of major crops did not change notably, whereas in the two decades that followed they increased markedly for all major crops; thus, between 1976 and 1997, wheat more than doubled in yield and maize more than tripled.

Observers like Lovell S. Jarvis et al. (2004) have argued that, ironically, the agrarian reforms laid the groundwork for this rapid transformation of Chilean agriculture after the economy wide policy reforms were instituted by the Pinochet regime in the late 1970s; that is, without the shock of the initial reform, and the subsequent distribution of land to small landholders in the counter-reform, there would not have been a favorable environment (especially a land market) for a more entrepreneurial class of farmers to take advantage of the deregulation, privatization, and trade reforms that followed. Antonio Bellisario (2007, 1) shares this view, noting that:

> Chile's agrarian reform was successful in expropriating (under the Frei and Allende administrations, 1964–1973) the great estates of the *hacienda* landed property system. The capitalist "partial" counter-reform then redistributed them . . . . CORA, the country's agency for agrarian reform, expropriated and subsequently redistributed 5809 estates of almost 10 million hectares, or 59 per cent of Chile's agricultural farmland. A large amount of the expropriated land (41 per cent) benefited 54 thousand peasant households with small-sized family farms and house-sites. The rest . . . benefited efficient and competitive commercial farmers and agro-business and consolidated medium-sized farms . . . . The redistribution of the agricultural land previously expropriated made possible the formation

of an agro-industrial bourgeoisie, small commercial farmers, an open land market and a dynamic agricultural sector.

The country returned to democracy in 1990. Eventually confronted with increasing opposition, including at the international level,[162] Pinochet legalized political parties in 1987 and called for a referendum to determine whether he would remain in power until 1997. He lost this 1988 vote by fifty-six percent to forty-four percent. By that time, he had done much to protect his own future. The transitional provisions of the 1980 constitution allowed him to remain as Commander-in-Chief of the Army until March 1998. He was then sworn in as a senator-for-life, which granted him immunity from prosecution in Chile. That immunity did not extend to other countries, and he was arrested in 1998 in the United Kingdom, on an extradition request issued by Spanish judge Baltasar Garzón and based on the murder of Spaniards under his regime. Eventually, he was allowed to return to Chile. Later evidence emerged on millions of dollars received through illicit means, tax fraud, and so on. Legal cases surrounded him and his family in Chile for the rest of his life.

## The 1970s Legacy of Growth, Inequality, and Poverty

At the time of the 1973 coup, the Chilean economy was depressed, under fiscal strain, and suffering hyperinflation, partly due to ongoing chaos as the government expropriated Chilean and foreign businesses, against heavy opposition. In response, the new government laid out a set of free-market reforms, drawn up by the "Chicago Boys."[163] After some macroeconomic mismanagement over the rest of that decade, those market principles were applied effectively and generated fast and sustained growth. Much privatization took place, including of the mining industry, much of the health care sector, and some of the education sector. All this came with rising inequality

[162] Another suggested reason for Pinochet's decision to call for elections was the April 1987 visit of Pope John Paul II to Chile. According to Weigel (2003), he held a meeting with Pinochet and pushed him to accept a democratic opening and he may even have called for his resignation.

[163] Pinochet had no particular knowledge or leanings within economics but was happy to climb onto this bandwagon, which got a strong and early start from the fact that various Chileans had recently undertaken graduate work at the University of Chicago, with its famous market-oriented and anti-government leanings.

and, according to some, deepening poverty, as they negatively impacted the wages, benefits and working conditions of Chile's working class.[164]

One of the more reliable studies of inequality trends, albeit only for greater Santiago,[165] reports a significant rise in the Gini coefficient[166] from around 0.45 from 1957 to 1966 to about 0.5, then a drop back to 0.45 by 1973/1974, then a dramatic increase to a peak of 0.6 in 1987, followed by a drop to the range of 0.5–0.52 over most of the 1990s (Ruiz-Tagle 1998).[167] Neither the causes nor the precise timing of the pre-1967 increase are clear. The country was experiencing an import substitution phase of development, and the mechanization and labor displacement trends within agriculture were likely contributing factors. The falling Gini between the late 1960s and 1974/1975 fits the broad expectations that the land reform plus other steps of the Frei and Allende governments, such as the nationalization of the mining industry which would have lowered national inequality,[168] but because it refers only to Santiago it does not provide direct evidence on the impacts for the rural population. A similar picture comes from possibly the most reliable data for greater Santiago reaching back into the 1960s, those for consumption per household for 1969, 1978, and 1988, which show dramatically falling shares for the bottom quintile of 7.6 percent, 5.2 percent, and 4.5 percent, respectively, and rising shares for the top quintile of 44.5 percent, 51.0 percent, and 54.9 percent, implying ratios of per capita consumption between the top and bottom quintiles rising from 5.8 to 9.8 and on to 12.5 respectively (Ffrench-Davis 1999, 267).[169] All the evidence thus points to a large increase in inequality, however measured, from the coup until the late 1980s or 1990;[170]

[164] According to Foxley (2001), by the end of Pinochet's reign about forty-four percent of Chilean families were living below the poverty line.

[165] That the respective Gini coefficients were quite similar between Greater Santiago and Chile when both became available does suggest that the Greater Santiago figures probably gave a relatively accurate picture of how the national Gini was behaving earlier.

[166] Whether for family income or per capita income.

[167] This study uses data from a University of Chile survey beginning in 1957.

[168] Estimates by Atria et al. (2018, 13) for the share of the top one percent nationally do show a sharp decline from seventeen percent in 1971 to a low of a little over eleven percent in 1974, before starting to rise.

[169] The respective peaks in the late 1980s were 6.0 for Greater Santiago in 1987 (Ruiz-Tagle 1998) and 57.2 for Chile in 1987 (World Bank n.d.) with the former at 0.45 during the period from 1957 to 1966.

[170] Atria et al. (2018, 14) discuss the data problems around the crisis years and the large-scale destabilization of the early 1970s. Data for 1982 to 1989 are missing, raising the suspicion that this may have been a deliberate step by the dictatorship. Their data show the share of the top one percent rising from 11.5 percent in 1974 to twenty percent in 1981, although the former was probably

the Gini coefficient of per capita income rose by as much as eighteen percentage points, from around 0.45 from 1973 to 1975 to its peak of 0.63 in 1988 (Ruiz-Tagle 1998, 9). For the top one percent, Atria et al. (2018) report a share rising from 11.5 percent in 1974 to 20 percent in 1981 and possibly higher over the next few years.[171]

A major issue is whether the predictable increase in inequality as the neoliberal policies took hold was then followed by a significant decline after the late 1980s as policies became less extreme and/or the political context moved back toward the middle, with centrist presidents such as Ricardo Lagos or left-leaning ones, like former torture-victim Michelle Bachelet. On this, the evidence is mixed. Household survey-based series do point to such a decline, but when information from tax returns and undistributed corporate profits are added, it appears that overall inequality may not have fallen at all (see Appendix 6.1). Thus, as noted earlier in the case of Colombia, the appearance of better statistics on top incomes has forced a revision of conclusions on recent inequality trends and especially on the share of those at the top. In summary, by a more optimistic interpretation the Gini coefficient in Chile was near 0.6 for only a few years before falling back close to its level of the 1960s; by a less optimistic but presumably more accurate one it did not. Hopefully, future research will throw more light on exactly what happened.

## Remaining Political and Economic Issues

Chile experienced a high-profile intervention by the US, akin to those in Guatemala and Iran. The fact that all three countries were led by democratically elected presidents (or prime ministers) made it necessary that the intervention be handled secretly. In each case, evidence has continued to emerge as to what actually happened. In Chile, covert US planning to block the election of Allende began weeks before his September 4 victory, according to recently declassified minutes of an August 19, 1970, meeting of the high-level interagency committee chaired by National Security Advisor Henry

affected by the crisis. Their data gap for 1982 to 1989 corresponds to the years for which Sanhueza and Mayer (2011) report the highest inequality.

171 The figure for 1974 was probably affected by the crisis.

Kissinger, who asked that action plans to prevent the Chilean Congress from ratifying an Allende victory "be as precise as possible and include what orders would be given on September 5, to whom, and in what way" (Kornbluh 2014).

Was US intervention in Chile inevitable? Key elements of the answer involve what a Democratic president, or perhaps just a different president (from Nixon) with a different foreign policy advisor (from Kissinger), would have done, and what a different Chilean military (within the range of possibilities) would have done. That it matters who is US President is suggested by the fact that all three of the cited interventions occurred under strongly anti-communist Republican regimes (Eisenhower, advised by the Dulles Brothers) in Guatemala and Iran, and Nixon (with Kissinger) in Chile. Given the usually markedly stronger anti-communist leanings of Republicans this is no surprise. The stance of Latin America's military establishments has also been related to/affected by US foreign policy. Among other links, several military leaders received their training in the US Army School of the Americas, created in Panama in 1946, which later came under considerable political attack for having trained students who went on to become dictators (as with Galtieri of Argentina, Noriega of Panama, and others), members of death squads, or other dubious operators. Pinochet studied in Chile, but the country's military was greatly influenced by America's anti-communist ideology.

Chile's reforms of the 1960s and 1970s were not candidates for remaking the country's development path the way those of Korean and Taiwan did. It was a less agricultural country than nearly all of the other cases considered here, heavily dependent on mining, relatively urbanized, and with a notably democratic history. By the 1950s, the injustices and abuses around its agriculture were of modest proportions compared to those of Guatemala, Bolivia, Colombia, Brazil, and others. It could thus not have been a "major success story" with huge gains on many fronts and a "transformation" of the country. The case is of special interest, however, as one in which a significant distributional improvement could have been achieved within the agricultural sector in a democratic country with good follow-up and reasonable continuity after the event. Probably this would have come, as it did at the time of the reform, with the nationalization of large foreign companies. Had the US government and the Chilean military and other elements of the hard right been moderately less aggressive, might the reform have been followed by a maintenance of economic and political stability and democratic practice? Had this happened, subsequent growth might have been good, although probably lower than that actually achieved. The main gain, however, would have taken the form of a much lower level of inequality. The agrarian reform might have provided useful lessons to other countries, especially those of Latin America. Arguably, the main damages resulting from the coup that ended the reform were the lives lost (probably three thousand to four thousand), the other human rights abuses (with perhaps forty thousand to fifty thousand victims),[172] and the failure to achieve a decent level of equality in the society.

Among the great unanswered questions around this reform and its aftereffects in the form of the 1973 coup, the "counter-reform," and the fast but highly unequal growth that followed are whether, in their absence, poverty and the welfare of those toward the bottom of the socio-economic hierarchy would have wound up higher or lower. Although the counter-reform in agriculture certainly contributed to rising inequality, it was not presumably a dominant factor, given the relatively small size of the agricultural sector and the fact that land inequality wound up fairly similar after the counter-reform as before the reforms. Among the most interesting counterfactuals are no reform beyond the sort implanted by Allesandri, or a significant reform but directed as much as possible at creating small independent farm units à la Japan et al.

A final question involves what would have happened in agriculture had the Allende reform not been terminated by the coup. Most reforming countries which made the mistake of opting for cooperatives and communes or state farms rather than small independent farmers have corrected that mistake later. Chile's sector involved crops with more economies of scale or more direct attachment to international markets than the average country, so the classically small farmer producing for the local market would not, under fairly free markets, have constituted as big a share of agriculture as was the case in most other countries.

[172] Numbers on human rights abuses have risen as examinations have proceeded since 1990 when democracy returned. As of 2011, the Commission on Human Rights raised the number from over twenty-seven thousand to over forty thousand, after examining another thirty-two thousand cases, most of them involving torture or other abuses. Only 3,065 were listed as "killed or disappeared." Survivors get lifetime pensions of US$260 per month. Michelle Bachelet, later to be President, was one of the survivors. Many left-wing oriented people fled the country after the coup.

## Costa Rica: Modest Redistribution without Violence

Costa Rica's reform experience is given added importance by its being the only country in Latin America which, without having a high availability of land per person (as do Argentina and Uruguay), has moved through the agrarian phase of its development in a relatively calm and successful fashion, thereby creating the foundation for one of the region's most advanced countries in economic, social, and political terms. Its low levels of violence and conflict are especially eye-catching in the context of its Central American neighbors, which (except for smallish Panama) have experienced such violent recent histories. Democracy was established in 1889. In 1948, the government did away with the military. Today it aspires to be the first country in the world to achieve a neutral impact on the environment through its management of carbon emissions.

Perhaps the most striking aspect of Costa Rica's twentieth-century history is how early it moved seriously toward social democracy (i.e., government chosen by votes and accompanied by relative equality and by decent support systems in the areas of education, health, etc.) despite a dramatic and difficult patch over the 1930s and 1940s. Costa Rica's nineteenth-century (and earlier) history provided some of the building blocks for such a system. Lacking the riches like gold and silver that attracted conquistadores, the country was lucky from the 1820s onward to have coffee as a key exportable product, a labor-intensive crop that does not lend itself to mechanization and thus ensures good job creation. Much of the production was carried out by small farms. Although the level of land concentration at that time is not known with precision, it seems unlikely that it ever approached those of Brazil, Mexico, or Colombia.[173] Ethnic homogeneity no doubt helped to create a more egalitarian society, as did good leaders at some key junctures. The lack of conflict was at times a matter of good luck; when, during the nineteenth century, some small coffee farmers were losing out to bigger producers, they were able to get work in the newly flourishing banana sector (Seligson 1980). In the twentieth century, when other outlets became less available, the *campesinos* did begin to colonize land that was unused by large landowners; this led to conflict and to the formation of *campesino* leagues.

[173] Bhattacharya and Ulubasoglu (2010) report a 1960 Gini coefficient of 0.78, one of the lowest of Latin America (Albertus 2021, 84).

The 1930s and 1940s turned out to be decisive for the future of the country. In the context of the Great Depression, movements representing groups from right-wing large landholders to communists arose. A brief civil war in 1948 cost two thousand lives. Two of the key factors in things turning out well were a strong and relatively unconcentrated coffee industry with a political presence, and a strong union movement with broad influence. A turning point on the latter front was the large 1934 strike against the banana-producing United Fruit Company, supported by the communists; it gave the country's union movement a big boost, and in 1938 the company felt obliged to sign an agreement with it. Although then and subsequently United Fruit had conflicts with the union, it behaved much less badly than elsewhere in the region, a fact that reflected the more democratic make-up of Costa Rica than of its neighboring countries. Its small farm character contributed to its democratic credentials and vice versa. A third element of the Costa Rica "model" came about with the government of Rafael Ángel Calderón Guardia from 1940 to 1944, which introduced a social security system, and that of José María Figueres (1948–1949, 1953–1958), which nationalized the banks and insurance companies, promulgated a new constitution establishing free education, a public health system and pensions, and terminated the military.

Within the coffee industry, a sort of petty bourgeoisie had considerable political influence (Gudmundson 1989, 255). Although dominated by the larger producers, the industry, supported by the National Liberation Party (*Partido Liberación Nacional*, PLN), founded in 1951 and a political platform for President Figueres, developed a model involving cooperative processing and marketing of coffee, which increased the benefits to the producers. It did not take direct account of or seek the support of the landless or the poor. Important proponents of small-scale production included Rodrigo Facia (1942), who saw it as contributing to the social development of the country. These producers developed an anti-Marxist and anti-labor program for the sector, which relied on state involvement. Yields rose substantially, due to public incentives for replanting, the use of fertilizers, and the development of hybrid varieties.

Costa Rica's land reform was of quite modest proportions but it was well executed and, as a result, beneficial. Pressure for reform grew from the turbulent times of the Great Depression and World War II, leading first to some distribution of state-owned land in frontier zones, then to a reform proposal defeated by the large landholders in the 1950s, and finally to another passed in 1961. Because it required full compensation, it could only proceed slowly.

As Mitchel Seligson (1980, 133–134) notes, it required that new projects be located on existing farms and be demonstrably viable; recipients were self-selected. At first the expropriation focused on areas of rural unrest. By the 1980s, it had become less reactive, more development oriented, and more focused on building settlements and providing infrastructure and credit (Picado and Silva 2002, 132–133).

In the 1960s and 1970s, nearly fifteen percent of the landless population received land (Seligson 1984, 34).[174] Beneficiaries did very well, outperforming national yield averages on a number of crops. Relatively unmechanized banana production grew fast on reform farms, becoming their single largest value crop by the mid-1970s while the government negotiated their participation in multinational operations. The two-decade period from 1960 to 1980 was one of very rapid overall economic growth, to which these developments contributed, and the country has, since 1960, greatly outperformed Latin America as a whole. The rural–urban divide in incomes and indicators of life quality is small. The share of farms with under five hectares rose from thirty-six percent in 1963 to fifty-five percent in 2014, and the share with over fifty hectares fell from fifteen percent to nine percent (Albertus 2021, 191). Overall income inequality is lower than before the land reform.

In summary, virtually everything went right in Costa Rica's land reform experience. The gravity of the challenge was far less than in most other countries considered here, and the government handled it quite competently. The Central American region's violent history over the last two centuries lends added interest to how and why things turned out so differently in Costa Rica. Dominant elements of politics elsewhere in the region have been the power of large landholders and the heavy involvement of the US, which mediated frequent intra-elite conflicts to assure stability, and sometimes collaborated with local elites to suppress opposition. The US involvement helped to impart an intensely reactionary and despotic character to most of the Central American regimes. Because Costa Rica was never as dominated by a small agrarian elite as were the other countries—it featured instead a substantial small-farm sector—it was not as natural an object of exploitation/intervention either by American firms like United Fruit or by the US government. The presence of the communists as a pressure group was not much of a threat to the political process and did contribute to the development of unions

[174] By 1910 about six percent of cultivable land had been redistributed.

and the advance on social policy. Probably the anti-Marxist and anti-union leaning of the small coffee producers was a stroke of luck as it made them less open to right-wing and American suspicion.

## Comparisons and Overview for Latin America

Agrarian reform attempts and the unrest that precedes them are part of the history of inequality. High land concentration, accompanied by some version of feudalism, leads eventually to tension/conflict, which then plays out in various ways along a spectrum from a highly successful reform, in the style of Japan, Korea, and Taiwan, through partial reforms that alleviate pressures but do not deliver their full potential (Mexico, Bolivia, Peru, and others), through continuing conflict with little if any progress toward serious reform (Brazil and Colombia), through continued heavy repression of the sort witnessed in Babylonia in the days of Hammurabi.

With the partial exception of Cuba, no country in Latin America has experienced a major and transformative agrarian reform. In that case, modifications over time in the way the sector was organized had much in common with the other communist countries discussed above; a broad majority of the rural population benefited and the reform was part of a permanent restructuring of society which greatly lowered inequality in at least the medium term. Unlike the Soviet Union and China, that positive effect carried into the long term as well. Unlike them, land came mainly from large agro-industrial corporations, mostly American, and very few people lost their lives. Latin America provides no examples of lasting distributional equity after a major land reform, and in that case the reform's impact was lessened by agriculture's relatively small share of employment and by the fact that the key was the broader shift to a socialist economic structure. Costa Rica provides another case of lasting equality, probably facilitated by timely but modest provisions of land to small landholders and by other special conditions as discussed. All of the region's other reforms have been partial, both in not transferring a high enough share of the land and in not bringing a sufficiently marked shift toward those non-agricultural policies which might have significantly lowered income inequality. Most reforms have simply been too small to produce such an impact; Mexico would be the most plausible exception because its revolution occurred a century ago, early in the country's development process, and over time redistributed up to about half of the cultivated land. But neither in that case nor in any other did a more democratic voting public, an industrial bourgeoisie with an interest in shrinking the agricultural elite, or a progressive military come to power in time to make a transformative difference.

On the key question of their short- and medium-term impacts on the income and welfare of the poor, the story is much more positive. A serf-like existence was ended for many millions, mainly in Mexico, Bolivia, and Peru. Income and economic security were improved for a comparably large and overlapping group, and mostly from these same countries. Entry into small agriculture brought a range of other quality-of-life advantages. Many peasants felt that only when they were granted a land title did they become real citizens of their country. By weakening the power of landlords and other dominant groups in the countryside, agrarian reforms encouraged a greater organizational and participatory presence for the peasantry in both local and national affairs. Bolivia and Mexico illustrate the permanent impacts of significant reforms. Even if partial, they contributed to a new more civilized normality which is hard to undo. The predatory behavior which helped to create the *latifundia* would have been hard to repeat a century later.[175]

For the beneficiaries, gaining control over the land they operated was the direct key to improved economic welfare. A higher average income depended on some combination of having more land, raising land productivity, and securing a bigger share of the income generated. Although the evidence on how production changed when land was redistributed is partial, the facts that (i) it appears generally to have either risen or remained about constant, and (ii) a higher share of the benefits now accrued to the new small landholders mean that most benefited economically, sometimes quite substantially.[176] In Mexico, while data for the reform period itself are not available, as of a

[175] Colombia has been an exception to this rule, with displacements even more common during the recent wave of violence than that of "*La Violencia*."

[176] If, prior to the reform, a tenant's rent amounted to thirty percent of output, then income would rise unless production fell by at least that same thirty percent. In no case do available data suggest such an outcome. Although relative to their initially low incomes, the resulting economic benefits to reform beneficiaries are typically substantial, inequality at the national level, as measured by indicators like the Gini coefficient, tends to show little change because the share of the GDP transferred to reform beneficiaries is usually quite low, say one to two percent. With the bottom decile of the overall income distribution, mostly made up of potential beneficiaries, having, say, one percent of national income, a doubling for them involves only transferring one percent of that national income from others.

few decades later the *ejido* units were, on average, doing relatively well. In Bolivia, output was generally higher after the reform. Small farms also typically have ecological advantages, given the major negative impacts that frequently accompany large-scale agriculture, especially the damage wrought on the forest and the ecosystem.

All of these issues can weigh significantly on whether the ultimate social payoff is likely to be greater when a country takes the conservative path of partial reforms like those of the market-assisted variety, in expectation of modest benefits for those at the bottom but no major shift in the allocation of land resources or in the pattern of inequality, as opposed to the more radical approach aiming at a major reallocation of land and large income and welfare benefits for the beneficiaries but bringing the risk of conflict and other possibly serious downsides.

The medium-term benefits of agrarian reforms have depended a good deal on the accompanying social policy changes. In Cuba, for example, the greater redistributive impact than in most other reforming countries reflected the fact that health and education policies targeted the rural poor. Bolivia's reform brought a less dramatic but still important improvement in rural education. Marked changes, albeit complicated ones, also followed the revolution in Mexico.

Kay (1998, 13) concludes that:

> The greatest contribution of agrarian reforms may lie in the stimulus given to institution-building in the countryside. Reformist governments have facilitated the organization of the peasantry into trade unions and cooperatives of various kinds, such as producer, marketing and credit associations, which helps to integrate them into the national economy, society and polity. Prior to reform, insurmountable obstacles usually blocked peasants from creating their own organizations. After the agrarian reforms, or sometimes in response to pressure for them, political parties began to vie for the peasant vote and extended their networks to rural areas where in the past reformist and left-wing political parties in particular had often been excluded by the landed oligarchy. Peasant participation in civil society was much enhanced. Thus, although agrarian reforms have usually been restricted in scope and/or thwarted by opposition forces, where transformation went deepest and where poverty and social exclusion were significantly reduced, social stability and political integration were advanced and economic development facilitated.

The potential benefits from well-executed and broad-coverage reforms are huge, but outcomes have often involved major negative effects as well. By its nature, involuntary land expropriation involves conflict. The most obvious cost of that conflict is the loss of lives. Three countries stand out—Mexico, Colombia, and Peru; however, their experiences have differed greatly. Mexico was the site of an agrarian revolution, although land was not the only issue of contention; about 1.5 million people lost their lives, approximately ten percent of the population. Peru's toll over several decades of conflict has been estimated at seventy thousand or more, about 0.4 percent of its eighteen million people as of the early 1980s. Colombia's violence has been more chronic than in any other case. Summing the toll of the wave in the 1940s and 1950s and the more recent one beginning in the 1980s, the figure approaches one million which, when compared to the population level of 16.1 million in 1960 amounts to about 6.2 percent, or compared to the 33.1 million in 1990 to about three percent. The Peru–Colombia contrast is striking; the dramatic *Sendero Luminoso* episode in Peru is more famous and better known around the world than Colombia's nearly continuous experience of violence, but took a much smaller toll in human lives, whether in absolute terms or in relation to the population.

One way in which many reforms have fallen short of potential has been the typically unequal benefits among subgroups of agricultural workers. Direct beneficiaries have typically not been the poorest component of rural society. Except in Cuba, they have not usually included the *minifundistas*, seasonal wage laborers, *comuneros*, or members of the indigenous communities who often account for the largest share of the rural poor. In Guatemala and Peru groups of indigenous peoples were either left out or treated less favorably than people of Spanish or mixed descent. In Peru, sugar plantation employees on the coast, already the best paid of rural workers, benefited the most while *comuneros*, the largest and poorest group among the peasantry, benefited the least (Kay 1983). The Mexican, and to some extent the Bolivian, reforms did redistribute land to indigenous communities. Overall, even if not the poorest, most recipients in most countries were certainly poor. Such "internal inequality" meant that most reforms raised overall welfare less than would have been possible. So did allocations which did not give somewhat more land to the most efficient farmers.[177] In many cases, benefits

[177] As argued by Adamopoulos and Restuccia (2020) in the case of the Philippines, and discussed by Ravallion and van der Walle (2008) in that of Vietnam.

were held down by bad government decisions, as with the initial choice in Peru to switch to cooperatives and the excessive control from above when officials typically knew less about farming than the operators themselves (as in Mexico).

As to what sorts of government offer the most promise, intra-regional contrasts among Brazil, Colombia, Mexico, Bolivia, and Peru throw up some hypotheses. Brazil and Colombia illustrate the difficulties of achieving much under more or less democratic conditions. Mexico achieved what it did due to a revolution and an aftermath of autocratic party rule. Peru did so through a progressive military government. Cuba was an autocracy. Only in Colombia was the military never close to staging a coup after 1910. Brazil's military was notoriously hardline, aligned with the oligarchs and not at all progressive.

The role of the US and the Cold War played out quite differently across the countries. At the time of the Mexican Revolution, US concerns were mainly business-related, and it was not a central actor, partly due to the Franklin Roosevelt government's Good Neighbor Policy. In Bolivia, it seemed to feel confident that things were unlikely to get out of hand if left mainly to internal forces, and its business concerns were not major. The Guatemalan tragedy featured the period of maximum US hysteria about communism, a government (Eisenhower and the Dulles brothers) susceptible to it, and the interests of the United Fruit Company with its close ties to the government. The failure in Brazil through the 1964 military coup was a case in which things might have worked out much better had the stance of either the US or the Goulart government been somewhat more flexible. The American preference for reforms that would not greatly alter power structures figured strongly in its reactions to the fairly radical plans of Allende in Chile and even to the moderate plans of Árbenz in Guatemala.

As the countries of Latin America today are mainly urban, their legacies of land concentration during the earlier phases of development are woven into this later history. However optimistic or pessimistic one is on these fronts, though, it is clear that agriculture can no longer be the venue for the correction of the economy-wide inequality problem to which it gave rise historically. It is now too small to perform the role it might have had major reforms been carried out before mid-century when it still dominated the economy and the labor force. The current and future challenge is to identify policies to reduce the high overall income inequality bequeathed by that history. One aspect is to rein in the political and societal corruption that goes with the classist-racist agriculture of the past, and to limit its transfer to the urban setting.

# Appendix 6.1

## Complementary Data on Inequality in Mexico, Brazil, and Chile

### Income Inequality Trends after Mexico's Land Reform

It is unclear how overall inequality has changed during the decades since the Revolution, but it was clearly high then and remains so. Felix (1977, 112) posits a Gini coefficient of 0.61 at the end of the *Porfiriato* period in 1910.[178] The best estimates for around 2020 are similar. There are no reliable data for the period during the first drawn-out redistribution but it is plausible to assume that it fell, as argued by Felix (1977); how much remains a matter of speculation.[179] As growth proceeded apace from the 1940s through the 1970s, other factors will naturally have been at play. Felix's estimate that the Gini rose by sixteen percent between the 1950s and the 1960s was necessarily guesswork. Drawing on SEDLCA data,[180] Krozer and Moreno-Brid (2014, 2) report a sky-high Gini coefficient of 0.59 in 1968, falling sharply to 0.52 in 1977 and then remaining in the range of 0.47–0.54 from 1977 to 2012 with a general downward trend since 2000.[181] For the period since 2001, the World Inequality Database reports a worsening as the share of the top one percent jumped from twenty-one percent in 2002 to twenty-eight to thirty percent for most years since 2008, one of the highest figures in the world. Thus, while many details remain to be sorted out, there is no doubt that inequality has been very high in recent decades.

If the cited 1968 figure of 0.59 is not overestimated, overall inequality was very high around that time. That it rose sharply in the preceding decade or so would suggest that it fell as the reform was occurring but began to rise as redistribution came close to a halt and industrial growth took off. In that scenario, the equality benefits of the reform were short-lived.[182] As for the impacts of the

[178] This is a very rough guess, not based on contemporary data (Felix 1977, 113). Still, something in this range is not implausible.

[179] Data prior to mid-century are scanty and must be interpreted with special caution until at least the 1970s.

[180] SEDLAC is the Socioeconomic data base for Latin America and the Caribbean, a joint venture between CEDLAS at Universidad de la Plata (Argentina) and the World Bank's Poverty and Gender Group for Latin America and the Caribbean. It draws on household survey microdata made available by the countries.

[181] A recent analysis by Sandoval (2015), designed to capture underreporting in the standard household surveys on which inequality is usually estimated, comes up with a higher level than reported in those figures, but still probably below the true values due to failure to include illegal income, underreporting of capital income and other problems.

[182] If so, the parallel with China and some other reform experiences is of interest, through the impact of rural–urban migration as industrial (or post-agricultural) growth accelerated. China's deliberate limiting of that migration clearly pushed inequality up. In Mexico, a combination of the *ejido*

liberalizing reform of the 1990s, they are unclear, and would not seem to have been large.[183]

## Brazil

Orlando Sotomayor (2007, 1280) notes that around the beginning of the present century the income of the ninetieth percentile in Brazil was sixteen times that of the tenth percentile; in Germany that ratio was 3.0, in the UK it was 4.7, and in the US it was 5.8. Using another measure of the top to bottom gap in Brazil, Pablo Astorga Junquera (2016, 59) estimates that the ratio of the top decile's per capita income to that of the bottom forty percent has varied from a low of about twenty-five-to-one around 1940 to a high of over seventy-to-one around 1990 (when that decile's share peaked at about sixty percent), before falling back to about forty-five-to-one by 2010.[184] Policies imposed during military rule probably helped to push inequality toward its historic high, including not only the strong support for large agriculture in its conflict with the small landholders and the landless, but also the banning or restriction of union membership and the reduced coverage of the minimum wage, a combination that increased labor market flexibility. For most of the last half century or so, during which household surveys have provided the bulk of the data, Sotomayor (2007) reports modest change, with the income of the top decile about 42.5 times that of the bottom one in 1977, rising to about forty-nine times in 2003.

A temporary base for optimism that inequality was finally on the wane did come from an apparent drop over the last couple of decades, as the household survey-based Gini coefficient of income fell from something around 0.6 during most of the period from 1970 to 2000 to 0.53 by 2012 (Robles 2018, 5).[185] But household surveys miss a good deal of income for those people at the top of the hierarchy; revised estimates designed to include them show inequality to be much higher and not falling, at least through 2016. Whereas the household survey data suggest that the share of the top ten percent fell gradually from about forty-seven percent in 2001 to about forty percent in 2015—a notable decline, the more complete data show (i) that the share is much higher, at fifty-five to fifty-six percent, and (ii) that it rose marginally during this period (World Inequality Lab 2018, based on Morgan 2017).[186] The increased share of income accruing to the top ten percent reflected

system's discouraging its members from leaving and a possibly lower tendency of indigenous than non-indigenous people to do could both have been at work.

[183] It is generally assumed that adjustment of the SEDLAC figures to allow for unreported income leads to an increasing gap between the former and the true figures, in which case it is quite likely that overall inequality has risen since the early 1990s. This is not surprising because any positive effect of this reform would not likely be very great, while other factors pushing inequality up were more powerful.

[184] A partially comparable picture emerges from preliminary estimates of the income share of the top one percent over the period from 1928 to 2012 by Souza and Medeiros (2015, 129).

[185] Azevedo et al. (2013) attribute an observed decline in inequality across a group of fourteen Latin countries to relatively strong growth of labor income for lower income workers; another important factor has been the positive impact of government transfers. The data used do not include correction for underreporting at the top of the income hierarchy.

[186] This conclusion is also reached by WID (2018) who note that when they combine survey and income tax data, the decline in the Gini coefficient from 2006 to 2012 all but disappears; it is virtually constant at an astronomically high 0.7.

their rising capital incomes (inadequately captured in the household survey).[187] The bottom fifty percent did experience a small increase in share from about 11.5 percent to a little over twelve percent. The gains in share at the top and the bottom came at the expense of the middle forty percent.

## Chile

Household survey-based series point to a decline in inequality since the Pinochet years; for example, those of the World Bank (based on the CASEN surveys) show a national Gini coefficient of around 0.55–0.56 from 1987 to 1998, with a peak of 0.57.2 in 1990, followed by a marked and continuous decline to 0.44 in 2015, and stability from then until 2022 (World Bank, n.d.). When, however, the household survey data are adjusted for underreporting,[188] they suggest a much more modest decline from around 0.57 in the early 1990s to 0.53 in 2006 (Hourton 2012, 15).[189] This is broadly consistent with results provided by Atria et al. (2018, 18) for trends in the share of the top one percent. After adding information from tax returns and undistributed corporate profits, they find that the best estimate share of that top one percent fell from about twenty-four percent in 1990 to under nineteen percent in 2003, then rose back to a peak of twenty-nine percent in 2010 and an average of over twenty-five percent since 2005. In short, they conclude that over the first years of the past decade, the share of that top one percent was sky high, comparable to Brazil's and above that of Colombia in 2010 (ibid., 22).

[187] According to Morgan (2017) the surveys captured only 57.1 percent as much as the more completely sourced data. For the bottom fifty percent, this share was about seventy-four percent; for the middle forty percent, it was eighty-nine percent; and for the top ten percent, it was just 41.7 percent. Meanwhile, Souza and Madeiros (2015, 127) conclude that the level of inequality in Brazil has been far more stable than often previously thought. Their estimates suggest no trend in the share of the top one percent between 1928 and 2012, with a Gini of around 0.7. There may be some upward bias in their methodology.

[188] As judged by comparison of the household survey results with the national accounts—a methodology which mainly corrects for underreporting of capital income.

[189] This series tracks that of the World Bank until 1996, after which they begin to diverge, something to be expected if, as concluded by Atria et al., the impact of undistributed profits comes mainly after 2000.

# 7

# Twentieth-Century Land Reforms in the East Asian Tigers, India, the Middle East, and the Philippines

## Varying Levels of Success

The land reforms of Japan, Korea, and Taiwan have set a standard for success. While providing an obviously important model, the special context in which they were undertaken suggests that few other cases were likely to be so successful. Two of the other three countries treated in this chapter come from the Middle East. In parallel to Guatemala and Chile, Iran's experience illustrates just how consequential a setting can be in which their own economic interests weigh very heavily in the policy choice of outsiders, choices which reflected both a fear of communism and a lack of in-depth knowledge about a country that might have allowed a better guess as to how its future would be affected by a reform. Egypt falls in the category of reasonably successful experiences which, however, have occurred in a context where the chance to spur fast overall growth was slight because there was simply too little land. Improving its distribution was, as in most other places, important to the economic and general well-being of many people, but it could not by itself provide very high incomes for them. The Philippines reform history provides, on the one hand, a natural comparator to the East Asian successes due to the many structural similarities, and, on the other hand a set of lessons for the many Sub-Saharan Africa (SSA) countries suffering from high population growth and severe land scarcity.

### The Exceptionality of the Southeast Asia Model

The reforms which brought all the potential economic benefits, including fast agricultural and overall growth, significant income increases for the new

*The Great Curse*. Albert Berry, Oxford University Press. © Oxford University Press 2024.
DOI: 10.1093/oso/9780197782675.003.0008

peasantry, and lasting income equality, have been very few. The widely accepted recipe is that provided by Japan, Korea, and Taiwan after their post-World War II land reforms. The economic payoff was accompanied by a base for solid democracies. Their success naturally raises the question of whether some SSA countries and others, which still rely heavily on agriculture for employment, can follow this path to lasting economic and political success. And, if so, can they thereby avoid the costs of high land concentration, if they do not now suffer it, or put an end to those costs if they do?

## Japan's Transition

These signal successes, beginning with Japan's, occurred at a special moment in world politics when Japan's new government, the US administration, and post-war Supreme Commander General MacArthur were all persuaded that an equalizing reform was needed. Internal pressures for reform had been building, as a long history of peasant movements had gradually weakened the landlord system, and various controls imposed during the war furthered the process. The biggest single episode in that pre-war trend was the rice riots of 1918, involving ten million people and bringing increasing national attention to class issues. The Russian Revolution of the previous year had provided a big impetus for the rice riots. The many tenant farmers who took part were motivated by having to deliver about half of their crops to the landlords as rent and then running short for their own needs and having to buy at high prices. This setting owed much to the Land Tax Reform of 1873 as the Meiji government increasingly based its vigorous industrialization program on land taxes, which constituted three-quarters of total government revenues (Dore 1959, 15); on rice land, those taxes amounted to about thirty-five percent of the average crop value, putting increasing pressure on the farmers and helping to push many peasant families into tenancy. From 1920 onward, the Ministry of Agriculture and Forestry had taken some steps to promote an owner–operator system (Takigawa 1972, 292). In December 1945, immediately after the end of the war, the Ministry presented a Land Reform Bill, with the objective of easing the critical food situation and the prevailing unrest in rural communities. The Bill was rejected by the Allied General Headquarters as incomplete and insufficient. Based on its recommendations, the Ministry then prepared a second Agricultural Reform Law, which was enacted in October 1946 and then implemented quickly and efficiently.

One of the ideological backstops to the post-war land reform was a sort of physiocratic one, described by Ronald P. Dore (1959, 56) as "agriculture-is-the-base-ism, an ideology which helps to establish and stabilize the life of peasants whose self-reliance and self-management is based on their assiduous labour, and who are necessary for the existence of a state." It constituted a sort of philosophy of small farm ownership (Takigawa 1972, 308).[1] However exactly one interprets the causality around this reform, and those in Korea and Taiwan, they did set the standard for success and they illustrated how well economies and societies can perform in their wake.

The combination of circumstances that led to success in Japan was certainly unusual. A country with a still economically oppressive agricultural system, characterized by a high concentration of land ownership and with a recent history of internal pressure for reform, was defeated in war by one whose local representative (General Douglas McArthur) believed that a land reform creating a political base of yeoman farmers was needed to turn the country into a stable democracy and protect it from communism.[2] This belief owed something to family history, as McArthur's father Arthur, as military governor of the Philippines after the Spanish–American War, had pursued a similar scheme but had been blocked by Washington (Montgomery 1975). In contributing to the reform in Japan, General McArthur was advised by one of the century's greatest students and supporters of reform, Wolf Ladejinsky.[3] Once in motion, and backstopping a burst of rapid overall economic growth, the new agrarian structure contributed to a new *status quo*. It greatly reduced rural tensions and did indeed lay part of the groundwork for Japan's democracy. Favorable conditions helped it to achieve robust growth; these conditions included a relatively well-educated peasantry capable of implementing new technologies as they came along. In an earlier effort to raise agricultural productivity beginning in the 1880s, Japan had learned some useful lessons. After a failed attempt to introduce Western methods of

[1] Although some foreign scholars, including Tuma (1965, 136), have claimed that the reform was essentially imposed from the outside, this is clearly oversimplistic. Kapstein (2017) agrees with Takigawa that it was not imposed by the United States on a reluctant Japan, and that it was the Japanese government that actually drove the effort.

[2] By 1947, the Communist Party of Japan had one hundred thousand members. In the 1949 election, it polled ten percent of all votes. The level of inequality, both in agriculture and overall, was a natural target for the party.

[3] It may have been another stroke of luck that McArthur favored the reform, given his reputation for insubordination, his lack of interest in details, and his choice of incompetent staff members (Ellman 2023). His biggest military mistake was to undertake a move in the Koran War which brought China into the fray in 1951; this led to his firing by President Truman.

large-scale farming in the 1870s, it had focused on raising the productivity of the small operating units (Johnston 1970, 61).

By 1945, seventy percent of Japanese farmers were renting all or part of their land, frequently at exorbitant rates that could reach eighty percent of the value of their crops.[4] In 1946, the government acquired about a one-third of all agricultural land and about seventy percent of that cultivated by tenants (Takigawa 1972, 290–291). It went to three million agricultural households, about one-half of the total. Some additional land was transferred by the end of 1952. The structure of the sector changed substantially; in 1947, as the reform began, owner-cultivated land constituted 61.5 percent of the total and land cultivated by tenants made up 39.5 percent; by 1950, these figures were 89.2 percent and 10.8 percent respectively. In 1970, tenant farmers were a negligible 1.6 percent of all operators, compared to 80 percent for owners.

The land reform, following on wartime restrictions on landlords' rights, contributed to the sharp decline in income inequality, although it was only one of several important factors working in that direction. A drastic deconcentration at the top of the hierarchy occurred from 1938 to 1945 (essentially, the war years)[5] and inequality has remained relatively low ever since (with a Gini coefficient often around 0.35), despite a long period of famously fast income growth (Moriguchi and Saez 2006).[6] Along with the end of high land concentration, other factors contributing to the fall between the pre- and post-war periods included limits on the practice of high dividend payments by large firms to shareholders, and a reduction in the relative compensation of very highly paid managers of large corporations. Wartime regulations on these fronts were the first step. Reforms undertaken under the US occupation from 1945 to 1952 included the development of unions and the break-up of some of the large monopolies that underpinned the extremely high incomes of top business executives. Inflation reduced the compensation paid to landlords to a fraction of the actual land value. Heavy and progressive property taxation was imposed. While significant, these postwar steps appear to have played a secondary role compared to the impact of World War II and the war-time policies of the Japanese government; US

[4] Levels close to the latter number were credible from an economic perspective given the scarcity of land and the abundance of labor.

[5] The share of the top one percent plummeted from about twenty percent of the national income in the late 1930s to seven to eight percent by 1945.

[6] These authors base their analysis on top income shares and top wage income shares; their source is the tax statistics.

occupation reforms were, in many ways, a continuation of Japan's wartime policies.

Japan's experience offers valuable lessons for developing countries aspiring to deal with the very high levels of inequality that typically stem from high land concentration and monopolization in other industries. The importance of curtailing cronyism in the high echelons of business and government is emphasized by the role that such anti-competitive and anti-meritocratic behavior has played, not only in pre-war Japan, but also in recent cases of extreme inequality in the US, Russia, and China. Its impact on the rate of growth is unclear but plausibly negative given its negative effect on the quality of leaders and the common monopoly practice of squeezing out smaller-scale competitors. Japan's great burst of growth came after the cronyism was reined in and a system of progressive taxation was instituted—the great fortunes of the earlier period had been accumulated when such taxation hardly existed. In contrast to most other countries, Japan undertook other institutional changes, including the abolition of primogeniture and reforms to corporate and union structure; this made the quick deconcentration difficult to reverse. Many other countries saw a major decline in the income share of the very rich during either World War I or the Great Depression, but few have been able to maintain that lower level.[7] The permanence of the changes presumably also owes something to the country's post-war political structure, based initially on the middle-class and the farmers, the bedrock of the Liberal-Democratic party which has ruled almost continuously since then.

## Taiwan and Korea

Although the Japanese land reform was successful in contributing directly to the welfare of many people and to long-term growth, its role in this already semi-industrialized country was less than in its former colonies of Taiwan and Korea. As in Japan, the size of producing units in Taiwan did not change significantly with the reform, but both productivity and incomes went up dramatically, something Shirley W. Y. Kuo (1983) attributes to rapid

[7] Piketty and Saez (2013) note that, in Switzerland, which neither suffered the travails of the war nor instituted very progressive taxes, the wealth share of the top one percent has remained in the thirty-five-to-forty-percent range since 1915. In Ireland, which did not suffer the severe shocks of war but did institute the progressive taxes, top income shares did not fall during the war, but they were significantly reduced later.

increases in multiple cropping and in crop diversification during the 1950s and 1960s transition period. The multiple cropping index rose from 172 in 1952 to its peak of 190 in 1966. The working-days-per-hectare jumped from about 170 in the 1948–1950 period to 260 in the 1963–1965 period.

The Korean and Taiwanese reforms also played out in quite special conditions, including having been colonies of the Japanese Empire. Both had higher land concentration and tenancy rates than did China. Thus, in the 1930s, South Korean landlords accounted for 2.7 percent of farm households but owned 64 percent of the arable land (Cho 1964, 21). A considerable share of land in both countries had been owned by large landholders with Japanese links, making it an inviting target for transfer to small farmers after the war; it was important to the incoming governments (the Kuomintang of Chiang Kai-Shek in Taiwan) to destroy rival power through the reform. Post-war economic performance benefited from the heavy pre-war investments of the Japanese, including that in education and in farmers' associations which, according to Yhi Min Ho (1966), were key to achieving the rapid productivity increases later, including those of the post-land reform period. In Taiwan, for example, those associations, together with agricultural co-operatives, co-managed the extension service (thirteen thousand workers in the late 1920s and early 1930s) and the agricultural advisors working with small agricultural units at the village level (nine thousand). The governments of both Korea and Taiwan responded to threats of foreign attack and of local unrest and communist infiltration by quickly building expert-based, coherent bureaucracies that could spur national development (Albertus 2021, 282).

The East Asian cases offer clear evidence of the lasting benefits of small-farm agriculture under the right circumstances. The post-reform agricultural performances of Korea and Taiwan are among the greatest ever recorded. After essentially putting all of the usable land into the hands of small family farmers, they experienced historically high rates of agricultural growth (at four percent per year and more), a strongly equalizing impact on income inequality and, as a joint product of those two factors, a very rapid growth of the income of those at the bottom of the hierarchy—a rate that fell in the range of six-to-eight percent per year in Taiwan over about two decades, essentially eradicating poverty over that short period. This contrasts, for example, with an average wage growth in Colombia (from 1950 to 2015) of about 1.0–1.4 percent per year (Berry 2017). Thus, over twenty years, the incomes of those working on small farms in Taiwan almost quadrupled while paid agricultural workers in Colombia achieved only a doubling over sixty-five years. Along with their strong performances in agriculture, the success of Korea and Taiwan in achieving growth with equity reflected the quality and egalitarian structure of their educational systems and their labor-intensive growth strategies.[8]

## Why So Few Big Wins?

Much was in play globally during the early post-World War II period and the subsequent Cold War; with a little additional good luck and/or good management, substantially greater reform benefits might have been achieved. The most important lost opportunity was that in China. What the efforts of Ladejinsky and partners might have borne had a hurriedly organized 1949 Sino–American project been launched sooner cannot be known. His proposed reform was similar to that in Japan, but before it could get beyond small experimental demonstrations, the Communists had pushed the Nationalist army and government over to Taiwan (then Formosa).[9] Ladejinsky judged that, had this effort begun ten years sooner, the outcome of China's civil war and the subsequent history might have been quite different. The following two decades saw enormous loss of life as Mao remade the agricultural system into a version of the Soviet one, with perhaps thirty-eight million people dying as a result,[10] mainly due to the starvation following his government's bad policy choices for agriculture. Over twenty years later, in the early 1980s, those mistakes were largely corrected when President Deng transferred more decision-making power to the farmers, helping to usher in the period of dramatically rapid growth in China and the historic fall in poverty. That reduction could have been achieved a couple of decades sooner had someone like Deng been in charge of agricultural policy or had Ladejinsky's proposals been implemented.

Soon after the China attempt, Ladejinsky was working on reform in South Vietnam from 1955 to 1961 but left when he became convinced that President Ngo Dinh Diem was not serious about it. Dysfunction within the US government led it to block many reform efforts.[11] The extraordinary

[8] Watkins (1998) credits these factors, together with the initially more equal distribution of income and assets, for the greater success in achieving growth with equity than that of the countries of Latin America.

[9] As advisor to President Chiang, he did help to implement the famously successful reform there.

[10] Leitenberg (2006).

[11] The degree of confusion in the US government around this issue is laid out by Rorty (1955).

character of the set of conditions in post-war Japan, Korea, and Taiwan is thus underlined by their fleeting nature; the absence of comparably successful experiences in the developing world after World War II; and the fact that, even for the US, this was a short moment of insight by parts of its government into the potential benefits of serious land reform. The impressive stance taken in East Asia was a historic outlier for a country which later, in the context of the Cold War and its fervid anti-communist mentality, came to totally block promising reforms in Guatemala, Iran, and elsewhere. The world was probably lucky to have Ladejinsky's skills on display in the right place at the right time. Despite, and perhaps partly because of, his outstanding skills and knowledge, he had to deal with plenty of opposition at home. He lived through the McCarthy period and Secretary of Agriculture Ezra Taft Benson temporarily blocked his taking up a position with the Foreign Operations Administration on the grounds that he was a security risk. The US battle against communism was always a factor in its attitude to reforms; in Japan, Korea, and Taiwan it was a positive one, but in almost all other places it played a negative role.

The high land concentration that is the historical norm in most places comes under pressure most obviously from its internal victims, who foment revolutions or push for reform by other means. The world's powerful non-communist countries may, on occasion, welcome such reforms on moral or philosophical grounds, but have usually been primarily or exclusively motivated by military/security/business considerations; the goal is stability and a Western-friendly style of government. In Japan, Korea, and Taiwan, those security issues were central. General McArthur was persuaded that a prosperous and stable peasantry would give Japan a stable polity. Ladejinsky promoted the economic benefits of reform as well by arguing that it would raise income levels and the economic security of the vast majority of the farming population and help to make them a stabilizing influence. Stability and freedom from leftist political threats were central goals in the US intervention against reform in Chile; in Guatemala, it was minor national economic interests (United Fruit Company) accompanied by implausible security concerns. Both cases involved right-wing governments (Nixon and Eisenhower, respectively). In Iran, it was mainly economic interests.

As the dominant economic model in the West came to be the neo-liberal one, the idea of reform through expropriation became a harder sell and reform through markets a more natural one, with the World Bank backing five such reforms in the 1980s and 1990s (Deininger 1999). By that time, in any case, whether land reforms were implemented in developing countries was seldom seen as having potentially important fallout in world politics.

## Indian Reforms

As the highest population country to experience colonialism, and as a democracy many of whose leaders espoused left-of-center ideologies and friendship with communist countries (in this case the USSR), India's land reform experience is of special interest here. Its states have considerable independence and have made significantly different decisions on land and other major policy issues. Some reform efforts have been initiated by non-governmental groups, like the Bhoodan (Land gift movement).[12] A significant part of India experienced and benefited importantly from the Green Revolution, with the states of Kerala and west Bengal figuring most prominently.

### The Setting at Independence

Indian agriculture at Independence (in 1945) reflected a past in which the typical farm was very small and productivity was low. One restraint on raising productivity, developing new land, or reducing poverty was the high rents received by some landowners who leased out scattered plots to sharecroppers for up to sixty to seventy percent of the gross product (Frankel 1978, 320). In addition, many families were vulnerable to moneylenders, who exploited their weak bargaining position, in effect keeping them as bonded laborers. Rural poverty was closely tied to landlessness or small unviable holdings. These conditions paralleled those of many other countries where small groups of landowners exercised great social and political power. But India's caste system was a particularly rigid social hierarchy, magnifying the challenge of moving rapidly toward an economically and socially egalitarian system. In such a situation, while progressive land legislations were passed to implement long standing promises in the political manifestos, the actual

[12] This movement, also known as the Bloodless Revolution, was initiated by Gandhian Vinoba Bhave in 1951 in an attempt to persuade wealthy landowners to voluntarily give a percentage of their land to landless people. Limited scope and the institutional barriers faced kept its impact quite small.

implementation was severely diluted as a result of the pressures exerted by the vested interests (Saxena 1990, 138).

## Plans and Execution at the National Level

The World War II backdrop for Japan's famously successful land reform also coincided with the end of European colonialism in Asia and Africa. With the second largest population in the world, and around eighty percent of its labor force employed in agriculture, what was to happen next in India certainly mattered to the welfare of a huge number of people. But an outcome similar to Japan's was, to put it mildly, an unlikely prospect. The departing colonial power had less policy sway, lacked the penchant for egalitarian agriculture of those in charge of US policy at that time, and was not motivated by the fear of a major world power ending up in or allied with the communist camp. Although the United Kingdom fostered democracy in India, it did not see significant land redistribution as a helpful step. As a colonial power, its administrative style had been to collaborate with the top echelons of the local society. And, in contrast to Japan, the peasantry was poorly educated; around mid-century, the literacy rate in rural India was under twenty percent for males and under ten percent for females. Whereas Japan had decades of experience in raising the productivity of small farms, India did not; only with the Green Revolution, dating from the 1960s, was there real potential for rapid productivity growth. Whether democracy was a final outcome was no doubt seen to be less important in India and other former colonies than in Japan, a just defeated military power whose collaboration or military neutrality during the post-war was seen as important.

After World War II and India's independence, there was plenty of internal debate around land reform and many promises were made, with a few serious attempts at implementation. But for the country as a whole, little was achieved in altering the pattern of power, the economic disparities, or the hierarchical character of the society that governed economic life. And, as per the standard historical pattern, a country that does not make a dent in its inequality by reducing the concentration of land-based income early in its development trajectory then bequeaths a high and often rising level of inequality to its post-agricultural phase. While never as high as in such extreme cases as Brazil, Colombia, and South Africa, India's inequality has remained serious and, by the 1990s, was rising as the country entered a fast growth phase. The slow growth of incomes in agriculture was reflected in an extremely rapid increase in non-agricultural informal activities; by 2001, with employment in the primary sector a little over fifty percent of the total, the informal sector accounted for about forty-three percent, with only seven percent in the formal sector (Berry 2018, 33).

Soon after Independence, Prime Minister Nehru laid out his plan for the country's future: that it be socialist with the means of production socially owned and controlled for the benefit of society, that industrialization be fostered by an import substitution strategy, and that rising consumer demands be satisfied mainly by an expansion of village and small-scale industries (Frankel 1978, 117). He believed the best option to provide the needed increase in food production was for one- or two-acre farmers to become landowners and be supported by the services of village multipurpose cooperative societies (Frankel 1978, 119). He concluded that "it is true from the economic point of view, a large farm will also be very productive. But once we give up these large farms and have relatively small holdings or farms, it becomes inevitable for cooperation between a number of small farmers. This is the economic aspect. From the social point of view, cooperative farming is equally necessary."[13] He believed that economies of scale did exist and that cooperative activities were needed to achieve them in the absence of large farms. In short, he suffered from some of the same partially mistaken beliefs as have many other leaders, but at the same time recognized that the small farm was essential for the medium-term future.

Francine R. Frankel (1978, 132) saw a contradiction between the goals of rapid industrialization and gradual agrarian reform. A growing provision of public support for farmers with little land and little education posed a challenge quite different from that in Japan, Korea, and Taiwan. Between the first and second five-year plans (1951 to 1956 and 1956 to 1961, respectively), the share of public outlays going to agriculture fell from 34.6 percent to 17.5 percent, while that going to industry and mining rose from 7.6 percent to 18.5 percent. While productivity did increase modestly, total agricultural output growth was not strong, falling from over three percent annually from 1951/1952 to 1960/1961 to around or below 2.5 percent over the next two decades, before rising to 3.3 percent from 1981 to 1991[14], as the green revolution had its impacts. Early pressures for reforms were manifested in

[13] Nehru (1957), cited by Frankel (1978, 119).
[14] Our World in Data (2023).

large-scale food riots in 1967. In response, a "high yields varieties program," which had by then covered only four million acres was quickly expanded to twenty-one million acres by 1968/1969.

In the first three decades after Independence, reform remained high in the stated agenda of governments and state administrations. As elsewhere, land reform policy had two main objectives: removing those impediments to higher agricultural productivity built into the existing agrarian structure, and curbing its exploitation and social injustice, thereby providing security to the tiller.[15] The most revolutionary step was probably the early 1950s abolition of the feudal zamindari system of large estates run by rent-collecting intermediaries, who had been given control of much of North India's land in return for payments to the British Raj. This step had strong political support because of the zamindars' close alliance with the British colonial government; it increased the security of millions of tenants and freed them from many illegal exactions, although the beneficiaries were not typically among the poorest (Lanjouw and Stern 1998).

On the other reform fronts, however, success has been modest, at best. Since 1947, India has arguably enacted more land reform legislation than any other country in the world, but it has failed to change the deep economic disparities or the traditional hierarchical nature of intergroup relationships in village society. For the country as a whole, the redistribution of land rights and improvement of terms of tenancy has been quite limited. By the end of 2005, state governments across India had declared 7.34 million acres to be above ceiling (1.8 percent of India's agricultural land). Of that land, the governments had taken possession of 6.5 million acres and distributed 5.4 million acres to 5.6 million households. The total acreage distributed amounts to approximately one percent of India's agricultural land, with the beneficiaries being as few as four percent of rural households (Binswanger-Mkhize et al. 2009, 247). This very limited achievement was concentrated in a few states with West Bengal alone accounting for about forty percent of the country's ceiling beneficiaries. Ceilings laws did provide an incentive for some sales by the better off to those with less land.[16] A number of factors

[15] The six main categories of reforms have been (i) abolition of intermediaries (rent collectors under the pre-Independence land revenue system), (ii) tenancy regulation (to improve the contractual terms including the security of tenure), (iii) a ceiling on landholdings (to redistribute surplus land to the landless), (iv) consolidation of disparate landholdings, (v) encouragement of cooperative joint farming, and (vi) settlement and regulation of tenancy.

[16] These and other policy steps were factors, although presumably not dominant ones, in the continuous decrease in farm size in India; between 1960/1961 and 2002/2003 the share of operated land

made the true reach of land redistribution less than even the official numbers would suggest. For one thing, redistributed land was often of poor quality; many recipients were members of scheduled casts and tribes (Saxena 1990, 124–126). Poor rural households have been allotted 14.7million acres of government wasteland.

Success has been greater, at least on paper, in the area of tenancy rights—12.4 million tenants, or about five percent of households, have been given rights over 15.6 million acres, comprising, again, five percent of agricultural land (Hanstad et al. 2009). But many field studies have demonstrated that even these modest gains overstate the actual achievement. Large landholders benefited from numerous exemptions, such as those given to bogus religious, educational, and charitable trusts. They distributed land to their relatives, they let go only of their most marginal lands, or they continued to retain possession of many of these lands through fraud and force (Herring 2008). Harsh Mander (2013, 13) reports that the "culturable wastelands" were often actually being cultivated by large, upper-caste landowners and allotments to scheduled caste and scheduled tribe (SC/ST) landless households often remained on paper, as allottees were forcefully evicted or not allowed to take possession. Tenancy was also widely subverted by misuse of the provision for repossessing land for "personal cultivation," by large-scale eviction of tenants, by collusion with local land authorities to ensure that their tenancy was not recorded, and even by forceful dispossession of legal right-holders after the transfer of legal titles to them. P. S. Apus (1996) estimated that as many as one-third of tenant household in rural India were evicted from the lands that they cultivated to evade tenancy reform laws (Mander 2013, 13–14).

How did such a failure to achieve significant poverty reduction through land reform emerge despite the political attention to it? In summary, there have been many promises, much less legislation, and very partial implementation of that which has been enacted. This democratic country, with large inter-group differences in political influence, shared many features with other countries. For one thing, politicians simply promise much more than they deliver; the promises give them political points. Andrew Q. Philips (2020) contends that the enactment of land policies is a "strategically timed signal"

in units of ten hectares or more fell from twenty-nine percent to about twelve percent, while the share in units of zero to one hectares rose from 6.9 percent to about twenty-two percent (Lipton 2009, 95) although the Gini coefficient changed little.

to voters used before elections. "Policy passage is more likely to occur the year before an election and is a clear signal to voters of incumbent competence, responsiveness to voter demands, and the desire to win over additional supporters. Land reform issues remain salient over time, even when reforms have been passed in a state . . . . Designed to win over rather than reward constituents, land reform is an ideal policy due to its low fiscal cost relative to other government policies, as well as its high visibility among landless rural voters."[17] Policy implementation, carried out by bureaucratic agents, may differ across ideologies, or bureaucracies may be influenced by political considerations in choosing to regulate and enforce certain policies. For instance, in the context of land reform, bureaucratic agents may reward loyal supporters with faster implementation, or they might try to win over swing voters.

That campaigning politicians offered more than was later delivered, owed something to institutional patterns. K. B. Saxena (1990, 138), in his detailed discussion of land and poverty in India, describes the role and administrative style of the Indian bureaucracy:

> A good officer is one who avoids conflict and can settle things tactfully and amicably. Such an officer accomplishes "token" implementation and does not pursue real change which requires persistence and facing conflicts. A typical example is the Collectors who would allot land to the rural poor but will avoid intervention when allotted land is taken back by force or legal harassment. Such a style of functioning, accomplishing "token" administration, is efficient on paper, and appreciated by vested interests.

He notes that potential losers from land reform, especially successful middle-sized farmers, emphasize the unfairness of taking rural properties but not urban ones.

As of a decade ago, India still had the largest number of rural poor and of landless households in the world. Landlessness remains a strong indicator of rural poverty. Land can provide not only economic security, but also social status, identity, and dignity. John Harriss (2013) affirms that even though

[17] This supports earlier findings in Venezuela (Albertus 2012) and Kenya (Boone 2012) that redistributive land reform was seen as a good tool to increase political support. It also supports previous work that finds reforms are politically salient (Teofilo and Garcia 2003). This salience is not limited to India; in 2003 an estimated forty percent of the non-urban population in Asia lived under informal land ownership (Deininger et al. 2003). In Africa, this figure is fifty percent.

semi-feudal forms of landlordism no longer exist in the current more capitalist framework of agriculture, there remains a strong case for redistributivist land reform because landed power remains such a major factor in India's politics and society.

## Reforms at the State Level

The most notable and successful reforms have been implemented in West Bengal and Kerala, in each case by a Communist government. In West Bengal, such administrations (1967 to 1971 and 1977 to 2011) undertook major reforms. The result was a more equitable distribution of land among the landless farmers, and the enumeration of landless farmers—without which they could be dangerously invisible. These achievements ensured an almost lifelong loyalty from the farmers, and they led to the communists' lengthy stay in power.

In their analysis of the effect of agricultural tenancy laws implemented in the late 1970s, Abhijit Banerjee et al. (2002, 275) concluded that Operation Barga (a program designed to implement and enforce long-dormant agricultural tenancy laws that regulated rents and protected the tenure security of sharecroppers) raised average rice productivity by twenty percent through the combination of a "bargaining power effect" that tended to raise the crop-share of tenants and a "security of tenure effect" that encouraged investment by the tenant, but eliminated the use of eviction threats by the landlord as an incentive. Radwan Ali Shaban (1987) had earlier estimated that, controlling for land quality, a change in contractual status from sharecropper-cultivated to owner-cultivated increased productivity by sixteen percent. Banerjee et al. (2002) suspect that the difference between the two estimates may reflect their measurement's inclusion of the effect of additional investment resulting from the shift in property rights.

Kerala, the only other large state where the Communist Party came to power, has arguably carried out the most extensive land, tenancy, and agrarian labor wage reforms in the non-socialist, late-industrializing world (Heller 1999). By its quick abolition of a system of serfdom and slavery, it cut the incidence of poverty notably (Herring 2001). The share of land and of agricultural families transferred or affected was considerable. The reforms have attracted attention not only for the scope of their goals, but also for the perceived efficiency with which they have been administered.

Ironically, this did not lead to a strong and rapidly expanding agricultural economy. The sector's role was outpaced by the expansion of emigration from Kerala to the Middle East and the sharp increase in wage rates that resulted. Rice acreage fell sharply, especially over the 1980s, and output did as well, but from 1965/1966 to 1995/1996 there was a sharp rise in yield by sixty-three percent, or 1.6 percent per year; it was thus a leader in India's Green Revolution. The fall in area and output was due to the rising scarcity of labor due to extensive migration to the Arabian Gulf region. The amount of rice purchasable from a day's wages skyrocketed from the mid-1970s to the end of the century (Balakrishnan 2002, 53, 62).

Although they took different routes, the more serious reform attempts, like those of Kerala and West Bengal, appear to have paid off quite well in terms both of agricultural productivity and rural welfare.

## Micro-level Evidence of Impacts Where Reforms Occurred

To the small extent that land reforms have actually been implemented on the ground outside Kerala and West Bengal, what has been their impact on the lives of those who received land allotments?

On balance, the many studies undertaken to assess the impacts of specific reform efforts make it clear that the potential for economic and welfare benefits from widespread reforms was high. The previously discussed analyses of Banerjee et al. (2002, 275) and Shaban (1987) for West Bengal point to such promise. In a more general look at the impacts of reform in the sixteen main states of India and a rare attempt to distinguish the various forms of reform and the various possible effects, Timothy Besley and Robin Burgess (2000, 424) conclude that "there is robust evidence of a link between poverty reduction and two kinds of land reform legislation-tenancy reform and abolition of intermediaries.... Although the effects on poverty are likely to have been greater if large-scale redistribution of land had been achieved, our results are nonetheless interesting as they suggest that partial, second-best reforms which mainly affect production relations in agriculture can play a significant role in reducing rural poverty." Many field studies also show that possession of land adds to their social standing and self-confidence, even though the landholders were often unable to cultivate it because supporting credit or grants were not available for land development and input costs

(Iyer 1997). Land reform can also benefit those with little or no land through its indirect effect of raising agricultural wages.

## Overall Socio-economic Advance and Associated Factors

As implicit in the above scenario, advancement in the rural population was modest and gradual over the post-Independence decades. Average productivity was eventually boosted by the Green Revolution, but it did not reflect the potential contributions of the various types of land reform as these were too infrequently undertaken; some were, in any case, badly designed and/or badly implemented. Longitudinal village studies reviewed by Peter Lanjouw and Rajshir Jayaraman (1999, 24–25) support the household survey-based conclusion that during the 1970s and 1980s India did experience a slow and irregular decline in rural poverty; the considerable movement in and out of poverty was attributable to harvest fluctuations, personal calamities, and other factors: "Low caste status and agricultural wage labor are associated with long-term poverty. Even where poverty does not appear to have fallen, increased ownership of consumer durables, shifts toward consumption of higher quality goods, and self-reported perceptions point to gradually improving living conditions." The rural poor often identify reduced dependence on patrons as an important improvement in their living conditions. The slowly rising incomes and poverty reduction were attributed to the modest agricultural productivity gains, based mainly on the broad package of new inputs involved in the Green Revolution, in particular, irrigation. The new technologies do not appear to have favored large farmers, despite their better access to credit for the purchase of new inputs; the expansion of irrigation can be quite progressive when only large farmers had access to it before. No general trend in landlessness was apparent. Land markets were usually inactive, but this changed when canal irrigation greatly altered productive potential. Resulting land sales often involved transfers from formerly well-endowed but non-cultivating households to cultivating castes; the small and vulnerable farmers were thus not necessarily the ones losing their land in these transactions.

Land legislation had both positive and negative effects on land distribution and on welfare. The beneficial effects were usually indirect, such as when farmers were encouraged to invest in new technologies. On the downside, a very common response to "land-to-the-tiller" legislation was the eviction of tenants, increasing both landlessness and the size of the agricultural wage labor force. Overall, tenancy appeared to be evolving along with the new cultivation practices; fixed-rent contracts became increasingly frequent, as did cost-sharing by landlords and "reverse tenancy" where small landholders rent to larger operators, reflecting the spread of modern technologies. Lanjouw and Jayaraman (1999) conclude that the persistence of tenancy as an institution suggests that it fulfills a useful purpose—permitting the cultivation of land by those who can put it to most productive use, without requiring a full transfer of property rights.

The rising trend in non-agricultural employment has benefited rural households, both through the incomes received and the security provided against losses from agricultural fluctuations. These benefits have gone disproportionately to the better off, with regular non-farm employment apparently linked to personal contacts, as well as to payment of bribes. At an aggregate level, growing non-agricultural employment "tightened" rural agricultural labor markets and raised agricultural wages in many villages. Given this scenario it is not clear how many small landholder cultivators are being pushed out of agriculture by declining returns or shrinking access to land, and how many are being pulled away by new opportunities in the non-agricultural sector; the frequent background of rising real agricultural wages suggests that pull factors may be more important.

Rural growth and, in particular, the integration of the village economy into the wider rural economy, has eroded the traditional caste structure in many villages and weakened the link between ritual status and economic status. In many villages, the traditionally dominant, non-cultivating caste was overtaken economically by households of other castes, usually traditional cultivators who have taken the greatest advantage of the new agricultural opportunities. But the lowest castes often remain easily distinguishable from the rest of village society by their very low material well-being and their limited opportunities. In addition, there has also been little evidence of improvement in gender relations. A decline in the already very low female–male population ratio suggests that gender-based inequality may be increasing. Sanskritization may play a role in this, in that women are often required to observe behaviors associated with higher castes, such as full *purdah* or withdrawal from wage labor activity.

Although rising agricultural productivity has clearly brought widespread, if very gradual, benefits, the same cannot be said of public spending over the last decades of the 20th century. Jean P. Dreze, Lanjouw, and Naresh Sharma (1998) review public spending in the municipality of Palanpur (Gujarat) from 1957/1958 to 1993, including the building of public schooling facilities, the implementation of the Integrated Rural Development Programme and other credit programs, the youth employment program, and the provision of widows' pensions. They conclude that, except for the modest success of a program providing two water handpumps near the low-caste quarters, the resulting benefits have been extremely disappointing. Privileged individuals or groups systematically direct the benefits of programs to themselves at the expense of other village members. This pattern induces them to ponder "whether high inequality within villages, and in particular the lack of strong village cohesion, present major obstacles to the successful implementation of policies in Indian villages. The answer could have important implications for the design of policies, especially policies that seek to avoid the recognized pitfalls of centralized delivery by exploiting the potential of decentralized mechanisms." (Dreze, Lanjouw and Sharma, 1998, Page?? ).

Few signs of changing inequality emerged in these studies, and serious inequalities persisted within villages. As noted, land reform itself was far too limited in its impacts to leave a legacy of low inequality in the country. Beginning in the 1990s, a period of increasing inequality took place (Deaton and Dreze 2002). In Kerala, however, inequality and poverty are much below the Indian average; the land reform was one factor, along with the opportunity to raise income through emigration and the state's progressive social policies in education, health, and so forth.

## Iran

Iran's agrarian reform history unfolded in the midst of a complicated political drama dominated by the battle for control of its oil. From the perspective of Iran's, and arguably the world's, future, it was a case of great consequence. As in Guatemala, failure to achieve land and other reforms when an opportune moment arose led to a disastrous long-term outcome. Unlike Guatemala, land reform was never the main source of contention, and when it did not proceed under Mohammad Mossadegh, it was undertaken only a decade later by Mohammed Reza Shah in a way that was probably not greatly different from what a Mossadegh government would have done. What was lost with Mossadegh's overthrow was not so much the benefits of an earlier land reform, but the possibility of a stable political future for this important Middle Eastern country. An optimal outcome would have required many things to go right; what did happen was the result of many things going wrong that could have turned out better.

The backdrop featured the dominant presence of Britain and the Anglo-Persian Oil Company (later British Petroleum) in the key oil industry, and the considerable unrest against a variety of perceived injustices, including those of exploited peasants against landlords. Mossadegh's popularity brought him to the Prime Minister's office in 1951; he was well known as an honest, democracy-oriented politician trying, among other things, to increase the power of the people against that of the crown. When, among other reforms, he nationalized the oil company in 1951, the British were very angry. Harry S. Truman's administration in the US was not sympathetic to that cause; Secretary of State Dean Acheson concluded that the British were "destructive and determined on a 'rule or ruin' policy in Iran" (Saikal 1980). Then, with the change to Dwight Eisenhower's administration in 1952, Prime Minister Winston Churchill plied the administration with the idea that Mossadegh, despite his open disgust for communism, would wind up being dependent on the pro-Soviet Tudeh Party (Schanzer 2004). The Dulles brothers, who personified the US administration's obsessive anti-communism slant, organized two coups to overthrow Mossadegh; Kermit Roosevelt (grandson of Theodore) was in Tehran to direct the second one. The Shah was afraid to go along and had to be persuaded—through bribery and other means—to sack Mossadegh. In the midst of turmoil, the Shah fled to Italy; the CIA believed the coup was failing and sent a cable to Roosevelt to call it off.[18] He ignored the cable and the coup proceeded successfully. The major impact of the US-orchestrated coup was to lay the ground for the Shah's ouster, decades later, in the Shia Revolution of 1979 and for the creation of one of the world's most repressive theocracies. That ouster caught the CIA, and the US more generally, off guard due to their underestimation of the degree of discontent under the Shah's rule. In 2000, Secretary of State Madeleine Albright voiced her regret for the coup against Mossadegh. Had the US administration not switched to an obsessively anti-communist one at the key point in time and had Kermit Roosevelt not ignored the cited cable, the outcome might have been much better for Iran and for the world.

[18] As revealed in documents declassified in 2017.

For many Iranians, Mossadegh has remained a revered figure. His brief administration introduced a wide range of social reforms, most notably the freeing of peasants from virtual serfdom and the requirement that landlords turn over twenty percent of their revenues, with half going to their tenants and half to a fund to pay for development projects such as public baths, rural housing, and pest control. A range of other social reforms included unemployment compensation and benefits to sick and injured workers.

In the event, the actual implementation of the country's land reform began in 1962 under the Shah. Unlike nearly all other reforms of significance, it was not a direct result of a revolution or pressure from below, but rather the decision of an authoritarian government not beholden to the country's agrarian interests. Fear that a communist revolution would be triggered by the great existing inequality was a major motivator, and the available revenues from oil made it easier to maintain a degree of control over all social groups. Between 1962 and the mid-1970s, about 2.3 million peasant families were direct beneficiaries of the replacement of the prior system, under which eighty percent of the farming population were either sharecroppers or landless workers and in which the landlords took huge shares (up to sixty to eighty percent) of the crop and benefited from free labor and other services in the off season. The expropriations had a major equalizing effect on the distribution of land. Growth of agricultural output accelerated from around 2.75 percent per year in the 1950s to a very high 4.6 percent from 1963 to 1978 (Majd 1991, 74). The reform was accompanied by a healthy expansion of rural non-agricultural employment, which contributed further to rapidly rising farm family incomes. One factor in the fast growth of such employment was probably the substantially greater land productivity of the smaller farms created by the reform than of the larger ones decreased or terminated by it.[19]

In short, this experience shared aspects of the classic reforms on the East Asian model; in the short-term, it brought all of the typical benefits. It has not entered the pantheon of great successes, partly because it has been less studied and there has been some debate about its effects,[20] partly because

[19] As of 1975, the farms of under ten hectares (81.7 percent of the total, with average size 2.7 hectares) produced fifty-eight percent of the output on thirty-three percent of the land; farms of ten to ninety-nine hectares produced 17.9 percent of output on fifty-two percent of land, while those of over one hundred hectares produced six percent on fifteen percent of the land (Majd 1991, 73). The land productivity of the small farms was thus 4.4 times greater than that of this last group.

[20] The reform was criticized by some for not doing enough and even for leading to an increase in inequality. Majd and Nowshirvani (1993) conclude that these criticisms were invalid and resulted primarily from a misreading of the data. The inclusion of much new land between 1960 and 1974 in the form of large holdings gave rise to the idea that the reform was not an equalizing one. The

it did not spell the end for large farms, and partly because it did not influence the medium-term economic and political trajectory of the country in the way that the reforms in Korea and Taiwan did. Although a clear success in the decade-plus following the reform, it did not set the course of future economic development; that path was determined primarily by oil. Nearing mid-century, Iran still depended on agriculture for the bulk of its employment; seventy-five percent of the workforce was so engaged in 1946. But this share then fell at an accelerating pace, to a little over fifty percent in 1960, and to thirty-four percent in 1976. The reform's effects thus coincided with a very sharp drop in agriculture's share of employment and a smaller decline in its absolute employment. Nor did this experience lay the base for a democratic society.

While the reform brought great economic and social benefits, the derailing of the one planned by Mossadegh a decade earlier had disastrous and long-lasting political and social effects, exemplifying the often-complicated interactions of land reform, internal politics, and international politics.

## Egypt

The Egyptian reform, which was begun in 1952 by General Gamal Abdul Nasser, became one of the twentieth century's better-known reforms, although its effects and the reasons for them have been the source of considerable debate. The setting had been created by the rise of commercial agriculture in the nineteenth century, which transformed a rural society where land was held in common by a village and granted in usufruct to individual families into a world of private ownership. The process generated a small class of wealthy absentee landowners; a somewhat larger class of relatively prosperous medium-sized farmers; and an enormous group of small farmers, sharecroppers, and landless laborers. As of 1950, just before the reform, the 1.5 percent of holdings with over fifty *feddans* (twenty-one hectares) had 39.1 percent of the land while the 9.3 percent with over ten *feddans* (4.2 hectares) had 63.5 percent. The median holding was about two feddans (0.85 hectares) (Adams 1985, 712).

government not only created a new peasant agriculture, via the reform, but also created the base for a new capitalist one made up of these large units in newly opened terrain.

The agrarian reform law of 1952 imposed an upper limit of 190 *feddans* (about eighty hectares), which the landholder could either farm himself or rent under specified conditions. Up to ninety-five additional *feddans* (forty hectares) might be held if the owner had children; any additional land had to be sold to the government. In 1961, the upper limit was reduced to one hundred *feddans* (forty-two hectares), with no one allowed to lease more than fifty *feddans* (twenty-one hectares). Compensation to former owners was in bonds bearing a low rate of interest, redeemable within forty years. A 1969 law further reduced the maximum holding to fifty *feddans*. This series of measures redistributed a little under fifteen percent of the arable land to about ten percent of the rural population.[21] Small peasant proprietors were the main beneficiaries.

Many early judgments (e.g., Warriner 1957) concluded that the series of reforms raised both the income and the morale and status of many peasant families. A good number of more recent assessments are also quite positive; thus Reem Saad (2002, 122) judged that in recent Egyptian history no other act was more empowering to the poor. This broad consensus was based on the idea that the land reform systematically destroyed the exploitative feudal system that had dominated Egyptian agriculture for generations. Many later views have been less positive. While it is likely that the non-economic benefits were substantial, the empirical evidence suggests that the economic ones were modest. To begin with, the amount of land that changed hands appears simply to have been too small to achieve major and widespread benefits. M. R. El-Ghonemy (2003, 6) contrasts the high ceilings original landholders were allowed to keep, even in the later reforms, with those of Korea's reform. The ceiling in Egypt as of 1964 was forty hectares and the average size of redistributed units was one hectare. The much more stringent Korean reforms of 1945 and 1950 established a ceiling of three hectares; the average beneficiary size was one hectare, with sixty-five percent of all arable land being redistributed among seventy-six percent of all agricultural households. The three-to-one ratio between the allowable retention limit and the average size of allocation to the beneficiaries contrasts with the forty-to-one ratio in Egypt as of the 1961 reform. The reported Gini coefficient

[21] As Lipton (2009, 294) notes, the high ceiling for the redistribution in 1961 meant that only a small share of farmland was redistributed; the value of the land not distributed was relatively high because virtually all of it was irrigated. By the mid-1980s, ninety percent of all land titles corresponded to holdings of less than five *feddans* (2.1 hectares) and about three hundred thousand families, or eight percent of the rural population, had received land under the program.

of land inequality fell in Egypt from 0.61 in 1952 to 0.46 in 1975, whereas that in Korea fell from 0.73 before the reform to 0.30 in 1970.[22] El-Ghomeny (1990, table 6.11, 209) estimated that the incidence of rural poverty fell in both cases, in Egypt from 56.1 percent in 1951 to 23.8 percent in 1965, and in Korea from sixty to eleven percent. In both countries, household income distribution was improved by land redistribution in a labor surplus setting and by wider access to education. The decline in poverty was similarly due to multiple factors at work; much of it in the form of off-farm earnings. Although Egypt's story may seem unimpressive when contrasted with Korea's, the numbers do leave open the possibility that the gains were quite significant.

Whether and how the Egyptian reforms affected productivity remains somewhat unclear,[23] but it is widely presumed that total output and income were not much affected, given the modest scale of redistribution and the fact that agriculture already operated in a very intensive fashion. Limitations placed on what the beneficiaries could do with the land have also been blamed for limiting benefits or even causing losses. Bent Hansen (1991) emphasizes that yields were already very high by international standards, so it was not to be expected that they would rise much, if at all, due to the reform. Since the period from the first reform in 1952 up to 1966 did see substantial increases, it was natural that some observers would credit these, at least in part, to the reform and such complementary measures as the regulation of land tenure and rent control.[24]

Did the Egyptian reform significantly raise the incomes of the beneficiaries and improve overall life quality? The rapid decline in poverty between 1951 and 1965 suggests that it did; however, other factors were clearly at work, too. Adams (1985) concludes that by the 1980s the limited possible further

[22] Data for Egypt presented by Hansen (1991, 219) show a more modest decline in inequality of the distribution of land. Interestingly, although the Gini coefficient of holdings (cultivated units) falls markedly from 0.68 to 0.48 from 1950 to 1977/1978, that of ownership drops only marginally, from 0.74 to 0.66. Hansen (1991) notes a presumed equalizing bias in the data, as a result of phenomena like fake contracts to avoid the reform laws, which were believed to be widespread.

[23] Probably the first quantitative analysis of the reform's effects was that of Gadalla (1962), who studied changes in the incomes of three hundred beneficiary farmers drawn randomly from three former estates with three hundred from matched estates not subject to expropriation and redistribution. From 1953 to 1956, he found that the former had a net farm income twenty percent above that of the latter.

[24] Hansen (1991, 106) notes that annual yield gains, after averaging 1.2 percent over the 1930s, slowed to 0.4 percent from 1940 to 1960, with most of the increase occurring in the late 1950s, possibly due to delayed effects of pre-war investments; another substantial increase (three year moving average increase of eleven percent, or 3.5 percent per year) took place from 1959 to 1966 mainly due, in his view, to the effects of the Aswan High Dam.

increases in land and labor inputs constrained the sector's future contribution. Continuing population growth and rising production costs had eroded many of the reform's benefits. Inheritance tended to fragment already small holdings, and the number of landless people had increased. Longer-term impacts on economic inequality at the national level also appear to have been modest; expenditure data suggest that it did not change much between 1958/1959 and 1982.[25] Judging by these estimates, Egypt was a middle equality country, well behind Korea and Taiwan but well ahead of most of Latin America.

Among those looking at the reform from the perspective of the 1980s or 1990s, a fairly broad consensus has been that, although it benefited a significant number of farm families and helped to end the earlier feudal practices, it did not produce a major short-term economic boost (because its scope was too limited) or a long-term positive impact on income distribution. One complicated and still open question involves the impacts of restrictions imposed on beneficiaries' cropping choices and the freedom to sell or divide their land on agricultural efficiency and on the distribution of income. El-Ghonemy (1992) found that the dominant path to land ownership was non-market transactions, including inheritance, interfamily marriage, and the land reform laws of 1952 and 1961. Samir Radwan and Eddie Lee (1986) reported that only fourteen percent of all households had ever purchased agricultural land and that they were predominantly larger landowners. Sellers were mainly very small landowners in the farm-size group of less than 0.4 hectares who sold under stress and became landless workers. In their recent analysis, Steven Brooke and Gabriel Koehler-Derrick (2020) conclude that restrictions on beneficiaries' decisions in these areas have been the unintentional source of continuing and avoidable poverty,[26] another illustration of how much things other than the redistribution of land can matter to a reform's impacts.

[25] Depending on the source, there was a small or a middling decline between 1958/1959 and 1964/1965 but then a return to the initial level (with the Gini coefficient in the mid-to-high 0.30s) for expenditure distribution (Hansen 1991, 221). The figure for income inequality was probably four to six points higher.

[26] They highlight the historic influence of the *'izba*, an "ubiquitous and coercive local agricultural institution that emerged in the early 1800s to facilitate the industrial-scale production of cotton, and lasted until a series of land reforms in the 1950s" (Brooke and Koehler-Derrick 2020) and, based on current regional differences in family incomes, conclude that the reform's land grants and the new co-op system to manage agricultural production combined to systematically depress the earning potential of former *'izba* residents. Further studies will presumably throw more light on this contention.

In such a land-scarce country as Egypt, eradication of poverty cannot rely mainly on agriculture; this gives special importance to non-agricultural activities that can be effectively undertaken along with farming. Richard H. Adams (2002) concluded that to further reduce poverty and improve income distribution in rural Egypt, policy makers needed to pay more attention to non-farm income, which then accounted for almost sixty percent of the total per capita income of the rural poor (defined as those in the lowest income quintile). One component of the non-farm income—income from unskilled labor in such fields as construction, brick making, and ditch-digging—accounted for over twenty-three percent of such income and had an important inequality-reducing impact.

## The Philippines

The backdrop for the Philippines's agrarian reform history has much in common with Latin American nations where the *hacienda* system was implanted, with its high level of land concentration. The recent setting shares much with SSA and other nations that are still substantially agricultural. The country is severely overpopulated due to a twentieth-century demographic explosion; as recently as 2000, population growth had only fallen to about two percent per year, and is now at just under 1.4 percent, after reaching 3.6 percent around 1950—one of the highest rates ever recorded anywhere, and comparable to a few SSA cases at or near their own peaks. Average farm size is, accordingly, extremely small and has fallen sharply—from 3.6 hectares in 1971 to 2.84 in 1980 and to 1.29 in 2012 (Philippine Statistics Authority 2021). This rate of shrinkage has probably slowed in the last few years with the declining growth of the agricultural labor force.[27] Agriculture no longer dominates the economy as it did in the early 1970s, when it accounted for half of all employment. By the first decade of the present century, agricultural employment in the Philippines had begun to shrink in absolute terms, and by 2018 it was down to twenty-six percent of the total. The sector's output growth has averaged 2.5 percent per year from 1970 to 2020; it was fastest during the 1970s, at 4.0 percent and from 2000 to 2010 at 3.5 percent. It was slowest during the 1980s, at 1.15 percent and through the last decade at 1.7 percent.

[27] The Philippines's experience invites comparison and contrast with that of Japan, another extremely heavily populated country but whose rate of population growth reached very low levels over the twentieth century and whose growth in per capita income took off.

As of 2012, with thirty-two percent of the labor force (twelve million people) engaged in agriculture, the agricultural census reported 5.56 million farms with 7.89 million parcels; about forty percent of the farms had less than one hectare and twenty-seven percent of all parcels were "home plots" (i.e., producing essentially for home consumption). About one-third of parcels had irrigation facilities, which covered one-quarter of all land. The one percent of farms with ten hectares or more had 17.1 percent of all the land and the 11.1 percent with three hectares and up had 51.5 percent (Philippine Statistics Authority 2015, 3). The thirty-nine percent with less than half a hectare averaged only 0.13 hectare; as a result, generating a reasonable level of earnings thus called for extremely intensive farming, usually accompanied by non-agricultural income. Some families, in effect, had only their home plots. "Effective landlessness"[28] was thus common; the United States Agency for International Development (USAID) (2011) estimated it at seventy percent of all farmers.[29] Among those who operate land, the level of concentration appears to have remained constant from the 1950s into the present century, with a modest Gini coefficient of 0.5–0.55 (Lipton 2009, 285).

Land has been increasingly degraded by a combination of population growth, conversion of marginal lands into production, increasing use of chemicals, and other practices. With the available land per person falling continuously, many poor rural families have been pushed to ill-suited uplands. Agricultural intensification has raised land productivity but also damaged the land (Briones 2005). The rate of deforestation has been one of the fastest in the world, driven not only by agricultural conversion but also by large scale logging for export. Results include destroyed topsoil, disrupted water flows, and frequent landslides.

Although the country has achieved good GDP growth—an average of 4.3 percent since 1965—per capita income growth has been much slower, at a modest 1.9 percent, as over one-half of the total economic growth has been "eaten up" by the demographic explosion. With the latter finally slowing, it is now a less serious impediment to increasing living standards.

[28] Use of this term reflects the inevitable ambiguity with respect to how much land a family needs to not be defined as landless. Space sufficient only for a small vegetable garden may preclude a family's engagement in any other agricultural activities.

[29] Among information anomalies is the fact that the 2012 census reported about one-quarter less land than did those of 1980, 1991, and 2002, with declines registered in all size categories above one hectare. The share of holdings with above ten hectares fell from 2.08 percent to 0.99 percent, and their share of total area fell from 20.31 percent to 17.13 percent. The share of holdings with less than one hectare rose from 40.1 percent to 56.9 percent. Methodological changes between the 2012 and earlier censuses are likely the cause of these apparent inconsistencies.

Overpopulation and the saleable skills of many citizens have laid the groundwork for massive emigration over recent decades, peaking at over three hundred thousand in 2010, or about twenty percent of the natural population increase. The rate of emigration has since dropped and now amounts to only about five percent of the population growth. Remittances from family abroad have recently accounted for around ten percent of GDP.

The Philippines has been and remains a country with a high level of income inequality. World Bank (2018, 24) data point to a modest decline in the Gini coefficient of household per capita income from 2006 to 2015 from about 0.48 to about 0.44. Apart from one sharp upward spike around 1997, there has been little measured change over the whole period during which household surveys have been available (1961 and onward).[30] Inequality within the agricultural sector provided the main historical base for enduring inequality at the national level; the absence of a major agrarian reform helps to explain why it has not fallen significantly. While not as high as in the world's extreme cases, it still accounts for much avoidable poverty as average income has been low—a parallel with pre-revolutionary China.

As elsewhere, the effort and success in redistributive land reform has depended essentially on political factors. The Philippines has featured democratic elections most of the time since the end of the American colonial period and the Japanese rule during World War II, but it has typically suffered from serious corruption[31] and policymakers have been beholden to a powerful agricultural oligarchy.[32]

It appears that the possible benefits from a well-designed and executed land reform could have been substantial. In its 1973 Mission report, the International Labour Organization (ILO) (1974, 491) estimated that, at a maximum, a total expropriation of large units would lower the Gini coefficient for income by about four percentage points (e.g., from 0.50 to 0.46); an intermediate guess might have put the impact at half as much.[33] A significant reform might have effected a net transfer of two to three percent of

[30] See Berry (1978) and Estudillo (1997) for studies of different time frames within that period. Both report very little change.

[31] In 2020, it was ranked at number 115 out of 180 countries on the corruption perceptions index.

[32] For critical analyses of the politics of land at different points of time see Putzel (1992) and Putzel and Morales (2002).

[33] The assumed transfer of income came from the richest twenty percent of urban dwellers (to which the landlords belonged) and was equally shared among the lower forty percent of rural dwellers (to which the rice and maize tenant farmers mainly belonged). The assumption of this much income being transferred is a very optimistic one.

the national income.[34] Potential productivity gains were less obvious than distributional ones but, by the 1970s, they were coming to be recognized by students of agriculture as evidence of the relatively high land productivity of small farms emerged.[35]

Compared to other countries, debate around agrarian structure and productive efficiency in the Philippines has focused less on size structure, where the gap between large and small is not as dramatic as in many Latin American countries—and more on the form of tenure and the efficiency of the rental market. In a system with much sharecropping and/or land rental, access to ownership by the sharecroppers and renters can imply a large net increase in their income. The impact on total agricultural output depends on how tenure affects productivity. Where the main goal is not to raise aggregate output but to redistribute income, and where the current share of the owner (explicit in share-cropping or implicit in rental fees) is high, then small differences in productivity may not be a major issue.

## Reforms and Their Effects

Need and pressure for reform has long been apparent in the Philippines. Perhaps the best opportunity lost was in the aftermath of the Spanish–American War of 1898, when the military governor Arthur MacArthur was pushing for reform.[36]

The Philippines has retained its agrarian-based elite and its violence ever since, despite various attempts at reform (Puntzel 1992) and reasonable expectations that such reform would raise total agricultural output

[34] From 1970 to 2020, the share of value added in agriculture fell from about thirty percent to about ten percent. During the 1970s and 1980s, when it was closer to the former level, a transfer of ten percent of agricultural income would thus have implied a transfer of 3.0–4.5 percent of national income.

[35] One source was the ILO (1974, special paper 5 on agrarian reform). A strong IR was reported later by Hayami et al. (1990). Berry and Cline (1979, 73–74) note that, in the absence of data on land quality by size, there is ambiguity as to the presence or strength of a quality-constant IR, but they also note that the provinces with larger farm sizes record lower land value per hectare. Larger farms leave more land fallow, in permanent pasture, and in forest. When these lands are excluded, crop output per cultivated area is essentially constant between units of 0.5 hectares and those close to one hundred hectares, although for palay rice the yields are much higher for very small farms of under 0.5 hectares. Yield differentials were not marked apart from this, even though smaller farms had an advantage in coconuts and larger ones in sugar cane. The strong negative association between production and size (unadjusted for quality) comes from the much higher ratio of animal products per non-cropped area on the smaller units (Berry and Cline 1979, 86).

[36] Future president William Howard Taft, then Civilian Governor in the Philippines, and McArthur clashed frequently.

as well as greatly improving the distribution of income (Berry and Cline 1979). At the time of the Spanish–American War, some internal forces in the US were pushing for it to nudge the Philippines toward democracy, while President Theodore Roosevelt's own initial inclination was more toward empire-building. The urgent need for reform has not abated over time as agricultural employment grew, total land available per person shrunk, and governments did little to correct the high level of concentration, although rising land productivity and the growth of non-agricultural employment opportunities did ease the stress. Some of the reform efforts have incorporated useful and promising components. Over the years, the country has pioneered efforts to devolve control of rural development to farmers, including participatory irrigation efforts in the 1970s, it has achieved early successes with community-based coastal resource management on Apo and Sumilon islands, and it has passed legislation on social and community forestry that provided models for much of Asia (Gollin and Kho 2002). But reform has generally been too limited in scale and/or too inefficiently implemented to meet the challenge, a result of both political opposition and bureaucratic incompetence/corruption.

Failures dating far back in time illustrate the many obstacles in the way. In response to tenant farmers' complaints about the sharecropping system, President Quezon implemented the Rice Share Tenancy Act of 1933 to establish minimum standards. It provided for a fifty–fifty sharing of the crop, regulation of the interest rate at a maximum of ten percent per year, and a safeguard against arbitrary dismissal by the landlord (Manapat 1961). But its use required that the majority of municipal councils in a province petition for it. With landowners typically controlling those councils, no province ever did so. Quezón then ordered that the act be mandatory in all Central Luzon provinces; but contracts were only of one year's duration and by simply refusing to renew them, landlords were able to evict tenants. During the period of post-war US control, the military helped to curtail peasant protests (Puntzel 1992). When independence came in 1946, there was much pressure on the democratically elected government to undertake some redistribution. The Agricultural Land Reform Code (RA 3844) enacted in 1963 under President Diosdado Macapagal included sensible objectives and aimed at establishing an owner–cultivator system of family-based agriculture. But, with many of the democratically elected officeholders being landowners themselves or coming from land-owning families, major advance was not forthcoming.

One of the pivotal regimes for those hopeful for serious reform was that of Corazon Aquino, who came to power through the "People's Power Revolution" when her predecessor Ferdinand Marcos tried to steal an election in 1985; she put that goal at the center of her social agenda.[37] In 1988, the Comprehensive Agrarian Reform Law (CARP) paved the way for the redistribution of agricultural lands to tenant-farmers, with landowners to be paid "just compensation" and allowed to retain a maximum of five hectares. A total of 10.3 million hectares was programmed for distribution over a ten-year period, of which 6.5 million hectares of public alienable lands and forest areas were to be distributed by the Department of Environment and Natural Resources (DENR) while 3.8 million hectares of private agricultural lands and resettlement areas were to be allotted by the Department of Agrarian Reform (DAR).[38] After twelve years of implementation, the program was reported to have redistributed 5.33 million hectares of land or 53.4 percent of all farmland and about 3.1 million rural poor households, constituting about forty-two percent of the total agricultural population, were said to have benefited directly (Moreno and Evangelista 2011, 13). In December 2017, DAR announced that of a total area of 5.4 million hectares that fell under CARP's scope, the government had distributed 4.8 million hectares. Such positive numbers stand in dramatic contrast with various alternative estimates; for example Michael Lipton (2009), while accepting that the amount of land titled had been large, guessed that only three hundred thousand hectares, or about 2.5 percent of cultivable land, had actually been redistributed, with between 8.5 and eleven million rural workers remaining essentially landless. Such discrepancies are partly due to the unreliability of official figures, the result of some combination of deception and inefficiency; meanwhile unofficial estimates necessarily suffer from a good deal of guesswork. Considerable uncertainty thus remains both with respect to what has happened on the reform front and how beneficial it has

[37] After the assassination of her husband, prominent Marcos critic Senator Benigni Aquino Jr. in 1983, she emerged as leader of the opposition and ran against Marcos in a 1985 election. When he was proclaimed winner despite serious allegations of fraud, she mounted a non-violent mass demonstration movement—the cited "People's Power Revolution"—which, aided by defections from the Armed Forces and support from the Philippine Catholic Church, successfully ousted Marcos in February 1986. Soon, however, her family background and social class as a privileged daughter of a wealthy, landed clan became a lightning rod of criticisms against her land reform agenda.

[38] The 1991 agricultural census recorded a total of 4.6 million holdings and 9.9 million hectares. Thus, the cited 3.8 million hectares would have constituted thirty-eight percent of that land.

been. While no one sees the reforms as having solved the land problem, some do believe that they have made a significant contribution while others do not.

Several studies have concluded that over its initial decade the CARP program had a positive impact on land ownership and poverty reduction (FAO 2002; Binswanger-Mkhize et al. 2009). A survey conducted by the Philippines Institute of Agrarian Studies found that incomes of agrarian reform beneficiaries had increased by twenty-one percent from their 1989 levels (Moreno and Leones 2011, 11). Prudencia U. Gordoncillo (2012) doubts that the results were so positive.[39] Many outcomes have probably reflected both reform efforts and other agricultural and related policies.

The evolution of TFP provides one measure of how much the sector has advanced (e.g., as a result of research and development of better varieties). But here, too, the picture remains somewhat unclear. There has been a general presumption among students of Philippine agriculture, and those comparing its performance with those of other ASEAN countries, that progress has been slow.[40] As noted, agricultural growth has been modest at an average of 2.5 percent per year from 1970 to 2010, consistent with a slow TFP advance.

The combination of policies directed at agriculture since the 1970s have, by and large, failed to meet the needs of the agricultural population. Land redistribution has not occurred on a large scale, and productivity has not risen rapidly. Despite the positive-leaning picture painted by various governments—whether of their plans or their achievements—nothing like a solution to the agrarian problem has been achieved. Agricultural census data do show a trend toward smaller farms over time and a decreasing share of area in large ones; presumably, the reforms have contributed something to this trend. But in such a heavily populated country even a significant positive contribution is not inconsistent with failure to resolve the problem; that

[39] Gordoncillo (2012) questions earlier results based on simple over time comparisons of income and poverty as between beneficiaries and non-beneficiaries, on the grounds that missing variables may have biased their results. With a more complete econometric approach and the inclusion of other variables like wealth and expenditures, the economic benefits no longer emerged as statistically significant.

[40] A more positive assessment comes from Teruel and Dumagan (2011, 11) who estimate an average TFP growth of 2.2 percent per year from 1974 to 2004. This, however, appears implausible in light of the fact that agricultural output growth averaged only 2.1 percent per year over that period.

challenge may simply have been too big for anything but a total overhaul to bring success.[41]

Apart from the simple magnitude of the challenge, other explanations for failure of the reform to meet its goals have been focused on weak design; in particular, the focus on titling rather than on redistribution despite evidence that titling does not guarantee land's successful use by the intended recipient. Another factor has been the lack of adequate support for the small-farm sector in general and especially for new farmers; while the number of small farms has increased over the decades, financial and technical support have not. Banks must comply with a requirement that they direct a minimum amount of credit to agriculture, but they have done so by lending mostly to large agribusinesses. In the worst cases, where land was distributed but no complementary services were provided, farmers with little experience in management have ended up leasing or selling it and becoming landless again. A third factor has been the general inefficiency of administration around the reform. These problems reflect the continuing resistance of the larger farmers, some of whom are not very large in absolute terms themselves.

The value of land titling in situations of informal control and use has been argued by Hernan de Soto (2000) and others on the grounds that formal titles spur investment by the owner and facilitate efficiency-inducing land markets. But a focus on titling, rather than on actual land redistribution, has been widely criticized as a design flaw by experts in land reform, among them Klaus Deininger and Hans Binswanger (1999). In the Philippines context, Jeffrey D. Michler and Gerald E. Shively (2015, 166) find no evidence that the provision of land titles has contributed to efficient land markets. At the same time, they find that, despite their informal nature, land rental contracts appear to be secure and do not lower efficiency. The CARP Law thus failed in its objective of generating more effective land rental markets.[42] The Philippines's experience thus exemplifies the limitations of formal titles

[41] The closest recent parallel to the Philippines, in terms of land scarcity, has probably been Vietnam (see Chapter 5). Its overall success provides a dramatic contrast to the Philippines experience.

[42] Their analysis of agricultural census data and additional survey data leads Adamopoulos and Restuccia (2020) to conclude that the 1988 reform was a failure because it had a negative impact (seventeen percent) on labor productivity and on average farm size (thirty-four percent). The use of labor productivity as the measure of efficiency makes this study non-comparable to most others; these impacts are not inconsistent with rising efficiency measured by land productivity or by correctly measured TFP. (How analysis of labor productivity fits into the efficiency questions is discussed in more detail in Chapter 3.) Despite its different focus, this study points to many ways in which a reform like that in the Philippines could curtail sectoral efficiency.

in providing, by themselves, a secure base for agricultural activities and investment in contexts where such titles are not in fact secure. It shares much with cases like Colombia, where security is a very complex matter. Its experience is highly relevant to many countries of SSA as they transition toward formal rights.

Along with such key design flaws as the excessive focus on titling, the programs have been riddled with inefficiencies, many of course benefiting the landlords through their ability to operate extra-legally. Outdated land administration laws, an inefficient land administration and adjudication infrastructure, and a poor information system have contributed to fraudulence, to overlapping and duplication of titles, and to widespread land-grabbing. They have also contributed to high transaction costs in securing, registering, and transferring property rights, and to tenure insecurity. Opportunism plays a role, as does bureaucratic inefficiency and dishonesty.[43] Activists say officials have accepted thousands of fraudulent claims. As usual, individuals within various institutions involved have been aware of the shortcomings and have made attempts to resolve them. But for many of these problems, the best possible option is only a partial solution.[44] Thus, even after a recent attempt to develop a transaction scheme more favorable to beneficiaries, the process still tends to favor landlords (Tadem 2015). Congress has typically kept available funding down to avoid[45] coverage of the lands owned by senators. Because of the unwillingness to tamper with large corporate producers, especially those which export, as most do, the reform program has had different impacts across regions; some areas with huge plantations have remained virtually untouched.

One factor that might have been expected to facilitate a more positive outcome on the agricultural front has been the Philippines's relatively high level of education given its stage of economic development.[46] Within a strong family-farm system, education can be a source of many benefits, among them faster productivity growth as new technologies become available. An analysis by Leonardo Lanzona (2013) suggests that this was the case when

[43] CARP allowed landowners to retain up to five hectares, in addition to three hectares for each heir. Landowners filed petitions for exemptions and are alleged to have installed fraudulent beneficiaries on their land.

[44] Moreno and Leones (2011) describe many of the problems and the attempted solutions for them.

[45] CARP allowed landowners to retain up to five hectares, in addition to three hectares for each heir. Landowners filed petitions for exemptions and are alleged to have installed fraudulent beneficiaries on their land.

[46] The Philippines ranks high on years of education relative to income per capita, but low on PISA scores, with many critics arguing that it is not very successful in teaching students how to think.

the new Green Revolution varieties were introduced in the 1970s.[47] The insecurities around the land reform attempts probably kept those benefits lower than they might have been.

## The Price of Falling Short

The inadequacy of Philippines's reform efforts has imposed a high cost. As noted above, although growth of the GDP has been relatively good over the last half century, the GDP per person has been substantially less so. Agrarian structure remains a barrier to social and economic progress, as evidenced by the still low incomes of most people who work there and the continuing land conflict. Relative to reasonable goals, the combination of policies directed at the sector since 1980 have, by and large, failed. Land redistribution has not occurred on a large scale and implementation has never been effective enough to bring most of its potential benefits. The Philippines exemplifies the inability of formal titles to provide a secure base for agricultural activities and investment in them when such titles are in fact not secure. The experience shares much with cases like Colombia in the complexity of achieving tenure security. Conflict remains a serious problem, now against a backdrop of drug-related violence and encouraged, during the recent Duterte government, by extra-judicial killings.

As the USAID (2011, 3) noted a decade ago: "Unequal access to land and natural resources by poor people is a key driver of conflict and an obstacle to national development, fueling social unrest and armed uprisings. Indigenous peoples are marginalized and have been pushed out of their ancestral lands by the government for infrastructure projects, and by private farming interests and natural resource concession holders." Recent years have seen a continuation of the ever-present friction, despite government efforts, some more serious and some less so. Most reform beneficiaries have continued to live below the poverty line. Over the years, many protesters have been treated as criminals and their demands answered with violence. Harassment, incarceration, and the murder of farmers asserting their rights

[47] The author used survey data from the Bicol region for 1978 and 1994; the former year coincided with the introduction of the modern Green Revolution varieties. He finds significant positive productivity impacts from both college and high school education of family members in 1978 but not in 1994. When total value of production was the dependent variable, the advantage of college was estimated at twenty-one percent in 1978 but only 4.8 percent in 1994 (Lanzona 2013, 19).

to land have continued (Tadem 2016). Clashes have appeared when land plots have been reallocated from small landholders to landless farmers.

As in Brazil, the Philippines's reform processes have encouraged farmers to fight for their rights to land. Some who have brought their claims to court have succeeded, but many are blocked when landowners file complaints against them on often trumped-up charges. Small farmers tend to lose their cases even when they have sufficient supporting evidence, as landlords exert their influence on the judiciary (Olea 2014). According to rights groups, hundreds of farmers were arrested, and at least 114 killed amid a rural crackdown during Rodrigo Duterte's presidency from 2016 to 2022. His simplistic, hard-line approach to crime—famous for its disregard for human rights—garners considerable support among part of the population in a setting of physical insecurity, a parallel to Bolsonaro's popularity in Brazil.[48]

Overall, and despite the long-standing need for and pressure to undertake serious land reform and the fact that a modest amount of redistribution has taken place, it has failed to bring the major benefits that it might have. Millions of lives have been less rewarding than they might have in terms of income, economic security, and other advantages. Population growth has remained higher than it might have due to low rural incomes. In a case like this one, where the political corruption and elite control that prevented substantial land reform has probably also held the country back economically in other ways and has kept overall poverty high, that failure has brought negative multiplier effects.

All this makes the case additionally relevant to SSA, where countries are transitioning toward formal rights. In its combining very small farms—with size shrinking over time—and very rapid population growth, the Philippines presents a close parallel to many SSA countries, especially those where population is densest. Its higher income inequality than most of those countries and its lack of political capacity to choose an equitable growth path built more firmly around the small family farm shines a threatening light on what may go wrong in a number of SSA countries.

[48] Chandran (2018) quotes Lito Lao, chairperson of the agricultural workers' union in Mindanao, to the effect that, "Thirty years after the law was passed, land has not been given to peasant farmers who have tilled the land for generations. Instead, farmers are getting killed for demanding their right to land, and dummy beneficiaries have been settled by landlords on land meant for the landless."

# SECTION III

# IMPLICATIONS OF PAST GLOBAL HISTORY FOR THE FUTURE IN SUB-SAHARAN AFRICA AND ELSEWHERE

In this section of the book, Chapter 8 reviews the current state of agriculture in Sub-Saharan Africa (SSA) and the implications of earlier land reform experiences for this part of the world, on the grounds that it is most relevant there. Chapter 9 then summarizes the main conclusions.

# 8

# The Last Battleground for Rural Land Issues

## Sub-Saharan Africa

### Historical and Ecological Backgrounds to the Present Challenges

The lessons of agrarian history from the now-industrialized world and from the relatively advanced developing countries (e.g., Latin America and East Asia) have their greatest current relevance in the still largely agricultural countries of the world, especially those of Sub-Saharan Africa (SSA). A different history, interrupted in the nineteenth century by European colonialism, with its heyday of conquest in the 1880s, has left a post-independence legacy in which the pattern, so prevalent elsewhere, of very high land concentration accompanied by serfdom, slavery, share-cropping, or other mechanisms for the subjection of labor to large landholders has been infrequent.[1]

During their presence in SSA, the European colonial powers could be seen as playing the "landlord role" in a system of serfdom, leaving legacies similar to those found elsewhere. Like the landlord classes everywhere, the colonials saw their African underlings as inferior, and also needful of strict and sometimes harsh treatment to make sure they did the work assigned to them. It was generally not presumed, or even comprehensible, that they could be quite competent farmers on their own. One of the great surprises for some colonials as they began to produce and export crops like cocoa was that African peasants could do it just as well; to prevent such unwanted competition, they were sometimes banned from exporting or producing the items. Like those with power in other unequal systems, the interlopers pushed

[1] The main relatively recent exceptions on this count have been Ethiopia, with its long and relatively uninterrupted history, and former European colonies like South Africa.

*The Great Curse*. Albert Berry, Oxford University Press. © Oxford University Press 2024.
DOI: 10.1093/oso/9780197782675.003.0009

peasants off land that they themselves wanted; a storied example was Kenya in the 1930s. Among European colonials, Belgium's King Leopold became particularly famous for the cruelty inflicted under his watch. He thought of the Belgian Congo as his own fiefdom and he is sometimes identified, together with Hitler, Stalin, and Mao, as one of the four great perpetrators of death over the century from 1880 to 1980. Each of the others was responsible for the loss of at least twenty million lives; Leopold's legacy includes an estimated ten million lives lost through a combination of violence, hunger, and famine (Hochschild 1998). As the European powers gradually retreated from their African colonies in the post-World War II period, Belgium was the least willing to do so.

Nineteenth-century European colonialism disrupted the larger and more powerful African powers that did exist and forced the rest of the continent into subservience. The region had earlier been victimized by the international slave trade, in which some local groups participated as intermediaries; that phase of its history also left many negative legacies.[2] But, except for a few countries, slavery or pseudo-slavery has not been a prominent feature of society since its independence, and most of it does not involve agriculture.[3] Nor is land concentration typically high by developing country standards, although it appears to be rising in a number of countries. The vast majority of people who earn their living mainly from agriculture operate small farms. Looking ahead, the big challenge on this front is to avoid the injustices and inequality that have accompanied land concentration in other parts of the world. While there are no obvious economic obstacles to achieving this goal in most countries of the region, there are many political ones. Developing strong research and diffusion systems for new technologies to help small farmers raise their productivity, once a big challenge in the region due to lack of funds and technical skills, is now much more feasible. It can still be blocked, however, by a political preference to serve larger farms, an already

[2] Nunn (2007, 2008) traces many of present-day SSA's societal problems to the slave trade.

[3] Mauritania was the last nation to officially abolish the practice (in 2007), although by one recent estimate 4.3 percent of its population still remained enslaved. In Niger, a 2008 law which threatened to bring the practice back appears to have had little or no effect. A number of other nations have also *de facto* retained the practice. But, by most definitions, this region is not a major center of slavery. Kevin Bales, co-founder of *Free the Slaves*, defines modern slavery as being present "when a person is under control of another person, who applies violence and force to maintain that control, and the goal of that control is exploitation." By this definition, the *Walk Free Foundation* estimated that, in 2016, the world had about 45.8 million slaves, or about 0.6 percent of the population, with fifty-eight percent of them living in five countries—India, Pakistan, China, Bangladesh, and Uzbekistan. Only a small share were male agricultural laborers. Many were females and children.

existing tendency that has been strengthened in some countries by a recent expansion of the number in the medium- and large-size farms (above five hectares) and in some instances by their good production performance. Then there are the business interests that benefit from selling their fertilizers and seeds, the latter often of the non-reproducing type designed to force the user to purchase new seeds each year. These interests typically prefer dealing with, and thus they favor, larger farms.

Colonialism left an unpromising political legacy of centralized and authoritarian governments, a tradition from which the region has only slowly begun to emerge. This history shares much with that of Latin America, where the shift toward democracy began around the beginning of the twentieth century and took most of that century to become fairly complete. Authoritarian regimes have facilitated corruption, long-term personal rule, and use of the military to retain power.[4] As a result, there has been little space for local government or for the direct participation by most people. This, in turn, has limited agricultural progress because those in national governments, even in the unusual cases where they have some knowledge of agriculture in general, are typically unaware of the degree to which settings vary by region and of the corresponding need to proceed differently according to locale.

The agricultural history of SSA has been very tied to its ecology. As Ewout Frankema (2014, 19) puts it, "few scholars would dispute that Africa offered a comparatively inhospitable environment for sustaining large concentrations of people. Apart from the high incidence of tropical diseases such as malaria, there were a number of barriers to the development of sedentary agriculture." The region is not well-endowed with navigable rivers. The bulk of its cultivable land lies in the tropics and, although many edible crops can be produced in rain forests, food cannot be stored for long in such warm and moist climates, limiting the processing and trading of food items. Tropical soils, although fertile, become exhausted quickly; this favors systems of extensive land use and day-to-day harvests of roots, tubers, and starchy fruit, such as plantain, for immediate consumption, along with the production of cereal grains. The tsetse fly, which causes sleeping sickness in people and kills cattle and horses, leaves much cultivable land in the tropical forests unsuitable for mixed farming. The fly further hampers the intensification and commercialization of agriculture by:

[4] For a recent study of Benin, see Bourguignon (2023).

> "limiting ox-plough cultivation, reducing the animal manure available for soil regeneration, limiting sources of animal protein, and curbing the use of cattle and horses for transportation purposes. Hence, unlike Eurasia where a considerable part of the energy used in soil preparation and transportation was supplied by animals, in tropical Africa the energy came from scarce human labour. The hoe remained the principle tool for soil preparation and humans were directly responsible for moving goods over large distances. Large parts of the African savannah outside the tsetse-infested forest zone cope with prolonged periods of drought. The highly erratic rainfall patterns caused by the Asian-Australian monsoon system, turn the cultivation decisions of many East African farmers into a repeated gamble" (Frankema 2014, 19)

Poverty in Africa was rooted historically in the high exposure to tropical diseases and pre-mature death, but those who survived were relatively well nourished. Cattle herders, with unusual access to animal protein and dairy in exceptional quantities, were exceptionally tall for pre-industrial standards (Moradi 2012). A rinderpest epidemic that swept across East and Southern Africa in the 1890s killed about ninety percent of all cattle. Pastoral groups, such as the Masai in Kenya, starved to death in large numbers as well. This became the first animal disease to be wiped out. (The World Health Organization [WHO] declared the disease to be eradicated on June 28, 2011.)

Early independent African states were fiscally weak, their bureaucracies were understaffed and undereducated, and there was a widespread incapacity to support economic policymaking with reliable statistical information. State policies designed to serve the national interests were paralyzed by a mosaic of ethnic, religious, and tribal identities. If early independent African states were able to secure a monopoly on the use of violence in the first place, it tended to be an unstable one (Frankema 2014, 20). It has been widely argued that the creation of "states without nations" (i.e., without a sense of solidarity, usually built on ethnicity and history) was among the worst of the long-term legacies of European colonial rule in Africa. The crux of the problem, both under colonial rule and afterward, was how to integrate relatively isolated and mobile groups of people, scattered across large spaces, under a central state administration with taxing capacity. Because control over people, rather than land, was key to achieving political ambitions, there was little incentive to formalize institutions for land tenure; exceptions included alienation of land for European settlers in Southern and Eastern Africa, and the concession of large tracts of land in Central Africa for private companies and missionaries. In parts of West Africa, European land ownership was discouraged, or even prohibited (Frankema 2014, 21). The improvement of subsistence agriculture was given no priority and, in some cases, also suffered from the withdrawal of labor to spur the more profitable sectors of the colonial economy. The lack of well-defined rules of land tenure led to increasing conflicts with the rapid closing of the land frontier in the twentieth century. Thus, as the Green Revolution emerged in Asia, African states were unlikely beneficiaries; in fact, that Green Revolution became an obstacle to agricultural advance in SSA. The increasing supply of food grains, and especially rice, flooded the world market in the midst of a long-term trend of falling food prices since the mid-nineteenth century; real food prices dropped by ten to fifteen percent between the 1967 and 1992. Cheaper than ever before, imported food benefited the urban population but also relieved the pressure on African governments to strengthen their agricultural development programs. The food price hikes of recent years, which have led to some food riots, suggest that the era of cheap food has come to an end. This is a boon to African food producers; however, even with this reversal, it would be unrealistic to expect it to foster a repetition of the Asian Green Revolution in Africa. The variety in Africa's ecological conditions and historical development trajectories is one broad barrier.[5]

Timing is a crucial aspect of revolutions. The standard narrative portrays the Green Revolution as a technological breakthrough in the development of new, high-yielding varieties of cereal grains, especially wheat, rice, and maize, between the early 1940s and the late 1970s. The new varieties were designed to transform higher inputs of water and artificial fertilizer into a larger number of kernels per ear. "Heavier ears were made to grow on shorter and stronger stems in order to prevent the plants from lodging. The cultivation of new varieties was complemented by an intensified use of machinery, irrigation, and a wide range of insecticides, pesticides and herbicides"

[5] Countries do differ, of course. As Frankema (2014, 23) states, "though one can be more optimistic about West African coastal countries such as Ghana, Senegal and Benin, with a comparatively strong historical record of commercialization but less so about landlocked countries in the interior such as Niger, Chad, or the Central African Republic. The more densely populated countries with a historical legacy of intensification, such as Rwanda, Burundi and Uganda are in a more favourable position than giant colonial constructs such as the Democratic Republic of Congo."

(Frankema 2014, 18). Most of the elements of the Green Revolution, like fertilizer, had been available for quite some time. So, the real change was not so much technological as its overall rapid diffusion. Asian governments channeled substantial public resources into the development of rural infrastructure and credit facilities, and they subsidized and coordinated technical support to farmers. They offered infant-industry protection to emerging fertilizer industries and, in some cases, went as far as to distribute micro-packages of hybridized seed and fertilizer to encourage farmers to grow new cultivars.

"The political momentum that pushed Asian governments into such a pro-active role had been building up during the Cold War. The Americans, in particular, feared that the impoverished masses in Asia would act as a magnet to socialist propaganda. The term 'Green Revolution' was introduced to contrast America's foreign policy with the violence associated with Red guerilla movements; green was the color of peace" (Frankema 2014, 19). Peaceful scientific progress was presented as the capitalist alternative to combat hunger, poverty, and inequality (Cullather 2010).

## The Current Setting

Because of the region's unusual historical experience, land concentration issues play out in a different context from those discussed in earlier chapters. Only a few reforms have been undertaken. More important than the success or failure of those attempts are (i) preventing land concentration from rising to an undesirable level and (ii) sorting out how this goal fits into the broader challenge of achieving large and widely distributed benefits from agricultural growth over the coming decades.

Looking to the future, optimists note that, whatever other burdens these newly independent countries have had to bear, extreme inequality of land distribution, with the associated extractive landlords and income inequality[6]

[6] Information remains inadequate to identify income distribution trends in most SSA countries, but most available point-of-time estimates suggest inequality levels far below those of the Latin American cases associated historically with a high concentration of land (see Hall et al. 2021). It appears safe to assume that this was true previously as well. Some countries or regions (e.g., today's Ethiopia) have had strongly hierarchical governments at various times in the past. Land concentration was no doubt high, and conditions exploitative, factors that led to the land reform under the communist government from 1974 to 1991. How that pre-1970s land concentration would compare with that of Latin countries is unknown. Few, if any, regions in SSA have experienced a long and

has not been a major one; many African societies have been built more around tribe and extended family, with a good deal of mutual support built into those patterns. Customary rights to land have been a historical norm; one result has been the relative absence of landless rural families, in contrast to both Asia and Latin America. All this makes the region a historical anomaly. Pessimists, drawing on tragic experiences like the Rwandan genocide, judge that the frequent conflict between tribes and ethnic groups in the same country has the potential to replay the world's earlier historic pattern of violent conflict for control of land, or the more recent stories, like that of Colombia.[7] They note the ever-present role of political corruption in ongoing land accumulation in SSA as a parallel with other regions. And the countries where income inequality has at some point become high, particularly in South Africa, manifest the universal pattern that it tends to stay high even when an important initial cause (in this case, the racial divide) wanes in importance. Coming later than other countries to given stages of development and of labor scarcity, they are more likely to introduce labor-displacing mechanization; early newer technological options mean that, for some types of production, less labor is needed than at similar phases of agricultural development elsewhere. This is bad if it costs many agricultural workers their jobs without raising output. It is good if it creates an opening for small farmers to mechanize their own plots, raise productivity and incomes on the farm, and free some of the family's labor to take productive jobs elsewhere, as was the case with the introduction of the two-wheel tractor in Japan. Both phenomena are apparent in SSA.

Today's agricultural challenge in SSA is to achieve rapid output growth, maintain a relatively egalitarian distribution of income, and foster income and food security, which, as evidenced by the successful experiences elsewhere, feeds into fast overall growth, rising education, and falling birth and population growth rates. Slower population growth and faster agricultural and overall economic growth contribute to both rapidly rising income

stable agricultural ruling class over hundreds of years. Land concentration rose quickly in a few cases in which Europeans invaded and took control of much territory. Recent income inequality data put countries like Ethiopia, with a Gini coefficient of 0.33 or 0.35 according to the World Bank, far below those of most Latin American countries, which fall into the range of 0.45 to 0.50 (World Bank n.d.).

[7] As with Colombia, Rwanda's conflict has been widely understood as essentially ethnic in nature, but there, too, conflict over access to land naturally plays a very significant role as well (Takeuchi and Marara 2011).

levels and a decreasing incentive to emigrate to other countries. Egalitarian growth requires avoiding a sharp increase in land concentration. Although at present that concentration does appear to be much less marked than it has long been in most of the Latin American countries, increases are now under way, at varying rates according to the country, and are now a real threat in some of them. The typical scarcity of land, together with the still-rising rural population in most countries, portends an increasing risk of conflict in future.

The arrival of the COVID-19 pandemic highlighted many of the region's problems and the economic insecurity of many families, in particular their precarious access to food. The Food and Agricultural Organization's (FAO) annual hunger report cited a dramatic increase in severe hunger between 2019 and 2020, by up to twenty-five percent, and a rise in moderate or severe food insecurity from fifty-one percent in 2014 to sixty-six percent in 2020 (FAO et al. 2021). In a recent and telling policy brief, Michael Fakhri, the UN Special Rapporteur on the right to food, criticizes the September 2021 UN Food Systems Summit as neglecting the real challenges facing marginal populations in SSA and elsewhere, and instead focusing exclusively on raising production while disregarding people's access to food and what determines it (United Nations Human Rights Special Procedures 2021). He notes that hunger, malnutrition, and famine are caused by political failures and shortcomings of governance more than by food scarcity. With its focus on raising production sustainably through new technologies, the Summit played down "the root causes of the failures in our food systems" and the "challenges of ensuring better and more equitable access—questions of how food is produced, by whom, and who reaps most of the benefits from its processing and trade. Even at the peak of the pandemic, the greatest threat to food security and nutrition was not because food was unavailable."[8] He decries the failure to address the extreme concentration of power in the hands of a set of private actors in food systems, which makes those entities "co-responsible for malnutrition, biodiversity loss and climate crises." A commonly noted weakness of many UN agencies is their need to avoid provoking criticism from some

[8] This view echoes the breakthrough insight of Sen (1981) when he identified lack of purchasing power, rather than an overall shortage of food, as the main factor in famines.

governments. As a result, they tend to focus on the positive and leave aside the negative in their official pronouncements, even when insiders are well aware of the latter.

Finding itself in this mixed but very challenging setting, an awareness of what was amiss on the land front in much of Latin America and many other developing countries and of what went right in Japan, Korea, Taiwan, and a few others, is important to the future of SSA. The Latin American syndrome involves large agricultural units that generate very little employment per hectare; recreating such a structure in SSA would be disastrous in light of the demographic overload and the severe land shortage. Such an extreme and wasteful concentration is not an immediate threat, given the few large cattle farms in SSA and the generally smaller differences in product composition by size of farm than are often found in Latin America. Still, small-scale agriculture typically outperforms medium-sized farms substantially in the creation of decent jobs; even without approaching the Latin extremes. As a result, morphing toward a larger farm structure could thus be quite costly. SSA will not have the sort of outlet the UK had for population made redundant by rising land concentration; neither a major industrial revolution creating many jobs, nor a comparable wave of emigration is on the horizon.

In broad terms, the colonial experience of SSA has been defined by the predominantly rural and agriculture-based economic systems, relatively low average incomes, and high levels of poverty. A number of the countries have experienced usually short-lived economic booms, but until recently the region as a whole had advanced slowly, especially in per capita terms. Population growth accelerated toward a peak of about three percent per year in the 1980s, a level never experienced in any other major region; as of 2020, it was still at nearly 2.5 percent (World Bank, n.d.). This demographic explosion was, until recently, accompanied by the developing world's slowest and most delayed path of agricultural productivity increase (Evenson 2008). That cereal yields had increased only twenty-nine percent in the forty-three years between 1961–1965 and 2003–2005, compared to 177 percent in developing Asia and 144 percent in Latin America, led to calls for an African Green Revolution (Djurfeldt et al. 2005, Diao et al. 2008) aimed at reversing this trend, particularly in light of the limited scope for further area expansion in most areas of SSA without serious environmental consequences.

As previously noted, that revolution was, in fact, designed mainly for Asian conditions, in part because in the early post-war years the bulk of the world's poverty was located there and Western countries worried about its political impact in the existing Cold War setting, and in part because of the relative availability of irrigation, which made it easier to reap benefits from what was in fact a seed–fertilizer–water model for productivity growth. Asia's dominant crop was rice and the Asian Green Revolution focused heavily on it; SSA had a wide range of staple crops, so raising aggregate productivity posed a bigger challenge. On top of this, the capacity to participate heavily in the research and dissemination of new technologies was naturally limited in a low-income region, including many small countries, and one that was early in its political development, given how recently the new nations had been created as colonialism came to an end. Today's challenges arise in a particularly difficult current setting in which agriculture remains the dominant activity, population continues to grow rapidly, considerable forest loss has already been suffered, and most governments are not yet able or willing to apply some of the strong regulations that might be needed to limit environmental damage. As a final challenge, parts of SSA are now suffering significant negative impacts of global warming on agricultural productivity.

Although a dramatic impact like that of the Asian Green Revolution cannot reasonably be expected in SSA, important advance in agriculture is both feasible and very important to overall socio-economic success. SSA agriculture currently provides about fifty-five to sixty-five percent of all jobs in the region,[9] and a considerably higher share in some of the lower-income countries.[10] The vast majority of those earning their living mainly from agriculture are on small farms. Although SSA's rural areas amount to 20.3 million square kilometers of land, only twenty-five percent is arable. There are probably about sixty million to sixty-five million farms,[11] of which just over sixty percent have one hectare or less, accounting for about eighteen percent of

[9] Estimates of this share vary with the source (https://cmail.chass.utoronto.ca/src/download.php?passed_id=158417&mailbox=INBOX&ent_id=4&absolute_dl=true).

[10] Because many people work in more than one sector, the proportion depending wholly or partly on agriculture is larger.

[11] The recent review by Lowder et al. (2016) reported about fifty-one million farms in SSA, but due to missing countries and others for which data were outdated, that figure is clearly too low. The actual number probably lies in the cited range.

the land. The average (mean) size of holding likely falls in the two- to three-hectare range. With an estimated rural population of 620 million people in 2017, the region is, on average, sparsely populated, at thirty-one people per square kilometer. But roughly seventy-two percent of that population resides on only ten percent of the land;[12] for this majority, the average density is a high 223 people per square kilometer. Therefore, even though in a geographic sense most of SSA might be considered land abundant and sparsely populated, a relatively large proportion of rural Africans face severe land scarcity, now increasingly accompanied by rapidly rising land prices and perceptions of tenure insecurity.[13] For farm families to have an average of ten hectares each would require that the bulk (sixty-seven to eighty percent) of those currently employed in the sector leave it, which can only happen if and when the non-agricultural sector flourishes for a number of decades. This basic logic helps to underpin the idea that the small farm will remain essential for a lengthy period and should, for the foreseeable future, be the main focus of policy support.

## The Possible Broad Paths Ahead

This combination of factors creates a difficult scenario. If agricultural output rises too slowly, there will continue to be aggregate food shortages. If the output increases do not come mainly from small farmers, poverty will rise or decrease more slowly than might be hoped. If technology is not green enough, the region will contribute that much more to global warming and/or to its own climate, water, and soil pollution problems. Rapid population growth, together with stagnant land productivity, creates a natural push to expand the agricultural frontier. This is particularly problematic in the densely populated countries with few forests left; in them, agricultural growth must come mainly from intensification, with the attendant environmental , including overuse of chemicals and declining soil quality. Where population is less dense, agricultural expansion will cause some forest loss, and logging and other resource exploitation will bring in new roads

[12] Jayne, Chamberlin, and Headey (2014).

[13] For example, rural land values in favorable market access areas of Tanzania doubled in real terms between 2009 and 2013, rising more rapidly than wage rates or other inputs into agricultural production (Jayne & Wineman 2018).

which invite farmers, large and small, to set up beside them.[14] At the same time, there will be less pressure to move quickly to a chemical-intensive agriculture.

Several qualitatively different paths for SSA's agriculture and its economies over the coming decades can be imagined, reflecting different policy choices and how the degree of land concentration enters the picture. The best option would be the nearest possible replay of the East Asian success stories. In it, the small farms are central; both productivity and income generated will rise fast, especially for those at the bottom of the income hierarchy. Rapid agricultural growth spurs fast growth of rural non-agricultural activities and, in due course, urbanization. Education rises, birth rates fall, and the rate of population growth declines, helping to alleviate the demographic overload now characterizing most of the region.

Toward the other end of the spectrum is a path in which land concentration rises markedly and overall economic growth is weak to modest. The growing land concentration raises income inequality which, coupled with the slowish economic growth and continuing fast population growth, pushes up poverty rates. The positive spinoff effects of the previous case are absent, so education advances more slowly and birth rates fall more slowly. Urbanization may be slower because non-agriculture is doing less well, or it could be faster because falling rural incomes have the effect of pushing people out. Slow agricultural growth may reflect low land productivity on larger units and/or misallocated public spending, such as when input subsidies crowd out R&D. Selection of a path favoring larger producers is a natural upshot of their political power, together with a lack of awareness by policymakers of the positive potential of smaller farms and of the negative labor market impact of this second approach. To the degree that countries opt for it, they run the risk of suffering the English experience in which the later enclosures, referred to by Robert C. Allen (1992) as the "landlord's enclosures" hastened urbanization and held down both urban and overall wages.

[14] Slash-and-burn agriculture has destroyed much of the ancient coastal forest in Eastern Africa and has accentuated human–wildlife conflict. This coastal zone, one of the continent's most biologically diverse, is under threat from unregulated investment in commercial agriculture. Forest loss has been great in Mozambique, Tanzania, and Zambia through over-harvesting for timber and fuelwood.

A third possibility is that agriculture be increasingly dominated by larger units but without leaving a lasting legacy of overall income inequality. If growth is fast enough so that the sectoral transition toward nonagriculture is well advanced before income inequality within agriculture gets too high, then that sector will not so firmly imprint its internal inequality on the economy as a whole, as it did in the UK and in developing countries like Brazil, Colombia, and the Philippines. The main mechanism whereby large farm dominance might produce faster agricultural output growth is a greater willingness of the state to support the sector when large farms dominate it; economies of scale seldom play a very significant role. While the worst-case scenario just discussed would see slow agricultural and overall growth, accentuating the inequality of the distribution of land and income and raising poverty, the recent evidence of medium and larger farms achieving good land productivity—sometimes even higher than that on small farms—suggests that a modestly greater role for them need not deter growth and may even promote it under certain circumstances. And differences in the labor-to-land ratio vis-à-vis small farmers seem to be much less in those cases than in their Latin American counterparts, where this gap has often been enormous. In such cases, a partial shift in structure toward larger units need not greatly reduce the total demand for labor; income distribution outcomes, while not as good as those in Korea or Taiwan, might still be considerably better than those in Latin America.

Given the relative lack of definitive research on which systems and policies may be expected to perform the best, much debate about the optimal agricultural path for SSA is understandable, both locally and in the international community. Many ideas on policy are based on experiences elsewhere, but given the big differences of context, such experiences only provide options to be considered, not plans for straightforward implementation.

The overall policy challenge is accentuated by the fast population growth. The vicious circle of population growth, poverty, and environmental degradation is most threatening in this region. Low incomes—driven by low land productivity in agriculture—deter both urbanization and educational advance, which in turn helps to maintain the region's still high fertility rates, which is currently at 4.8 births per woman at a time when the figure for the rest of the world taken together is just a little over 2 births per woman. Factors explaining that high number include not only the low urbanization, education, and income levels which are correlates of high fertility everywhere, but also social characteristics like the importance of the extended family and the strong ties of first-generation urban residents to their home villages.

An increasing share of SSA's population lives in densely populated countries—around seventy-two percent by one recent estimate.[15] Emigration can ease domestic population pressure a little, but in the industrial countries (ICs) the politics of immigration are becoming increasingly negative, especially for people who look or act different from the existing population. SSA emigration to Organisation for Economic Co-operation and Development (OECD) countries did indeed rise sharply between 1960 and the 2010s, reaching around three hundred thousand in 2012 (González et al. 2016, 6) and leading to projections that half of Europe's 2050 population would be of African descent. The political reaction to high immigration in host countries has been marked, so this exit door cannot be assumed to stay open, especially in the context of the aftermath of COVID-19. And even in the peak period of emigration from the region, it only corresponded to a tiny share of population growth.[16] As of 2019, the number of Africans living outside the region was about 18.3 million, and had risen by an average of 2.2 million per year over the previous four years, about six percent of the annual population growth.[17] Some migration can and does occur between SSA countries, but this, too, is a frequent source (or result) of conflict, so it cannot be expected to provide much relief against the intensifying over-population of the region as a whole. A sharp drop in fertility is thus sorely needed. Some grounds for optimism do exist. As Williams (2017) notes, fertility in a few countries (including South Africa) has already fallen below replacement level, and some others have recorded marked declines in recent years. Rwanda's average fertility rate fell by about two children between 2005 and 2014, and it is particularly interesting that the decline coincided with the dramatic surge of economic growth beginning soon after the country's 1994 genocide. Rapid economic growth was accompanied by a sharp increase in (gross) primary

[15] Based on figures from Lowder et al. (2016).

[16] For Africa as a whole, including the countries north of the Sahara, one estimate put emigration at about 2.5 percent of population growth (OECD 2008).

[17] See the figures from International Organization for Migration (2020). An estimate for 2006 was very similar, putting the emigration at one-twentieth of the population growth (OECD 2008).

school attendance[18] from eighty percent in 1992 to 110 percent by the late 1990s, when many of those entering the child-bearing age between 2005 and 2014 were in school.

In this complex and demanding context, the ongoing debates about African agricultural policy involve two key questions: (i) how should technological advance be pursued (e.g., degree of emphasis on chemicals versus greener inputs, importance of self-reproducing seeds, optimal level and type of extension service, etc.) and, more generally, how can the ecological quality of the agricultural system be improved; and (ii) to what extent should the small family farm be the main focus of policy and, as part of that issue, whether having some medium or large farms may be helpful in achieving good overall productivity gains.

The possible need for land reform to lower existing inequality has arisen, especially in Ethiopia and in those countries where European colonists became engaged in farming. In many others, the main challenge on the concentration front is to prevent it from rising unduly in the next few decades. Agrarian structure and the degree of land concentration may be seen as medium-term concerns in most SSA countries; current inequality of access appears substantially lower than in the extreme cases of Latin America, although some of the same concentrating forces are indeed present. Uncertainty remains for two main reasons: the lack of agricultural censuses or other sources that can give an accurate picture of size structure, and the (related) fact that, in some countries, well-placed politicians are known to have extensive landholdings but details are not available. At Independence, a number of leaders made off with large amounts, including Jomo Kenyatta, the first president of Kenya (whose son was recently president and in possession of that land); this pattern is reminiscent of that observed in the early post-independence periods in various countries of Latin America, when well-placed people took advantage of the lack of controls on land acquisition. In some SSA countries foreign firms also hold large amounts of land.

The IR between size and land productivity appears, on average, to be weaker/less universal in SSA than in Latin America, implying a smaller threat of lower agricultural production from a high level of concentration.

[18] The ratio of children in school to children in the normal age range for school. It can exceed one when some students repeat years.

The tendency not to focus public policy sufficiently on the smaller farmers is often marked (and may be one reason the IR is weaker). The same pro-large farm bias that helped to produce several unsuccessful governmental efforts to advance toward what was thought of as large-scale modern agriculture is still very present. Some of the features of the seed and fertilizer policy package will inevitably have a tendency to concentrate land. Corruption and lack of fairness have already done so in a good number of countries.

With respect to agrarian structure, the main medium-term challenge has been, and remains, preventing land concentration from rising to seriously detrimental levels. Where high concentration already exists, the challenge is to correct it through some type of redistribution. The fact that few, if any, regions in SSA have long-standing agricultural ruling classes may make these tasks easier. Concentration did rise quickly in a few cases where Europeans invaded and took control of much territory; sometimes this has left an indirect legacy of large landholdings in the hands of the Africans who then appropriated that land.

Possibly the biggest immediate danger is that in many countries the intensification of agriculture seen as necessary to fulfill food requirements will further accentuate chemical-based environmental damage; at worst, the sector could be trapped in the vicious circle of a highly polluting Green Revolution, fostered by the involvement of large chemical firms which are able, in the absence of strong and capable governments, to twist policy to favor their own products and interests. Much of the global importance of how African agriculture develops is linked to that issue. Any approach involving the heavy use of chemicals poses direct ecological threats; the pertinent question is whether failure to take that route would slow agricultural progress, overall economic growth, and poverty reduction.

Current policy debates often begin with how to interpret the low productivity problem of SSA agriculture, as reflected in its much lower yields than elsewhere and their lethargic growth over most of the last half-century. The average maize yield in the US has more than doubled since 1960 and thereby widened the already wide gap with SSA to about five-to-one; China produces three times as much per hectare. This large productivity deficit is interpreted by the Alliance for a Green Revolution in Africa (AGRA)—an institution through which large business interests exert pressure—as a powerful argument in favor of its Green Revolution model for Africa, built around the seeds and fertilizers of those large suppliers. Most agricultural economists see the productivity gap as a more general reflection of inadequate past efforts in the areas of research and diffusion of more productive technologies to the small farmers,[19] of the relative scarcity of irrigation as compared to East Asia, and the greater diversity of settings and of crops in SSA. Agroecologists see it as a challenge which, if approached using that science, will leave much less environmental damage than they see emerging from the cited Green Revolution model. Many argue that the biggest problem, one that underlies things like inadequate R&D, has been badly designed policies;[20] there is no doubt that those policies could have been a good deal better, although much of the problem has arguably been an inevitable result of scarce financial resources and the relative political inexperience of newish countries.

Against a background featuring many difficult challenges, the last few decades have seen significant improvements (depending on the country), leading to the historically fast growth of output from 2000 to 2015, with associated increases in land productivity. Policymakers need now to understand not only the many ongoing sources of worry but also the factors behind these advances. And, although some recent trends do give new grounds for optimism, they are also cause for concern. For one thing, the post-2015 period has seen a slow-down of output growth. And, while a number of countries appear to have achieved rapid productivity increases which bode well for aggregate agricultural performance, at least in the short-term, some of the associated trends suggest risks on both the income distribution and the environmental fronts. Rising land concentration is increasingly accompanied by rapidly mounting land prices and perceptions of tenure insecurity. Despite this, those countries still having land that can be opened up to agriculture typically invite large investors to undertake the task. Where communal land rights are losing ground to more open markets, a new threat to small farmers arises. Urban owners are getting control of more and more land. Any approach that substantially favors larger farms creates a danger that, in already poor and overpopulated countries, the greatest source of productive

[19] Mellor (2014) emphasizes that research on new varieties has been inadequate, particularly in taking account of the very diverse soil types found in countries and regions of SSA. He also stresses the complexity of "fertilizer economics" in Africa as compared to Asia. In the use of that input in Africa, simple general rules are unlikely to provide many benefits.

[20] Policy has been questionable in many other areas as well.

employment—small agriculture—will be squeezed, with resulting negative impacts on the wages and earnings of the lower income groups.

## The Future Role of the Small Family Farm

The evidence needed to compare the performances of SSA farms by size and to assess their relative potential remains limited, albeit increasing. Most in-depth analyses report the standard IR. In some countries, including Ethiopia, Rwanda, Malawi, Nigeria, and Tanzania, the differentials appear quite marked (Owusu 2019). In others, however, the IR holds only up to the middle-size range (five to ten hectares), after which productivity rises with size (e.g., Zambia, Kenya);[21] this recently identified phenomenon has not yet been deeply probed nor is it known in how many other cases it is present. With a higher productivity on larger units, land concentration would not have the downward impact on aggregate output arguably present in countries like Brazil and Colombia. Given the much smaller differences in employment per hectare, a very negative impact on employment might be avoided as well. In most of the land-scarce SSA countries, however, land productivity does appear to be much higher on the smaller farms, so the logic of basing future agricultural development mainly on them remains very strong. But it still confronts a deeply ingrained belief from outside the small circle of those familiar with the relevant empirical research, that large-scale production is more efficient. An approach favoring the bigger units predictably gets support from the large farm interests themselves. Because they tend to interact closely with politicians, policies favoring them and their expansion at the expense of smaller producers are hard to avoid. A recent burst of land acquisitions in medium and larger farms has been widely noted; some involve investors from outside the countries, but more are by nationals with economic bases outside agriculture, and many are by successful small farmers moving up the size scale (Jayne et al. 2019, 84). A modest growth in the number of medium-sized farms, much of it due to the cited scaling up, is probably not cause for much concern, whereas that of large units is more likely to be.

In any case, a battle of ideas is underway between supporters of the small family farm model on the one hand, and the politicians, farmers' unions

[21] Data for Kenya are provided by Muyanga and Jayne (2019).

(typically dominated by larger farmers), and skeptics of the potential of that model on the other (Jayne et al. 2019). This battle overlaps the differences between ecologists and the backers of a chemical-intensive agriculture that relies on seeds developed by large agribusinesses like Monsanto. The argument for a heavy emphasis on the small farm draws on its success elsewhere, especially in South and East Asia, where over ninety percent of farms were smaller than two hectares at the beginning of the original Green Revolution (Jayne et al. 2019); on the empirical evidence of higher land productivity on smaller farms than on large ones (i.e., the IR); and on the presumption that it is the best model to create employment and reduce poverty because such farms are more labor-intensive than larger ones and that a higher (often much higher) share of the income generated on them goes to lower income workers than in the case of larger units. Another stylized fact from Asia's agricultural development experience is that overall rural development proceeds faster when land distribution is not concentrated; small landholders have a higher propensity to spend their money in the local rural economy, thereby stimulating growth linkages between the farm and non-farm sectors (Mellor 1995). If a few large-scale farmers dominate production but spend their money outside that rural economy—such as when they are urban dwellers—the local growth multipliers are likely to be weaker (Johnston and Kilby 1975). Consistent with all of this is the finding that agricultural growth is, in general, the most effective way to reduce poverty in a country (e.g., Byerlee et al. 2009). But because most of these conclusions come from experiences outside Africa, to be fully convincing they must receive empirical confirmation within that context as well.

Helping to explain why so many agricultural economists have accepted that a small landholder-led strategy is the best fit for the region[22] is the cited fact that small farms currently constitute the vast majority of the total, making them a natural building block. The fact that the large-scale model has not fared well in the major experiments carried out so far adds weight to this view; various post-independence attempts by SSA countries to modernize their agricultural sectors through government-promoted large-scale farming projects supported by subsidized credit, machinery, and ready access to land have generally failed or fallen short of expectations.[23]

[22] For example, Hazell et al. (2010).

[23] See Eicher and Baker (1992). The attempts include Nigeria's large-scale mechanized irrigated wheat schemes of the 1970s and 1980s, which were eventually largely abandoned (Andrea and

Investment in large farm projects, like the Gezira scheme in the Sudan, has reflected the widespread belief in the importance of economies of scale.[24] All, or nearly all, of the earlier failures occurred against a backdrop of policy distortions which discouraged (export) agriculture, and of generally low public investment in rural areas. Policy improvements over the past two or three decades have created a better setting and renewed international investor interest in large commercial farming. In any case, the tendency to expect large farms to perform well remains widespread. Even Ethiopia, a country known for the very small size of the great majority of its farms in the densely populated highlands, has for some years been trying unsuccessfully to develop big, modern, machinery-intensive agriculture in its sparsely settled province of South Omo.[25] Problems have included a lack of capital, along with incompetent and corrupt investors, many of them linked to the ruling party (Kamski 2019). Meanwhile the overall development of such regions is seldom taken seriously by the central government, which starves them for funds and makes it harder for the existing agriculture to advance.

Underlying or contributing to such policies is the almost universal failure to understand the relevant economics, and in particular to believe that high labor productivity and mechanization go with efficiency, when in fact they often signal just the opposite (see Appendix 3.1).

Beckman 1985), and Sudan's unfulfilled plans for major mechanized sorghum and sesame production.

[24] Goelnitz and Al-Saidi (2020) emphasize the problems of management which is too distant from the users of the water provided by the system, insufficiently competent and knowledgeable about the needs, failing to take account of what the users know and believe, and other problems like conflicts among using groups. The issue here is not so much whether there are potential economies of scale at the physical level but whether there are diseconomies of scale at the management level. They discuss the merits of Irrigation Management Transfers, whereby management is shifted from government to the farmers.

[25] In 2012, Fri-EI, an Italian conglomerate, signed a lease with the state government for thirty thousand hectares to produce palm oil. It was envisaged as a paradigm of development but it quickly came up against the reality that there was not enough water. As a result, cotton became the new product of choice. Much was left unpicked due to labor shortages because Omo is a sparsely settled zone; the hope had been that nomads who use some of the land would convert to laborers on the large farms. In 2018, less than three percent of the one hundred thousand hectares leased to investors in three of the province's districts was actually being farmed. Some leased areas were too big, given a dearth of capital, to develop them. Some investors were incompetent, as confessed by an estate manager who said, "We didn't know what to do, we're not farmers" (Kamski 2019). Some were crooks. Many deals involved individuals linked to the ruling party. Despite a record of such failures, officials have recently hinted that the government wants again to promote huge farms there.

Recent evidence suggesting that medium and larger farms (in most SSA countries, this would be seen as those with five hectares or more) have been achieving better results and thus may deserve a bigger role helps to validate already existing skepticism about the small-farm model and to fuel efforts to nurture the large-scale variant. In every part of the world most proponents of larger farms believe firmly in economies of scale and doubt the potential of traditional farmers, regardless of the empirical evidence. The patchy progress of African small landholder agriculture over a lengthy period does give rise to more legitimate doubts as to whether an African Green Revolution based, like the Asian one, on very small farms can achieve comparable success. Some recent pessimism has stemmed from micro evidence of the slow uptake of modern inputs, of the shrinking size of most smallholder farms due to rural population growth and rising land scarcity, and of widespread land degradation. Given that the core mechanism of any green revolution is the development of better seeds and the availability of complementary inputs (e.g., water, fertilizer, etc.), the most legitimate worry is that many African governments may not be able to improve their support systems for small farms the way the successful Asian countries did, or they may not be willing to make the effort needed to do so. All these concerns suggest to some people that larger farms are a better bet.

Most serious analysts do not see the size question as black or white, but rather a matter of the optimal mix of sizes in a given setting and the degree of policy preference which should be given to one or another group of farms, something which depends partly on which has greater capacity to raise output quickly in that specific setting, whether the IR between farm size and agricultural income accruing to lower income families—almost universal elsewhere—is strong, and hence whether the income generated on small farms has a greater poverty-reducing effect. The most fervent proponents of the seed-fertilizer revolution see it as the key to success and view the size question as secondary; to them, whichever type of farm can best be the vehicle for that inputs-based revolution should be favored. At the extreme are those who tout the potential of seeds and fertilizer by themselves to raise yields whatever the setting; they include the policymakers and commentators who appear to take literally the advice of large seed and chemical companies; AGRA falls in this latter category. While few people question the importance of new seeds, chemicals, and fertilizers, many do claim that success requires complementary steps and that, if badly executed, an approach built solely around them can bring more harm than good. Some are concerned especially with the ecological fallout from an unnuanced version of the chemicals-focused approach. In any case, judgment should be based on as current a reading of the current state of SSA agriculture as possible, as there have been significant changes over time.

## The Evolving Setting

SSA agriculture has undergone increasing change over the last few decades. From a low land-productivity base and a period of modest growth of output from 1970 to 2000 (2.4 percent per year), the pace picked up to 3.6 percent from 2000 to 2015; it then slowed to 2.1 percent from 2015 to 2021 (2.4 percent from 2015 to 2019 and 1.6 percent from 2019 to 2021) (see Table 8.1). Land productivity and yields advanced only slowly; cereal yields, for example, rose only twenty-nine percent in the forty-three years between 1961/1963 and 2003/2005, compared to 177 percent in developing Asia and 144 percent in Latin America (FAO, 2019).

**Table 8.1** Level and Growth of Agricultural Output in Sub-Saharan Africa, 1961–2021

| Year | Value of output[a] | Average growth between years[b] |
|---|---|---|
| 1961 | 74.53 | — |
| 1970 | 99.14 | 3.22 |
| 1980 | 113.5 | 1.28 |
| 1990 | 153.9 | 3.09 |
| 2000 | 202.1 | 2.76 |
| 2010 | 290.3 | 3.68 |
| 2015 | 341.2 | 3.28 |
| 2019 | 375.1 | 2.40 |
| 2020 | 385.1 | 2.65 |
| 2021 | 387.1 | 0.53 |

[a] In constant US dollars of 2014–2016.

[b] Average annual growth from the previous year shown to the present one. Thus, the figure 2.40 gives the average annual growth from 2015 to 2019.

*Source*: FAO Statistical Yearbook (2022)

Although agricultural production rose in absolute terms over the last half of the twentieth century, this was mainly because growing numbers of small landholders were bringing more land under cultivation. In the majority of African countries, per capita production of food declined from the 1960s through the 1990s. According to the 2013 FAO statistics, thirty out of fifty-three African countries produced less food per head than they had in the early 1960s (FAOSTAT 2013), a result of slow or modest output growth, fast population growth, and increasing access to food imports through the export of mineral and other items. Whereas historically food shortages had been caused by climate shocks, disease epidemics, or military conflict (Iliffe 1987), by the late twentieth century more were the result of international trade fluctuations. Large-scale famines became increasingly associated with Africa (Frankema 2014, 18).

Fortunately, there is a renewed focus of national and international agencies on rural development in Africa. The World Bank, after a period of neglect during the structural adjustment programs of the 1980s and 1990s, now increasingly recognizes Africa's economic, geographic, and institutional diversity. In addition, there is an marked ambition to avoid the environmental costs of the original Green Revolution in terms of water and soil pollution, land erosion, and loss of biodiversity. Indeed, the call for a "doubly green revolution" stresses the need to combine agricultural productivity growth with more sustainable forms of natural resource management (Conway 1998, cited by Frankema 2014, 23).

## Agricultural Intensification versus Involution

It is clear that agricultural output must rise relatively quickly in the future for a good overall outcome to be achieved, and that it must be achieved mainly by an intensification that raises output per unit of land. The big policy issue and research question is how best to achieve this goal. One of the standing questions is how population growth fits in. Although normally seen as an obstacle, for example, to rising food output *per capita*, it has also been seen historically by some analysts as contributing to a healthy intensification. Rapid population growth has indeed contributed to an intensification of agriculture in SSA and elsewhere (e.g., South Asia), raising the question of whether its effects will on balance be negative, in the sense of making life harder for those working there, or positive through the sort of virtual circle portrayed by Ester Boserup (1965) and Hans P. Ruthenberg (1980) whereby rising population and increasing market access lead to rapid intensification. Over the past two decades, rapid population growth in SSA has put farming systems under new pressures, while rapid urbanization and economic growth have provided new market opportunities. Hans P. Binswanger-Mkhize and Sara Savastana (2017) argue that the patterns of intensification across countries are only partially consistent with the Boserup and Ruthenberg predictions: "Fallow areas have disappeared, but cropping intensities remain very low. The use of organic and chemical fertilizers is too low to maintain soil fertility. Investments in irrigation are inadequate." This pattern is similar to that reported by Clifford Geertz (1963) in Java prior to the Green Revolution and to which he applied the term "agricultural involution." Since the 1960s, biological technical change in SSA has been lagging behind the rest of the world, and so have fertilizer use, mechanization, and investment in irrigation (World Bank 2009).

The literature on agricultural intensification in Africa has developed significantly since the 1980s. In most areas studied, intensification has progressed qualitatively along the lines predicted by Boserup and Ruthenberg, with clear evidence of involution confined to a few areas. However, Derek Headey and Thomas S. Jayne (2014), using cross country data, have shown that rises in population density have been associated with reduced fallow and more intensive use of fertilizer, but not with more mechanization or irrigation, a combination that, in their judgment, would make involution very likely.

In their review of available information for six African countries—Ethiopia, Malawi, Niger, Nigeria, Uganda. and Tanzania, —Binswanger-Mkhize and Savastana (2017, 39) reach a similar conclusion:

> Given the rise in population pressure in all these African countries, the improvements in infrastructure and the growing urban demand, land use intensity, consistent with BR predictions, has reached permanent cropping in all of the countries. Fallow areas have virtually disappeared. Under permanent agriculture, high doses of organic and inorganic fertilizers are required to maintain or restore the soil nutrients taken out by the plants. Except for Malawi and Ethiopia, the proportion of households using chemical fertilizers is clearly too low to do so. Nor is this compensated for by the high proportion of households using organic fertilizer, which is relatively high only in Niger and Ethiopia. The

> BR theory also predicts that, under pressure from population growth and market access, irrigation investment and other modern technologies would be used more intensively to increase yields. However, these factors did not trigger significant irrigation investments, even in semi-arid areas where the payoff to irrigation is high. Unfortunately, we do not have data on other land investments, or on mechanization, to judge whether expected intensification responses have occurred with respect to these important investments. However, the descriptive analysis suggests that the BR impacts of population pressure and market access have triggered an inadequate response of the farming systems with respect to irrigation and technology use.

Leaving aside the matter of whether population growth figures positively or negatively, the process of what one may call "positive intensification"—intensification that brings an overall benefit to the farm family—is complicated because any short-term productivity and income gains must outweigh risks to family food and/or income security and to the environment. The existing empirical literature includes mixed results on the effect of adopting modern varieties and technologies, with debate on the causes of their limited performance and on the environmental effects of modern varieties, whose diffusion threatens the conservation of local diversity, which constitutes a valuable genetic stock to preserve for future crop breeding efforts and to assist in the battle with climate change.

In the presence of both market failures and agro-ecological threats, farmers have relied on a range of local strains as part of an agricultural risk minimization strategy. In their assessment of the economic and environmental effects of switching from traditional to modern species in Uganda as of 2009/2010, Manuela Coromaldi et al. (2015, 355) find that some farmers do benefit from the adoption of modern varieties—typically the "larger owners of land of good soil quality, better educated, and less credit and market constrained. Their farms are located in temperate agroecological zones and are thus less exposed to agricultural shocks or extreme climate." In contrast, local varieties tend to perform better than modern ones in marginalized and climatic vulnerable areas, confirming the now widespread fear that modern varieties are being dispersed too widely and too fast. "Crop biodiversity plays a fundamental role in farmers' risk minimizing strategies when the available modern varieties are not adaptable to the local context and not supported by the required level of agro-intensification. Rural development policies should consider the heterogeneity in the adoption returns and support diversity conservation as a national strategic asset for a suitable bioprospecting and a best-fitting agricultural system implementation." (Coromaldi et al, 2015, 346). Overall, they find that adopters do not wind up better off compared to non-adopters; both income from crop cultivation and food expenditure per capita would have, on average, been higher if adopters had not adopted. This could be due to the superior resistance of traditional varieties to local agro-ecosystem conditions and agricultural stresses in marginal lands. "Farmers who conserve a diversified set of local varieties support natural agricultural processes that can substitute for external agrochemicals inputs in the soil nutrient management. To maximize their welfare, adopters should supply land with the appropriate combination of different inputs, but vulnerability to market prices and lack of access to credit leave farmers with a sub-optimal level of intensification, and consequently results in underperformance compared to non-adopters." (Coromaldi et al, 2015, 355).

The potential benefits from the increased use of external inputs, such as agrochemicals, are limited. Above a threshold level of intensification, their economic payoff is restrained by the often low adaptability of available modern varieties to poor soils conditions, local climate, and random agricultural shocks. This stems from the heterogeneous distribution of adoption costs and benefits across the rural population and creates the need for a "best fitting" strategy at the farm level. Such a strategy is preferable to the indiscriminate dissemination of genetically standardized major crops that farmers, once adopted, are not able to sustain with the required intensification level as long as they are economically vulnerable (Coromaldi et al. 2015, 355). The effects of adoption of modern seeds on crop diversity are negative, although varying by agro-ecological zone and soil quality; the higher the intensification, the stronger the reduction of local crop biodiversity.

In terms of policy interventions, Coromaldi et al. (2015, 355–356) note that the availability of agricultural extension services provided by the government or NGO's to marginalized farmers is a main driver of higher rates of adoption. In this context, where both adopters and non-adopters react to agro-climatic shocks and variability of input prices by increasing crop richness and evenness, they conclude that:

> While it is necessary to target food security by increasing the availability of high yielding varieties, incentivizing the adoption, irrespective of their

adaptability to local agro-ecosystems, leads to shortcomings incurred by financially vulnerable farmers who, in turn, cannot afford the intensification strategy. Exploiting the stock of local varieties, sustaining marginalized farmers with capacity building in best-fitting agricultural practices, should be not only a transitional strategy until the countries reach modernization in agriculture, but a permanent program to enhance rural livelihood and facing climate shocks. Further, governments, supporting diversity conservation by those farmers with lower opportunity costs, could focus on capitalizing the adaptability characteristics of local landraces. An R&D public investment on new varieties bioprospecting, genetically based on attractive landraces' traits, should provide countries with a structure for a modern agricultural system founded on a unique crops portfolio suitable for farmers' knowledge, local tradition, and agro-climatic exposure, and thus capable to compete in international food markets.

Meanwhile, however, the structure and internal dynamics of the sector remain less understood than elsewhere in the developing world; past information gaps have given rise to oversimplifications and, in some cases, to myths. A recent burst of research has clarified some issues and provided a starting point for more in-depth analysis on others.[26] It helps to explain both the still modest advance of productivity in some of the regions, the significant structural changes of the last decade or so in some countries, and the remaining threats to a successful medium- and longer-term performance. Among other things, this analysis has revealed:

(i) a sharp recent increase in the number of middle- and large-sized farms and, related to it, a sizeable and rising share of agricultural land controlled by urban-based households (Jayne et al. 2019). This phenomenon may be altering the strength and character of growth links to the nonfarm rural economy. It is not directly government-promoted, as were various earlier experiments featuring large-farm models.

(ii) a land market that is playing an increasing role, both in the rise of medium and large farms and more generally. As population density rises and land becomes scarcer in many areas, tenure security is increasingly important because it generally promotes long-term land

[26] See Christiaensen and Demery (2018), Jayne et al. (2019), and Wise (2019), among others.

investments and agricultural productivity, as well as contributing to a family's overall economic security and well-being. In the allocation of customary land there has been a notable shift away from the rights-based approach that has guaranteed access for the local-born toward market-based approaches in which land becomes a commodity for rent or sale. The early presumption of many observers from developed countries that the shift toward formal land titles would improve economic efficiency was generally based on an overestimate of their effectiveness in settings where they were not the historical norm, and an underestimate of the effectiveness of traditional and communal tenure systems. Empirical studies from the 1980s and earlier have identified this error. David A. Atwood (1990) summarized much of the evidence from around Africa calling this standard view into question, and arguing both that the costs of land titling could be high and that its effects could be the opposite of those expected.[27] Recent thinking (to be discussed later in this chapter) recognizes both the complexity of this issue and the fact that modifications may be important both because of weaknesses of existing systems and the implications of rapidly changing settings.

(iii) an increasing use of modern inputs, which is a significant modification from earlier times when African farmers applied them very little. Formal credit does not yet finance much of that use, even in the case of the larger farms, but rural financial markets are gradually improving, and more generally enabling people to purchase or lease land, invest in irrigation and soil conditioning, and intensify the use of cash inputs such as fertilizers and improved seeds. These processes in turn alter the distribution of farms by size (Jayne et al. 2019).[28]

(iv) rapid improvements in transportation and communication infrastructure including roads, transport equipment, electricity,

[27] Members of Wisconsin's Land Tenure Center, including John Bruce and Peter Dorner (Bruce 1986; Bruce and Dorner 1982) were important early contributors on these issues.

[28] In four SSA countries studied, only six percent of farmers used any form of credit; the idea that fertilizer use is uneconomically low was tested in detail in Nigeria and found to be untrue in the case of maize. Liverpool-Tasie et al. (2017) find that fertilizer use is not particularly profitable there, which explains its relatively low use and contradicts the common view that it is profitable but farmers are not sufficiently aware of this fact.

and information and communication technologies (ICT), allow for better domestic market integration. Whereas in 1990 only one percent of Africans had a subscription to a mobile or fixed telephone connection, today nearly every African adult has one. New communication technologies offer real-time market information to farmers at very low costs, they enable instant financial transactions, and they facilitate new forms of credit, saving, and insurance (Frankema 2014, 22).

(v) reasonably diversified rural household incomes, with an increasing share (now about one-third) from outside agriculture. For such households in many other parts of the developing world the comparable figure is now two thirds, a difference that mainly reflects their being at different points on the same structural trajectory. Most off-farm income comes from informal activities, often closely related to agriculture (Davis et al. 2018); such a reliance on informal activities is no surprise given their dominance within the urban areas of these economies.

(vi) labor productivity in agriculture not far below that outside it,[29] contradicting the common view of serious malfunction in the way the market allocates labor across sectors;

(vii) the importance of trees to the livelihood of many farm families; on that one-third of farms where they are grown, they provide seventeen percent of the gross income, in addition to their contribution to soil and water conservation and to biodiversity (Christiaensen and Demery 2018, 8).

(viii) the increasing problem of drought in parts of SSA, although it is not yet as serious a source of economic insecurity as are price fluctuations. For both problems, the main coping mechanism is family savings.

(ix) post-harvest losses that do not appear to be excessively large, as has often been claimed.

These findings suggest that in certain respects today's small-farm agriculture in SSA resembles its counterparts elsewhere at comparable stages of

[29] National accounts can show differences of up to six-to-one, but these are large exaggerations due to measurement problems (McCullough 2017).

economic development. Many of the findings mirror those of fifty to seventy years ago within the small-scale subsector of Latin countries or thirty to forty years ago in Asian countries, when most of those countries' R&D and extension systems were nascent. In Latin America, the idea that such systems should serve small agriculture as well as large was then a relatively novel one and seen by many as eccentric. The formal financial system also provided little support to the small farmer, who was often wary of it in any case. In contrast to the state of near stagnation often used to characterize SSA agriculture, Jayne et al. (2019) refer to profound farm-level transformation in parts of the region, suggesting that the ongoing changes may even be fast by the historical standards of other regions. Still, as previously noted, the ecological setting of SSA does differ substantially from other regions, as does its institutional history and, now, the challenge of global warming.

The relative roles of the various factors contributing to rapid change in SSA agriculture, and when and where those changes have been fastest, remain to be fully sorted out. One such factor is the region's overall growth of per capita income, which experienced an unusual spurt (at an average of over five percent per year) over the century's first decade, well above anything achieved before, and due in part to the developments within agriculture. But growth over the next decade (from 2010 to 2022) slowed to 3.1 percent (and, from 2010 to 2020 it was only 1.9 percent), only marginally better than the 1.6 percent from 1990 to 2000. Growth in agriculture followed a similar pattern. Even without the complicating effects of COVID-19, it would appear optimistic to expect that the dynamism of 2000 to 2010 will quickly be recaptured.

The changing distribution of land in SSA is also playing itself out against an evolving political context with impacts on policy choices. After a decade of frequent disagreement (from about 1985 to 1995) between African governments and international lenders over the course of agricultural policy, local interests tended to regain control starting in the early 2000s, often in a setting of emerging multiparty political systems (Jayne et al. 2019). Parties have frequently championed such populist stances as the provision of free or subsidized inputs and price supports for products, which they justify as a way to guarantee food self-sufficiency. National farmers' unions, ostensibly lobbying in the interest of the farming community as a whole, have a greater voice and influence than before, but because specific policies affect distinct groups of farmers in different ways, those with less influence can wind up losing. In some countries these unions lobby forcefully for agricultural subsidies and land allocations that favor relatively large farms. Larger operators are also favored by the support policies that raise food prices (because the biggest gains go to those farmers with the largest marketable surpluses); they benefit from input and credit subsidy programs in which they participate disproportionately, and they promote the conversion of land from customary tenure to statutory land. Thus, as of a decade ago, the approximately fifty percent of the Zambian government's agricultural budget going into subsidy programs mainly benefited the most privileged five percent of farmers (Jayne, Mather, and Mghenyi 2010). Similarly, despite extensive public rhetoric in support of "progressive farmers with the entrepreneurial experience to transform African agriculture," attempts to facilitate land market transactions are mainly designed to give large investors access to more land. Their support for such efforts suggests that some of the unions have been, in effect, captured by this group (Sitko and Jayne 2014), whose higher levels of education and more extensive social connections with traditional and state authorities give them advantages in getting access to land from either customary or statutory land institutions (Jayne et al. 2019).

Larger farmers have benefited from the rising local demand for food products due to population growth and rising incomes, and from the boom in global food prices starting in 2006, which led to a highly publicized burst of investment in African farmland by foreigners. Less noted was the much larger entry of African professionals, entrepreneurs, civil servants, and retirees, accompanied by relatively successful small-scale farmers who expanded into the lower end of the medium- and large-scale farm category (operating five to twenty hectares).[30] Many had accumulated wealth from non-farm jobs, which they then invested in land to become either part-time or full-time farmers. Many of those who live in rural areas have political or social influence with the traditional authorities. Some retain jobs in the cities and hire managers to take care of their farms. In the last few years, such outside investor interest appears to have lessened as food prices dropped from their 2006 to 2012 high, and most of the new entrants to medium-scale farming seem to be successful former small-scale farm

[30] In Ghana, Zambia, Tanzania, and Kenya, the amount of land acquired by these medium-scale African farmers since 2000 has far exceeded the amount acquired by foreign investors (Jayne et al. 2019).

households. The increasing dynamism of the markets for land, labor, finance, agro-inputs, and machinery may have fostered this upward mobility. Removal of restrictions on private movement of food commodities across district borders and the development of both formal and informal land markets has made it easier for individuals with money and resources to acquire property.

Large-farm investment, especially when coming from outside the country, interacts with the political world in many self-reinforcing ways; for example, boosting private agricultural investment typically requires accompanying infrastructural development. Tom Lavers and Festus Boamah (2016, 94) contend that in situations of overlapping authority between state and societal organizations—a common condition in Africa—this complementarity may provoke changes in power relations between state and society with important implications for both. They contrast "two countries that have figured prominently in the 'land grab' literature but where land tenure regimes and state–society relations take markedly different forms." In Ghana, chiefs have taken advantage of increased demand from private investors in an attempt to (re-)assert their authority over land vis-à-vis the state and other societal organizations. In Ethiopia, an already highly centralized and hierarchical state has sought to capitalize on the demand from those investors to pursue its developmental and state-building strategy, including the enhancing of federal control over lowland regions in the west and south of the country. Ethiopia exemplifies the causal chain in which the private purchase of public land on a large scale is attractive to the state because it enriches it (sometimes in terms of foreign exchange) and, through its power to invest and choose the direction of investment, enhances its control over the land and its inhabitants. Allocating land to small farmers cannot normally bring in the same revenue. An increasing role for large farms is usually seen as beneficial for efficiency reasons as well, partly based on the belief that they are more efficient than small ones[31] and partly that they can be helpful to overall agricultural progress through spillover benefits to smaller ones.

Medium-scale farms have recently become a significant and even a major force in the agriculture of some African countries, especially where there was

[31] The much higher land productivity on small farms that emerges in Owusu's (2018) study throws much doubt on this proposition.

previously a good deal of undeveloped land. Since 2000, their share of food production has risen rapidly in countries like Tanzania and Zambia, where they now account for roughly forty percent of marketed surplus.[32] In land-constrained, densely populated countries like Kenya, Uganda, and Rwanda, small-scale farms still account for the bulk of agricultural output and the share of land in medium-scale farms does not appear to have been rising (Jayne et al. 2019, 5).

Based on the few studies undertaken so far, Jayne et al. (2019) identify both positive and potentially negative effects from the rapid acquisition of land by medium- and large-scale farmers. Where they are doing well, several factors appear to be at work, including early adoption of new technical innovations and practices. This creates the possibility that they may also be helping smaller farmers to test new options, as suggested by evidence that small farmer productivity is higher when they operate in the presence of medium-sized farms.[33] Such positive spillover benefits, assuming this is what they are, appear to be less marked in districts with a relatively high share of land controlled by larger farms of over ten hectares. Medium-scale farmers share many social and economic ties with small farm households and thus may be more likely to have mutually beneficial economic synergies; many large farms, in contrast, are controlled by people of other ethnic backgrounds or who reside outside the area and are thus less likely to have strong social ties in the local community (Chamberlin and Jayne 2018). The presence of medium-scale farms tends to improve small farmers' access to agricultural inputs and services and to attract private investment in value chains (e.g., by large-scale grain buyers), which boosts the market access of nearby small landholders (Sitko et al. 2018). Thus, small Tanzanian farms are much more likely to have access to mechanization services (e.g., tractor rental) in areas with a high concentration of medium-scale farms,[34] allowing them to reduce

[32] Between the first and most recent surveys (generally a period of six to ten years), the share of national marketed crop output value accounted for by medium-scale farms rose from twenty-three to forty-two percent in Zambia, from seventeen to thirty-six percent in Tanzania, and from seven to eighteen percent in Nigeria.

[33] In Ghana, Zambia, Tanzania, and Kenya, the amount of land acquired by these medium-scale African farmers since 2000 has far exceeded the amount acquired by foreign investors (Jayne et al. 2019).

[34] Although only three percent of small-scale farms rent tractors in the twenty-one regions of mainland Tanzania with the lowest concentration of medium-scale farms, twenty-three percent rent mechanization services in the five regions with the highest concentration of medium-scale farms (Van der Westhuisen et al. 2018). Other differences across the regions than the presence of medium-scale farms may account for some of the observed variation.

their labor on the farm and reallocate some to higher-return, non-farm activities.[35] Medium-scale farmers spend in the local economy, contributing to the off-farm employment opportunities of those formerly dependent on subsistence farming alone (Chamberlin and Jayne 2018). But Daniel Ayaleu Ali et al. (2019) report that,

> In Ethiopia, a rapid expansion of investment in large-scale agriculture has been justified partly by the expectation that nearby smallholders would benefit from positive spillovers. But a relatively uncoordinated process of commercial farm establishment over 2004–2014 created at best modest spillovers for neighboring smallholders in terms of technology, input market access, and resilience to shocks, while bringing no job creation benefits. Spillover effects on yields, input market access, and resilience were largely limited to maize, a crop where technology used by large and small farms is similar and large farm density is sufficiently high to allow interaction with small farmers.[36]

The production and income levels of commercialized medium-scale farms also represent an opportunity for governments and local communities to raise revenues to finance local public goods like infrastructure, but this has yet to happen beyond a few cases.

How then should the very recent evidence of positive contributions from medium or large farms affect thinking about the region's agricultural future? Despite the possible cited benefits, there remains much professional skepticism about attempts to jump-start agricultural growth through the promotion of medium- and large-scale farming. Whether the small family farm should be the focus of future SSA agricultural development or whether medium and larger farms (e.g., those up to and above twenty hectares) should play a substantially bigger role than their present one depends on how size is related to current economic efficiency, to the

[35] Other studies in this emerging "spillovers" literature tend to find positive synergies in some cases and no clear statistical relationship in others (Jayne et al. 2019). Some note that displaced small landholders, especially younger ones, tend to leave the land in search of other sources of employment.

[36] They note that the large farm data relate to units above fifty hectares that cultivate field crops. This matters because commercial farms in the ten-to-twenty-hectare category achieve higher yields than those larger than fifty hectares in virtually all crops and may therefore provide more potential for spillovers.

potential for productivity increase over time, to willingness and capability of governments to provide support for each category of farmers, to capacity for poverty reduction through job creation, and to ecological impacts. The available evidence suggests that, at least in some cases, the larger-size category has the advantage on the first two counts; this can be virtually assumed to be the case on the third one, as nearly all governments cater to that group. When, as is usually the case, ecological considerations and potential for poverty reduction favor smaller units, then a shift toward larger farms is desirable from a societal point of view only if their economic efficiency is substantially higher now and/or if they have substantially greater potential to improve over time. An increasing body of information is available on each of these matters.

The most complicated issue involves the indirect effects on welfare through the broader labor market and the wage rate, and how the contribution of larger farms to overall success depends on their relative labor intensity. The SSA countries are noted for the very high share of urban employment found in the informal sector, an indication that well-paying formal jobs are still very scarce there, just as they are in agriculture, and a finding consistent with the fact, noted above, that labor earnings do not differ greatly as between jobs in agriculture and jobs elsewhere. The capacity to create a large amount of reasonably productive employment will thus remain for some time a major criterion against which to judge any sector's contribution to economic success. Just as the gap in single factor productivity by size seems to be smaller in much of SSA than in the "Latin American syndrome" countries, so the gap in labor intensity appears to be smaller and less of a barrier to larger farms making a positive contribution. In countries and regions where farms are smallest and incomes lowest, the impact on income distribution and poverty is most important; the higher share of the income generated on small units that goes to lower income families remains a big advantage for them under such circumstances. Thus, even if the IR did not exist, the small farm would still sometimes be the best bet because of its superior contribution to poverty reduction.

Two questions always remain: can small units raise productivity fast enough to make them a good medium- and longer-term bet, and will governments be both able and willing to provide the needed support to those units? A real dilemma would arise if the IR were strong but the smaller farmers could not raise their productivity and incomes much over time. Such an outcome seems implausible, however, in light of the intensity with which they typically manage their farms, and of the experience elsewhere in the world. Unfortunately, there are few, if any, SSA studies of farms by size that look jointly at current productivity, at how productivity is changing over time, and at who gets the income generated.

## The Evidence on Size and Productivity in SSA

Although many studies in SSA countries do report the standard IR between farm size and land productivity that is widely observed elsewhere, the evidence remains partial and hence open to some debate.[37] Presumably the range of results reflects differences of setting (e.g., in degree of land scarcity), probably also the pace of change within agriculture, as well as measurement problems and differing methodologies. In the dozen or so countries where in-depth studies have been carried out, two patterns stand out.[38] First, IR is reported by studies in all or nearly all of those countries—including Ethiopia, Ghana, Malawi, Nigeria, Tanzania, Rwanda, Madagascar, and Uganda[39]—although in some of them other studies do not find that result. Obed Owusu (2018) presents recent and comparable evidence on the association between plot size and land productivity for five countries—Ethiopia, Ghana, Malawi, Nigeria, and Tanzania—with all but Ghana showing a land productivity advantage of at least 2.4:1 between small plots of two hectares or less and larger ones;[40] for Ghana the ratio was 1:28.[41] As in other parts of the world, the IR in these countries appears to depend heavily on higher

[37] As of a few years ago, Nkonde et al. (2015) concluded that there was no systematic pattern.

[38] Most studies not only present descriptive data on how the productivity of land and of labor vary by farm size, but also undertake statistical analysis aimed at explaining the role of such factors as land quality, purchased inputs used, education of household head, and others.

[39] For the case of Uganda, Carletto et al. (2013, 260) report that typical measurement errors in household surveys involve over reporting of plot size by small farmers while the larger groups under-report on average. As a result, estimates of the IR based on the household survey data understate it. This result was also found by Groote and Traoré (2005) for Mali.

[40] In focusing on plot size rather than farm size, Owusu's work contrasts with most other studies; his results are thus not fully comparable, even though plot size and farm size are correlated.

[41] Another recent study of three densely populated countries—Malawi, Tanzania and Uganda—broadly supports Owusu's (2018) results (Julien et al. 2019). For low-income, land scarce Rwanda, Ali and Deininger (2014) report "a strong negative relationship between farm size and per hectare gross output that does not disappear if plot characteristics or household attributes are controlled for." They conclude that more intensive labor use by smaller farms is a key underlying reason. For Tanzania and Uganda, Kilic et al. (2016) confirm the presence of the IR and conclude that it is strengthen by a better measurement technique they employ (see Chapter3).

labor/land ratios—labor productivity thus rises with size; higher fertilizer usage per unit of land on the small plots appears also to play a role.[42] Where reported, the IR appears usually to be less marked than in extreme cases from Latin America, like Colombia and Brazil, probably because its main source in those latter cases—different product composition by size—is much less present in SSA. Second, studies in a few countries, including Kenya and Zambia, reveal a U-shaped relationship whereby land productivity falls with size near the bottom of the size distribution and then rises in the medium-to-large range.[43] Where this pattern does occur,[44] land is typically less scarce than in countries like Malawi or Rwanda. For Kenya, Milu Muyanga and Jayne (2019) employ three measures—land productivity, profits per hectare, and total factor productivity—in each case finding a U-shaped relationship with size. The standard inverse relationship holds within the range of zero to three hectares, between three and five hectares there is no clear pattern, and in the five-to-seventy-hectare range there is a strong positive relationship. Farms in the twenty-to-seventy-hectare range are on average substantially more productive per unit of land operated (fifty to sixty percent, depending on the measure) than those of less than five hectares.[45] In contrast to the typical pattern in Latin American countries, in which the strong IR between size and land productivity reflects much greater labor intensity on the small farms and an accompanying difference in product composition (with small farms focusing on higher value labor-intensive items while large ones do the opposite), the evidence to date from Tanzania, Kenya, and Nigeria suggests

[42] For low-income, land-scarce Rwanda, Ali and Deininger (2014) report "a robust negative relationship between farm size and per hectare gross output . . . that does not disappear if plot characteristics or household attributes are controlled for. More intensive labour use by smaller farms is a key underlying reason. On another controversial size-related matter, they report fragmentation of a farm's land into a number of plots does not reduce its productivity."

[43] The U-shaped results showing up in a number of countries inside and outside SSA are interpreted by Foster and Rosenzweig (2018), drawing on Indian data, as being the result of imperfect factor markets and economies of scale in machinery use.

[44] There has until recently been little evidence for farms of above five hectares or so because so few fall in that range. It is widely suspected that the true share of farms and of land in these larger units is greater than often reported, due among other things to the questionable way in which the land has been procured.

[45] In the case of Zambia, total labor days (mostly family in all cases) per hectare operated rise from 83.72 to 136 (Muyanga and Jayne 2019, 34) as between farms in the zero-to-five-hectare range and in the fifty-to-one hundred-hectare range (Nkonde et al. 2015, 16), a dramatic contrast to the pattern in the Latin countries where the inverse relationship is strong. The role of roots and tubers does go down sharply with size.

that the cropping patterns of medium- and larger-scale farms do not differ greatly from those of small ones (Jayne et al. 2019, 83).

Another complication in the assessment of links between size and productivity arises from the fact that smaller farms use a higher proportion of their land, a typical pattern in most other places as well. This creates further ambiguity about the size–productivity relationship because, even when land productivity per hectare operated rises it may fall with amount of land owned. This was the case recently in Zambia, where the share of owned land that is operated fell from eighty-six percent for farms with under five hectares to sixty-one percent for those with five to twenty hectares and down to twenty-five percent for those in the fifty-to-one hundred-hectare range (Nkonde et al. 2015, 16). Taking all land into account, productivity would fall by as much as two-to-one or more between the smallest category and the largest. Because these medium and large farms have been appearing quickly in recent years, it may be presumed that the share operated does tend to rise over time, as the landholders indicate in surveys (Muyanga and Jayne 2019) but it remains unclear how rapidly this will happen. New information noting whether the uncultivated land is of lower quality than that cultivated land will also be needed to better understand this issue. In the interim, none of the limited data available suggests a strong positive relationship between productivity and land held.[46] In summary, the existing pattern between farm size and productivity in SSA appears to vary considerably across countries, with most (perhaps all) having a lower size range within which land productivity falls with size (the IR) but some having a range higher up in the distribution where productivity rises with amount of land operated, but not necessarily with total land owned.

Meanwhile, estimates of TFP typically vary only modestly, by say ten to twenty-five percent, across size categories, sometimes favoring the larger farmers and sometimes the smaller.[47] In the five countries analyzed by Owusu (2018), both the smaller and the larger plots exhibit a high average level of technical inefficiency,[48] producing, on average, about fifty percent

[46] In fact, there is a risk that awareness of the positive correlation with size operated may create the impression of a productivity advantage which in fact does not exist or may only exist in the future.

[47] For a discussion of the problems inherent to the measurement of TFP, see Appendix 3.1.

[48] The technical efficiency of a production unit (like a plot or farm) is traditionally defined as the ratio of its output per unit of inputs used (i.e., TFP) in relation to that of the most productive unit in its category (as defined by size or whatever characteristics are used in the analysis). Its productivity is thus compared to that of the best practice units in its category. The level of technical inefficiency is the percent by which a unit's productivity falls short of the best practice unit.

below potential (i.e., relative to the "best practice" plots in the same survey). These low levels are consistent with other indications that average productivity is lower in SSA agriculture than elsewhere; on the positive side, they suggest a good deal of room to raise performance. It is worth noting, however, that the measurement of both TFP and of technical efficiency is theoretically complex and hence subject to considerable error (see Appendix 3.1).

Given that major aggregate productivity increases are necessary if SSA agriculture is to help resolve the region's economic challenges, the potential of the various types of farms to raise productivity is arguably more important than current differentials, especially in light of the generally modest TFP gaps that appear to exist at this time. For land productivity or TFP to double over, say, twenty-five years, it would have to rise by nearly three percent per year, an impressive rate in any situation, albeit one that was surpassed at the height of the Asian Green Revolution experiences. Given the need for such a large overall increase, an initial negative gap of fifteen to twenty percent would not weigh too heavily against a given category's potential to be as productive as others in the medium-term future, although a gap of fifty percent or more would.

Unfortunately, there is much less evidence available on changes over time in land productivity or TFP by size of farm than on differences at a point of time, but for medium and large farms in some countries the scattered evidence on this count is mainly positive. Although little evidence is available for small farms, experiences like that of Ethiopia are encouraging. In a scenario of continuing worry mixed with some hope about the future of agriculture, a burst of growth began around the turn of the century and largely invalidated the pessimism built around a long period of stagnation and the small size of most farms. The country registered a six percent real average annual agricultural growth from 2000 to 2015,[49] a growth that was largely small landholder-led (Jayne et al. 2019). That fertilizer use is now substantially higher on smaller farms, which also have much higher land productivity than do larger ones, strongly suggests that the period during which such use has increased also saw sharply rising productivity on these smaller units and very possibly a strengthening of the IR.[50] Their productivity growth was made possible by solid government support, including improved infrastructure; agricultural R&D; extension; and diverse farmer

[49] Based on "World Bank Development Indicators."

[50] From 2004 to 2009, Savastano and Pasquale (2017, 7) report a growth of twenty-three percent or 4.2 percent per year in a set of farms sampled.

support services, such as soil testing—in short, similar conditions to those that fueled the East Asian successes. The potential of the small farmer is illustrated by details like the remarkably fast spread of improved chickpea varieties; within just seven years, the adoption rate rose from thirty to eighty percent (Verkaart et al. 2019). Their attraction lay in superior returns and disease resistance. The chickpea was already an important crop for rural households, for both cash income and consumption. Good access to markets[51] and to extension services helped to speed the adoption. Such experiences illustrate the importance of tailoring agricultural innovations to the realities and needs of rural households and of recognizing that the benefits of adoption need to be substantial for it to occur, particularly in the case of resource-poor, small landholders.

Comparably encouraging is the recent record of small-scale agriculture in Rwanda. As part of the economy's dramatic burst of growth (at an average of 8.1 percent from 2000 to 2012), agriculture expanded at over five percent per year (reaching 5.7 percent from 2006 to 2012). Average farm size is very small; it has been recently reported at 0.33 hectares (Republic of Rwanda 2014). The present government, noted for its dedication to economic development, has been implementing a plan that includes many of the features recommended by specialists, including irrigation, better land management, better access to inputs like improved seeds and fertilizers, expansion of advisory services, protection against erosion, and so on. Despite the lack of detailed data on output and income growth by farm size, it may be presumed, as in Ethiopia, that with aggregate agricultural growth occurring so rapidly and the sector so heavily dominated by very small units, that category of farms must have been doing very well. As will be discussed, however, there are worrisome questions as to whether some of the growth achieved will not be sustainable or will have serious environmental costs.

## Risks Accompanying Excessive Expansion of the Medium and Large Farm Sector

As noted, medium-scale farms have accounted for a significant portion of recent agricultural output growth in a number of SSA countries. Their rise is

[51] The stress on market access, which is fostered by better rural infrastructure and other factors, mirrors the conclusion reached by Webb (2013) in the context of a remote region of highland Peru.

affecting the region in various other ways as well. Although they can be a positive driver of a more general agricultural transformation, Jayne et al. (2019) emphasize that this does not reduce the importance of support for small farms, including improvement of their land tenure security. In some places the pattern of large farm growth includes mechanisms that have contributed to the Latin American syndrome of land concentration, including the marginalization of would-be small landholders, often with the help of political and/or legal manipulation and other unfair practices and at the limit the use of force; policy support focused on the larger farms; and resulting income inequality. But many elements of this SSA story remain to be analyzed in depth or are still playing themselves out.

The origins of the current medium-scale farms are revealing of the political connections often involved. Studies for Zambia, Kenya, Ghana, Nigeria, and Malawi, covering recall periods between 2005 and 2013, reported that fewer than twenty-five percent of the new medium-sized farmers had started as small operators with farming as their main source of income and then graduated into medium-scale status (Jayne et al. 2016); Ghana was the sole exception. In Zambia, Kenya, and Tanzania, the majority had been engaged in non-farm activities; many were relatively wealthy or privileged rural residents (civil servants, rural businesspeople, extension agents, religious leaders, traditional headmen, chiefs, etc.) or urban dwellers. Owners residing in urban areas and hiring managers to run their farms became relatively common. Urban-based individuals thus came to control a significant proportion of total land in these five countries; in almost all cases that proportion increased between the first and most recent survey. Later evidence from 2017/2018 suggests a less worrisome pattern; studies in Zambia, Senegal, and Nigeria indicate that perhaps sixty percent of the now medium-scale farmers had "stepped up" from small-scale status (Jayne et al. 2019, 84).

The surge of investment in larger farms up to about 2010 bore out widespread apprehensions, including (i) weak land governance and an associated failure to recognize, protect, or—when voluntary transfer can be agreed upon—properly compensate local communities' land rights (Alden-Wily 2010); (ii) a lack of capacity to process and effectively manage large-scale investments, including participatory consultations that result in clear and enforceable agreements; (iii) a prevalence of investor proposals that were non-viable technically; and (iv) resource conflicts giving rise to negative distributional and gender effects. Implementation was often well behind schedule, such that local people suffered asset losses but received few or none of the promised benefits (Deininger and Byerlee 2012).

In their recent update on some of the warning signs, Jayne et al. (2019) emphasize the "squeeze effect" on traditional small-farm families of this trend toward larger units. As the customary land tenure system becomes less dominant—estimates put its current share of land at about three-quarters—its capacity to protect individual rights to land diminishes. As local land market activity rises, small landholders feel more at risk of losing land through private disputes or expropriation by the government.[52] Even when it occurs at fair market prices, the sale of land by traditional authorities to outside investors makes access more difficult for young people from these communities and increases the likelihood that they will have to leave farming. Poor rural households in Africa have differed historically from their Asian counterparts in having some rights to land; now, landlessness is increasingly present there as well. Medium-scale investors from outside the community are sometimes the main source of tenure insecurity, but members of the local community can be as well, for example, when they constitute a threat to local indigenous groups.

A central question is how the balance between benefits reaped and damage suffered by small farmers changes as the share of land in medium- and large-scale farms rises. If there are too few medium and large farms, both output gains and potentially beneficial spillover effects on the small-scale sector may be lost; if there are too many, the land left for the small farmers may be so little that almost no one can benefit. The issue is thus one of optimal proportions. When political factors are taken into account, the problem becomes more complex because currently having the optimal share of land in the hands of medium farmers from a purely economic point of view may set in motion political processes (alluded to previously) which then guarantee that their share will eventually overshoot that optimal level, at the expense of the small-scale sector. Politics are the key.

From a technical perspective the needed policy package is straightforward enough: better seeds, fewer but more beneficial (efficient) chemicals, investment in rural infrastructure (roads, irrigation works, etc.), and investment in education. Among the political challenges are keeping big, vested interests under control. Jayne et al. (2019, 92) conclude that, if the rise of the middle and large farm group is to bring widespread benefits to

[52] See Ghebru and Lambrecht's (2017) analysis for Ghana, Nigeria, and Mozambique.

SSA's rural populations, then improvements in technology, infrastructure, and institutions must be accompanied by better land governance and property rights, as well as community access to information and the ability to negotiate; in their absence, land will often be given away for free or go to large scale rent-seekers. Small landholders and their organizations should be provided with advisory and business development services. Limited public sector capacity makes it more important that, where possible, larger farms help small farmers get access to finance, markets, and technology, especially in situations where the former achieve much larger yields than the latter.

As the balance of political power shifts toward the larger and richer farmers, the risk intensifies that this will steer countries away from the small-farm strategy they need to achieve growth together with a wide distribution of its benefits. Even if the rise of medium and large farms has, on balance, been beneficial to a given rural society thus far, this may not continue to be the case in that country or region. A quick, major shift toward larger units is unlikely to be desirable when both the impacts on aggregate output and on the welfare of the lower income families are taken into account. This issue has been very little researched in SSA and is now a key area deserving focus.

## Optimal Directions for Future Policy

Few technical or economic factors stand in the way of successful small farm-led agricultural transformation strategies in most or all of SSA, as long as governments provide sustained support for small landholders through appropriately targeted policies and public expenditures. Ethiopia and Rwanda appear to have achieved good, and perhaps impressive, success with such a strategy, although in Ethiopia it does not extend to all parts of the country. Yet, as the political power of commercialized medium- and large-scale farmers continues to rise, the risk that they will increasingly dominate the content and design of policy rises (e.g., by allocating unused land to them rather than to smaller farmers). Where competition for land is not intense, the apparently positive synergies between small and larger farms support the view that it is not necessarily a matter of "either/or." However, in the more common setting of densely populated regions where small-scale farms predominate and little land is available to bring under cultivation, the priority is clear: raising the productive potential of small farms.

While consensus is rare on some details as to how SSA agriculture should best evolve, there is broad agreement that, as elsewhere, seed improvements and fertilizer use are essential for sustainable productivity growth. Several related questions arise. First, who should be in charge of developing (or importing) the new technologies and, more generally, what are the desirable roles of government, private companies, and farmers themselves? Second, what types of support are most effective in inducing farmers to adopt the best technologies, as among extension workers, dispersion of information (pamphlets, radio, etc.), and temporary subsidies to provide the incentive to try a new technology?

Even while agreeing on the importance of better seeds and appropriate fertilizer use, there are many ways to get the surrounding policy package wrong, either by prioritizing some elements too highly and others too little, or by implementing them inefficiently. The much-debated input subsidy programs (ISPs) used in a number of countries shine a light both on the real potential of such a policy and on the two cited dangers—excessive weight and weak implementation. Begun in the 1960s and 1970s, these programs were, for various reasons, phased out during the 1980s and 1990s;[53] a new wave was then introduced in the early 2000s, designed to avoid earlier failings. They have achieved the goal of raising the use of modern inputs, like new seeds and chemicals, at least in the short-term. But the empirical record is also increasingly clear that they "are not sufficient by themselves to achieve profitable, productive, and sustainable farming systems in most parts of Africa" (Jayne et al. 2018). A broader and more balanced set of policies is needed, including a rapid scaling up of the capacities of government and other relevant institutions to contribute directly to progress and to rein in the vested interests pursuing their own profit line, even when it comes at the expense of the farmers, the countries, and the world.

Although ISPs can sometimes raise food production quickly, their overall benefits tend to be smaller and shorter-lived than expected because, among other reasons, they suffer from elite capture along distribution channels, which reduces the benefits to the small farmers.[54] They often distribute

[53] For a review of this history, see Kato and Greeley (2016).

[54] In Tanzania, Pan and Christiaensen (2012) found sixty percent of households receiving input vouchers included a village official, and that households with elected officials and voucher committee members were up to four times more likely to receive input vouchers than others. Evidence from Zambia and Malawi also suggests that households with links to traditional authorities are more likely to receive input subsidies.

fertilizer to beneficiaries who had regularly purchased it in the past, thereby reducing those farmers' reliance on commercial markets and implying that the total increase in fertilizer use is less than it appears to be. Most important, the yield response to fertilizer on small landholder-managed fields is typically less than expected because a large proportion of the farmers operate under adverse agro-ecological conditions in terms of the physical, chemical, and biological makeup of their soils and because the quality of farm management differs; both factors contribute to a highly variable response which is, on average, substantially lower than that obtained in researcher-managed trials.[55] Probably due to these limiting factors, fertilizer subsidy programs typically fail to generate the dynamic growth that would be expected if (as is often argued) farmers, once introduced to them and in a position to weigh their merits, then proceed to buy them at market prices and thereby obviate any further need for subsidies. Subsidies which do become permanent have been shown in other places to morph into a major political dilemma because the pressure to continue them becomes great, even if they are not needed to induce the use of the input in question.[56] In the case of Mozambique, Michael Carter et al. (2014) found that farmers receiving a subsidy two years in a row experienced positive production and income impacts, but that those impacts seemed to decay afterward. A study in Malawi showed little impact on maize production even one year after farmers had graduated from the subsidy program following three years of participation (Ricker-Gilbert and Jayne 2016). Although it is plausible that well-designed subsidy systems could produce larger benefits, their effectiveness depends very much on institutional, political, and cultural contexts; the better-designed features of the recent wave of ISPs in Africa have frequently been watered down or cancelled out at the implementation stage, so it is unsurprising that expectations are not being met.

Despite their performance limitations and some decline in the political enthusiasm for them, public popularity and the fact that major benefiting groups will continue to lobby for subsidies suggests that they will persist for the foreseeable future, regardless of whether or not there are any net economic benefits. Those in Malawi, Nigeria, Tanzania, and Ghana have been at least temporarily discontinued or significantly downsized in recent years, often because governments have been unable to maintain them

[55] It is worth remembering that a significant yield gap between research station tests and application on the farm has always been the norm; it should be no surprise in the SSA context.

[56] India's experience with fertilizer subsidies is notorious in this regard.

when external funding ran out. After a trial in one region, Zambia was scheduled in 2016/2017 to go national with the transformation of its ISP into a flexible e-voucher program that would allow farmers to choose from a wide range of subsidized inputs; other national governments have also begun discussing reform options. Accordingly, Jayne et al. (2018) believe that this may be a good time for reforms or alternatives to these second-generation ISPs, designed to promote sustainable intensification and support for small landholder resilience to climate change, rather than simply encouraging the monocropping and continuous cultivation that runs the risk of exacerbating vulnerability to climate change, something a number of existing ISPs inadvertently do. Options of interest include: (i) offering farmers subsidies conditional on their adoption of such practices; (ii) subsidizing inputs that can directly contribute to sustainable intensification or resilience, such as legume seed and drought tolerant varieties of maize seed (Paymal, 2018); and (iii) limiting the time during which a farmer can receive the subsidy. Use of locally available organic resources (e.g., organic manure from commercial livestock and poultry operations) is desirable when viable.

In any case, the needed improvement in crop yields will require going well beyond even the better-designed ISP systems by greatly increasing public investment in agricultural research, development, and extension, and by emphasizing bi-directional learning between farmers and information providers, such as extension workers and researchers, to help adapt recommendations for inputs and management practices to local agro-ecological conditions and to incorporate local advances achieved by the farmers themselves. At present, heavy spending on ISPs sometimes crowds out such efforts (Ghins et al. 2017); when this effect is taken into account, the net impact of some ISPs may be not just be smaller than hoped, but substantially negative. Timothy Wise (2019a), Jayne et al. (2018), and others agree that the current focus on chemical inputs is excessive; that such chemicals can, on balance, be damaging; and that for the subsidies themselves to provide many benefits on the fertilizer front they must be complemented by steps that embed them in a more holistic strategy. At worst, they can cause severe environmental damage while generating only small and temporary productivity gains, and even less income benefits for small farmers; channeling too many resources in this direction and away from much more productive uses, such as research, extension, and rural infrastructure is thus another big mistake. Second-generation African ISPs have clearly given too much attention to inducing farmers to use fertilizer and too little to helping them to do so efficiently and profitably. But reform will face strong political pressure both from the users and from the producers of the inputs, as well as from the politicians who benefit from overseeing such programs.

The wide range of scenarios within which farmers operate multiplies the importance of their direct participation in the search for better ways to do things. Farmers know much that no one else does, especially how their own situation differs from that of others (the "diversity of setting" issue), how and why they make the decisions they do, and how they are responding to ongoing changes of setting, such as those due to global warming. Among Uganda's 1.7 million small coffee farmers, for example, climate adaptation reflects such factors as rainfall, household size, whether the household decision maker is a woman, and whether bananas or maize (or both) are grown alongside the coffee. This makes it unrealistic to expect to implement any given solution across a large area. Catherine Mulinde, a student of climate risks and other drivers of adaptation, emphasizes that success depends on local communities playing a central role in the design and implementation of solutions. Because they are already adapting to climate shocks, much of what is needed involves upscaling and diffusing their existing knowledge (Arriens 2019). Mulinde found that when coffee farmers were connected to social groups like farming cooperatives, they were more likely to implement such beneficial forms of adaptation as fertilizer use.[57]

While the process of productivity enhancement in SSA has, by definition, much in common with experiences elsewhere, it also involves several features either special to the region or more marked there, albeit sometimes also differing widely across countries. One is the magnitude of the challenge, as described above. Initial poverty levels are similar to those in some of the Asian countries, but the physical context tends to be more challenging—less reliable sources of water, a greater range of staple crops, and the like. Another is the relative lack of experience in handling the challenge of raising productivity in comparatively new countries with a short supply of highly trained

[57] Locally-led adaptation is a focus area of the Global Commission on Adaptation. Managed by World Resources Institute and the Global Center on Adaptation, this Commission works to accelerate such modification and to increase political support for climate resilience. Its locally led Action Track aims to empower and scale up planning, implementation and learning from local adaptation. The Commission aims to expand the quality and quantity of financial resources available to those working at the local level, including community-based organizations and local governments.

personnel. A shortage of skills to handle the scientific aspects of moving forward contributes to an inability to control/influence other players, especially the large international companies in the seed and fertilizer business. Finally, there are the ecological concerns, which are greater—typically much greater—than they were at comparable stages of agricultural progress in other parts of the developing world; mistakes made relatively early in that trajectory will continue to do damage longer into the future here than elsewhere. The importance of advancing in the area of seeds and other inputs interfaces with the need to prevent foreign interests from dominating that process in ways that are ultimately damaging to the countries and the farmers, an interface illustrated by all too many events of the last decade or so in SSA. Advocates of small-scale agriculture and of agroecology support the broad outlines of the multi-faceted technology push just described, as opposed to a narrower seed-and-chemicals focus.[58] Timothy Wise, a specialist in African agriculture, agrees that such a push is sorely needed to fulfill legitimate national and international goals, but is skeptical of success because of the power of the corporate interests pushing the narrower focus on their seeds and their chemicals, feeling threatened by ecology-based approaches, and hijacking government policies all over the world to advance their own interests.

Some analysts who accept that SSA agriculture will remain mainly small farm-based do argue that a degree of consolidation of plots will be important so that more families will have the means to invest in machinery and other inputs where scale matters (Giller et al. 2021). When being on the margin of subsistence makes food and income security inconsistent with significant investments or with running the risks implicit in testing new technologies, and where governments do not help farmers much in confronting these challenges, such consolidation may be necessary. This issue arises, for example, in Malawi, for which Muyanga et al. (2020) provide a balanced and realistic assessment of an extremely challenging setting. Farm size is already quite small, with seventy-six percent of farmers operating less than one hectare and about thirty percent struggling on less than half a hectare of land. The population continues to grow. Despite the relatively high intensity of fertilizer use, agricultural productivity is low due to soils degraded by continuous cultivation without fallowing. Non-agricultural wage jobs are unlikely

[58] Parmentier (2014) presents a detailed explanation and defense of agroecology and a critique of genetically modified seeds and the institutions that push them.

to provide employment for a large share of the youth, so the great majority will depend on farming and agricultural-related informal sector jobs. Raising agricultural productivity is the only realistic way to raise incomes. The country suffers a large yield gap in virtually all crops. Evidence suggests that the greatest payoff to investment will come from research and development, from education (especially to improve extension services) and from infrastructure (especially roads and electricity). Shoring up land rights and tenure laws incentivizes long-term investments in soil health, which could also enable sustainable intensification of the limited land resource. Secure land rights can also facilitate mutually beneficial transfers of land toward the most productive uses. The country will also need to deal with some of the already known challenges, such as an unpredictable policy environment featuring frequent ad hoc decision-making that threatens agricultural commercialization, a lack of coordination between government policy and public and private investment decisions, and a limited voice for private sector and civil society in the policy-making processes.

## The Governance Threat to Good Policy

For perhaps the first time in history, a large, self-interested seed-and-fertilizer company, Monsanto, has had such power over local decision-making as to be able to participate directly in writing a nation's rule book on seeds. This recently occurred in Malawi,[59] a low-income country where equitable growth through rising productivity on small farms is crucially important. Monsanto works in league with AGRA, an institution founded in 2006 with the stated goals of doubling yields and incomes for thirty million small-scale farm households while halving food insecurity by 2020. With the Gates Foundation as main sponsor and the heavy backing of agribusiness, it has encouraged African governments to spend big shares of their agricultural budgets to subsidize the purchase of commercial seeds and synthetic fertilizers.[60] Wise (2019), like many others, worries that increased monocropping and the use of synthetic fertilizers have aggravated

[59] See Wise (2019).

[60] The Gates Foundation is justly famous for having funded many good projects. Its erring on this one may reflect a tendency to focus on major technological breakthroughs rather than on apparently less revolutionary advances. In this case the many small things that can add up to major productivity growth benefiting the small farmers and preserving the environment appear to be a much safer bet

acidification and reduced much-needed organic matter, and that costly input subsidies have shifted land use from drought-tolerant, nutritious crops like sorghum and millet to commercial alternatives, with crop and diet diversity lessening as a result. Advocates of agroecology, who favor a multi-faceted technology push rather than one focused exclusively on non-reproducible seeds and chemicals, see a major threat from the dominance of large agribusiness companies that monopolize the sales of seeds, fertilizers, and other chemicals in a way which gives near total weight to the profit line and essentially none to environmental concerns or, despite its rhetoric, to the welfare of the agricultural population, nearly all of whom work on small farms.

The AGRA story has the makings of a pseudo-scam morphing into a tragedy. In 2006 AGRA put forward its "model," allegedly designed to achieve great progress within a decade or so. Predictably, given an apparent lack of familiarity with the economics of small-scale agriculture and its dynamics, the program has fallen far short of its stated objectives, possibly even doing more harm than good. Now facing serious criticism, the interests behind AGRA are doubling down. Some presumably believe the line of argument espoused; others are primarily concerned with their firms' bottom lines; many politicians have provided support as a route to power and financial gain. The four features that AGRA has most clearly manifested thus far—lack of in-depth knowledge, a non-scientific approach that has not included the appropriate test trials since it was initiated, aggressive marketing of the model, and a lack of transparency manifested in a sort of cover-up designed presumably to prevent criticism from rising too rapidly and spreading too widely—suggest that the more completely it can be removed from the playing field of SSA agriculture the better.[61]

In a detailed critique of what he calls the existing Green Revolution model of input-intensive agriculture in SSA, Wise (2019a) specifically targets

than the allegedly big breakthrough spearheaded by AGRA. The Foundation has shown wisdom in some other cases by backing away from its initial support for an institutional innovation that then proved less successful than expected or claimed.

[61] Among historical counterparts, the roles of Stalin in Russia and Mao in China in contributing to poor agricultural performance leading to unnecessary poverty and death come to mind (see Chapter 5). In those cases, the damage resulted from the leaders' unwillingness to listen to real scientists or to ascribe any skills and knowledge to farmers themselves, together with their own self-confidence and their partnering with pseudoscientists. In the case of AGRA, these faults are accompanied by the powerful force of profit-seeking. The great students of farming, like Chayanov in Russia, do recognize the wisdom built into some of the traditional farming practices. SSA needs its Chayanovs rather than its Monsantos. Hopefully, they are being and will be listened to more than Chayanov was.

AGRA, which highlighted the goals of doubling crop yields and the incomes of thirty million small landholder households within fourteen years-implying annual yield increases of an impressive 3.1 percent. The approach has fallen far short of those objectives, even with many African governments spending big shares of their agricultural budgets to subsidize the purchase of Green Revolution inputs of commercial seeds and synthetic fertilizers through the ISPs previously discussed.[62] In fact, just as AGRA's influence was rising, the growth of agriculture in SSA was slowing, from an impressive 5.5 percent per year from 2000 to 2010 to 3.4 percent from 2010 to 2020. With a population still growing at an astronomic rate of 2.7 percent per year, the increase in agricultural output per person was marginal and that of food per person was probably negative for the region as a whole and certainly in many of its countries.

The above-cited criticisms of the ISPs are part of a growing skepticism among experts as to AGRA's capacity to facilitate large output gains in the medium term, given its lack of a persuasive plan, its lack of transparency, and its disregard for the environment. Those with financial interests in the input-intensive system respond with attacks on the capacity of agroecology to raise agricultural output fast enough (or at all). Wise (2019b) contradicts this latter view, citing the recent FAO expert report (FAO 2019) to the effect that, "the approach has been shown to improve soil fertility, increase crop and diet diversity, raise total food productivity, improve resilience to climate change, and increase farmers' food and income security while decreasing their dependence on costly inputs. The predominant input-intensive approach to agricultural development can hardly claim such successes, which is precisely why international institutions are actively seeking alternatives." He notes that much of the discourse around the issue is ill-informed about the technical innovations that agroecology can offer to small-scale farmers; a dismissive article by a researcher associated with a pro-biotechnology institute in Uganda recently equated agroecology to traditional agriculture and, on that basis, labeled it as a step backward. Meanwhile, under the banner of AGRA, agribusiness lobbies governments to subsidize the increasing use of fossil-fuel-based fertilizers and commercial seeds. In Malawi, forty to sixty percent of the government's agricultural budget has gone to these

[62] The very successful experiences of Rwanda and Ethiopia, previously discussed, might be seen as evidence that, at least in some places, AGRA's goals are being met. But in both cases, success appears to be substantially due to the pursuit of the more holistic approach.

subsidies, without which many farmers could not afford the inputs because they typically do not raise yields enough to pay their full cost.[63] Meanwhile, the land becomes more acidic and less fertile. Monsanto's sales, which include fifty percent of Malawi's commercial corn seeds, are highly dependent on the subsidies.[64] The company's other (long-standing) tactic is to actively hinder farmers from saving seeds from their last harvest, which the majority still do. One draft of Malawi's national seed policy, in whose preparation a Monsanto executive participated, threatened to outlaw a farmer's rights to save, exchange, or sell their seeds. Although Wise (2019b) reports that farm groups were able to remove some of the worst provisions of that program, the bill still threatened the sale of farm-saved seed. At one local seed fair, these guidelines led to the exclusion of a highly productive variety of native orange maize developed by a local group of farmers; the authorities refused to categorize it as a "seed," but instead labeled it as a "grain." Such an incident, and the experience of Malawi more generally, illustrates an extreme version of the common mismatch between weak local governments and powerful foreign firms pushing their profitable lines, with the assistance of groups like AGRA. Malawi's decision-makers appear insufficiently aware of the economics of agriculture to contradict the intuitive idea that traditional farmers are, by definition, unreceptive to technological advance. The top-down model pushed by Monsanto leaves no room for the farmer participation judged so important by Mulinde and scores of other close observers of rural reality. The societal cost of losing this battle will be greatest in low-income countries like Malawi, because how well family farms do is likely to remain the central determinant of advances in their national well-being for some decades; an early bias toward an overly chemical-intensive agriculture that does not benefit

[63] This contention is consistent with the finding, reported above, that the benefits of ISPs do not seem to last much beyond the period of subsidization.

[64] Monsanto and fellow agro-giants have campaigned to open Mexico to the cultivation of genetically modified corn. An injunction stalled the effort for some years, and in early 2021, President Lopez Obrador issued a decree to phase out use of the herbicide glyphosate and the cultivation of genetically modified corn (Doran 2021). Later he clarified that the government would also phase out GM corn imports in three years, including not just corn for human consumption but also yellow corn destined primarily for livestock. Lopez Obrador's step can be seen as signaling that the president's agricultural policies "have begun to favour Mexican producers, particularly small-scale farmers, and protect consumers alarmed by the rise of obesity and chronic diseases associated with high-fat, high-sugar processed foods" (Wise 2021b). Under NAFTA, the United States saw a four hundred percent increase in corn exports to Mexico, the vast majority of which were genetically modified yellow dent corn. Citizens and farmers have complained that the release of such corn, which pollinates through the wind, would threaten the integrity of Mexico's remarkable repository of some twenty-three thousand varieties of native corn that have evolved over millennia. Such crop diversity is important both for commercial crop breeding and for the kind of land management the Inter-governmental Panel on Climate Change (IPCC) is recommending (Wise 2019).

the small family farmer or protect the ecology will have a bigger social cost than it would in already-rich countries and ones less subject to the impact of climate change. Among mistaken economic policies, this one is unusual in the degree of acceptance not only by bureaucrats but even by some experts in related areas like plant science. The latter are seldom well-schooled on the economic issues involved, nor naturally inclined to expect much of relatively uneducated farmers unless they have had a chance to work with them. And they are only gradually becoming conscious of the societal costs of chemical use. Monsanto takes great pains to fend off critics of chemical-based water pollution, wherever they appear.[65]

In contrast to the widespread damage that can be wrought by a system in which the technology giants play such a dominating role, a more holistic approach, including agroecology, offers many of the innovations small-scale farmers need to increase soil fertility, raise productivity, improve food and nutrition security, and build climate resilience. These include biological pest control;[66] push–pull technology, such as when a scientifically proven mix of crops keeps pests away from food crops, allowing farmers to reduce pesticide use while increasing productivity; participatory plant breeding, where agronomists work with farmers to identify the most productive and desirable seed varieties and improve them through careful seed selection and farm management, a process in which degraded local varieties are improved or replaced with locally adapted alternatives; agro-forestry, where scientists have demonstrated the soil-building potential of incorporating trees and cover crops on small-scale farms, allowing nitrogen fixing in the soil, cutting erosion, and giving farmers another cash crop while degraded land is restored; incorporation of small livestock like goats or fowl to provide farmers with a sustainable source of manure while adding needed protein to local diets; and science-driven production of compost which can dramatically improve soil quality (Wise 2019b).[67] Many innovative farmers in

[65] In 2017, the editor of northern Iowa's *Storm Lake Times*, Art Cullen, won a Pulitzer Prize for uncovering a secret agribusiness fund, bankrolled by Monsanto, Koch Fertilizer, and other companies, whose purpose was to defeat a lawsuit seeking to reduce water pollution from agriculture in the area around Storm Lake and other districts along the state's Upper Raccoon River. The lawsuit was brought by the Des Moines Water Works and aimed to force agriculture to regulate/control the sort of chemical applications the IPCC has been denouncing (Wise 2019).

[66] Scientist Hans Herren won a World Food Prize for halting the spread of a cassava pest in Africa by introducing a wasp that naturally controlled the infestation.

[67] These innovations and many others are explored in depth in the *High Level Panel of Experts on Food Security and Nutrition (HLPE)* report of 2017 (FAO-HLPE 2019).

southern Africa grow a mix of crops, which helps insure against disaster if one of them fails, as well as providing the families with a diverse and healthier diet. Using composted manure instead of synthetic fertilizer, they simultaneously improve the fertility of their soils and reduce their carbon footprints.

The global conflict between chemical-intensive agriculture and ecologically safer approaches is playing out most starkly in this SSA scenario, where the need to raise production and yields is greatest. The short-term yield increases achieved under programs like AGRA's have at times been substantial but, as noted, the subsidies do not seem to have put farmers on a path to permanent improvement, the productivity increases have generally been limited and diminishing over time, and they have come with considerable ecological damage. Worst of all, subsidies like the ISPs crowd out government spending where it is most essential: on technological research, diffusion and infrastructure. They also multiply the risk of benefits being quite concentrated among the already better-off.

In illuminating AGRA's trajectory, Wise (2020a, 2021b) highlights a string of dubious behavior patterns:[68]

> Fourteen years into this billion-dollar donor initiative to revolutionize African farming, and now past the 2020 endpoint for its goals of doubling yields and incomes for 30 million smallholder farmers, AGRA finally published internal country monitoring and evaluation reports from early last year. I reviewed all 1,365 pages of those documents, unearthed in Freedom of Information Act requests to the U.S. Agency for International Development after AGRA refused to provide them. They show no progress toward AGRA's top-line goals. The absence of impact data in AGRA's 11 recent country Outcome Monitoring reports, with no reference to results from its first ten years of Green Revolution promotion, suggests either that those results are so poor the organization does not want to reveal them or that it has never bothered to track progress toward its main goals. It is hard to know which is worse. If AGRA is concealing evidence that its well-funded interventions, backed by massive African government subsidies for farmers to purchase commercial seeds and fertilizers, are failing to produce the intended results, it is defrauding donors, participating governments, and most of all, farmers.

[68] See Wise (2020b) for a more detailed assessment of AGRA.

> AGRA refused to provide data on its beneficiaries for our 2020 report, False Promises. Using national-level data we showed that crop yields were growing slowly—just 18% staple yield growth over 12 years. Poverty remained high and the number of undernourished people in AGRA's 13 countries had increased 30% from 2006 to 2018.
>
> If . . . AGRA has not gathered the data to monitor its expensive interventions, it would be hard to think of another billion-dollar enterprise that is so unaccountable, failing even to track progress toward its top-line goals.

Some AGRA-backed efforts have produced impressive looking numbers. Thus, from 2004/2006 to 2016/2018, Rwanda achieved a fourfold increase in maize production, with a sixty-six percent increase in yields (4.3 percent per year). Rice output doubled, although yields fell by nineteen percent (Wise 2020b, 25). For staples as a whole, yields rose by twenty-four percent or 1.8 percent per year. The focus on selected crops was quite deliberate; recent accounts indicate that the Ministry of Agriculture fined farmers if they did not plant maize and other approved program crops (Dawson 2020). They were compelled to use fertilizer, which the government heavily subsidized. This enforced planting regimen cut dramatically into traditional practices of intercropping and reduced the diversity of food crops. The campaign met resistance from farmers and, with President Paul Kagame facing an election in 2017, some restrictions were relaxed, leading to somewhat more diverse cropping patterns (Wise 2020b, 26). What the medium- and longer-term impacts of this growth burst are will be an important topic of analysis in future.

Wise (2020b, 26) cites Mali's impressive record as a stark contrast to most other AGRA countries, suggesting that it may well be due:

> to its government's more careful approach to widespread promotion of the Green Revolution technology package. Farmer and other non-governmental organizations actively mobilized to stop AGRA from imposing its model there. Since democratic government was restored in the 1990s, farmers groups have played a role in government policy, even drafting the 2004 Agricultural Orientation Law, the country's overall agricultural framework. Mali's Coalition to Protect African Genetic Resources convened organizations from all over Africa to engage with AGRA and

dissuade governments from collaborating with it, launching a 2007 campaign "Agroecological Alternatives to AGRA."

AGRA entered a SSA scenario featuring a long-standing dearth of the solid empirical information needed to permit quick and accurate quantification of the benefits and costs of alternative strategies for a given locale. This is now changing; there is much professional support for the view that the small farmer must remain a central player and that undue focus on "industrial agriculture" is dangerous. But it was inevitable that some corporate and philanthropic leaders would respond to the challenge of feeding growing populations by calling for major investments in that type of agriculture, with the corporate interests attacking agroecology or whatever else stood in the way. The common defenses of the now substantially embedded system reflect both the widely held belief of non-experts that traditional systems are not and cannot be made efficient, and the fact that a more agroecological approach would be a threat to the business profits now being reaped. Some advocates of this industrial approach have probably recognized that it is important to influence policy early—before additional information either raises doubts about their preferred pathway or confirms the benefits of ecology or other competing options. Smoothing the way for this defense is the fact that reports emanating from UN agencies like FAO tend to avoid "getting into politics" by commenting on the challenge implicit in the power of agribusiness. While the business group is naturally expected to push solutions that favor its own interests, it is worrisome that most others in a position to influence outcomes, including some philanthropic interests and many government officials in both ICs and DCs, share some of its views and provide practical support. In such a scenario, good policy on agriculture in SSA will likely be an even harder sell than good policy on greenhouse gas (GHG) emissions has been. With time, the fact that something is affecting our climate has become more and more obvious to an increasing share of the population. It is far less evident, and in fact counter-intuitive to most people not close to the issues, that to solidify the future availability of food for all in SSA in a way consistent with environmental sustainability, family farmers with self-propagating seeds and modest usage of fertilizers and other chemical inputs are a better bet than large mechanized producers because those farmers can both achieve high food production and guarantee that everyone has access to it.

The government practice of dictating to farmers without knowing very well (or at all) what underlies farmers' preferred behavior has been a scourge nearly everywhere, albeit in varying degree. Parts of Africa are now replaying this sad litany with the help of outsiders. While Malawi and Brazil may be extreme cases of policies that combine bad economics and bad ecology, they are far from the only ones. Inside SSA, few people understand the character and severity of this threat; outside SSA, almost no one is aware of what is going on there.

Despite recent advances in the analysis of SSA agriculture, much still must be learned. The net economic benefits from the AGRA approach are clearly in question, and there is much evidence that fertilizer subsidies have not thus far led to systematic and lasting productivity gains. At the same time, it remains unclear exactly how far and how fast a more small-farm *cum* ecological focus can take the region. A much better thought-out approach is needed in each country—one that prioritizes the welfare of small farmers and other low-income groups together with environmental sustainability, and one that builds in strong learning processes, among other things, by facilitating the diffusion of new findings and experiences.[69] Raising productivity in environmentally friendly ways relies on better crop rotation, less tilling, and varieties that do not require heavy doses of fertilizer or other chemicals. Sometimes it will mean starting with traditional seeds and improving them in line with these criteria. Sometimes it may mean starting with existing chemical-guzzling varieties to test the extent to which they can be modified to wean them off the more damaging input levels now applied. A key is making sure that the process, and those involved in it, understand that a new and more complex set of objectives has replaced that of simply raising yields or, even worse, raising fertilizer use and the profits of the input producing companies.

R&D should thus have three goals, with the advantages of each weighed off against the advantages of the others: productivity gains, including those coming from choice of higher value products; environmental protection; and a greater share of benefits going to lower income people (mainly small-farm families). A main lesson of experience to date is that few private firms

[69] On this front, the radio has proven valuable in many settings. An important contribution comes from Canada-based Farm Radio International, founded in 1979 as the first international non-profit organization to work alongside radio broadcasters with the goal of improving food security and agricultural methods for small-scale farmers in African countries.

can be trusted to act in the societal interest, either in raising the incomes of poorer farmers or in advancing ecological protection; in a context as complicated as that of SSA, they could, in any case, not be expected to understand what furthers the welfare of the rural population, even were they inclined to try. To the extent that the term "modernization" is used to include the high productivity chemical-intensive approach together with mechanization, it is clear that the three cited objectives are not at all synonymous with it. It has long been recognized that mechanization is often damaging to the welfare of the poor when it occurs on large farms and displaces labor, a fact of which the World Bank became officially conscious back in the 1970s (McInerney and Donaldson 1975). Where, because of economies of scale, mechanization encourages the concentration of land in fewer hands, its effects are again usually perverse; it is, however, desirable when it occurs on small family farms as labor scarcity reaches the point where the farmers opt to replace their own manual labor with machines. In the agrarian successes of Japan, Korea, and Taiwan, this mechanization phase involved the two-wheeled tractor, now part of the process occurring in parts of SSA.

The diversity of context within SSA and within each of its countries is one of the main challenges to widespread success. The many ways in which climate change alters existing scenarios, and the ways in which farmers respond, adds a newish dimension of diversity and another reason to make sure that farmers themselves are involved in and listened to as new technologies develop. In most SSA countries, an important factor is the continuing lack of personnel who can provide strong support for small farmers; this is one reason why they must sort so many things out on their own. Malawi, already a tricky case because of overpopulation and the heavy presence of Monsanto and AGRA, exemplifies this complexity. Farmers have themselves been coming up with new seeds, but in the case cited above the authorities attempted to brush it off. Although Malawians are among the most climate-aware of African people,[70] it can be hard to get politicians to see the phenomenon as an immediate threat.

The climate change challenge interacts with that of improving the situation of female farmers. Gender inequality is a major issue in SSA agriculture generally. Women do much work but have less access to resources, including land and other inputs. In their detailed discussion of these challenges in the

[70] As noted by Declan Conway of the London School of Economics, a member of the Future Climate for Africa Project (*The Economist*, September 21, 2019).

context of two regions of Malawi—Nkhamenya and Kabudula—Murray et al. (2016, 140–141) note that female small landholders have extremely limited access to agricultural productivity-enhancing inputs and resources. Even if they are motivated to adopt green practices, they may not have the power to do so. Participatory technology development and adaptation approaches are needed to increase the access to and the utility of such practices for them. As the effects of climate change intensify, markets are expected to expand for products and services that support climate resilience, and it is crucial that the poor (many of whom are women) have access to sustainable energy pathways.

## Tenure Complexity and Land Markets

The social and agrarian history of SSA has left a varied and complicated set of arrangements with respect to land tenure. They have been the topic of much discussion and many suggestions for reform. The dialogue has evolved over time as understanding has deepened and settings have changed. Two related themes have been prominent: first, the implications of past and current tenure regimes for productivity, distribution of income and welfare, and the pursuit of output increases through investment and the use of modern inputs; and second, the potential of a greater role for land markets (rental and purchase) in improving these outcome.

Competition and conflict over land are increasing in many parts of SSA as farm families feel the need to produce more; civil servants and others with outside employment also want a land base, as do many politicians, wealthy nationals, and foreign companies; environmental groups and some national governments try to extend the area under conservation; and the increasing exploitation of resources, such as minerals, wildlife, water, trees, and so on, squeezes the supply of land. Such rising pressures on the available land create many problems, even more so when rights to land are complicated by the overlap between current systems with their various communal aspects and more formal Western-type systems (Cousins 2009). Peters (2004, 278) sees a key "socio-cultural dynamic of differentiation" emerging within social units such as the family, lineage, village, tribe ethnically defined group, with the definition of "belonging" becoming more exclusive.

The term "communal tenure" has confused this discussion as, for some people, it suggests joint or collective ownership and use of all land and natural resources; in fact, most African systems include clearly defined individual or family rights to some types of land. On the other hand, these systems generally do involve the conferral of rights on the basis of accepted group membership, and a degree of group control or supervision over land matters, which "relativizes" individual rights to a greater degree than in systems of private property. John Bruce (1986) saw "communal tenure" systems as mixed regimes, comprising variable bundles of individual, family, subgroup, and larger group rights and duties in relation to a variety of natural resources. Their distinguishing feature is that they derive their authority from the community where they operate rather than from the nation-state. He notes, however, that post-colonial African governments had been "remarkably activist" in their attempts to reform traditional patterns of land holding (Bruce 1993, 13). Recent thinking has increasingly favored a pragmatic, "adaptationist" approach rather than the radical replacement of existing regimes attempted, mostly unsuccessfully, in the past. Ben Cousins (2009, 9) suggests that the core needs in adapting the dominant model are explicit recognition of indigenous tenure rules, legal protection for land held under them, strengthening of local institutions which administer those rules, and recognition or provision of mechanisms for resolving disputes. This perspective acknowledges that private title does not necessarily bring security of tenure to the landholder, let alone to the community; in fact, "unsuccessful attempts to substitute state titles for customary entitlements may reduce security by creating normative confusion, of which the powerful may take advantage" (Bruce and Mighot-Adholla 1994, 260).

In many settings, there are no easy solutions to this challenge. Local institutions, such as village committees, are not by definition "open and neutral" fora for managing any tenure reform which may greatly alter the existing system; authority and regulation are basically political issues. Positive reform calls for the capacity to clarify multiple claims to land and to resolve conflicting claims of "prior occupancy" while balancing these against existing use rights. A combination of community and state regulation may be required, but defining it is difficult, among other things, because it must anticipate "how the different players . . . will try to use that framework . . . and attempt to distort it to their own advantage" (Lavigne Delville 1999, 19–22). Another challenge is that few at the national government level are ready to go beyond rhetoric and devolve real authority over land to the local level (partly because of resistance by the political and administrative class), and that few states have the real capacity to carry through serious reform.

The simple formalization of land rights tends to override the complexities of marginalized, common access, and multiple rights, and often has a built-in bias toward individual and exclusive rights. Codification,[71] if extended to cover the rights of marginalized groups such as pastoralists, can possibly help to protect informal rights under threat. Protecting "custom" under the authority of state trusteeship is not feasible given that the state itself all too often becomes the instrument of interest groups. Decentralization of land administration and management to the community level is, by itself, insufficient because it does not resolve the issue of authority and representation at the local level where conflicts of interest arise, the disadvantaged often lack voice, and some outside interventions (e.g., by state agricultural projects) cannot be dealt with at village level alone. For these reasons, decentralization requires the central government to take responsibility for providing the broad framework and principles underlying tenure, and for ensuring the transparency and accountability of local structures (Toulmin 2000).

More than a decade ago, Cousins (2009, 11) saw a degree of convergence in recommendations for tenure reform. There was a general call for greater recognition in law of the rights observed under "customary" systems, and thus for legal protection of the rights of vulnerable groups, as well as of the secondary and multiple rights to land and resources which are often ignored in current statutory law. Given the frequently predatory nature of the contemporary state and the interest groups able to use state power for their own ends, these protections are partly designed to keep the state itself at bay. There was also a focus on strengthening local institutions of land administration and management, on the subsidiarity principle[72] (thus saving on costs) and because of the advantages of local definition and flexibility in the application of rules. However, because local institutions are themselves vulnerable to the power plays of elites, as well as to a "politics of exclusion" (Lavigne Delville 1999, 14), transparency and accountability (i.e., democratization), underwritten by central

[71] "Codification" refers to the collection and systematic arrangement of the laws of a state or country, or the statutory provisions, rules, and regulations that govern a specific area or subject of law or practice. It rearranges and displaces/supersedes prior statutes and case decisions. Codification of an area of law generally constitutes the whole source that is relied upon for a legal question in that area.

[72] Subsidiarity is a principle of social organization holding that social and political issues should be dealt with at the most immediate or local level consistent with their resolution.

government, were also seen as necessary. Thirdly, because conflicts over land rights are inevitable, there is a need for institutions and procedures to mediate, arbitrate, and negotiate, particularly at the local level (Toulmin 2000). This involves defining clear roles both for customary mechanisms and institutions on the one hand, and for state authorities on the other; accountability and transparency are again important. All this said, much of the detailed sorting out of just how legal recognition of "customary" rights should be structured remains to be done. Enduring features include the often greater trust that populations put in local chiefs than in national governments; the former are seen as more trustworthy, less corrupt, and better at their jobs than politicians.[73] This contrast underlines why local participation can be very important, or even essential, to the implementation of positive national policies. Boone (2014) notes how politicians who preside over state-dominated land tenure systems push for settlement of new communities in regions with already existing populations in order to mobilize them for political ends.[74]

Whatever the gradual and limited progress in confronting these complexities, more recent thinking on tenure issues reflects the rapid change of setting in most SSA countries as population explodes, farm size shrinks, off-farm activities of farm families increase, and the pressure on land increases. Sources of economic efficiency which may have appeared both less urgent and less feasible some decades ago are now important. Unfortunately, the existing SSA literature on the relationship between property rights in land, agricultural investment, and land use patterns is often confusing. A link between land tenure and agricultural investment has long been taken for granted by many economists, but James Fenske (2011) notes that empirical studies have failed to systematically identify it in SSA.[75] This result is probably due to (i) oversimplistic hypotheses, either that Western-type property rights are always beneficial or that traditional systems always do a good job; (ii) a failure to take due account of differences in settings and among farmers;

[73] Based on a survey of Afrobarometer in twenty-eight countries, cited by *The Economist*, October 14, 2023, "Custom Redesigned."

[74] Given the complexity of rights issues in SSA, it is unsurprising that most empirical analyses of the impacts of weak or unclear rights to land have been undertaken in other regions. Many of the same phenomena observed elsewhere with respect to state control are present here as well. Albertus (2021) discusses some of these.

[75] The parallel with the results of such studies in economic history as Allen (1992) are noteworthy (see Chapter 2).

and (iii) methodological problems, often inevitable due to incomplete and/or inaccurate data.[76]

In his review of the now numerous studies on this issue, Fenske (2011) concludes that it has become possible to distinguish types of investment and measures of land tenure for which there is a robust link, and those for which it is not.[77] For example, studies that have searched for a link between tenure and fallow have almost all found one. This literature does, however, leave many questions open, as well as showing how complex the patterns of causation may be. In their study, Markus Goldstein and Christopher Udry (2008) have shown, through a context-specific study of one particular region of Ghana, that investment outcomes are determined by the interaction of gender, political status, and land acquisition, and that their combined impact is large. While most of the studies cited have been careful to take local details into account, it is unclear whether the impacts of land tenure they have found operate solely for certain types of individuals in specific circumstances.

Fenske (2011, 154) draws several conclusions from his survey: "First, while land rights in West Africa may often provide adequate security for investment, rights are only secure conditional on use. Land left fallow may be lost; this shortens the fallow period in some contexts and lengthens the time between fallow periods in others, depending on the farming system." The productivity increase attainable through investment in fallow is the most vulnerable to expropriation; such loss has the most negative effects on security. Second, tree planting may enhance rights, but these, too, are affected by the nature of land tenure. Finally, tenure does not generally affect short-lived investments and inputs such as labor, fertilizer, manure, and insecticide. Taken together, these conclusions "suggest that if African agriculture becomes more input-intensive in the future, tenure security will become less important."

The potential role of markets has been given more attention in recent decades. Thus, Klaus Deininger et al. (2017, 78), using data from six countries—Ethiopia, Malawi, Niger, Nigeria, Tanzania, and

[76] On methodological issues Fenske (2011, 137) comments that "Studies with small sample sizes, those that use binary investment measures, and those that control for household fixed effects are less likely to find a statistically significant link between land tenure and investment. Self-reported tenure security has been a poor predictor of investment outcomes."

[77] He also notes that it is possible to identify how the econometric techniques these studies use have affected their outcomes.

Uganda—conclude that such markets have great potential to increase productivity and equalize factor input ratios across farms by transferring land to land-poor and labor-rich producers, while noting that their operation may be constrained by ill-defined or insecure rights and by policy restrictions. Such potential benefits reflect not only differences in factor proportions due to imperfect factor markets for land and labor, but also considerable productivity variation among small landholders for other reasons. And because customary systems are often biased against women, "in particular restricting their ability to inherit land and thus their bargaining power within the household," a freer market can bring benefits on this front.[78] These various benefits are likely to rise as land becomes scarcer, putting traditional institutions under greater stress to deal with more land disputes. The growth of the rural non-farm economy, increasing dispersion of skills, diversification of income sources, and rural–urban migration together "increase the scope for efficiency-enhancing transactions as, investment becomes more profitable, and land from those joining the non-agricultural sector can be leased to those specializing in agriculture. In such situations, rental markets can provide advantages by equalizing factor endowments and allowing gains from specialization." A consistent finding across the six countries is that land markets contribute to equalization of land endowments, especially in Malawi, Nigeria, and Uganda, where overall land pressure is high, and rather modestly in Tanzania, Niger, and Ethiopia. Land market performance seems to be lower where implicit or explicit restrictions on land rental exist, where perceived threats of uncompensated expropriation reduce subjective tenure security, and where policies to document existing land rights exist but are not implemented or are implemented in an ad hoc manner or in a way that leaves out specific groups of landholders, in particular women, or is unaffordable to them (ibid. 89).

## Land Reform Experiences Thus Far in Sub-Saharan Africa

Most of the region's few agrarian reforms have involved transferring land from colonialists to the local population (e.g., South Africa and Zimbabwe); the main exception has been Ethiopia's reform. Sorting out how much the

[78] See Murray et al. (2016).

transfer of land has redistributed income and cut poverty has, as usual, been difficult; settings vary enormously, many factors are at work, and the available data is usually scanty.

Zimbabwe's experience is arguably the most disappointing of these three. Land reform was a pledge of the country's liberation movement and a promising beginning came quickly when the new government took over in 1980; it recorded several years of high activity before winding down by 1990 (Kinsey 2004, 1671). About one-tenth of communal area households had benefited and these resettled farmers were generating perhaps two to two-and-a-half times as much income as those not moved.[79] By 2000, the "Golden Age" of resettlement had come to an end, initial goals were being sidetracked and land was increasingly being passed to members of a wealthy political elite—a process that was both cause and effect of the country's descent into violence and state failure. Contributing to the change, ironically, were ill-informed and unduly negative assessments of the reform as it unfolded in the 1980s. No careful studies had, at that time, detected the considerable benefits and some expectations were unreasonable (Kinsey 2004, 1672). The country's macroeconomic failure has since then made success in both agriculture and the surrounding activities more difficult.

A more historically "normal" type of reform occurred in 1975 in Ethiopia, a country with a tradition of strongly top-down government whose population density and agrarian hierarchy made its setting for reform more similar to those elsewhere in the world than in the case of almost any other country of SSA. By the time the communist military council (the *Derg*) took over in 1974, land concentration and exploitative conditions were creating much pressure for a comprehensive reform (Cohen and Weintraub 1975).[80]

> The land reform of 1975 was an important landmark in the socio-economic evolution of rural Ethiopia, not only as an economic but also as a political-administrative point of transition. It came as the culmination of a popular

[79] After controlling for relevant and identifiable differences (Deininger et al. 2000). As Kinsey (2004, 1682–1685) discusses in detail, the data have some weaknesses, but leave no real doubt that both productivity and incomes were much higher in the resettlement areas.

[80] It is not possible to compare the land concentration prior to that 1974 revolution with that of the extreme Latin American cases for lack of adequate data (see Cohen and Weintraub 1975; Sobhan 1993). Although it was probably less extreme, its impact on poverty was accentuated by the great shortage of land in most of the country, in that sense paralleling the case of China. Recent income inequality data put countries like Ethiopia, with a Gini coefficient of 0.33 or 0.35, far below those of most Latin American countries, typically in the range of 0.45–0.50 (World Bank n.d.).

> movement against the legacy of a political-economic system that ended with the rule of Emperor Haile Selassie. (Baye 2013, 154)

It aimed at effecting a major transformation of both the country's complex land tenure system and its social and political structure as well, destroying the feudal order and changing landowning patterns, particularly in the south, in favor of peasants and small landowners.

Its arrival "opened the floodgates of rural discontent, allowing the peasants to take over the land and encouraging them to organize into peasant associations" (Ottaway 1977), as the government did not seriously attempt to control the process. Peasant associations were, in principle, allowed to decide whether to redistribute land among their members or to enter into collective forms of operation. Its wide scope and the suddenness with which the reform was announced and implemented led most observers, even many radical Ethiopians and diplomats from socialist countries, to forecast economic disaster and social breakdown. Thousands lost their lives in the associated turmoil. There was a short-term increase in production, although this was due mostly to favorable weather and a tangible improvement in peasant living conditions (Dalton 1975). The urban population, however, suffered because of the sharp price increases that resulted from the disruption of the marketing system and an increase in on-farm consumption (Holmberg 1976). The longer-term effects of the reform are unclear due to major differences by region, changing settings over time, accompanying violence and famine, and a lack of in-depth analyses.

Historically, Ethiopia has been divided into the northern highlands, constituting the core of the old Christian kingdom and the bulk of the nation's population, and the southern highlands, most of which were brought under imperial rule by conquest. In the northern regions, the major form of ownership was a communal system known as *rist*, under which all descendants (both male and female) of an individual founder were entitled to a share. Most peasants held at least some *rist* land; absentee landlords were rare. In the southern provinces, however, few farmers owned the land they cultivated. The land ownership patterns developed after the Ethiopian conquest in the late nineteenth and early twentieth centuries, when officials divided land equally among the state, the church, and the existing population. The loss of two-thirds of their land to the new landlords and the church turned many people into tenants, who accounted for between sixty-five to eighty percent of the holdings; tenant payments to landowners averaged as much as fifty percent of output (Wubne 1991).

By the mid-1960s, many sectors of Ethiopian society favored land reform. In a partial parallel with Mexico's Revolution, university students were among its strongest advocates. By1974, it was widely believed that the archaic land tenure system was playing a major role in the backwardness of Ethiopian agriculture. The reform was thoroughgoing; it nationalized rural land without compensation, abolished tenancy, forbade the hiring of wage labor on private farms, kept all commercial farms under state control, and granted each peasant family so-called "possessing rights" to a plot of land not to exceed ten hectares. The Ethiopian Church lost all its land, and its clergy and lay people had to rely on stipends from the *Derg* to live (Wubne 1991). Tenant farmers in southern Ethiopia naturally welcomed the reform. In the northern highlands, where *rist* tenures dominated and large landholdings and tenancy were exceptions, many people resisted it and remained suspicious of the new government's intentions.

The political-administrative structure in rural areas was radically altered by the reform and by the establishment of peasant associations. Although these were, in principle, designed to give more political and policy influence to the peasants, authors like Temesgen Gebeyehu Baye (2013) have argued that the state used them as instruments of control rather than letting them evolve into genuine local governments, and that this caused or exacerbated rural grievances.[81]

Subsequent agrarian history has been complicated and, at times, violent and hectic. The reform coincided with the beginning of the 1974 to 1991 civil war in Ethiopia and present-day Eritrea, between the Ethiopian military junta's communist governments and the Ethio-Eritrean anti-government rebels. The worst famine in a century (lasting from 1983 to 1985) occurred a decade into that civil war, leaving 1.2 million dead, prompting four hundred thousand refugees to leave the country, and internally displacing 2.5 million people. Its impacts were magnified by the war. Soviet support for the Communist government ended when the USSR broke up at the end of the 1980s.

It is no surprise that, in the midst of conflict and famine, the government should have failed to set up a good support system for small farmers. Population growth continued and farms became smaller. Questionable policies typical of new governments were also part of the story. One

[81] The grievances to which he refers were primarily those of the land-owning classes, many of whose members were forced, in 1975, to flee to remote and inaccessible areas, from which they began an organized resistance against the government. Whether the government could have walked the fine line between making more land available to those with too little and upsetting these members of the gentry is a major question.

component of the *Derg*'s agricultural policy was developing large-scale state farms; it was planned that by 1994 these state farms would account for 6.4 percent of cultivated land (Mulato 1991), and it was hoped that they would reverse the drop in post-revolution/reform food production, or at least in sales to urban centers. Dictator Mangiest Haile Mariam and his advisors thought the state farms could do better than the peasantry, and greatly favored the former in the provision of access to needed inputs.[82] Although accounting for only a small share of total output (six percent in 1987), those farms did manage to provide much of the urban food supply (sixty-five percent) (Wubne 1991).[83]

Agriculture naturally suffered during this period of conflict, as well as during periodic rainfall shortages. Since the return of peace, much internal debate on how the sector should be organized has been encouraged by its initially low productivity, the extent of rural poverty, and the apparent defects of the system created by the reform. By the early years of this millennium, the slow advance of productivity and output had strengthened the view that underperformance might have roots in an excessively egalitarian land distribution, or in the failure to give farmers the right to buy and sell land (Devereux et al. 2005). With the exception of a brief period at the end of imperial rule, when some farmers did enjoy a kind of private property right (freehold), Ethiopian peasants have never held entitlements that would clearly classify them as owners (Crewett et al. 2008, 10).[84] Ruling regimes have been reluctant to hand over the full range of rights, and the peasantry itself has manifested significant support for that approach; farmers' stated preferences reveal that tenure security is more important than the particular form it takes (Nega et al. 2003). That most farmers have not been keen on unrestricted freehold is reflected in the large share who identify state ownership with secured rights as their preferred choice among options presented.[85] Much direct evidence points to lack of tenure security as a barrier to raising

[82] From 1982 to 1990, these farms received about forty-three percent of the government's agricultural investment. In 1983, they received seventy-six percent of the total allocation of chemical fertilizers, ninety-five percent of the improved seeds, and eighty-one percent of agricultural credit (Wubne 1991).

[83] In the sensitivity of reform success and beliefs about it to the adequacy of the urban food supply, this case parallels the Bolivian reform of 1953 (see Chapter 6).

[84] For example, under the taxonomy proposed by Schlager and Ostrom (1992).

[85] Accordingly, Nega et al. (2003, 14) believe that a flexible landholding system centered around security of tenure and allowing for local sensibilities and including a mixture of private, state, and communal holdings would be preferred to one "fixated by the public/private dichotomy that characterizes the current debate in the country."

productivity,[86] and survey data suggest that government action to increase both tenure security and transferability of land rights could significantly enhance rural investment and productivity. Farmers' *de facto* involvement in land transactions, despite the legal restrictions on them, suggest that a suitable land policy could help formal land markets to improve allocation; Deininger et al. (2003) found that land rental markets outperformed administrative reallocation in both terms of efficiency and poverty reduction.

Although recognizing that the post-reform system had serious failings, post-*Derg* governments have been reluctant to effect major changes (Nega et al. 2003). Policymakers have pointed to China, where small producing units and public ownership did not hinder agricultural growth (Gebresalassie 2006, 4). They had considerable confidence that, if it could be expanded and strengthened, an extension program begun in 1994 would bring increases in small landholder productivity.[87] In fact, a burst of growth did finally begin, largely invalidating the pessimism resulting from the long period of stagnation, the small size of most farms, and whatever else contributed to it. From 2000 to 2015, the country registered a six percent growth rate of agricultural output, for a total increase of about 140 percent.

Ethiopia's experience with land reform is indeed a complicated one. Only a quarter century after the 1975 reform did major income gains appear for a large proportion of the small farmers. Factors in the delay included internal turmoil, famine, weather fluctuations, and modest initial levels of support from the public sector. Whether a greater role for larger farms would have brought faster overall productivity and output growth during that interim cannot be known, but it seems extremely unlikely that it would have brought greater income gains for the bottom half of the rural population. The final outcome is a clear confirmation of the potential of small farm systems when the right conditions are present.

An issue of interest with respect to the experience of *South Africa*, the most industrial country of SSA, is whether, at its stage of development, land reform has been or is still one of the more promising instruments with which to rein in the country's extremely high level of inequality, or if it is even a useful instrument at

[86] There is no discernable link between sustainability practices and size of plot, but feelings of security are markedly linked (Nega et al. 2003, 12). The weight given by small farmers to economic security has been widely recognized around the world.

[87] As of 2001, the number of farmers not included in the extension program (sixty-three percent) was still far greater than those who were, and net farm income per hectare was only 5.8 percent higher for those participating in it. On the other hand, per capita food production was about one-third higher and total earnings were twenty-six percent higher.

all. Agricultural employment now accounts for less than ten percent of the total, sources of inequality other than land concentration clearly dominate, and the country is already rich enough and capable enough to apply other remedies for inequality. The evidence does, however, point clearly to land redistribution still being a useful component of the policy package.

When apartheid ended in 1994, eighty-seven percent of commercial farmland was owned by whites, and just thirteen percent by blacks—the inverse of their shares of the population. The dispossession of the land rights of South Africa's majority population had been a central feature of colonial policy and the apartheid era that followed. The land reform program launched in 1994 by the first democratically elected government had the objective of redistributing thirty percent of white-owned farmland to poor blacks. As of 2009, only about five percent of this goal had been achieved.

Earlier land dispossession had all but eliminated the peasant small landholder class around which the typical reform is built. In the beginning, the major reform goal was the restitution of legal rights rather than the pursuit of economic benefits (Keswell and Carter 2013, 2). The slow uptake led the government to create the Land Redistribution for Agricultural Development (LRAD) program in 2001. Styled on the willing buyer–willing seller market-assisted land reform model, LRAD aims to provide land to black South Africans (especially women) with an interest in farming. Applicants must live on or near the land they wish to acquire through the program. Individuals who hold public office, civil servants, or relatives of such individuals are ineligible. The program features a grant and a matching contribution from the intended beneficiary. Like other market-assisted programs, it was meant to rely on beneficiary self-selection to ensure that resources would be channeled to those most interested in farming and best able to benefit from it. Although generally well designed, it has failed to reach a significant number of families, as well as suffering from other common weaknesses of land reform efforts.[88] Keswell and Carter (2013) report a good average payoff for beneficiary families; although their per-capita consumption initially drops, after three to four years it rises to twenty-five to fifty percent above the pre-transfer level, probably closer to the upper figure.[89] Comparing this result to estimates of the long-term earnings impact of cash transfers (eight

[88] Gandidzanwa et al. (2021) is a recent study of which factors have helped or hurt its performance.

[89] This outcome provides a close parallel to that of Helfand et al. (2019) in their analysis of the MALF in Brazil.

percent) and of South Africa's Child Support Grant (three percent),[90] they conclude that LRAD's identifiable long-term impacts are much larger than those of such alternatives.[91] While the model can clearly bring substantial benefits, the "willing seller" aspect has made the transfer of land expensive in monetary terms.

Most other land reform efforts have been less successful. Binswanger (2014, 253) judged the country's overall performance in this area to have been weak in terms of the number of beneficiaries and the improvements in livelihoods and agricultural output: "Even though there are islands of success, for the past twenty years the Land Reform Programme has not satisfied these criteria. Implementation has been poor and farm workers' and farm dwellers' rights have not been protected. This failure is primarily attributed to the use of group or co-operative farming; inadequate participation by the beneficiaries; the absence, late arrival or poor quality of post-settlement support; and capacity problems in the civil service." In fact, "the programme has failed to stem the eviction of farm workers and farm dwellers" and has increasingly opted for "fewer and fewer beneficiaries getting larger and larger amounts of land, in the hope that they will bring farming skills and capital to develop and sustain the farms" (Binswanger 2014, 267). He lays out a recipe for success, based primarily on the family farm model and on intensive participation of the beneficiaries or their groups in the identification, planning, implementation, and financial management of their projects.

Although agricultural employment constitutes a small and declining share of the total, the high levels of poverty and inequality and the low employment-creating capacity of the mining sector keep land reform among the better available options to ease those problems, were it possible to improve implementation. Both this setting and the inadequate scope of reform can be traced, in large part, to politics, with elite capture and cronyism at work to steer programs in the wrong direction (Cousins 2013), and with the disinterest in providing adequate funding for the purchase and operation of the programs presumably reflecting the severe level of state corruption, especially during the governments of Jacob Zuma (2007–2017).

[90] For example, the early childhood nutritional impacts of that cash grant would increase adult earnings by about three percent in the long term.

[91] Each of these three interventions may have either positive or negative indirect effects on future income trends. One issue is whether the increases in family well-being from the land redistribution program spill over into the kinds of investment in child human capital detected in conditional and unconditional cash transfer programs.

South Africa's relative failure on this front, where the post-apartheid government had plenty of incentive to succeed, has many possible lessons for other SSA countries. One is the ever-present danger of promising institutions falling victim to downward spirals that lead to much less positive outcomes than might have been expected. Levy et al. (2021) explore this process in South Africa and consider ways to reverse the cycle. For many democracies, a critical weakness or challenge lies in the complexity of addressing challenges of inequality and exclusion.

## Agricultural Policy in Sub-Saharan Africa: Summing Up

Where do the ongoing debates surrounding land use, food security, poverty reduction, and climate change in SSA leave us? Is what Wise (2020a) refers to as the "Green Revolution input-output model" as bad as much evidence suggests or, at the other end of the spectrum, are some aspects of it essential to keep people supplied with enough food? How much potential does an agro-ecological approach have to outdo the productivity of the existing system while avoiding its increasingly obvious environmental costs?

SSA was long a source of special concern given its combination of the slowest agricultural growth among the major developing regions and fastest population growth anywhere. Keeping the food-to-population ratio rising has thus been a major and continuing challenge (Eicher 1982). For many reasons, a Green Revolution like Asia's was not going to come early or easily. Only over the decade from 2000 to 2010 did agricultural output per capita rise to over two percent (2.8 percent), but then it slipped back to 0.7 percent during the last decade. In planning for the future, analysts now draw on the region's experience to date—a good deal of failure and some success, the record elsewhere in the developing world, and the specific conditions now found in the countries of SSA. With the bulk of the population still in, or dependent on, agriculture and working on small farms, that sector must continue to play a central role, especially in poverty reduction. A number of countries have or might achieve faster economic growth as mineral exports come on the scene, but such accelerated growth is by no means guaranteed due to "natural resource curse" mechanisms. Poverty reduction is even less assured because the mineral sector not only creates few jobs itself but it usually erases more in other sectors through the imports it finances; it also invites massive levels of corruption such that little or no additional income may get through to the poor, even if overall economic growth is good—often the poor are, in fact, made worse off.[92] So it must be presumed that agriculture will remain the dominant employment sector for a substantial period and that how it progresses will be the main determinant of the rate of poverty reduction. In some African countries, there is a relatively ample supply of land, but in most it is a very scarce resource.

Among the broad and complex issues needing attention are the role of markets and that of government, including its regulation of the private sector. The playing out of the African puzzle well exemplifies the motto "never expect either governments or unregulated markets, left to themselves, to effectively advance the interest of the population; rather, strive to combine the positive potential of both and recognize that markets work best when governments are most capable of setting and enforcing good rules". Large-scale private enterprise is likely to work particularly badly in the sort of SSA setting under discussion because the public sector's capacity to regulate it effectively is low (this being a skill that usually takes both time and dedication to develop). There is a power imbalance between dominant private foreign firms and inexperienced local governments, and members of government can, as elsewhere, easily be subject to bribery, pressure, or threat. This component of the private sector must now be expected to behave particularly badly because awareness of the environmental costs of chemicals and climate change has, for the most part, arisen since giant firms got into this line of activity in the African countries. No easy success can be expected on the regulatory front; the challenge is to do the best possible under the circumstances. There is no reason, in principle, why the contribution of private sector input firms could not become much more positive, but it would probably call for a major change in their *modus operandi*,[93] which might require a high degree of international collaboration and pressure. In a parallel to the suggestion

[92] The damage from mineral exporting follows from the fact that, on the trade front, that industry outcompetes other more socially beneficial ones, such as agriculture and manufacturing, a reality that only came to be well understood over the last twenty-five years, most prominently in the paradoxical conclusion of Sachs and Warner (2001) that countries well-endowed with natural resources grew more slowly than others not so blessed. The economic and political factors that contribute to the frequency of bad economic and social outcomes in mineral-exporting countries have been widely addressed. See Ross (2015) for a discussion of the politics of the "curse."

[93] The fact that the profit-seeking seed firms do not have the public interest as their goal does not mean that they cannot, under some circumstances, be helpful. But those circumstances usually include a near total skepticism with respect to anything they say (i.e., it must be verified independently) and a capacity to wield much control over them.

of James Hansen et al. (2017) that in controlling GHG emissions the pollution tax be imposed on the producing firm or the importing country rather than on the final consumer (Hansen et al, 2017), a promising approach here is to reward seed firms more (or penalize them less) the higher yielding their seeds are, the better they can self-pollinate, the less environmentally damaging they are, and the better they can adjust to the rising temperature, drier conditions, and more erratic weather that accompany climate change. In line with this strategy, the equivalent of a carbon tax aimed at curbing the use of environmentally damaging chemicals would, where possible, be imposed at point of sale rather than point of use. Needless to say, success with such a regulatory apparatus would depend on reasonably efficient and honest governments that draw on the evolving expertise in their own countries, in international institutions, and so forth. Countries would benefit from agencies overseeing the whole operation. International institutions like the World Bank can and do play a major role in both designing the needed policies and in helping the relevant agencies to implement them. It may be desirable to implement some of the central elements of policy before others; for example, a tax on environmentally damaging chemicals whose implementation would be simpler than subsidizing firms to develop good seeds.

Agricultural policy thinking in SSA countries was, for some decades, focused substantially on the small farmers, a tendency probably helped along by the success of that approach elsewhere in the world and, perhaps a little, by the failures of nearly all of the large-farm projects launched within SSA. But the small farm focus eventually came under greater attack, due in part to the enduring belief among non-experts that larger farms could be more efficient, together with the small farm sector's lack of obvious progress in SSA (even though many would argue that it had not been given a serious chance) and, especially after about 2000, the rapid growth of medium and larger farms, particularly in the more land-abundant countries, and the renewed development of agricultural subsidies to which access became a "vested interest" for well-connected farmers. A series of political mechanisms reminiscent of the Latin American story have come into play since that time. Some have contributed to concerns that concentration of land, of subsidies, and of other benefits from the public sector would move the systems farther in that direction and increasingly squeeze out the poorer families with little land. This fear gives urgency to the conclusion of most detailed analyses that small agriculture should remain the principal target of public policy, that policy needs to be carried out much more effectively in the future than in the past, and that politics should not be allowed to twist it inordinately toward the medium- and large-farm sector.

The purely economic arguments for the small farmer remain powerful. With the exception of plantation crops, as long as policies create a level playing field, family farms combine efficiency with high levels of employment generation and a positive poverty impact (Deininger and Byerlee 2012).[94] An inclusive small landholder form of agricultural growth will clearly generate more employment in both farm and non-farm sectors than a comparable rate of agricultural growth concentrated among a few large farms.[95]

The higher land productivity on medium and large farms than on small ones reported in several recent studies must be probed for its implications. It could reflect any number of advantages that larger units typically have, including greater capacity or willingness to take risks, greater access to credit or to own funds, and easier access to up-to-date information. Usually, public sector services are directed preferentially to larger farms rather than to smaller ones. Although marketing services often come first to places where medium and large farms are generating large surpluses, rising productivity in smaller units means that eventually considerable surpluses show up there as well, so the observed differences in market access between settings with mainly medium and large farms and those without have, in many places, been a passing phenomenon. Such factors were no doubt at work in producing early advantages for larger farms in the course of the Asian Green Revolution; but, in a context where large potential increases in productivity are possible, the smaller and often more risk-averse farmers can quickly (e.g., within ten years) close the gap, as they did in the Philippines. Case-specific details determine the speed and degree to which this happens. One major impediment can be different patterns of production between the larger and the smaller farms where public sector support is channeled to the larger; if all sizes produce the same items and with reasonably similar technologies, the small farmers may still progress reasonably well even when receiving little direct attention from extension workers.

Economic grounds for optimism notwithstanding, the political challenges to achieving broad-based inclusive agricultural development remain daunting. The interests and policy preferences of the larger farmers present a major threat to the welfare of the rest. So do the large input producers, whose actions are often both anti-environmental and contrary to the interests of small farmers. Environmental considerations should be woven tightly into

[94] See also Lipton (2009).

[95] Pioneering work by Mellor & Johnston (1984) contrasting employment effects from small landholder Asia versus *latifundia*-based Latin America, as well as more recent work (Christiaensen et al. 2011) show that inclusive forms of agricultural growth generate much bigger output and employment multipliers than does agricultural growth generated by relatively few large farms.

policymaking, which is difficult when there is so little precedent for doing so. The whole agricultural policy apparatus should incorporate ecological knowledge and interact with the environmental policy institutions. There is little doubt that with good policy on R&D, infrastructural development, selective use of subsidies, removal of market imperfections, and all the other elements of a technically strong policy package, things would work out well. But an ever-present complication is that what may be a good policy when well administered can become not just ineffective but perverse, as when the benefits of productivity growth are captured by an elite whose success squeezes out everyone else. A current example is input subsidies, which in other settings have been helpful when provided only for a limited period and to the right producers, but not when they become permanent (as in the famous case of India) or are disproportionately channeled to better-off farmers, as is now occurring in a number of SSA countries.

Whatever conclusions emerge from the current wave of research on the absolute and relative efficiency of small farms in traditional economic terms, it is highly unlikely that those results will provide an argument for a major increase in the number of larger units given the typically much better distribution of the income earned on smaller ones. On these and many other points, policy options and likely best choices vary considerably with the degree of land abundance or scarcity of a country or region. Where much land remains to be put into cultivation, a reasonable number of medium and larger farms can be a boon, allowing testing of new seeds and modes of cultivation, and providing spillover benefits to other farmers. The "socio-economic distance" between these new, larger farms and the small ones has, thus far, been less in SSA than in Latin America's historically bimodal pattern, suggesting greater positive externalities between them. Still, the political mechanisms tending to promote concentration are very much present, as the inside group takes advantage of its preferential access to benefits.

## A Brief Summary of What We Know

The gradually unfolding evidence on how agriculture is changing in SSA and about the best options for the future leave a number of things at least fairly clear.

(i) Continued growth in the productivity of land is essential, given its severe scarcity in most places.

(ii) In light of the enormous diversity found in the region and within most countries, that growth needs to be pursued through many avenues and in settings that differ widely (e.g., by soil characteristics, by water availability, etc.).

(iii) While the appropriate role of ecologically friendly sources of productivity increase in the bigger picture remains to be sorted out in detail, it is clearly significant; many advances must bear fruit on the productivity front and be ecologically sustainable as well, otherwise there will be disasters.

(iv) The increasing role of medium-sized farms in some settings raises the overall performance of agriculture and brings positive spinoffs to small farmers. In other settings this is not the case and the latter group is made worse off.

(v) The hub of agriculture must remain the small farmer because such a high share of families currently fall in that category. Getting to a situation in which the typical farm is middle-sized (e.g., ten hectares) without quickly forcing the great majority of families out of agriculture is impossible, given the limited amount of land available.

(vi) Accordingly, it is important that land concentration not rise, especially through theft and other unfair mechanisms that put small farm families in distress.

(vii) With enough resources invested in R&D and complementary diffusion efforts, productivity advancements can be substantial over an extended period of time-for example the twenty to thirty years needed to bring performance to a level that greatly reduces poverty.

Two broad political dangers stand in the way of success:

(i) the lack of the governance quality needed to set countries on the path just described, through some combination of failure to understand what is needed, an incapacity to undertake the needed support activities like R&D, and a vulnerability to pressure groups and/or corruption; and

(ii) the power and persuasiveness of pressure groups, including agribusiness companies, large farm groups, farmers unions, and others.

These two "danger" factors have, for example, led to the provision of excessive subsidies for the purchase of inputs, encouraged both by agribusiness and by farmers' unions, and the (related) excessively narrow focus on a certain set of seeds and inputs as the ones to be supported.

The success or failure in SSA agriculture will have major ramifications both inside and outside the region. A performance two-thirds as good as that achieved in Southeast Asia would lead to more rapid income increases within the sector and overall,[96] falling inequality, and probably somewhat more rapid urbanization as rising rural incomes would create demand for urban-produced goods, rising education, and falling birth and population growth rates.[97] This scenario is likely to improve political performance and, with even higher likelihood, decrease the urge for people to leave the region for Europe and elsewhere. If growth is slow, these positive trends will either be absent or less in evidence. If it is reasonably rapid, but substantially based on either capital-intensive mining or on larger-scale agriculture, the benefits will go to a small minority of people, so inequality will tend to increase, poverty reduction will be slower or absent, the economies will remain highly informal in economic structure, and popular dissatisfaction will be rampant.

If reasonably egalitarian democracy early in the process of agricultural development is the only way to prevent land concentration,[98] will many SSA countries achieve that goal? Will authoritarian populists sometimes limit such concentration? Under what conditions can the needs, wants, and arguments of small farmers carry enough weight? Can the empirical evidence on which agrarian structures and which policies raise economic efficiency make much difference? When can small farmers be a better political and economic complement and support for the emerging bourgeoisie than larger ones? Will the historically unusual power of foreign agribusiness corporations continue to warp policy seriously away from where it should be?

[96] Those cases saw small farmers' income grow at six percent per year for one to two decades; a four percent income growth would be a major achievement in SSA countries.

[97] If urbanization were central to a country's success in raising educational levels and cutting population growth, and if a focus on large-scale agriculture, through its immiserating effect on the bulk of the rural population, pushed them into the city and added to the poverty there, it is possible that the suffering of this generation could pay off in the future by cutting population growth, but this requires that falling population growth be the major single factor in achieving a degree of overall success. The immiseration effect would be a replay of what the enclosures did in the UK; but a quite differential access to education and to contraception for poorer people depending on whether they live in rural or urban areas has characterized a number of countries.

[98] As argued by Herring (2009).

# 9

# Land Concentration and Agrarian Reform in Recent World History

## Successes, Failures, and Lessons

### The Twentieth-Century Setting: Land Reform on the Path to Civilization

High levels of land concentration arise through an inequality of power within societies and are maintained by the natural inertia of situations in which those at the top set the rules and then enforce them. Pressures for change arise naturally from the inherent inequality and injustice of those situations and from their sometime economic inefficiency. Such pressures have been important—whether leading to major change or not—in countries that together account for the majority of the world's population. Most of the major reforms have been undertaken by post-revolutionary Communist governments (China, Soviet Union, Vietnam, and Cuba) as part of broader social restructurings. In those cases, internal politics determined the details of the reform (e.g., the degree of collectivization, etc.). Reforms undertaken in capitalist settings were, of course, not automatic and their political underpinnings varied; foreign pressures came into play frequently, usually to prevent them or tone them down considerably, but, in a few cases, to support serious reforms.

Most large societies in history have been strongly hierarchical, with those at the top controlling much or all of the land. Although that control is originally based on outdoing others through greater physical/military power, theft is used as needed by the winning group against the losing one. But when wealth concentration has been achieved, then "justice"—in particular, rules against theft of property—becomes useful. Such intra-group justice (justice among members of the group) helps to make any society function

*The Great Curse*. Albert Berry, Oxford University Press. © Oxford University Press 2024.
DOI: 10.1093/oso/9780197782675.003.0010

more smoothly, regardless of how hierarchical it may be. Those at the top benefit particularly because it helps to protect the assets they now have (even if they were obtained "unjustly") and to maintain order in the rest of the society. The elite may then give up the *de facto* right to take what they want from anyone else in the society because this helps to keep the other tiers in line, and because they themselves no longer need that power to concentrate the wealth into their own hands. Aspirants to elite status, however, may continue to prey on others if permitted. Any society's elite tends to develop a sense of fairness that only goes back far enough to cover the period since they themselves were the aggressors/thieves. Lower levels of society come to accept that what they have in terms of assets and rights is fair, even if some other groups have more.

The long sweep of history has seen some shifts away from land and wealth inequality toward more egalitarian arrangements, but overall progress has obviously been quite incomplete. "Empire building" at the expense of others still exists, even as it has come to be less a matter of physical takeover and more of gaining/expanding control through other mechanisms. The continuing presence and value of physical aggressiveness is partly due to the fact that undefended groups cannot easily survive in a world where physical power remains so important. The twentieth-century capitalism–communism rift acted as a spur to international conflict by inserting a new element of political/social ideology. Then, along with conflicts between powers, there are the internal battles within them. As long as those at the top of a wealth (land) hierarchy can continue to set the rules for that society, they tend to stay there, designing the rules to achieve that end. When their combination of economic and political dominance is, for whatever reason, reduced, a more egalitarian and arguably more "civilized" society may emerge. But even as countries strive toward civilization internally, the world does not abide by the rules appropriate to it; preparing to defend against "less civilized" powers remains necessary.

Lowering the concentration of landholding and eliminating slavery/serfdom—the standard goals of agrarian reform—are two components in the advance toward civilization. They are expected to reduce both socio-political and economic inequality. Land reform usually contributes by enhancing food security for the bulk of the population and sometimes by speeding economic growth, effects achieved through its potential to raise agricultural and aggregate economic output and to bring a better distribution of income. That potential is discussed in some detail in Chapter 4.

## Potential and Actual Benefits of Land Reform and the Prevention of Concentration: The Changing Twentieth-Century Economic and Political Background

During most of history economies have been essentially agricultural, with small (ten to twenty percent) shares of the labor force engaged in other activities. In the case of the Roman Empire, arguably the most "developed" economy prior to the Industrial Revolution, the share in non-agricultural activities is estimated to have reached the range of fifteen to twenty percent. The degree of land concentration has varied greatly by time and place. When it did fall or when the abuse of labor was curtailed, such advances tended to be transitory. Chinese history reflects this pattern over the millennia. In the Roman Empire, land concentration had increased by the second century BCE as the nobility usurped public lands; subsequent attempts to lower land concentration did not get very far. Progress toward a prosperous democratic civilization was not continuous either on the economic front, toward a higher income and less agriculture-based economy, or on the political front, toward a more equal distribution of influence. Advance toward these goals has become steadier in Europe and a few other places over recent centuries.

Things changed dramatically in the twentieth century, during which essentially all economies became richer and less agricultural than before. Outcomes were more mixed on the political front, but there too a general pattern of progress appeared. In short, the twentieth century stands out in history for the advances achieved at the global level. The world economy grew much faster than at any previous time, poverty was greatly reduced, and life expectancy greatly extended—increasing from about thirty years in 1900 to 66.5 years in 2000. Political progress manifested a rise from about three to about fifty percent of the world's population living in more or less democratic countries, with reasonably free processes to elect governments. The century saw the later stages of the transition from feudal agricultural arrangements to more market-based ones as, in Karl Polanyi's terms, the labor-market became a central feature of economic systems. With the Industrial Revolution in England came the Poor Laws (Temin 2004, 513), reflecting the fact that the degree of economic security implicit in the earlier rentier-based agriculture was absent in the developing market economy.

The potential benefits and losses from the land reforms on which this study focuses include (i) improved economic conditions for the lower income workers in agriculture, primarily in terms of higher income and greater economic security; (ii) improved quality of life for this group due to the reduction of abuse associated with their previously subservient status and to improvements in their children's education; (iii) effects on total agricultural output and on overall economic growth, which can be either positive or negative; (iv) usually positive effects on overall income distribution; (v) suffering and loss of life before, during, and after the direct conflicts associated with reform; and (vi) effects on the environment.

In any discussion of benefits and losses from a specific land reform one reference point is what would have happened in the reform's absence;[1] another is the outcome under the best possible reform, as defined by favorable economic and political conditions, together with effective implementation. The actual outcome is always inferior to this latter outcome, and is hopefully, but not necessarily, superior to the "no reform" trajectory. Actual outcomes differ from the "ideal condition" outcomes due to both gains being less than they might have been and to losses being greater. Both changes around the time of the reform and those occurring later are part of the story.

The potential benefits of land reform or the prevention of land concentration have changed greatly over time, especially during the twentieth century. Whether, when, and how reforms occurred was affected by the many changes of scenario. Central among them were (i) the declining role of agriculture and the rising level of urbanization; (ii) within the large-farm category, the gradual replacement of the traditional *hacienda*-type farms by agribusiness; (iii) changes in the political landscape, including the end of European colonialism, the important presence of autocratic communist countries, and the increasing share of the world's population living in democracies or near-democracies; (iv) the arrival, increasing intensity, and then calming of the Cold War between communist and non-communist countries; (v) globalization, with its increased mutual economic dependency across countries and, toward the end of the century, the increasing popularity of market-based policies; and (vi) internal political changes in many countries, most importantly the US, where the government's concern with and fear of communism fluctuated over time according to the trajectory of the Cold War and which party was in power.

With countries decreasingly reliant on agriculture, the potential benefits from lowering land concentration or preventing its rise are now typically less than in the past. The associated rise of industrialization and urbanization

[1] For a more detailed discussion, see Chapter 4 and the discussion around Figure 4.1.

also changes the alternative policy options available to reduce poverty and income inequality.

## The Big Lessons from Twentieth-Century Reforms

The main objective of the preceding chapters has been to gauge how much progress toward a better world has been achieved through egalitarian land systems, through the land reforms that contribute to them, and what can be learned from that history for the benefit of countries still confronting major land issues. Knowledge of what has gone right and what has gone wrong in the past is particularly relevant in today's Sub-Saharan Africa (SSA), as it is now the world's most agricultural region, it still suffers from fast population growth, and it is the site both of some recent success stories and also of some worrisome trends which are a threat not only to the region's future, but to that of the world.

A plausible reading of twentieth-century history, as summarized in the earlier chapters, is that reforms have more often than not failed or fallen far short of their goals or potential. Michael Lipton, a leader in this field, has taken a more positive view, and notes that "small farms share of land is rising in most of Africa and Asia" and that "this is driven not (as widely claimed) by growth in rural population or farm productivity, but by the relative efficiency of small farms, and in some cases by land reform" (Lipton 2009, frontispiece). He judges such reform to have been "more successful than is widely believed" (ibid., 7) affecting well over a billion people dependent on agriculture, and he argues that the large decline in world poverty from 1950 to 2005 from one-half to one-quarter was due less to the Green Revolution (although it was important) than to land reform. As for the future, Lipton judges that wherever agriculture continues to be central to the lives of the poor, as it does in many countries, the role of reform will not diminish for at least the next half century (ibid, 10).

Where does the truth lie between pessimistic and optimistic takes on land reform and on the state of small-farm agriculture? Many of the worrisome aspects of SSA agricultural development have come to light only in the last decade or so, including in a number of countries a rising share of land in medium and large farms, and their faster productivity growth in some cases. At the same time, the Alliance for a Green Revolution in Africa (AGRA) and its allies (e.g., Monsanto) advocate for an African Green

Revolution which would feature a heavy reliance on chemical fertilizers and the non-reproducing seeds that firms such as Monsanto sell. However, they fail to appreciate the potential role of small-farmer knowledge, just as their counterparts in Russia, China, and many other countries did, at great cost to the effectiveness of their plans and to the future of their countries. AGRA's own plans for the region appear to be based more on wishful thinking than on any professional understanding of SSA agriculture, and these plans have been defended by obfuscation and often with inaccurate statements. However, these plans gain support from many local politicians. On the relative role of the original (mainly Asian) Green Revolution, Lipton's (2009) point is a crucial one. The societal payoff to any revolution that raises yields quickly and significantly depends on the size structure of farms (see Chapter 4). The payoff is greatest in an egalitarian, small-farm agricultural system; it may be modest, or even negative, in a large-farm system where few of the benefits accrue to those in the lower levels of the income hierarchy.

Whatever the past record, a good deal has been learned about the benefits of various types of reform, and about how they may be best carried out, especially about which options work best to reduce inequality of income and raise societal welfare. Because it is likely to be easier to prevent land concentration than to correct it, learning how to do so is very important, especially for those countries—many of them in SSA—where such concentration is not yet close to the highs experienced elsewhere. Unfortunately, much less attention has been given to the economics and politics of prevention.

At the world level, land reforms with all, or nearly all, of the major potential economic and social benefits and that have occurred early enough in the development process to leave a large long-term positive legacy have been very few, both in number and in share of the world population affected. They are the ones that not only ended exploitation/serfdom, curtailed the degree of land inequality, and created small farm owner-operators, but also raised total agricultural output—all this when countries were still in the agricultural phase of their development. They raised the demand for labor in agriculture and in the economy as a whole, and thus boosted wage rates all around and left low levels of inequality, which tended to endure over time.

When reforms creating large-scale collective or state farms are added to the picture, the share of world population that has been affected is much greater, probably in the range of seventeen to twenty-five percent.[2] Over the

[2] Estimates for each country correspond to the time when the reform was undertaken; these are then summed up.

first six decades of the twentieth century, hundreds of millions of people in Russia, China, North Vietnam, Mexico, Egypt, Iran, and elsewhere were made better off. But many millions died in the process, especially in China, Russia, and Mexico. Some, while not dying, were made worse off through things like associated conflict and chaos and bad planning. Former landowners also suffered economic losses, but the number of people involved was small. After 1960, the cases involving many beneficiaries have been few, most notably South Vietnam, Ethiopia, and Iran. Rough estimates of relevant numbers for the major countries studied are presented in Table 9.1.[3]

As noted, two of the most important potential reform benefits are poverty reduction through rising income[4] and improvement in quality of life as serf-like status and the associated abuses are ended. Those benefiting in the latter way, beginning with the cases of China, Russia, and Mexico, have been in the hundreds of millions (probably 330 million to five hundred million), or about thirteen to twenty percent of the contemporary world population. The number of people pulled quickly and permanently out of poverty has been substantially less because the two highest-population cases—China and the Soviet Union—were the context of much economic chaos. The largest experience of quick post-reform poverty-reduction occurred in China, but within two decades a huge number had died in the famine resulting from faulty policy choices by the reform government. Another especially complicated case is Ethiopia; there, too, the reform probably brought many out of poverty, but it was soon followed by a famine that was partly induced by conflict. Vietnam's reform helped to pull many millions out of poverty. Japan's reform brought significant benefits to many and brought many out of poverty, although less than would have been the case in a lower-income country. Korea and Taiwan were big successes on this front.

By far the biggest reform by almost any dimension, and also the source of many lessons, was that of the new Communist government in China. In a still highly agricultural country (about eighty-three percent of employment

[3] All numbers are approximations, including those referring to beneficiaries and deaths. The wide ranges are due to the numerical approximations involved and to the fact that explicit or implicit definitions of the "beneficiary" category vary from country to country. The country discussions of earlier chapters add information on this latter front.

[4] In many cases a reform brings some people out of poverty at the time and brings others out of poverty before they would otherwise have made that transition.

Table 9.1 Quantitative Impacts of Major Twentieth-Century Land Reforms

| Country and time period[a] | Percent of world population[a] | Percent of country's employment in agriculture | Beneficiaries as percent of agricultural employment | Beneficiaries (millions) | Beneficiaries as percent of world population | Related deaths | Related deaths/ beneficiaries (percent) |
|---|---|---|---|---|---|---|---|
| China, around 1950 | 21.8 | 83 | 55–80[b] | 250–360[b] | 10–15[b] | 30–35M | 8.3–14 |
| Soviet Union, 1930s | 7.3 | About 60% | 15–25[c] | 14–24[c] | 0.65–1.1[c] | About 10M | 42–71 |
| Mexico, 1930s | 0.84 | 65 | 35 | 10 | 0.55 | 1M | 10 |
| Vietnam, 1970 | 1.22 | 80 | 60–80 | 20–30 | 0.55–0.85 | 15–20k | 0.05–0.10 |
| Japan, 1945 | 3.2 | 50 | 50 | 20 | 0.82 | Tiny | Tiny |
| Colombia, circa 1970 | 0.58 | 50 | 15–20[d] | 0.27–0.30[d] | Tiny | 1M | 3–4 |
| Ethiopia, 1975 | 0.80 | 90 | 30–50 | 9–15 | 0.07–0.12 | Unclear | Unclear |

[a] At time of reform.

[b] The case of China is special because the number of beneficiaries in the short term was much greater than in the medium term, by which time the Great Famine had taken its toll. The figure here corresponds to the short-term, pre-Famine period.

[c] The figures for the Soviet Union are highly speculative, both because available information on who was affected in what way are very partial, and because numbers would vary considerably according to the precise definition of beneficiary. Many families benefited at some point in the couple of decades after the reform began, but then suffered losses at other points. In addition, it should be remembered that many former serfs did benefit greatly from the 1861 "Emancipation" undertaken by Tsar Alexander II.

[d] Estimates based on a variety of sources.

was located in that sector as of 1950), with the world's largest population, and with the majority of agricultural families coming out ahead in the short term, probably ten to fifteen percent of the world's population (i.e., 250 million to 360 million people) benefited. Some experienced larger increases in land and in income than others, so the wide range of benefits meant that, for some, they were quite small.[5] The number of unnecessary deaths, including those killed during the reform and those who died in the great famine caused by the ill-conceived Great Leap Forward of 1958 to 1962, most likely fell in the range of thirty million to thirty-five million. If those who experienced significant gains were half of all the beneficiaries—or a little more, with a best guess of 150 million—this group is 4.3 to five times larger than the probable number of direct deaths (to which should be added the probably greater number who suffered from starvation and severe food shortage). Many arguments could be mounted against these numbers,[6] but they point to the possibility that this reform did as much harm as good, at least in the medium term.

The second major message from the Chinese reform thus relates to damage sustained and loss of potential benefits due to policy errors. In the epitome of ironies, the human destruction wrought by Great Famine came as an indirect result of the reform because of government overconfidence in the success of its policies. Meanwhile, major potential benefits were lost by the choice of a collective farming system. Had the new government opted from the beginning for small family farms, life for the agricultural workers would have been better from the start. Output would have been substantially higher, food consumption greater, food security much better, and the overall quality of life would have been much better, as well. Possibly some lives would still have been lost through a food shortage at the time of what became the Great Famine, but the toll would have been much less. The implementation of this sort of reform before the Communists could take over, as per Wolf Ladejinsky's plan, would similarly have led to a much superior outcome than what actually unfolded, with faster productivity and greater income gains, and the saving of a huge number of lives-in short, something akin to the Taiwanese experience but on a much bigger scale. Within a decade of the late-1940s reform, productivity and incomes would have been rising apace,

[5] Further complicating the measurement of benefits is the matter of whether welfare after the reform was affected positively or negatively by the change of context from a more family-based life to a more communal-based one.

[6] Blaming it for all of the deaths in the Great Famine may be extreme, for example.

spurred, as in Taiwan, by the rapid growth of rural non-agricultural activities. A famine a few years later would have been virtually impossible.

The Soviet Union's earlier reform followed the same broad pattern as China's. Again, if fifty to eighty percent of agricultural families were in a position to be made better off by a reasonably successful reform, this would have amounted to about fifty-five million to eighty-five million people. But, in fact, many became worse off due to the ongoing chaos and conflict, and perhaps ten million lives were lost in the collectivization process (Stalin's figure). In both countries, a first question is how many "beneficiaries" wound up with more income and food in light of what happened to total output and to their share of it. In Russia, where the early stages of reform coincided with almost continuous conflict, the government did not give primacy to making this group better off. Instead, it prioritized the welfare of the urban population and the military. In both countries, the Marxist line of thinking naturally favored the industrial working class, so mistreatment of the peasantry by a socialist regime was less surprising than it might otherwise have seemed. Although the urban population was clearly favored by policy, at times (such as in Russia from 1918 to 1920) it suffered more from food shortages than did the rural areas where the food originated. As in China, the violent deaths during the lead-in to the reform (Revolution, other conflicts), its implementation, plus the deaths and suffering through famine and weak economic performance complicate any attempt to assess the reform experience in the Soviet Union. Had the late nineteenth-century gains in quality of life been used as a base on which to build—along the lines espoused by Alexander Chayanov, for example—the overall outcome would no doubt have been dramatically better.

Arguably the two reforms leaving the clearest positive effects on large numbers of people without great human costs have been those of Japan and Vietnam. In the former case, essentially nothing went wrong. The share of total population that benefited amounted to about one-quarter, or about twenty million people. (Around one-half of all agricultural families fell in this category.). In Vietnam, with its high reliance on agriculture at the time of reform implementation, the number of beneficiaries was probably in the range of twenty million to thirty million people, or forty to sixty percent of the total population. As in the other communist countries, there were many violent deaths—perhaps fifteen thousand to twenty thousand—but those deaths were still a tiny number compared to the experiences of China and Russia.

In the medium- or longer-term, both Russia/USSR and China failed to maintain the impressive equality achieved by their respective revolutions and reforms and they now suffer higher levels of inequality than before those events. To date, although much less time has elapsed, Vietnam has maintained a relatively low level of inequality.

Also worthy of note for the large numbers of people involved are the experiences of Ethiopia and Mexico, where the conflict-laden settings make assessment of the reforms' overall contributions especially difficult. In Ethiopia, a highly agricultural country at the time (with about ninety percent of employment in that sector), the available evidence remains partial as to the number benefiting, in what ways, and for how long. The ownership structure was unusually complicated to begin with, and the violence and famines have further confused the picture. Had thirty to fifty percent of agricultural families benefited, the number of people impacted would have nine million to fifteen million. Mexico's revolution was a case study in large quality-of-life benefits soon after the reform, much violent loss of life during the associated revolution, and a modest (at most) long-term effect on income inequality. Redistribution of land continued over the whole period from the 1920s until 1950, so new beneficiaries were spread out over several decades; the total number was probably about ten million, or a little over one-third of the 1950 population.[7] Bolivia's reform brought major quality of life benefits without much loss of life and, like Mexico's reform, failed to greatly impact overall inequality and/or maintain the lower level initially attained. In both Mexico and Ethiopia, the reforms were accompanied by high levels of violence that led either to famine (Ethiopia) or to widespread starvation (Mexico). Lack of food and starvation can be powerful contributors to uprisings; conflict and the resulting chaos typically lowers food production, and so causation also goes in the other direction.

Colombia and Guatemala stand out for their enormous human tolls unaccompanied by major benefits. The efforts made in these two cases, and especially in Guatemala's, could be argued to have backfired to the point of making things worse, even though the outcomes would probably have been quite bad even had no attempts been made. The most likely "alternative route" in Guatemala would have involved a continuation of pseudo-serfdom,

[7] Judging by the fact that agriculture accounted for a little under sixty percent of employment (Reynolds 1970, 386) and that *ejidatarios* appeared to have constituted about two-thirds of agricultural families (Yates 1978, vol. 1, 519), they thus accounted for nearly forty percent of the population.

transitioning eventually into exploitation through low wages, and probably continuing up to the present; this far-from-attractive outcome would presumably have been much better than what actually happened given the war of reprisal unleashed by a particularly vicious military over the decades. In the case of Colombia, the picture is more ambiguous—much depends on the extent to which guerrillas, drug lords, paramilitaries, and corruption within the military would have increased in the absence of the reform attempts. A striking lesson from that case is the role played in later conflicts by the lasting sense of grievance felt by the descendants of peasants who had much earlier been dispossessed of land they considered theirs. Today's Colombia illustrates how far into a country's subsequent history such previous land conflicts can inflict huge societal costs. In both Colombia and Guatemala, whatever potential benefits of reform were foregone by its modest dimensions (Colombia), or absence (Guatemala), have been overshadowed by the tremendous costs which probably could have been avoided had it been carried out successfully. Guatemala has probably suffered over 350,000 deaths with over one million people displaced; Colombia has had about one million deaths over land conflicts since the 1930s and many millions displaced. How many of these deaths and displacements could have been avoided by a timely reform in Colombia remains a point of debate, but a reasonable guess would be the majority of them—perhaps even nearly all. In Guatemala's case, the answer is straightforward because about three hundred thousand deaths alone resulted from the installation of the anti-reform government in the wake of President Arbenz's reform effort.

In Iran, benefits to recipients were delayed by about a decade between the overthrow of Mossadegh's government and the later reform of the Shah, but the failure of the former attempt to proceed was part of a tragic sequence leading to the highly authoritarian/repressive government of the Shah and, later, the clerical one, each of which imposed major costs of a different sort. Agrarian reform was not central to Mossadegh's overthrow. As with Guatemala, this was a case of major damage resulting from self-interested foreign economic involvement.

Given the huge loss of life in and around land reforms, any assessment of their effects must take into account whose lives are lost. This varies greatly from case to case, but most have been peasants; the great majority of those dying in famines or in conflict with repressive governments before, during, or after reform attempts have fallen into this category. A smallish number in relation to the total have been rich landlords (because there are never very many of them), and a moderate number have been rich peasants. Disproportionate numbers have been indigenous peoples (as in Mexico and, especially, Guatemala) or other victimized groups.

General lessons provided by the twentieth-century experience around land concentration and land reform include the following:

(i) Potential economic and social benefits from reforms have been enormous because, as the century began, most countries were heavily agricultural and much of the agricultural population still suffered in one degree or another from the abuses of feudalism or semi-feudalism.[8] But only in a rather small number of countries have large, net economic benefits been a realistic possibility due to political constraints, the choice of inferior policy options, and weak implementation. In many of the countries that are most in need of reform to their agrarian systems, achieving even modest benefits without suffering serious costs has not been a realistic prospect. The most likely alternative in many cases has been the continuation of existing oppression, at least for a time. Large net benefits have been achieved only in that small number of places where reform has been carried out effectively; of these, the only two relatively large countries have been Japan and Vietnam.

(ii) Arguably the most striking benefits have taken the form of the general improvement in the quality of life that comes with freedom from serfdom, abuse, and the economic and other insecurities that go with it, as witnessed by the assessments of anthropologists and others in cases like Bolivia and Mexico. Such impacts in Russia and China also appear to have been very large, with those in Russia occurring mainly with the Emancipation Act of 1861. In many other countries as well, the reduction of abuse has been a major social benefit, although its magnitude is hazy because of the lack of detailed information about how good or bad life was under slavery/serfdom or conditions approaching these. At times, the underclass was very badly treated and, at other times, much less so. But it is plausible to guess that, on average, life was, to put it mildly,

[8] About two hundred years ago, with about sixty percent of the world's labor force in agriculture and the majority of them in that status, their share of world population was probably in the range of forty-five to fifty percent, as noted in Chapter 4.

not very good. The improvement in the quality of post-reform life has, in many countries, been accompanied by marked advances in children's education (Mexico, Bolivia, Russia, China, etc.), which may safely be assumed to bring long-term benefits for the contemporary and future generations.

(iii) Several of the cases featuring large social benefits (the ending of the abuse associated with a feudal system, as in Bolivia, Mexico, Egypt, Iran, and others) and significant economic gains to direct beneficiaries have probably only experienced small (if any) benefits in terms of aggregate output and its growth.

(iv) The gap between actual and potential net benefits of implemented reforms can be enormous, much of it due to losses rather than to unrealized potential gains, as evidenced in the experiences of China and Russia. In both countries, the two major mistakes were to shift to large production units and to overestimate the future path of output and then conclude that resources could be moved rapidly to other sectors of the economy. The mortality tolls of the conflicts around these and other reforms illustrate the range of dangers. By far the biggest unnecessary loss, whether in absolute or relative terms, was a result of the policy errors behind the Great Leap Forward in China, although its relationship with the land reform is complicated. Mao's bigger plans, focusing on industrialization, were arguably as much to blame for the loss of life in the Great Famine as was anything about the reform itself.

(v) Apart from the selection of an ineffective production system, a range of other problems have plagued many reforms, among them incompetent and unnecessarily large administrative bureaucracies notably uninterested in learning from the peasants themselves (e.g., Peru and many others), lack of support through new technologies and infrastructure (in most cases), and badly designed land transfer mechanisms and counterproductive limitations on what beneficiaries could do (e.g., which crops they could grow).

(vi) It has not been uncommon for both (gross) benefits and (gross) losses to be great, as in China, Russia, Mexico, and a few other cases; in all of these instances, the losses have involved many deaths associated with a revolution (Mexico) and/or the implementation or aftereffects of the reform.

(vii) Some reforms have not only brought the anticipated economic benefits to the direct beneficiaries (e.g., higher income, greater economic security) but have also helped to spur overall economic growth and left a long-term legacy of low inequality (Japan, Korea, Taiwan, and Vietnam are the best-known cases).

(viii) A number of countries have experienced significant economic gains in the incomes of the farmers and in aggregate agricultural output, without significant losses, but these gains have been insufficient to change the pattern of growth toward a markedly more egalitarian one or to accelerate that growth (Iran, Egypt, and others).

(ix) A few reforms outside of East Asia have put countries on a good short-term path but the potential lasting benefits have, for various reasons, not been forthcoming. Even as its first agrarian reform bore fruit, Iran was in the process of rapidly becoming an oil economy, with all that this implied both for its economy and for its polity; as a result, there was no possibility of the story unfolding like the East Asian cases. During that phase when the share of the labor force found in agriculture was falling from over fifty percent (around 1960) to thirty-four percent (1976), the reform probably contributed as much as it could. In Egypt, the reform brought modest benefits that were limited by the small share of land redistributed (fifteen percent of the land to an estimated ten percent of the rural population) and, arguably, by restrictions on its sale. With yields already high and the population growing fast, it was certainly not enough to effect a major change in the country's development path.

(x) Reform planning has seldom been systematically linked to environmental protection, partly because concern with the environment was still a minor issue until a few decades ago. An equitable distribution of land has been shown to bring benefits in some cases, and it probably does so in general. Small farmers' greater concern for the natural environment is one factor at work. In countries like Brazil and Colombia, the lack of reform facilitated the deforestation carried out by large agro-industrial and forestry enterprises. The environmental damage implicit in the policies pursued by AGRA in SSA has been evident in recent years.

(xi) The cost of failure to achieve significant reforms can be enormous, as evidenced most dramatically in the cases of Guatemala and

Colombia, where deaths, conflict, and other impacts have been huge, and in Iran, where reform was part of the broad package proposed by Mossadegh; its blocking by outside forces has had great political cost to the country and the world from then to the present.

(xii) Some reforms or attempted reforms have arguably caused more harm than good in the form of abuse, suffering, or death, whether of those fighting against the reform, those who do not follow the rules, or those who die because it is managed incompetently. How one accounts for the sources of damage becomes important; if they are, in fact, inherent parts of the reform process, for example, if the only group capable of pulling off the reform are firm believers in moving to an inefficient and damaging production arrangement, then the two may be inseparable.

The usually deeply embedded patterns of injustice that accompany land concentration and the (related) power of the forces that protect them mean that both unusual circumstances and special people (or groups) are necessary to tackle them successfully. The associated confrontation is likely to bring heavy costs. Thus, the single key message from history is to *avoid land concentration if at all possible, especially early in the stages of economic development.* A related message is to *never miss a promising opportunity for reform but be realistic as to what defines such an opportunity.*

## Explaining the Outcomes

Agrarian performance and agrarian policy involve two main interrelated aspects: (i) the distribution of land among small owner-operated farms, small rented or sharecropped farms, large private farms and large state managed farms, and (ii) the system of support for agriculture, in terms of research and the dissemination of new technologies, provision of infrastructure and support for useful institutions like property rights.

Available empirical evidence suggests that small owner-operated units produce the best outcomes for the agricultural population as a whole, as long as they are provided with a decent level of support by the state. Large units, whether state or privately owned, typically perform less well, especially in terms of employment creation and labor earnings; exceptions are those unusual cases in which there are significant economies of scale in production, and those much more common situations in which capitalist governments are less willing to provide support to small farms than to large ones.

Because a fully successful agrarian reform is one that creates prosperous small farmers or allocates more land to existing ones, effective design and implementation require a good understanding of what contributes to prosperous small-scale agriculture. Weak understanding, both of the pluses of small-scale agriculture and of how best to support it, has been a major stumbling block both in the land reforms themselves and in agricultural policy more generally. Probably the most general misconception, shared typically by communists and capitalists, is simply that larger is better. It complements and accentuates the overconfidence shared by many policymakers that they understand agriculture, including the small-farm component of it, well enough to design good policy. In fact, that understanding does not come easily; three recipes for error are the beliefs that it operates the same way as large-scale agriculture (or large non-agriculture) but on a smaller scale, that it is the same everywhere, and that the operators collectively know less than they actually do. Few policymakers avoid all of these errors.

The shortcomings of agrarian reform over the twentieth century have been due in considerable degree to ineffective policymaking and implementation by governments sincerely pursuing societal advance. Master politicians who maneuvered their way into power but lacked the capacity to deal with policy challenges in this area bear much of the blame. A new government dominated by people of overconfident (Mao) and/or paranoid (Stalin) temperament was not a good bet. In cases where land reform was part of a bigger plan to correct harmful features of the existing socio-economic structure, many progressive people were involved but they tended to be pushed aside by aggressive political manipulators, who often featured other bad characteristics as well. Thus, neither revolutions nor major structural reforms tend to wind up under the guidance of thoughtful team players, even when many such people are involved in the earlier stages. At worst, nasty dictators play a big role, with predictable effects on how things unfold. Mexico was an exception in that, within a decade of the revolution, Lazaro Cardenas was in charge with a socially positive project in mind, and the PRI governments that followed managed to discourage the remaining agricultural elite from fighting back too much and too quickly.

While the political and economic elite usually constitutes the main barrier to improving agrarian systems by preventing, weakening, or distorting reforms, a significant and complementary role is often played by misbeliefs about agriculture. Land policy, including land reform, is typically determined by politics rather than by the understanding of economists who specialize in the area.[9] The technical/economic arguments for a system of small(ish) family farms are almost always stronger than those for larger farms; the tendency to favor the latter draws on some combination of inadequate knowledge and weak intuition, leading to a belief in the dominance of economies of scale and the inability of relatively uneducated people to farm effectively.

Interacting with the preference for size has been an ideological dedication to communal or collective organization of production. This tendency within egalitarian socialist thinking has systematically reduced the potential economic gains from reforms undertaken after socialist revolutions. When the respective governments do become aware of the inefficiencies of large collective or state units of production, they have usually returned that control to the operators and scaled down the size of the production unit, a step that was in the interest of both the agricultural workers and the economy as a whole. The preference for large-scale collective production usually involves not only the belief in economies of scale, but also the idea that working together contributes to a better life. But a good deal of the empirical evidence suggests that small farm systems have an advantage on this front, partly because within such systems the most beneficial collaboration is self-generated, reflecting the interests and needs of the farm families themselves, whereas the nature of the collaboration within a collective farm is applied top-down and is decided upon by outsiders unaware of "peasant mentality."[10]

Recently the pro-cooperative bias suffered by many earlier reforms has been overtaken by the pro-market thinking prominent during the period of globalization since the 1970s. And a new role for outsiders is that of the World Bank, whose involvement assures a market-based approach (e.g., Market-Assisted Land Reform, MALR) and helps to guard against incompetent implementation. Results have generally been positive (as in Brazil), but their scope usually means that the impact is modest; for it to be large would call for a major fiscal contribution from the governments in question.

The belief of most policymakers that larger farms systematically outperform smaller ones on the economic front has a variety of sources. Many involve a misunderstanding of basic economics, as when devotees of free

[9] As macroeconomic policy, for example, is much more likely to be.

[10] Robert Frost, the famous American poet, prominently noted that "good fences make good neighbors."

markets assume that private profitability signals economic and social efficiency, or when efficiency is judged by labor productivity, even when that input is in surplus supply. This latter idea owes much to the fact that in rich industrial countries where labor is relatively scarce, its productivity is a reasonable proxy for a firm's impact on the GDP. Another misunderstanding is the acceptance of GDP as an adequate indicator of aggregate economic performance instead of a more comprehensive measure that also takes account of poverty reduction, economic security, and other desirable outcomes.[11] These various errors usually come with a failure to realize that alternative indicators of performance can rank agrarian structures quite differently. In particular, high profit levels due to mechanization and a lowering of the demand for labor tend to be inversely related to poverty reduction/income of the poor.

Lack of knowledge and weak economics are frequently mixed together with predispositions based on self-interest (e.g., the view of chemical companies that agriculture should use a lot of their products) or self-respect, such as when the middle class in a country believes itself intellectually superior to the agricultural working class. Misbeliefs can be innocent, as when they result simply from a person's overconfidence in whatever they believe has merit, a tendency often correlated with success in the political and business worlds. Both great purveyors of human disaster in land reform contexts, Stalin and Mao, suffered from such overconfidence. They seemed to have little feel for what they did not know, they did not dig around carefully to fill their knowledge gaps, and they were hostile to those who disagreed with them. The costly mistakes they made were not accidents or bad luck.

Group behavior often adds an additional element of confidence because one's views are shared by many others. This mix can underpin the aggressive pursuit of a way of thinking and of doing things. Perhaps the most dangerous example in today's developing world is AGRA. As discussed in Chapter 8, those involved seem to be collectively guilty of many of the misconceptions common to this area, which leads to choosing the wrong model (or an inferior one), proceeding with overconfidence/hubris, and responding with aggressive defense of those actions when met with

[11] Lipton (2009) draws the distinction between private efficiency (private return to capital and other resources used) by which criterion larger farms are often or usually efficient, and social efficiency, which takes account of the fact that smaller farms often use resources that are in excess supply, especially labor, which implies that when inputs are (correctly) valued at their social opportunity costs, the smaller farms often have the efficiency advantage.

opposition. A facilitating role is played by those who go along with such policies, even if they are worried about them, and by politicians on the make, who are attracted to foreign power and funding and to the local political benefits it may bestow on them.

Pursuit of bad or questionable policy packages usually comes with a persuasive "narrative." The political and social dialogue/debate around land begins with each group's perceived self-interest, particularly that of the large owners. Moving from interest to belief involves the selective use of facts (helped by the various biases in the sources of information at hand). Narratives are selected on the basis of a combination of the purveyor's beliefs and persuasiveness; the former are more important for honest people and in cases where the beliefs involved are in any case highly persuasive. For those without much concern for the truth, persuasiveness becomes the key in choice of the narrative, which may be designed differently for different target groups. Ignorance of the facts can be useful for narrative creators and users because it widens the scope of beliefs one can honestly push (e.g., that peasants are ignorant and incompetent). The arguments for and against land reform or land concentration have necessarily changed with the evolving settings, and the effective narratives trace those changes.[12]

Reforms playing out in a capitalist context have generated a much wider range of results than those in communist settings. When large landowners still have strong political influence, there is pressure to limit the redistribution of land, to have it taken from public lands rather than the large landholders, and to continue to focus public support on large-scale agriculture. The governments involved try to achieve a politically acceptable balance between the large landholders and the peasants. The only total successes, in the sense of winding up in the best possible place from the perspective of the agricultural population, are those few in capitalist countries where policymakers opted for small family farms and, in so doing, contributed both to good economic outcomes and to democratic polities. The socialist countries, after erring in their selection of large collective or state farms, typically corrected this mistake later. Some that eventually wound up in a good position did, however, pay a huge price before they got there—especially China.

The power and influence of foreign nations in the reform experience (or lack of it) has frequently been evident. As with internal actors, their

[12] The idea that large-scale mechanization makes everyone better off because it is "modern," even as it displaces many workers, can appeal to people captivated by "modernity."

stance reflects the distribution of power and influence within their own countries and their current belief systems. The Cold War was the dominant political conflict of the second half of the twentieth century, and, accordingly, it played a major role in many reforms. The USSR provided support to Ethiopia's reform and to some of the reforms in Latin America (most notably Cuba's). The US supported a few, tried to control the direction of many, and worked to prevent others, depending on the circumstances and the type of reform involved and depending on who was in power at home. US participation (in the case of Iran, in alliance with Britain) has been consequential in many cases, including its support for major successes (Japan, Korea, and Taiwan); the cases where potentially very positive outcomes did not emerge because the support came too late—as in China in the 1940s and in South Vietnam around 1970; the cases where US influence was important or pivotal in blocking a promising reform (Guatemala, Iran, and Brazil); and the in-between cases where the impact was either not definitive or not apparently very great (Bolivia, Colombia, and others). All these interactions have lessons both for world powers and for reforming countries.

While many factors determine the success of a reform, luck can play a significant role as well. A well-executed Chinese or Russian reform could have generated very large net benefits. Any one of several prominent Russian post-Revolutionary leaders who were more humane, better-informed, and more willing to listen to experts than Stalin would likely have produced a much better outcome. In China, there was bad luck in the timing of the Communist victory which precluded the country's implementation of a Ladijinsky-type reform. The biggest dose of good luck came in Japan, Korea, and Taiwan. Among reforms that took place or almost took place, those plagued by the worst luck included Guatemala (a different US president could have made a huge difference), China (with either Ladejinsky or some of Mao's associates calling the shots and thereby avoiding the Great Famine), and around Mossadegh in Iran (had Kermit Roosevelt followed the orders in the cable sent to him, the coup might not have taken place).

There is no satisfactory way to sum up the gross or net benefits resulting from land reforms or to identify with any precision the relative importance of the different factors involved. But two things are clear. First, there is no credible technical or economic excuse for the failure of reforms or the prevention of land concentration; such failure is due to political opposition and administrative weakness. Second, other things than the redistribution of land can matter a great deal, including the rights attached to the land, the provision of support to beneficiaries, and the presence and effects of progressive taxes. It is also noteworthy that some of the typical benefits from a land reform tend to come later anyway, if and as a country becomes more civilized. This is especially the case with the human rights components. But some of those benefits are unlikely to come quickly in the absence of reform. Economic and social equality may be greatly delayed—perhaps by a hundred years or so—when it is not brought about early and strongly by such reform.

## The Concentration Challenge: How Does Concentration Increase and How Can It Be Blocked?

Land concentration is encouraged by a range of factors, including:

(i) a high demand on the part of present and aspiring owners to acquire more land, something that depends on its economic, political, and social value to them. Economic value depends both on productivity and on other possible advantages like items (iii) and (iv) below;
(ii) a weak system of justice, which facilitates dispossession of land operated by small landholders to the benefit of the powerful;
(iii) high levels of corruption in the political and judicial worlds, which make it easier for the "in-group" to access land, either from the state, from communities, or from individuals. Corruption can be activated more effectively by the better-off against the landless and the small landholders operating on lands not formally titled (true of many) who are particularly vulnerable to such corruption;
(iv) a favorable tax treatment for large landholders, in absolute terms and in relation to small landholders;
(v) good public sector support on the infrastructural and technological fronts for large landholders, in absolute terms and in relation to small landholders;
(vi) a lack of organized local opposition that can pressure against each of the above facilitating factors;
(vii) a lack of international pressure against the sorts of personal and environmental abuses often engaged in by large landholders; and
(viii) widespread misunderstanding of the economic merits of small farms and the weaknesses of large ones.

Concentration is discouraged by putting constraints on each of the facilitating factors at work (items i to v) and encouraging the controlling ones (items vi, vii, and viii).

The history of reform attempts teaches us much about the opposing forces and their tactics, some of which, in the absence of those attempts, lead to increasing concentration, but the analysis of how to best prevent or slow concentration is much less developed.[13] Success on this front will be especially important in SSA. The outsider's role has not been very present thus far in efforts to prevent concentration, which typically call for a more gradual and continuous effort and one that requires forethought more than reaction, making it less likely to generate outsider involvement. Some sway is exercised not by governments but by international agencies (like the World Bank) and the flow of ideas. Thus, the knowledge and literature on the potential benefits of progressive land taxes is available to interested parties. Knowledge of the socio-economic advantages of small-scale agriculture, which provides an argument for governments to support that agriculture with technology, infrastructure, and the like, also fits into this category. Outside assistance with things like technical advance and infrastructure may, without necessarily being planned, influence the size question.

## Implications of What Has Been Learned for the Future in Sub-Saharan Africa and Elsewhere

Given its major relevance to SSA, learning on the 'prevention' front is arguably more important today than that on the 'curative' front, though concentration may have reached high levels in some countries. Also clearly relevant is learning about the potential of 'alternatives' to land reform as ways to lower inequality, poverty and mistreatment of those at the bottom.

With the economies of SSA most similar to those of Latin America in their dependence on natural resources for international competitiveness, rather than on extremely high labor availability as is the case in most of Asia, the story of Latin America is the most likely to be of relevance, and is thus worth summarizing with a view to how its negative features may best be avoided.

[13] Some ideas are implicit in the reform literature (e.g., as where concentration is an unplanned result of reforms efforts).

The widely held view that the age of redistributive agrarian reform has come to an end has been based largely on this experience. There, most countries now have only small shares of the labor force in agriculture; even where land concentration remains very high, near-serfdom has been greatly diminished and replaced by paid labor. Further, globalization and a general shift toward a greater role for markets have affected the institutional setting. The first two factors mean that future reforms could not have as great a short-term welfare-increasing impact as they did over the earlier decades of the last century. The import of the third one is less clear as the popularity of the market, free trade, and so on has waned over the last couple of decades. As Cristóbal Kay (2019, 753-4) notes:

> The traditional hacienda or latifundia system has largely disappeared because of earlier land reforms and/or its modernization (sometime as a consequence of land reform). Thus, today we have capitalized and technically advanced capitalist farms dominating Latin America's countryside. These agribusinesses employ far less labor than the large estates of the past, when most workers lived on the farm and had access to a plot of land for their subsistence. These tenant workers have largely disappeared as the modernized capitalist farms employ wageworkers under precarious labor conditions. Most live outside the farm in nearby towns and cities, some are migrant workers, and labor contractors increasingly provide the required workers for agribusiness. Hence, it becomes increasingly difficult to organize rural laborers, and even more so to mobilize them for a land reform, as the main demands of many are better employment conditions and higher wages. There are few mass mobilizations demanding land reform as compared to those before the new millennium. The peasants of today have to confront agribusinesses, which are more powerful than the traditional landlords of the past as they are interlinked in a complex web with industrial, financial, and commercial capital, as well as with foreign capital. Furthermore, this modernization forced more peasants to migrate to the cities or abroad. As urbanization continued to grow, the rural vote has become less important. With the end of the Cold War, and with the threat of communist insurgency no longer on the horizon, neither the dominant capitalist class nor its allies in the United States or elsewhere feel compelled to tackle the remaining and newly emerging inequalities that have arisen with neoliberal globalisation. The main reason why I think that governments, even of a progressive kind, are not inclined to undertake major land reforms is their firm conviction

> that these modernized, large-scale farm enterprises are more productive than peasant farmers and hence more likely to satisfy the country's food requirements in the domestic markets. Moreover, the agro-export boom governments have come to depend on the export revenue generated by agribusiness.

The accentuating ecological crisis adds a new twist to the current context, and it transforms issues of national agrarian structure into a global problem. Miguel Carter (2015, 425), in alerting readers to the environmental and health costs of corporate agriculture and highlighting the need to shift to agro-ecological peasant farming, detects an increasing recognition among leading scientists and global policy makers of "the kernels of ecological wisdom found among the alleged 'backward people' and 'historical residues' of modernity—the peasants, indigenous communities, forest gatherers, artisanal fisher-folk and nomadic pastoralists." This sentiment underpins *La Via Campesina* and its campaign for a new global food system based on "food sovereignty." Kay (2019, 755) judges that "A redistributive land reform on a global scale would be required to achieve such aims. Whether this is desirable and possible is a matter for debate but one that is acquiring increasing urgency." If much redistribution does occur from now on in Latin America, it may occur as part of such a world event.

As agricultural policy in SSA evolves, the settings in terms of inequality of access to land are less dire than in most historic cases of revolution or reform, but a major similarity is the imbalance within the political discourse between the recognition of the efficiency advantages of smaller farms and the widely alleged and accepted advantages of larger ones. Accessibility to relevant evidence on the advantages of smaller units is now easier than it was in Latin American countries when they contemplated or undertook reform. On the other hand, the power of large, self-interested foreign companies to affect policy is also greater. Its impact may be more on the choice of seeds and on avoiding being penalized for environmental damage than directly on the size structure of farms. But an implicit preference for larger, "more modern" units is there. This farm-size drama remains to be fully played out, with major impacts in the region and in the world. As Gregory Clark (1991) notes in the context of the English history, it takes a long time for the pro-small farm argument to get any political traction, if it ever does, although it does not seem implausible that some politicians, including populist ones, would under some circumstances buy this argument.

The relative role of *latifundia*-type units has been much less in SSA than in Latin America and many other places, but the ongoing rise of large corporate-style farms promises to have the same qualitative effects of squeezing out small farmers, lowering the demand for labor, and keeping wages down. It is likely to be fostered by the influence of large input firms and of global food supply chains.

In any case, the potential future role of agrarian reform, or more generally of support for a small farm-based agrarian structure, remains especially pertinent in SSA. Many of its countries are still heavily agricultural, are experiencing rapid population and labor force growth, have very large informal sectors whose size reflects the lack of adequate employment opportunities outside agriculture, and have high rates of poverty. All these conditions make it key that the small family farm remain dominant within agriculture for up to several decades, depending on the country. On this continent, the large farm threat comes less from centuries-long historical patterns, but it does share with Latin America and some other regions the tendency for politicians to favor that route, partly because they themselves have gained or could gain access to large amounts of land, partly because they are favorably disposed to large-scale foreign investments which can bring direct benefits to them, partly because they share the widespread misbelief in the economic superiority of large farms, and partly because they have powerful allies in foreign companies producing inputs (e.g., seeds, chemical fertilizers, etc.) and because their countries do not yet have strong extension systems that can quickly foster the development of increasingly efficient small farms. There are factors working on the other side as well, but this list implies a great danger that SSA will follow too closely the unhappy Latin American route.

# Bibliography


Adamopoulos, Tasso. 2007. "Land Inequality and the Transition to Modern Growth." *Review of Economic Dynamics* 11: 257–282.

Adamopoulos, Tasso, and Diego Restuccia. 2014. "Size Distribution of Farms and International Productivity Differences." *American Economic Review* 104, no. 6: 1667–1697.

Adamopoulos, Tasso, and Diego Restuccia. 2020. "Land Reform and Productivity: A Quantitative Analysis with Micro Data." *American Economic Journal: Macroeconomics* 12, no. 3: 1–39.

Adams, Richard H. 1985. "Development and Structural Change in Rural Egypt, 1952 to 1982." *World Development* 13, no. 6: 705–724.

Adams, Richard H. Jr. 2002. "Nonfarm Income, Inequality, and Land in Rural Egypt." *Economic Development and Cultural Change* 50, no. 2: 339–365.

Akram-Lodhi, A. Haroon. 2010. "Review Essay: Land, Labour and Agrarian Transition in Vietnam." *Journal of Agrarian Change* 10, no. 4: 564–580.

Alameda, Raul. 1962. "Las investigaciones socio-economicas en el Ministerio de Agricultura" y "Un estudio comparativo preliminar de cuatro comunidades agrıcolas." [Socio-economic Research of the Ministry of Agriculture and a Preliminary Comparative Study of Four Agricultural Communities]. Princeton University Library microfiche collection, call number MICROFILM 06159.

Albertus, Michael. 2012. "Vote Buying with Multiple Distributive Goods." *Comparative Political Studies* 46, no. 9: 1082–1111.

Albertus, Michael. 2015. *Autocracy and Redistribution: The Politics of Land Reform*. New York: Cambridge University Press.

Albertus, Michael. 2020. "Land Reform and Civil Conflict: Theory and Evidence from Peru." *American Journal of Political Science* 64, no. 2: 256–274.

Albertus, Michael. 2021. *Property without Rights: Origins and Consequences of the Property Rights Gap*. New York: Cambridge University Press. Albertus, Michael, Thomas Brambor, and Ricardo Ceneviva. 2018. "Land Inequality and Rural Unrest: Theory and Evidence from Brazil." *Journal of Conflict Resolution* 62, no. 3: 557–596.

Albertus, Michael, Alberto Diaz-Cayeros, Beatriz Magaloni, and Barry R. Weingast. 2016. "Authoritarian Survival and Poverty Traps: Land Reform in Mexico." *World Development* 77: 154–170.

Albertus, Michael, and Oliver Kaplan. 2013. "Land Reform as a Counterinsurgency Policy: The Case of Colombia." *Journal of Conflict Resolution* 57, no. 2: 198–231.

Ali, Daniel Ayaleu, and Klaus Deininger. 2014. "Is There a Farm Size–Productivity Relationship in African Agriculture? Evidence from Rwanda." World Bank Research Paper #6770. Washington, DC: The World Bank.

Ali, Daniel Ayaleu, Klaus Deininger, and Anthony Harris. 2019. "Does Large Farm Establishment Create Benefits for Neighboring Smallholders? Evidence from Ethiopia." *Land Economics* 95, no. 1: 71–90.

Allen, Robert C. 1992. *Enclosure and the Yeoman: The Agricultural Development of the South Midlands 1450–1850*. Oxford: Clarendon Press.

Allen, Robert C. 1999. "Tracking the Agricultural Revolution in England." *Economic History Review* L11, no. 2: 209–235.

Alvaredo, Facundo, Denis Cogneau, and Thomas Piketty. 2020. "Income Inequality under Colonial Rule: Evidence from French Algeria, Cameroon, Tunisia, and Vietnam and comparisons with British colonies 1920–1960." WID.world WORKING PAPER N° 2020/ 14. Washington, D.C: Center for Economic Policy Research.

Alvaredo, Facundo, and Leonardo Gasparini. 2013. "Recent Trends in Inequality and Poverty in Developing Countries." Documento de Trabajo No. 151. Centro de Estudios Distributivos, Laborales y Sociales (CEDLAS) [Centre for Studies on Distribution, Labour and Social Issues]. Universidad Nacional de la Plata.

Amnesty International. 1992. *BRAZIL Impunity and the Law: The Killing of Street Children in Rio de Janeiro State.* Amnesty International.

Andrea, Gunila, and Bjorn Beckman. 1985. *The Wheat Trap: Bread and Underdevelopment in Nigeria.* London: Zed Books.

Applebaum, Anne. 2017. *Red Famine: Stalin's War on Ukraine.* New York: Penguin.

Apus, P. S. 1996. *Land Reforms in India: A Survey of Policy, Legislation and Implementation.* Vikas: New Delhi.

Aresvik, Oddvar. 1976. *The Agricultural Development of Iran.* New York: Praeger.

Arias, Diego, Pedro Abel Vieira, Elisio Contini, Barbara Farinelli, and Michael Morris. 2017. *Agriculture Productivity Growth in Brazil: Recent Trends and Future Prospects.* Brazil Productivity Growth Flagship Report. Washington, D.C: World Bank Group.

Aristizabel-Ramirez, María, Gustavo Canavire-Bacarreza, and Michael Jetter. 2015. "Income Inequality in Bolivia, Colombia, and Ecuador: Different Reasons." IZA Discussion Paper No. 9210. Bonn, Germany: Institute for the Study of Labor.

Ashton, Basil, Kenneth Hill, Alan Piazza, and Robin Zeitz. 1984. "Famine in China, 1958–61." *Population and Development Review* 10, no. 4: 613–645.

Assies, Willem. 2008. "Land Tenure and Tenure Rights in Mexico: An Overview." *Journal of Agrarian Change* 8, no. 1: 33–63.

Atkinson, L. Jay. 1970. *Agricultural Productivity in Colombia.* Washington, DC: United States Department of Agriculture, Economic Research Service, Foreign Development and Trade Division.

Atria, Jorge, Ignacio Flores, Ricardo Mayer, and Claudia Sanhueza. 2018. "Top Incomes in Chile: A Historical Perspective of Income Inequality (1964–2015)." WID world Working Paper Series No. 2018/11.

Atwood, David A. 1990. "Land Registration in Africa: The Impact on Agricultural Production." *World Development* 18, no. 5: 659–672.

Aybar de Soto, José. 1978. *Dependency and Intervention: The Case of Guatemala in 1954.* Boulder, CO: Westview Press.

Azevedo, J. P., G. Inchauste, and V. Sanfelice. 2013. "Decomposing the Recent Inequality Decline in Latin America." Policy Research Working Paper 6715. Washington, D.C.: The World Bank

Azevedo, Joao Pedro, María Eugenia Dávalos, Carolina Díaz-Bonilla, Bernardo Atuesta and Raúl Andrés Castañeda 2013. "Fifteen Years of Inequality in Latin America: How Have Labor Markets Helped?" World Bank, Policy Research Working Paper 6384. Washington: The World Bank.

Babiarz, Kimberly Singer, Karen Eggleston, Grant Miller, and Qiong Zhang. 2015. "An Exploration of China's Mortality Decline under Mao: A Provincial Analysis, 1950–80." *Population Studies* 69, no. 1: 39–56.

Babiarz, Kimberly Singer, Karen Eggleston, Grant Miller, and Qiong Zhang. 2014. "An Exploration of China's Mortality Decline Under Mao: A Provincial Analysis, 1950–80." *Population Studies* 69, no. 1: 39–56.

Bagley, Bruce. 1979. "Political Power, Public Policy and the State in Colombia: Case Studies of the Urban and Agrarian Reforms during the National Front, 1958–1974." Ph.D. diss., University of California, Los Angeles.

Balakrishnan, Pulapre. 2002. "Why Did a Slump Follow Land Reforms in Kerala?" *South Asia Economic Journal* 3, no. 1: 51–66.

Banerjee, Abhijit V., Paul J. Gertler, and Maitreesh Ghatak. 2002. "Empowerment and Efficiency: The Economics of Agrarian Reform. *Journal of Political Economy* 110, no. 2: 239–280.

Banister, Judith. 1987. *China's Changing Population*. Redwood City, CA: Stanford University Press.

Barraclough, Solon. 1973. *Agrarian Structure in Latin America*. Lexington, MA: D.C. Heath.

Barraclough, Solon, and Arthur Domike. 1970. "Agrarian Structure in Seven Latin American Countries." In *Agrarian Problems and Peasant Movements*, edited by Rodolfo Stavenhagen, 41–100. New York: Anchor Books.

Barros, Ricardo Paes de. 2009. *Succesos e Desafios para a Politica Social Brasileiro (apresentacao) Instituto de Pesquisa Economica Aplicada*. Brasilia: IPEA.

Bauluz, Luis, Yajna Govind, and Filip Novokmet. 2020. "Global Land Inequality." World Working Paper No. 2020/10, June 2020 version. World Inequality Database (WID). World Inequlaity Lab, Paris School of Economics.

Baye, Temesgen Gebeyehu. 2013. "Peasants, Land Reform and Property Right in Ethiopia: The Experience of Gojjam Province, 1974 to 1997." *Journal of African Studies and Development* 5, no. 6: 145–156.

Becker, Jasper. 1997. *Hungry Ghosts: Mao's Secret Famine*. New York: Free Press.

Bellisario, Antonio. 2007. "The Chilean Agrarian Transformation: Agrarian Reform and Capitalist 'Partial' Counter-Agrarian Reform, 1964–1980." *Journal of Agrarian Change* 7: 1–34.

Bellon, Mauricio R., and Jean Risopoulos. 2001. "Small-scale Farmers Expand the Benefits of Improved Maize Germplasm: A Case Study from Chiapas, Mexico." *World Development* 29, no. 5: 799–81

Benjamin, Dwayne, Loren Brandt, John Giles, and Sangui Wang. 2008. "Income Inequality in the Transition Period." In *China's Great Economic Transition: Origins, Mechanisms, and Consequences*, edited by Loren Brandt and Thomas Rawski, 729–775. Cambridge: Cambridge University Press.

Benjamin, Dwayne, Loren Brandt, and Brian McCaig. 2017. "Growth with Equity: Income Inequality in Vietnam, 2002–14." *Journal of Economic Inequality* 15, no. 1: 25–46.

Berbecel, Dan. 2018. "The Politics of Policy Stability: Explaining the Levels of Volatility in Economic Policymaking in Argentina and Brazil between 1990 and 2010." *Canadian Journal of Latin America and Caribbean Studies* 43, no. 1: 18–46.

Berdegue, Julio A., and Ricardo Fuentealba. 2011. "Latin America: The State of Smallholders in Agriculture." Paper presented at the IFAD Conference on New Directions for Smallholder Agriculture, January 24–25.

Berg, Andrew G., and Jonathan D. Ostry. 2011. "Inequality and Unsustainable Growth: Two Sides of the Same Coin." IMF Staff Discussion Note.

Bernstein, Henry. 2002. "Land Reform: Taking a Long(er) View." *Journal of Agrarian Change* 2, no. 4: 433–463.

Berry, Albert. 1971. "Land Reform and the Agricultural Income Distribution." *Pakistan Development Review* 11, no. 1, 30–44.

Berry, Albert. 1978. "Income and Consumption Trends in the Philippines 1950–1970." *Review of Income and Wealth* June: 313–331.

Berry, Albert. 1984. "Land Reform and the Adequacy of World Food Production." In *International Dimensions of Land Reform*, edited by John D. Montgomery, 63–87. Boulder, CO: Westview Press.

Berry, Albert. 1985. "Trends in Brazilian Agriculture during 1960–1098." Unpublished paper.

Berry, Albert. 1989a. "Agricultural and Rural Policies for the Poor." In *Government Policy and the Poor in Developing Countries*, edited by Richard Bird and Susan Horton, 173–213. Toronto: University of Toronto Press.

Berry, Albert. 1989b. "Income Distribution and Foreign Trade: The Case of Peru." In *External Trade and Income Distribution*, edited by Francois Bourguignon and Christian Morrisson, 197–237. Paris: OECD.

Berry, Albert. 1997. *Avance y fracaso en el agro colombiano, siglos XX y XXI*. Bogota: Universidad del Rosario.

Berry, Albert. 2013. "Inequality, Poverty, and Employment: What We Know." *Revue Interventions Economiques* 47: 1–29.

Berry, Albert. 2015. "Agriculture, Rural Development, and the Attempts at Land Reform in Colombia: Prelude to the 21st Century." In *Colombia's Political Economy at the Outset of the 21st Century: From Uribe to Santos and Beyond*, edited by Bruce Bagley and Jonathan Rosen, 33–48. Washington, DC: Lexington Books.

Berry, R. Albert. 2017a. "Reflections on Injustice, Inequality and Land Conflict in Colombia." *Canadian Journal of Latin American and Caribbean Studies/Revue canadienne des études latino-américaines et caraïbes* 42, no. 3: 277–297.

Berry, Albert. 2017b. *Avance y fracaso en el agro colombiano, siglos XX y XXI*. Bogota: Universidad del Rosario.

Berry, Albert. 2018. "India's 1970s–1990s Step-wise Growth Acceleration: Causes and Impacts." *Journal of Development Innovations* 2, no. 1: 14–38.

Berry, Albert. n.d. "The Toll of Land Concentration in Twentieth-century Colombia." Unpublished paper.

Berry, Albert. Forthcoming. *Environmental Insanity and the Economic Misunderstandings that Underlie It.*

Berry, R. Albert, and William R. Cline. 1979. *Agrarian Structure and Productivity in Developing Countries*. Baltimore, MA: Johns Hopkins University Press.

Berry, Albert, and John Serieux. 2007. "Riding the Elephants: The Evolution of World Economic Growth and Income Distribution at the End of the 20th Century." In *Flat World, Big Gaps*, edited by K. S. Jomo, with Jacques Baudot, 74–98. London: Zed Books.

Berry, Wendell. 2009. *Bringing It to the Table: On Farming and Food*. Berkeley, CA: Counterpoint Press.

Besley, Timothy, and Robin Burgess. 2000. "Land Reform, Poverty Reduction, and Growth: Evidence from India." *Quarterly Journal of Economics* 115, no. 2, 389–430.

Bhalla, Surjit S., and Prannoy Roy. 1988. "Mis-Specification in Farm Productivity Analysis: The Role of Land Quality." *Oxford Economic Papers* 40: 55–73.

Bhattacharya, Prasad, and Mehmet Ulubasoglu. 2010. "How Do Legal Systems Affect Land Distribution? A Long-Run Disaggregated Analysis." Working paper.

Binder, Carola. 2015. "De Janvry on Mexico's Second Land Reform." *Berkeley Review of Latin American Studies*: 1–9. Spring. Center for Latin American and Caribbean Studies.

Binswanger, Hans, Karl Deininger, and Gershon Feder. 1995. "Power, Distortions, Revolt and Reform in Agricultural Land Relations." In *Handbook of Development Economics, Vol. 111*, edited by Jere Behrman and T. N. Srinivasan, 2659–2772. Amsterdam: Elsevier.

Binswanger-Mkhize, Hans P. 2014. "From Failure to Success in South African Land Reform." *African Journal of Agricultural and Resource Economics* 9, no. 4: 253–269.

Binswanger-Mkhize, Hans P., Camille Bourguignon, and Rogier J. E. van den Brink, ed. 2009. *Agricultural Land Redistribution: Toward Greater Consensus*. Washington, DC: World Bank.

Binswanger-Mkhize, Hans P., and Sara Savastano. 2017. "Agricultural Intensification: The Status in Six African Countries." *Food Policy* 67: 26–40.

Birn, Anne-Emanuelle, Yogan Pillay, and Timothy H. Holtz. 2009. *Textbook of International Health: Global Health in a Dynamic World*. New York: Oxford University Press.

Blum, Jerome. 1961. *Lord and Peasant in Russia from the Ninth to the Nineteenth Century*. Princeton, NJ: Princeton University Press.

Blum, Jerome. 1967. *Lord and Peasant in Russia*. Princeton University Press.

Bonifaz, Miguel. 1955. *Legislación Agrario-Indígenal*. Cochabamba, Bolivia: Impresa Universitaria.

Boone, Catherine. 2012. "Land Conflict and Distributive Politics in Kenya." *African Studies Review* 55, no. 1: 75–103.

Boone, Catherine. 2014. *Property and Political Order: Land Rights and the Structure of Politics in Africa*. New York: Cambridge University Press.

Boserup, Ester. 1965. *The Conditions of Agricultural Growth*. Chicago: Aldine.

Bourguignon, Francois. 2019. "Crime, Violence and Inequitable Development." Paper prepared for the Annual World Bank Conference on Development Economics.

Bourguignon, Francois. 2023. *State Capture and Rent-Seeking in Benin*. New York: Cambridge University Press.

Bowen, Gordon L. 1983. "U.S. Foreign Policy Toward Radical Change: Covert Operations in Guatemala, 1950–1954." *Latin America Perspectives* 10, no. 1: 88–102.

Boyle, James. 2003. "The Second Enclosure Movement and the Construction of the Public Domain." *Law and Contemporary Problems* 66: 33–74.

Briones, Nicomedes D. 2005. "Environmental Sustainability Issues in Philippine Agriculture." *Asian Journal of Agriculture and Development* 2, no. 1–2: 67–78.

Brittain, James J. 2005. "A Theory of Accelerating Rural Violence: Lauchlin Currie's Role in Underdeveloping Colombia." *The Journal of Peasant Studies* 32, no. 2: 335–360.

Brocheux, Pierre. 2000. *Du comflit d'Indochine aux conflits indochinois*. Bruxelles: Complexe.

Brockett, Charles D. 1988. *Land, Power and Poverty: Agrarian Transformations and Political Conflict in Central America*. New York: Unwin Hyman.

Bromley, David W. 2008a. "Formalizing Property Relations in the Developing World: The Wrong Prescription for the Wrong Malady." *Land Use Policy* 26: 20–27.

Bromley, David W. 2008b. "Resource Degradation in the African Commons: Accounting for Institutional Decay." *Environment and Development Economics* 13: 539–563.

Brooke, Steven, and Gabriel Koehler-Derrick. 2020. "When Redistribution Exacerbates Poverty: Evidence from Gamal Abdel Nasser's Land Reforms." Harvard University Paper prepared for the 2020 AALIMS Conference (v. April 6, 2020) Working Paper.

Bruce, John. 1986. *Land Tenure Issues in Project Design and Strategies for Agricultural Development in Sub-Saharan Africa*. Madison, WI: University of Wisconsin, Land Tenure Center.

Bruce, John W. 1993. "The Variety of Reform: A Review of the Recent Experiences with Land Reform and the Reform of Tenure, with Particular Reference to the African Experience." In *Institutional Issues in Natural Resource Management*, edited by H. Secher Marcussen. Roskilde, 13–56. Denmark: International Development Studies, Roskilde University.

Bruce, John, and Peter Dorner. 1986. "Agricultural Land Tenure in Zambia: Perspectives, Problems and Opportunities." Land Tenure Research Paper No. 76. Madison, WI: University of Wisconsin, Land Tenure Center.

Bruce John W., and Shem E. Mighot-Adholla, eds. 1994. *Searching for Land Tenure Security in Africa*. Washington: World Bank.

Bunzel, Ruth. 1940. "The Role of Alcoholism in Two Central American Cultures." *Psychiatry* 3, no. 3: 361–387.

Burke, Melvin. 1971. "Land Reform in the Lake Titicaca Region." In *Beyond the Revolution: Bolivia Since 1952*, edited by James M. Malloy and Richard S. Thorn, 301–339. Pittsburgh, PA: University of Pittsburgh Press.

Bustos, Paula, Bruno Caprettini, and Jacopo Ponticelli. 2016. "Agricultural Productivity and Structural Transformation: Evidence from Brazil." *American Economic Review* 106, no. 6: 1320–1365.

Byerlee, Derek, Xinshen Diao, and Chris Jackson. 2005. "Agriculture, Rural Development, and Pro-Poor Growth." World Bank, Agriculture and Rural Development Paper 21.

Calderon, Cesar. 2022. *Boosting Productivity in Sub-Saharan Africa: Policies and Institutions to Promote Efficiency*. Washington, DC: World Bank.

Cant, Anna. 2012. "'Land for Those Who Work It': A Visual Analysis of Agrarian Reform Posters in Velasco's Peru." *Journal of Latin American Studies* 44, no. 1: 1–37.

Carletto, Calogero, Sara Savastano, and Alberto Zezza. 2013. "Fact or Artifact: The Impact of Measurement Errors on the Farm Size–Productivity Relationship." *Journal of Development Economics* 103: 254–261.

Carr, Barnes. 2020. *The Lenin Plot: The Unknown Story of America's War against Russia.* New York: Pegasus.

Carter, Michael R., Rashid Laajaj, and Dean Yang. 2014. "Subsidies and the Persistence of Technology Adoption Field Experimental Evidence from Mozambique." NBER Working Paper No. 20465. Cambridge, MA: NBER.

Carter, Miguel, ed. 2015. *Challenging Social Inequality: The Landless Rural Workers Movement and Agrarian Reform in Brazil.* Durham, NC: Duke University Press.

Castellano, Daniel J. 2006. "Assessment of CIA Activities in Chile (1962–1973)." https://arcaneknowledge.org.histpoli/cia-chile-htm.

Central Intelligence Agency (CIA). 2000. "CIA Activities in Chile." https://irp.fas.org/cia/product/chile/index.html.

Centro Económico para América Latina y el Caribe (CEPAL). 2018. *Medición de la pobreza por ingresos Actualización metodológica y resultados.* Santiago: CEPAL.

Centro Nacional de Memoria Histórica. 2013. *Informe General: Basta Ya! Colombia: Memorias de guerra y dignidad.* Bogotá: CNMH.

Cepeda, Fernando. 2015. "Corruption in Colombia." In *Colombia's Political Economy at the Outset of the Twenty-first Century: From Uribe to SANTOS and Beyond,* edited by Bruce M. Bagley and Jonathan D. Rosen. 51–70. Lanham, Boulder, New York, London: Lexington Books.

Chandran, Rina. 2018. "Philippine Peasants Fight for Land 30 Years After Reform." *Reuters.* May 30. https://www.reuters.com/article/idUSKCN1IW04J/.

Chayanov, Alexander V. 1966. *The Theory of Peasant Economy,* edited and introduced by Daniel Thorner, Basile Kerblay, and R. E. F. Smith. Homewood, IL: Richard D. Irwin Inc.

Chenery, Hollis, Montek S. Ahluwalia, C. G. H. Bell, John Duloy, and Richard Jolly. 1974. *Redistribution with Growth: Policies to improve Income Distribution in Developing Countries in the Context of Economic Growth.* New York: Oxford University Press.

Cho, Chae-hong. 1964. "Post 1945 Land Reforms and Their Consequences in South Korea." PhD diss., Indiana University.

Christiaensen, Luc, and Lionel Demery, ed. 2018. *Agriculture in Africa.* Washington, D.C.: World Bank Group.

Christiaensen, Luc, Lionel Demery, and Jesper Kuhl. 2011. "The (Evolving) Role of Agriculture in Poverty Reduction—An Empirical Perspective." *Journal of Development Economics* 96, no. 2 (November): 239–254.

Christian, David. 1997. *Imperial and Soviet Russia.* London: Macmillan Press Ltd.

Chu, Ke-young, Hamid R. Davoodi, and Sanjeev Gupta. 2000. "Income Distribution, Tax, and Government Social Spending Policies in Developing Countries." Working paper Number 214. Helsinki: World Institute for Development Economics Research, The United Nations University.

Cipollina, Maria, Nadia Cuffaro, and Giovanna D'Agostino. 2018. "Land Inequality and Economic Growth: A Meta-Analysis." *Sustainability* 10: 1–20.

Clark, Gregory. 2009. "Review of Mark Overton 'Agricultural Revolution in England: The Transformation of the Agrarian Economy 1500–1850.'" *Journal of Economic History* 58, no. 2: 576–578.

Clark, Gregory. 1991. "Labor Productivity and Farm Size in English Agriculture before Mechanization: A Note." *Explorations in Economic History* 28, no. 2: 248–257.

Clark, Ronald J. 1968. "Land Reform and Peasant Market Participation on the Northern Highlands of Bolivia." *Journal of Land Economics* XLIV (May): 153–173.

Climate Diplomacy. 2012. "Land Conflict in the Philippines." https://climate-diplomacy.org.case-studies/land-conflict-philippines.

Cline, William R. 1970. *Economic Consequences of a Land Reform in Brazil.* Amsterdam: North Holland.

Cohen, John M., and Dov Weintraub. 1975. *Land and Peasants in Imperial Ethiopia: The Social Background of a Revolution*. Assen, The Netherlands: Van Gorkum.

Cohen, Stephen F. 1985. *Rethinking Soviet Experience: Politics and History since 1917*. New York: Oxford University Press.

Collier, Paul, Anke Hoeffler, and Dominic Rohner. 2019. "Beyond Greed and Grievance: Feasibility and Civil War." *Oxford Economic Papers* 61, no. 1: 1–27.

Conquest, Robert. 1986. *The Harvest of Sorrow: Soviet Collectivization and the Terror-famine*. New York: Oxford University Press.

Conway, Gordon. 1998. *The Doubly Green Revolution: Food for All in the Twenty-first Century*. New York: Cornell University Press.

Coromaldi, Manuela, Giacomo Pallante, and Sara Savastano. 2015. "Adoption of Modern Varieties, Farmers' Welfare and Crop Biodiversity: Evidence from Uganda." *Ecological Economics* 119: 346–358.

Coronado, Sergio. 2019. "Rights in the Time of Populism: Land and Institutional Change amid the Resurgence of Right-Wing Authoritarianism in Colombia." *Land* 8, no. 119. www.mdpi.com/journal/land.

Council on Hemispheric Affairs (COHA). 2007. "Bolivia's Agrarian Revolution: Hanging In." November 16. https://coha.org/agrarian-revolution/.

Council on Hemispheric Affairs (COHA). 2008. "The Rise and Fall of Shining Path." https://coha.org/the-rise-and-fall-of-shining-path/.

Courville, Michael, and Raj Patel. 2006. "The Resurgence of Agrarian Reform in the Twenty-first Century." In *Promised Land: Competing Visions of Agrarian Reform*, edited by Peter Rosset, Raj Patel, and Michael Courville, 3–22. Oakland, CA: Food First Books.

Cousins, Ben. 2009. "Potential and Pitfalls of 'Communal' Land Tenure: Experience in Africa and Implications for South Africa." Paper presented at World Bank Conference on "Land Governance in support of the MDGs: Responding to new challenges." Washington, DC. March 9–10.

Cousins, Ben. 2013. "Land Redistribution, Populism and Elite Capture: New Land Reform Policy Proposals Under the Microscope." *Journal of the Helen Suzman Foundation* 70: 11–19.

Cox, Terry. 2002. "The New History of the Russian Peasantry: Review Essay." *Journal of Agrarian Change* 2, no. 4 (October): 570–586.

Cramer, Christopher. 2003. "Does Inequality Cause Conflict?" *Journal of international Development* 15: 397–412.

Crewett, Wibke, Ayalneh Bogale, and Benedikt Korf. 2008. "Land Tenure in Ethiopia: Continuity and Change, Shifting Rulers, and the Quest for State Control." International Food Policy Research Institute, Policy Paper. Washington, DC.

Cullather, Nick. 2010. *The Hungry World: America's Cold War Battle against Poverty in Asia*. Cambridge, MA: Harvard University Press.

Currie, Lauchlin. 1966. *Accelerating Development: The Necessity and the Means*. New York: McGraw Hill.

Dacy, Douglas C. 1986. *Foreign Aid, War, and Economic Development: South Vietnam 1955–1975*. Austin: University of Texas Press.

Dahlman, Carl J. 1980. *The Open Field System and Beyond*. New York: Cambridge University Press.

Dalton, John. 1975. "Report on Prospects of the Ethiopian Harvest of 1968 E.C. (1975–76 G.C.)." Prepared for the Relief and Rehabilitation Commission of the Government of Ethiopia and the United Nations Development Program. Addis Ababa, mimeo.

Dangl, Ben. 2007. *The Price of Fire: Resource Wars and Social Movements in Bolivia*. Stirling, UK: AK Press.

Davies, R. W., and Stephen G. Wheatcroft. 2004. *The Years of Hunger: Soviet Agriculture, 1931–1933*. New York: Palgrave Macmillan.

Dawson, Neil. 2020. "Why the 'Green Revolution' Is Making Farmers Poorer in Rwanda." *The Conversation.* http://theconversation.com/why-the-green-revolution-is-making-farmers-poorer-in-rwanda.

Deacon, Angus, and Jean Dreze. 2002. "Poverty and Inequality in India, A Re-examination." *Economic and Political Weekly*. September 7.

De Groote, Hugo, and Oumar Traoré. 2005. "The Cost of Accuracy in Crop Area Estimation." *Agricultural Systems* 84: 21–38.

Deininger, Klaus. 1999. "Making Negotiated Land Reform Work: Experience from Colombia, Brazil and South Africa." *World Development* 27, no. 4: 651–672.

Deininger, Klaus, and Hans Binswanger. 1999. "The Evolution of the World Bank's Land Policy: Principles, Experiences and Future Challenges." *World Bank Research Observer* 14: 247–276.

Deininger, Klaus, and Ernest Feder. 2009. "Land Registration, Governance, and Development. Evidence and Implications for Policy." *World Bank Research Observer* 24, no. 2: 233–266.

Deininger, Klaus, Gerson Feder, G. Gordillo de Anda, and Paul Munro-Faure. 2003. "Land Policy to Facilitate Growth and Poverty Reduction." In *Land Reform: Land Settlement and Cooperatives*, edited by Paolo Groppo, vol. 3, 5–18. Rome: United Nations Food and Agriculture Organization.

Deininger, Klaus, H. Hoogeveen, and Bill H. Kinsey. 2000. "Productivity and Equity Impacts of Land Reform: The Case of Zimbabwe." Paper presented at the Mini Symposium on Improving Land Access and Asset Ownership by the Poor Through Land Reform: Empirical Evidence and Polity Implications, at the XXIV International Conference of Agricultural Economists. Berlin, 13–18.

Deininger, Klaus W., and Pedro Olinto. 2000. "Asset Distribution, Inequality, and Growth." World Bank Policy Research Working Paper #2375.

Deininger, Klaus, Sara Savastano, and Fang Xia. 2017. "Smallholders' Land Access in Sub-Saharan Arica: A New Landscape?" *Food Policy* 67: 78–92.

Deininger, Klaus, Songqing Jin, Berhanu Adenew, Samuel Gebre-Selassie, and Mulat Demeke. 2003. "Market and Non-market Transfers of Land in Ethiopia—Implications for Efficiency, Equity, and Non-farm Development." Policy Research Working Paper Series 2992. The World Bank.

de Janvry, Alain. 1981. *The Agrarian Question and Reformism in Latin America.* Baltimore: Johns Hopkins University Press.

de Janvry, Alain, Kyle Emerick, Marco Gonzalez-Navarro, and Elisabeth Sadoulet. 2015. "Delinking Land Rights from Land Use: Certification and Migration in Mexico." *American Economic Review* 105, no. 10): 3125–3149.

de Jesus, Carolina Maria. 1962. *Child of the Dark: The Diary of Carolina Maria de Jesus.* Boston: E.P. Dutton.

Deng, Zhong, and Donald J. Treiman. 1997. "The Impact of the Cultural Revolution on Trends in Educational Attainment in the People's Republic of China." *American Journal of Sociology* 103, no. 2: 391–428.

Dennison, Tracy, and Steven Nafziger. 2012. "Living Standards in Nineteenth-century Russia." *Journal of Interdisciplinary History* 43, no. 3: 397–441.

Departamento Nacional de Planeación (DNP). 1972. *Guías para una nueva estrategia.* Bogotá: DNP.

DeShazo, Peter. 1972. "The Colonato System on the Bolivian Altiplano from Colonial Times to 1952." Land Tenure Center, University of Wisconsin, Publication #83.

de Soto, Hernan. 2000. *The Mystery of Capitalism: Why Capitalism Triumphs in the West and Fails Everywhere Else.* New York: Basic Books.

Devereux, Stephen, Amdissa Teshome, and Rachel Sabates. 2005. "Too Much Inequality or Too Little? Inequality and Stagnation in Ethiopian Agriculture." *IDS Bulletin* 36, no. 2 (June): 121–126.

Diao, Xinshen, Derek Headey, and Michael Johnson. 2008. "Toward a Green Revolution in Africa: What Would It Achieve, and What Would It Require?" *Agricultural Economics* 8 (December): 539–550.

Dixit, Avinash K. 2004. *Lawlessness and Economics: Alternative Modes of Governance.* Princeton, NJ: Princeton University Press.

Dixit, Avinash K., and Joseph E. Stiglitz. 1977. "Monopolistic Competition and Optimum Product Diversity." *American Economic Review* 67, no. 3 (June): 297–308.

Djurfeldt, Goran, H. Holmen, and M. Jirstroml, eds. 2005. *The African Food Crisis: Lessons from the Asian Green Revolution.* Wallingford, Oxon: CABI Publishing.

Doran, Tom. 2021. "Mexico Bans GMO Corn: 2024 Deadline Includes Elimination of Glyphosate Herbicide." *Agrinews.* January 18.

Dore, Elizabeth, and John Weeks. 2007. "Up from Feudalism." *NACLA: Reporting on the Americas since 1967.* https://nacla.org/article/feudalism.

Dore, Ronald P. 1959. *Land Reform in Japan.* New York: Oxford University Press.

Dorner, P. 1992. *Latin American Land Reforms in Theory and Practice: A Retrospective Analysis.* Madison, WI: University of Wisconsin Press.

Dorsey, Joseph F. 1975. "A Case Study of Ex-Hacienda Toralapa in the Tiraque Region of the Upper Cochabamba Valley." Research Paper Number 64, Land Tenure Center, University of Wisconsin, Madison.

Dreze, Jean P., Peter Lanjouw, and Naresh Sharma. 1998. "Economic Development, 1957–93." In *Economic Development in Palanpur over Five Decades,* edited by Peter Lanjouw and Nicholas Stern, 114–238. Oxford: Oxford University Press.

Duff, E. 1968. *Agrarian Reform in Colombia.* New York: Praeger.

Eagleton, Terry. 2016. "Utopias, Past and Present: Why Thomas More Remains Astonishingly Radical." *Utopian Studies* 27, no. 3: 412–417.

Eckstein, Schlomo, Gordon Donald, Douglas Horton, and Thomas Carroll. 1978. "Land Reform in Latin America: Bolivia, Chile, Mexico, Bolivia and Venezuela." World Bank Staff Working Paper No. 275.

Economic Commission for Latin America and the Caribbean (ECLAC). 1984. *Social Panorama of Latin America.* Santiago: ECLAC.

Eicher, Carl K., and Desmond C. Baker. 1992. "Research on Agricultural Development in Sub-Saharan Africa: A Critical Survey." Michigan State University International Development Paper #1.

El-Ghonemy M. R. 1992. "The Egyptian State and the Agricultural Land Market. *Journal of Agricultural Economics* 43, no. 2: 175–190.

El-Ghonemy M. R. 2003. "Land Reform Development Challenges of 1963–2003 Continue into the Twenty-first Century." *Land Reform* 2: 33–42.

Elliott, David. 2003. *The Vietnamese War: Revolution and Social Change in the Mekong Delta, 1930–1975.* New York: Routledge.

Ellman, James. 2023. *MacArthur Reconsidered: General Douglas MacArthur as a Wartime Commander.* Mechanicsburg, Pennsylvania: Stackpole Books.

Estrem, David J. 2016. "The Catholic Church and Politics in Colombia: A Shifting Foundation." MA Thesis, The Naval Postgraduate School, Monterrey, California.

Estudillo, Jonna P. 1997. "Income Inequality in the Philippines, 1961–91." *Developing Economies* XXXV, no. I: 68–95.

Evans, M. D. R., Juhua Yang, and Jonathan Kelly. 2016. "Family Background and Education: China in Comparative Perspective." *Comparative Sociology* 15, no. 1: 41–84.

Evenson, Robert E. 2008. "The Green Revolution." In *International Handbook of Development Economics, Volume 1,* edited by Amitava Krishna Dutt and Jaime Ros, 453–469. Edward Elgar Publishing.

Faguet Jean-Paul, Fabio Sánchez, and Marta-Juanita Villaveces. 2020. "The Perversion of Public Land Distribution by Landed Elites: Power, Inequality and Development in Colombia." *World Development* 136.

Fajnzylber, Pablo, Daniel Lederman, and Norman Loayza. 2002. "Inequality and Violent Crime." *Journal of Law & Economics* 45, no. 1: 1–39.

Fals Borda, Orlando. 1955. *Peasant Society in the Colombian Andes: A Sociological Study of Saucío.* Gainesville: University of Florida Press.

FAO-HLPE. 2019. *High Level Panel of Experts on Food Security and Nutrition (HLPE) report of 2017: Agroecological and other innovative approaches for sustainable agriculture and food systems that enhance food security and nutrition.* Rome: FAO.

FAO, IFAD, UNICEF, WFP, and WHO. 2021. *The State of Food Security and Nutrition in the World 2021. Transforming Food Systems for Food Security, Improved Nutrition and Affordable Healthy Diets for All.* Rome: FAO. https://doi.org/10.4060/cb4474en.

FAOSTAT. 2013. http://faostat.fao.org/site/291/default.aspx.

Felix, David. 1977. "Income Inequality in Mexico." *Current History* 72, no. 425: 111–116.

Felstehausen, Herman. 1969. "Fitting Agricultural Extension to the Development Needs of Colombia." *Wisconsin Land Tenure Center Papers*, Ino. 57: 1–18.

Fenske, James. 2011. "Land Tenure and Investment Incentives: Evidence from West Africa." *Journal of Development Economic* 95, no. 2: 137–156.

Ferragut, Casto. 1961. "Principales características de las colonias agrícolas de Bolivia y querencias para una política de colonización." Food and Agricultural Organization. July (mimeo). La Paz. "Reforma Agraria Boliviana." *Revista Interamericana de Ciencias Sociales* II, no. 1: 78–151.

Ffrench-Davis, Ricardo. 1999. *Entre el Neoliberalismo y el Crecimiento con Equidad: Tres décadas de política económica en Chile.* S.A. Santiago: Dolmen Ediciones.

Figueroa, Adolfo. 1984. *Capitalist Development and the Peasant Economy in Peru.* New York: Cambridge University Press.

Fitz, Dylan. 2018. "Evaluating the Impact of Market-assisted Land Reform in Brazil." *World Development* 103: 255–267.

Flores, Thomas Edward. 2014. "Vertical Inequality, Land Reform, and Insurgency in Colombia." *Peace Economics, Peace Science and Public Policy* 20, no. 1: 5–31.

Flores Perez, Carlos Antonio. 2015. "The Eternal Conflict: Land, Peasants, and the Military in Mexico." *CMI Insight, Chr. Michelsen Institute,* no. 33 (May): 1–8.

Fogel, Robert William, and Stanley L. Engerman. 1974. *Time on the Cross: The Economics of American Negro Slavery.* 2 vol. New York: W.W. Norton and Company.

Food and Agriculture Organization (FAO). 2003. *Impact of Access to Land on Food Security and Poverty: The Case of the Philippines.* Rome: FAO.

Forero Alvarez, Jaime, Juan Andrés Galarza, Luz Elba Torres, and José Luis Forero. 2002. "La economía campesina colombiana, 1990–2001." *Cuadernos Tierra y Justicia*, no. 2: 1–32.

Foster, Andrew D., and Mark R. Rosenzweig. 2018. "Learning by Doing and Learning from Others: Human Capital and Technical Change in Agriculture" *Journal of Political Economy* 103, no. 6, 1176–1209.

Foxley, Alejandro. 2001. "Interview, Conducted for The Commanding Heights: The Battle for the World Economy Series." *PBS*. March 26. https://www.pbs.org/wgbh/commandingheights/shared/minitextlo/int_alejandrofoxley.html.

Frankel, Francine R. 1978. *India's Political Economy, 1947–1977: The Gradual Revolution.* Princeton, NJ: Princeton University Press.

Frankema, Ewout. 2014. "Africa and the Green Revolution: A Global Historical Perspective." *NJAS-Wageningen Journal of Life Sciences* 70–71: 17–24.

Fritzen, Scott. 2002. "Growth, Inequality and the Future of Poverty Reduction in Vietnam." *Journal of Asian Economics* 13: 635–657.

Fuentes, Federico. 2013. "Bolivia's Communitarian Socialism." In *Latin America's Turbulent Transitions: The Future of Twenty-First Century Socialism*, edited by Roger Burbach, Michael Fox, and Federico Fuentes, 78–96. London, UK: Zed Books.

Gadalla, Saad M. 1962. *Land Reform in Relation to Social Development in Egypt.* Columbia: University of Missouri Press.

Galan, Juan Sebastian. 2020. "Tied to the Land? Intergenerational Mobility and Agrarian Reform in Colombia." Unpublished paper.

Galvis, Juan Pablo. 2009. "Developing Exclusion: The Case of the 1961 Land Reform in Colombia." *Development and Change* 40, no. 3: 509–529.

Gandidzanwa, Colleta, Aart Jan Verschoor, and Thabo Sacolo. 2021. "Evaluating Factors Affecting Performance of Land Reform Beneficiaries in South Africa." *Sustainability* 13: 1–15.

Gasperini, Lavinia. 1999. "The Cuban Educational System: Lessons and Dilemmas." *Country Studies Education Reform and Management Publication* 1, no. 5. The World Bank. https://documents1.worldbank.org/curated/fr/549011468746733557/pdf/multi0page.pdf.

Gates, Marilyn. 1981. "Partial Proletarization and Reinforcement of Peasantry in the Mexican Ejido." *Canadian Journal of Latin America Studies* VI, no. 12: 63–80.

Gauster, Susana, and S. Ryan Isakson. 2007. "Eliminating Market Distortions, Perpetuating Rural Inequality: An Evaluation of Market-assisted Land Reform in Guatemala." *Third World Quarterly* 28, no. 8: 1519–1536.

Gebreselasie, Samuel. 2006. "Land, Policy and Smallholder Agriculture in Ethiopia: Options and Scenarios." Future Agricultures, Discussion Paper.

Geertz, Clifford. 1963. *Agricultural Involution*. Berkeley: University of California Press.

Gerschenkron, Alexander. "Agrarian Policies and Industrialization, Russia 1861–1917." In *The Cambridge Economic History of Europe (VI). The Industrial Revolutions and After: Incomes, Population and Technological Changes (2)*, edited by H. J. Habakkuk and M. Postan, 706–800. Cambridge: Cambridge University Press, 1965.

Ghai, Dharam P., Cristóbal Kay, and Peter Peek. 1988. *Labour and Development in Rural Cuba*. Basingstoke, UK: Macmillan.

Ghebru, Hosaena, and Isabel Lambrecht. 2017. "Drivers of Perceived Land Tenure (in) Security: Empirical Evidence from Ghana." *Land Use Policy*, 66: 293–303.

Ghins, Léopold, Alban Mas Aparisi, and Jean Balié. 2017. "Myths and Realities About Input subsidies in sub-Saharan Africa." *Development Policy Review* 35, no. 52, 214–233.

Giller, Ken E., Thomas Delaune, João Vasco Silva, Katrien Descheemaeker, Gerrie van de Ven, Antonius G. T. Schut et al. 2021. "The Future of Farming: Who Will Produce Our Food?" *Food Security* 13: 1073–1099.

Gleijeses, Piero. 1989. "The Agrarian Reform of Jacobo Arbenz." *Journal of Latin American Studies* 21, no. 3: 453–480.

Gleijeses, Piero. 1991. *Shattered Hope: The Guatemalan Revolution and the United States, 1944–54*. Princeton, NJ: Princeton University Press.

Goelnitz, Anna, and Mohammad Al-Saidi. 2020. "Too Big to Handle, Too Important to Abandon: Reforming Sudan's Gezira Scheme." *Agricultural Water Management* 241: 1.

Goldstein, Markus, and Christopher Udry. 2008. "The Profits of Power: Land Rights and Agricultural Investment in Ghana." *Journal of Political Economy* 116, no. 6: 981–1022.

Gollin, Douglas. 2018. "Farm Size and Productivity: Lessons from Recent Literature." *IFAD Research Series* 34: 1–40.

Gollin, Karin L., and James L. Kho. 2002. "After the Romance: Communities and Environmental Governance in the Philippines." The Ford Foundation (draft).

Golley, Jane, and S. T. Kong. 2013. "Inequality in Intergenerational Mobility of Education in China." *China and World Economy* 21, no. 2, 15–37.

Gomez Sarmiento, Isabella. 2019. "How Evo Morales Made Bolivia a Better Place . . . Before He Fled the Country." *National Public Radio*. November 26.

Gonzalez-Garcia, Jesus, Ermal Hitaj, Montfort Mlachila, Arina Viseth, and Mustafa Yenic. 2016. *Sub-Saharan African Migration Patterns and Spillovers*. New York: International Monetary Fund.

Gordoncillo, Prudencia U. 2012. "The Economic Effects of the Comprehensive Agrarian Reform Program in the Philippines." *ISSAAS* 18, no. 1: 76–86.

Grantham, George. 1993. "Divisions of Labour: Agricultural Productivity and Occupational Specialization in Pre-Industrial France." *Economic History Review* 46: 478–502.

Greenwood, David J. 1973. "The Political Economy of Peasant Family Farming: Some Anthropological Perspectives on Rationality and Adaptation." Cornell University Rural Development Committee, Occasional Paper No. 2.

Gregory, Paul R. 1994. *Before Command: An Economic History of Russia from Emancipation to the First Five-Year.* Princeton, NJ: Princeton University Press.

Grindle, Merilee, and Pilar Domingo, eds. 2003. *Proclaiming Revolution: Bolivia in Comparative Perspective.* Cambridge, MA: David Rockefeller Centre for Latin American Studies.

Gustafson, Richard F. 1986. *Leo Tolstoy: Resident and Stranger.* Princeton, NJ: Princeton University Press.

Gutierrez-Malaxechebarria, Álvaro. 2014. "Viabilidad de la agricultura familiar con riego informal en montaña." Tesis doctoral, Pontificia Universidad Javeriana.

Hall, Olaa, Goran Djurfeldt, and Niklas Boke-Olen. 2021. "Gini and Wealth in 34 Sub-Saharan Countries from 1990." Unpublished article.

Hamilton, Edith. 1993. *The Greek Way.* New York: W.W. Norton and Company.

Hamilton, Nora. 1982. *The Limits of State Autonomy: Post Revolutionary Mexico.* Princeton, NJ: Princeton University Press.

Handy, Jim. 1994. *Revolution in the Countryside: Rural Conflict and Agrarian Reform in Guatemala, 1944–1954.* Chapel Hill: University of North Carolina Press.

Hannum, Emily. 1999. "Political Change and the Urban–Rural Gap in Basic Education in China, 1949–1990." *Comparative Education Review* 43, no. 2: 193–211.

Hansen, Bent. 1991. *The Political Economy of Poverty, Equity, and Growth: Egypt and Turkey.* New York: Oxford University Press.

Hansen, James, *Makiko* Sato, Pushker Kharecha, Kaarina von Schuckmann, David J. Beerling, Junji Cao et al. 2017. "Young People's Burden. Requirement of Negative CO2 Emissions." *Earth System Dynamics*, 8, no. 3: 577–616.

Hanstad, T., R. Nielsen, D. Vhugen, and T. Haque. 2009. "Learning from Old and New Approaches to Land Reform in India." In *Agricultural Land Redistribution: Toward Greater Consensus*, edited by Hans P. Binswanger-Mkhize, Camille Bourguignon, and Rogier J. E. van den Brink, 241–263. Washington, DC: World Bank.

Hao, Rui, and Wei Zheng. 2009. "Measuring Inter-provincial Income Inequality in China: A Sensitivity Analysis." *Journal of Chinese Economic and Business Studies* 7, no. 1: 55–76.

Hardin, Garrett. 1968. "The Tragedy of the Commons." *Science* 162, no. 3859: 1243–1248.

Harrison, Mark. 1975. "Chayanov and the Economics of the Russian Peasantry." *Journal of Peasant Studies* 2, no. 4: 389–417.

Harrison, Mark, and Andrei Markevich. 2012. "Russia's Home Front, 1914–1922: The Economy." https://ssrn.com/abstract=2001002 or http://dx.doi.org/10.2139/ssrn.2001002.

Harriss, John 2013. "Does Landlordism Still Matter? Reflections on Agrarian Change in India." *Journal of Agrarian Change*, 13, no.3: 351–364.

Hayami, Yujiro, Agnes R. Quisumbing, and Lourdes Adriano. 1990. *Towards an Alternative Land Reform Paradigm: A Philippine Perspective.* Manila: Ateneo de Manila University Press.

Havinden, Michael A. 1961. "Agricultural Progress in Open-Field Oxfordshire." *Journal of Agricultural History* 9: 73–83.

Hazell, Peter, Colin Poulton, Steve Wiggins, and Andrew Dorward. 2010. "The Future of Small Farms: Trajectories and Policy Priorities." *World Development* 38, no. 10: 1349–1361.

Headey, Derek, and Thomas S. Jayne. 2014. "Adaptation to Land Constraints: Is Africa Different?" *Food Policy* 48 (October): 18–33.

Heath, John Richard. 1992. "Evaluating the Impact of Mexico's Land Reform on Agricultural Productivity." *World Development* 20, no. 5: 695–711.

Helfand, Steven M., Marcelo Magalhaes, and Nicholas Rada. 2015. *Brazil's Agricultural Total Factor Productivity Growth by Farm Size.* Washington, DC: Inter-American Development Bank.

Helfand, Steven M., Vilma H. Sielawa, and Deepak Singhania. 2019. "A Matter of Time: An Impact Evaluation of the Brazilian National Land Credit Program." *Journal of Development Economics* 141.

Helfand, Steven M., and Matthew P. H. Taylor. 2020. "The Inverse Relationship Between Farm Size and Productivity: Refocusing the Debate." *Food Policy*.

Heller, Patrick. 1999. *The Labor of Development*. Ithaca, NY: Cornell University Press.

Helliwell, John F., Richard Layard, Jeffrey Sachs, and Jan-Emmanuel De Neve, eds. 2020. *World Happiness Report 2020*. New York: Sustainable Development Solutions Network.

Heredia, Beatriz, Leonilde Medeiros, Moacir Palmeira, Rosângela Cintrão, Sérgio Pereira Leite, and Miles Forest. 2005. "An Analysis of the Regional Impacts of Land Reform in Brazil." *Estudos Sociedade e Agricultura* 1: 1–27.

Herring, Ronald J. 2000. "Political Conditions for Agrarian Reform and Poverty Alleviation." Institute of Development Studies, Discussion Paper 375.

Herring, Ronald J. 2001. "Contesting the Great Transformation; Local Struggles with the Market in South India." In *Agrarian Studies: Synthetic Work at the Cutting Edge*, edited by James C. Scott and Nina Bhatt, 235–263. New Haven, CT: Yale University Press.

Herring, Ronald. 2008. "Agrarian Reform for a Liberal Pattern of Society?" In *Development in Karnataka: Challenges of Governance, Equity and Empowerment*, edited by Gopal K Kadekodi, Ravi Kanbur, and Vijayendra Rao, 253–290. New Delhi: Academic Foundation.

Herring, Ronald. 2009. "Beyond the Political Impossibility Theorem of Agrarian Reform." In *Changing Paths: International Development and the New Politics of Inclusion*. 2nd ed. edited by Peter P. Houtzager and Michael Peter Moore, 58–87. Ann Arbor, Michigan: University of Michigan Press.

Higgins, Sean, and Claudiney Pereira. 2009. "The Effects of Brazil's Taxation and Social Spending on the Distribution of Household Income." *Public Finance Review* 42, no. 3: 346–367.

Himka, John-Paul. 2013. "Encumbered Memory: The Ukrainian Famine of 1932-33." *Kritika: Explorations in Russian and European History* 14, no. 2: 441–436.

Hirschman, Albert O. 1963. *Journeys toward Progress: Studies of Economic Policy-making in Latin America*. New York: Twentieth Century Fund.

Ho, Samuel P. S. 1978. *Economic Development of Taiwan, 1860–1970*. New Haven, CT: Yale University Press.

Ho, Yhi Min. 1966. *Agricultural Development of Taiwan, 1903–1960*. Nashville: Vanderbilt University Press.

Hollander, Samuel. 1985. *The Economics of John Stuart Mill, Vol. 2: Political Economy*. Hoboken, NJ: Blackwell.

Hollinger, Frank. 1999. "Del mercado de tierras al mercado de reforma agraria." In *El mercado de tierras en Colombia*, edited by Absalón Machado and Ruth Suárez, 137–196. Bogotá: Tercer Mundo Editores.

Holmberg, Johan. 1976. "Pricing Strategies for Agricultural Produce in a Changing Society: Rural-Urban Contradictions in Ethiopia." Paper presented at the 19th Annual Meeting of the African Studies Association, Boston.

Horton, Susan. 1994. "Bolivia." In *Labor Markets in an Era of Adjustment, Volume 2, Case Studies*, edited by Susan Horton, Ravi Kanbur and Dipak Mazumdar, 99–136. Washington, DC: The World Bank, Economic Development Institute, EDI Development Studies.

Hough, Phillip A. 2011. "Disarticulation and Commodity Chains: Cattle, Coca, and Capital Accumulation Along Colombia's Agricultural Frontier." *Environment and Planning A*, 43: 1016–1034.

Hourton, Alain. 2012. "Income Inequality in Chile: 1990–2006." Kyoto University, Graduate School of Economics, Discussion Paper No. E-12-004.

Hua, Gao. 2011. "Food Augmentation Methods and Food Substitutes during the Great Famine." In *Eating Bitterness: New Perspectives on China's Great Leap Forward and Famine*, edited by Kimberley Ens Manning, Felix Wemheuer and Gao Hua, 171–196. Vancouver: University of British Columbia Press.

Hussain, Sajidin, and Derek R. Byerlee. 1995. "Education and Farm Productivity in Post-'Green Revolution' Agriculture in Asia." 1994 Conference, August 22–29, 1994, Harare, Zimbabwe 183412, International Association of Agricultural Economists.

Ibáñez, Anna María, and Carlos Eduardo Vélez. 2007. "Civil Conflict and Forced Migration: The Micro Determinants and Welfare Losses of Forced Displacement in Colombia." *World Development* 36, no. 4, 659–676.

Ibáñez, Ana María. 2008. *El desplazamiento forzoso en Colombia: Un camino sin retorno a la pobreza.* Bogotá: Universidad de los Andes, Facultad de Economía.

Ibáñez, Ana Maria, Juan Carlos Muñoz-Mora, and Margarita Gafaro. 2012. *Atlas de la Distribución de la Propiedad Rural en Colombia.* Bogotá: Universidad de Los Andes.

Iliffe, John. 1987. *The African Poor: A History.* African Studies Series 58. New York: Cambridge University Press.

INCORA. n.d. "Funcion de la Reforma Agraria." *Carta Informativa* 4: 1.

INCORA. 1974. *La colonización en Colombia: Una evaluación del proceso.* Bogotá: IICA.

INCORA. 1988. *25 años de reforma agraria en Colombia.* Bogotá: INCORA.

Instituto Geográfico Agustín Codazzi (IGAC) and Centro de Estudios Sobre el Desarrrollo (CEDE), Universidad de Los Andes. 2012. *Atlas de la Distribución de la Propiedad Rural en Colombia.* Bogota: Instituto Geográfico Augustin Codazzi.

International Bank for Reconstruction and Development. 1950. *The Basis of a Development Program for Colombia: Report of a Mission Headed by Lauchlin Currie and Sponsored by the International Bank for Reconstruction and Development in Collaboration with the Government of Colombia.* Washington, DC: International Bank for Reconstruction and Development.

International Labour Organization. 1974. *Sharing in Development: A Programme of Employment, Equity and Growth for the Philippines.* Geneva: ILO.

International Organization for Migration. 2020. *World Migration Report 2020.* New York: United Nations.

Ish-Shalom, Piki. 2006. "Theory Gets Real, and the Case for a Normative Ethic: Rostow, Modernization Theory, and the Alliance for Progress." *International Studies Quarterly* 50, no. 2: 287–311.

Ituassu, Arthur. 2010. "Brazil: Democracy vs Poverty." *Open Democracy.* July 29. https://www.opendemocracy.net/en/brazil-democracy-vs-poverty/.

Jamison, Dean T., and Laurence L. Lau. 1982. *Farmer Education and Farm Efficiency.* Baltimore: Johns Hopkins University Press.

Jaramillo, Carlos Felipe. 1998. *Liberalization, Crisis and Change in Colombian Agriculture.* Boulder, CO: Westview Press.

Jarvis, Lovell S., J. Cancino, and E. Vera-Toscano. 2004. "The Agricultural Effects of Land and Economic Reforms in Chile, 1965–2000." Davis: Department of Agricultural Economics, University of California.

Jayne, Thomas S., Jordan Chamberlin, Lulama Traub, Nicholas Sitko, Milu Muyanga, Felix K. Yeboah, Ward Anseeuw, Antony Chapoto, Ayala Wineman, Chewe Nkonde, and Richard Kachule. 2016. "Africa's Changing Farm Size Distribution Patterns: The Rise of Medium-Scale Farms." *Agricultural Economics* 47, no. 51: 197–214.

Jayne, Thomas, Nicole M. Mason, William J. Burke, and Joshua Ariga. 2018. "Review: Taking Stock of Africa's Second-generation Agricultural Input Subsidy Programs." *Food Policy*, 75: 1–14.

Jayne, Thomas S., Milu Muyanga, Ayala Wineman, Hosaena Ghebru, Caleb Stevens, Mercedes Stickler et al. 2019. "Are Medium-scale Farms Driving Agricultural Transformation in Sub-Saharan Africa?" *Agricultural Economics* 50: 75–95.

Jayne, Thomas, and Ayala Wineman. 2018. "Land Prices Heading Skyward? An Analysis of Farmland Values in Tanzania." *The Journal Applied Economics Perspectives and Policy (AEPP)* 40, no. 2, 187–214.

Johnson, Ian. 2018. "Who Killed More: Hitler, Stalin or Mao?" *New York Review of Books.* February 5.

Johnson, J. K. 1990. "Land Policy and the Upper Canada Elite Reconsidered: The Canada Emigration Association, 1840–1841." In *Old Ontario: Essays in Honour of J. M. S. Careless*, edited David Keane and Colin Read, 217–233. Toronto: Dundurn Press.

Johnston, Bruce F. 1970. "The Japanese 'Model' of Agricultural Development: Its Relevance to Developing Nations." In *Agriculture and Economic Growth: Japan's Experience*, edited by Kazushi Ohkawa, Bruce F. Johnston and Hiromitsu Kaneda, 58–102. Princeton, NJ: Princeton University Press.

Jorgenson, H. 1963. "End-of-Tour-Report submitted by Mr. Harold T. Jorgenson, Agrarian Reform Advisor (Agricultural Advisor)." US Department of State (mimeo). (Obtained and cited by Galvis, 2009).

Julien, Jacques C., Boris E. Bravo-Ureta, and Nicholas E. Rada. 2019. "Assessing Farm Performance by Size in Malawi, Tanzania and Uganda." *Food Policy* 84, no. 9: 153–164.

Junquera, Pablo Astorga. 2016. "The Haves and the Have-Nots in Latin America in the 20th Century." *Revista de Economía Mundial* 43: 47–68.

Kamski, Benedikt. 2019. "Water, Sugar, and Growth: The Practical Effects of a 'Failed' Development Intervention in the Southwestern Lowlands of Ethiopia." *Journal of Eastern African Studies* 13, no. 4: 621–641.

Kandell, Jonathan. 2023. "Emmanuel Le Roy Ladurie, 94, Dies; Looked at History from Bottom Up." *New York Times*, November 29.

Kapstein, Ethan B. 2017. *Seeds of Stability: Land Reform and U.S. Foreign Policy.* New York: Cambridge University Press.

Karakacili, Eona. 2004. "English Agrarian Labor Productivity Rates Before the Black Death: A Case Study." *Journal of Economic History* 64, no. 1: 24–60.

Kato, Tamahi, and Martin Greeley. 2016. "Agricultural Input Subsidies in Sub-Saharan Africa." *IDS Bulletin* 47, no. 2: 33–48.

Kawano, Shigeto. 1970. "Effects of the Land Reform on Consumption and Investment of Farmers." In *Agriculture and Economic Growth: Japan's Experience*, edited by Kazushi Ohkawa, Bruce F. Johnston and Hiromitsu Kaneda, 374–397. Princeton, NJ: Princeton University Press.

Kay, Cristóbal. 1981. "Agrarian Change and Migration in Chile." In *The Agrarian Situation in Latin America*, edited by Miguel Murmis, Gonzalo Arroyo, Silvio Gomes de Almeida, Jean Marc vonder Weid and Cristobal Kay, 63–86. Latin American Research Unit Studies (LARU). Toronto, Canada: York University.

Kay, Cristóbal. 1988a. "The Landlord Road and the Subordinate Peasant Road to Capitalism in Latin America." *Etudes Rurales* 77: 5–20.

Kay, Cristóbal. 1988b. "Cuban Economic Reforms and Collectivisation." *Third World Quarterly* 10, no. 3: 1239–1266.

Kay, Cristóbal. 1998. "Latin America's Agrarian Reform: Lights and Shadows"." *Food and Agricultural Organization* Bulletin 2: 1–22.

Kay, Cristóbal. 2019. "Land Reform in Latin America: Past, Present and Future." *Latin America Research Review* 54, no. 3: 747–755.

Kenez, Peter. 1999. *A History of the Soviet Union from Beginning to End.* New York: Cambridge University Press.

Keswell, Malcolm, and Michael R. Carter. 2014. "Poverty and Land Redistribution." *Journal of Development Economics* 110 (September): 250–261.

Kilic, Talip, Alberto Zezza, Calogero Carletto, and Sara Savastano. 2016. "Missing(ness) in Action: Selectivity Bias in GPS-Based Land Area Measurements." *World Development* 92: 143–157.

Kindleberger, Charles P. 1996. *World Economic Primacy: 1500–1990.* New York: Oxford University Press.

Kinsey, Bill H. 2004. "Zimbabwe's Land Reform Program: Underinvestment in Post-Conflict Transformation." *World Development* 32: 1669–1696.

Klaus, Kathleen, and Matthew I. Mitchell. 2015. "Land Grievance and the Mobilization of Electoral Violence: Evidence from Côte d'Ivoire and Kenya." *Journal of Peace Research* 52, no. 5: 622–635.

Knight, Alan. 1994. "Cardenismo: Juggernaut or Jalopy?" *Journal of Latin American Studies* 26, no. 1: 73–107.

Knight, John. 2013. "Inequality in China: An Overview." *World Bank Research Observer* 29, no. 1: 1–19.

Kolchak, Peter. 1987. *Unfree Labor: American Slavery and Russian Serfdom*. Cambridge, MA: Harvard University Press.

Kompas, Tom. 2002. "Market Reform, Productivity and Efficiency in Vietnamese Rice Production." https://crawford.anu.edu.au/pdf/crawford_seminar/ap01_tkompas.pdf.

Kopsidis, Michael, Katja Bruisch, and Daniel W. Bromley. 2015. "Where Is the Backward Russian Peasant? Evidence Against the Superiority of Private Farming, 1883–1913." *Journal of Peasant Studies* 42, no. 2): 425–447.

Kornbluh, Peter. 2014. *The Pinochet File: A Declassified Dossier on Atrocity and Accountability*. Washington, DC: A National Security Archive Book.

Korovkin, Tanya. 1990. *Politics of Agricultural Co-Operativism in Peru: A Country Study*. Vancouver: University of British Columbia Press.

Kotsonis, Yanni. 1999. *Making Peasants Backward: Agricultural Cooperatives and the Agrarian Question in Russia, 1861–1914*. Basingstoke, UK: Macmillan.

Krozer, Alice, and Juan Carlos Moreno-Brid. 2014. "Inequality in Mexico." *World Economics Association Commentaries* 4, no. 5: 4–6.

Kuo, Shirley W. Y. 1983. *The Taiwan Economy in Transition*. Boulder, CO: Westview Press.

Kuznets, Simon. 1955. "Economic Growth and Income Inequality." *American Economic Review* 45: 1–28.

Ladejinsky, Wolf. 1977. *Agrarian Reform as Unfinished Business: The Selected Papers of Wolf Ladejinsky*. Edited by L. J. Walinsky. London: Oxford University Press for the World Bank.

Ladurie, Emmanuel Le Roy. 1975. *Montaillou, village occitan de 1294 à 1324*. Paris: Ediciones Gallimard.

LaFeber, Walter. 1993. *Inevitable Revolutions: The United States in Central America*. New York: W.W. Norton.

Lahoti, Rahul, Arjun Jayadev, and Sanjay Reddy. "The Global Consumption and Income Project (GCIP): An Overview." *Journal of Globalization and Development* 7, no. 1: 61–108.

Lambais, Guilherme B. R. 2008. "Land Reform in Brazil: The Arrival of the Market Model." Paper presented at presented at the XXVIII ILASSA (The Institute of Latin American Studies Student Association) Conference at the University of Texas in February 2008.

Lanjouw, Peter, and Nicholas Stern, eds. 1998. *Economic Development in Palanpur over Five Decades*. Oxford: Oxford University Press.

Lanjouw, Peter, and Rajshri Jayaraman. 1999. "The Evolution of Poverty and Inequality in Indian Villages." *World Bank Research Observer* 14, no. 1: 1–30.

Lanzona, Leonardo A. Jr. 2013. *Productivity Growth in Philippine Agriculture: Human Capital and Agricultural Productivity: The Case of the Philippines*. Laguna, Philippines: SEARCA, Bureau of Agricultural Research and the Philippine Rice Research Institute.

Lastarria-Cornhiel, Susana. 1989. "Agrarian Reforms of the 1960s and 1970s in Peru." In *Searching for Agrarian Reform in Latin America*, edited by William Thiesenhusen, 156–187. Boston: Unwin Hyman.

Laszlo, Sonia. 2008. "Education, Labour Supply and Market Development in Rural Peru." *World Development* 36, no. 11: 2421–2439.

Lavers, Tom, and Festus Boamah. 2016. "The Impact of Agricultural Investments on State Capacity: A Comparative Analysis of Ethiopia and Ghana." *Geoforum* 72: 94–103.

Lavigne, Delville Phillipe. 1999. "Harmonising Formal Law and Customary Land Rights in French-speaking West Africa." IIED Issue Paper No. 86. June. London: International Institute for Environment and Development.

Leech, Garry. 2011. *The FARC: The Longest Insurgency*. New York: Zed Books Ltd.

Legrand, Catherine. 1986. *Frontier Expansion and Peasant Protest in Colombia, 1850–1936*. Albuquerque: University of New Mexico Press.

Lehman, David. 1978. "The Death of Land Reform: A Polemic." *World Development* 6, no. 3: 339–345.

Leitenberg, Milton. 2006. "Deaths in Wars and Conflicts in the 20th Century." Cornell University Peace Studies Program, Occasional Paper #29, 3rd ed.

Leonard, Carol S. 2011. *Agrarian Reform in Russia: The Road from Serfdom*. Cambridge: Cambridge University Press.

Levine, Daniel H. 1981. *Religion and Politics in Latin America: The Catholic Church in Venezuela and Colombia*. Princeton, NJ: Princeton University Press.

Levy, Brian, Alan Hirsch, Vinothan Naidoo, and Musa Nxele. 2021. "South Africa: When Strong Institutions and Massive Inequalities Collide." *Carnegie Endowment for International Peace*. https://carnegieendowment.org/research/2021/03/south-africa-when-strong-institutions-and-massive-inequalities-collide?lang=en.

Lewis, W. Arthur. 1954. "Economic Development with Unlimited Supplies of Labour." *The Manchester School* 22, no. 2 (May): 139–191.

Li, Chao, and John Gibson. 2013. "Spatial Price Differences and Inequality in the People's Republic of China: Housing Market Evidence." Working Paper 06/13, Department of Economics, University of Waikato.

Li, Shi, Hiroshi Sato, and Terry Sicular. 2013. *Rising Inequality in China: Challenges to a Harmonious Society*. New York: Cambridge University Press.

Lin, Justin Yifu. 1990. "Collectivization and China's Agricultural Crisis in 1959–1961." *Journal of Political Economy* 98, no. 6: 1228–1252.

Lin, Justin Yifu. 1992. "Rural Reforms and Agricultural Growth in China." *American Economic Review* 82, no. 1: 34–51.

Lindert, Peter H., and Jeffrey G. Williamson. 2011. "American Incomes Before and After the Revolution." *Journal of Economic History* 73, no. 3: 725–765.

Lippit, Victor. 1974. *Land Reform and Economic Development in China, A Study of Institutional Change and Development Finance*. White Plains, NY: International Arts and Sciences Press.

Lipton, Michael. 2009. *Land Reform in Developing Countries: Property Rights and Property Wrongs*. New York: Routledge.

Liu, Ts'ui Jung, and John C. H. Fei. 1977. "An Analysis of the Land Tax Burden in China, 1650–1865." *Journal of Economic History* XXXVII, no. 2: 359–381.

Liverpool-Tasie, Lenis Saweda Onipede, Bolarin T. Omonona, Awa Sanou, and Wale O. Ogunleye. 2017. "Is Increasing Inorganic Fertilizer Use for Maize Production in SSA a Profitable Proposition? Evidence from Nigeria." *Food Policy* 67, 41–51.

Lleras, Alberto. n.d. "El problema de la tierra" (The Land Problem). Speech delivered by the President of the Republic, before the National Peasant Congress. Princeton University Library microfiche collection, call number MICROFILM 06159.

Lopez, Alejandro. 1927. *Problemas Colombianos*. Columbia: Editorial Paris-America.

López, Alfonso. 1961. "Hacia una verdadera reforma que complete la 'Revolución en Marcha'" [Towards a True Reform that Completes the "Marching Revolution"]. In *Tierra: 10 ensayos sobre la reforma agraria en Colombia*, edited by Carlos Lleras, 83–104. Bogotá: Ediciones Tercer Mundo.

López-Uribe, Maria del Pilar, and Fabio Sanchez Torres. 2018. *On the Agrarian Origins of Civil Conflict in Colombia*. London: London School of Economics.

Lowder, Sarah, Jakob Skoet, and Terri Raney. 2016. "The Number, Size, and Distribution of Farms, Smallholder Farms, and Family Farms Worldwide." *World Development* 87: 16–29.

Lucassen, Jan. 2021. *The Story of Work: A New History of Mankind*. New Haven, CT: Yale University Press.

Luong, Hy Van. 1985. "Agrarian Unrest from an Anthropological Perspective: The Case of Vietnam." *Comparative Politics* 17: 153–174.

Lynch, Michael. 2008. *The People's Republic of China, 1949–76*. 2nd ed. London: Hodder Education.

Machado, Absalon. 1984. "Reforma Agraria: Una mirada retrospective." *Economıa Colombiana* 160–161: 55–69.

Magalhães, Marcelo Marques de, Hildo Meirelles de Souza Filho, Miguel Rocha de Sousa, José Maria F. J. da Silveira, and Antônio Márcio Buainain. 2011. "Land Reform in NE Brazil: A Stochastic Frontier Production Efficiency Evaluation." *Revista de Economia e Sociologia Rural* 49, no. 1: 9–30.

Majd, Mohammed G. 1991. "The Political Economy of Land Reform in Iran." *Land Use Policy,* 8, no. 1: 69–76.

Majd, Mohammed G., and Vahid Nowshirvani. 1993. "Land Reform in Iran Revisited: New Evidence on the Results of Land Reform in Nine Provinces." *Journal of Peasant Studies* 20: 442–458.

Malesky, Edmund, Regina Abrami, and Yu Zheng. 2011. "Institutions and Inequality in Single-Party Regimes: A Comparative Analysis of Vietnam and China." *Comparative Politics* 43, no. 4 (July): 401–419.

Manapat, Carlos. 1961. *Economics, Taxation, and Agrarian Reform.* Quezon City: C&E Publishers.

Mançano Fernandes, Bernardo. 2013. "Re-peasantization, Resistance and Subordination: The Struggle for Land and Agrarian Reform in Brazil." *Agrarian South: Journal of Political Economy* 2, no. 3: 1–21.

Mander, Harsh. 2013. "Reviving Land Reforms?" *Economic and Political Weekly* 48, no. 35 (August 31): 13–15.

Markevich, Andrei. 2018. "Russia in the Great War: Mobilisation, Grain, and Revolution." In *The Economics of the Great War: A Centennial Perspective,* edited by Stephen Broadberry and Mark Harrison. 103–108: Paris and London: CEPR Press.

Markevich, Andrei, and Ekaterina Zhuravskaya. 2018. "The Economic Effects of the Abolition of Serfdom: Evidence from the Russian Empire." *American Economic Review* 108, no. 4–5: 1074–1117.

Martinez-Torres, María Elena, and Peter M. Rosset. 2010. "La Vía Campesina: The Birth and Evolution of a Transnational Social Movement." *Journal of Peasant Studies* 37, no. 1: 149–175.

Martins, Jose de Souza. 2002. "Representing the Peasantry? Struggles For/About Land in Brazil." *Journal of Peasant Studies* 29, no. 3–4: 300–335.

McCaa, Robert. 2001. "Missing Millions: The Human Cost of the Mexican Revolution." *Mexican Studies* 19, no. 2. http://users.pop.umn.edu/~rmccaa/missmill/mxrev.htm.

McCaig, Brian, Dwayne Benjamin, and Loren Brandt. 2009. "The Evolution of Income Inequality in Vietnam, 1993–2006." Unpublished paper.

McClintock, Cynthia. 1981. *Peasant Cooperatives and Political Change in Peru.* Princeton, NJ: Princeton University Press.

McCloskey, Deirdre. 1991. "The Prudent Peasant: New Findings on the Open Fields." *Journal of Economic History* 51, no 2: 343–355.

McCullough, Ellen B. 2017. "Labor Productivity and Employment Gaps in Sub-Saharan Africa." *Food Policy,* 67, 133–152.

Mcelwee, Pamela. 2007. "From the Moral Economy to the World Economy: Revisiting Vietnamese Peasants in a Globalizing Era." *Journal of Vietnamese Studies* 2, no. 2: 57–107.

McEwan, William J. 1975. *Changing Rural Society: A Study of Communities in Bolivia.* New York: Oxford University Press.

McMillan, John, John Whalley, and Lijing Zhu. 1989. "The Impact of China's Economic Reforms on Agricultural Productivity Growth." *Journal of Political Economy* 97, no. 4: 781–807.

Melo, Jorge Orlando. 2012. "El axioma de Carimagua." Ámbito Jurídico September 3: 1–2.

Mellor, John. 1976. *The New Economics of Growth.* Ithaca: Cornell University Press.

Mellor, John W. 2014. "High Rural Population Density Africa – What are the Growth Requirements and Who Participates?" *Food Policy* 48: 66–75.

Mellor, John W., and Johnston, Bruce F. 1984. "The World Food Equation: Interrelations Among Development, Employment, and Food Consumption." *Journal of Economic Literature* 22, no. 2: 531–574.

Melmed-Sanjak, Jolyne S., and Michael R. Carter. 1991. "The Economic Viability and Stability of 'Capitalised Family Farming': An Analysis of Agricultural Decollectivization in Peru." *Journal of Development Studies* 27, no. 2: 190–210.

Mendes Pereira, João Márcio, and Dario Fajardo. 2015. "The World Bank's 'Market Assisted Land Reform' in Colombia and Brazil (1994–2002)." *Revista Brasileira de História* 35, no. 70: 157–180.

Meng, Xin, Nancy Qian, and Pierre Yared. 2010. "The Institutional Causes of China's Great Famine, 1959–61." NBER Working Paper No. 16361.

Meng, Xin, Kailing Shen, and Sen Xue. 2013. "Economic Reform, Education Expansion, and Earnings Inequality for Urban Males in China, 1988–2009." *Journal of Comparative Economics* 41, no. 1, 227–244.

Michler, Jeffrey D., and Gerald E. Shively. 2015. "Land Tenure, Tenure Security and Farm Efficiency: Panel Evidence from the Philippines." *Journal of Agricultural Economics* 66: 155–169.

Miles, Tshombe. 2019. "Reflecting on the Legacy of Brazilian Slavery and Reimaging Afro-Brazilian Agency." *Black and Latino Studies History Compass* 17, no. 1: 1–8.

Mill, John Stuart. 1848. *The Principles of Political Economy.* London: John W. Parker.

Mironov, Boris N. 1991. "The Development of Literacy in Russia and the USSR from the Tenth to the Twentieth Centuries Author." *History of Education Quarterly* 31, no. 2: 229–252.

Moise, Edwin. 2001. "Land Reform in North Vietnam, 1953–1956." Paper presented at the 18th Annual Conference on SE Asian Studies, Center of SE Asian Studies, University of California, Berkeley, February.

Molano, Adolfo. 2015. *A lomo de mula. Viajes al corazón de la FARC.* Bogotá: Editorial Aguilar.

Monteiro, Carlos Agusto, Wolney Conde, and Silvia Konno. 2006. "Analise do inquerito Chamada Nutricional 2005." *Cadernos de Estudos,* no. 4: 29–36.

Montgomery, John. 1972. "Allocation of Authority in Land Reform Programs: A Comparative Study of Preform Administrative Processes and Output." *Administrative Science Quarterly* 17 (March): 62–75.

Montgomery, Paul L. 1975. "Wolf Ladejinsky, Land Reformer Dies; Helped to Break Feudal System in Japan." *New York Times,* July 4.

Moon, David. 1999. *The Russian Peasantry, 1600–1930: The World the Peasants Made.* London: Longman.

Moore, Barrington, Jr. 1966. *Social Origins of Dictatorship and Democracy: Lord and Peasant in the Making of the Modern World.* Boston: Beacon Press.

Moradi, Alexander. 2012. "Climate, Height, and Economic Development in Sub-Saharan Africa." *Journal of Anthropological Sciences* 90: 225–228.

More, Thomas. 1891. *Utopia.* New York: Columbian Publishing Company. (Original work published in 1516)

Moreno, Frede G., and Susana Evangelista Leones. 2011. "Agrarian Reform and Philippine Political Development." http://world.bepress.com/frede_moreno/9/.

Morgan, Marc. 2017. "Extreme and Persistent Inequality: New Evidence for Brazil Combining National Accounts, Survey and Fiscal Data." World Inequality Lab., Working Paper Series (No. 2017/12).

Morrisson, Christian, and Wayne Snyder. 2000. "The Income Inequality of France in Historical Perspective." *European Journal of Economic History* 4: 59–83.

Motta, Marcia Maria Menendes. 2013. "Classic Works of Brazil's New Rural History: Feudalism and the Latifundio in the Interpretations of the Left (1940/1964)." *Historia Crítica* 51: 121–144.

Mulato, Wubne. 1991. "Agriculture." In Ethiopia, a *Country Study,* edited by Thomas P. Ofcansky and LaVerle Berry, 162–182. Washington, DC: Library of Congress Federal Research Division.

Muriel, Beatriz, and Luis Carlos Jemio. 2010. "Mercado laboral y reformas en Bolivia." In *Desafíos Laborales En América Latina Después De Dos Décadas De Reformas Estructurales: Bolivia, Paraguay y Perú, 1997–2008,* edited by José Rodríguez and Albert

Berry, 273–356. Lima: Instituto de Estudios Peruanos, Fondo Editorial de la Pontificia Universidad Católica del Perú.

Murray, Una, Zewdy Gebremedhin, Galina Brychkova, and Charles Spillane. 2016. "Smallholder Farmers and Climate Smart Agriculture: Technology and Labor-productivity Constraints amongst Women Smallholders in Malawi." *Gender, Technology and Development* 20, no. 2: 117–148.

Musgrave, Richard A. 1981. *Fiscal Reform in Bolivia: Final Report of the Bolivian Mission on Tax Reform*. New Haven, CT: Harvard Law School, International Tax Program.

Muyanga, M., and Thomas Jayne. 2019. "Revisiting the Farm Size-Productivity Relationship Based on a Relatively Wide Range of Farm Sizes: Evidence from Kenya." *American Journal of Agricultural Economics* 101, no. 4: 1140–1163.

Muyanga, Milu, Zephania Nyirenda, Yanjanani Lifeyo, and William J. Burke. 2020. "The Future of Smallholder Farming in Malawi." MwAPATA Institute Working Paper No. 20.

Mwabu, Germano, and Erik Thorbecke. 2004. "Rural Development, Growth and Poverty in Africa." *Journal of African Economies* 13, no. suppl_1: 116–165.

Nafziger, Steven. 2008. "Communal Institutions, Resource Allocation, and Russian Economic Development: 1861-1905." *Journal of Economic History* 68, no. 2: 570–575. (Dissertation Summary)

Nafziger, Steven. 2016. "Communal Property Rights and Land Redistributions in Late Tsarist Russia (2016)." *Economic History Review* 69, no. 3: 773–800.

Nafziger, Steven. 2017. "Quantification and the Economic History of Imperial Russia." *Slavic Review* 76, no. 1: 30–36.

Nafziger, Steven, and Peter Lindert. 2013. "Russian Inequality on the Eve of Revolution." Working paper.

Nash, Manning. 1966. *Primitive and Peasant Economic Systems*. Oxford: Chandler Publishing.

Nassar, Carlos Camacho. 2010. "La cuestión agraria, los derechos de los indígenas a la tierra y el fracaso del proceso de paz en Guatemala." *Cuadernos de Antropología*, no. 20: 1–25.

Naughton, Barry. 2003. "Communist China." In *The Oxford Encyclopedia of Economic History, Volume 1*, edited by Joel Mokyr, 435–438. New York: Oxford University Press.

Nega, B., B. Adenew, and S. Gebre Sellasie. 2003. "Current Land Policy Issues in Ethiopia." Ethiopian Economic Policy Research Institute, Addis Ababa, Ethiopia.

Nehru, Jawaharlal. 1957. *Fortnightly Letters to the Chief Ministers, 1948–63*. May 5 (unpublished).

Nieto-Matiz, Camilo. 2019. "Democracy in the Countryside: The Rural Sources of Violence against Voters in Colombia." *Journal of Peace Research* 56, no. 2: 264–278.

Nkonde, Chewe, Thomas S. Jayne, Robert B. Richardson, and Frank Place. 2015. "Testing the Farm Size-Productivity Relationship Over a Wide Range of Farm Sizes: Should the Relationship be a Decisive Factor in Guiding Agricultural Development and Land Policies in Zambia?" *World Bank Conference On Land And Poverty*, Washington, DC.

Nunn, Nathan. 2007. "Historical Legacies: A Model Linking Africa's Past to its Current Underdevelopment." *Journal of Development Economics* 83, no. 1: 157–175.

Nunn, Nathan. 2008. "The Long-Term Effects of Africa's Slave Trades." *Quarterly Journal of Economics* 123, no. 1: 139–176.

Nurkse, Ragnar. 1953. *Problems of Capital Formation in Underdeveloped Countries*. New York: Oxford University Press.

Olea, Ronalyn V. 2014. "Farmers Hit Proposed Extension of Agrarian Reform Law, Call for Aquino's Ouster." *Bulatlat*. June 30.

Olinto, Pedro, Klaus Deininger, and Benjamin Davis. 2000. "Land Market Liberalization and the Access to Land by the Rural Poor: Panel Data Evidence of the Impact of the Mexican Ejido Reform." World Bank Discussion Paper.

Open Democracy. 2021. "Four Years Later: Colombia's Peace Agreement Advances at a Snail's Pace." January 6. from https://www.opendemocracy.net/en/democraciaabierta/colombia-peace-agreement-advances-snail-pace/.

Organization for Economic Cooperation and Development (OECD). 2008. *World Migration 2008*. London, UK: Hammersmith Press.

Orwell, George. 1945. *Animal Farm: A Fairy Story*. London: Secker and Warburg.

Ospina Vásquez, Luis. 1955. *Industria y Protección en Colombia, 1810–1939*. Medellín: Editorial S.F.

Ostrom, Elinor. 1990. *Governing the Commons: The Evolution of Institutions for Collective Action*. Cambridge: Cambridge University Press.

Ottaway, Marina. 1977. "Land Reform in Ethiopia, 1974–1977." *African Studies Review* 20, no. 3: 79–90.

Overton, Mark. 1996. "Re-establishing the English Agricultural Revolution." *Agricultural History Review* 44, no. 1: 1–20.

Owusu, Obed. 2018. "Subsistence Agriculture and Labour Reallocation in Developing Countries." PhD diss., Dalhousie University.

Oxfam International. 2014. "Beyond Safe Land: Why Security of Land Tenure is Crucial for the Philippines Post-Haiyan Recovery." Oxfam Briefing Paper.

Ozanne, Adam. 1999. "Perverse Supply Response in Peasant Agriculture: A Review." *Oxford Development Studies* 27, no. 2: 251–270.

Palacios, Marco. 2006. *Between Legitimacy and Violence: A History of Colombia, 1875–2002*. Durham, North Carolina: Duke University Press.

Pallot, Judith. 1999. *Land Reform in Russia 1906–1917: Peasant Responses to Stolypin's Project of Rural Transformation*. Oxford: Oxford University Press.

Pan, Lei, and Luc Christiaensen. 2012. "Who is Vouching for the Input Voucher? Decentralized Targeting and Elite Capture in Tanzania" *World Development* 40, no. 8, pp. 1619–1633.

Parmentier, Stephane. 2014. "Scaling up Agroecological Approaches: What, Why and How?" Oxfam Discussion Paper, Oxfam-Solidarity, Belgium.

Pearson, Ross. 1963. "Land Reform, Guatemalan Style." *American Journal of Economics and Sociology* 22, no. 2: 225–234.

Peart, Sandra. 1984. "John Stuart Mill on Irish Development: Some Modern Development Issues in a Nineteenth-century Context." Essay submitted in Economics 2700 (Economic Development), University of Toronto.

Peinado, Marcelo. 1969. "Land Reform in Three Communities of Cochabamba, Bolivia." PhD diss., University of Wisconsin-Madison.

Pereira, Anthony W. 2018. "The US Role in the 1964 Coup in Brazil: A Reassessment." *Bulletin of Latin American Research* 37, no. 1: 5–17, 20.

Pereira, João Márcio Mendes. 2007. "The World Bank's 'Market-Assisted' Land Reform as a Political Issue: Evidence from Brazil (1997–2006)." *European Review of Latin American and Caribbean Studies* 82: 21–24.

Pereira, Pedro A. Arraes, Geraldo B. Martha Jr., Carlos A. M. Santana, and Eliseu Alves. 2012. "The Development of Brazilian Agriculture: Future Technological Challenges and Opportunities." *Agriculture & Food Security* 1: article 4.

Peres-Cajías, José Alejandro. 2017. "The Expansion of Public Spending and Mass Education in Bolivia: Did the 1952 Revolution Represent a Permanent Shock?" In *Has Latin American Inequality Changed Direction?*, edited by L. Bértola and J. Williamson, 195–218. New York: Springer Link.

Peritore, N. Patrick, and Anna Karina Galve Peritore. 1990. "Brazilian Attitudes toward Agrarian Reform: A Q-Methodology Opinion Study of a Conflictual Issue." *Journal of Developing Areas: Macomb* 24, no. 3: 377–406.

Perkins, Dwight. 1975. *China's Modern Economy in Historical Perspective*. Stanford: Stanford University Press.

Perkins, Dwight. 1986. *China, Asia's Next Economic Giant*. Seattle: University of Washington Press.

Peters, Pauline. 2004. "Inequality and Social Conflict Over Land in Africa." *Journal of Agrarian Change* 4, no. 3: 269–314.

Philippines Statistics Authority. 2015. *Special Report—Highlights of the 2012 Census of Agriculture (2012 CA).* Quezon City: Philippines Statistics Authority.

Philipps, Andrew Q. 2020. "Just in Time: Political Policy Cycles of Land Reform." *Politics* 40, no. 2: 207–226.

Picado, Wilson, and Margarita Silva. 2002. *De la colonización al desarrollo rural.* San José: Instituto de Desarrollo Agrario.

Piketty, Thomas, and Emmanuel Saez. 2013. "Top Incomes and the Great Recession: Recent Evolutions and Policy Implications." *IMF Economic Review* 61, no. 3: 456–478.

Piketty, Thomas, Li Yang, and Gabriel Zucman. 2019. "Income Inequality is Growing Fast in China and Making It Look More Like the US." *LSE Newsletter*, April 1.

Piketty, Thomas. 2014. *Capital in the Twenty-First Century.* Cambridge, Massachusetts: Harvard University Press.

Pinheiro, Armando Castelar, Indermit S. Gill, Luis Servén, and Mark Roland Thomas. 2004. "Brazilian Economic Growth, 1900–2000: Lessons and Policy Implications." Inter-American Development Bank.

Polanyi, Karl. 1944. *The Great Transformation: The Political and Economic Origins of Our Time.* New York: Farrar & Rinehart.

Polanyi, Karl. 1957. *The Great Transformation: The Political and Economic Origins of Our Time.* Boston: Beacon Press.

Pollock, John C. 1975. "Violence, Politics and Elite Performance: The Political Sociology of La Violencia in Colombia." *Studies in Comparative International Development* X, no. 2: 22–50.

Powelson, John P., and Richard Stock. 1987. *The Peasant Betrayed: Agriculture and Land Reform in the Third World.* Boston: Oelgeschlager, Gunn and Hain.

Preece, Warren E., ed. 2010. "Serfdom." In *New Encyclopedia Britannica, Vol. 16*, 858. Chicago: Encyclopedia Britannica.

Prosterman, Roy L. 1967. "Land Reform in South Vietnam: A Proposal for Turning the Tables on the Viet Cong." *Cornell Law Review* 53 (November): 26–44. http://scholarship.law.cornell.edu/clr/vol53/iss1/3.

Prosterman, Roy L., and Jeffrey M. Riedinger. 1987). *Land Reform and Democratic Development.* Baltimore: Johns Hopkins University Press.

Proyect, Louis. 1998. "Class and Indigenous Roots of the Guatemalan Revolution." http://www.columbia.edu/~lnp3/mydocs/indian/guatemala.htm.

Pryor, Frederic L. 1992. *The Red and the Green: The Rise and Fall of Collectivized Agriculture in Marxist Regimes.* Princeton, NJ: Princeton University Press.

Putzel, James. 1992. *A Captive Land: The Politics of Agrarian Reform in the Philippines.* London: Catholic Institute for International Relations.

Putzel, James, and Horacio Morales Jr., eds. 2002. *Power in the Village: Agrarian Reform, Rural Politics, Institutional Change and Globalisation.* Quezon City: University of Philippines Press.

Radwan, Samir, and Eddy Lee. 1986. *Agrarian Change in Egypt: An Anatomy of Rural Poverty.* London: Croom Helm.

Ramirez, Maria Teresa, and Irene Salazar. 2007. "The Emergence of Education in the Republica de Colombia in the 19th Century: Where Did We Go Wrong?" *Presentation at the International Seminar on the Economic History of Colombia in the 19th Century*, Bogotá, Banco de la Republica.

Raup, Philip M. 1967. "Land Reform and Agricultural Output." In *Agricultural Development and Economic Growth*, edited by Herman F. Southworth and Bruce F. Johnston, 267–314. Ithaca, NY: Cornell University Press.

Ravallion, Martin, and Dominique van de Walle. 2008. *Land in Transition: Reform and Poverty in Rural Vietnam.* Washington, DC: The World Bank.

Rawski, Thomas G. 1979. *Economic Growth and Employment in China.* New York: Oxford University Press.

Raymond, Chad. 2008. "No Responsibility and No Rice": The Rise and Fall of Agricultural Collectivization in Vietnam." *Agricultural History* 82, no. 1: 43–61.

Reveiz, Edgar. 2007. *El Estado Lego y la Fractura Social.* Bogotá: Academia Colombiana de Ciencias Económicas (ACCE) y Centro Colombiano de Responsabilidad Empresarial (CCRE).

Reyes, Alejandro. 2008. *Guerreros y campesinos: El despojo de la tierra en Colombia.* Bogotá: FESCL, Grupo Editorial Norma.

Reyes, Alejandro. 2016. "Fedegan y el procurador contra la restitución de tierras." *Razón Publica.* May 2.

Reynolds, Clark W. 1970. *The Mexican Economy: Twentieth Century Structure and Growth.* New Haven, CT: Yale University Press.

Richardson, Nan, Stephen Ferry, and Gonzalo Sanchez. 2012. *Violentology: A Manual of the Conflict in Colombia.* New York: Umbrage Editions.

Ricker-Gilbert, Jacob, and Thomas S. Jayne. 2016. "Estimating the Enduring Effects of Fertiliser Subsidies on Commercial Fertiliser Demand and Maize Production: Panel Data Evidence from Malawi." *Journal of Agricultural Economics* 68, no. 1, 70–9.

Robles, Wilder. 2018. "Revisiting Agrarian Reform in Brazil, 1985–2016." *Journal of Developing Societies* 34, no. 1: 1–34.

Robles, Wilder, and Henry Veltmeyer. 2015. "Agrarian Reform under Sarney and Collor de Mello-Franco." In *The Politics of Agrarian Reform in Brazil. Social Movements and Transformation*, edited by W. Robles and K. A. Loparo, 85–104. New York: Palgrave Macmillan.

Rocha, Cecilia, Luciene Burlandy, and Renato Maluf. 2012. "Small Farms and Sustainable Rural Development for Food Security: The Brazilian Experience." *Development Southern Africa* 29, no. 4: 519–529.

Rodríguez, A. R. 1960. "La colonización agrícola y algunos problemas de la tenencia y uso de la tierra en Colombia" [Agricultural Colonization and Some Problems with Land Use and Land Tenure in Colombia]. Rome: FAO (mimeo).

Rorty, James. 1955. "The Dossier of Wolf Ladejinsky: The Fair Rewards of Distinguished Civil Service." *Commentary Magazine.* April. https://www.commentary.org/articles/james-rorty/the-dossier-of-wolf-ladejinskythe-fair-rewards-of-distinguished-civil-service/.

Rosenstein-Rodan, Paul. 1961. "Notes on the Theory of the 'Big Push.'" In *Economic Development for Latin America*, edited by Howard S. Ellis and Henry C. Wallich, 57–81. London: Palgrave Macmillan.

Roser, Max. 2016. "Democracy." *Our World in Data.* https://ourworldindata.org/democracy.

Ross, Michael L. 2015. "What Have We Learned about the Resource Curse?" *American Review of Political Science* 18: 239–259.

Rosstat—Federal State Statistical Service, Moscow. 2008. *Statistical Yearbook of the Russian Federation 2007.* Chapter 14, p. 445 et seq. http://www.gks.ru/ > Публикации > Электронные версии публикаций статистический ежегодник (2007г. in Russian).

Rostow, Walter W. 1960. *The Stages of Economic Growth: A Non-Communist Manifesto.* Cambridge: Cambridge University Press.

Rozman, Stephen L. 1970. "The Evolution of the Political Role of the Peruvian Military." *Journal of InterAmerican Studies and World Affairs* 12, no. 4: 539–564.

Ruiz-Tagle V., and A. Jaime. 1998. "Chile: 40 Años de Desigualdad de Ingresos." Departamento de Economía, Universidad de Chile.

Ruthenberg, Hans P. 1980. *Farming Systems in the Tropics.* Oxford: Clarendon Press.

Rytkonen, Paulina. 2004. *Fruits of Capitalism: Modernization of Chilean Agriculture, 1950–2000*, 43–48. Lund Studies in Economic History Stockholm: Almquist & Wiksell International.

Saad, Reem. 2002. "Egyptian Politics and the Tenancy Law." In *Counter-Revolution in Egypt's Countryside: Land and Farmers in the Era of Economic Reform*, edited by Ray Bush, 103–125. London: Zed Books.

Saavedra, Jaime, Roberto Melzi-Ríos, and Arturo Miranda Blanco. 1997. "Financiamiento de la educación en el Perú." Lima: GRADE, Documento de Trabajo, 24. https://www.grade.org.pe/publicaciones/24-financiamiento-de-la-educacion-en-el-peru/.

Sachs, Jeffrey D., and Andrew. M. Warner. 2001. "The Curse of Natural Resources." *European Economic Review* 45: 827–838.

Saffon, Maria Paula. 2015. "When Theft Becomes Grievance: Dispossession as a Cause of Redistributive Land Claims in 20th-century Latin America." PhD diss., Columbia University.

Saikal, Amin. 1980. *The Rise and Fall of the Shah.* Princeton, NJ: Princeton University Press.

Sánchez, Gonzalo. 1977. *Las ligas campesinas en Colombia.* Bogotá: Ediciones Tiempo Presente.

Sanderson, Susan Walsh. 1984. *Land Reform in Mexico, 1910–1980.* Orlando: Academic Press.

Sandilands, Roger. 1990. *The Life and Political Economy of Lauchlin Currie.* Durham, NC: Duke University Press.

Sandoval Olascoaga, Sebastián. 2015. "The Distribution of Top Incomes in Mexico: How Rich are the Richest?" Master's diss., Paris School of Economics.

Sanhueza, Claudia, and Ricardo Mayer. 2011. "Top Incomes in Chile Using 50 Years of Household Surveys: 1957–2007." *Estudios de economía* 38, no. 1: 169–193.

Savastano, Sara, and Pasquale L. Scandizzo. 2017. "Farm Size and Productivity." World Bank Group, Policy Research Working Paper 8127.

Saxena, K. B. 1990. "Access to Land as Instrument of Poverty Alleviation." *Journal of Rural Development* 9, no. 1: 115–143.

Schanzer, Jonathan. 2004. "Review of *All the Shah's Men*: An American Coup and the Roots of Middle East Terror." *Middle East Quarterly*. June 1.

Schlager, E., and Elinor Ostrom. 1992. "Property-Rights Regimes and Natural Resources: A Conceptual Analysis." *Land Economics* 69, no. 3: 249–262.

Schlesinger, Stephen C., and Stephen Kinzer. 1983. *Bitter Fruit: The Story of the American Coup in Guatemala.* New York: Anchor Books.

Schran, Peter. 1969. *The Development of Chinese Agriculture, 1950–1959.* Urbana: University of Illinois Press.

Schuler, Friedrich E. 1999. *Mexico between Hitler and Roosevelt: Mexican Foreign Relations in the Age of Lazaro Cardenas, 1934–1940.* Alburquerque: University of New Mexico Press.

Schultz, Theodore. 1964. *Transforming Traditional Agriculture.* New Haven, CT: Yale University Press.

Schumacher, Ernst F. 1973. *Small is Beautiful: A Study of Economics as if People Mattered.* London, UK: Blond and Briggs.

Scott, C. D. 1997. "Poverty Among Small Farmers Under Frei and Pinochet, 1968–1986." *Bulletin of Latin American Research* 16, no. 1 (January): 57–69.

Scott, James C. 1976. *The Moral Economy of the Peasant: Rebellion and Subsistence in Southeast Asia.* Yale University Press.

Scott, James C. 2017. *Against the Grain: A Deep History of the Earliest States.* New Haven, CT: Yale University Press.

Seers, Dudley. 1969. "The Meaning of Development." *International Development Review* 11, no. 4: 3–4.

Seligson, Mitchell. 1980. *Peasants of Costa Rica and the Development of Agrarian Capitalism.* Madison, WI: University of Wisconsin Press.

Seligson, Mitchell. 1984. "Implementing Land Reform: The Case of Costa Rica." *Managing International Development* 1, no. 2: 29–46.

Sen, A. K. 1962. "An Aspect of Indian Agriculture." *Economic Weekly* 14, no. 4-5-6: 243–246. Annual Number.

Sen, Amartya. 1981. *Poverty and Famines: An Essay on Entitlement and Deprivation.* New York: Oxford University Press.

Shaban, Radwan Ali. 1987. "Testing between Competing Models of Sharecropping." *Journal of Political Economy* 95: 893–920.

Sicular, Terry, Yue Ximing, and Bjorn Anders Gustafsson. 2007. "The Urban–Rural Income Gap and Income Inequality in China." In *Understanding Inequality and Poverty in China: Methods and Applications*, edited by Guanghua Wan, 30–71. London, UK: Palgrave Macmillan.

Siekmeier, James F. 2011. *The Bolivian Revolution and the United States, 1952 to the Present.* Philadelphia: Pennsylvania State University Press.

Skidmore, Thomas E. 1988. *The Politics of Military Rule in Brazil, 1964–85.* New York: Oxford University Press.

Smith, Gavin. 1991. *Livelihood and Resistance: Peasants and the Politics of Land in Peru.* Berkley: University of California Press.

Smith, Stansfield. 2018. "Eleven Years of the 'Process of Change' in Evo Morales' Bolivia." Council on Hemispheric Affairs. January 3. https://coha.org/eleven-years-of-the-process-of-change-in-evo-morales-bolivia/.

Smith, William C., ed. 2009. *Latin American Democratic Transformations: Institutions, Actors, and Processes.* New York: John Wiley & Sons.

Sobhan, Rehman. 1993. *Agrarian Reform and Social Transformation.* London: Zed Books.

Sotomayor, Orlando. 2007. "The Distribution of Household Income in Brazil: Unequal and Immutable?" *World Development* 36, no. 7: 1280–1293.

Souza, Pedro H. G. F., and Marcelo Medeiros. 2015. "Top Income Shares and Inequality in Brazil, 1928–2012." *Sociologies in Dialogue* 1, no. 1: 119–132.

Staatz, John M., and Niama Nango Dembélé. 2008. "Agriculture for Development in Sub-Saharan Africa." Background paper for World Development Report 2008. Washington, DC: World Bank.

Stavis, Ben. 1978. "China and the Comparative Analysis of Land Reform." *Modern China* 4, no. 1: 63–78.

Stepan, Alfred, ed. 1973a. *Authoritarian Brazil: Origins, Policies, and Future.* New Haven, CT: Yale University Press.

Stepan, Alfred. 1973b. "The New Professionalism of Internal Warfare and Military Role Expansion." In *Authoritarian Brazil: Origins, Policies, and Future*, 47–65. New Haven, CT: Yale University Press.

Stephens, Evelyne Huber. 1983. "The Peruvian Military Government, Labor Mobilization, and the Political Strength of the Left." *Latin American Research Review* 18, no. 2: 57–93.

Tadem, Eduardo Climaco. 2015. "Philippine Agrarian Reform in the 21st Century." Presentation at a "Land Grabbing, Conflict and Agrarian-environmental Transformations: Perspectives from East and Southeast Asia." Conference at Chiang Mai University, June 5–6.

Takeuchi, Shinichi, and Jean Marara. 2011. "Conflict and Land Tenure in Rwanda." Japan International Cooperation Agency (JICA-RI) Working Paper.

Takigawa, Tsutomu. 1972. "Historical Background of Agricultural Land Reform in Japan." *The Developing Economies* 10, no. 3: 390–410.

Tamayo, Héctor. 1970. *La Reforma Agraria en Colombia: Una Base apara su Evaluación.* Bogotá: Universidad Nacional de Colombia.

Tauger, Mark. 2004a. "Soviet Peasants and Collectivization: Resistance and Adaptation." *Journal of Peasant Studies* 31, no. 3–4: 427–456.

Tauger, Mark. 2004b. "The Years of Hunger: Soviet Agriculture, 1931–1933." https://eh.net/book-reviews/the-years-of-hunger-soviet-agriculture-1931-1933/.

Tauger, Mark. 2018. "Review of Anne Applebaum's 'Red Famine: Stalin's War on Ukraine.'" *History News Network.* https://historynewsnetwork.org/article/169438.

Taylor, Sally. 1990. *Stalin's' Apologist.* New York: Oxford University Press.

Temin, Peter. 2004. "The Labor Market of the Early Roman Empire." *Journal of Interdisciplinary History* XXXIV, no. 4: 513–538.

Teofilo, Edson, and D. Prado Garcia. 2003. "Brazil: Land Politics, Poverty and Rural Development." In *Land Reform: Land Settlement and Cooperatives, Vol. 3*, edited by Paulo Groppo, 19–39. Rome: United Nations Food and Agriculture Organization.

Teruel, Romeo G., and Jesus C. Dumagan. 2011. "Measuring and Explaining Total Factor Productivity (TFP) Growth and Patterns in Philippine Agriculture: A Regional Panel Data Framework." Paper presented at the 7th Asian Society of Agricultural Economists (ASAE) Conference, Hanoi, Vietnam, October 13–15.

Thiesenhusen, William C. 1995. *Broken Promises: Agrarian Reform and the Latin American Campesino*. Boulder, CO: Westview Press.

Thirsk, Wayne. 1976. "The Distribution of Land Reforms Benefits in Colombia." *Land Economics* 52, no. 1: 77–87.

Thornton, William Thomas. 2019. *A Plea for Peasant Proprietors: With the Outlines of a Plan for Their Establishment in Ireland*. London, UK: Wentworth Press. (Originally published in 1843)

Thoumi, Francisco E. 2015. *Debates y paradigmas de las políticas de drogas en el mundo y los desafíos para Colombia*. Bogotá: Academia colombiana de Ciencias Económicas.

Thoumi, Francisco E. 2021. "La necesidad de repensar el fenómeno de las drogas en Colombia desde una perspectiva de complejidad y atendiendo el contexto interno." Unpublished paper.

Torres Alarcon, Juan David. 2020. "Shaping Inequality? Agrarian Institutions, Property Rights, and Landlord Empowerment." MA thesis, Universidad de Los Andes.

Toulmin, Camilla. 2000. "Evolving Land Rights, Tenure and Policy in Sub-Saharan Africa." In *Evolving Land Rights in Africa*, edited by Camilla Toulmin and Julian Quan, 1–30. London: UK Department for International Development.

Toynbee, Arnold. 1884. *Lectures on the Industrial Revolution in England: Public Addresses, Notes and Other Fragments, Together with a Short Memoir by B. Jowett*. London: Rivington's.

Trefzger Douglas W. 2002. "Guatemala's 1952 Agrarian Reform Law: A Critical Reassessment." *International Social Science Review* 77, no. 1/2: 32–46.

Tucker, Spencer C., ed. 1998. *Encyclopedia of the Vietnam War*. New York: Oxford University Press.

Tullis, F. LaMond. 1970. *Lord and Peasant in Peru: A Paradigm of Political and Social Change*. Cambridge, MA: Harvard University Press.

Tuma, Elias H. 1965. *Twenty-six Centuries of Agrarian Reform: A Comparative Analysis*. Berkeley: University of California Press.

Tutino, John. 1986. *From Insurrection to Revolution in Mexico: Social Bases of Agrarian Violence, 1750–1940*. Princeton, NJ: Princeton University Press.

Unger, Jonathan. 1984. "Severing the Links Between School Performance and Careers: The Sobering Experience of Chinese Urban Schools, 1968–1976." *Comparative Education* 20, no. 1: 93–103.

Unger, Jonathan. 1985. "The Decollectivization of the Chinese Countryside: A Survey of Twenty-eight Villages." *Pacific Affairs* 58, no. 4: 585–606.

United Nations Commission for Historical Clarification. 1999. *Guatemala: Memory of Silence*. New York: United Nations.

United Nations Human Rights Special Procedures. 2021. "Policy Brief: Last Chance to Make the Food Systems Summit Truly a 'People's Summit.'" Geneva, Switzerland: United Nations.

Uphoff, Norman, and Milton Esman. 1974. *Local Organization for Rural Development in Asia*. Ithaca, NY: Cornell University Rural Development Committee.

USAID. 2011. "Philippines: Country Profile." Property Rights and Resource Governance. https://www.usaid.gov/philippines/document/usaid-philippines-country-profile#.

Utuassu, Arthur. 2010. "Brazil: Democracy versus Poverty." *Instituto de Pesquisa Econômica Aplicada (IPEA)*. July 22.

Valdés, Alberto, and William Foster. 2014. "The Agrarian Reform Experiment in Chile: History, Impact, and Implications." IFPRI Discussion Paper 01368.

Van der Ploeg, Jan, and Ye Jingzhong. 2016a. *China's Peasant Agriculture and Rural Society*. Oxford: Routledge.

Van der Ploeg, Jan, and Ye Jingzhong. 2016b. "The Rise of Capitalist Modes of Farming." In *China's Peasant Agriculture and Rural Society*, 107–129. Oxford Routledge.

van der Westhuizen, Duan, Thomas Jayne, Ferdinand Meyer, and Arno J. van Niekerk. 2018. "Causes and Consequences of Rising Tractor Use in Sub-Saharan Africa: Evidence from Tanzania." *Paper presented at the International Conference of Agricultural Economists*, Vancouver, Canada, July 30, 2018.

Vargas, Jonathan M. Fortum. 2012. "The Sources of Inequality in Bolivia." *International Journal of Trade, Economics and Finance* 3, no. 5: 374–380.

Vargas, Jose P. Mauricio, and Santiago Garriga. 2015. "Explaining Inequality and Poverty Reduction in Bolivia." IMF Working Paper WP/15/265.

Vergara, Wilson, and Julio Zainea. 2019. "La relación entre el tamaño de la finca y la productividad agrícola. Evidencias de Colombia." Unpublished paper.

Verkaart, Simone, Kai Mausch, Lieven Claessens, and Ken E. Giller. 2019. "A Recipe for Success? Learning from the Rapid Adoption of Improved Chickpea Varieties in Ethiopia." *International Journal of Agricultural Sustainability* 17, no. 1: 34–48.

Villaveces Niño, Juanita, and Fabio Sánchez. 2015. "Tendencias históricas y regionales de la adjudicación de baldíos en Colombia." Facultad de Economía, Universidad del Rosario, Serie Documentos de Trabajo No. 179. February.

Viscidi, Lisa. 2004. "Land Reform and Conflict in Guatemala." *Counterpunch.org*. https://www.counterpunch.org/2004/09/08/land-reform-and-conflict-in-guatemala/.

von Humboldt, Alexander. 1811. *Political Essay on the Kingdom of New Spain, Vol. 1*. Translated by John Black. London: Longman, Hurst, Rees, Orme, and Brown.

Wagner, Maria Luise. 1989a. "The *Sexenio* (1946–52)." In *Bolivia: A Country Study*, edited by Rex A. Hudson and Dennis M. Hanratty, 33–34. Washington, DC: Library of Congress Federal Research Division.

Wagner, Maria Luise. 1989b. "Radical Reforms." In *Bolivia: A Country Study*, edited by Rex A. Hudson and Dennis M. Hanratty, 35–36. Washington, DC: Library of Congress Federal Research Division.

Wang, Xiaolu, and Wing Thye Woo. 2011. "The Size and Distribution of Hidden Household Income in China." *Asian Economic Papers* 10, no. 1: 1–26.

Warriner, Doreen. 1939. *Economic Problems of Peasant Farming*. London, New York: Oxford University Press.

Warriner, Doreen. 1957. *Land Reform and Development in the Middle East: A Study of Egypt, Syria and Iraq*. London: Institute of International Affairs.

Warriner, Doreen. 1964. *Economics of Peasant Farming*. New York: Routledge.

Warriner, Doreen. 1969. *Land Reform in Principle and Practice*. Oxford: Clarendon Press.

Watkins, Kevin. 1998. *Economic Growth with Equity: Lessons from East Asia*. New York: Oxford University Press.

Webb, Richard. 1977. *Government Policy and the Distribution of Income in Peru, 1963–1973*. Cambridge, MA: Harvard University Press.

Webb, Richard. 2013. *Conexión y Despegue Rural* [Connection and rural takeoff]. Lima, Peru: Universidad de San Martin de Porres (USMP).

Webb, Richard, and Adolfo Figueroa. 1975. *Distribución del Ingreso en el Perú*. Lima: Instituto de Estudios Peruanos.

Webber, Jeffery R. 2016. "Evo Morales, Transformismo, and the Consolidation of Agrarian Capitalism in Bolivia." *Journal of Agrarian Change* 17: 330–347.

Webster, Paul Christopher. 2012. "Colombian Gold-mining Village Fights to Stay Put." *National Catholic Reporter*. March 2.

Wegren, Stephen K. 1998. *Land Reform in Russia Institutional Design and Behavioral Responses*. New Haven, CT: Yale University Press.

Wei, Chen, Xilu Chen, Chang-Tai Hsieh, and Zheng Song. 2019. "A Forensic Examination of China's National Accounts." *Brookings Papers on Economic Activity*. Spring.

Weigel, George. 2003. *Biografía de Juan Pablo II—Testigo de Esperanza*. Barcelona: Editorial Plaza & Janés.

Welch, Cliff. 2006. "Globalization and the Transformation of Work in Rural Brazil: Agribusiness, Rural Labor Unions, and Peasant Mobilization." *International Labor and Working-Class History* 70, no. 1: 35–60.

Welch, Clifford Andrew, and Sérgio Sauer. 2015. "Rural Unions and the Struggle for Land in Brazil." *Journal of Peasant Studies* 42, no. 6: 1109–1135.

Wesson, Robert G. 1982. *Democracy in Latin America: Promise and Problems*. New York: Praeger.

Williams, Eunice Mueni. 2017. "Opening up the Demographic Dividend Window in Sub-Saharan Africa: How Did Low-Fertility Countries Do It?" *Paper Presented at the Annual Meeting of the Population Association of America.*

Wilson, Charles 1984. England's Apprenticeship, 1603–1763. 2nd edn. London: Longman.

Wilson, Judith. 2020. "Tolstoy vs. the Police." *New York Times*. August 2.

Wineman, Ayala, and Thomas Jayne. 2018. "Land Prices Heading Skyward? An Analysis of Farmland Values Across Tanzania." *Applied Economic Perspectives and Policy* 40, no. 2: 187–214.

Wise, Timothy A. 2019. "Opinion: Agroecology as Innovation." *Sustainable Agriculture*. https://foodtank.com/news/category/sustatinable-agriculture.

Wise, Timothy A. 2020a. *False Promises: The Alliance for a Green Revolution in Africa (AGRA)*. Thika, Kenya: Biodiversity and Biosafety Association of Kenya (BIBA) formerly the Kenya Biodiversity Coalition (KBioC) SACDEP Training Centre, Upper Hill Road.

Wise, Timothy A. 2020b. "Failing Africa's Farmers: An Impact Assessment of the Alliance for a Green Revolution in Africa." Global Development and Environment Institute, Working Paper No. 20–01.

Wise, Timothy A. 2021a. "Mexico to Ban Glyphosate, GM Corn: Presidential Decree Comes Despite Intense Pressure from Industry, US Authorities." *Inter Press Service News*. February 24.

Wise, Timothy A. 2021b. "Africa's Green Revolution: Few Gains, No Transparency." *Nairobi Star*. March 8.

Wise, Timothy A. 2021c. "AGRA Update: Throwing Good Money After Bad." *IATP Blog*. July 1. https://www.iatp.org/throwing-good-money-after-bad.

Wong, John. 1973. *Land Reform in the People's Republic of China, Institutional Transformation in Agriculture*. New York: Praeger.

World Bank. 1975. *Land Reform-Sector Policy Paper*. Washington: World Bank.

World Bank. 1978. *Land Reform in Latin America: Bolivia, Chile, Mexico, Peru and Venezuela*. Staff Working Paper # 275. Washington, DC.

World Bank. 1997. "Economic Growth and Income Inequality: Reexamining the Links." *Finance and Development*, March.

World Bank. 2003a. *Rural Poverty Alleviation in Brazil: Toward an Integrated Strategy*. Report N° 26760. Washington, DC: The World Bank.

World Bank. 2003b. *Land Policies for Growth and Poverty Reduction*. Washington, DC: World Bank.

World Bank. 2009. *Agriculture for Development, World Development Report, 2008*. Washington, DC: World Bank.

World Bank. 2014. *Taking Stock: An Update on Vietnam's Recent Economic Developments (July 2014)—Key Findings*. Washington, DC: World Bank.

World Bank. 2018. *Making Growth Work for the Poor: A Poverty Assessment for the Philippines*. Washington, DC: The World Bank.

World Income Inequality Database. n.d. "UNU-WIDER." https://www/\.wider.unu.edu/.

World Inequality Lab. 2018. *World Inequality Report 2018*. Paris: Paris School of Economics.

Xie, Yu, and Xiang You. 2014. "Income Inequality in Today's China." *Proceedings of the National Academy of Sciences of the United States of America* 111, no. 19: 6928–6933.

Xu, Weibin. 2000. "Education and Economic Growth: Evidence from China and Policy Implications." Dissertations available from ProQuest. AAI9989672.https://repository.upenn.edu/dissertations/AAI9989672.

Xue, Jinjun. 2012. "Growth with inequality: An international comparison on income distribution." *World Scientific*. Japan: Nagoya University.

Xue, Jinjun, and Wenshu Gao. 2012. "How Large is the Urban-Rural Income Gap in China?" *Paper Presented at the World Economy Conference Organised by RCIE at the University of Washington, KIET, APEA, and UIBE, Seattle.*

Yang, Jisheng. 2021. *The World Turned Upside Down*. New York: Farrar, Straus and Giroux.

Yates, Paúl Lamartine. 1978. *El Campo Mexicano*. México, DF: Ediciones El Caballito, S.A.

Yates, Paul Lamartine. 1981. *Mexico's Agricultural Dilemma*. Tucson, Arizona: University of Arizona Press.

You, J. 2014. "Land Reform, Inequality, and Corruption: A Comparative Historical Study of Korea, Taiwan, and the Philippines." *Korean Journal of International Studies* 12–1: 191–224.

Young, Arthur. 1771. *A Six Months Tour through the North of England*. 2nd ed. London.

Yue, Ximing, Shi Li, and Terry Sicular. 2010. Are the High Salaries of Employees in Monopoly Industries Justified? (in Chinese). *Social Sciences in China* 171, no.3: 77–93.

Zhou, Yixiao, and Ligang Song. 2016. "Income Inequality in China: Causes and Policy Responses." *China Economic Journal* 9, no. 2: 186–208.

# Index

*For the benefit of digital users, indexed terms that span two pages (e.g., 52–53) may, on occasion, appear on only one of those pages.*

Tables and figures are indicated by an italic *t* and *f* following the page number.

The manufacturer's authorised representative in the EU for product safety is Oxford University Press España S.A. of el Parque Empresarial San Fernando de Henares, Avenida de Castilla, 2 – 28830 Madrid (www.oup.es/en).

Printed in the USA/Agawam, MA
December 10, 2024

878627.004